Microsoft® Office
Excel® 2007:
Data Analysis and
Business Modeling

Wayne L. Winston

PUBLISHED BY
Microsoft Press
A Division of Microsoft Corporation
One Microsoft Way
Redmond, Washington 98052-6399

Library of Congress Control Number: 2007924648

Printed and bound in the United States of America.

5 6 7 8 9 10 11 12 13   QGT   5 4 3 2 1 0

Distributed in Canada by H.B. Fenn and Company Ltd.

A CIP catalogue record for this book is available from the British Library.

Microsoft Press books are available through booksellers and distributors worldwide. For further information about international editions, contact your local Microsoft Corporation office or contact Microsoft Press International directly at fax (425) 936-7329. Visit our Web site at www.microsoft.com/mspress. Send comments to mspinput@microsoft.com.

Acquisitions Editor: Juliana Aldous Atkinson
Developmental Editor: Sandra Haynes
Project Editor: Kathleen Atkins
Editorial Production Services: Online Training Solutions, Inc.
Technical Reviewer: Jason Lee; Technical Review services provided by Content Master, a member of CM Group, Ltd.

Body Part No. X13-68388

Table of Contents

What do you think of this book? We want to hear from you!

Microsoft is interested in hearing your feedback so we can continually improve our books and learning resources for you. To participate in a brief online survey, please visit:

www.microsoft.com/learning/booksurvey/

What do you think of this book? We want to hear from you!

Microsoft is interested in hearing your feedback so we can continually improve our books and learning resources for you. To participate in a brief online survey, please visit:

www.microsoft.com/learning/booksurvey/

Preface

Whether you work for a Fortune 500 corporation, a small company, a government agency, or a not-for-profit organization, if you're reading this preface the chances are you use Microsoft Office Excel in your daily work. Your job probably involves summarizing, reporting and analyzing data. It might also involve building analytic models to help your employer increase profits, reduce costs, or manage operations more efficiently.

Since 1999, I've taught thousands of analysts at organizations such as 3M, Bristol-Myers Squibb, Cisco Systems, Eli Lilly, Ford, General Electric, General Motors, Intel, Microsoft, NCR, Owens Corning, Pfizer, Proctor & Gamble, the U.S. Army, the U.S. Department of Defense, and Verizon how to use Excel more efficiently and productively in their jobs. Students have often told me that the tools and methods I teach in my classes have saved them hours of time each week and provided them with new and improved approaches for analyzing important business problems. Most of these classes used Excel 2003. With the added power of Excel 2007, you can be more productive than you ever dreamed! To paraphrase Alicia Silverstone in the movie *Clueless*, Excel 2003 is so five years ago.

I've used the techniques described in this book in my own consulting practice to solve many business problems. For example, we use Excel to help the Dallas Mavericks NBA basketball team evaluate referees, players, and lineups. By the way, during the last five seasons the Mavericks have won more games than any other NBA team! During the last 15 years I have also taught Excel business modeling and data analysis classes to MBA students at Indiana University's Kelley School of Business. (As proof of my teaching excellence, I have won MBA teaching awards for 26 consecutive years, and have won the school's overall MBA teaching award five times.) I would like to also note that 95 percent of MBA students take my spreadsheet modeling class even though it is an elective.

The book you have in your hands is an attempt to make these successful classes available to everyone. Here is why I think the book will help you learn how to use Excel more effectively:

- The materials have been tested while teaching thousands of analysts working for Fortune 500 corporations and the U.S. Army.

- I've written the book as though I am talking to the reader. This approach hopefully transfers the spirit of a successful classroom environment to the written page.

- I teach by example, which makes concepts easier to master. These examples are constructed to have a "real-world" feel. Many of the examples are based on questions sent to me by employees of Fortune 500 corporations.

- For the most part, I lead you through the approaches I take to set up and answer a wide range of data analysis and business questions in Excel. You can follow along with my explanations by referring to the sample worksheets that accompany each example. However, I have also included template files for the book's examples on the companion CD.

If you wish, these templates allow you to work directly with Excel and complete each example on your own.

- For the most part, the chapters are short and organized around a single concept. You should be able to master the content of most chapters with at most two hours of study. By looking at the questions that begin each chapter, you'll gain an idea about the types of problems you'll be able to solve after mastering a chapter's topics.

- In addition to learning about Excel formulas, you will learn some important math in a fairly painless fashion. For example, you'll learn about statistics, forecasting, optimization models, Monte Carlo simulation, inventory modeling, and the mathematics of waiting in line. You will also learn about some recent developments in business thinking such as real options, customer value, and mathematical pricing models.

- At the end of each chapter, I've provided a group of practice problems (over 500 in total) that you can work through on your own. These problems will help you master the information in each chapter. Answers to all problems are included on the book's CD. Many of these problems are based on actual problems faced by business analysts at Fortune 500 companies.

- Most of all, learning should be fun. If you read this book, you will learn how to predict U.S. presidential elections, how to set football point spreads, how to determine the probability of winning at craps, and how to determine the probability of a specific team winning an NCAA tournament. These examples are interesting and fun, and they also teach you a lot about solving business problems with Excel.

- To follow along with this book **you must have Excel 2007.** The previous version of this book can be used with Excel 97 or Excel 2003.

What You Should Know Before Reading this Book

To follow the examples in this book you do not need to be an Excel guru. Basically, the two key actions you should know how to do are the following:

- **Enter a formula.** You should know that formulas must begin with an equal sign (=). You should also know the basic mathematical operators. For example, you should know that an asterisk (*) is used for multiplication, a forward slash (/) is used for division and the caret key (^) is used to raise a quantity to a power.

- **Work with cell references.** You should know that when you copy a formula that contains a cell reference such as $A$4 (an absolute cell reference, which is created by including the dollar signs), the formula will still refer to cell $A$4 in the cells you copy it to. When you copy a formula that contains a cell reference such as $A4 (a mixed cell address) the row will remain fixed, but the column will change. Finally, when you copy a formula that contains a cell reference such as A4 (a relative cell reference), both the row and the column of the cells referenced in the formula will change.

How to Use this Book

As you read along with the examples in this book, you can take one of two approaches:

- You can open the template that corresponds to the example you are studying and complete each step of the example as you read the book. You will be surprised how easy this process is and amazed with how much you learn and retain. This is the approach I use in my corporate classes.

- Instead of working in the template, you can follow my explanations as you look at the final version of each sample file.

Using the Companion CD

The CD-ROM that accompanies the book contains the sample files you use in the book's examples (both the final Excel workbooks and starting templates you can work with on your own). The workbooks and templates are organized in folders named for each chapter. The answers to all chapter-ending problems in the book are also included on the book's CD. Each answer file is named so you can identify it easily. For example, the file containing the answer to Problem 2 in Chapter 10 is named s10_2.xlsx.

To use the CD, first insert it into your CD-ROM drive. If AutoRun is not enabled on your PC, browse to the root folder of the CD and double-click the StartCD file. You will be presented with a licensing agreement that you need to accept before you can install the files from the CD. By default, the sample files will be installed to your folder Documents\Microsoft Press\Excel 2007 Data Analysis folder.

The CD also contains an electronic version of this book in PDF format. Adobe Reader is required to view the PDF version of the book. The CD includes a link to Adobe's Web site, where you can choose to download a copy of Adobe Reader if you do not already have a copy installed on your computer. (You can download Adobe Reader free of charge.)

Support Information

Every effort has been made to ensure the accuracy of this book and the contents of the companion CD. To provide feedback on the book's contents or the companion CD, you can send e-mail to mspinput@microsoft.com or write to us at the following address:

Microsoft Excel Data Analysis and Business Modeling Editor

Microsoft Press/Microsoft Learning

One Microsoft Way

Redmond WA 98052

Microsoft Press provides corrections for books through the World Wide Web at *www.microsoft.com/learning/support/*. To connect directly to the Microsoft Press Knowledge Base and enter a query or question on an issue you may have, go to *www.microsoft.com /learning/support/search.asp*. For Excel technical support information, you can connect to Microsoft Technical Support on the Web at *support.microsoft.com*.

Acknowledgments

I am eternally grateful to Jennifer Skoog and Norm Tonina, who had faith in me and first hired me to teach Excel classes for Microsoft finance. Jennifer in particular was instrumental in helping design the content and style of the classes on which the book is based. Keith Lange of Eli Lilly, Pat Keating and Doug Hoppe of Cisco Systems, and Dennis Fuller of the U.S. Army also helped me refine my thoughts on teaching data analysis and modeling with Excel. The capable people at OTSI, reviewer Jason Lee, and Microsoft Press Editor Kathleen Atkins helped shepherd the project to completion.

I am grateful to my many students at the organizations where I've taught and at the Kelley School of Business. Many of them have taught me things I did not know about Excel.

Alex Blanton of Microsoft Press championed the project and shared my vision of developing a user-friendly text designed for use by business analysts.

Finally, my lovely and talented wife Vivian and my wonderful children Jennifer and Gregory put up with my long weekend hours at the keyboard.

Introduction to Excel 2007: What's New?

- What is the Ribbon?
- What is the Quick Access Toolbar?
- What is the Mini toolbar?
- How can I easily find useful keystroke combinations?
- Can I create larger worksheets in Excel 2007 than in Excel 2003?
- What is Formula AutoComplete?
- What is the Microsoft Office Button?
- What are themes?
- What is SmartArt?
- How do I change the zoom level for a worksheet?
- How do I display multiple copies of a workbook at the same time?
- Are there new ways to look at my spreadsheet before I print it?
- My friend does not have Excel 2007. How can I send her files she can use?
- What else has changed?

Microsoft Office Excel 2007 is truly new and improved. At first the new interface and new features may confuse experienced users, but when you are familiar with the new interface, you will never want to use an earlier version of Excel! If you are a novice user of Excel, the new interface will make it much easier for you to locate the more complex and useful features of Excel 2007. In this introductory chapter we will briefly describe the changes in Excel 2007. Our book's main focus is on using Excel for business modeling and data analysis, so we will not spend much time on visually oriented features such as SmartArt and Themes. For more information about these features, we refer the reader to *Microsoft Office Excel 2007 Inside Out* by Mark Dodge and Craig Stinson.

What is the Ribbon?

When the Excel team asked Excel users what they typically had trouble doing in Excel, they found that over 90 percent of the features people wanted but couldn't find were already available in Excel 2003. The problem was that many great features such as Data Tables, Data Consolidate, and Solver were hard to find. To make it easier for users to find and learn about all the wonderful features of Excel and other Microsoft Office programs, the Office team created the Ribbon. (See Figure 0-1 on the next page.)

Figure 0-1   The Ribbon: Home tab

The options available from the Ribbon depend on which tab is selected:

❑ **Home.** This tab contains most worksheet editing and formatting commands (such as font type and cell alignment) as well as clipboard commands (such as Paste and Paste Special).

❑ **Page Layout.** This tab contains commands that control the printing of your worksheets as well as worksheet appearance (for example, do I want gridlines to show?)

❑ **Insert.** Use commands on this tab when you want to insert things such as clip art, charts, and PivotTables into a worksheet.

❑ **Data.** Commands on this tab pertain to data analysis features such as sorting and filtering.

❑ **Formulas.** Use commands on this tab when you want to name a range of cells, gain access to the wonderful Excel functions, control calculation options, or audit the structure of a worksheet.

❑ **Review.** Use commands on this tab to manage worksheet comments, protect worksheets, check spelling, track worksheet changes, or perform related tasks.

❑ **View.** Use commands on this tab to control how your worksheet is viewed. You can freeze panes, tile and arrange windows, and control the page layout (more on this later in this section).

❑ **Developer.** Commands on this tab are used primarily to develop Excel macros. You can also insert user forms and controls (discussed in Chapter 25, "Spin Buttons, Scroll Bars, Option Buttons, Check Boxes, Combo Boxes, and Group List Boxes"). If this tab is not visible, click the Microsoft Office Button (see Figure 0-2), click Excel Options, and then on the Popular page, check the Show Developer Tab In The Ribbon box.

❑ **Add-Ins.** Excel Add-Ins such as the Solver or Analysis Toolpak are available from this tab. The tab is visible only when at least one add-in is installed.

Figure 0-2   Microsoft Office Button

The tabs and Ribbon make it much easier to see what Excel has to offer. If you think the Ribbon takes up too much space, you can hide it (or redisplay it) by pressing Ctrl+F1, double-clicking any tab, or right-clicking the Ribbon and then clicking Minimize The Ribbon.

What is the Quick Access Toolbar?

There are probably many commands that you use more often than others. Having to switch between tabs to find the command you want could really slow you down. Excel now provides you with the Quick Access Toolbar which allows you to collect your favorite commands in one place. The default location of the Quick Access Toolbar is above the Ribbon in the upper-left portion of the screen. See Figure 0-3.

Figure 0-3   Quick Access Toolbar

You can add a command to the Quick Access Toolbar by simply right-clicking the command and choosing Add To Quick Access Toolbar. You can also add commands by clicking the Microsoft Office Button, clicking Excel Options, and then displaying the Customize page (shown in Figure 0-4). After choosing a command you want to add just select Add and click OK. You may remove any command from the Quick Access Toolbar by right-clicking the command and then clicking Remove From Quick Access Toolbar. You may move the Quick Access Toolbar below the Ribbon by right clicking on the toolbar and selecting Show below the Ribbon.

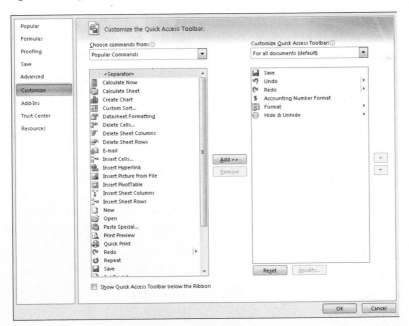

Figure 0-4   You can add, remove, and arrange commands on the Quick Access Toolbar.

What is the Mini toolbar?

When you select the contents of a cell or right-click a cell or a cell range the Mini toolbar appears. See Figure 0-5. The Mini-toolbar gives you quick access to the most commonly used formatting tools.

If you want to prevent the Mini toolbar from appearing, click the Microsoft Office Button followed by Excel Options. Then on the Popular page, clear the Show Mini Toolbar On Selection check box.

Figure 0-5   The Mini toolbar

How can I easily find useful keystroke combinations?

Press the Alt key once to display the available tab-level keyboard shortcuts (and again to hide them). Pressing the key that represents the tab on which the command you want is located displays that tab and all its command-level shortcuts. For example, Alt+M displays the Formulas tab. Alt+H+H displays the Fill Color gallery, and so on.

Can I create larger worksheets in Excel 2007 than in Excel 2003?

Excel 2003 has a worksheet size limit of 64,000 rows and 256 columns. Excel 2007 allows up to 1,048,576 rows and 65,536 columns. To test this, click F5 (which allows you to go to any cell), type in *CAT1000000* for example, and click OK. Excel sends you to cell CAT1000000! Excel 2007 was also designed to perform calculations on large worksheets much more quickly. In fact, if your computer has *n* processors, then certain operations can be performed close to *n* times as quickly as Excel 2003 because Excel 2007 is programmed to take advantage of multiple processors.

Many other limits have been improved in Excel 2007, such as these:

❑ 4.3 billion available colors

❑ Unlimited levels of conditional formatting

❑ Sorting on up to 64 columns

❑ 100 levels of Undo allowed

❑ 8,000 characters allowed in a formula

❑ 32,000 characters allowed in a cell

What is Formula AutoComplete?

Suppose you start typing in a formula to average a range of cells. You would begin by typing in *=AV*. Then the new Formula AutoComplete feature appears. See Figure 0-6. Instead of typing *average* all you need do is press Tab or double-click AVERAGE. Excel then enters *=Average(* into your formula.

If you use range names (see Chapter 1, "Range Names") or the new Table feature (see Chapter 24, "Tables") you will really see the benefits of Formula AutoComplete.

Figure 0-6   Formula AutoComplete feature

What is the Microsoft Office Button?

We have already briefly discussed the Microsoft Office Button. From the menu that appears when you click the Microsoft Office Button, you can:

- ❑ Perform key file-level tasks such as Save, Close, Open, and Print.
- ❑ Customize various aspects of Excel (by clicking Excel Options).
- ❑ Install Excel add-ins (by clicking Excel Options and then displaying the Add-Ins page).

What are themes?

Themes let you control the colors, fonts, and special effects used in your worksheets. Themes apply to your entire workbook. To select a theme, simply click the Page Layout tab and then in the Themes group, click Themes. You will be presented with many theme choices, some of which are shown in Figure 0-7. When you point to a theme, the Office Live Preview feature shows you how things will look if you select that theme. Alternatively, by making selections from the Colors, Fonts, and Effects lists, you can create your own customized theme and save it for later use. Any customized themes you create will appear in the Custom category.

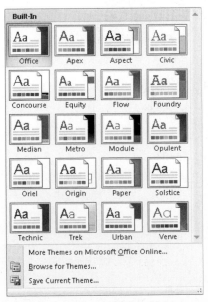

Figure 0-7   Theme choices

What is SmartArt?

SmartArt gives you many neat shapes and effects that go beyond the usual circles, rectangles, and arrows. To see how SmartArt works, open a new workbook and on the Insert tab, in the Illustrations group, click SmartArt. You will see the options shown in Figure 0-8.

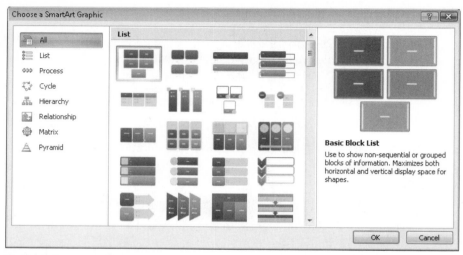

Figure 0-8   SmartArt choices

We chose the first option and entered in the text for each block the name of a starting member of the Dallas Mavericks NBA team. We obtained the figure shown in Figure 0-9.

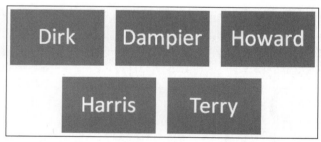

Figure 0-9   SmartArt example

How do I change the Zoom level for a worksheet?

Excel 2007 makes it a snap to zoom in and out of a worksheet by moving the Zoom slider located in the lower-right corner of your screen. See Figure 0-10.

Figure 0-10   Zoom slider

Are there new ways to look at my spreadsheet before I print it?

The Workbook Views group on the View tab displays the possible views shown in Figure 0-11.

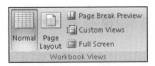

Figure 0-11   Workbook view options

Normal view is your usual worksheet view. Page Layout view shows individual pages and lets you add headers and footers, adjust margins, and so on. Page Break Preview shows and allows you to adjust page breaks.

How do I display multiple copies of a workbook at the same time?

Suppose your workbook contains a worksheet for each month of the year. You might want to perform computations that involve different months, so it would be helpful to see different worksheets of the workbook on the screen at the same time. To see multiple views of your workbook, click the View tab and then repeatedly click New Window to bring up enough views of the spreadsheet (for example, if you want three views, click New Window twice). Then click Arrange All and choose how you want the copies of your workbook displayed. Displaying a different worksheet in each window makes it easier to develop formulas involving more than one worksheet.

My friend does not have Excel 2007. How can I send her files she can use?

If your friend has Office 97, Office 2000, Office XP or Office 2003, save the file in the Excel 97-2003 Workbook file format. If your friend has Office 95, save the file in the Microsoft Excel 5.0/95 Workbook file format. The default file format for Excel 2007 files is Excel Workbook, which creates a file with the *.xlsx* extension.

> **Note**   If you use certain new features of Excel 2007, your workbook may not be entirely compatible with earlier versions of Excel.

To determine whether your workbook is compatible with earlier Excel versions you can run the Excel Compatibility checker. Click the Microsoft Office Button, point to Prepare, and then click Run Compatibility Checker. For the workbook containing the SmartArt shown in Figure 0-9 on the next page, the Compatibility Checker would inform us that our SmartArt is not compatible with earlier versions of Excel.

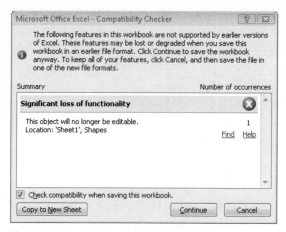

Figure 0-12   Compatibility Checker

What else has changed?

The new features of Excel discussed in this chapter do not pertain to business modeling and data analysis, so we gave only a brief explanation of these features. The following new features of Excel 2007 are very important in data analysis and business modeling so they will be covered in great detail.

❑ The method for creating range names has been greatly improved. See Chapter 1 for details.

❑ Conditional formatting options have been greatly expanded. You will be amazed by the new visually oriented conditional formatting choices that can be used to help you better understand your data (data bars, icons and color scales). See Chapter 22, "Conditional Formatting," for a complete discussion of conditional formatting.

❑ Sorting and filtering have been vastly improved. You can even sort on cell or font color! Excel 2007 also makes it easy to remove duplicates. See Chapter 23, "Sorting in Excel," and Chapter 40, "Filtering Data and Removing Duplicates," for more details.

❑ The new Table feature will revolutionize spreadsheet modeling. Proper use of the Table feature will cause your formulas, formatting, and charts to automatically update as you add new data to your workbook. See Chapter 24 for a complete discussion of the Table feature.

❑ Pivot tables have been revamped and improved. See Chapter 38, "Using Pivot-Tables to Describe Data," for a detailed discussion of this important data analysis feature.

❑ The appearance of Excel charts has been improved. This will become clear as you glance at the Excel charts included in the book.

❑ The new IFERROR function (see Chapter 11, "IF Statements") will make it easier to modify the dreaded #REF and #N/A error messages that often make spreadsheet calculations a nightmare!

❑ The new COUNTIFS (Chapter 18, "The COUNTIF, COUNTIFS, COUNT, COUNTA, and COUNTBLANK Functions") and SUMIFS and AVERAGEIFS (Chapter 19, "The SUMIF, AVERAGEIF, SUMIFS, and AVERAGEIFS Function") will make it much easier to summarize data sets.

Chapter 1
Range Names

- I want to total sales in Arizona, California, Montana, New York, and New Jersey. Can I use a formula to compute total sales in a form such as *AZ+CA+MT+NY+NJ* instead of *SUM(A21:A25)* and still get the right answer?

- What does a formula like Average(A:A) do?

- What is the difference between a name with workbook scope and one with worksheet scope?

- I really am getting to like range names. I have started defining range names for many of the workbooks I have developed at the office. However, the range names do not show up in my formulas. How can I make recently created range names show up in previously created formulas?

- How can I easily select a cell range?

- How can I paste a list of all range names (and the cells they represent) into my worksheet?

You have probably worked with worksheets that use formulas such as *SUM(A5000:A5049)*. Then you have to find out what's contained in cells A5000:A5049. If cells A5000:A5049 contain sales in each U.S. state, wouldn't the formula *SUM(USSales)* be easier to understand? In this chapter, I'll teach you how to name individual cells or ranges of cells. I'll also show you how to use range names in formulas.

How Can I Create Named Ranges?

There are three ways to create named ranges:

- By entering a range name in the Name Box.

- By clicking Create From Selection in the Defined Names group on the Formulas tab.

- By clicking Name Manager or Define Name in the Defined Names group on the Formulas tab.

Using the Name Box to Create a Range Name

The Name Box is located directly above the label for column A, as you can see in Figure 1-1. (To see the Name Box, you need to display the Formula bar.) To create a range name in the Name Box, simply select the cell or range of cells that you want to name, click in the Name Box, and then type the range name you want to use. Press Enter, and you've created the range name. Clicking the Name arrow displays the range names defined in the current workbook. You can display all the range names in a workbook by pressing the F3 key to open the Paste Name dialog box. When you select a range name from the Name Box, Microsoft Office Excel selects the cells corresponding to that range name. This enables you to verify that you've chosen the cell or range that you intended to name.

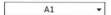

Figure 1-1 You can create a range name by selecting the cell range you want to name and then typing the range name in the Name Box.

For example, suppose we want to name cell F3 *east* and cell F4 *west*. See Figure 1-2 and the file Eastwest.xlsx. We simply select cell F3, type east in the Name Box, and then press Enter. Then we select cell F4, type west in the Name Box, and press Enter. If we now reference cell F3 in another cell, we will see =*east* instead of =F3. This means that whenever we see the reference *east* in a formula, Excel will insert whatever is in cell F3.

	A	B	C	D	E	F
1						
2						
3					east	5
4					west	10
5						
6						

Figure 1-2 Naming cell F3 east and F4 west

Suppose we want to assign a rectangular range of cells (such as A1:B4) the name *Data*. Simply select the cell range A1:B4, type Data in the Name Box, and press Enter. Now a formula such as =*AVERAGE(Data)* would average the contents of cells A1:B4. See the file Data.xlsx and Figure 1-3.

	A	B	C	D
1	1	2		
2	3	2		
3	1	1		
4	2	-1		
5			1.375	
6		cell C5	=AVERAGE(data)	
7		contains		

Figure 1-3 Naming range A1:B4 Data

Sometimes we want to name a range of cells made up of several noncontiguous rectangular ranges. For example, in Figure 1-4 and the file Noncontig.xlsx we might want to assign the name *Noncontig* to the range consisting of cells B3:C4, E6:G7 and B10:C10. To assign this name, select any one of the three rectangles making up the range (we chose B3:C4). Hold down the Ctrl key and select the other two ranges (E6:G7 and B10:C10). Now release the Ctrl key, type the name Noncontig in the Name Box, and press Enter. Using *Noncontig* in any formula will now refer to the contents of cells B3:C4, E6:G7 and B10:C10. For example, entering the formula *=AVERAGE(Noncontig)* in cell E10 yields 4.75 (because the 12 numbers in our range add up to 57 and *57/12=4.75*).

	A	B	C	D	E	F	G
1							
2							
3		1	2				
4		3	4				
5							
6					6	7	10
7					8	9	1
8							
9							
10		2	4				
11					4.75		
12					Cell E11 contains formula		
13					=AVERAGE(noncontig)		

Figure 1-4   Naming a noncontiguous range of cells

Creating Named Ranges by Using the Create from Selection Option

The worksheet States.xlsx contains sales during March for each of the 50 U.S. states. Figure 1-5 shows a subset of this data. We would like to name each cell in the range B6:B55 with the correct state abbreviation. To do this, select the range A6:B55, and click Create From Selection in the Defined Names group on the Formulas tab (see Figure 1-6 on the next page). Then check the Left Column box, as indicated in Figure 1-7 on the next page.

	A	B
1		
2		
3		
4		
5	State	
6	AL	$915.00
7	AK	$741.00
8	AZ	$566.00
9	AR	$754.00
10	CA	$687.00
11	CO	$757.00
12	CT	$786.00
13	DE	$795.00
14	FL	$944.00
15	GA	$624.00
16	HI	$663.00
17	ID	$895.00
18	IL	$963.00

Figure 1-5   By naming the cells that contain state sales with state abbreviations, you can use the abbreviation when you refer to the cell rather than the cell's column letter and row number.

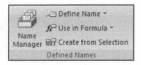

Figure 1-6   Select Create From Selection

Figure 1-7   Select the Left Column check box

Excel now knows to associate the names in the first column of the selected range with the cells in the second column of the selected range. Thus, B6 is assigned the range name *AL*, B7 is named *AK*, and so on. Note that creating these range names in the Name Box would have been incredibly tedious! Click the Name arrow to verify that these range names have been created.

Creating Range Names by Using the Name Manager Option

If you click Name Manager on the Formulas tab and then choose New, the New Name dialog box shown in Figure 1-8 opens.

Figure 1-8   The New Name dialog box before creating any range names

Suppose you want to assign the name *range1* (range names are not case sensitive) to the cell range A2:B7. Simply type range1 in the Name box and then point to the range or type =A2:B7 in the Refers To area. Click OK, and you're done. The New Name dialog box will now look like Figure 1-9.

Figure 1-9   New Name dialog box after creating a range name

If you click the Scope arrow, you can select the option Workbook or any worksheet in your workbook. We will discuss this decision later, so for now just choose the default Scope of Workbook. You can also add, if desired, comments for any of your range names.

The Name Manager

If you now click in the Name arrow the name *range1* (and any other ranges you have created) will appear in the Name Box. In the 2007 Microsoft Office System there is an easy way to edit or delete your range names that was not present in earlier versions of Office. Simply open the Name Manager by selecting Formulas and then clicking Name Manager. You will now see a list of all range names. For example, for the file States.xlsx the Name Manager dialog box will look like Figure 1-10.

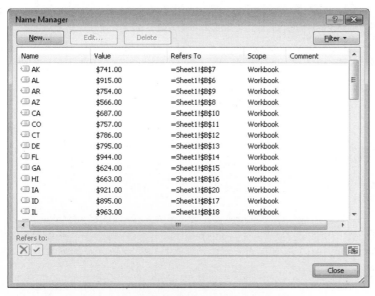

Figure 1-10   Name Manager dialog box for States.xlsx

To edit any range name, simply select the range name and click Edit. Then you can change the name of the range, the cells the range refers to, or the scope of the range.

To delete any subset of range names, simply select the range names you want to delete. If the range names are listed consecutively, simply select the first listed range name, hold down the Shift key, and select the last listed range name. If the range names are not listed consecutively, you can select any range name you want to delete and then hold down the Ctrl key while you select the other range names for deletion. Then press the Delete key to delete the selected range names.

Now let's look at some specific examples of how to use range names.

I want to total sales in Arizona, California, Montana, New York, and New Jersey. Can I use a formula to compute total sales in a form such as *AZ+CA+MT+NY+NJ* instead of *SUM(A21:A25)* and still get the right answer?

Let's return to the file States.xlsx in which we assigned each state's abbreviation as the range name for the state's sales. If we want to compute total sales in Alabama, Alaska, Arizona, and Arkansas, we could clearly use the formula *SUM(B6:B9)*. We could also point to cells B6, B7, B8, and B9, and the formula would be entered as *=AL+AK+AZ+AR*. The latter formula is, of course, much easier to understand.

As another illustration of how to use range names, look at the file Historicalinvest.xlsx, shown in Figure 1-11, which contains annual percentage returns on stocks, T-Bills, and bonds. (Some rows aren't visible; the data ends in row 81.)

	A	B	C	D	E	F	G
6		Annual Returns on Investments in					
7	Year	Stocks	T.Bills	T.Bonds			
8		1928	43.81%	3.08%	0.84%		
9		1929	-8.30%	3.16%	4.20%		
10		1930	-25.12%	4.55%	4.54%		
11		1931	-43.84%	2.31%	-2.56%		
12		1932	-8.64%	1.07%	8.79%		
13		1933	49.98%	0.96%	1.86%		
14		1934	-1.19%	0.30%	7.96%		0.1205
83		stocks	tbills	bonds			
84	averages	12.05%	3.96%	5.21%			

Figure 1-11   Historical investment data

After selecting the cell range B7:D81 and choosing Formulas, Create From Selection, we choose to create names in the top row of the range. The range B8:B81 is named *Stocks*, the range C8:C81 *T.Bills*, and the range D8:D81 *T.Bonds*. Now we no longer need to remember where our data is. For example, in cell B84, after typing *=AVERAGE(*, we can press F3 and the Paste Name dialog box appears, as shown in Figure 1-12.

Figure 1-12   You can add a range name to a formula by using the Paste Name dialog box.

Then we can select Stocks in the Paste Name list and click OK. After entering the closing parenthesis, our formula, =*AVERAGE(Stocks)*, computes the average return on stocks (12.05 percent). The beauty of this approach is that even if we don't remember where the data is, we can work with the stock return data anywhere in the workbook!

We would be remiss if we did not mention the exciting new AutoComplete capabilities of Excel 2007. If you begin typing =*Average(T* then Excel will show you a list of range names and functions that begin with T. Then you can simply click T.Bills to complete the entry of the range name. See Figure 1-13.

Figure 1-13   Example of AutoComplete feature

What does a formula like Average(A:A) do?

If we use a column name (in the form A:A, C:C, and so on) in a formula, Excel treats an entire column as a named range. For example, entering the formula =*AVERAGE(A:A)* will average all numbers in column A. Using a range name for an entire column is very help-ful if you frequently enter new data into a column. For example, if column A contains monthly sales of a product, as new sales data is entered each month, our formula com-putes an up-to-date monthly sales average. I caution you, however, that if you enter the formula =*AVERAGE(A:A)* in column A, you will get a circular reference message because the value of the cell containing the average formula depends on the cell containing the average. You will learn how to resolve circular references in Chapter 10, "Circular References." Similarly, entering the formula =*AVERAGE(1:1)* will average all numbers in row 1.

What is the difference between a name with workbook scope and one with worksheet scope?

The file Sheetnames.xlsx will help us to understand the difference between range names that have workbook scope and range names that have worksheet scope. When we create names with the Name Box, the created names have workbook scope. For example, suppose we use the Name Box to assign the name *sales* to the cell range E4:E6 in Sheet3 and these cells contain the numbers 1, 2, and 4, respectively. Then if we enter a formula such as =SUM(*sales*) in any worksheet, we will obtain an answer of 7. This is because the Name Box creates names with workbook scope and so anywhere in the workbook where we refer to the name *sales* (which has workbook scope) the name refers to cells E4:E6 of Sheet3. In any worksheet if we now enter the formula =SUM(*sales*) we will obtain 7 because anywhere in the workbook Excel will link *sales* to cells E4:E6 of Sheet3.

Now suppose that we type 4, 5, and 6 in cells E4:E6 of Sheet1, and 3, 4, and 5 in cells E4:E6 of Sheet2. Next we go to the Name Manager, give the name jam to cells E4:E6 of Sheet1, and define the scope of this name as Sheet1. Then we move to Sheet2, go to the Name Manager, and give the name jam to cells E4:E6, and define the scope of this name as Sheet2. Our Name Manager dialog box now looks like Figure 1-14.

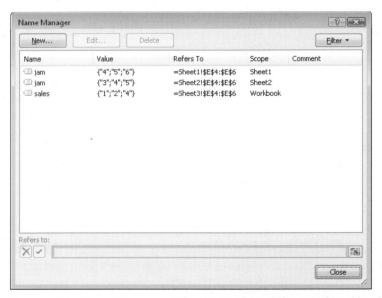

Figure 1-14   Name Manager dialog box with worksheet and workbook names

Now what if we enter the formula =SUM(*jam*) in each sheet? In Sheet 1, =SUM(*jam*) will total cells E4:E6 of Sheet1. Because those cells contain 4, 5, and 6, we obtain 15. In Sheet2 =Sum(*jam*) will total cells E4:E6 of Sheet2, yielding *3 + 4 + 5=12*. In Sheet3, however, the formula =SUM(*jam*) will yield a *#NAME?* error because there is no range named *jam* defined in Sheet3! If we enter anywhere in Sheet3 the formula =SUM(Sheet2!jam) then Excel will recognize the worksheet-level name that represents cell range E4:E6 of Sheet2 and yields a result of *3 + 4 + 5 =12*. Thus, prefacing a worksheet-level name by its sheet name followed by an exclamation point (!) will allow us to refer to a worksheet-level range in a worksheet other than the sheet in which the range is defined.

I really am getting to like range names. I have started defining range names for many of the workbooks I have developed at the office. However, the range names do not show up in my formulas. How can I make recently created range names show up in previously created formulas?

Let's look at the file Applynames.xlsx. See Figure 1-15.

	A	B	C	D	E	F
1						
2						
3					price	$5.00
4					demand	8500
5					unitcost	$4.00
6					fixed cost	$3,000.00
7					profit	$5,500.00
8						
9						

Figure 1-15   How to apply range names to formulas

We have entered the price of a product in cell F3, and product demand of =10000−300*F3 in cell F4. Our unit cost and fixed cost are entered in cells F5 and F6, respectively. Our profit is computed in cell F7 with the formula =F4*(F3−F5)−F6. We have just used Formulas, Create from Selection, choosing the Left Row option to name cell F3 *price*, cell F4 *demand*, cell F5 *unit cost*, cell F6 *fixed cost*, and cell F7 *profit*. We would like these range names to show up in our cell F4 and cell F7 formulas. To apply our range names, first select the range where you want the range names applied (in our case F4:F7). Now go to the Defined Names area on the Formulas tab, click the Define Name arrow, and then click Apply Names. Highlight the Names you want to apply, and click OK. Note that cell F4 now contains the formula =10000−300*price and cell F7 contains the formula =demand*(price−unitcost)−fixed_cost, as desired.

By the way, if you want the range names to apply to the entire worksheet, simply select the entire worksheet by clicking the Select All button at the intersection of the column and row headings.

How can I easily select a named range?

If you have selected a cell within a named range, press Ctrl+* to select the entire range.

How can I paste a list of all range names (and the cells they represent) into my worksheet?

Press F3 to display the Paste Name box, and then click the Paste List button. A list of range names and the cells each corresponds to will be pasted into your worksheet, beginning at the current cell location.

Remarks

■ Excel does not allow you to use the letters *r* and *c* as range names.

■ If you use Create from Selection to create a range name, and your name contains spaces, Excel inserts an underscore (_) to fill in the spaces. For example, the name *Product 1* is created as *Product_1*.

■ Range names cannot begin with numbers or look like a cell reference. For example, *3Q* and *A4* are not allowed as range names. Because Excel 2007 has over 16,000 columns, a range name such as *cat1* would not be permitted because there is a cell CAT1. If you try and name a cell *CAT1*, Excel tells you the name is invalid. Probably your best bet is to name the cell cat1_.

■ The only symbols allowed in range names are periods (.) and underscores (_).

Problems

1. The file Stock.xlsx contains monthly stock returns for General Motors and Microsoft. Name the ranges containing the monthly returns for each stock, and compute the average monthly return on each stock.

2. Open a worksheet and name the range containing the cells A1:B3 and A6:B8 as *Red*.

3. Given the latitude and longitude of any two cities, the file Citydistances.xlsx computes the distance between any two cities. Define range names for the latitude and longitude of each city and ensure that these names show up in the formula for total distance.

Chapter 2

Lookup Functions

- How do I write a formula to compute tax rates based on income?

- Given a product ID, how can I look up the product's price?

- Suppose that a product's price changes over time. I know the date the product was sold. How can I write a formula to compute the product's price?

Syntax of the Lookup Functions

Lookup functions enable you to "look up" values from worksheet ranges. Microsoft Office Excel allows you to perform both vertical lookups (by using the VLOOKUP function) and horizontal lookups (by using the HLOOKUP function). In a vertical lookup, the lookup operation starts in the first column of a worksheet range. In a horizontal lookup, the operation starts in the first row of a worksheet range. Because the majority of formulas using lookup functions involve vertical lookups, we'll concentrate on VLOOKUP functions.

VLOOKUP Syntax

The syntax of the VLOOKUP function is as follows. The brackets ([ ]) indicate optional arguments.

```
VLOOKUP(lookup value,table range,column index,[range lookup])
```

- *Lookup value* is the value that we want to look up in the first column of the table range.

- *Table range* is the range that contains the entire lookup table. The table range includes the first column, in which we try and match the lookup value, and any other columns in which we will look up formula results.

- *Column index* is the column number in the table range from which the value of the lookup function is obtained.

- *Range lookup* is an optional argument. The point of range lookup is to allow you to specify an exact or approximate match. If the range lookup argument is *True* or omitted, the first column of the table range must be in ascending numerical order. If the range lookup argument is *True* or omitted and an exact match to the lookup value is found in the first column of the table range, Excel bases the lookup on the row of the table in which the exact match is found. If the range lookup argument is *True* or omitted and an exact match does not exist, Excel bases the lookup on the largest value in the first column that is less than the lookup value. If the range lookup argument is *False* and an exact match to the lookup value is found in the first column of the table range, Excel bases the lookup on the row of the table in which the exact match is found. If no exact match is obtained, Excel returns an #N/A response (Not Available). Note that a range lookup argument of *1* is equivalent to TRUE whereas a range lookup argument of *0* is equivalent to FALSE.

HLOOKUP Syntax

In an HLOOKUP function, Excel tries to locate the lookup value in the first row (not the first column) of the table range. For an HLOOKUP function, use the VLOOKUP syntax and change "column" to "row."

Let's explore some interesting examples of lookup functions.

How do I write a formula to compute tax rates based on income?

The following example shows how a VLOOKUP function works when the first column of the table range consists of numbers in ascending order. Suppose that the tax rate depends on income, as shown in the following table.

Income level	Tax rate
$0–$9,999	15%
$10,000–$29,999	30%
$30,000–$99,999	34%
$100,000 and over	40%

To see an example of how to write a formula that computes the tax rate for any income level, open the file Lookup.xlsx, shown in Figure 2-1.

	C	D	E	F	G
3	Lookup Tables				
4					
5		Income	Tax rate		Lookup=D6:E9
6		0	0.15		
7		10000	0.3		
8		30000	0.34		
9		100000	0.4		
10					
11			TRUE	FALSE	
12		Income	Rate		
13		-1000	#N/A	#N/A	
14		30000	0.34	0.34	
15		29000	0.3	#N/A	
16		98000	0.34	#N/A	
17		104000	0.4	#N/A	

Figure 2-1   Using a lookup function to compute a tax rate. The numbers in the first column of the table range are sorted in ascending order.

I began by entering the relevant information (tax rates and break points) in cell range D6:E9. I named the table range D6:E9 *lookup*. I recommend that you always name the cells you're using as the table range. If you do so, you need not remember the exact location of the table range, and when you copy any formula involving a lookup function, the lookup range will always be correct. To illustrate how the lookup function works, I entered some incomes in the range D13:D17. By copying from E13:E17 the formula *VLOOKUP(D13,Lookup,2,True)*, we computed the tax rate for the income levels listed in D13:D17. Let's examine how the lookup function worked in cells E13:E17. Note that because the column index in the formula is 2, the answer always comes from the second column of the table range.

- ❏ In D13, the income of –$1,000 yields #N/A because –$1,000 is less than the lowest income level in the first column of the table range. If you wanted a tax rate of 15 percent associated with an income of –$1,000, simply replace the 0 in D6 by a number that is –1,000 or smaller.

- ❏ In D14, the income of $30,000 exactly matches a value in the first column of the table range, so the function returns a tax rate of 34 percent.

- ❏ In D15, the income level of $29,000 does not exactly match a value in the first column of the table range, which means the lookup function stops at the largest number less than $29,000 in the first column of the range–$10,000 in this case. This function returns the tax rate in column 2 of the table range opposite $10,000, or 30 percent.

- ❏ In D16, the income level of $98,000 does not yield an exact match in the first column of the table range. The lookup function stops at the largest number less than $98,000 in the first column of the table range. This returns the tax rate in column 2 of the table range opposite $30,000–34 percent.

- ❏ In D17, the income level of $104,000 does not yield an exact match in the first column of the table range. The lookup function stops at the largest number less than $104,000 in the first column of the table range, which returns the tax rate in column 2 of the table range opposite $100,000–40 percent.

- ❏ In F13:F17, we changed the value of the *range lookup* argument from *True* to *False* and copied from F13 to F14:F17 the formula *VLOOKUP(D13,Lookup,2,False)*. Cell F14 still yields a 34 percent tax rate because the first column of the table range contains an exact match to $30,000. The other entries in F13:F17 all display #N/A because none of the other incomes in D13:D17 have an exact match in the first column of the table range.

Given a product ID, how can I look up the product's price?

Often, the first column of a table range does not consist of numbers in ascending order. For example, the first column of the table range might list product ID codes or employee names. In my experience teaching thousands of financial analysts, I've found that many people don't know how to deal with lookup functions when the first column of the table range does not consist of numbers in ascending order. In these situations, you need to remember only one simple rule: use *False* as the value of the range lookup argument.

Here's an example. In the file Lookup.xlsx (see Figure 2-2), you can see the prices for five products, listed by their ID code. How do you write a formula that will take a product ID code and return the product price?

	H	I	J
9			Lookup2=H11:I15
10	Product ID	Price	
11	A134	$ 3.50	
12	B242	$ 4.20	
13	X212	$ 4.80	
14	C413	$ 5.00	
15	B2211	$ 5.20	
16			
17	ID	Price	
18	B2211	3.5	
19	B2211	5.2	

Figure 2-2   Looking up prices from product ID codes. When the table range isn't sorted in ascending order, enter False as the last argument in the lookup function formula.

Many people would enter the formula as I have in cell I18: *VLOOKUP(H18,Lookup2,2)*. However, note that when you omit the fourth argument (the range lookup argument), the value is assumed to be *True*. Because the product IDs in the table range *Lookup2* (H11:I15) are not listed in alphabetical order, an incorrect price ($3.50) is returned. If we enter the formula *VLOOKUP(H18,Lookup2,2,False)* in cell I18, the correct price ($5.20) is returned.

You would also use *False* in a formula designed to find an employee's salary using the employee's last name or ID number.

By the way, you can see in Figure 2-2 that we hid columns A-G. To hide columns in Excel 2007, you begin by selecting the columns you want to hide. Click the Home tab on the Ribbon. In the Cells group, click Format, point to Hide & Unhide (under Visibility), and then click Hide Columns.

Suppose that a product's price changes over time. I know the date the product was sold. How can I write a formula to compute the product's price?

Suppose the price of a product depends on the date the product was sold. How can you use a lookup function in a formula that will pick up the correct product price? More specifically, suppose the price of a product is as shown in the following table.

Date sold	Price
January-April 2005	$98
May-August 2005	$105
September-December 2005	$112

We'll write a formula to determine the correct product price for any date on which the product is sold in the year 2005. For variety, we'll use an HLOOKUP function. I've placed the dates when the price changes in the first row of the table range. See the file Datelookup.xlsx, shown in Figure 2-3.

	A	B	C	D
1				
2	Date	1/1/2005	5/1/2005	8/1/2005
3	Price	98	105	112
4				
5			Lookup:B2:D3	
6				
7		Date	Price	
8		1/4/2005	98	
9		5/10/2005	105	
10		9/12/2005	112	
11		5/1/2005	105	

Figure 2-3   Using an HLOOKUP function to determine a price that changes depending on the date it's sold.

I copied from C8 to C9:C11 the formula *HLOOKUP(B8,lookup,2,TRUE)*. This formula tries to match the dates in column B with the first row of the range B2:D3. At any date between 1/1/05 and 4/30/05, the lookup function will stop at 1/1/05 and return the price in B3; for any date between 5/01/05 and 7/31/05, the lookup stops at 5/1/05 and returns the price in C3; and for any date later than 8/01/05, the lookup stops at 8/01/05 and returns the price in D3.

Problems

1. The file Hr.xlsx gives employee ID codes, salaries, and years of experience. Write a formula that takes a given ID code and yields the employee's salary. Write another formula that takes a given ID code and yields the employee's years of experience.

2. The file Assign.xlsx gives the assignment of workers to four groups. The suitability of each worker for each group (on a scale from 0 to 10) is also given. Write a formula that gives the suitability of each worker for the group to which the worker is assigned.

3. You are thinking of advertising Microsoft products on a sports telecast. As you buy more ads, the price of each ad decreases as shown in the following table.

Number of ads	Price per ad
1–5	$12,000
6–10	$11,000
11–20	$10,000
More than 20	$9,000

For example, if you buy 8 ads, you pay $11,000 per ad, but if you buy 14 ads, you pay $10,000 per ad. Write a formula that yields the total cost of purchasing any number of ads.

4. You are thinking of advertising Microsoft products on a popular TV music program. You pay one price for the first group of ads, but as you buy more ads, the price per ad decreases as shown in the following table.

Ad number	Price per ad
1–5	$12,000
6–10	$11,000
11–20	$10,000
20 or higher	$9,000

For example, if you buy 8 ads, you pay $12,000 per ad for the first 5 ads and $11,000 for each of the next 3 ads. If you buy 14 ads, you pay $12,000 for each of the first 5 ads, $11,000 for each of the next 5 ads, and $10,000 for each of the last 4 ads. Write a formula that yields the total cost of purchasing any number of ads. Hint: You will probably need at least three columns in your table range and your formula might involve two lookup functions.

5. The annual rate your bank charges you to borrow money for 1, 5, 10, or 30 years is shown in the following table.

Duration of loan	Annual loan rate
1 year	6%
5 years	7%
10 years	9%
30 years	10%

If you borrow money from the bank for any duration from 1 through 30 years that's not listed in the table, your rate is found by interpolating between the rates given in the table. For example, let's say you borrow money for 15 years. Because 15 years is one quarter of the way between 10 years and 30 years, the annual loan rate would be calculated as follows:

$$\frac{1}{4}(10) + \frac{3}{4}(9) = 9.25\%.$$

Write a formula that will return the annual interest rate on a loan for any period between 1 and 30 years.

6. The distance between any two U.S. cities (excluding cities in Alaska and Hawaii) can be approximated by the formula

$$69 * \sqrt{(lat\,1 - lat\,2)^2 + (long\,1 - long\,2)^2}$$

The file Citydata.xlsx contains the latitude and longitude of selected U.S. cities. Create a table that gives the distance between any two of the listed cities.

7. In the file Pinevalley.xlsx, the first worksheet contains the salaries of several employees at Pine Valley University, the second worksheet contains the age of the employees, and the third worksheet contains the years of experience. Create a fourth worksheet that contains the Salary, Age, and Experience for each employee.

8. The file Lookupmultiplecolumns.xlsx contains information about several sales made at an electronics store. A salesperson's name will be entered in B17. Write an Excel formula that can be copied from C17 to D17:F17 that will extract each salesperson's Radio sales to C17, TV sales to D17, Printer sales to E17, and CD sales to F17.

Chapter 3
The INDEX Function

- I have a list of distances between U.S. cities. How do I write a function that returns the distance between, for example, Seattle and Miami?
- Is there a way I can write a formula that references the entire column containing the distances between each city and Seattle?

Syntax of the INDEX Function

The INDEX function allows you to return the entry in any row and column within an array of numbers. The most commonly used syntax for the INDEX function is:

```
INDEX(Array,Row Number,Column Number)
```

To illustrate, the formula INDEX(A1:D12,2,3) would return the entry in the second row and third column of the array A1:D12. This entry is the one in cell C2.

I have a list of distances between U.S. cities. How do I write a function that returns the distance between, for example, Seattle and Miami?

The file Index.xlsx (see Figure 3-1) contains the distances between eight U.S. cities. The range C10:J17, which contains the distances, is named Distances.

	A	B	C	D	E	F	G	H	I	J
1										
2										
3										
4		Boston-Denver	1991			T Dist to Seattle	15221			
5		Seattle- Miami	3389							
6										
7										
8										
9			Boston	Chicago	Dallas	Denver	LA	Miami	Phoenix	Seattle
10	1	Boston	0	983	1815	1991	3036	1539	2664	2612
11	2	Chicago	983	0	1205	1050	2112	1390	1729	2052
12	3	Dallas	1815	1205	0	801	1425	1332	1027	2404
13	4	Denver	1991	1050	801	0	1174	2100	836	1373
14	5	LA	3036	2112	1425	1174	0	2757	398	1909
15	6	Miami	1539	1390	1332	2100	2757	0	2359	3389
16	7	Phoenix	2664	1729	1027	836	398	2359	0	1482
17	8	Seattle	2612	2052	2404	1373	1909	3389	1482	0

Figure 3-1 You can use the INDEX function to calculate the distance between cities.

Suppose that you want to enter the distance between Boston and Denver in a cell. Because distances from Boston are listed in the first row of the array named Distances, and distances to Denver are listed in the fourth column of the array, the appropriate formula is *INDEX(distances,1,4)*. The results show that Boston and Denver are 1991 miles apart. Similarly, to find the (much longer) distance between Seattle and Miami, you would use the formula *INDEX(distances,6,8)*. Seattle and Miami are 3389 miles apart.

Imagine that the Seattle SuperSonics basketball team is embarking on a road trip in which they play games in Phoenix, Los Angeles, Denver, Dallas, and Chicago. At the conclusion of the road trip, the Sonics return to Seattle. Can we easily compute how many miles they travel on the trip? As you can see in Figure 3-2, we simply list the cities the Sonics visit (8-7-5-4-3-2-8) in the order they are visited, starting and ending in Seattle, and copy from D21 to D26 the formula *INDEX(distances,C21,C22)*. The formula in D21 computes the distance between Seattle and Phoenix (city number 7), the formula in D22 computes the distance between Phoenix and Los Angeles, and so on. The Sonics will travel a total of 7112 miles on their road trip. Just for fun, I used the INDEX function to show that the Miami Heat travel more miles during the NBA season than any other team.

	C	D
19	Road Trip!!	
20	City	Distance
21	8	1482
22	7	398
23	5	1174
24	4	801
25	3	1205
26	2	2052
27	8	
28	Total	7112

Figure 3-2   Distances for a Seattle Sonics road trip

Is there a way I can write a formula that references the entire column containing the distances between each city and Seattle?

The INDEX function makes it easy to reference an entire row or column of an array. If we set the row number to 0, the INDEX function references the listed column. If we set the column number to 0, the INDEX function references the listed row. To illustrate, suppose we want to total the distances from each listed city to Seattle. We could enter either of the following formulas:

```
SUM(INDEX(distances,8,0))
```

```
SUM(INDEX(distances,0,8))
```

The first formula totals the numbers in the eighth row (Row 17) of the Distances array; the second formula totals the numbers in the eighth column (Column J) of the Distances array. In either case, we find the total distance from Seattle to the other cities is 15,221 miles, as you can see in Figure 3-1.

Problems

1. Use the INDEX function to compute the distance between Los Angeles and Phoenix, and the distance between Denver and Miami.

2. Use the INDEX function to compute the total distance from Dallas to the other cities.

3. Mark Cuban and the Dallas Mavericks are embarking on a road trip that takes them to Chicago, Denver, Los Angeles, Phoenix, and Seattle. How many miles will they travel on this road trip?

4. The file Product.xlsx contains monthly sales for six products. Use the INDEX function to compute the sales of Product 2 in March. Use the INDEX function to compute total sales during April.

5. The file Nbadistances.xlsx shows the distances between any pair of NBA arenas. Suppose you begin in Atlanta, visit the arenas in the order listed, and then return to Atlanta. How far would you travel?

Chapter 4
The MATCH Function

- Given monthly sales for several products, how do I write a formula that returns the sales of a product during a specific month? For example, how much of Product 2 did I sell during June?

- Given a list of baseball players' salaries, how do I write a formula that yields the player with the highest salary? How about the player with the fifth-highest salary?

- Given the annual cash flows from an investment project, how do I write a formula that returns the number of years required to pay back the project's initial investment cost?

Suppose you have a worksheet with 5000 rows containing 5000 names. You need to find the name *John Doe*, which you know appears somewhere (and only once) in the list. Wouldn't you like to know a formula that would return the row number at which John Doe is located? The Microsoft Office Excel 2007 MATCH function enables you to find within a given array the first occurrence of a "match" to a given text string or number. You should use the MATCH function instead of a lookup function in situations in which you want the position of a number in a range rather than the value in a particular cell. The syntax of the match function is:

```
Match(lookup value,lookup range,[match type])
```

In the explanation that follows, we'll assume that all cells in the lookup range are located in the same column. In this syntax:

- *Lookup value* is the value you're trying to match in the lookup range.

- *Lookup range* is the range you're examining for a "match" to the lookup value.

- *Match type=1* requires the lookup range to consist of numbers listed in ascending order. The MATCH function then returns the row location in the lookup range (relative to the top of the lookup range) that contains the largest value in the range that is less than or equal to the lookup value.

- *Match type=-1* requires the lookup range to consist of numbers listed in descending order. The MATCH function returns the row location in the lookup range (relative to the top of the lookup range) that contains the last value in the range that is greater than or equal to the lookup value.

- *Match type=0* returns the row location in the lookup range that contains *the first exact* match to the lookup value (we will discuss how to find the second or third match in Chapter 19). When no exact match exists *and match type=0, Excel returns* #N/A. Most MATCH function applications use *match type=0,* but if *match type* is not included, *match type=1* is assumed. Thus, we use Match type 0 when the cell contents of the lookup range is unsorted. This is the situation we usually face.

The file Matchex.xlsx, shown in Figure 4-1, contains three examples of the MATCH function's syntax.

	A	B	C	D	E	F	G
1							
2							
3							
4		Boston			-5		6
5		Chicago			-4		5
6		Dallas			-3		4
7		Denver			-1		3
8		LA			3		-1
9		Miami			4		-3
10		Phoenix			5		-4
11		Seattle			6		-5
12				last number<=0	4	last number>=-4	7
13	Boston	1					
14	Phoenix	7					
15	Pho*	7					

Figure 4-1 Using the MATCH function to locate the position of a value in a range.

In cell B13, the formula *MATCH("Boston",B4:B11,0)* returns 1 because the first row in the range B4:B11 contains the value *Boston.* Text values must be enclosed in quotation marks (""). In cell B14, the formula *MATCH("Phoenix",B4:B11,0)* returns 7 because cell B10 (the seventh cell in B4:B11) is the first cell in the range that matches *"Phoenix."* In cell E12, the formula *MATCH(0,E4:E11,1)* returns 4 because the last number that is less than or equal to 0 in the range E4:E11 is in cell E7 (the fourth cell in the lookup range). In cell G12, the formula *MATCH(-4,G4:G11,-1)* returns 7 because the last number that is greater than or equal to -4 in the range G4:G11 is contained in cell G10 (the seventh cell in the lookup range).

The MATCH function can also work with an inexact match. For example, the formula *MATCH("Pho*",B4:B11,0)* returns 7. The asterisk is treated as a wildcard, which means that Excel searches for the first text string in the range B4:B11 that begins with *Pho.* Incidentally, this same technique can be used with a lookup function. For example, in the price lookup exercise in Chapter 2, "Lookup Functions," the formula *VLOOKUP("x*",lookup2,2)* would return the price of product X212 ($4.80).

If the lookup range is contained in a single row, Excel returns the relative position of the first match in the lookup range, moving from left to right. As shown in the following examples, the MATCH function is often very useful when it is combined with other Excel functions, such as VLOOKUP, INDEX, or MAX.

Given monthly sales for several products, how do I write a formula that returns the sales of a product during a specific month? For example, how much of Product 2 did I sell during June?

The file Productlookup.xlsx (shown in Figure 4-2) lists sales of four NBA bobble-head dolls from January through June. How can we write a formula that computes the sales of a given product during a specific month? The trick is to use one MATCH function to find the row in which the given product is located, and another MATCH function to find the column in which the given month is located. We can then use the INDEX function to return the product sales for the month.

	A	B	C	D	E	F	G
1							
2							
3		January	February	March	April	May	June
4	Shaq	831	685	550	965	842	804
5	Kobe	719	504	965	816	639	814
6	MJ	916	906	851	912	964	710
7	T-Mac	844	509	991	851	742	817
8							
9	Product	Month	Row # of product	Column # of month	Product Sales		
10	Kobe	June	2	6	814		

Figure 4-2   The MATCH function can be used in combination with functions such as INDEX and VLOOKUP.

We have named the range B4:G7, which contains sales data for the dolls, as *Sales*. We enter the product we want to know about in cell A10, and the month in cell B10. In C10, we use the formula *MATCH(A10,A4:A7,0)* to determine which row number in the range *Sales* contains sales figures for the Kobe doll. Then, in cell D10, we use the formula *MATCH(B10,B3:G3,0)* to determine which column number in the range *Sales* contains June sales. Now that we have the row and column numbers that contain the sales figures we want, we can use the formula *INDEX(Sales,C10,D10)* in cell E10 to yield the piece of sales data we want. For more information on the INDEX function, see Chapter 3, "The INDEX Function."

Given a list of baseball players' salaries, how do I write a formula that yields the player with the highest salary? How about the player with the fifth-highest salary?

The file Baseball.xlsx (see Figure 4-3 on the next page) lists the salaries paid to 401 major league baseball players during the 2001 season. The data is not sorted by salary, and we want to write a formula that returns the name of the player with the highest salary as well as the name of the player with the fifth highest salary.

To find the name of the player with the highest salary we proceed as follows:

- ❏ Use the MAX function to determine the value of the highest salary.

- ❏ Use the MATCH function to determine the row that contains the player with the highest salary.

- ❏ Use a VLOOKUP function (keying off the data row containing the player's salary) to look up the player's name.

We have named the range C12:C412, which includes the players' salaries, as *Salaries*. We've named the range used in our VLOOKUP function (range A12:C412) as *Lookup*.

	A	B	C	D
6		name	Alex Rodriguez	dl-Derek Jeter
7			highest	5th highest
8		player position	345	232
9		amount	22000000	12600000
10				
11		name	salary	
12	1	dl-Mo Vaughn	13166667	
13	2	Tim Salmon	5683013	
14	3	Garret Anderson	4500000	
15	4	Darin Erstad	3450000	
16	5	Troy Percival	3400000	
17	6	Ismael Valdes	2500000	
18	7	Pat Rapp	2000000	
19	8	Glenallen Hill	1500000	
20	9	Troy Glaus	1250000	
21	10	Shigetoshi Hasegawa	1150000	
22	11	Scott Spiezio	1125000	
23	12	Orlando Palmeiro	900000	
24	13	Alan Levine	715000	
25	14	Mike Holtz	705000	
26	15	Jorge Fabregas	500000	
27	16	Benji Gil	350000	
28	17	Ben Molina	350000	
29	18	dl-Gary DiSarcina	320000	

Figure 4-3 This example uses the MAX, MATCH, and VLOOKUP functions to find and display the highest value in a list.

In cell C9, we begin by finding the highest player salary ($22 million) with the formula *MAX(Salaries)*. Next, in cell C8, we use the formula *MATCH(C9,Salaries,0)* to determine the "player number" of the player with the highest salary. We use *match type=0* because the salaries are not listed in either ascending or descending order. We find that player number 345 has the highest salary. Finally, in cell C6, we use the function *VLOOKUP(C8,Lookup,2)* to find the player's name in the second column of the lookup range. Not surprisingly, we find that Alex Rodriguez was the highest paid player in 2001.

To find the name of the player with the fifth-highest salary, we need a function that yields the fifth-largest number in an array. The LARGE function does that job. The syntax of the LARGE function is *LARGE(cell range,k)*. When the LARGE function is entered this way, it returns the kth-largest number in a cell range. Thus, the formula *LARGE(salaries,5)* in cell D9 yields the fifth largest salary ($12.6 million). Proceeding as before, we find that Derek Jeter is the player with the fifth-highest salary. (The *dl* before Jeter's name indicates that at the beginning of the season, Jeter was on the disabled list.). The function *SMALL(salaries,5)* would return the fifth-lowest salary.

Given the annual cash flows from an investment project, how do I write a formula that returns the number of years required to pay back the project's initial investment cost?

The file Payback.xlsx, shown in Figure 4-4, shows the projected cash flows for an investment project over the next 15 years. We assume that in Year 1, the project required a cash outflow of $100 million. During Year 1, the project generated a cash inflow of $14 million. We expect cash flows to grow at 10 percent per year. How many years will pass before the project pays back its investment?

The number of years required for a project to pay back an investment is called the *payback period*. In high-tech industries, the payback period is often used to rank investments. (You'll learn in Chapter 7, "Evaluating Investments by Using Net Present Value Criteria," that payback is flawed as a measure of investment quality because it ignores the value of money over time.) For now, let's concentrate on how to determine the payback period for our simple investment model.

	A	B	C	D	E
1	Year 1 cash flow	14			Payback Period
2	Growth	0.1			6
3	Initial Invetsment	-100			
4	Year	Annual Cash flow	Cumulative cash flow		
5	0	-100	-100		
6	1	14	-86		
7	2	15.4	-70.6		
8	3	16.94	-53.66		
9	4	18.634	-35.026		
10	5	20.4974	-14.5286		
11	6	22.54714	8.01854		
12	7	24.801854	32.820394		
13	8	27.2820394	60.1024334		
14	9	30.01024334	90.11267674		
15	10	33.01126767	123.1239444		
16	11	36.31239444	159.4363389		
17	12	39.94363389	199.3799727		
18	13	43.93799727	243.31797		
19	14	48.331797	291.649767		
20	15	53.1649767	344.8147437		

Figure 4-4   Using the MATCH function to calculate an investment's payback period.

To determine the payback period for the project, we proceed as follows:

- ❑   In column B, we compute the cash flows for each year.

- ❑   In column C, we compute the cumulative cash flows for each year.

We use the MATCH function (with *match type=1*) to determine the row number of the first year in which cumulative cash flow is positive. This calculation gives us the payback period.

We gave the cells in B1:B3 the range names listed in A1:A3. Our Year 0 cash flow (−Initial_investment) is entered in cell B5. Our Year 1 cash flow (Year_1_cf) is entered in cell B6. Copying from B7 to B8:B20 the formula *B6*(1+Growth)* computes the cash flow for Years 2 through 15.

To compute the Year 0 cumulative cash flow, we enter the formula *B5* in cell C5. For later years, we calculate cumulative cash flow by using a formula such as *Year t cumulative cash flow=Year t−1 cumulative cash flow+Year t cash flow*. To implement this relationship, simply copy from C6 to C7:C20 the formula *=C5+B6*.

To compute the payback period, we use the MATCH function (with *match type=1*) to compute the last row of the range C5:C20 containing a value less than 0. This calculation will always give us the payback period. For example, if the last row in C5:C20 that contains a value less than 0 is the sixth row in the range, that means the seventh value marks the cumulative cash flow for the first year the project is paid back. Because our first year is Year 0, the payback occurs during Year 6. Therefore, the formula in cell E2, *MATCH(0, C5:C20,1)*, yields the payback period (6 years). If any cash flows after Year 0 were negative, this method would fail because our range of cumulative cash flows would not be listed in ascending order.

Problems

1. Using the distances between U.S. cities given in the file Index.xlsx, write a formula using the MATCH function to determine (based on the names of the cities) the distance between any two of the given cities.

2. The file Matchtype1.xlsx lists in chronological order the dollar amounts of 30 transactions. Write a formula that yields the first transaction for which total volume to date exceeds $10,000.

3. The file Matchthemax.xlsx gives the product ID codes and unit sales for 265 products. Use the MATCH function in a formula that yields the product ID code of the product with the largest unit sales.

4. The file Buslist.xlsx gives the amount of time between bus arrivals (in minutes) at 45th Street and Park Avenue in New York City. Write a formula that, for any arrival time after the first bus, gives the amount of time I have to wait for a bus. For example, if I arrive 12.4 minutes from now, and buses arrive 5 minutes and 21 minutes from now, I wait *21−12.4=8.6* minutes for a bus.

Chapter 5
Text Functions

■ I have a worksheet in which each cell contains a product description, a product ID, and a product price. How can I put all the product descriptions in column A, all the product IDs in column B, and all the prices in column C?

■ Every day, I receive data about total U.S. sales, which is computed in a cell as the sum of East, North, and South regional sales. How can I extract East, North, and South sales to separate cells?

■ At the end of each school semester, my students evaluate my teaching performance on a scale from 1 to 7. I know how many students gave me each possible rating score. How can I easily create a bar graph of my teaching evaluation scores?

When someone sends you data or you download data from the Web, it often isn't formatted the way you want. For example, when downloading sales data, dates and sales amounts might be in the same cell, but you might need them to be in separate cells. How can you manipulate data so that it appears in the format you need? The answer is to become good at using the Microsoft Office Excel 2007 text functions. In this chapter, I'll show you how to use the following Excel text functions to magically manipulate your data so it looks the way you want:

■ LEFT

■ RIGHT

■ MID

■ TRIM

■ LEN

■ FIND

■ SEARCH

■ REPT

■ CONCATENATE

■ REPLACE

- VALUE
- UPPER
- LOWER
- CHAR

Text Function Syntax

The file Reggie.xlsx, shown in Figure 5-1, includes examples of text functions. You'll see how to apply these functions to a specific problem later in the chapter, but let's begin by describing what each of the text functions does. Then we'll combine the functions to perform some fairly complex manipulations of data.

	A	B	C	D
1	Reggie	Miller		
2				
3	Reggie Miller	Left 4	Regg	
4		Right 4	ller	
5		Trim spaces	Reggie Miller	
6		Number of characters	15	
7		Number of characters in trimmed res	13	
8		5 characters starting at space 2	eggie	
9		Find first space	7	
10		Find first r (case sensitive)	15	
11		Find first r (not case sensitive)	1	
12		Combining first and Last Name	Reggie Miller	Reggie Miller
13		Replace g with n	Rennie Miller	
14	Text 31	Number 31		
15	31	31		

Figure 5-1   Examples of text functions

The LEFT Function

The function *LEFT(text,k)* returns the first *k* characters in a text string. For example, cell C3 contains the formula *LEFT(A3,4)*. Excel returns *Regg*.

The RIGHT Function

The function *RIGHT(text,k)* returns the last *k* characters in a text string. For example, in cell C4, the formula *RIGHT(A3,4)* returns *ller*.

The MID Function

The function *MID(text,k,m)* begins at character *k* of a text string and returns the next *m* characters. For example, the formula *MID(A3,2,5)* in cell C8 returns characters 2–6 from cell A3, the result being *eggie*.

The TRIM Function

The function *TRIM(text)* removes all spaces from a text string except for single spaces between words. For example, in cell *C5* the formula *TRIM(A3)* eliminates two of the three spaces between Reggie and Miller and yields *Reggie Miller*. The TRIM function also removes spaces at the beginning and end of the cell.

The LEN Function

The function *LEN(text)* returns the number of characters in a text string (including spaces). For example, in cell *C6*, the formula *LEN(A3)* returns 15 because cell A3 contains 15 characters. In cell C7, the formula *LEN(C5)* returns 13. Because the trimmed result in cell C5 has two spaces removed, cell C5 contains two less characters than the original text in A3.

The FIND and SEARCH Functions

The function *FIND(text to find,actual text,k)* returns the location at or after character *k* of the first character of *text to find* in the *actual text*. FIND is case sensitive. SEARCH has the same syntax as FIND, but it is not case sensitive. For example, if we enter *FIND("r",A3,1)* in cell C10, Excel returns 15, the location of the first lowercase *r* in the text string *Reggie Miller*. (The uppercase *R* is ignored because FIND is case sensitive.) Entering *SEARCH("r",A3,1)* in cell C11 returns 1 because SEARCH matches *r* to either a lowercase character or an uppercase character. Entering *FIND(" ",A3,1)* in cell C9 returns 7 because the first space in the string *Reggie Miller* is the seventh character.

The REPT Function

The REPT function allows you to repeat a text string a desired number of times. The syntax is *REPT(text,number of times)*. For example *REPT("|",3)* will produce the output | | |.

The CONCATENATE and & Functions

The function *CONCATENATE(text1,text2, . . .,text30)* can be used to join up to 30 text strings into a single string. The & operator can be used instead of CONCATENATE. For example, entering in cell C12 the formula *A1&" "&B1* returns *Reggie Miller*. Entering in cell D12 the formula *CONCATENATE(A1," ",B1)* yields the same result.

The REPLACE Function

The function *REPLACE(old text,k,m,new text)* begins at character *k* of *old text* and replaces the next *m* characters with *new text*. For example, in cell C13, the formula *REPLACE(A3,3,2,"nn")* replaces the third and fourth characters (*gg*) in cell A3 with *nn*. This formula yields *Rennie Miller*.

The VALUE Function

The function *VALUE(text)* converts a text string that represents a number to a number. For example, entering in cell B15 the formula *VALUE(A15)* converts the text string *31* in cell A15 to the numerical value 31. You can identify the value 31 in cell A15 as text because it is left-justified. Similarly, you can identify the value 31 in cell B15 as a number because it is right-justified.

The UPPER and LOWER Functions

The function *UPPER(text)* will change the text to all uppercase. Thus if cell A1 contains jan then *UPPER(A1)* will yield JAN. Similarly the function *LOWER(text)* will change text to lowercase. Thus if A1 contains JAN then *LOWER(A1)* will yield jan.

The CHAR Function

The function *CHAR(number)* will yield (for a number between 1 and 255) the ASCII character with that number. For example, *CHAR(65)* yields A, *CHAR(66)* yields B, and so on.

Text Functions in Action

You can see the power of text functions by using them to solve some actual problems that were sent to me by former students working for Fortune 500 corporations. Often, the key to solving problems is to combine multiple text functions into a single formula.

I have a worksheet in which each cell contains a product description, a product ID, and a product price. How can I put all the product descriptions in column A, all the product IDs in column B, and all the prices in column C?

In this example, the product ID is always defined by the first 12 characters, and the price is always indicated in the last 8 characters (with two spaces following the end of each price). Our solution, contained in the file Lenora.xlsx and shown in Figure 5-2, uses the LEFT, RIGHT, MID, VALUE, TRIM, and LEN functions.

It's always a good idea to begin by trimming excess spaces, which we do by copying from B4 to B5:B12 the formula *TRIM(A4)*. The only excess spaces in column A turn out to be the two spaces inserted after each price. To see this put the cursor in cell A4 and select F2 to edit the cell. If you move to the end of the cell, you will see two blank spaces. The results of using the TRIM function are shown in Figure 5-2. To prove that the TRIM function removed the two extra spaces at the end of cell A4, you can use the formulas =*LEN(A4)* and =*LEN(B4)* to show that cell A4 contains 52 characters and cell B4 contains 50 characters.

	A	B
1	length of A4	length of B4
2	52	50
3	Untrimmed	Trimmed
4	32592100AFES CONTROLLERPENTIUM/100,(2)1GB H 3	32592100AFES CONTROLLERPENTIUM/100,(2)1GB H 304
5	32592100JCP9 DESKTOP UNIT 225.00	32592100JCP9 DESKTOP UNIT 225.00
6	32592700899O DESKTOP VINDOVS NT 4.0 SERVER 23	325927008990 DESKTOP VINDOVS NT 4.0 SERVER 232.
7	325926008990 DESKTOP VINDOVS NT 4.0 VKST 232.0	325926008990 DESKTOP VINDOVS NT 4.0 VKST 232.00
8	325921008990 DESKTOP, DOS OS 232.00	325921008990 DESKTOP, DOS OS 232.00
9	325922008990 DESKTOP, VINDOVS DESKTOP OS 232.	325922008990 DESKTOP, VINDOVS DESKTOP OS 232.0
10	325925008990 DESKTOP, VINDOVS NT OS 232.00	325925008990 DESKTOP, VINDOVS NT OS 232.00
11	325930008990 MINITOVER, NO OS 232.00	325930008990 MINITOVER, NO OS 232.00
12	32593000KEYY MINI TOVER 232.00	32593000KEYY MINI TOVER 232.00

Figure 5-2   Using the TRIM function to trim away excess spaces.

To capture the product ID, we need to extract the 12 leftmost characters from column B. We copy from C4 to C5:C12 the formula *LEFT(B4,12)*. This formula extracts the 12 leftmost characters from the text in cell B4 and the following cells, yielding the product ID, as you can see Figure 5-3.

	B	C	D	E	F
1	length of B4				
2	50				
3	Trimmed	Product ID	Price	Product Description	Concatenation
4	32592100AFES CONTROLLERPENTIUM/100,(2)1GB H 304.	32592100AFES	304	CONTROLLERPENTIUM/100,(2)1GB H	32592100AFES CONTROLLERPENTIUM/100,(2)1GB H 304
5	32592100JCP9 DESKTOP UNIT 225.00	32592100JCP9	225	DESKTOP UNIT	32592100JCP9 DESKTOP UNIT 225
6	325927008990 DESKTOP VINDOVS NT 4.0 SERVER 232.00	325927008990	232	DESKTOP VINDOVS NT 4.0 SERVER	325927008990 DESKTOP VINDOVS NT 4.0 SERVER 232
7	325926008990 DESKTOP VINDOVS NT 4.0 VKST 232.00	325926008990	232	DESKTOP VINDOVS NT 4.0 VKST	325926008990 DESKTOP VINDOVS NT 4.0 VKST 232
8	325921008990 DESKTOP, DOS OS 232.00	325921008990	232	DESKTOP, DOS OS	325921008990 DESKTOP, DOS OS 232
9	325922008990 DESKTOP, VINDOVS DESKTOP OS 232.00	325922008990	232	DESKTOP, VINDOVS DESKTOP OS	325922008990 DESKTOP, VINDOVS DESKTOP OS 232
10	325925008990 DESKTOP, VINDOVS NT OS 232.00	325925008990	232	DESKTOP, VINDOVS NT OS	325925008990 DESKTOP, VINDOVS NT OS 232
11	325930008990 MINITOVER, NO OS 232.00	325930008990	232	MINITOVER, NO OS	325930008990 MINITOVER, NO OS 232
12	32593000KEYY MINI TOVER 232.00	32593000KEYY	232	MINI TOVER	32593000KEYY MINI TOVER 232

Figure 5-3   Using text functions to extract the product ID, price, and product description from a text string.

To extract the product price, we note that the price occupies the last six digits of each cell, so we need to extract the rightmost six characters from each cell. I copy from cell D4 to D5:D12 the formula *VALUE(RIGHT(B4,6)*. I use the VALUE function to turn the extracted text into a numerical value. Without converting the text to a numerical value, you couldn't perform mathematical operations on the prices.

Extracting the product description is much trickier. By examining the data, we can see that if we begin our extraction with the 13th character and continue until we are 6 characters from the end of the cell, we can get the data we want. Copying from E4 to E5:E12 the formula *MID(B4,13,LEN(B4)−6−12)* does the job. *LEN(B4)* returns the total number of characters in the trimmed text. This formula (MID for Middle) begins with the 13th character and then extracts the number of characters equal to the total number less the 12 characters at the beginning (the product ID) and the 6 characters at the end (price). This subtraction leaves only the product description!

Now suppose we are given the data with the product ID in column C, the price in column D, and the product description in column E. Can we put these values together to recover our original text?

Text can easily be combined by using the CONCATENATE function. Copying from F4 to F5:F12 the formula *CONCATENATE(C4,E4,D4))* recovers our original (trimmed) text, which you can see in Figure 5-3.

The concatenation formula starts with the product ID in cell C4. Next we add the product description from cell E4. Finally, we add the price from cell D4. We have now recovered the entire text describing each computer! Concatenation can also be performed by using the & sign. We could recover the original product ID, product description, and price in a single cell with the formula *C4&E4&D4*. Note that cell E4 contains a space before the product description and a space after the product description. If cell E4 did not contain these spaces then the formula *C4&" "&E4&" "&D4* would have inserted the necessary spaces. Note that the space between each pair of quotes results in the insertion of a space.

If the product IDs did not always contain 12 characters, this method of extracting the information would fail. We could, however, extract the product IDs by using the FIND function to discover the location of the first space. Then we could obtain the product ID by using the LEFT function to extract all characters to the left of the first space. The example in the next section will show how this approach works.

If the price did not always contain precisely six characters, extracting the price would be a little tricky. See Problem 15 for an example of how to extract the last word in a text string.

Every day I receive data about total U.S. sales, which is computed in a cell as the sum of East, North, and South regional sales. How can I extract East, North, and South sales to separate cells?

This problem was sent to me by an employee in the Microsoft finance department. She received a worksheet each day containing formulas such as *=50+200+400, =5+124+1025*, and so on. She needed to extract each number into a cell in its own column. For example, she wanted to extract the first number (East sales) in each cell to column C, the second number (North sales) to column D, and the third number (South sales) to column E. What makes this problem challenging is that we don't know the exact location of the character at which the second and third numbers start in each cell. In cell A3, the North sales begin with the fourth character. In cell A4, the North sales begin with the third character. The data we're using in this example is in the file Salesstripping.xlsx, shown in Figure 5-4. We can identify the locations of the different regions' sales as follows:

- ❏ East sales are represented by every character to the left of the first plus sign (+).

- ❏ North sales are represented by every character between the first and second plus signs.

- ❏ South sales are represented by every character to right of the second plus sign.

By combining the FIND, LEFT, LEN, and MID functions, we can easily solve this problem as follows:

- ❏ Use the Edit, Replace command to replace each equal sign (=) with a space. To remove the equal signs, select the range A3:A6. Then on the Home tab in the Editing group, click Find & Select, and then click Replace. In the Find What field, enter an equal sign (=) and leave Replace With blank. Then click Replace All. This converts each formula into text by replacing the = sign by a space.

❑ Use the FIND function to locate the two plus signs in each cell.

	A	B	C	D	E	F	G
1	Extracting Sales in Three Regions						
2	East+North+South	First +	Second +	East	North	Total Length	South
3	10+300+400	3	7	10	300	10	400
4	4+36.2+800	2	7	4	36.2	10	800
5	3+23+4005	2	5	3	23	9	4005
6	18+1+57.31	3	5	18	1	10	57.31

Figure 5-4   Extracting East, North, and South sales with a combination of the FIND, LEFT, LEN, and MID functions.

We begin by finding the location of the first plus sign for each piece of data. By copying from B3 to B4:B6 the formula *FIND("+",A3,1)*, we can locate the first plus sign for each data point. To find the second plus sign, we begin *one character* after the first plus sign, copying from C3 to C4:C6 the formula *FIND("+",A3,B3+1)*.

To find East sales, we use the LEFT function to extract all the characters to the left of the first plus sign, copying from D3 to D4:D6 the formula *LEFT(A3,B3-1)*. To extract the North sales, we use the MID function to extract all the characters between the two plus signs. We begin one character after the first plus sign and extract the number of characters equal to *(Position of 2nd plus sign)−(Position of 1st plus sign) − 1*. If you leave out the −1, you'll get the second + sign. (Go ahead and check this.) So, to get the North sales, we copy from E3 to E4:E6 the formula *MID(A3,B3+1,C3−B3−1)*.

To extract South sales, we use the RIGHT function to extract all the characters to the right of the second plus sign. South sales will have the number of characters equal to *(Total characters in cell) − (Position of 2nd plus sign)*. We compute the total number of characters in each cell by copying from F3 to F4:F6 the formula *LEN(A3)*. Finally, we obtain South sales by copying from G3 to G4:G6 the formula *RIGHT(A3,F3-C3)*.

Extracting Data by Using the Text To Columns Wizard

There is an easy way to extract East, North, and South sales (and data similar to this example) without using text functions. Simply select cells A3:A6, and then on the Data tab of the Ribbon, click Text to Columns. Then select Delimited, click Next, and fill in the dialog box as shown in Figure 5-5 on the next page.

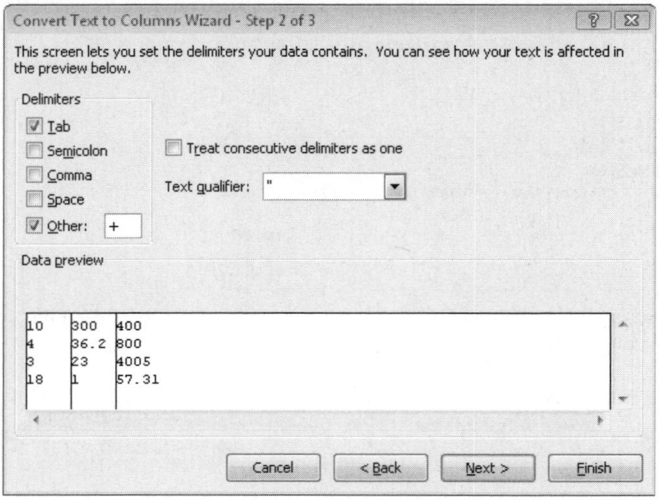

Figure 5-5 Text To Columns Wizard dialog box

Entering the plus sign in the Delimiters area directs Excel to separate each cell into columns, breaking at each occurrence of the plus sign. Note that there are options given for breaking data at tabs, semicolons, commas, or spaces. Now click Next, select the upper-left corner of your destination range (we chose cell A8), and click Finish. The result is shown in Figure 5-6.

	A	B	C
8	10	300	400
9	4	36.2	800
10	3	23	4005
11	18	1	57.31
12			
13	Results of Data Text to Columns		

Figure 5-6 Result of Text To Columns Wizard

At the end of each school semester, my students evaluate my teaching performance on a scale from 1 to 7. I know how many students gave me each possible rating score. How can I easily create a bar graph of my teaching evaluation scores?

The file Repeatedhisto.xlsx contains my teaching evaluation scores (on a scale from 1 through 7). Two people gave me scores of 1, three people gave me scores of 2, and so on. Using the REPT function we can easily create a graph to summarize this data. Simply copy from D4 to D5:D10 the formula =REPT("|",C4). This formula places in column D as many "|" as the entry in column C. Figure 5-7 makes clear the preponderance of good scores (6s and 7s) and the relative rarity of poor scores (1s and 2s). Repeating a character such as | enables us to easily mimic a bar graph or histogram. See Chapter 36, "Summarizing Data with Histograms," for further discussion of how to create histograms with Excel.

	B	C	D
3	Score	Frequency	
4	1	2	||
5	2	3	|||
6	3	6	||||||
7	4	7	|||||||
8	5	9	|||||||||
9	6	33	|||||||||||||||||||||||||||||||||
10	7	28	||||||||||||||||||||||||||||

Figure 5-7 Using the REPT function to create a frequency graph.

Problems

1. Cells B2:B5 of the workbook Showbiz.xlsx contain the fictitious addresses of some of our favorite people. Use text functions to extract each person's name to one column and each person's street address to another.

2. The workbook IDprice.xlsx contains the product ID and prices for various products. Use text functions to put the product IDs and prices in separate columns. Then use the Text To Columns command on the Data tab of the Ribbon to accomplish the same goal.

3. The workbook Quarterlygnpdata.xlsx contains quarterly GNP data for the United States (in billions of 1996 dollars). Extract this data to three separate columns, where the first column contains the year, the second column contains the quarter number, and the third column contains the GNP value.

4. The file Textstylesdata.xlsx contains information about the style, color, and size for a variety of shirts. For example, the first shirt is style 100 (indicated by digits between the colon and the hyphen). Its color is 65, and its size is L. Use text functions to extract the style, color, and size of each shirt.

5. The file Emailproblem.xlsx gives first and last names of several new Microsoft employees. To create an e-mail address for each employee, we follow the first letter of their first name by their last name and add @microsoft.com to the end. Use text functions to efficiently create the e-mail addresses.

6. The file Lineupdata.xlsx gives the number of minutes played by five player combinations (lineups). (Lineup 1 played 10.4 minutes, and so on.) Use text functions to put this data into a form suitable for numerical calculations; for example, transform 10.4m into the number 10.4.

7. The file Reversenames.xlsx gives the first names, middle names or initials, and last names of several people. Transform these names so that the last name appears first, followed by a comma, followed by the first and middle names. For example, transform Gregory William Winston into Winston, Gregory William.

8. The file Incomefrequency.xlsx contains the distribution of starting salaries for M.B.A. graduates of Faber College. Summarize this data by creating a frequency graph.

9. Recall that *CHAR(65)* yields the letter A, *CHAR(66)* yields the letter B, and so on. Use these facts to efficiently populate cells B1:B26 with the sequence A, B, C, and so on through Z.

10. The file Capitalizefirstletter.xlsx contains various song titles or phrases such as "The rain in Spain falls mainly in the plain." Ensure that the first letter of each song title is capitalized.

11. The file Ageofmachine.xlsx contains data in the following form:

    S/N: 160768, vib roller,84" smooth drum,canopy Auction: 6/2–4/2005 in Montgomery, Alabama

    Each row refers to the purchase of a machine. Determine the year that each machine was purchased.

12. When downloading corporate data from the Security and Exchange Commission's EDGAR site, you often obtain data for a company that looks something like this:

    Cash and Cash Equivalents $31,848 $ 31,881

    How would you efficiently extract the Cash and Cash Equivalent for each company?

13. The file Lookuptwocolumns.xlsx gives the model, year, and price for each of a series of cars. Set up formulas that enable you to enter the model and year of a car, and return its car price.

14. The file Moviedata.xlsx contains the names of several movies followed by the number of copies of the movie DVD purchased by a local video store. Extract the title of each movie from this data.

15. The file Moviedata.xlsx contains the names of several movies followed by the number of copies of the movie DVD purchased by a local video store. For each movie extract the number of copies purchased from this data. Hint: You will probably want to use the SUBSTITUTE function. The syntax of the Substitute function is *SUBSTITUTE(text,old_text, new_text,[instance_num])*. If instance *num* is omitted, then every occurrence of old text in text is replaced by new text. If instance *num* is given, then only that occurrence of old text is replaced by new text. For example, *SUBSTITUTE(A4,1,2)* would replace each 1 in cell A4 with a 2, but *SUBSTITUTE(A4,1,2,3)* would only replace the third occurrence of a 1 in cell A4 with a 2.

Chapter 6
Dates and Date Functions

- When I enter dates into Excel, I often see a number such as 37625 rather than a date such as 1/4/2003. What does this number mean, and how do I change it to a normal date?

- Can I use a formula to automatically display today's date?

- How do I determine a date that is 50 workdays after another date? What if I want to exclude holidays?

- How do I determine the number of workdays between two dates?

- I have 500 different dates entered in an Excel worksheet. How do I write formulas can I use to extract from each date the month, year, day of the month, and day of the week?

- My business has purchased and sold machines. For some, I have the date the machine was purchased and the date the machine was sold. Can I easily determine how many months we kept each machine?

To illustrate the most commonly used month-day-year formats in Microsoft Office Excel 2007, suppose today is January 4, 2004. We could enter this date as any of the following:

- 1/4/2004

- 4-Jan-2004

- January 4, 2004

- 1/4/04

If you enter only two digits to represent a year, and the digits are 30 or higher, Excel assumes the digits represent years in the twenty first century; if the digits are lower than 30, Excel assumes they represent years in the twentieth century. For example, 1/1/29 is treated as January 1, 2029, but 1/1/30 is treated as January 1, 1930. Each year, the year treated as dates in the twenty first century increases by one.

If you want to walk through the explanations for the problems in this chapter in Excel, open the file Dates.xlsx.

When I enter dates into Excel, I often see a number such as 37625 rather than a date such as 1/4/2003. What does this number mean, and how do I change it to a normal date?

The way Excel treats calendar dates is sometimes confusing to the novice. The key is understanding that Excel can display a date in a variety of month-day-year formats, or it can display a date in *serial format*. A date in serial format, such as 37625, is simply a positive integer that represents the number of days between the given date and January 1, 1900. Both the current date and January 1, 1900 are included in the count. For example, Excel displays January 3, 1900, in serial format as the number 3, which means there are three days between January 1, 1900, and January 3, 1900 (including both days).

> **Note**   Excel assumes that 1900 was a leap year containing 366 days. In reality, 1900 contained only 365 days.

Figure 6-1 shows the worksheet named *Serial Format* in the file Dates.xlsx. Suppose you are given the dates shown in cells D5:D14 in serial format. For example, the value 37622 in cell D5 indicates a date that is 37,622 days after January 1, 1900 (including both January 1, 1900, and the current day). To display these dates in month-day-year format, copy them to E5:E14. Select the cell range E5:E14, right-click the selection, and choose Format Cells. Now select the date format you want from the list shown in Figure 6-2. The dates in E5:E14 will be displayed in date format, as you can see in Figure 6-1. If you want to format dates in the serial number format, select E5:E14, right-click the selection, and choose Format Cells General.

	D	E
4	Dates	Reformatted
5	37622	1/1/2003
6	37623	1/2/2003
7	37624	1/3/2003
8	37625	1/4/2003
9	37626	1/5/2003
10	37627	1/6/2003
11	37628	1/7/2003
12	37629	1/8/2003
13	37630	1/9/2003
14	37631	1/10/2003

Figure 6-1   Use the Format Cells command to change dates from serial number format to month-day-year format.

Simply changing the date format of a cell to General will yield the date in serial format. Another way to obtain the date in serial format is to use the DATEVALUE function, and enclose the date in quotation marks. For example, in the *Date Format* worksheet of file Dates.xlsx, cell I5 contains the formula *DATEVALUE("1/4/2003")*. Excel yields 37625, which is the serial format for January 4, 2003.

Can I use a formula to automatically display today's date?

Displaying today's date with a formula is easy, as you can see by looking at cell C13 of the *Date Format* worksheet shown in Figure 6-3. Entering the *TODAY()* function in a cell will display today's date. Of course, whenever you open the workbook, the cell displays the current date, but if you update a worksheet every day and want to display the current date, use *TODAY()*.

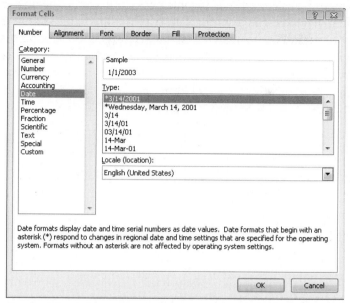

Figure 6-2   Reformatting a serial number to month-day-year format.

	B	C	D	E	F	G	H	I
							Putting date	Serial
4			Year	Month	Day	Day of Week	together	Number
5	1/4/2003	1/4/2003	2003	1	4	7	1/4/2003	37625
6	2/1/1901	2/1/1901	1901	2	1	6	2/1/1901	398
7	4-Jan-2003	4-Jan-03	2003	1	4	7	1/4/2003	
8	January 4, 2003	4-Jan-03	2003	1	4	7	1/4/2003	
9	1/4/03	4-Jan-03	2003	1	4	7	1/4/2003	
10		3-Jan-01	1900	1	0	7	1/0/1900	3
11								
12								
13	Today's date	3/6/2007	50 workdays from start	excluding holidays				
14	Start date	1/3/2003	3/14/2003	3/17/2003				
15	Later date	8/4/2003						
16					Holidays			
17	Workdays between (excluding holidays)	150			7/4/2003			
18	Workdays between (excluding holid	152			1/20/2003			

Figure 6-3   You can use the DATEVALUE function to format a date in serial format.

How do I determine a date that is 50 workdays after another date? What if I want to exclude U.S. holidays?

The function *WORKDAY(start_date,#days,[holidays])* displays the date that is the number of workdays indicated by *#days* (a workday is a nonweekend day) after a given start date. *Holidays* is an optional argument for the function that allows you to exclude from the calculation any dates that are listed in a cell range. Thus, entering the formula *WORKDAY(C14,50)* in cell D14 of the *Date Format* worksheet tells us that 3/14/2003 is 50 workdays after 01/03/2003. If we believe that the only two holidays that matter are

Martin Luther King Day and Independence Day, we can change the formula to *WORK-DAY(C14,50,F17:F18)*. With this addition, Excel does not count 01/20/2003 in its calculations, making 03/17/2003 the 50th workday after 01/03/2003. We note that instead of referring to the holidays in other cells, they may be directly entered in the WORKDAY formula with the serial number of each holiday enclosed in { }. For example, *WORK-DAY(38500,10,{38600,38680,38711})* would find the tenth workday after the date with serial number 38500, ignoring Labor Day, Thanksgiving, and Christmas of 2005.

How do I determine the number of workdays between two dates?

The key to solving this problem is to use the NETWORKDAYS function. The syntax for this function is *NETWORKDAYS(start_date,end_date,[holidays])*, where *holidays* is an optional argument identifying a cell range that lists the dates you want to count as holidays. The NETWORKDAYS function returns the number of working days between *start_date* and *end_date* excluding weekends and any listed holidays. As an illustration of the NETWORKDAYS function, look at cell C18 in the *Date Format* worksheet, which contains the formula *NETWORKDAYS(C14,C15)*. This formula yields the number of working days between 1/3/2003 and 8/4/2003, which is 152. The formula *NETWORK-DAYS(C14,C15,F17:F18)* in cell C17 yields the number of workdays between 1/3/2003 and 8/4/ 2003 excluding Martin Luther King Day and Independence Day. The answer is 152−2=150.

I have 500 different dates entered in an Excel worksheet. How do I write formulas that will extract from each date the month, year, day of the month, and day of the week?

The *Date Format* worksheet (see Figure 6-3) lists several dates in the cell range C5:C10. In C5 and C7:C9, I've used four different formats to display January 4, 2003. In columns D:G, I've extracted the year, month, day of the month, and day of the week for each date. By copying from D5 to D6:D10 the formula *YEAR(B5)*, we extract the year for each date. By copying from E5 to E6:E10 the formula *MONTH(B5)*, we extract the month (1=January, 2=February, and so on) portion of each date. By copying from F5 to F6:F10 the formula *DAY(B5)*, we extract the day of the month for each date. Finally, by copying from G5 to G6:G10 the formula *WEEKDAY(B5,1)*, we extract the day of the week for each date.

When the last argument of the Weekday function is 1, then 1=Sunday, 2=Monday, and so on. When the last argument is 2, then 1=Monday, 2=Tuesday, and so on. When the last argument is 3, then 0=Monday, 1=Tuesday, and so on.

Suppose you are given the year, month, and day of the month for a date. Is there an easy way to recover the actual date? The DATE function, whose arguments are *DATE(year,month,day)*, will return the date with the given year, month, and day of the month. In the *Date Format* worksheet, copying from cell H5 to cells H6:H10 the formula *DATE(D5,E5,F5)* recovers the dates we started with.

My business has purchased and sold machines. For some, I have the date the machine was purchased and the date the machine was sold. Can I easily determine how many months we kept each machine?

The DATEDIF function can easily determine the number of complete years, months, or days between two dates. In file Datedif.xlsx (see Figure 6-4), we see that a machine was bought on 10/15/2006 and will be sold on 4/10/2008. How many complete years, months, or days was the machine kept? The syntax of the DATEDIF function is *DATEDIF(startdate,enddate,time unit)*. If unit is written as "y," we get number of complete years between the start and end dates; if unit is written as "m," we get the number of complete months between the start and end dates; if unit is written as "d," we get the number of complete days between the start and end dates. Thus, entering *DATEDIF(D4,D5,"y")* in cell D6 shows that the machine was kept for one full year. Entering the formula *DATEDIF(D4,D5,"m")* in cell D7 shows the machine was kept for 17 complete months. Entering the formula *DATEDIF(D4,D5,"d")* in cell D7 shows the machine was kept for 543 complete days.

	C	D
4	bought	10/15/2006
5	sold	4/10/2008
6	years	1
7	months	17
8	days	543

Figure 6-4   Using the DATEDIF function.

Problems

1. What is the serial format for January 25, 2006?

2. What is the serial format for February 14, 1950?

3. To what actual date does a serial format of 4526 correspond?

4. To what actual date does a serial format of 45000 correspond?

5. Determine the day that occurs 74 workdays after today's date (including holidays).

6. Determine the day that occurs 74 workdays after today's date (including holidays but excluding the current year's Christmas, New Year's Day, and Independence Day).

7. How many workdays (including holidays) are there between July 10, 2005, and August 15, 2006?

8. How many workdays (including holidays but excluding Christmas, New Year's Day, and Independence Day) are there between July 10, 2005, and August 15, 2006?

Note   The file Datep.xlsx contains several hundred dates. Use this file for the next set of problems.

9. Determine the month, year, day of the month, and day of the week for each date.

10. Express each date in serial format.

11. A project will begin on December 4, 2005. The project consists of three activities: Activities 1, 2, and 3. Activity 2 can start the day after Activity 1 finishes. Activity 3 can start the day after Activity 2 finishes. Set up a worksheet that will accept as inputs the duration (in days) of the three activities and output both the month and year during which each activity is completed.

12. We bought a stock on July 29, 2005, and we are going to sell it on December 30, 2005. The stock exchange will be closed on Labor Day, Christmas, and Thanksgiving. Create a list of dates the stock market will be open during the time we own the stock.

13. The file Machinedates.xlsx contains dates on which several machines were bought and sold. Determine how many months and years each machine was kept.

14. Given any date, find a way to have Excel compute the day of the week of the first day of the date's month.

15. Given any date, find a way to have Excel compute the last day of the date's month. Hint: DATE(2005,13,1), surprisingly, returns 1/1/2006.

Chapter 7

Evaluating Investments by Using Net Present Value Criteria

- What is net present value (NPV)?
- How do I use the Excel NPV function?
- How can I compute NPV when cash flows are received at the beginning of a year or in the middle of a year?
- How can I compute NPV when cash flows are received at irregular intervals?

Consider the following two investments, whose cash flows are listed in the file NPV.xlsx and shown in Figure 7-1 on the next page.

- Investment 1 requires a cash outflow of $10,000 today and $14,000 two years from now. One year from now, this investment will yield $24,000.
- Investment 2 requires a cash outflow of $6,000 today and $1,000 two years from now. One year from now, this investment will yield $8,000.

Which is the better investment? Investment 1 yields total cash flow of $0, whereas Investment 2 yields a total cash flow of $1,000. At first glance, Investment 2 appears to be better. But wait a minute. Most of the cash outflow for Investment 1 occurs two years from now, while most of the cash outflow for Investment 2 occurs today. Spending $1 two years from now doesn't seem as costly as spending $1 today, so maybe Investment 1 is better than it first appears. To determine which investment is better, we need to compare the values of cash flows received at different points in time. That's where the concept of net present value proves useful.

	A	B	C	D	E	F
1						
2						
3		r	0.2			
4	NPV	Time	0	1	2	Total cf
5	277.7778	Investment 1 Cash flow	-10000	24000	-14000	0
6	-27.7778	Investment 2 Cash Flow	-6000	8000	-1000	1000
7		Present V alue Inv 1	-10000	20000	-9722.22	
8		Present Value Inv 2	-6000	6666.667	-694.444	
9						
10		Present Value beginning of Year				
11		Investment 1	$277.78	$277.78		
12		Investment 2	($27.78)	($27.78)		
13		Present Value End of Year				
14		Investment 1	$231.48			
15		Investment 2	($23.15)			
16		Present Value Middle of year				
17		Investment 1	$253.58			
18		Investment 2	($25.36)			

Figure 7-1   To determine which investment is better, we need to calculate net present value.

What is net present value?

The net present value (NPV) of a stream of cash flow received at different points in time is simply the value *measured in today's dollars*. Suppose we have $1 today and we invest this dollar at an annual interest rate of *r* percent. This dollar will grow to $1+r$ dollars in the first year, $(1+r)^2$ dollars in two years, and so on. We can say in some sense that $1 today equals $\$(1+r)$ a year from now and $\$(1+r)^2$ two years from now. In general, we can say that $1 today is equal to $\$(1+r)^n$ *n* years from now. As an equation, we can express this calculation as follows:

$1 now=$\$(1+r)^n$ received n years from now

If we divide both sides of this equation by $(1+r)^n$, we get the following important result:

$1/(1+r)^n$ now=$1 received n years from now

This result tells us how to compute (in today's dollars) the NPV of any sequence of cash flows. You can convert any cash flow to today's dollars by multiplying the cash flow received *n* years from now (*n* can be a fraction) by $1/(1+r)^n$.

You then add up the value of the cash flows (in today's dollars) to find the investment's NPV. Let's assume *r* is equal to 0.2. We could calculate the NPV for the two investments we're considering as follows:

$$Investment1NPV = -10,000 + \frac{24,000}{(1+0.20)^1} + \frac{-14,000}{(1+0.20)^2} = \$277.78$$

$$Investment2NPV = -6,000 + \frac{8,000}{(1+0.20)^1} + \frac{-1,000}{(1+0.20)^2} = \$-27.78$$

On the basis of NPV, Investment 1 is superior to Investment 2. Although total cash flow for Investment 2 exceeds total cash flow for Investment 1, Investment 1 has a better NPV because a greater proportion of Investment 1's negative cash flow comes later and the NPV criterion gives less weight to cash flows that come later. If we use a value of .02 for r, Investment 2 has a larger NPV because when r is very small, later cash flows are not discounted as much and NPV returns results similar to those derived by ranking investments according to total cash flow.

> **Note**   I randomly chose the interest rate $r=0.2$, skirting the issue of how to determine an appropriate value of r. You would need to study finance for at least a year to understand the issues involved in determining an appropriate value for r. The appropriate value of r used to compute NPV is often called the company's cost of capital. Suffice it to say that most U.S. companies use an annual cost of capital between 0.1 (10 percent) and 0.2 (20 percent). If the annual interest rate is chosen according to accepted finance practices, projects with NPV>0 increase the value of a company, projects with NPV<0 decrease the value of a company, and projects with NPV=0 keep the value of a company unchanged. A company should (if it had unlimited investment capital) invest in every available investment having positive NPV.

To determine the NPV of Investment 1 in Excel, I first assigned the range name $r\_$ to the interest rate (located in cell C3). I then copied the Time 0 cash flow from C5 to C7. I determined the NPV for Investment 1's Year 1 and Year 2 cash flows by copying from D7 to E7 the formula $D5/(1+r\_)\wedge D\$4$. The caret symbol (^), located over the number 6 on the keyboard, raises a number to a power. In cell A5, I computed the NPV of Investment 1 by adding the NPV of each year's cash flow with the formula $SUM(C7:E7)$. To determine the NPV for Investment 2, I copied the formulas from C7:E7 to C8:E8 and from A5 to A6.

How do I use the Excel NPV function?

The Excel NPV function uses the syntax $NPV(rate,range\ of\ cells)$. This function determines the NPV for the given rate of the cash flows in the range of cells. The function's calculation assumes that the first cash flow is one period from now. In other words, entering the formula $NPV(r\_,C5:E5)$ will not determine the NPV for Investment 1. Instead, this formula (entered in cell C14) computes the NPV of the following sequence of cash flows: −$10,000 a year from now, $24,000 two years from now, and −$14,000 three years from now. Let's call this Investment 1 (End OF Year). The NPV of Investment 1 (End of Year) is $231.48. To compute the actual cash NPV of Investment 1, I entered the formula $C7+NPV(r\_,D5:E5)$ in cell C11. This formula does not discount the Time 0 cash flow at all (which is correct because Time 0 cash flow is already in today's dollars), but first multiplies the cash flow in D5 by $1/1.2$ and then multiplies the cash flow in E5 by $1/1.2^2$.

The formula in cell C11 yields the correct NPV of Investment 1, $277.78.

How can I compute NPV when cash flows are received at the beginning of a year or in the middle of a year?

To use the NPV function to compute the net present value of a project whose cash flows always occur at the beginning of a year, you can use the approach we followed to determine the NPV of Investment 1: separate out the Year 1 cash flow and apply the NPV function to the remaining cash flows. Alternatively, observe that for any year n, $1 received at the beginning of year n is equivalent to $\$(1+r)$ received at the end of year n. Remember that in one year, a dollar will grow by a factor $(1+r)$. Thus, if we multiply the result obtained with the NPV function by $(1+r)$, we can convert the NPV of a sequence of year-end cash flows to the NPV of a sequence of cash flows received at the beginning of the year. We can also compute the NPV of Investment 1 in cell D11 with the formula $(1+r\_)*C14$. Of course, we again obtain an NPV of $277.78.

Now suppose the cash flows for an investment occur in the middle of each year. For an organization that receives monthly subscription revenues, we can approximate the 12 monthly revenues received during a given year as a lump sum received in the middle of the year. How can we use the NPV function to determine the NPV of a sequence of mid-year cash flows? For any year n,

$$\$\sqrt{1+r}$$

received at the end of year n is equivalent to $1 received at the middle of year n because in half a year $1 will grow by a factor of

$$\sqrt{1+r}$$

If we assume the cash flows for Investment 1 occur mid year, we can compute the NPV of the mid-year version of Investment 1 in cell C17 with the formula $SQRT(1+r\_)*C14$. We obtain a value of $253.58.

How can I compute NPV when cash flows are received at irregular intervals?

Cash flows often occur at irregular intervals, which makes computing the NPV or internal rate of return (IRR) of these cash flows more difficult. Fortunately, the Excel XNPV function makes computing the NPV of irregularly timed cash flows a snap.

The XNPV function uses the syntax $XNPV(rate,values,dates)$. The first date listed must be the earliest, but other dates need not be listed in chronological order. The XNPV function computes the NPV of the given cash flows assuming the current date is the first date in the sequence. For example, if the first listed date is 2/15/03, the NPV is computed in February 15, 2003 dollars.

To illustrate the use of the XNPV function, look at the example on worksheet *NPV as of first date* in the file XNPV.xlsx, which is shown in Figure 7-2. Suppose that on April 8, 2001 we paid out $900. Later we receive the following amounts:

❑ $300 on August 15, 2001

❑ $400 on January 15, 2002

❑ $200 on June 25, 2002

❑ $100 on July 3, 2003

If the annual interest rate is 10 percent, what is the NPV of these cash flows? We enter the dates (in Excel date format) in D3:D7 and the cash flows in E3:E7. Entering the formula *XNPV(A9,E3:E7,D3:D7)* in cell D11 computes the project's NPV in April 8, 2001 dollars because that is the first date listed. This project would have an NPV, in April 8, 2001 dollars, of $20.63.

	A	B	C	D	E	F	G
2	XNPV Function		Code	Date	Cash Flow	Time	df
3			36989.00	4/8/2001	-900		1
4			37118.00	8/15/2001	300	0.353425	0.966876
5			37271.00	1/15/2002	400	0.772603	0.929009
6			37432.00	6/25/2002	200	1.213699	0.890762
7			37805.00	7/3/2003	100	2.235616	0.808094
8	Rate						
9		0.1					
10				XNPV	Direct		
11				20.62822	20.628217		

Figure 7-2   Using the XNPV function

The computations performed by the XNPV function are as follows:

1. Compute the number of years after April 8, 2001, that each date occurred. (We did this in column F.) For example, August 15 is 0.3534 years after April 8.

2. Discount cash flows at the rate $1/(1+rate)^{years\ after}$.

    For example, the August 15, 2001 cash flow is discounted by

    $$\frac{1}{(1 + 0.1)^{.3534}} = 0.967$$

3. Sum up in cell E11 overall cash flows: *(cash flow value)*(discount factor)*.

Suppose that today's date is actually February 14, 2001. How would you compute the NPV of an investment in today's dollars? Simply add a row with today's date and 0 cash flow and include this row in the range for the XNPV function. (See Figure 7-3 and the *Today* worksheet.) The NPV of the project in today's dollars is $20.34.

	A	B	C	D	E	F
1						
2	XNPV Function		Code	Date	Cash Flow	Time
3				2/14/2001	0	
4			36989.00	4/8/2001	-900	
5			37118.00	8/15/2001	300	0.353425
6			37271.00	1/15/2002	400	0.772603
7			37432.00	6/25/2002	200	1.213699
8			37805.00	7/3/2003	100	2.235616
9	Rate					
10		0.1				
11				XNPV		
12				20.3447		

Figure 7-3   NPV converted to today's dollars.

Problems

1. An NBA player is to receive a $1,000,000 signing bonus today and $2,000,000 one year, two years, and three years from now. Assuming $r=0.10$ and ignoring tax considerations, would he be better off receiving $6,000,000 today?

2. A project has the following cash flows:

Now	One year from now	Two years from now	Three years from now
−$4 million	$4 million	$4 million	−$3 million

    If the company's cost of capital is 15 percent, should it proceed with the project?

3. Beginning one month from now, a customer will pay their Internet provider $25 per month for the next five years. Assuming all revenue for a year is received at the middle of a year, estimate the NPV of these revenues. Use $r=0.15$.

4. Beginning one month from now, a customer will pay $25 per month to their Internet provider for the next five years. Assuming all revenue for a year is received at the middle of a year, use the XNPV function to obtain the exact NPV of these revenues. Use $r=0.15$.

5. Consider the following set of cash flows over a four-year period:

Year	1	2	3	4
	-$600	$550	-$680	$1,000

    Determine the NPV of these cash flows if $r=0.15$ and cash flows occur at the end of the year.

6. Solve problem 5 assuming cash flows occur at the beginning of each year.

7. Consider the following cash flows:

Date	Cash flow
-12/15/01	−$1,000
1/11/02	$300
4/07/03	$600
7/15/04	$925

    If today is November 1, 2001, and $r=0.15$, what is the NPV of these cash flows?

8. After earning an MBA, a student will begin working at an $80,000-per-year job on September 1, 2005. She expects to receive a 5 percent raise each year until she retires on September 1, 2035. If the cost of capital is 8 percent a year, determine the total present value of her before-tax earnings.

Chapter 8
Internal Rate of Return

- How can I find the IRR of cash flows?

- Does a project always have a unique IRR?

- Are there conditions that guarantee a project will have a unique IRR?

- If two projects each have a single IRR, how do I use the projects' IRRs?

- How can I find the IRR of irregularly-spaced cash flows?

- What is the MIRR and how do I compute it?

The net present value (NPV) of a sequence of cash flows depends on the interest rate (r) used. For example, if we consider cash flows for Projects 1 and 2 (see the worksheet *IRR* in the file IRR.xlsx, shown in Figure 8-1), we find that for $r=0.2$, Project 2 has a larger NPV, and for $r=0.01$, Project 1 has a larger NPV. When we use NPV to rank investments, the outcome can depend on the interest rate. It is the nature of human beings to want to boil everything in life down to a single number. The internal rate of return (IRR) of a project is simply the interest rate that makes the NPV of the project equal to 0. If a project has a unique IRR, the IRR has a nice interpretation. For example, if a project has an IRR of 15 percent, we receive an annual rate of return of 15 percent on the cash flow we have invested. In this chapter's examples, we'll find that Project 1 has an IRR of 47.5 percent, which means that the $400 we have invested at Time 1 is yielding an annual rate of return of 47.5 percent. Sometimes, however, a project might have more than one IRR or even no IRR. In these cases, speaking about the project's IRR is useless.

	A	B	C	D	E	F	G	H	I	J	K
1		Time		1	2	3	4	5	6	7	NPV r=.2	NPV r=.01
2	Project 1			-400	200	600	-900	1000	250	230	$268.54	$918.99
3	Project 2			-200	150	150	200	300	100	80	$297.14	$741.07
4	Project 1	IRR Proj 1 No Guess	IRR Proj 2 No Guess								
5	no guess	47.5%	80.1%								
6											
7	guess	Guess Proj 1	Guess proj 2								
8	-0.9	47.5%	80.1%								
9	-0.7	47.5%	80.1%								
10	-0.5	47.5%	80.1%								
11	-0.3	47.5%	80.1%								
12	-0.1	47.5%	80.1%								
13	0.1	47.5%	80.1%								
14	0.3	47.5%	80.1%								
15	0.5	47.5%	80.1%								
16	0.7	47.5%	80.1%								
17	0.9	47.5%	80.1%								

Figure 8-1 Example of the IRR function

How can I find the IRR of cash flows?

The Microsoft Office Excel 2007 IRR function calculates internal rate of return. The function has the syntax IRR(range of cash flows,[guess]), where guess is an optional argument. If you do not enter a guess for a project's IRR, Excel begins its calculations with a guess that the project's IRR is 10 percent, and then varies the estimate of the IRR until it finds an interest rate that makes the project's NPV equal 0 (the project's IRR). If Excel can't find an interest rate that makes the project's NPV equal 0, Excel returns #NUM. In cell B5, I've entered the formula IRR(C2:I2) to compute Project 1's IRR. Excel returns 47.5 percent. Thus, if we use an annual interest rate of 47.5 percent, Project 1 will have an NPV of 0. Similarly, we find that Project 2 has an IRR of 80.1 percent.

Even if the IRR function finds an IRR, a project might have more than one IRR. To check whether a project has more than one IRR, you can vary the initial guess of the project's IRR (for example, from −90 percent to 90 percent). I varied the guess for Project 1's IRR by copying from B8 to B9:B17 the formula IRR($C$2:$I$2,A8). Because all the guesses for Project 1's IRR yield 47.5 percent, we're fairly confident that Project 1 has a *unique* IRR of 47.5 percent. Similarly, we can be fairly confident that Project 2 has a unique IRR of 80.1 percent.

Does a project always have a unique IRR?

In the worksheet *Multiple IRR* in the file IRR.xlsx (see Figure 8-2), you can see that Project 3 (cash flows of −20, 82, −60, 2) has two IRRs. I varied the guess about Project 3's IRR from −90 percent to 90 percent by copying from C8 to C9:C17 the formula IRR($B$4:$E$4,B8).

	A	B	C	D	E	F
1	Multiple IRR's					
2						
3		1	2	3	4	
4	Project 3	-20	82	-60	2	
5			plain irr	-9.6%		
6						
7		guess				
8		-0.9	-9.6%		npv at -9.6%	($0.01)
9		-0.7	-9.6%		npv at 216.1%	$0.00
10		-0.5	-9.6%			
11		-0.3	-9.6%			
12		-0.1	-9.6%			
13		0.1	-9.6%			
14		0.3	-9.6%			
15		0.5	216.1%			
16		0.7	216.1%			
17		0.9	216.1%			

Figure 8-2   Project with more than one IRR

Note that when a guess is 30 percent or less, the IRR is −9.6 percent. For other guesses, we find an IRR of 216.1 percent. For both these interest rates, Project 3 has an NPV of 0.

In the worksheet *No IRR* in the file IRR.xlsx (shown in Figure 8-3), you can see that no matter what guess we use for Project 4's IRR, we receive the #NUM message. This message indicates that Project 4 has no IRR.

When a project has multiple IRRs or no IRR, the concept of IRR loses virtually all meaning. Despite this problem, however, many companies still use IRR as their major tool for ranking investments.

	A	B	C	D
2		No IRR		
3				
4		0	1	2
5	Project 4	10	-30	35
6				
7		guess		
8		-0.9	#NUM!	
9		-0.8	#NUM!	
10		-0.7	#NUM!	
11		-0.6	#NUM!	
12		-0.5	#NUM!	
13		-0.4	#NUM!	
14		-0.3	#NUM!	
15		-0.2	#NUM!	
16		-0.1	#NUM!	
17		0	#NUM!	
18		0.1	#NUM!	
19		0.2	#NUM!	
20		0.3	#NUM!	
21		0.4	#NUM!	
22		0.5	#NUM!	
23		0.6	#NUM!	
24		0.7	#NUM!	
25		0.8	#NUM!	
26		0.9	#NUM!	

Figure 8-3   Project with no IRR

Are there conditions that guarantee a project will have a unique IRR?

If a project's sequence of cash flows contains exactly one change in sign, the project is guaranteed to have a unique IRR. For example, for Project 2 in worksheet *IRR*, the sign of the cash flow sequence is – + + + + +. There is only one change in sign (between Time 1 and Time 2), so Project 2 must have a unique IRR. For Project 3 in worksheet *Multiple IRR*, the signs of the cash flows are – + – +. Because the sign of the cash flows changes three times, a unique IRR is not guaranteed. For Project 4 in worksheet *No IRR*, the signs of the cash flows are + – +. Because the signs of the cash flows change twice, a unique IRR is not guaranteed in this case either. Most capital investment projects (such as building a plant) begin with a negative cash flow followed by a sequence of positive cash flows. Therefore, most capital investment projects will have a unique IRR.

If two projects each have a single IRR, how do I use the projects' IRRs?

If a project has a unique IRR, we can state that the project increases the value of the company *if and only if* the project's IRR exceeds the annual cost of capital. For example, if the cost of capital for a company is 15 percent, both Project 1 and Project 2 would increase the value of the company.

Suppose two projects are under consideration (both having unique IRRs), but we can undertake at most one project. It's tempting to believe that we should choose the project with the larger IRR. To illustrate that this belief can lead to incorrect decisions, look at Figure 8-4 on the next page and the *Which Project* worksheet in IRR.xlsx. Project 5 has an IRR of 40 percent, and Project 6 has an IRR of 50 percent. If we rank projects based on

IRR and can choose only one project, we would choose Project 6. Remember, however, that a project's NPV measures the amount of value the project adds to the company. Clearly, Project 5 will (for virtually any cost of capital) have a larger NPV than Project 6. Therefore, if only one project can be chosen, Project 5 is it. IRR is problematic because it ignores the scale of the project. Whereas Project 6 is better than Project 5 on a per-dollar-invested basis, the larger scale of Project 5 makes it more valuable to the company than Project 6. IRR does not reflect the scale of a project, whereas NPV does.

	B	C	D	E
2	Project	Time 0	Time 1	IRR
3	5	-100	140	40%
4	6	-1	1.5	50%

Figure 8-4   IRR can lead to an incorrect choice of which project to pursue.

How can I find the IRR of irregularly spaced cash flows?

Cash flows occur on actual dates, not just at the start or end of the year. The XIRR function has the syntax *XIRR(cash flow, dates, [guess])*. The XIRR function determines the IRR of a sequence of cash flows that occur on any set of irregularly spaced dates. As with the IRR function, *guess* is an optional argument. For an example of how to use the XIRR function, look at Figure 8-5 and worksheet *XIRR* of the file IRR.xlsx.

	A	B	C	D	E
1					Project 7
2	XIRR Function			Date	Cash Flow
3				4/8/2001	-900
4				8/15/2001	300
5				1/15/2002	400
6				6/25/2002	200
7				7/3/2003	100
8				XIRR	
9				12.97%	

Figure 8-5   Example of the XIRR function

The formula *XIRR(E3:E7, D3:D7)* in cell D9 shows that the IRR of Project 7 is 12.97 percent.

What is the MIRR and how do I compute it?

In many situations the rate at which a company borrows funds is different than the rate at which the company reinvests funds. IRR computations implicitly assume that the rate at which a company borrows and reinvests funds is equal to the IRR. If we know the actual rate at which we borrow money and the rate at which we can reinvest money, then the modified internal rate of return (MIRR) function computes a discount rate that makes the NPV of all our cash flows (including paying back our loan and reinvesting our proceeds at the given rates) equal to 0. The syntax of MIRR is *MIRR(cash flow values,borrowing rate,reinvestment rate)*. A nice thing about MIRR is that it is always unique! Figure 8-6 in worksheet *MIRR* of file IRR.xls contains an example of MIRR. Suppose we borrow $120,000 today and receive the following cash flows: Year 1: $39,000 Year 2: $30,000 Year 3: $21,000 Year 4: $37,000 Year 5: $46,000. Assume we can borrow at 10 percent per year and reinvest our profits at 12 percent per year.

After entering these values in cells E7:E12 of worksheet *MIRR* we find the MIRR in cell D15 with the formula *MIRR(E7:E12,E3,E4)*. Thus, our project has an MIRR of 12.61 percent. In cell D16 we computed the actual IRR of 13.07 percent.

	C	D	E
3		borrow	0.1
4		invest	0.12
5			
6		Year	Amt
7		0	-120000
8		1	39000
9		2	30000
10		3	21000
11		4	37000
12		5	46000
13			total
14			
15	MIRR	12.6094%	
16	IRR	13.0736%	

Figure 8-6   Example of the MIRR function

Problems

1. Compute all IRRs for the following sequence of cash flows:

Year 1	Year 2	Year 3	Year 4	Year 5	Year 6	Year 7
−$10,000	$8,000	$1,500	$1,500	$1,500	$1,500	−$1,500

2. Consider a project with the following cash flows. Determine the project's IRR. If the annual cost of capital is 20 percent, would you undertake this project?

Year 1	Year 2	Year 3
−$4,000	$2,000	$4,000

3. Find all IRRs for the following project:

Year 1	Year 2	Year 3
$100	−$300	$250

4. Find all IRRs for a project having the given cash flows on the listed dates.

1/10/2003	7/10/2003	5/25/2004	7/18/2004	3/20/2005	4/1/2005	1/10/2006
−$1,000	$900	$800	$700	$500	$500	$350

5. Consider the following two projects. Assume a company's cost of capital is 15 percent. Find the IRR and NPV of each project. Which projects add value to the company? If the company can choose only a single project, which project should it choose?

	Year 1	Year 2	Year 3	Year 4
Project 1	−$40	$130	$19	$26
Project 2	−$80	$36	$36	$36

6. 25-year-old Meg Prior is going to invest $10,000 in her retirement fund at the beginning of each of the next 40 years. Assume that during each of the next 30 years Meg will earn 15 percent on her investments and during the last 10 years before she retires, her investments will earn 5 percent. Determine the IRR associated with her investments and her final retirement position. How do you know there will be a unique IRR? How would you interpret the unique IRR?

7. Give an intuitive explanation of why Project 6 (on the worksheet *Which Project* in the file IRR.xlsx) has an IRR of 50 percent.

8. Consider a project having the following cash flows.

Year 1	Year 2	Year 3
−$70,000	$12,000	$15,000

Try to find the IRR of this project without simply guessing. What problem arises? What is the IRR of this project? Does the project have a unique IRR?

9. For the cash flows in Problem 1 assume we can borrow at 12 percent per year and invest profits at 15 percent per year. Compute the project's MIRR.

Chapter 9
More Excel Financial Functions

- You are buying a copier. Would you rather pay $11,000 today or $3,000 a year for five years?

- If at the end of each of the next 40 years I invest $2,000 a year towards my retirement, and earn 8 percent a year on my investments, how much will I have when I retire?

- I am borrowing $10,000 for 10 months with an annual interest rate of 8 percent. What are my monthly payments? How much principal and interest am I paying each month?

- I want to borrow $80,000 and make monthly payments for 10 years. The maximum monthly payment I can afford is $1,000. What is the maximum interest rate I can afford?

- If I borrow $100,000 at 8 percent interest and make payments of $10,000 per year, how many years will it take me to pay back the loan?

When we borrow money to buy a car or house, we always wonder if we are getting a good deal. When we save for retirement, we are curious how large a nest egg we will have when we retire. In our daily work and personal lives, financial questions similar to these often arise. Knowledge of the Excel PV, FV, PMT, PPMT, IPMT, CUMPRINC, CUMIPMT, RATE, and NPER functions makes it easy to answer these types of questions.

You are buying a copier. Would you rather pay $11,000 today or $3,000 a year for five years?

The key to answering this question is being able to value the annual payments of $3,000 per year. We will assume the cost of capital is 12 percent per year. We could use the NPV function to answer this question but the Excel PV function provides a much quicker way to solve this problem. A stream of cash flows that involves the same amount of cash outflow (or inflow) each period is called an *annuity*. Assuming that each period's interest rate is the same, an annuity can easily be valued using the Excel PV function. The PV function returns the value in today's dollars of a series of future payments under the assumption of periodic, constant payments and a constant interest rate. The syntax of the PV function is *PV(rate,#per,[pmt],[fv],[type])*, where *pmt, fv* and *type* are optional arguments.

> **Note**   When working with Microsoft Office Excel 2007 financial functions, we use the following conventions for the signs of Pmt (payment) and Fv (future value): money received has a positive sign and money paid out has a negative sign.

❑ *Rate* is the interest rate per period. For example if you borrow money at 6 percent per year and the period is a year then *rate=0.06*. If the period is a month then *rate=0.06/12=0.005*.

❑ *#per* is number of periods in the annuity. For our copier example, *#per=5*. If payments on the copier were made each month for five years then *#per=60*. Your rate must, of course, be consistent with #per. That is, if #per implies a period is a month you must use a monthly interest rate, whereas if #per implies a period is a year you must use an annual interest rate.

❑ *Pmt* is the payment made each period. For our copier example, *pmt=-$5,000*. A payment has a negative sign whereas money received has a positive sign. At least one of Pmt or Fv must be included.

❑ *Fv* is the cash balance (or future value) you want to have after the last payment is made. For our copier example, *fv=0*. For example, if we want to have a $500 cash balance after the last payment, then *fv=$500*. If we want to make an additional $500 payment at the end of a problem *fv=-$500*. If *fv* is omitted, it is assumed equal to 0.

❑ *Type* is either 0 or 1 and indicates when payments are made. When type is omitted or equal to 0 then payments are made at the end of each period. When *type=1*, payments are made at the beginning of each period. Note that you may also write True instead of 1 and False instead of 0 in all functions discussed in this chapter.

Figure 9-1 (see worksheet *PV* of file Excelfinfunctions.xlsx) indicates how to solve our copier problem.

	A	B
2	PMT	
3	Pay $3000 for 5 years end of year	$10,814.33
4	Pay $3000 for 5 years beginning of year	$12,112.05
5	Extra $500 payment end of year 5;end of year payments	$11,098.04

Figure 9-1   Example of PV function

In cell B3 we computed the present value of paying $3,000 at the end of each year for five years with a 12 percent cost of capital using the formula =PV(0.12,5,−3000,0,0) Excel returns a NPV of $10,814.33. By omitting the last two arguments, we obtained the same answer with the formula=PV(0.12,5,−3000). Thus it is a better deal to make payments at the end of the year than to pay out $11,000 today.

If we make payments on the copier of $3,000 at the beginning of each year for five years, the NPV of our payments is computed in cell B4 with the formula =PV(0.12,5,−3000,0,1). Note that changing the last argument from a 0 to a 1 changed the calculations from end of year to beginning of year. We find the present value of our payments to be $12,112.05. Therefore it is better to pay $11,000 today than make payments at the beginning of the year.

Suppose we pay $3,000 at the end of each year and we must include an extra $500 payment at the end of Year 5. We may now find the present value of all our payments in cell B5 by including a future value of $500 with the formula =PV(0.12,5,−3000−,500,0). Note the $3,000 and $500 cash flows have negative signs because we are paying out the money. We find the present value of all these payments to equal $11,098.04.

If at the end of each of the next 40 years I invest $2,000 a year towards my retirement, and earn 8 percent a year on my investments, how much will I have when I retire?

In this situation we want to know the value of an annuity in terms of future dollars (40 years from now) and not today's dollars. This is a job for the Excel FV (Future Value) function. The FV function gives the future value of an investment assuming periodic, constant payments with a constant interest rate. The syntax of the FV function is FV(rate,#per,[pmt],[pv],[type]), where pmt, pv and type are optional arguments.

- ❏ *Rate* is the interest rate per period. In our case, *rate=0.08*.

- ❏ *#per* is the number of periods in the future at which you want the future value computed. #per is also the number of periods during which the annuity payment is received. In our case, *#per=40*.

- ❏ *Pmt* is the payment made each period. In our case *pmt=−$2,000*. The negative sign indicates we are paying money into an account. At least one of Pmt or Pv must be included.

- ❏ *Pv* is the amount of money (in today's dollars) owed right now. In our case *pv=$0*. If today we owed someone $10,000, then *pv=$10,000* because they lent us $10,000 and we received it. If today we had $10,000 in the bank, then *pv=−$10,000* because we must have paid $10,000 into our bank account. If pv is omitted it is assumed to equal 0.

- ❏ *Type* is a 0 or 1 and indicates when payments are due or money is deposited. If *type=0* or is omitted, then money is deposited at the end of the period. In our case, *type* is 0 or omitted. If *type=1* then payments are made or money is deposited at the beginning of the period.

In worksheet *FV* of file Excelfinfunctions.xlsx (see Figure 9-2) we enter in cell B3 the formula =FV(0.08,40,–2000) to find that in 40 years our nest egg will be worth $518,113.04. Note that we entered a negative value for our annual payment. This is because we paid the $2,000 into our account. We could also have obtained the same answer by entering the last two unnecessary arguments with the formula *FV(0.08,40,–2000,0,0)*.

If deposits were made at the beginning of each year for 40 years, then the formula (entered in cell B4) =FV(0.08,40,–2000,0,1) would yield the value in 40 years of our nest egg: $559,562.08.

	A	B
2	FV	
3	Invest $2000 end of year for 40 years	$518,113.04
4	Invest $2000 beginning of year for 40 years	$559,562.08
5	We start with $30000 and invest $2000 per year at end of year for 40 years	$1,169,848.68

Figure 9-2   Example of FV function

Finally, suppose that in addition to investing $2,000 at the end of each of the next 40 years we initially have $30,000 to invest. If we earn 8 percent per year on our investments, how much money will we have when we retire in 40 years? We can answer this question by setting *pv=–$30,000* in the FV function. The negative sign is used because we have deposited or paid $30,000 into our account. In cell B5 the formula =FV(0.08,40,–2000,–30000,0) yields a future value of $1,169,848.68.

I am borrowing $10,000 for 10 months with an annual interest rate of 8 percent. What are my monthly payments? How much principal and interest am I paying each month?

The Excel PMT function computes the periodic payments for a loan assuming constant payments and a constant interest rate. The syntax of the PMT function is *PMT(rate, #per,pv,[fv],[type])*, where *fv* and *type* are optional arguments.

- *Rate* is the per-period interest rate of the loan. In our example we will use one month as a period, so *rate=0.08/12=0.006666667*.

- *#per* is the number of payments made. In our case, *#per=10*.

❑ *Pv* is the present value of all our payments. That is, pv is the amount of the loan. In our case, *pv=$10,000*. Pv is positive because we are receiving the $10,000.

❑ *Fv* indicates the final loan balance you want to have after making the last payment. In our case *fv=0*. If fv is omitted, Excel assumes it to equal 0. Suppose we have taken out a *balloon loan* where we make payments at the end of each month, but at the conclusion of the loan we pay off the final balance by making a $1,000 balloon payment. Then *fv=-$1,000*. The $1,000 is negative because we are paying it out.

❑ *Type* is a 0 or 1 and indicates when payments are due. If *type=0* or is omitted, then payments are made at the end of the period. We will first assume end-of-month payments so type is 0 or omitted. If *type=1*, then payments are made or money is deposited at the beginning of period.

In cell G1 of worksheet *PMT* of file Excelfinfunctions.xlsx (see Figure 9-3) we computed the monthly payment on a 10-month loan for $10,000, assuming an 8 percent annual interest rate and end-of-month payments with the formula=-*PMT(0.08/12,10, 10000,0,0)*. We find the monthly payment is $1,037.03. Note the PMT function by itself returns a negative value because we will be making the payment to the company giving us the loan.

If desired, we can use the Excel IPMT and PPMT functions to compute the amount of interest paid each month towards the loan and the amount of the balance paid down each month (this is called the payment on the principal).

	B	C	D	E	F	G	H
1			rate	0.00666667	payment	$1,037.03	
2	PMT,PPMT,IPMT Functions		months	10	end of month		
3	CUMPRINC CUMIPMT		loan amount	$10,000.00			
4							
5		Time	Beginning balance	Monthly Payment	Principal	Interest	Ending Balance
6		1	$ 10,000.00	$1,037.03	$970.37	$66.67	$9,029.63
7		2	$9,029.63	$1,037.03	$976.83	$60.20	$8,052.80
8		3	$8,052.80	$1,037.03	$983.35	$53.69	$7,069.45
9		4	$7,069.45	$1,037.03	$989.90	$47.13	$6,079.55
10		5	$6,079.55	$1,037.03	$996.50	$40.53	$5,083.05
11		6	$5,083.05	$1,037.03	$1,003.15	$33.89	$4,079.90
12		7	$4,079.90	$1,037.03	$1,009.83	$27.20	$3,070.07
13		8	$3,070.07	$1,037.03	$1,016.56	$20.47	$2,053.51
14		9	$2,053.51	$1,037.03	$1,023.34	$13.69	$1,030.16
15		10	$1,030.16	$1,037.03	$1,030.16	$6.87	($0.00)
16							
17		NPV of payment	$10,000.00				
18					cum int months 2-	cumprinc months 2-4	
19		payment beginning of each month	$1,030.16		-161.0125862	-2950.083682	
20		monthly payment if we make $1000 ending payment	$940.00				

Figure 9-3   Examples of PMT, PPMT, CUMPRINC, CUMIPMT, and IPMT functions

To determine the interest paid each month we use the IPMT function. The syntax of the IPMT function is *IPMT(rate,per,#per,pv,[fv],[type])*, where *fv* and *type* are optional arguments. The *per* argument indicates the period number for which you compute the interest. The other arguments mean the same as they did for the PMT function. Similarly, to

determine the amount paid towards the principal each month we use the PPMT function. The syntax of the PPMT function is *PPMT(rate,per,#per,pv,fv,type)*. The meaning of
each argument is the same as it was for the IPMT function. By copying from F6 to F7:F16
the formula =−PPMT(0.08/12,C6,10,10000,0,0), we compute the amount of each
month's payment that is applied to the principal. For example, during Month 1 we pay
only $970.37 towards the principal. As expected, the amount paid towards the principal
increases each month. The minus sign is needed because the principal is paid to the
company giving us the loan, and PPMT will return a negative number. By copying from
G6 to G7:G16 the formula =−IPMT(0.08/12,C6,10,10000,0,0), we compute the amount of
interest paid each month. For example, in Month 1 we pay $66.67 in interest. Of course,
the amount of interest we pay each month decreases.

Note that each month *(Interest Paid)+(Payment Towards Principal)=(Total Payment)*. Sometimes the total is off by a penny due to rounding.

We can also create our ending balances for each month in column H by using the relationship *(Ending Month t Balance)=(Beginning Month t Balance)−(Month t Payment towards
Principal)*. Note that in Month 1, *Beginning Balance=$10,000*. In column D, we create each
month's beginning balance by using the relationship (for *t=2, 3, ...10)(Beginning Month
t Balance)=(Ending Month t−1 Balance)*. Of course, *Ending Month 10 Balance=$0,* as it
should.

Our interest each month can be computed as *(Month t Interest)=(Interest rate)*(Beginning
Month t Balance)*.For example, our month 3 *interest payment* can be computed as
=(0.0066667)*($8,052.80)=$53.69.

Note of course, that the NPV of all our payments is exactly $10,000. We checked this in
cell D17 with the formula *NPV(0.08/12,E6:E15)*. (See Figure 9-3.)

If our payments were made at the beginning of each month, the amount of each payment
is computed in cell D19 with the formula =−PMT(0.08/12,10,10000,0,1). Note that
changing the last argument to 1 changes each payment to the beginning of the month.
Because our lender is getting her money earlier, our monthly payments will be less than
the end-of-month case. If we pay at the beginning of the month, our monthly payment is
$1,030.16.

Finally, suppose that we want to make a balloon payment of $1,000 at the end of 10
months. If we make our monthly payments at the end of each month, then the formula
=−PMT(0.08/12,10,10000,−1000,0) in cell D20 computes our monthly payment. Our
monthly payment turns out to be $940. Because $1,000 of our loan is not being paid
with monthly payments, it makes sense that our new monthly payment is less than our
original end-of-month payment of $1,037.03.

CUMPRINC and CUMIPMT Functions

We often want to accumulate the interest or principal paid during several periods. The CUMPRINC and CUMIPMT functions make this a snap.

The CUMPRINC function computes the principal paid between two periods (inclusive). The syntax of the CUMPRINC function is *CUMPRINC(rate,#per,pv,start period,end period,type)*. *Rate*, *#per*, *pv*, and *type* have the same meanings as described previously.

The CUMIPMT function computes the interest paid between two periods (inclusive). The syntax of the CUMIPMT function is *CUMIPMT(rate,#nper,pv,start period,end period,type)*. *Rate*, *#per*, *pv*, and *type* have the same meanings as described previously. For example, in cell F19 on the *PMT* worksheet we computed the interest paid during months 2 through 4 ($161.01) by using the formula *=CUMIPMT(0.08/12,10,10000,2,4,0)*. In cell G19 we computed the principal paid off in months 2 through 4 ($,2950.08) by using the formula *=CUMPRINC(0.08/12,10,10000,2,4,0)*

I want to borrow $80,000 and make monthly payments for 10 years. The maximum monthly payment I can afford is $1,000. What is the maximum interest rate I can afford?

Given a borrowed amount, the length of a loan, and the payment each period, the RATE function tells us the rate of the loan. The syntax of the RATE function is *RATE(#per,pmt,pv,[fv],[type],[guess])*, where *fv*, *type*, and *guess* are optional arguments. *#per*, *pmt*, *pv*, *fv*, and *type* have the same meanings as previously described. *Guess* is simply a guess at what the loan rate is. Usually this can be omitted. Entering in cell D9 of worksheet *Rate* of file Excelfinfunctions.xlsx the formula *=RATE(120,-1000,80000,0,0,)* yields .7241 percent as the monthly rate. We are assuming end-of-month payments. (See Figure 9-4.)

	D	E	F	G	H	I	J	K	L
6	BORROWING $80,000								
7	120 MONTHLY PAYMENTS OF $1000 PER MONTH								
8	WHAT IS MAX RATE YOU CAN HANDLE?						CHECK!		
9	0.72410%	=RATE(120,-1000,80000,0,0)				$80,000.08	=PV(0.007241,120,-1000,0,0)		
10	IF YOU CAN PAY $10,000 AT END								
11	WHAT IS MAX RATE YOU CAN HANDLE?								
12	0.818%								

Figure 9-4   Example of RATE function

In cell I9 we verified the RATE function calculation. The formula *=PV(.007241,120,-1000,0,0)* yields $80,000.08. This shows that payments of $1,000 at the end of each month for 120 months have a present value of $80,000.08.

Note that if you could pay back $10,000 during month 120, the maximum rate you could handle would be given by the formula *=RATE(120,-1000,80000,-10000,0,0)* . In cell D12, this formula yields a monthly rate of 0.818 percent.

If I borrow $100,000 at 8 percent interest and make payments of $10,000 per year, how many years will it take me to pay back the loan?

Given the size of a loan, the payments each period, and the loan rate, the NPER function tells us how many periods it takes to pay back a loan. The syntax of the NPER function is NPER(rate,pmt,pv,[fv],[type]), where *fv* and *type* are optional arguments.

Assuming end-of-year payments, the formula =NPER(0.08,–10000,100000,0,0) in cell D7 of worksheet *Nper* of file Excelfinfunctions.xlsx yields 20.91 years. (See Figure 9-5.) Thus, 20 years of payments will not quite pay back the loan, but 21 years will overpay the loan. To verify the calculation, in cells D10 and D11 we use the PV function to show that paying $10,000 per year for 20 years pays back $98,181.47, and paying back $10,000 for 21 years pays back $100,168.03.

Suppose that we are planning to pay back $40,000 in the final payment period. How many years will it take to pay back the loan? Entering in cell D14 the formula =NPER(0.08,–10000,100000,–40000,0) shows that it will take 15.90 years to pay back the loan. Thus, 15 years of payments will not quite pay off the loan, and 16 years of payments will slightly overpay the loan.

	C	D
3		Borrow $100000 8%
4		ANNUAL PAYMENTS OF $10,000 PER YEAR
5		END OF YEAR PAYMENT
6		HOW MANY YEARS?
7		20.91237188
8		20 YEARS WILL NOT PAY IT OFF; 21 WILL
9		CHECK
10	20 YEARS	$98,181.47
11	21 YEARS	$100,168.03
12		
13		IF WE PAY $40,000 AT END OF PROBLEM
14		15.9012328
15		15 YEARS WILL NOT PAY IT OFF; 16 YEARS WILL

Figure 9-5 Example of NPER function

Problems

Unless otherwise mentioned, all payments are made at the end of the period.

1. You have just won the lottery. At the end of each of the next 20 years you will receive a payment of $50,000. If the cost of capital is 10 percent per year, what is the present value of your lottery winnings?

2. A *perpetuity* is an annuity that is received forever. If I rent out my house and at the beginning of each year I receive $14,000, what is the value of this perpetuity? Assume an annual 10 percent cost of capital. (Hint: Use the PV function and let the number of periods be many!)

3. I now have $250,000 in the bank. At the end of each of the next 20 years I withdraw $15,000. If I earn 8 percent per year on my investments, how much money will I have in 20 years?

4. I deposit $2,000 per month (at the end of each month) over the next 10 years. My investments earn 0.8 percent per month. I would like to have $1 million in 10 years. How much money should I deposit now?

5. An NBA player is receiving $15 million at the end of each of the next seven years. He can earn 6 percent per year on his investments. What is the present value of his future revenues?

6. At the end of each of the next 20 years I will receive the following amounts:

Years	Amounts
1–5	$200
6–10	$300
11–20	$400

Use the PV function to find the present value of these cash flows if the cost of capital is 10 percent. Hint: Begin by computing the value of receiving $400 a year for 20 years then subtract the value of receiving $100 a year for 10 years, etc.

7. We are borrowing $200,000 on a 30 year mortgage with an annual interest rate of 10 percent. Assuming end-of-month payments, determine the monthly payment, interest payment each month, and amount paid towards principal each month.

Answer each question in Problem 7 assuming beginning-of-month payments.

8. Use the FV function to determine the value to which $100 accumulates in three years if you are earning 7 percent per year.

9. You have a liability of $1,000,000 due in 10 years. The cost of capital is 10 percent per year. What amount of money would you need to set aside at the end of each of the next 10 years to meet this liability?

10. You are going to buy a new car. The cost of the car is $50,000. You have been offered two payment plans:

   ❑ A 10 percent discount on the sales price of the car, followed by 60 monthly payments financed at 9 percent per year.

   ❑ No discount on the sales price of the car, followed by 60 monthly payments financed at 2 percent per year.

If you believe your annual cost of capital is 9 percent, which payment plan is a better deal? Assume all payments occur at the end of the month.

11. I presently have $10,000 in the bank. At the beginning of each of the next 20 years I am going to invest $4,000 and I expect to earn 6 percent per year on my investments. How much money will I have in 20 years?

12. A *balloon mortgage* requires you to pay off part of a loan during a specified time period and then make a lump sum payment to pay off the remaining portion of the loan. Suppose you borrow $400,000 on a 20 year balloon mortgage and the interest rate is .5 percent per month. Your end-of-month payments during the first 20 years are required to pay off $300,000 of your loan and 20 years from now you will have to pay off the remaining $100,000. Determine your monthly payments for this loan.

13. An adjustable rate mortgage (ARM) ties monthly payments to a rate index (say, the US T-Bill rate). Suppose we borrow $60,000 on an ARM for 30 years (360 monthly payments). The first 12 payments are governed by the current T-Bill rate of 8 percent. In years 2–5, monthly payments are set at the year's beginning monthly T-Bill rate + 2 percent. Suppose the T-Bill rates at the beginning of years 2–5 are as follows:

Beginning of year	T-Bill rate
2	10 percent
3	13 percent
4	15 percent
5	10 percent

Determine monthly payments during years 1–5 and each year's ending balance.

14. Suppose we have borrowed money at a 14.4 percent annual rate and we make monthly payments. If we have missed four consecutive monthly payments, how much should next month's payment be to catch up?

15. We want to replace a machine in 10 years and we estimate our cost will be $80,000. If we can earn 8 percent annually on our investments, how much money should we put aside at the end of each year to cover the cost of the machine?

16. We are buying a motorcycle. We pay $1,500 today and $182.50 a month for three years. If the annual rate of interest is 18 percent, what was the original cost of the motorcycle?

17. Suppose the annual rate of interest is 10 percent. We pay $200 a month for two years, $300 a month for a year, and $400 for two years. What is the present value of all our payments?

18. We can invest $500 at the end of each six-month period for five years. If we want to have $6,000 after five years, what is the annual rate of return we need on our investments?

19. I borrow $2,000 and make quarterly payments for two years. The annual rate of interest is 24 percent. What is the size of each payment?

20. I have borrowed $15,000. I am making 48 monthly payments and the annual rate of interest is 9 percent. What is the total interest paid over the course of the loan?

21. I am borrowing $5,000 and plan to pay back the loan with 36 monthly payments. The annual rate of interest is 16.5 percent. After one year, I pay back $500 extra and shorten the period of the loan to two years total. What will my monthly payment be during the second year of the loan?

22. With an Adjustable Rate Mortgage, you make monthly payments depending on the interest rates at the beginning of each year. We have borrowed $60,000 on a 30-year ARM. For the first year, monthly payments will be based on the current annual T-Bill rate of 9 percent. In years 2–5, monthly payments will be based on the following annual T-Bill rates +2 percent.

    ❑ Year 2: 10 percent

    ❑ Year 3: 13 percent

    ❑ Year 4: 15 percent

    ❑ Year 5: 10 percent

    The catch is that the ARM contains a clause which ensures that monthly payments can increase a maximum of 7.5 percent from one year to the next. To compensate the lender for this provision, the borrower adjusts the ending balance of the loan at the end of each year based on the difference between what the borrower actually paid and what he should have paid. Determine monthly payments during Years 1–5 of the loan.

23. You have a choice of receiving $8,000 each year beginning at age 62 and ending when you die, or receiving $10,000 each year beginning at age 65 and ending when you die. If you think you can earn an 8 percent annual return on your investments, which will net the largest amount?

24. You have just won the lottery and will receive $50,000 a year for 20 years. What rate of interest would make these payments the equivalent of receiving $500,000 today?

25. A bond pays a $50 coupon at the end of each of the next 30 years, and pays $1,000 face value in 30 years. If we discount cash flows at an annual rate of 6 percent, what would be a fair price for the bond?

26. You have borrowed $100,000 on a 40-year mortgage with monthly payments. The annual interest rate is 16 percent. How much will you pay over the course of the loan? With four years left on the loan, how much will you still owe?

27. I need to borrow $12,000. I can afford payments of $500 per month and the annual rate of interest is 4.5 percent. How many months will it take to pay off the loan?

Chapter 10
Circular References

- I often get a circular reference message from Excel. Does this mean I've made an error?
- How can I resolve circular references?

When Microsoft Office Excel displays a message that your workbook contains a circular reference, it means there is a "loop," or dependency, between two or more cells in a worksheet. For example, a circular reference occurs if the value in cell A1 influences the value in C2, the value in cell C2 influences the value in cell D2, and the value in cell D2 influences the value in cell A1. Figure 10-1 illustrates the pattern of a circular reference.

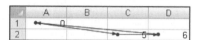

Figure 10-1   A loop causing a circular reference

As you'll soon see, you can resolve circular references by clicking the Microsoft Office Button followed by Excel Options. Then choose Formulas and check the Enable Iterative Calculation box.

I often get a circular reference message from Excel. Does this mean I've made an error?

A circular reference usually arises from a logically consistent worksheet in which several cells exhibit a "looping" relationship similar to that illustrated in Figure 10-1. Let's look at a simple example of a problem that cannot easily be solved in Excel without creating a circular reference. A small company earns $1,500 in revenues and incurs $1,000 in costs. They want to give 10 percent of their after-tax profits to charity. Their tax rate is 40 percent. How much money should they give to charity? The solution to this problem is in the file Circular.xlsx, shown in Figure 10-2.

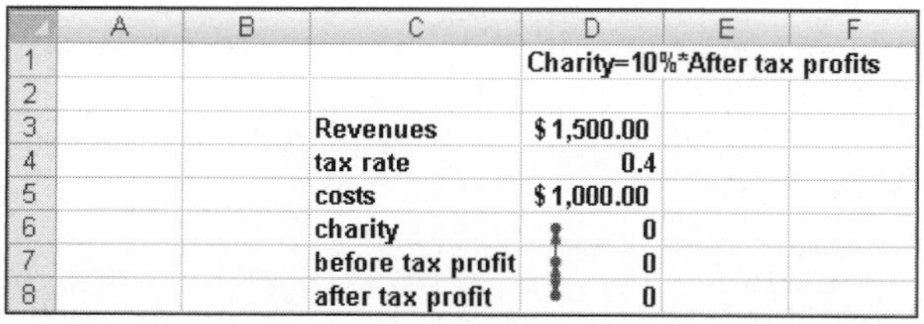

	A	B	C	D	E	F
1				Charity=10%*After tax profits		
2						
3			Revenues	$1,500.00		
4			tax rate	0.4		
5			costs	$1,000.00		
6			charity	0		
7			before tax profit	0		
8			after tax profit	0		

Figure 10-2   A circular reference can occur when you're calculating taxes.

We begin by naming the cells in D3:D8 with the corresponding names in cells C3:C8. Next we enter the firm's revenue, tax rate, and costs in D3:D5. To compute a contribution to charity as 10 percent of after-tax profit, we enter in cell D6 the formula *0.1*after_tax_profit*. Then we determine before-tax profit in cell D7 by subtracting costs and the charitable contribution from revenues. Our formula in cell D7 is Revenues–Costs–Charity. Finally, we compute after-tax profit in cell D8 as

(1–tax_rate)*before_tax_profit

Excel indicates a circular reference in cell D8 (see the bottom left-hand corner of file Circular.xlxs). What's going on?

1. Charity (cell D6) influences before-tax profit (cell D7).

2. Before-tax profit (cell D7) influences after-tax profit (cell D8).

3. After-tax profit (cell D8) influences charity.

Thus we have a loop of the form D6-D7-D8-D6 (indicated by the blue arrows in Figure 10-2), which causes the circular reference message. Our worksheet is logically correct; we have done nothing wrong! Still, we see from Figure 10-2 that Excel is giving us an incorrect answer for charitable contributions.

How can I resolve circular references?

Resolving a circular reference is easy. Simply click the Microsoft Office Button in the upper-left corner of the Ribbon, and then click Excel Options. Choose Formulas in the left pane, and check the Enable Iterative Calculation box in the Calculation Options section, as shown in Figure 10-3.

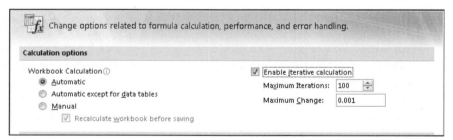

Figure 10-3   Use the Enable Iterative Calculation option to resolve a circular reference.

When you activate the Enable Iterative Calculation option, Excel recognizes that your circular reference has generated the following system of three equations with three unknowns:

```
Charity=0.1*(AfterTax Profit)
BeforeTax Profit=Revenue-Charity-Costs
AfterTax Profit=(1-Tax rate)*(BeforeTax Profit)
```

The three unknowns are *Charity*, *BeforeTax Profit*, and *AfterTax Profit*. When you activate the Enable Iterative Calculation option, Excel iterates (based on our limitation, 100 iterations will be used) to seek a solution to all equations generated by the circular reference. From one iteration to the next, the values of the unknowns are changed by a complex mathematical procedure (Gauss-Seidel Iteration). Excel stops if the maximum change in any worksheet cell from one iteration to the next is smaller than the Maximum Change value (0.001 by default). You can reduce the Maximum Change setting to a smaller number, such as 0.000001. If you do not reduce the Maximum Change to a smaller number, you might find Excel assigning a value of, for example, 5.001 to a cell that should equal 5, and this is annoying! Also, some complex worksheets might require more than 100 iterations before "converging" to a resolution of the circularity. For our example, however, the circularity is almost instantly resolved, and we see the solution given in Figure 10-4.

	C	D	E	F
1		Charity=10%*After tax profits		
2				
3	Revenues	$1,500.00		
4	tax rate	0.4		
5	costs	$1,000.00		
6	charity	28.301887		
7	before tax profit	471.69811		
8	after tax profit	283.01887		

Figure 10-4   Excel runs the calculations to resolve the circular reference.

Note that our charitable contribution of $28.30 is now exactly 10 percent of our after-tax profit of $283.01. All other cells in the worksheet are now correctly computed.

Here's one more example of a circular reference. In any Excel formula, you can refer to an entire column or row by name. For example, the formula *AVERAGE(B:B)* will average all cells in column B. The formula *=AVERAGE(1:1)* will average all cells in row 1. This shortcut is useful if you're continually dumping new data (such as monthly sales) into a column or row. Then our formula always computes average sales, and we do not need to ever change it. The problem is, of course, that if we enter this formula in the column or row that it refers to, we'll create a circular reference. By activating the Enable Iterative Calculation option, circular references such as these will be resolved quickly.

Problems

1. Before paying employee bonuses and state and federal taxes, a company earns profits of $60,000. The company pays employees a bonus equal to 5 percent of after-tax profits. State tax is 5 percent of profits (after bonuses are paid). Federal tax is 40 percent of profits (after bonuses and state tax are paid). Determine the amount paid in bonuses, state tax, and federal tax.

2. On January 1, 2002, I have $500. At the end of each month I earn 2 percent interest. Each month's interest is based on the average of the month's beginning and ending balances. How much money will I have after 12 months?

3. My airplane is flying the following route: Houston-Los Angeles-Seattle-Minneapolis-Houston. On each leg of the journey, the plane's fuel usage (expressed as miles per gallon) is *40–.02*(average fuel en route)*. Here, *average fuel en route* is equal to *.5*(initial fuel en route+final fuel en route)*. We begin in Houston with 1000 gallons of fuel. The distance flown on each leg of the journey is as follows.

Leg	Miles
Houston to Los Angeles	1200
Los Angeles to Seattle	1100
Seattle to Minneapolis	1500
Minneapolis to Houston	1400

4. How many gallons of fuel will remain when I return to Houston?

5. A common method used to allocate costs to support departments is the *reciprocal cost allocation method*. This method can easily be implemented by use of circular references. To illustrate, suppose Widgetco has two support departments: Accounting and Consulting. Widgetco also has two product divisions: Division 1 and Division 2. Widgetco has decided to allocate $600,000 of the cost of operating the Accounting department and $116,000 of the cost of operating the Consulting department to the two divisions. The fraction of accounting and consulting time used by each part of the company is as follows.

	Accounting	Consulting	Division 1	Division 2
Percentage of accounting work done for other parts of the company	0%	20%	30%	50%
Percentage of consulting work done for other parts of the company	10%	0%	80%	10%

How much of the accounting and consulting costs should be allocated to other parts of the company? We need to determine two quantities: total cost allocated to accounting and total cost allocated to consulting. Total cost allocated to accounting equals *$600,000+.1*(total cost allocated to consulting)* because 10 percent of all consulting work was done for the Accounting department. A similar equation can be written for the total cost allocated to consulting. You should now be able to calculate the correct allocation of both accounting and consulting costs to each other part of the company.

Chapter 11
IF Statements

- If I order up to 500 units of a product, I pay $3.00 per unit. If I order from 501 through 1200 units, I pay $2.70 per unit. If I order from 1201 through 2000 units, I pay $2.30 per unit. If I order more than 2000 units, I pay $2.00 per unit. How can I write a formula that expresses the purchase cost as a function of the number of units purchased?

- I've just purchased 100 shares of stock at a cost of $55 per share. To hedge the risk that the stock might decline in value, I purchased 60 six-month European put options. Each option has an exercise price of $45 and costs $5. How can I develop a worksheet that indicates the six-month percentage return on my portfolio for a variety of possible future prices?

- Many stock market analysts believe that moving-average trading rules can outperform the market. A commonly suggested moving-average trading rule is to buy a stock when the stock's price moves above the average of the last 15 months, and to sell a stock when the stock's price moves below the average of the last 15 months. How would this trading rule have performed against the Standard & Poor's 500 Stock Index (S&P)?

- In the game of craps, two dice are tossed. If the total of the dice on the first roll is 2, 3, or 12, you lose. If the total of the dice on the first roll is 7 or 11, you win. Otherwise, the game keeps going. How can I write a formula to determine the status of the game after the first roll?

- In most pro forma financial statements, cash is used as the plug to make assets and liabilities balance. I know that using debt as the plug would be more realistic. How can I set up a pro forma statement having debt as the plug?

- When I copy a VLOOKUP formula to determine salaries of individual employees, I get a lot of #NA errors. Then when I average the employee salaries, I cannot get a numerical answer because of the #NA errors. Can I easily replace the #NA errors with a blank space so I can compute average salary?

- My worksheet contains quarterly revenues for Wal-Mart. Can I easily compute the revenue for each year and place it in the row containing the first quarter's sales for that year?

- IF statements can get rather large. How many IF statements can I nest in a cell? What is the maximum number of characters allowed in an Excel formula?

The eight situations listed above seem to have little, if anything, in common. However, setting up Microsoft Office Excel 2007 models for each of these situations requires the use of an IF statement. I believe that the IF formula is the single most useful formula in Excel. IF formulas let you conduct conditional tests on values and formulas, mimicking (to a limited degree) the conditional logic provided by computing languages such as C, C++, and Java.

An IF formula begins with a condition such as *A1>10*. If the condition is true, the formula returns the first value listed in the formula; otherwise, we move on within the formula and repeat the process. The easiest way to show you the power and utility of IF formulas is to use them to help answer each of our eight questions.

If I order up to 500 units of a product, I pay $3.00 per unit. If I order from 501 through 1200 units, I pay $2.70 per unit. If I order from 1201 through 2000 units, I pay $2.30 per unit. If I order more than 2000 units, I pay $2.00 per unit. How can I write a formula that expresses the purchase cost as a function of the number of units purchased?

You can find the solution to this question on the *Quantity Discount* worksheet in the file Ifstatement.xlsx. The worksheet is shown in Figure 11-1.

	A	B	C	D
1		cutoff	price	
2	cut1	500	$ 3.00	price1
3	cut2	1200	$ 2.70	price2
4	cut3	2000	$ 2.30	price3
5			$ 2.00	price4
6				
7				
8	order quantit	cost	per unit cost	
9	450	$1,350.00	$ 3.00	
10	900	$2,430.00	$ 2.70	
11	1450	$3,335.00	$ 2.30	
12	2100	$4,200.00	$ 2.00	

Figure 11-1   You can use an IF formula to model quantity discounts.

Suppose cell A9 contains our order quantity. We can compute an order's cost as a function of the order quantity by implementing the following logic:

❑ If A9 is less than or equal to 500, the cost is *3*A9*.

❑ If A9 is from 501 through 1200, the cost is *2.70*A9*.

❑ If A9 is from 1201 through 2000, the cost is *2.30*A9*.

❑ If A9 is more than 2000, the cost is *2*A9*.

We begin by linking the range names in A2:A4 to cells B2:B4, and linking the range names in cells D2:D5 to cells C2:C5. Then we implement this logic in cell B9 with the following formula:

```
IF(A9<=_cut1,price1*A9,IF(A9<=_cut2,price2*A9,IF(A9<=_cut3,price3*A9,price4*A9)))
```

To understand how Excel computes a value from this formula, recall that IF statements are evaluated from left to right. If the order quantity is less than or equal to 500 (*cut1*), the cost is given by *price1*A9*. If the order quantity is not less than or equal to 500, the formula checks to see whether the order quantity is less than or equal to 1200. If this is the case, the order quantity is from 501 through 1200, and the formula computes a cost of *price2*A9*. Next, we check whether the order quantity is less than or equal to 2000. If this is true, the order quantity is from 1201 through 2000, and our formula computes a cost of *price3*A9*. Finally, if the order cost has not yet been computed, our formula defaults to the value *price4*A9*. In each case, the IF formula returns the correct order cost. Note that I typed in three more order quantities in cells A10:A12 and copied our cost formula to B10:B12. For each order quantity, our formula returns the correct total cost.

An IF formula containing more than one IF statement is called a *nested IF formula*.

I've just purchased 100 shares of stock at a cost of $55 per share. To hedge the risk that the stock might decline in value, I purchased 60 six-month European put options. Each option has an exercise price of $45 and costs $5. How can I develop a worksheet that indicates the six-month percentage return on my portfolio for a variety of possible future prices?

Before tackling this problem, I want to review some basic concepts from the world of finance. A European put option allows you to sell at a given time in the future (in this case, six months) a share of a stock for the exercise price (in this case, $45). If our stock's price in six months is $45 or higher, the option has no value. Suppose, however, that the price of the stock in 6 months is below $45. Then you can make money by buying a share and immediately reselling the stock for $45. For example, if in 6 months our stock is selling for $37, you can make a profit of $45–$37, or $8 per share, by buying a share for $37 and then using the put to resell the share for $45. You can see that put options protect you against downward moves in a stock price. In this case, whenever the stock's price in six months is below $45, the puts start kicking in some value. This cushions a portfolio against a decrease in value of the shares it owns. Note also that the percentage return on a portfolio (we will assume that no dividends are paid by the stocks we own) is computed by taking the change in the portfolio's value (*final portfolio value–initial portfolio value*) and dividing that number by the portfolio's initial value.

With this background, let's look at how the six-month percentage return on our portfolio, consisting of 60 puts and 100 shares of our stock, varies as the share price varies between $20 and $65. You can find this solution on the *Hedging* worksheet in the file Ifstatement.xlsx. The worksheet is shown in Figure 11-2 on the next page.

The labels in A2:A7 are linked to cells B2:B7. The initial portfolio value is equal to *100($55)+60($5)=$5,800*, shown in cell B7. By copying from B9 to B10:B18 the formula *IF(A9<exprice,exprice–A9,0)*Nputs*, we compute the final value of our puts. If the six-month price is less than our exercise price, we value each put as *exercise price–six-month price*. Otherwise, each put will in six months have a value of $0. Copying from C9 to C10:C18 the formula *Nshares*A9*, we compute the final value of our shares. Copying from D9 to D10:D18 the formula *((C9+B9)–startvalue)/startvalue)* computes the percentage return on our hedged portfolio. Copying from E9 to E10:E18 the formula

(C9–Nshares*pricenow)/(Nshares*pricenow) computes the percentage return on our portfolio if we are unhedged (that is, buy no puts).

	A	B	C	D	E
2	Nputs	60			
3	Nshares	100			
4	exprice	$ 45.00			
5	pricenow	$ 55.00			
6	putcost	$ 5.00			
7	startvalue	$5,800.00			
8	final stock price	final put value	final share value	percentage return hedged	percentage return unhedged
9	$ 20.00	$1,500.00	$2,000.00	-39.7%	-63.6%
10	$ 25.00	$1,200.00	$2,500.00	-36.2%	-54.5%
11	$ 30.00	$ 900.00	$3,000.00	-32.8%	-45.5%
12	$ 35.00	$ 600.00	$3,500.00	-29.3%	-36.4%
13	$ 40.00	$ 300.00	$4,000.00	-25.9%	-27.3%
14	$ 45.00	$ -	$4,500.00	-22.4%	-18.2%
15	$ 50.00	$ -	$5,000.00	-13.8%	-9.1%
16	$ 55.00	$ -	$5,500.00	-5.2%	0.0%
17	$ 60.00	$ -	$6,000.00	3.4%	9.1%
18	$ 65.00	$ -	$6,500.00	12.1%	18.2%

Figure 11-2   Hedging example that uses IF statements

In Figure 11-2, you can see that if the stock price drops below $45, our hedged portfolio has a larger expected return than our unhedged portfolio. Also note that if the stock price does not decrease, the unhedged portfolio has a larger expected return. This is why the purchase of puts is often referred to as *portfolio insurance*.

Many stock market analysts believe that moving-average trading rules can outperform the market. A commonly suggested moving-average trading rule is to buy a stock when the stock's price moves above the average of the previous 15 months and to sell a stock when the stock's price moves below the average of the previous 15 months' price. How would this trading rule have performed against the Standard & Poor's 500 Index?

In this example, we'll compare the performance of the moving-average trading rule (in the absence of transaction costs for buying and selling stock) to a buy-and-hold strategy. The strength of a moving-average trading rule is that it helps you follow market trends. A moving-average trading rule lets you ride up with a bull market and sell before a bear market destroys you. Our data set contains the monthly value of the S&P 500 Index for the time period January 1871 through October 2002. To track the performance of our moving-average trading strategy, we need to track the following information each month:

❑ What is the average of the S&P 500 Index over the last 15 months?

❑ Do we own stock at the beginning of each month?

❑ Do we buy stock during the month?

❑ Do we sell stock during the month?

❑ What is our cash flow for the month (positive if we sell stock, negative if we buy stock, and 0 otherwise)?

Our worksheet for this situation requires us to scroll down many rows. We would like to keep columns A and B as well as the headings in row 8 visible as we scroll down. To do this, in the file Matrade.xlsx, we move the cursor to cell C9, click View on the Ribbon, and then click Freeze Panes. This presents us with the choices shown in Figure 11-3.

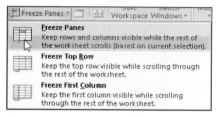

Figure 11-3   Freeze Panes options

We chose the Freeze Panes option. This allows us to keep columns A and B and rows 6–8 visible as we scroll through the worksheet. The Freeze Top Row option (new in Excel 2007) lets us keep just the top row visible while scrolling through the rest of the worksheet. For example, if the top visible row is row 6, then we will see row 6 no matter how far down we scroll. If we choose the Freeze First Column option (also new in Excel 2007), we will always see the leftmost column as we scroll through the worksheet. Selecting Unfreeze Panes from the menu returns us to normal worksheet view.

The file Matradingrule.xlsx, shown in Figure 11-4, includes the formulas needed to track the effectiveness of a moving-average strategy. Tackling this problem requires several IF formulas, and some of the IF formulas will require an AND operator. For example, we'll buy the stock during a month if and only if we don't own the stock at the beginning of the month and the current month's price is larger than the 15-month moving average for the stock's price. The first month for which we can compute a 15-month moving average is April 1872, so we begin our calculations in row 24.

	A	B	C	D	E	F	G
6		S&P				MA profit	$1,319.75
7		Comp.				Buy and hold profit	$849.45
8	Date	P	Own?	MA	Buy?	Sell?	Cash flow
24	1872.04	5.18	Yes	4.7386667	no	no	0
25	1872.05	5.18	Yes	4.788	no	no	0
26	1872.06	5.13	Yes	4.8333333	no	no	0
27	1872.07	5.1	Yes	4.868	no	no	0
28	1872.08	5.04	Yes	4.892	no	no	0
29	1872.09	4.95	Yes	4.904	no	no	0
30	1872.1	4.97	Yes	4.9126667	no	no	0
31	1872.11	4.95	Yes	4.9286667	no	no	0
32	1872.12	5.07	Yes	4.9393333	no	no	0
33	1873.01	5.11	Yes	4.9546667	no	no	0
34	1873.02	5.15	Yes	4.9893333	no	no	0
35	1873.03	5.11	Yes	5.0233333	no	no	0
36	1873.04	5.04	Yes	5.048	no	yes	5.04
37	1873.05	5.05	no	5.06	no	no	0
38	1873.06	4.98	no	5.0713333	no	no	0

Figure 11-4   Moving-average trading rule beats buy and hold!

Let's assume we first owned the stock in April 1872, so we entered Yes in cell C24.

❑ By copying from D24 to D25:D1590 the formula *AVERAGE(B9:B23)*, we compute the 15-month moving average for each month.

> **Note**   An easy way to copy the formula from D24 to D25:D1590 is to point at the lower right corner of cell D24 (the pointer is displayed as a crosshair) and then double-click the left mouse button. Double-clicking copies the formula in a column to match the number of filled rows in the column to the left of the current column. This trick can also be used to copy formulas in multiple columns.

❑ By copying from E24 to E25:E1590 the formula *IF(AND(C24="No",B24>D24),"yes", "no")*, we determine for each month whether our S&P share is purchased during the month. Remember that we purchase the share only if we did not own the stock at the beginning of the month and the current value of the S&P exceeds its 15-month moving average. Notice the AND portion of the formula. It contains two conditions (more than two are allowed) separated by a comma. If both conditions are satisfied, the formula returns *Yes*; otherwise, it returns *No*. For an IF formula to recognize text, you need to place quotation marks (" ") around the text.

❑ By copying from F24 to F25:F1590 the formula *IF(AND(C24="Yes",B24<D24),"yes", "no")*, we determine for each month whether our S&P share is sold. The stock is sold if and only if we owned the S&P share at the beginning of the month and the current value of the S&P share is below the 15-month moving average. April 1873 is the first month in which we sell our S&P stock.

❑ During any month before October 2002, if we buy a share of the S&P during the month, our cash flow is negative the value of the S&P share we bought. If we sell a share of the S&P during the month, our cash flow equals the value of the S&P. Otherwise, the cash flow is 0. During October 2002, we sell any S&P share we own to get credit for its value. Therefore, by copying from G24 to G25:G1589 the formula *IF(E24="yes",–B24,IF(F24="yes",B24,0))*, we record our cash flow for all months before October 2002. Entering in cell G1590 the formula *IF(C1590="yes", B1590,0)* gives us credit for selling any stock we own at the beginning of the last month.

❑ In cell G6, we compute our total profit from the moving-average trading strategy with the formula *SUM(G24:G1590)*. We find the 15-month moving average strategy earns a profit of $1,319.75.

❑ The profit from buying and holding shares is simply the October 2002 S&P value minus the April 1872 S&P value. We compute the profit from the buy-and-hold strategy in cell G7 with the formula B1590–B24. We find that the buy and hold profit of $849.45 is far worse than the profit from the moving-average trading rule. Of course, we ignored the transaction costs incurred in buying and selling stocks. If transaction costs are large, then this might wipe out the excess profits earned by the moving-average trading strategy.

In the game of craps, two dice are tossed. If the total of the dice on the first roll is 2, 3, or 12, you lose. If the total of the dice on the first roll is 7 or 11, you win. Otherwise, the game keeps going. How can I write a formula to determine the status of the game after the first roll?

The fact that you lose in craps if you throw a 2, 3, or 12 can be conveniently modeled by placing an OR formula within an IF formula. In cell B5 of the *Craps* worksheet, shown in Figure 11-5 and found in the file Ifstatement.xlsx, we enter the formula IF(OR(A5=2, A5=3,A5=12),"lose",IF(OR(A5=7,A5=11),"win","keep going")). This formula is then copied from B5 to B6:B7. The formula displays *lose* if a 2, 3, or 12 is entered in cell A5. It displays *win* if a 7 or 11 is entered, and it displays *keep going* for any other value.

	A	B
2	Craps	
3		
4	Toss	Result
5	3	lose
6	7	win
7	9	keep going

Figure 11-5   Using IF statements to model the first roll in craps

In most pro forma financial statements, cash is used as the plug to make assets and liabilities balance. I know that using debt as the plug would be more realistic. How can I set up a pro forma statement having debt as the plug?

A pro forma is basically a prediction of a company's financial future. A pro forma requires construction of a company's future balance sheets and income statements. The balance sheet provides a snapshot of the company's assets and liabilities at any point in time. An income statement tells us how the company's financial status is changing at any point in time. Pro forma statements can help a company determine its future needs for debt and are also key parts of valuation models that stock analysts use to determine whether a stock is properly valued. In the file Proforma.xlsx, I've generated the free cash flows (FCFs) for a company for the next four years. Figure 11-6 on the next page shows the balance sheet, and Figure 11-7 on the next page shows the income statement.

	B	C	D	E	F	G	H
3	Sales growth	SG	0.02		CA/Sales		0.15
4	Initial sales	IS	1,000.00		CL/Sales		0.07
5	Interest rate on debt	IRD	0.10		NFA/Sales		0.60
6	Dividend payout	DIV	0.05		GFA/Sales		0.90
7	Tax rate	TR	0.53				
8	COGS/Sales	COGS	0.75				
9	Depreciation rate	DEP	0.10				
10	Liquid asset interest rate	LAIR	0.09				
11	Balance sheet						
12			0.00	1.00	2.00	3.00	4.00
13	Cash and marketable securities			0.00	0.00	0.00	52.56
14	Current assets		150.00	153.00	156.06	159.18	162.36
15	Gross fixed assets		900.00	1,001.33	1,115.29	1,243.29	1,386.93
16	Acc. dep.		300.00	400.13	511.66	635.99	774.68
17	Net fixed assets		600.00	601.20	603.62	607.30	612.24
18	Total assets		750.00	754.20	759.68	766.48	827.17
19							
20	Current liabilities		70.00	71.40	72.83	74.28	75.77
21	Debt		180.00	118.96	59.33	1.80	0.00
22	Stock		400.00	400.00	400.00	400.00	400.00
23	Retained earnings		100.00	163.84	227.52	290.39	351.40
24	Equity		500.00	563.84	627.52	690.39	751.40
25	Total liabilities		750.00	754.20	759.68	766.48	827.17

Figure 11-6   Pro forma assumptions and balance sheet

	B	C	D	E	F	G	H
27	Income statement		0.00	1.00	2.00	3.00	4.00
28	Sales		1,000.00	1,020.00	1,040.40	1,061.21	1,082.43
29	Cost of goods sold		700.00	765.00	780.30	795.91	811.82
30	Depreciation			100.13	111.53	124.33	138.69
31	Operating income			154.87	148.57	140.97	131.92
32	Interest income			0.00	0.00	0.00	4.73
33	Interest expense			11.90	5.93	0.18	0.00
34	Income before taxes			142.97	142.64	140.79	136.65
35	Taxes			75.77	75.60	74.62	72.42
36	Net income			67.20	67.04	66.17	64.22
37							
38	Beg. retained earnings			100.00	163.84	227.52	290.39
39	Dividends			3.36	3.35	3.31	3.21
40	Ending retained earnings			163.84	227.52	290.39	351.40

Figure 11-7   Pro forma income statement

Column D contains information about the company's current status (during year 0). Our basic assumptions are as follows:

- ❑ Sales growth (SG) is 2 percent per year.

- ❑ Initial sales are $1,000.

- ❑ Interest rate on debt is 10 percent.

- ❑ Dividend payout is 5 percent of net income.

- ❑ The tax rate is 53 percent.

- ❑ Cost of goods sold (COGS) are 75 percent of sales.

- ❑ Depreciation is 10 percent of gross fixed assets.

- ❑ Liquid assets earn 9 percent.

- ❑ Current assets are 15 percent of sales.

- ❑ Current liabilities are 7 percent of sales.

- ❑ Net fixed assets are 60 percent of sales.

I've assigned the names in the cell range C3:C10 to the cells in the range D3:D10. Then, during each Year *t*, basic finance and accounting imply the following relationships, which are then implemented in a series of formulas:

❑ Formula 11.1: *Year t+1 sales=(Year t sales)*(1+SG)*. I've computed sales during each year by copying from E28 to F28:H28 the formula *D28*(1+SG)*.

❑ Formula 11.2: *Year t COGS=COGS*(Year t sales)*. Each year's COGS are computed by copying from E29 to F29:H29 the formula *COGS*E28*.

❑ Formula 11.3: If *Year t assets>Year t liabilities, Year t debt* must be set equal to *Year t total assets−Year t current liabilities−Year t equity*. Otherwise, *Year t debt=0*. I've computed each year's debt in E21:H21 with the formula *IF((E18>E20+E24,E18−E20−E24,0)*. If Year *t* total assets are greater than Year *t* total liabilities, this formula sets Year *t* debt to *Year t total assets−Year t current liabilities−Year t equity*. This equalizes, or balances, assets and liabilities. Otherwise, we set Year *t* debt equal to 0. In this case, Year *t* cash and marketable securities will be used to balance assets and liabilities.

❑ Formula 11.4: *Year t current liabilities=(CL/Sales ratio)*(Year t sales)*. In E20:H20, we use the formula *$H$4*E28* to compute current liabilities for each year (copying this formula from E20 to F20:H20).

❑ Formula 11.5: *Year t equity=Year t stock+Year t retained earnings*. In E24:H24, we compute equity by copying from E24 to F24:H24 the formula *SUM(E22:E23)*.

❑ Formula 11.6: If Year *t* debt is greater than 0, Year *t* cash and marketable securities equals 0. Otherwise, Year *t* cash and marketable securities equals *MAX(0,Year t total liabilities−Year t current assets−Year t net fixed assets)*. In E13:H13, I compute cash and marketable securities for each year by copying from E13 to F13:H13 the formula *IF(E21>0,0,MAX(0,E25−E14−E17))*. If Year *t* debt is greater than 0, we need not use Year *t* cash and marketable securities to balance assets and liabilities.
In this case, we set Year *t* cash and marketable securities equal to 0. Otherwise, we set Year *t* cash and marketable securities equal to *Year t total assets−Year t current liabilities−Year t equity*. This balances assets and liabilities if Year *t* assets (without cash and marketable securities) are less than Year *t* liabilities. If debt does not balance assets and liabilities, this creates liquid assets as the plug that does balance assets and liabilities.

❑ Formula 11.7: *Year t interest expense=(Year t Debt)*IRD*. In E33, I compute interest expense by using the formula *IRD*E21*, copying this formula again to F33:H33.

❑ Formula 11.8: *Year t interest income=(Year t cash and marketable securities)*LAIR*. In E32:H32, I compute interest income by copying from E32 to F32:H32 the formula *LAIR*E13*.

❑ Formula 11.9: *Year t operating income=Year t sales−Year t COGS−Year t depreciation.* In E31:H31, operating income is computed by copying from E31 to F31:H31 the formula *E28−E29−E30*.

❑ Formula 11.10: *Year t dividends=(Year t net income)*DIV.* In E39:H39, I copy from E39 to F39:H39 the formula *E36*DIV* to compute dividends for each year.

❑ Formula 11.11: *Year t+1 beginning retained earnings=Year t ending retained earnings.* I compute beginning retained earnings each year in F38:H38, copying from F38 to G38:H38 the formula *E40*.

❑ Formula 11.12: *Year t end of year retained earnings=Year t beginning retained earnings+Year t net income−Year t dividends.* In E40:H40, I compute each year's ending retained earnings by copying from E40 to F40:H40 the formula *E38+E36−E39*.

❑ Formula 11.13: *Year t income before taxes=Year t operating income−Year t interest expense+Year t cash income.* I compute income before taxes by copying from E34 to F34:H34 the formula *E31−E33+E32*.

❑ Formula 11.14: *Year t taxes=(Year t income before taxes)*TR.* I compute each year's taxes in E35:H35 by copying from E35 to F35:H35 the formula *TR*E34*.

❑ Formula 11.15: *Year t net income after taxes=(Year t income before taxes)−(Year t taxes).* In E36:H36, I compute each year's net income by copying from E36 to F36:H36 the formula *E34−E35*.

❑ Formula 11.16: *Year t net fixed assets=(Year t sales)*(NFA/Sales).* In E17:H17, I compute each year's net fixed assets by copying the formula *$H$5*E28* from E17 to F17:H17.

❑ Formula 11.17: *Year t gross fixed assets=Year t net fixed assets+Year t accumulated depreciation.* In cells E15:H15, I compute gross fixed assets for each year by copying the formula *E17+E16*.

❑ Formula 11.18: *Year t depreciation=(Year t net fixed assets)*DEP.* Each year, I use the formula *DEP*E15* to compute depreciation, copying the formula from E30 to F30:H30.

❑ Formula 11.19: *Year t accumulated depreciation=Year t−1 accumulated depreciation +Year t depreciation.* Each year, I use the formula *D16+E30* to compute accumulated depreciation by copying the formula from E16 to F16:H16.

❑ Formula 11.20: *Year t net fixed assets=Year t gross fixed assets−Year t accumulated depreciation.* In row 17, to compute net fixed assets, I copy from E16 to F16:H16 the formula *D15−D16*.

❑ Formula 11.21: *Year t total assets=Year t liquid assets+Year t net fixed assets+Year t cash and marketable securities.* By adding liquid assets, current assets, and net fixed assets, I compute our total assets by copying from E18 to F18:H18 the formula *SUM(E13,E14,E17)*.

❏ Formula 11.22: *Year t total liabilities=Year t current liabilities+Year t debt+Year t equity.* By copying from E25 to F25:H25 the formula *SUM(E20,E21,E24),* I compute total liabilities for each period. Each year will balance because of our debt and liquid asset statements.

Formulas 11.3 and 11.6 require the use of IF statements. This worksheet will also contain circular references. (For more information about solving circular references, see Chapter 10, "Circular References.") For example, the following relationships create a circular reference:

❏ Year *t* cash affects Year *t* total assets.

❏ Year *t* total assets affect Year *t* debt.

❏ Year *t* debt affects Year *t* cash.

Because our worksheet contains circular references, we need to select the Microsoft Office Button followed by Excel options. Then choose Formulas and check the Enable Iterative Calculations box. As explained in Chapter 10, "Circular References," this will enable Excel to resolve our circular references. Note that for each Year *t*, total assets in row 18 equal total liabilities in row 25. This shows the power of IF formulas and circular references.

When I copy a VLOOKUP formula to determine salaries of individual employees, I get a lot of #N/A errors. Then when I average the employee salaries I cannot get a numerical answer because of the #N/A errors. Can I easily replace the #N/A errors with a blank space so I can compute average salary?

The file Errortrap.xlsx (see Figure 11-8 on the next page) contains salaries and names of 5 employees in the cell range D3:E7. In D11:D15 we have a list of 5 people and we compute their salary by copying from E11 to E12:E15 the formula *=VLOOKUP(D11, $D3:$E$7,2,False).* Unfortunately in cells E13 and E14 we see an #N/A error. NA is short for "not available." Excel returns an #N/A error value when a formula cannot return an appropriate result. Because JR and Josh have no listed salary the VLOOKUP cannot return a salary value for them. Thus when we compute average salary in E16 with formula *=AVERAGE(E11:E15)* we get an #N/A error. Many people I have taught go through and manually replace the #N/A errors with spaces so their average formula will calculate properly (by ignoring the spaces). The *IFERROR* function (new in Excel 2007) makes replacing errors by a desired character (such as space or 0) a snap. The syntax of *IFERROR* is *IFERROR(value,value_if_error).*

The first argument is the formula you want calculated, and the second argument is the value inserted in the cell if your formula returns an error value (other common error values are #DIV/0, #NAME, #NUM, #REF, #VALUE; more on these later in the section). Therefore copying from F11 to F12:F15 the formula *IFERROR(VLOOKUP(D11, $D$3:$E$3:$E7,2,False)," ")* computes salary correctly for each actual employee and enters a blank space for people who are not actual employees. The formula =*AVERAGE(F11:F15)* now correctly computes the average salary for all listed employees.

	D	E	F	G
2		salary		
3	Jane	40		
4	Jack	60		
5	Jill	70		
6	Erica	34		
7	Adam	120		
8				
9				
10	Name	Salary	errortrapped	
11	Erica	34	34	
12	Adam	120	120	
13	JR	#N/A		
14	Josh	#N/A		
15	Jill	70	70	
16	average	#N/A	74.66667	

Figure 11-8   Error trapping formulas

The file Errortypes.xlsx, shown in Figure 11-9, contains examples of other common error values.

	B	C	D	E	F	G	H
1	Error Examples						
2							
3		5	0	#DIV/0!	=C3/D3		
4							
5							
6		5 jack		#VALUE!	=c6+d6		
7				#NAME?	=sum(sales)		
8				#NUM!	=sqrt(-1)		
9			#REF!		=SUM(A1:A3);DELETED COLUMN A		

Figure 11-9   Examples of Excel error values

❑   In cell D3, the formula =*C3/B3* yields a #DIV/0! value because we are dividing by 0.

❑   In cell D6, the formula =*C6+D6* yields a #VALUE! error because *Jack* is not the appropriate type of data for the entered formula. (Jack is text.)

❑   In cell D7, the formula =*SUM(Sales)* returns a #NAME? error indicating that the range name *Sales* referred to in the formula is not defined.

❑   In cell D8, the formula =*SQRT(−1)* results in a #NUM! error. The #NUM error results when you enter an unacceptable argument in a function. Because negative numbers do not have square roots, we receive the #NUM! error.

❑   In cell C9, we entered the formula *SUM(A1:A3)* and then deleted column A. This results in a #REF! error because the cells that we referred to in our formula (cells A1:A3) are no longer in the worksheet.

❑   The IFERROR function can be used to replace any of these error values by any desired number or text string,

My worksheet contains quarterly revenues for Wal-Mart. Can I easily compute the revenue for each year and place it in the row containing the first quarter's sales for that year?

The file Walmartrev.xlsx contains quarterly revenues (in millions of dollars) for Wal-Mart. (See Figure 11-10.) Rows 6, 10, 14, and so on contain the revenues for the first quarter of each year. In each of these rows, we would like to compute total revenues for the year in column E. In other rows, column E should be blank. We could enter in cell E6 the formula *SUM(D6:D9)* and copy this formula to E10, then E14, then E18, and so on. There must be a better way. Using an IF statement with two neat Excel functions, (*ROW()* and *MOD()*), gives us an easy way to enter our formula once and then copy the formula. The function *ROW(cell reference)* yields the row of reference. The function *=ROW(A6)* would yield a 6, whereas if we are in row 6 the *=ROW()* function would also yield a 6. The function *MOD(number,divisor)* yields the remainder when *number* is divided by *divisor*. For example, *MOD(9,4)* yields 1, whereas *MOD(6,3)* yields 0. Note that we want our formula to work only in rows that leave a remainder of 2 when divided by 4. Therefore, copying from E6 to E7:E57 the formula *=IF(MOD(ROW(),4)=2,SUM(D6:D9)," ")* will ensure that we add up revenues for the current year only in rows that leave a remainder of 2 when divided by 4. This means that we compute annual revenues only in the first quarter of each year, as desired.

	B	C	D	E
3	Wal-Mart revenues			
4				
5	Year	Quarter	revenue	Annual revenues
6	1991	1	9,281	43886.76096
7	1991	2	10,340	
8	1991	3	10,628	
9	1991	4	13,639	
10	1992	1	11,649	55483.59296
11	1992	2	13,028	
12	1992	3	13,684	
13	1992	4	17,122	
14	1993	1	13,920	67344.29593
15	1993	2	16,237	
16	1993	3	16,827	
17	1993	4	20,361	
18	1994	1	17,686	82493.89093
19	1994	2	19,942	
20	1994	3	20,418	
21	1994	4	24,448	
22	1995	1	20,440	93627
23	1995	2	22,723	

Figure 11-10

IF statements can get rather large. How many IF statements can I nest in a cell? What is the maximum number of characters allowed in an Excel formula?

In Excel 2007, you can nest up to 64 IF statements in a cell. In previous versions of Excel, you could nest a maximum of 7 IF statements. In Excel 2007, a cell can contain up to 32,000 characters. Previous versions of Excel allowed only 1000 characters in a cell.

Problems

1. Suppose the price of a product will change at dates in the future, as follows:

Date	Price
On or before February 15, 2004	$8
From February 16, 2004, through April 10, 2005	$9
From April 11, 2005, through January 15, 2006	$10
After January 15, 2006	$11

Write a formula that will compute the price of the product based on the date the product is sold.

2. The Blue Yonder Airline flight from Seattle to New York has a capacity of 250 people. The airline sold 270 tickets for the flight at a price of $300 per ticket. Tickets are non-refundable. The variable cost of flying a passenger (mostly food costs and fuel costs) is $30 per passenger. If more than 250 people show up for the flight, the flight is over-booked and Blue Yonder must pay overbooking compensation of $350 per person to each overbooked passenger. Develop a worksheet that computes Blue Yonder's profit based on the number of customers who show up for the flight.

3. A major drug company is trying to determine the correct plant capacity for a new drug. A unit of annual capacity can be built for a cost of $10. Each unit of the drug sells for $12 and incurs variable costs of $2. The drug will be sold for 10 years. Develop a worksheet that computes the company's 10-year profit given the chosen annual capacity level and the annual demand for the drug. We will assume demand for the drug is the same each year. You can ignore the time value of money in this problem.

4. Our drug company is producing a new drug. The company has made the following assumptions:

    ❑ During year 1, 100,000 units will be sold.

    ❑ Sales will grow for three years and then decline for seven years.

    ❑ During the growth period, sales will grow at a rate of 15 percent per year. During the decline, sales will drop at a rate of 10 percent per year.

    Develop a worksheet that takes values for year 1 sales, length of growth cycle, length of decline cycle, growth rate during growth cycle, and rate of decrease during decline cycle, and computes unit sales for years 1–11.

5. We are bidding on a construction project. The low bid will get the project. We estimate our project cost at $10,000. Four companies are bidding against us. It costs $400 to pre-pare the bid. Write a formula that (given the bids of our four competitors and our bid) computes our profit.

6. We are bidding on a valuable painting. The high bid will get the painting. We estimate the painting's value at $10,000. Four companies are bidding against us. It costs $400 to prepare the bid. Write a formula that (given the bids of our four competitors and our bid) determines whether we get the painting.

7. Our drug company believes a new drug will sell 10,000 units during 2004. They expect two competitors to enter the market. The year in which the first competitor enters, our company expects to lose 30 percent of its market share. The year in which the second competitor enters, the company expects to lose 15 percent of its market share. The size of the market is growing at 10 percent per year. Given values of the years in which the two competitors enter, develop a worksheet that computes the annual sales for the years 2004–2013.

8. A clothing store has ordered 100,000 swimsuits. It costs $22 to produce a swimsuit. They plan to sell them until August 31 at a price of $40 and then mark the price down to $30. Given values for demand through August 31 and after August 31, develop a worksheet to compute the profit from this order.

9. In a game of craps, on each roll of the dice after the first roll, the rules are as follows: If the game has not ended and the current roll matches the first roll, we win the game. If the game has not ended and the current roll is a 7, we lose. Otherwise, the game continues. Develop a worksheet that tells us (given knowledge of the first four rolls) the status of the game after four dice rolls.

10. On our S&P moving-average example, suppose we still buy shares if the current price exceeds the 15-month moving average, but we sell if the current price is less than the 5-month moving average. Is this strategy more profitable than selling when the current price is less than the 15-month moving average?

11. A European call option gives us the right to *buy* at a specified future date a share of stock for a given exercise price. A *butterfly spread* involves buying one call option with a low exercise price, buying one call option with a high exercise price, and selling two call options with an exercise price midway between the low and high exercise prices. Here is an example of a butterfly spread: The current stock price is $60. We buy a $54 six-month European call option for $9, buy a $66 six-month European call option for $4, and sell two $60 European call options for the price of $6. Compute the profit (in dollars, not percentage) for this transaction as a function of six-month stock prices ranging from $40–$80. When a trader purchases a butterfly spread, which type of movement in the stock price during the next six months is the trader betting on?

12. Suppose a stock is currently selling for $32.00. We buy a six-month European call option with an exercise price of $30.00 for $2.50 and sell a six-month European call option with an exercise price of $35.00 for $1.00. Compute the profit of this strategy (in dollars) as a function of a six-month stock price ranging from $25.00–$45.00. Why is this strategy called a *bull spread*? How would you modify this strategy to create a *bear spread*?

13. Let's reconsider our pro forma example. Suppose the interest rate on our debt depends on our financial well-being. More specifically, suppose that if our earnings before interest and taxes (EBIT) are negative, our interest rate on debt is 16 percent. If our interest expense is more than 10 percent of EBIT and EBIT is positive, our interest rate on debt is 13 percent. Otherwise, our interest rate is 10 percent. Modify our pro forma to account for this variable interest rate.

14. Do this problem independently of Problem 13. Suppose our firm wants a debt-to-equity ratio of 50 percent during each year. How would you modify our pro forma? Hint: You must keep each year's stock nonnegative and use stock and cash or marketable securities to balance assets and liabilities.

15. Martin Luther King Day occurs on the third Monday in January. Write a formula that computes (given the year) the date of Martin Luther King Day. Hint: First determine the day of the week for January 1 of the given year.

16. Thanksgiving occurs on the fourth Thursday in November. Write a formula that computes (given the year) the date of Thanksgiving. Hint: First determine the day of the week for November 1 of the given year.

17. The first quarter of the year is January–March; the second quarter, April–June; the third quarter, July–September; and the fourth quarter, October–December. Write a formula that returns (for any given date) the quarter of the year.

18. Write a formula that returns a person's age, given his or her date of birth.

19. Labor Day is the first Monday in September. Write a formula that determines the date of Labor Day for a given year.

20. File Nancybonds.xlsx gives the bond rating for several bonds in a previous and future month. You want to efficiently count how many bonds were downgraded. Unfortunately, each company is listed in more than one row. Assuming we have sorted the data on the company name, how would you determine the number of downgraded bonds?

21. The file Addresses.xlsx gives people's names on one line, their street address on the next line, and their city, state, and zip code on the following line. How could you put each person's information on one line?

22. The file FormattingDDAnum.xlsx gives a bunch of text strings such as DDA : D, DDA1250045, and so on. A cell is properly formatted if the first three characters are DDA and the last seven characters are a number 1 million or larger. Determine which cells are properly formatted.

23. Suppose the number of Group 1 members is listed in cell B1, the number of Group 2 members is listed in cell B2 and the number of Group 3 members is listed in cell B3. The total number of group members is always 100. Suppose that Group 1 has 50 members, Group 2 has 30 members, and Group 3 has 20 members. Efficiently place a "1" for each Group 1 member in column D, a "2" for each Group 2 member in column D, and a "3" for each Group 3 member in column D. Thus, column D should (in our example) have a "1" in D1:D50, a "2" in D51:D80 and a "3" in D81:D100.

24. The file Divideby0price.xlsx contains units sold of each product and total revenue. We want to determine the average price for each product. Of course, if units sold are 0, then there is no average price. Error-trap the file Divideby0price.xlsx to ensure that all products with 0 sales yield the message "no sales" instead of a #DIV!0 error.

25. The School of Fine Art has 100 lockers numbered 1–100. At present, all lockers are open. We begin by closing every locker whose number evenly divides by 3. Then we "toggle" (toggling means opening a closed locker and closing an open locker) each locker whose number is divisible by 4; then toggle each locker whose number is divisible by 5,…, and finally toggle each locker whose number is divisible by 100. How many lockers are now open?

26. The file Matchlist.xlsx contains a list of people who bought your product in February and a list of people who bought it in March. Determine how many of your February customers purchased your product in March.

27. Set up a "calendar worksheet" that takes a given month and year as inputs and tells you the day of the week on which each day of the month occurs.

Chapter 12

Time and Time Functions

- How do I enter times into Excel?

- How do I enter a time and date in the same cell?

- How does Excel do computations with times?

- How can I have my worksheet always display the current time?

- How can I use the TIME function to create times?

- How can I use the TIMEVALUE function to convert a text string to a time?

- How do I extract the hour, minute, or second from a given time?

- Given work starting and ending times, how do I determine the number of hours an employee worked?

- I added up the total time an employee worked and I never get more than 24 hours. What did I do wrong?

- How can I easily create a sequence of regularly spaced time intervals?

Recall from Chapter 6, "Dates and Date Functions," that Microsoft Office Excel 2007 gives a date of January 1, 1900 a serial number of 1, a date of January 2, 1900 a serial number of 2, and so on. Excel also assigns serial numbers to times (as a fraction of a 24-hour day). The starting point is midnight, so 3:00 A.M. has a serial number of .125, noon has a serial number of .5, 6:00 P.M. has a serial number of .75, and so on. If you combine a date and time in a cell, then the serial number is the number of days after January 1, 1900 plus the time fraction associated with the given time. Thus, entering January 1, 2007 in a cell yields (when formatted as General) a serial number of 39083, whereas January 1, 2007 6:00 A.M. yields a serial number of 39083.25.

How do I enter times into Excel?

To indicate times we enter a colon (:) after the hour and another colon before the seconds. For example, in file Time.xlsx (see Figure 12-1 on the next page), we entered in cell C2 the time 8:30 A.M. as either simply 8:30 or 8:30 A.M. In cell C3, we entered 8:30 PM as 8:30 PM. As shown in cell D3, we could also have entered 8:30 PM with 24-hour military time as 20:30. In cell A4, we entered 3:10:30 PM. This represents 30 seconds after 3:10 PM.

	A	B	C	D	E
2	8:30 AM	=TIME(8,30,0)	8:30 AM	8:30	
3	8:30 PM	=time(20,30,0)	8:30 PM	20:30	
4	3:10:30 PM	=TIME(15,10,30)	HOUR(A4)	Minute(a4)	SECOND(A4)
5	1:10:30 AM	=TIME(25,10,30)	15.00	10	30
6					
7	0.354166667	=TIMEVALUE("8:30")			
8					
9			start	finish	
10		JANE	9:00 PM	6:00 AM	
11		Jack	7:00 AM	3:30 PM	
12		elapsed time			
13		Jane	9.00		
14		Jack	8.50		
15					
16					
17	Start	5/12/2006 8:12	5/12/2006 8:12		
18	Finish	6/10/2006 12:30	6/10/2006 7:30		
19		29.18	28.97		

Figure 12-1 Examples of time formats

How do I enter a time and date in the same cell?

Simply put a space after the date and enter the time. In cell F13 of file Time.xlsx, we entered January 1, 2007 5:35. Of course, this represents 5:35 A.M. on January 1, 2007. Excel immediately reformatted this to 1/1/2007 5:35.

How does Excel do computations with times?

When Excel does computations with times involving differences in times the displayed result depends on the format used in the cell. Figure 12-2 displays the various Excel time formats.

	C	D	E	F	G	H	I
1					=NOW()	ASTIME	ASNUMBER
2	8:30 AM	8:30			3/7/2007 13:05	1:05 PM	0.55
3	8:30 PM	20:30					
4	HOUR(A4)	Minute(a4)	SECOND(A4)				
5	15.00	10	30	0.50	=C3-C2	12:00 PM	
6				0.50	=d3-d2	12:00	
7				###############	=D2-D3 PROBLEM!		
8				-0.50	CHANGE TO NUMBER FORMAT OK		

Figure 12-2 Excel time formats

In file Time.xlsx (see Figure 12-1), we took the difference between 8:30 PM and 8:30 A.M. in cells F5 and H5 with the formula =C3−C2. If we do not change the format, Excel thinks these times are 12 hours apart and enters 12:00 PM, as shown in cell H5. In most cases, we would like Excel to portray these times are .5 days apart. (Multiplying by 24, we could convert this time difference to hours.) To make Excel show .5 in cell F5 simply format cell F5 as a number.

In cell F7 we try to subtract an earlier time from a later time with the formula =D2−D3. If we do not reformat the cell, then Excel displays the dreaded #############. If we simply change the cell containing the formula to Number format (as in cell F8) we obtain the correct time difference −.5 days.

Cells B17 and C17 give the start times for two jobs whereas cells B18 and C18 give the finish times for the jobs. (See Figure 12-3.) If we want to calculate how many hours it takes to complete each job, simply copy from B19 to C19 the formula =*B18–B17* and reformat the cell as a Number. Thus, the first job took 29.18 days whereas the second job took 28.97 days.

	A	B	C
17	Start	5/12/2006 8:12	5/12/2006 8:12
18	Finish	6/10/2006 12:30	6/10/2006 7:30
19		29.18	28.97

Figure 12-3   Determining time needed to complete jobs

How can I have my worksheet always display the current time?

The Excel formula =*NOW()* gives today's date and the current time. For example, in cell G2 (see Figure 12-4) of file Time.xlsx, entering =*NOW()* yielded 3/7/2007 13:05 because I created the screen capture at 1:05 P.M. on March 7, 2007. To compute the current time, simply enter in cell H2 or I2 the formula =*NOW()–TODAY()*. Cell H2 is formatted to show a time (1:05 P.M.) whereas cell I2 is formatted to show a number (.55days). This represents the fact that 1:05 P.M. is 39 percent of the way between midnight of one day and midnight of the next day.

	G	H	I
1	=NOW()	ASTIME	ASNUMBER
2	3/7/2007 13:05	1:05 PM	0.55

Figure 12-4   Using the *Now()* and *Today()* functions

How can I use the TIME function to create times?

The TIME function has the syntax *TIME(hour,minute,second)*. Given an hour, minute, and second, the TIME function returns a time of day. *The TIME function will never return a value exceeding 24 hours.*

In cell A2 (see Figure 12-1), the formula =*TIME(8,30,0)* yields 8:30 A.M. In cell A3, the formula =*TIME(20,30,0)* yields 8:30 PM. In cell A4, the formula =*TIME(15,10,30)* yields 3:10:30 PM. Finally, note that in cell A5 the formula =*TIME(25,10,30)* treats the 25 like it is *25–24=1* and yields 1:10:30 A.M.

Of course, if the second amount does not show up in a cell, just select a Time format that displays seconds.

How can I use the TIMEVALUE function to convert a text string to a time?

The function TIMEVALUE has the syntax =*TIMEVALUE(timetext)* where *timetext* is a text string that gives a time in a valid format. Then TIMEVALUE returns the time as a fraction between 0 and 1. (This means that the TIMEVALUE function ignores any date in *timetext*.) For example, in cell A7 (see Figure 12-1) the formula =*TIMEVALUE("8:30")* yields 0.354166667 because 8:30 A.M. is 35.4 percent of the way between midnight of one day and midnight of the next day.

How do I extract the hour, minute or second from a given time?

The Excel HOUR, MINUTE, and SECOND functions will extract the appropriate time unit from a cell containing time. For example, (as shown in Figure 12-1) entering in cell C5 the formula =HOUR(A4) yields 15 (3:00 PM is 15:00 military time). Entering in cell D5 the formula =Minute(a4) yields 10 whereas entering =SECOND(A4) in cell E5 yields 30.

Given work starting and ending times, how do I determine the number of hours an employee worked?

In cells C10:D11, we entered the times that Jane and Jack started and ended work. We want to figure out how long each of them worked. (See Figure 12-5.) The problem is that Jane finished work the day after she started, so a simple subtraction will not give the actual number of hours she worked. Copying from C13 to C14 the formula =IF(D10>C10, 24*(D10–C10),24+24*(D10–C10)) yields the correct result. Of course, we formatted these cells as Number. If the finish time is after the start time, then subtracting the start time from the finish time and multiplying by 24 yields hours worked. If the finish time is before the start time, then 24*(finish time–start time) yields a negative number of hours, but adding 24 hours fixes things, assuming the end of the shift was one day later. Thus, Jane worked 9 hours and Jack worked 8.5 hours.

	A	B	C	D
9			start	finish
10		JANE	9:00 PM	6:00 AM
11		Jack	7:00 AM	3:30 PM
12		elapsed time		
13		Jane	9.00	
14		Jack	8.50	

Figure 12-5   Computing length of time worked by employees

I added up the total time an employee worked and I never get more than 24 hours. What did I do wrong?

In cells C31:D35, we give the number of hours (formatted as h:mm) an employee worked on each day of her workweek. (See Figure 12-6.) In cell D36, the formula =SUM(D31:D35) is used to compute the total number of hours worked during the week. Excel yields 14:48. This is clearly wrong! With the format h:mm, Excel will never yield a value exceeding 24 hours. In cell D38, we chose a format (38:48:00) which allows for more than 24 hours. Then summing up the hours worked each day yields the correct number of hours worked (38 hours and 48 minutes).

	C	D
31	mon	9:23
32	tues	8:30
33	wed	7:20
34	thur	9:40
35	fri	3:55
36	total	14:48
37	38 hours 48 min	
38	total reformatte	38:48:00

Figure 12-6   Determining total hours worked during the week

How can I easily create a sequence of regularly spaced time intervals?

Suppose a doctor takes appointments from 8:00 A.M. in 20 minute segments up to 5:00 PM. How can I enter in different rows the list of possible appointment times? Simply use Excel's great Auto Fill feature. (See Figure 12-7.) Simply enter the first two times (8:00 A.M. and 8:20 A.M.) in cells L15: L16. Now select cells L15: L16 and move the cursor to the lower-right corner of cell L16 until you see the black cross. Now drag the pointer down until you see 5:00 PM (the last appointment time). From cells L15: L16, Excel has guessed (correctly!) that you want to enter times that are 20 minutes apart. Of course, entering Monday in a cell and Tuesday below and using Auto Fill will yield the sequence Monday, Tuesday, Wednesday,..., eventually repeating Monday. Entering 1/1/2007 in one cell, 2/1/2007 in another cell, selecting these two cells, and using Auto Fill will yield a sequence of dates like 1/1/2007, 2/1/2007, 3/1/2007, and so on.

	L
14	sequence of times
15	8:00 AM
16	8:20 AM
17	8:40 AM
18	9:00 AM
19	9:20 AM
20	9:40 AM
21	10:00 AM
22	10:20 AM
23	10:40 AM
24	11:00 AM
25	11:20 AM
26	11:40 AM
27	12:00 PM
28	12:20 PM
29	12:40 PM
30	1:00 PM
31	1:20 PM

Figure 12-7   Entering a sequence of times

Problems

1. Write a formula that will return a time 18 hours after the current time.

2. The file Marathon.xlsx gives marathon race times for four runners. Problems a through c refer to this data. Compute the average time of the runners.

   a. How much faster was John than Jill?

   b. How many total minutes did each runner take?

   c. How many total seconds did each runner take?

3. The file Jobshop.xlsx gives the start time and date for several jobs and the time required to complete each job. Determine the completion time for each job.

Chapter 13
The Paste Special Command

- How can I move the results of calculations (not the formulas) to a different part of a worksheet?

- I have a list of names in a column. How can I make the list appear in a row instead of a column?

- I've downloaded U.S. T-Bill interest rates from a Web site into Excel. The data displays a 5 when the interest rate is 5 percent, 8 when the interest rate is 8 percent, and so on. How can I easily divide my results by 100 so that a 5 percent interest rate, for example, is displayed as .05?

With the Paste Special command in Microsoft Office Excel 2007, you can easily manipulate worksheet data. In this chapter, I'll show how you can use the Paste Special command to perform the following types of operations:

- Paste only the values in cells (not the formulas) to a different part of a worksheet.

- Transpose data in columns to rows and vice versa.

- Transform a range of numbers by adding, subtracting, dividing, or multiplying each number in the range by a given constant.

How can I move the results of calculations (not the formulas) to a different part of a worksheet?

In the *Paste Special Value* worksheet in the file Pastespecial.xlsx, the cell range E4:H9 contains the names, games, total points, and points per game for five 10–11-year-old basketball players from Bloomington, Indiana. In the cell range H5:H9, I've used the data in cells F5:G9 to compute each child's points per game, as shown in Figure 13-1 on the next page. Suppose we want to copy this data and the calculated points per game—but not the formulas that perform the calculations—to a different cell range (E13:H18, for example). All you do is select the range E4:H9, press Ctrl+C, and then move to the upper-left corner of the range where you want to copy the data (cell E13 in this example). Next, right-click the upper-left corner cell in the target range, click Paste Special, and then fill in the Paste Special dialog box as indicated in Figure 13-2 on the next page. After clicking OK, the range E13:H18 contains the data but not the formulas from the cell range E4:H9. You can check this by going to cell H16. You will see a value (7) but not the formula that was used to compute Gregory's average points per game. Note that if you use the Paste Special command, select Values, and then paste the data into the same range from which you copied the data, your formulas will disappear from the worksheet.

	E	F	G	H
4		Games	Points	Points/game
5	Dan	4	28	7.00
6	Gabe	4	28	7.00
7	Gregory	5	35	7.00
8	Christian	6	22	3.67
9	Max	6	15	2.50
10				
11				
12				
13		Games	Points	Points/game
14	Dan	4	28	7
15	Gabe	4	28	7
16	Gregory	5	35	7
17	Christian	6	22	3.66666667
18	Max	6	15	2.5

Figure 13-1   Using the Paste Special command to paste only values

Figure 13-2   The Paste Special dialog box with Values selected. Selecting Values pastes only values and not any formulas.

I have a list of names in a column. How can I make the list appear in a row instead of a column?

To realign data from a row to a column (or vice versa), copy the data and then use the Paste Special command with Transpose selected. Essentially, the Transpose option in the Paste Special dialog box "flips" selected cells around so that the first row of the copied range becomes the first column of the range you paste data into, and vice versa. For an example, look at the *Paste Special Transpose* worksheet in the file Pastespecial.xlsx, shown in Figure 13-3.

Suppose that you want to list the players' names in one row (starting in cell E13). Simply select the range E5:E9, and then press Ctrl+C to copy the data. Right-click cell E13, click Paste Special, and check Transpose in the Paste Special dialog box. After clicking OK, Excel transposes the players' names into one row.

	E	F	G	H	I	J
3						
4		Games	Points	Points/game		
5	Dan	4	28	7.00		
6	Gabe	4	28	7.00		
7	Gregory	5	35	7.00		
8	Christian	6	22	3.67		
9	Max	6	15	2.50		
10						
11						
12						
13	Dan	Gabe	Gregory	Christian	Max	
14						
15						
16						
17		Dan	Gabe	Gregory	Christian	Max
18	Games	4	4	5	6	6
19	Points	28	28	35	22	15
20	Points/game	7.00	7.00	7.00	3.67	2.50

Figure 13-3   Use the Transpose option in the Paste Special dialog box to transpose a row of data into a column or a column of data into a row.

Suppose you want to transpose the spreadsheet content in E4:H9 to a range beginning in cell E17. Begin by selecting the range E4:H9. Next, press Ctrl+C. Now move to the upper-left corner of the range where you want to put the transposed information (E17). Right-click and choose Paste Special, check Transpose, and then click OK. You'll see that the content of E4:H9 is transposed (turned on its side), as shown in Figure 13-3. Note that in F20:J20, Excel was smart enough to adjust the points-per-game formula so that the average for each player is now computed from data in the same column instead of the same row.

> **Note**   When you select Paste Special and click Paste Link instead of OK, the transposed cells are linked to the original cells, and changes you make to the original data are reflected in the copy. By changing the value in cell F5 to 7, the value in cell F18 becomes 7 as well, and cell F20 would display Dan's average as 4 points per game.

I've downloaded U.S. T-Bill interest rates from a Web site into Excel. The data displays a 5 when the interest rate is 5 percent, 8 when the interest rate is 8 percent, and so on. How can I easily divide my results by 100 so that a 5 percent interest rate, for example, is displayed as .05?

The *Paste Special Divide* Before worksheet in the file Pastespecial.xlsx (see Figure 13-4 on the next page) contains the annual rate of interest paid by three-month U.S. T-Bills for each month between January 1970 and February 1987. In January 1970, the annual rate on a three-month T-Bill was 8.01 percent. Suppose we want to earn annual interest on $1 invested at the current T-Bill rate. The formula to calculate the rate is *(1+(annual rate)/ 100)*. It would be easier to compute earned interest if our column of annual interest rates were divided by 100.

The Operations area of the Paste Special dialog box lets you add, subtract, multiply, or divide each number in a range by a given number, providing an easy way to divide each interest rate by 100. Here we want to divide each number in column D. To begin, I entered our divisor (100). You can enter it anywhere in the worksheet. I chose F5. With F5 selected, press Ctrl+C. You will see the "moving ants" surrounding cell F5. (See Figure 13-4.) Next, select the range of numbers you want to modify. To select all the data in column D, click in cell D10 and press Ctrl+Shift and then the Down Arrow key. This shortcut is a useful trick for selecting a "tall" cell range. (To select a "wide" set of data listed in one row, move to the first data point and then press Ctrl+Shift and the Right Arrow key.) Next, right-click and choose Paste Special, and then select Divide in the Paste Special dialog box, as shown in Figure 13-5.

	C	D	E	F
5				100
6				
7				
8				
9	date	3mo		
10	1.1970	8.01		
11	2.1970	7.01		
12	3.1970	6.48		
13	4.1970	7.03		
14	5.1970	7.04		
15	6.1970	6.52		
16	7.1970	6.43		
17	8.1970	6.38		
18	9.1970	6.03		
19	10.1970	5.96		
20	11.1970	5.07		
21	12.1970	4.9		
22	1.1971	4.17		
23	2.1971	3.43		
24	3.1971	3.64		
25	4.1971	4.04		
26	5.1971	4.38		
27	6.1971	5.12		
28	7.1971	5.31		

Figure 13-4   Data for using the Divide option in the Paste Special dialog box to divide a data range by a constant.

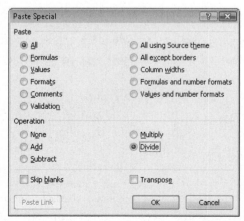

Figure 13-5   You can apply an option in the Operation area of the Paste Special dialog box to a range of cells.

After you click OK, Excel divides each selected number in column D by 100. The results are shown in Figure 13-6. If we had selected Add, D10 would have displayed 108.01; if we had selected Subtract, D10 would have displayed −91.99; and if we had selected Multiply, D10 would have displayed 801.

	C	D	E	F
5				100
6				
7				
8				
9	date	3mo		
10	1.1970	0.0801		
11	2.1970	0.0701		
12	3.1970	0.0648		
13	4.1970	0.0703		
14	5.1970	0.0704		
15	6.1970	0.0652		
16	7.1970	0.0643		
17	8.1970	0.0638		
18	9.1970	0.0603		
19	10.1970	0.0596		
20	11.1970	0.0507		
21	12.1970	0.049		
22	1.1971	0.0417		
23	2.1971	0.0343		
24	3.1971	0.0364		
25	4.1971	0.0404		

Figure 13-6   Results of using the Divide option in the Paste Special dialog box

Problems

1. The file Mavs.xlsx contains statistics for the great 2002–2003 Dallas Mavericks basketball team. Player names are listed in column A, statistical categories are listed in row 3, and statistical results are listed in rows 4–20. Change the worksheet so that all player names are listed in the same row and all statistical categories are listed in the same column.

2. Field goal percentage, free throw percentage, and three-point percentage are listed as decimals. For example, Steve Nash makes 91.9 percent of his free throws, which is listed as .919. Change the worksheet so that all shooting percentages are listed as a number from 1 through 100.

3. The file Productpaste.xlsx contains data on quarterly sales for four products. Copy this data to another range so that quarterly sales are read across instead of down. Link your copied data to the original data so your computation of annual sales in the copied data range will reflect changes entered in rows 5–8.

4. The file Productsalespaste.xlsx contains sales of products x, y, and z (in thousands of units). Convert this sales data to sales in actual units. Hint: Remember you can use the Ctrl key (as explained in Chapter 1, "Range Names") to select a non-contiguous range of cells.

Chapter 14
The Auditing Tool

- I've just been handed a 5000-row worksheet that computes the net present value (NPV) of a new car. In the worksheet, my financial analyst made an assumption about the annual percentage of the growth in the product's price. Which cells in the worksheet are affected by this assumption?

- I think my financial analyst made an error in computing Year 1 before-tax profit. Which cells in the worksheet model were used for this calculation?

- How does the auditing tool work when I'm working with data in more than one worksheet or workbook?

When we hear the word *structure*, we often think about the structure of a building. The structure of a worksheet model refers to the way our input assumptions (data such as unit sales, price, and unit cost) are used to compute outputs of interest, such as NPV, profit, or cost. The Microsoft Office Excel 2007 auditing tool provides an easy method for documenting the structure of a worksheet, which makes understanding the logic underlying complex worksheet models easier. To view the auditing options in Excel 2007, display the Formulas tab of the Ribbon, and then view the Formula Auditing group. (See Figure 14-1.)

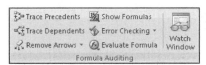

Figure 14-1   The Formula Auditing toolbar

We will discuss Trace Precedents, Trace Dependents, and Remove Arrows. These commands locate and display precedents and dependents for worksheet cells or formulas. A *precedent* is any cell whose value is needed to compute a selected formula's value. For example, if you were analyzing a direct mail campaign, you would make assumptions about the number of letters mailed and the response rate for the mailing. Then you could compute the number of responses as *response rate*letters mailed*. In this case, the response rate and total letters mailed are precedents of the cell containing the formula used to compute total responses. A *dependent* is any cell containing a formula whose values can't be computed without knowledge of a selected cell. In the previous example, the cell containing the total number of responses is a dependent of the cell containing the response rate. Excel marks precedents and dependents with blue arrows when you use the Auditing tool.

Let's apply the Auditing tool to some practical problems.

I've just been handed a 5000-row worksheet that computes the net present value (NPV) of a new car. In the worksheet, my financial analyst made an assumption about the annual percentage of the growth in the product's price. Which cells in the worksheet are affected by this assumption?

The *Original Model* worksheet in the file NPVaudit.xlsx contains calculations that compute the NPV of after-tax profits for a car expected to be available from the manufacturer for five years. (See Figure 14-2.) Price and cost are in thousands of dollars. The parameter values assumed for the analysis are given in cells C1:C8 (with associated range names listed in cells B1:B8). I've assumed that the price of the product will increase by 3 percent per year. Which cells in the worksheet are dependents of this assumption?

	A	B	C	D	E	F
1		taxrate	0.4			
2		Year1sales	10000			
3		Sales growth	0.1			
4		Year1price	$ 9.00			
5		Year1cost	$ 6.00			
6		intrate	0.15			
7		costgrowth	0.05			
8		pricegrowth	0.03			
9	Year	1	2	3	4	5
10	Unit Sales	10000	11000	12100	13310	14641
11	unit price	$ 9.00	$ 9.27	$ 9.55	$ 9.83	$ 10.13
12	unit cost	$ 6.00	$ 6.30	$ 6.62	$ 6.95	$ 7.29
13	Revenues	$ 90,000.00	$ 101,970.00	$115,532.01	$ 130,897.77	$ 148,307.17
14	Costs	$ 60,000.00	$ 69,300.00	$ 80,041.50	$ 92,447.93	$ 106,777.36
15	Before Tax Profit	$ 30,000.00	$ 32,670.00	$ 35,490.51	$ 38,449.83	$ 41,529.81
16	Tax	$ 12,000.00	$ 13,068.00	$ 14,196.20	$ 15,379.93	$ 16,611.92
17	Aftertax Profits	$ 18,000.00	$ 19,602.00	$ 21,294.31	$ 23,069.90	$ 24,917.89
18						
19	NPV	$70,054.34				

Figure 14-2 You can use the auditing tool to trace formulas in complex spreadsheets.

To answer this question, select cell C8 (the cell containing the assumption of 3 percent price growth) and then click the Trace Dependents button in the Formula Auditing group on the Formula tab. Excel displays the set of arrows shown in Figure 14-3, pointing to dependent cells.

By clicking the Trace Dependents button once, Excel points to the cells that *directly* depend on our price growth assumption. In Figure 14-3, you can see that only the unit prices for Years 2–5 depend directly on our price growth assumption. Clicking Trace Dependents repeatedly shows *all* formulas whose calculation requires the value for annual price growth, as shown in Figure 14-4.

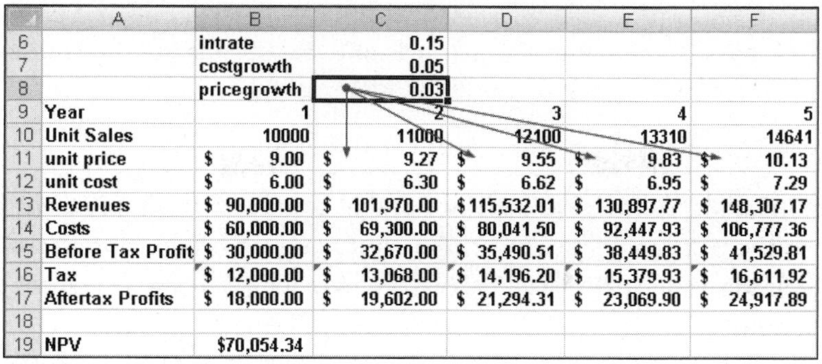

Figure 14-3   Tracing dependent cells

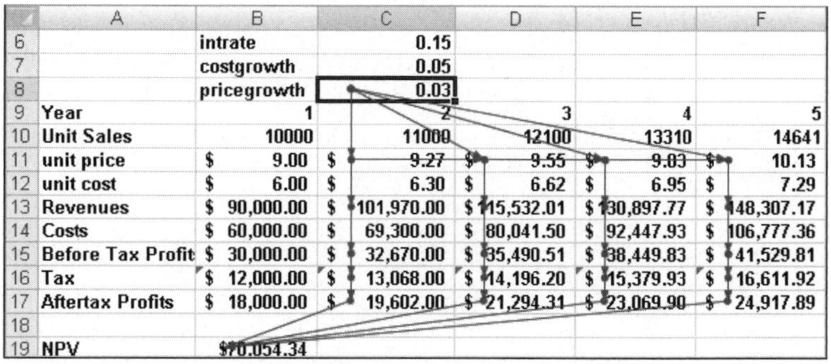

Figure 14-4   Clicking Trace Dependents repeatedly shows all the dependents of the price growth assumption.

You can see that in addition to unit price in Years 2–5, our price growth assumption affects Years 2–5 revenue, before-tax profits, tax paid, after-tax profits, and NPV. You can remove the arrows by clicking the Remove Arrows button.

I think my financial analyst made an error in computing Year 1 before-tax profit. Which cells in the worksheet model were used for this calculation?

Now we want to find the precedents for cell B15. These precedents are the cells needed to compute Year 1 before-tax profit. Select cell B15, and then click the Trace Precedents button once. You'll see the arrows shown in Figure 14-5.

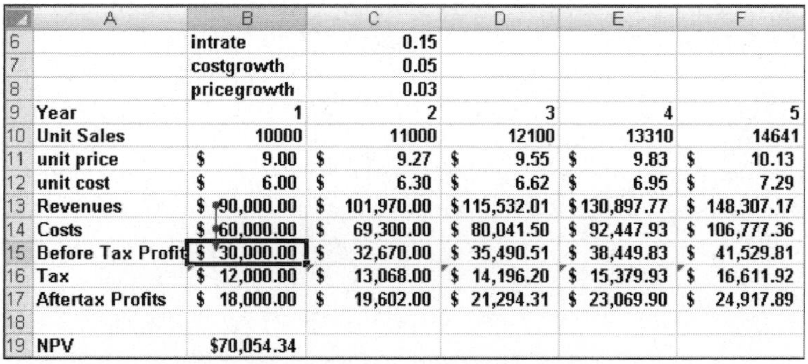

Figure 14-5   Direct precedents for Year 1 before-tax profit

We find that the cells directly needed to compute before-tax Year 1 profit are Year 1 revenues and Year 1 cost. (Before-tax Year 1 profit equals Year 1 revenue minus Year 1 cost.) Repeatedly clicking the Trace Precedents button yields all precedents of Year 1 before-tax profit, as shown in Figure 14-6.

	A	B	C	D	E	F
1		taxrate	0.4			
2		Year1sales	10000			
3		Sales growth	0.1			
4		Year1price	$ 9.00			
5		Year1cost	$ 6.00			
6		intrate	0.15			
7		costgrowth	0.05			
8		pricegrowth	0.03			
9	Year	1	2	3	4	5
10	Unit Sales	10000	11000	12100	13310	14641
11	unit price	$ 9.00	$ 9.27	$ 9.55	$ 9.83	$ 10.13
12	unit cost	$ 6.00	$ 6.30	$ 6.62	$ 6.95	$ 7.29
13	Revenues	$ 90,000.00	$ 101,970.00	$ 115,532.01	$ 130,897.77	$ 148,307.17
14	Costs	$ 60,000.00	$ 69,300.00	$ 80,041.50	$ 92,447.93	$ 106,777.36
15	Before Tax Profit	$ 30,000.00	$ 32,670.00	$ 35,490.51	$ 38,449.83	$ 41,529.81
16	Tax	$ 12,000.00	$ 13,068.00	$ 14,196.20	$ 15,379.93	$ 16,611.92
17	Aftertax Profits	$ 18,000.00	$ 19,602.00	$ 21,294.31	$ 23,069.90	$ 24,917.89
18						
19	NPV	$70,054.34				

Figure 14-6   Click Trace Precedents repeatedly to show all precedents of Year 1 before-tax profit.

We find that the only input assumptions that influence Year 1 before-tax profit are Year 1 sales, Year 1 price, and Year 1 cost.

How does the auditing tool work when I'm working with data in more than one worksheet or workbook?

Consider the simple worksheet model in the workbook Audittwosheets.xlsx, shown in Figure 14-7. The formula in the *Profit* worksheet computes a company's profit (*unit sales**(*price*–*variable cost*)–*fixed cost*) from information contained in the *Data* worksheet.

	A	B	C	D			C	D	E
6				Profit		4	Fixed cost	10000	
7				$2,900.00		5	Unit Sales	3000	
8						6	Price	$ 7.50	
9						7	Variable cost	$ 3.20	

Figure 14-7   Data for using the auditing tool with data on multiple worksheets

Suppose we want to know the precedents of the profit formula. Select cell D7 in the *Profit* worksheet, and then click Trace Precedents in the Formula Auditing group on the Formula tab. You'll see a dotted line, an arrow, and the worksheet icon shown in Figure 14-8.

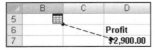

Figure 14-8   Results of tracing precedents with data on multiple worksheets

The worksheet icon indicates that the precedents of the profit formula lie in another worksheet. Double-clicking on the dotted line displays the Go To dialog box, shown in Figure 14-9.

Figure 14-9   With the Go To dialog box, you can audit data in multiple worksheets.

Now we can click any of the listed precedents (cells D4:D7 in the *Data* worksheet), and Excel will send us to the precedent we selected.

Problems

- In the car NPV example, determine the following:
  - ❑ The direct dependents and all dependents of the interest rate.
  - ❑ The direct dependents and all dependents of the tax rate.
  - ❑ The direct precedents and all precedents for Year 4 unit sales.
  - ❑ The direct precedents and all precedents for Year 3 costs.

Chapter 15
Sensitivity Analysis with Data Tables

- I'm thinking of starting a store in the local mall to sell gourmet lemonade. Before opening the store, I'm curious about how my profit, revenue, and variable costs will depend on the price I charge and the unit cost.

- I am going to build a new house. The amount of money I need to borrow (with a 15-year repayment period) depends on the price I sell my current house for. I'm also unsure about the annual interest rate I'll receive when I close. Can I determine how my monthly payments will depend on the amount borrowed and the annual interest rate?

- A major Internet company is thinking of purchasing another online retailer. The retailer's current annual revenues are $100 million, with expenses of $150 million. Current projections indicate that the retailer's revenues are growing at 25 percent per year and its expenses are growing at 5 percent per year. We know projections might be in error, however, and we would like to know, for a variety of assumptions about annual revenue and expense growth, the number of years before the retailer will show a profit.

Most worksheet models contain assumptions about certain parameters or inputs to the model. In our lemonade example, the inputs would include:

- The price for which a glass of lemonade is sold

- The variable cost of producing a glass of lemonade

- The sensitivity of demand for lemonade to price charged

- The annual fixed cost of running a lemonade stand

Based on input assumptions, we can compute outputs of interest. For the lemonade example, the outputs of interest might include:

- Annual profit

- Annual revenue

- Annual variable cost

Despite best intentions, assumptions about input values can be in error. For example, our best guess about the variable cost of producing a glass of lemonade might be $0.45, but it's possible that our assumption will be in error. *Sensitivity analysis* determines how a spreadsheet's outputs vary in response to changes to its inputs. For example, we might want to see how a change in product price affects yearly profit, revenue, and variable cost. A data table in Microsoft Office Excel 2007 makes it easy to vary one or two inputs and perform a sensitivity analysis. With a *one-way* data table, you can determine how changing one input will change any number of outputs. With a *two-way* data table, you can determine how changing two inputs will change a single output. Our three examples will show how easy it is to use a data table and obtain meaningful sensitivity results.

I'm thinking of starting a store in the local mall to sell gourmet lemonade. Before opening the store, I'm curious about how my profit, revenue, and variable costs will depend on the price I charge and the unit cost.

The work required for this analysis is in the file Lemonade.xlsx. (See Figures 15-1, 15-2, and 15-4.) Our input assumptions are are given in the range D1:D4. We're assuming that annual demand for lemonade (see the formula in cell D2) equals *65000–9000*price*. (Chapter 7, "Evaluating Investments by Using Net Present Value Criteria," contains a discussion of how to estimate a demand curve.) I've created the names in C1:C7 to correspond to cells D1:D7.

I computed annual revenue in cell D5 with the formula *demand*price*. In cell D6, I computed the annual variable cost with the formula *unit_cost*demand*. Finally, in cell D7, I computed profit by using the formula *revenue–fixed_cost–variable_cost*.

	C	D
1	price	$ 4.00
2	demand	29000
3	unit cost	$ 0.45
4	fixed cost	$ 45,000.00
5	revenue	$ 116,000.00
6	variable cost	$ 13,050.00
7	profit	$ 57,950.00

Figure 15-1   The inputs that change the profitability of a lemonade store

Suppose that I want to know how changes in price (for example, from $1.00 through $4.00 in $0.25 increments) affect annual profit, revenue, and variable cost. Because we're changing only one input, a one-way data table will solve our problem. The data table is shown in Figure 15-2.

To set up a one-way data table, begin by listing input values in a column. I listed the prices of interest (ranging from $1.00 through $4.00 in $0.25 increments) in the range C11:C23. Next, I moved over one column and up one row from the list of input values, and there I listed the formulas we want a data table to calculate. I entered the formula for profit in cell D10, the formula for revenue in cell E10, and the formula for variable cost in cell F10.

Now select the table range (C10:F23). The table range begins one row above the first input; its last row is the row containing the last input value. The first column in the table range is the column containing the inputs; its last column is the last column containing an output. After selecting the table range, display the Data tab of the Ribbon. In the Data Tools group, click What-If Analyis, and then click Data Table. Now fill in the Data Table dialog box as shown in Figure 15-3.

	B	C	D	E	F
9			profit	revenue	variable cost
10	price		57950	116000	13050
11		$ 1.00	$ (14,200.00)	$ 56,000.00	$ 25,200.00
12		$ 1.25	$ (2,000.00)	$ 67,187.50	$ 24,187.50
13		$ 1.50	$ 9,075.00	$ 77,250.00	$ 23,175.00
14		$ 1.75	$ 19,025.00	$ 86,187.50	$ 22,162.50
15		$ 2.00	$ 27,850.00	$ 94,000.00	$ 21,150.00
16		$ 2.25	$ 35,550.00	$ 100,687.50	$ 20,137.50
17		$ 2.50	$ 42,125.00	$ 106,250.00	$ 19,125.00
18		$ 2.75	$ 47,575.00	$ 110,687.50	$ 18,112.50
19		$ 3.00	$ 51,900.00	$ 114,000.00	$ 17,100.00
20		$ 3.25	$ 55,100.00	$ 116,187.50	$ 16,087.50
21		$ 3.50	$ 57,175.00	$ 117,250.00	$ 15,075.00
22		$ 3.75	$ 58,125.00	$ 117,187.50	$ 14,062.50
23		$ 4.00	$ 57,950.00	$ 116,000.00	$ 13,050.00

Figure 15-2   One-way data table with varying prices

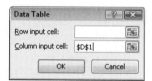

Figure 15-3   Creating a data table

As the column input cell, use the cell in which you want the listed inputs—that is, the values listed in the first column of the data table range—to be assigned. Because the listed inputs are prices, I chose D1 as the column input cell. After clicking OK, Excel creates the one-way data table shown in Figure 15-4.

	B	C	D	E	F
1		price	$ 4.00		
2		demand	29000		
3		unit cost	$ 0.45		
4		fixed cost	$ 45,000.00		
5		revenue	$ 116,000.00		
6		variable cost	$ 13,050.00		
7		profit	$ 57,950.00		
8					
9			profit	revenue	variable cost
10	price		57950	116000	13050
11		$ 1.00	$ (14,200.00)	$ 56,000.00	$ 25,200.00
12		$ 1.25	$ (2,000.00)	$ 67,187.50	$ 24,187.50
13		$ 1.50	$ 9,075.00	$ 77,250.00	$ 23,175.00
14		$ 1.75	$ 19,025.00	$ 86,187.50	$ 22,162.50
15		$ 2.00	$ 27,850.00	$ 94,000.00	$ 21,150.00
16		$ 2.25	$ 35,550.00	$ 100,687.50	$ 20,137.50
17		$ 2.50	$ 42,125.00	$ 106,250.00	$ 19,125.00
18		$ 2.75	$ 47,575.00	$ 110,687.50	$ 18,112.50
19		$ 3.00	$ 51,900.00	$ 114,000.00	$ 17,100.00
20		$ 3.25	$ 55,100.00	$ 116,187.50	$ 16,087.50
21		$ 3.50	$ 57,175.00	$ 117,250.00	$ 15,075.00
22		$ 3.75	$ 58,125.00	$ 117,187.50	$ 14,062.50
23		$ 4.00	$ 57,950.00	$ 116,000.00	$ 13,050.00

Figure 15-4   One-way data table with varying prices

In the range D11:F11, profit, revenue, and variable cost are computed for a price of $1.00. In cells D12:F12, profit, revenue, and variable cost are computed for a price of $1.25, and on through the range of prices. The profit-maximizing price among all listed prices is $3.75. A price of $3.75 would produce an annual profit of $58,125.00, annual revenue of $117,187.50, and an annual variable cost of $14,062.50.

Suppose I want to determine how annual profit varies as price varies from $1.50 through $5.00 (in $0.25 increments) and unit variable cost varies from $0.30 through $0.60 (in $0.05 increments). Because we're changing two inputs, we need a *two-way* data table. (See Figure 15-5.) I list the values for one input down the first column of the table range (I'm using the range H11:H25 for the price values), and the values for the other input in the first row of the table range. (In this example, the range I10:O10 holds the list of variable cost values.) A two-way data table can have only one output cell, and the formula for the output must be placed in the upper-left corner of the table range. Therefore, I placed the profit formula in cell H10.

	G	H	I	J	K	L	M	N	O
9			var cost						
10		57950	$ 0.30	$ 0.35	$ 0.40	$ 0.45	$ 0.50	$ 0.55	$ 0.60
11		$ 1.50	$16,800.00	$14,225.00	$11,650.00	$ 9,075.00	$ 6,500.00	$ 3,925.00	$ 1,350.00
12		$ 1.75	$26,412.50	$23,950.00	$21,487.50	$19,025.00	$16,562.50	$14,100.00	$11,637.50
13		$ 2.00	$34,900.00	$32,550.00	$30,200.00	$27,850.00	$25,500.00	$23,150.00	$20,800.00
14		$ 2.25	$42,262.50	$40,025.00	$37,787.50	$35,550.00	$33,312.50	$31,075.00	$28,837.50
15		$ 2.50	$48,500.00	$46,375.00	$44,250.00	$42,125.00	$40,000.00	$37,875.00	$35,750.00
16		$ 2.75	$53,612.50	$51,600.00	$49,587.50	$47,575.00	$45,562.50	$43,550.00	$41,537.50
17		$ 3.00	$57,600.00	$55,700.00	$53,800.00	$51,900.00	$50,000.00	$48,100.00	$46,200.00
18		$ 3.25	$60,462.50	$58,675.00	$56,887.50	$55,100.00	$53,312.50	$51,525.00	$49,737.50
19		$ 3.50	$62,200.00	$60,525.00	$58,850.00	$57,175.00	$55,500.00	$53,825.00	$52,150.00
20	price	$ 3.75	$62,812.50	$61,250.00	$59,687.50	$58,125.00	$56,562.50	$55,000.00	$53,437.50
21		$ 4.00	$62,300.00	$60,850.00	$59,400.00	$57,950.00	$56,500.00	$55,050.00	$53,600.00
22		$ 4.25	$60,662.50	$59,325.00	$57,987.50	$56,650.00	$55,312.50	$53,975.00	$52,637.50
23		$ 4.50	$57,900.00	$56,675.00	$55,450.00	$54,225.00	$53,000.00	$51,775.00	$50,550.00
24		$ 4.75	$54,012.50	$52,900.00	$51,787.50	$50,675.00	$49,562.50	$48,450.00	$47,337.50
25		$ 5.00	$49,000.00	$48,000.00	$47,000.00	$46,000.00	$45,000.00	$44,000.00	$43,000.00

Figure 15-5 A two-way data table showing profit as a function of price and unit variable cost

I select the table range (cells H10:O25), and display the Data tab. In the Data Tools group, click What-If Analysis, and then click Data Table. Cell D1 (price) is the column input cell, and cell D3 (unit variable cost) is the row input cell. This ensures that the values in the first column of the table range are used as prices, and the values in the first row of the table range are used as unit variable costs. After clicking OK, we see the two-way data table shown in Figure 15-5. As an example, in cell K19, when we charge $3.50 and the unit variable cost is $0.40, our annual profit equals $58,850.00. For each unit cost, I've highlighted the profit-maximizing price. Note that as the unit cost increases, the profit-maximizing price increases as we pass on some of the cost increase to our customers. Of course, we can only guarantee that the profit-maximizing price in the data table is within $0.25 of the actual profit-maximizing price. When we study the Excel Solver in Chapter 70, "Estimating a Demand Curve," you'll learn how to determine (to the penny) the exact profit-maximizing price.

Here are some other notes on this problem:

- ❏ As you change input values in a worksheet, the values calculated by a data table change, too. For example, if we increased fixed cost by $10,000, all profit numbers in the data table would be reduced by $10,000.

- ❏ You can't delete or edit a portion of a data table. If you want to save the values in a data table, select the table range, copy the values, and then right-click and select Paste Special. Then choose Values from the Paste Special menu. If you take this step, however, changes to your worksheet inputs will no longer cause the data table calculations to update.

- ❏ When setting up a two-way data table, be careful not to mix up your row and column input cells. A mix-up will cause nonsensical results.

- ❏ Most people set their worksheet calculation mode to Automatic. With this setting, any change in your worksheet will cause all your data tables to be recalculated. Usually, you want this, but if your data tables are large, automatic recalculation can be incredibly slow. If the constant recalculation of data tables is slowing your work down, click the Microsoft Office Button, click Excel Options, and then click the Formulas tab. Then select Automatic Except For Data Tables. When Automatic Except For Data Tables is selected, all your data tables recalculate only when you press the F9 (recalculation) key. Alternatively, you can click the Calculation Options button (in the Calculation group on the Formulas tab), and then click Automatic Except For Data Tables.

I am going to build a new house. The amount of money I need to borrow (with a 15-year repayment period) depends on the price I sell my current house for. I'm also unsure about the annual interest rate I'll receive when I close. Can I determine how my monthly payments will depend on the amount borrowed and the annual interest rate?

The real power of data tables becomes evident when you combine a data table with one of the Excel functions. In this example, we'll use a two-way data table to vary two inputs (the amount borrowed and the annual interest rate) to the Excel PMT function and determine how the monthly payment will vary as these inputs change. (The PMT function is discussed in detail in Chapter 9, "More Excel Financial Functions.") Our work for this example is in the file Mortgagedt.xlst, shown in Figure 15-6 on the next page.

Suppose we're borrowing money on a 15-year mortgage, where monthly payments are made at the end of each month. I've input the amount borrowed in cell D2, the number of months in the mortgage (180) in D3, and annual interest rate in D4. I've associated the range names in cells C2:C4 with the cells D2:D4. Based on these inputs, we compute our monthly payment in D5 with the formula:

```
-PMT(Annual_int_rate/12,Number_of_Months,Amt_Borrowed)
```

	C	D	E	F	G	H	I	J
3	Number of Months	180						
4	Annual int rate	6%						
5	Monthly Payment	$3,375.43						
6			Annual	Interest	Rate			
7	$3,375.43	5.0%	5.5%	6.0%	6.5%	7.0%	7.5%	8.0%
8	$ 300,000.00	2372.38088	2451.25	2531.57	2613.322	2696.485	2781.037	2866.956
9	$ 350,000.00	2767.777694	2859.792	2953.499	3048.876	3145.899	3244.543	3344.782
10	$ 400,000.00	3163.174507	3268.334	3375.427	3484.429	3595.313	3708.049	3822.608
11	$ 450,000.00	3558.57132	3676.876	3797.356	3919.983	4044.727	4171.556	4300.434
12	$ 500,000.00	3953.968134	4085.417	4219.284	4355.537	4494.141	4635.062	4778.26
13	$ 550,000.00	4349.364947	4493.959	4641.213	4791.091	4943.555	5098.568	5256.086
14	$ 600,000.00	4744.76176	4902.501	5063.141	5226.644	5392.97	5562.074	5733.913
15	$ 650,000.00	5140.158574	5311.042	5485.069	5662.198	5842.384	6025.58	6211.739

Figure 15-6 You can use a data table to determine how mortgage payments vary as the amount borrowed and the interest rate change.

We think the amount borrowed will range (depending on the price we sell our current house for) between $300,000 and $650,000 and that our annual interest rate will range between 5 percent and 8 percent. In preparation for creating a data table, I entered the amounts borrowed in the range C8:C15 and possible interest rate values in the range D7:J7. Cell C7 contains the output we want to recalculate for various input combinations. Therefore, I set cell C7 equal to cell D5. Next I select the table range (C7:J15), click What-If Analysis on the Data tab, and then click Data Table. Because numbers in the first column of the table range are amounts borrowed, the column input cell is D2. Numbers in the first row of the table are annual interest rates, so our row input cell is D4. After clicking OK, we see the data table shown in Figure 15-6. This table shows us, for example, that if we borrow $400,000 at an annual rate of 6 percent, our monthly payments would be just over $3,375. Our data table also shows us that at a low interest rate (for example, 5 percent), an increase of $50,000 in the amount borrowed raises our monthly payment by around $395, whereas at a high interest rate (such as 8 percent), an increase of $50,000 in the amount borrowed raises our monthly payment by about $478.

A major Internet company is thinking of purchasing another online retailer. The retailer's current annual revenues are $100 million, with expenses of $150 million. Current projections indicate that the retailer's revenues are growing at 25 percent per year and its expenses are growing at 5 percent per year. We know projections might be in error, however, and we would like to know, for a variety of assumptions about annual revenue and expense growth, the number of years before the retailer will show a profit.

We want to determine the number of years needed to break even, using annual growth rates in revenue from 10 percent through 50 percent and annual expense growth rates from 2 percent through 20 percent. Let's also assume that if the firm cannot break even in 13 years, we'll say "cannot break even." Our work is in the file Bezos.xlsx, shown in Figures 15-7 and 15-8.

I chose to hide columns A and B and rows 16–18. To hide columns A and B, select any cells in columns A and B (or select the column headings). Then display the Home tab. In the Cells group, click Format, point to Hide & Unhide, and select Hide Columns. To hide rows 16–18, select any cells in those rows (or select the row headings) and repeat the previous procedure, selecting Hide Rows. Of course, the Format Visibility options also include Unhide Rows and Unhide Columns. If you receive a worksheet with many hidden rows and columns and want to quickly unhide all of them, you can select the entire worksheet by clicking the Select All button at the intersection of the column and row headings. Now selecting Unhide Rows and/or Unhide Columns will unhide all hidden rows and/or columns in the worksheet.

In row 11, I project the firm's revenue out 13 years (based on the annual revenue growth rate assumed in E7) by copying from F11 to G11:R11 the formula *E11*(1+$E$7)*. In row 12, I project the firm's expenses out 13 years (based on the annual expense growth rate assumed in E8) by copying from F12 to G12:R12 the formula *E12*(1+$E$8)*. (See Figure 15-7.)

	C	D	E	F	G	H	P	Q	R
7	Revenue	1E+08	0.25						
8	Exp	1.50E+08	0.05						
9									
10			0	1	2	3	11	12	13
11		Rev	1E+08	1.25E+08	1.56E+08	1.95E+08	1.16E+09	1.46E+09	1.82E+09
12		Exp	1.5E+08	1.58E+08	1.65E+08	1.74E+08	2.57E+08	2.69E+08	2.83E+08
13		Breakeven		0	0	3	0	0	0
14									
15		Total	3						

Figure 15-7   You can use a data table to calculate how many years it will take to break even.

We would like to use a two-way data table to determine how varying our growth rates for revenues and expenses affects the years needed to break even. We need *one cell* whose value always tells us the number of years needed to break even. Because we can break even during any of the next 13 years, this might seem like a tall order.

I begin by using in row 13 an IF statement for each year to determine whether we break even during a year. The IF statement returns the number of the year if we break even during the year or 0 otherwise. I determine the year we break even in cell E15 by simply adding together all the numbers in row 13. Finally, I can use cell E15 as the output cell for our two-way data table.

I copy from cell F13 to G13:R13 the formula *IF(AND(E11<E12,F11>F12),F10,0)*. This formula reflects the fact that we break even for the first time during a year if, and only if, during the previous year, revenues are less than expenses *and* during the current year, revenues are greater than expenses. If this is the case, we enter the year number in row 13; otherwise, we enter 0.

Now, in cell E15, I can determine the breakeven year (if any) with the formula *IF(SUM (F13:R13)>0,SUM(F13:R13),"No BE")*. If we do not break even during the next 13 years, the formula enters the text string "No BE".

I now enter our annual revenue growth rates (10 percent through 50 percent) in the range E21:E61. I enter annual expense growth rates (2 percent to 20 percent) in the range F20:X20. I ensure that the year-of-breakeven formula is copied to cell E20 with the formula *=E15*. Next, I select the table range E20:X61, click What-If Analysis on the Data tab, and then click Data Table. I select cell E7 (revenue growth rate) as the column input cell and cell E8 (expense growth rate) as the row input cell. We obtain the two-way data table shown in Figure 15-8.

	D	E	F	G	H	P	Q	R	W	X
15	Total	3								
19				Exp growth						
20		3	0.02	0.03	0.04	0.12	0.13	0.14	0.19	0.2
21		0.1	6	7	8 No BE	No BE	No BE	No BE	No BE	No BE
22	Rev	0.11	5	6	7 No BE	No BE	No BE	No BE	No BE	No BE
23	growth	0.12	5	5	6 No BE	No BE	No BE	No BE	No BE	No BE
24		0.13	4	5	5 No BE	No BE	No BE	No BE	No BE	No BE
25		0.14	4	4	5 No BE	No BE	No BE	No BE	No BE	No BE
55		0.44	2	2	2	2	2	2	3	3
56		0.45	2	2	2	2	2	2	3	3
57		0.46	2	2	2	2	2	2	2	3
58		0.47	2	2	2	2	2	2	2	2
59		0.48	2	2	2	2	2	2	2	2
60		0.49	2	2	2	2	2	2	2	2
61		0.5	2	2	2	2	2	2	2	2

Figure 15-8   A two-way data table

Note, for example, that if expenses grow at 4 percent a year, a 10-percent annual growth in revenue will result in breaking even in eight years, whereas a 50-percent annual growth in revenue will result in breaking even in only two years! Also note that if expenses grow at 12 percent per year and revenues grow at 14 percent per year, we will not break even by the end of 13 years.

Problems

1. You've been assigned to analyze the profitability of Bill Clinton's new autobiography. The following assumptions have been made:

    ❏ Bill is receiving a one-time royalty payment of $12 million.

    ❏ The fixed cost of producing the hardcover version of the book is $1 million.

    ❏ The variable cost of producing each hardcover book is $4.

    ❏ The publisher's net from book sales per hardcover unit sold is $15.

    ❏ The publisher expects to sell 1 million hardcover copies.

    ❏ The fixed cost of producing the paperback is $100,000.

    ❏ The variable cost of producing each paperback book is $1.

    ❏ The publisher's net from book sales per paperback unit sold is $4.

    ❏ Paperback sales will be double hardcover sales.

    Use this information to answer the following questions.

    ❏ Determine how the publisher's before-tax profit will vary as hardcover sales vary from 100,000 through 1 million copies.

❏ Determine how the publisher's before-tax profit varies as hardcover sales vary from 100,000 through 1 million copies and the ratio of paperback to hardcover sales varies from 1 through 2.4.

2. The annual demand for a product equals $500-3p+10a^{.5}$ where p is the price of the product in dollars and a is hundreds of dollars spent on advertising the product. The annual fixed cost of selling the product is $10,000 and the unit variable cost of producing the product is $12. Determine a price (within $10) and amount of advertising (within $100) that maximizes profit.

3. Reconsider our hedging example in Chapter 11, "IF Statements." For stock prices in six months that range from $20.00 through $65.00 and the number of puts purchased varying from 0 through 100 (in increments of 10), determine the percentage return on your portfolio.

4. For our mortgage example, suppose you know the annual interest rate will be 5.5 percent. Create a table that shows for amounts borrowed from $300,000 through $600,000 (in $50,000 increments) the difference in payments between a 15-year, 20-year, and 30-year mortgage.

5. Currently, we sell 40,000 units of a product for $45 each. The unit variable cost of producing the product is $5. We are thinking of cutting the product price by 30 percent. We are sure this will increase sales by an amount from 10 percent through 50 percent. Perform a sensitivity analysis to show how profit will change as a function of the percentage increase in sales. Ignore fixed costs.

6. Let's assume that at the end of each of the next 40 years, we will put the same amount in our retirement fund and earn the same interest rate each year. Show how the amount of money we will have at retirement changes as we vary our annual contribution from $5,000 through $25,000 and the rate of interest varies from 3 percent through 15 percent.

7. The *payback period* for a project is the number of years needed for a project's future profits to pay back the project's initial investment. A project requires a $300 million investment at Time 0. The project yields profit for 10 years, and Time 1 cash flow will be between $30 million and $100 million. Annual cash flow growth will be from 5 percent through 25 percent a year. How does the project payback depend on the year 1 cash flow and cash flow growth rates?

8. A software development company is thinking of translating a software product into Swahili. Currently, 200,000 units of the product are sold per year at a price of $100 each. Unit variable cost is $20.00. The fixed cost of translation is $5 million. Translating the product into Swahili will increase sales during each of the next three years by some unknown percentage over the current level of 200,000 units. Show how the change in profit resulting from the translation depends on the percentage increase in product sales. You can ignore the time value of money and taxes in your calculations.

9. The file Citydistances.xlsx gives latitude and longitude for several U.S. cities. There is also a formula that determines the distance between two cities by using a given latitude and longitude. Create a table that computes the distance between any pair of of cities listed.

10. You have begun saving for your child's college education. You plan to save $5,000 per year, and want to know for annual rates of return on your investment from 4 percent through 12 percent the amount of money you will have in the college fund after saving for 10–15 years.

11. If we earn interest at percentage rate r per year and compound our interest n times per year, then in y years $1 will grow to $(1+(r/n))^{ny}$ dollars. Assuming a 10 percent annual interest rate, create a table showing the factor by which $1 will grow in 5–15 years for daily, monthly, quarterly, and semiannual compounding.

12. Assume I have $100 in the bank. Each year, I will withdraw x percent (ranging from 4 percent through 10 percent) of my original balance. For annual growth rates of 3 percent through 10 percent per year, determine how many years it will take before I run out of money. Hint: You should use the IFERROR function (discussed in Chapter 11, "IF Statements") because if my annual growth rate exceeds the withdrawal rate, I will never run out of money.

13. If we earn interest at an annual rate of x percent per year, then in n years $1 will become $(1+x)^n$ dollars. For annual rates of interest from 1 percent through 20 percent, determine the exact time (in years) in which $1 will double.

14. We are borrowing $200,000 and making payments at the end of each month. For an annual interest rate ranging from 5 percent through 10 percent and loan durations of 10, 15, 20, 25, and 30 years, determine the total interest paid on the loan.

15. You are saving for your child's college fund. You are going to contribute the same amount of money in the fund at the end of each year. Your goal is to end up with $100,000. For annual investment returns ranging from 4 percent through 15 percent and number of years investing varying from 5–15 years, determine your required annual contribution.

16. The file Antitrustdata.xlsx gives the starting and ending years for many court cases. Determine the number of court cases active during each year.

Chapter 16
The Goal Seek Command

- For a given price, how many glasses of lemonade does a lemonade store need to sell per year to break even?

- We want to pay off our mortgage in 15 years. The annual interest rate is 6 percent. The bank told us we can afford monthly payments of $2,000. How much can we borrow?

- I always had trouble with "story problems" in high-school algebra. Can Excel make solving story problems easier?

The Goal Seek feature in Microsoft Office Excel 2007 enables you to compute a value for a worksheet input that makes the value of a given formula match the goal you specify. For example, in our lemonade store example from Chapter 15, "Sensitivity Analysis with Data Tables," suppose we have fixed overhead costs, fixed per-unit costs, and a fixed sales price. Given this information, we can use Goal Seek to calculate the number of glasses of lemonade we need to sell to break even. Essentially, Goal Seek embeds a powerful equation solver in your worksheet. To use Goal Seek, you need to provide Excel with three pieces of information:

Set Cell
Specifies that the cell contains the formula that calculates the information you're seeking. In the lemonade example, the Set Cell would contain the formula for profit.

To Value
Specifies the numerical value for the goal that's calculated in the Set Cell. In the lemonade example, because we want to determine the sales volume that represents the breakeven point, the To Value would be 0.

By Changing Cell
Specifies the input cell that Excel changes until the Set Cell calculates the goal defined in the To Value cell. In the lemonade example, the By Changing Cell would contain annual lemonade sales.

For a given price, how many glasses of lemonade does a lemonade store need to sell per year to break even?

Our work for this section is in the file Lemonadegs.xlsx, which is shown in Figure 16-1. As in Chapter 15, I've assumed an annual fixed cost of $45,000.00 and variable unit cost of $0.45. Let's assume a price of $3.00. The question is how many glasses of lemonade we need to sell each year to break even.

	C	D
1	price	$ 3.00
2	demand	17647.05882
3	unit cost	$ 0.45
4	fixed cost	$ 45,000.00
5	revenue	$ 52,941.18
6	variable cost	$ 7,941.18
7	profit	$ -

Figure 16-1   We'll use this data to set up the Goal Seek feature to perform a breakeven analysis.

To start, insert any number for demand in cell D2. In the What-If Analysis group on the Data tab, click Goal Seek. Now fill in the Goal Seek dialog box shown in Figure 16-2.

Figure 16-2   The Goal Seek dialog box filled in with entries for a breakeven analysis

The dialog box indicates that we want to change cell D2 (annual demand, or sales) until cell D7 (profit) hits a value of 0. After clicking OK, we get the result that's shown in Figure 16-1. If we sell approximately 17,647 glasses of lemonade per year (or 48 glasses per day), we'll break even. To find the value we're seeking, Excel varies the demand in cell D2 (alternating between high and low values) until it finds a value that makes profit equal $0. If a problem has more than one solution, Goal Seek will still display only one answer.

We want to pay off our mortgage in 15 years. The annual interest rate is 6 percent. The bank told us we can afford monthly payments of $2,000. How much can we borrow?

You can begin to answer this question by setting up a worksheet to compute the monthly payments on a 15-year loan (we'll assume payments at the end of the month) as a function of the annual interest rate and a trial loan amount. You can see the work I did in the file Paymentgs.xlsx and in Figure 16-3.

In cell E6, the formula $-PMT(annual\_int\_rate/12,years,amt\_borrowed)$ computes the monthly payment associated with the amount borrowed, which is listed in cell E5. Filling in the Goal Seek dialog box as shown in Figure 16-4 calculates the amount borrowed that results in monthly payments equal to $2,000. With a limit of $2,000 for monthly payments, we can borrow up to $237,007.03.

	D	E
3	Years	180
4	Annual int rate	0.06
5	Amount borrowed	$ 237,007.03
6	Monthly payment	$2,000.00

Figure 16-3   You can use data such as this with the Goal Seek feature to determine the amount you can borrow based on a set monthly payment.

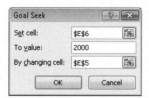

Figure 16-4   The Goal Seek dialog box set up to calculate the mortgage example

I always had trouble with "story problems" in high-school algebra. Can Excel make solving story problems easier?

If you think back to high-school algebra, most story problems required you to choose a variable (usually called it x) that solved a particular equation. Goal Seek is an equation solver, so perfectly suited to solving story problems. Here's a typical high-school algebra problem:

Maria and Edmund have a lover's quarrel while honeymooning in Seattle. Maria storms into her Mazda Miata and drives 64 miles per hour toward her mother's home in Los Angeles. Two hours after Maria leaves, Edmund jumps into his BMW in hot pursuit, driving 80 miles per hour. How many miles will each person have traveled when Edmund catches Maria?

You can find the Excel solution in the file Maria.xlsx, shown in Figure 16-5.

	C	D
2	Time Maria drives	10
3	Maria speed	64
4	Time Edmund drive:	8
5	Edmund speed	80
6	Maria distance	640
7	Edmund distance	640
8	Difference	0

Figure 16-5   Goal Seek can help you solve story problems.

Our Set Cell will be the difference between the distance Maria and Edmund have traveled. We will set this to a value of 0 by changing the number of hours Maria drives. Of course, Edmund drives two hours less than Maria.

I entered a trial number of hours that Maria drives in cell D2. Then I associated the range names in the cell range C2:C8 with cells D2:D8. Because Edmund drives two fewer hours than Maria, in cell D4 I've entered the formula *Time_Maria_drives*−2. In cells D6 and D7, we use the fact that *distance=speed*time* to compute the total distance Maria and Edmund travel. The difference between the distances traveled by Edmund and Maria is computed in cell D8 with the formula *Maria_distance−Edmund_distance*. Now I can fill in the Goal Seek dialog box as shown in Figure 16-6.

Figure 16-6   The Goal Seek dialog box filled in to solve an algebra story problem

We change Maria's hours of driving (cell D2) until the difference between the miles traveled by Edmund and Maria (cell D8) equals 0. We find that after Maria drives 10 hours and Edmund 8 hours, they will each have driven a distance of 640 miles.

Problems

1. From Problem 1 in Chapter 15, determine how many hardcover books must be sold to break even.

2. From the car net present value (NPV) example in Chapter 14, "The Auditing Tool," by what rate do annual sales need to grow for total NPV to equal $1 million?

3. What value of Year 1 unit cost would increase our NPV in the car example of Chapter 14 to $1 million?

4. In our mortgage example, suppose I need to borrow $200,000 for 15 years. If my maximum payments are limited to $2,000 per month, how high an annual interest rate can I tolerate?

5. How could I use Goal Seek to determine a project's internal rate of return (IRR)?

6. At the end of each of the next 40 years, I'm going to put $20,000 in my retirement fund. What rate of return on my investments do I need so that I will have $2 million available for retirement when I retire in 40 years?

7. I expect to earn 10 percent per year on my retirement investments. At the end of each of the next 40 years, I want to put the same amount of money in my retirement portfolio. How much money do I need to put in each year if I want to have $2 million in my account when I retire?

8. Consider two projects with the following cash flows:

	Year 1	Year 2	Year 3	Year 4
Project 1	−$1,000	$400	$350	$400
Project 2	−$900	$100	$100	$1,000

For what rate of interest will project 1 have a larger NPV? (Hint: Find the interest rate that makes both projects have the same NPV.)

9. I am managing a conference at my college. My fixed costs are $15,000. I must pay the 10 speakers $700 each, and the college union $300 per conference participant for food and lodging costs. I am charging each conference participant who is not also a speaker $900, which includes the conference fee and their food and lodging costs. How many paid registrants need to attend for me to break even?

10. I am buying 40 pounds of candy. Some of the candy sells for $10 per pound and some sells for $6 per pound. How much candy in each price should I buy to result in an average cost of $7 per pound?

11. Three electricians are wiring my new home. Electrician 1 by himself will need 11 days to do the job. Electrician 2 by himself will need 5 days to do the job. Electrician 3 by herself will need 9 days to do the job. If all three electricians work on the job, how long will the job take to complete?

12. To celebrate the Lewis and Clark Expedition, I am traveling 40 miles upstream and then 40 miles downstream in a canoe. The speed of the river current is 5 miles per hour. If the trip takes me 5 hours total, how fast do I travel if the the river has no current?

Chapter 17

Using the Scenario Manager for Sensitivity Analysis

■ I'd like to create best, worst, and most-likely scenarios for the sales of an automobile by varying the values of Year 1 sales, annual sales growth, and Year 1 sales price. Data tables for sensitivity analysis allow me to vary only one or two inputs, so I can't use a data table. Does Excel have a tool I can use to vary more than two inputs in a sensitivity analysis?

The Scenario Manager enables you to perform sensitivity analysis by varying as many as 32 input cells. With the Scenario Manager, you first define the set of input cells you want to vary. Next, you name your scenario and enter for each scenario the value of each input cell. Finally, you select the output cells (also called *result cells*) that you want to track. The Scenario Manager then creates a beautiful report containing the inputs and the values of the output cells for each scenario.

I'd like to create best, worst, and most-likely scenarios for the sales of an automobile by varying the values of Year 1 sales, annual sales growth, and Year 1 sales price. Data tables for sensitivity analysis allow me to vary only one or two inputs, so I can't use a data table. Does Excel have a tool I can use to vary more than two inputs in a sensitivity analysis?

Suppose we want to create the following three scenarios related to the net present value (NPV) of a car, using the example in Chapter 14, "The Auditing Tool."

	Year 1 sales	Annual sales growth	Year 1 sales price
Best case	$20,000	20%	$10.00
Most likely case	$10,000	10%	$7.50
Worst case	$5,000	2%	$5.00

For each scenario, we want to look at the firm's NPV and each year's after-tax profit. Our work is in the file NPVauditscenario.xlsx. Figure 17-1 shows the worksheet model (contained in the *Original Model* worksheet), and Figure 17-2 shows the scenario report (contained in the *Scenario Summary* worksheet).

	A	B	C	D	E	F
1		taxrate	0.4			
2		Year1sales	12000			
3		Sales growth	0.05			
4		Year1price	$ 7.50			
5		Year1cost	$ 6.00			
6		intrate	0.15			
7		costgrowth	0.05			
8		pricegrowth	0.03			
9	Year	1	2	3	4	5
10	Unit Sales	12000	12600	13230	13891.5	14586.075
11	unit price	$ 7.50	$ 7.73	$ 7.96	$ 8.20	$ 8.44
12	unit cost	$ 6.00	$ 6.30	$ 6.62	$ 6.95	$ 7.29
13	Revenues	$ 90,000.00	$ 97,335.00	$ 105,267.80	$ 113,847.13	$ 123,125.67
14	Costs	$ 72,000.00	$ 79,380.00	$ 87,516.45	$ 96,486.89	$ 106,376.79
15	Before Tax Profit	$ 18,000.00	$ 17,955.00	$ 17,751.35	$ 17,360.24	$ 16,748.88
16	Tax	$ 7,200.00	$ 7,182.00	$ 7,100.54	$ 6,944.10	$ 6,699.55
17	Aftertax Profits	$ 10,800.00	$ 10,773.00	$ 10,650.81	$ 10,416.15	$ 10,049.33
18						
19	NPV	$35,492.08				

Figure 17-1   The data on which the scenarios are based

	B	C	D	E	F	G
2	Scenario Summary					
3			Current Values:	Best	Most Likely	Worst
5	Changing Cells:					
6		Year1sales	12000	20000	10000	5000
7		Sales_growth	0.05	0.2	0.1	0.02
8		Year1price	$ 7.50	$ 10.00	$ 7.50	$ 5.00
9	Result Cells:					
10		$B$17	$ 10,800.00	$ 48,000.00	$ 9,000.00	$ (3,000.00)
11		$C$17	$ 10,773.00	$ 57,600.00	$ 9,405.00	$ (3,519.00)
12		$D$17	$ 10,650.81	$ 69,016.32	$ 9,741.10	$ (4,090.33)
13		$E$17	$ 10,416.15	$ 82,560.80	$ 9,980.12	$ (4,718.50)
14		$F$17	$ 10,049.33	$ 98,588.50	$ 10,087.17	$ (5,408.35)
15		$B$19	$35,492.08	$226,892.67	$32,063.83	($13,345.75)
16	Notes: Current Values column represents values of changing cells at					
17	time Scenario Summary Report was created. Changing cells for each					
18	scenario are highlighted in gray.					

Figure 17-2   The scenario summary report

To begin defining the best-case scenario, I display the Data tab, and then click Scenario Manager on the What-If Analysis menu. Then I click the Add button and fill in the Add Scenario dialog box as shown in Figure 17-3.

I enter a name for the scenario (Best) and select C2:C4 as the input cells containing the values that will define the scenario. After I click OK in the Add Scenario dialog box, I fill in the Scenario Values dialog box with the input values that define the best case, as shown in Figure 17-4.

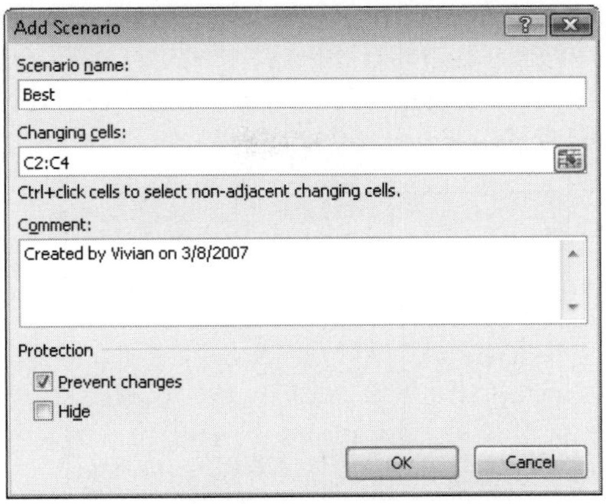

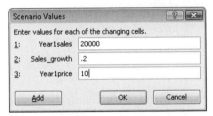

Figure 17-3   Data inputs for the best-case scenario

By clicking Add in the Scenario Values dialog box, I can enter the data for the most-likely and worst-case scenarios. After I've entered data for all three scenarios, I click OK in the Scenario Values dialog box. The Scenario Manager dialog box, shown in Figure 17-5, lists the scenarios I created. When I click Summary in the Scenario Manager dialog box, I can choose the result cells that will be displayed in scenario reports. Figure 17-6 on the next page shows how I indicated in the Scenario Summary dialog box that I want the scenario summary report to track each year's after-tax profit (cells B17:F17) as well as total NPV (cell B19).

Figure 17-4   Defining the input values for the best-case scenario

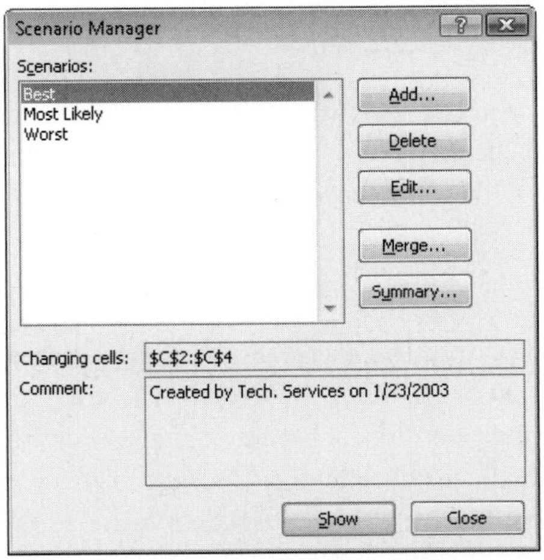

Figure 17-5   The Scenario Manager dialog box displays each scenario I defined.

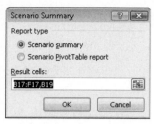

Figure 17-6 Use the Scenario Summary dialog box to select the result cells for the summary report.

Because the result cells come from more than one range, I've separated the ranges B17:F17 and B19 with a comma. (I could also have used the Ctrl key to select and enter multiple ranges.) After selecting Scenario Summary (instead of the PivotTable option), I click OK, and Microsoft Office Excel 2007 creates the beautiful Scenario Summary report pictured earlier in Figure 17-2. Notice that Excel includes a column, labeled *Current Values*, for the values that were originally placed in the worksheet. The worst case loses money (a loss of $13,345.75), whereas the best case is quite profitable (a profit of $226,892.67). Because the worst-case price is less than our variable cost, the worst case loses money in each year.

Remarks

- The Scenario PivotTable Report option on the Scenario Summary dialog box presents the scenario results in a PivotTable format.

- Suppose we select a scenario in the Scenario Manager dialog box and then click the Show button. The input cells' values for the selected scenario then appear in the worksheet, and Excel recalculates all formulas. This tool is great for presenting a "slide show" of your scenarios.

- It's hard to create a lot of scenarios with the Scenario Manager because you need to input each individual scenario's values. Monte Carlo simulation (see Chapter 60, "Introduction to Monte Carlo Simulation") makes it easy to create many scenarios. Using the Monte Carlo simulation method, you can find information such as the probability that the NPV of a project's cash flows is nonnegative—an important measure because it is the probability that the project adds value to the company.

- Clicking the minus (–) sign in row 5 of the Scenario Summary report will hide the Assumption cells and show only results. Clicking the plus (+) sign will restore the full report.

- Suppose you send a file to several people and each adds their own scenarios. After each person returns the file containing his or her created scenarios to you, you can merge all the scenarios into one workbook by opening each person's version of the workbook. Then click the Merge button in the Scenario Manager dialog box in the original workbook and select the workbooks containing the scenarios you want to merge. Excel will merge all the selected scenarios in the original workbook.

Problems

1. Delete the best-case scenario and run another scenario report.

2. Add a scenario named *High Price*, in which Year 1 Price equals $15 and the other two inputs remain at their most-likely values.

3. For the lemonade stand example in Chapter 15, "Sensitivity Analysis with Data Tables," use the Scenario Manager to display a report summarizing profit for the following scenarios:

Scenario	Price	Unit cost	Fixed cost
High cost/high price	$5.00	$1.00	$65,000.00
Medium cost/medium price	$4.00	$0.75	$45,000.00
Low cost/low price	$2.50	$0.40	$25,000.00

4. For the mortgage payment example in Chapter 15, use the Scenario Manager to create a report tabulating monthly payments for the following scenarios:

Scenario	Amount borrowed	Annual rate	Number of monthly payments
Lowest payment	$300,000	4%	360
Most-likely payment	$400,000	6%	240
Highest payment	$550,000	8%	180

Chapter 18

The COUNTIF, COUNTIFS, COUNT, COUNTA, and COUNTBLANK Functions

- Suppose I have a list of songs that are played on the radio. For each song, I know the singer, the date the song was played, and the length of the song. How can I answer questions such as these about the songs in the list:

  - How many were sung by each singer?

  - How many were not sung by my favorite singer?

  - How many were at least four minutes long?

  - How many were longer than the average length of all songs on the list?

  - How many were sung by singers whose last names begin with *S*?

  - How many were sung by singers whose last names contain exactly six letters?

  - How many were played after June 15, 2005?

  - How many were played before 2009?

  - How many were exactly four minutes long?

  - How many were sung by my favorite singer and were exactly four minutes long?

  - How many were sung by my favorite singer and were three to four minutes long?

- In a more general context, how do I perform operations such as the following:

  - Count the number of cells in a range containing numbers.

  - Count the number of blank cells in a range.

  - Count the number of nonblank cells in a range.

We often want to count the number of cells in a range that meet a given criterion. For example, if a worksheet contains information about makeup sales, we might want to count the number of sales transactions made by the salesperson named Jennifer, or the number of sales transactions that occurred after June 10. The COUNTIF function lets you count the number of cells in a range that meet criteria that are defined on the basis of a one row or column of the worksheet.

The syntax of the COUNTIF function is *COUNTIF(range,criterion)*.

- *Range* is the range of cells in which you want to count cells meeting a given criterion.
- *Criterion* is a number, date, or expression that determines whether to count a given cell in the range.

The syntax of COUNTIFS (new in Microsoft Office Excel 2007) is *COUNTIFS(range1, criterion1,range2,criterion2,...,range_n,criterion_n)*.

COUNTIFS will count the number of rows for which the *range1* entry meets *criterion1*, the *range2* entry meets *criterion2*, the *range_n* entry meets *criterion_n*, and so on. Thus, COUNTIFS allows the criteria to involve more than one column or multiple conditions in one column. Other functions that allow for multiple criteria are discussed in Chapter 19, "The SUMIF, AVERAGEIF, SUMIFS, and AVERAGEIFS Functions," and Chapter 39, "Summarizing Data with Database Statisitical Functions."

The key to using the COUNTIF function (and other similar functions) successfully is understanding the wide variety of criteria that Excel will accept. The types of criteria you can use are best explained through the use of examples. In addition to examples of the COUNTIF function, I'll provide examples of the COUNT, COUNTA, and COUNTBLANK functions:

- The COUNT function counts the number of cells in a range containing numbers.
- The COUNTA function counts the number of nonblank cells in a range.
- The COUNTBLANK function counts the number of blank cells in a range.

As an illustration of how to use these functions, consider a database that gives the following information for each song played on radio station WKRP:

- The singer
- The date the song was played
- The length of the song

The file Rock.xlsx, shown in Figure 18-1, shows a subset of the data.

	D	E	F	G
6	Song Number	Singer	Date	Minutes
7	1	Eminem	5/21/2004	4
8	2	Eminem	4/15/2004	2
9	3	Cher	1/28/2005	2
10	4	Eminem	1/28/2005	4
11	5	Moore	11/5/2004	2
12	6	Cher	9/18/2004	4
13	7	Spears	4/15/2004	3
14	8	Spears	3/17/2005	3
15	9	Manilow	1/16/2005	4
16	10	Eminem	4/10/2005	4
17	11	Madonna	2/15/2004	3
18	12	Eminem	1/10/2004	4
19	13	Springsteen	4/10/2005	2
20	14	Spears	4/15/2004	4
21	15	Moore	7/8/2004	3
22	16	Madonna	6/26/2004	4
23	17	Spears	5/28/2005	3
24	18	Mellencamp	7/27/2005	5
25	19	Spears	9/18/2004	5
26	20	Madonna	7/8/2004	4
27	21	Springsteen	9/6/2004	3
28	22	Madonna	6/2/2004	3

Figure 18-1   The song database we use for the COUNTIF examples

How many songs were sung by each singer?

To begin, I select the first row of the database, the range D6:G6. Then I select the whole database by pressing Ctrl+Shift+Down Arrow. Next, in the Defined Names group on the Formulas tab, I clicked Create From Selection, and then chose Top Row. We have now named the range D7:D957 *Song Numb*, the range E7:E957 *Singer*, the range F7:F957 *Date*, and the range G7:G957 *Minutes*. To determine how many songs were sung by each singer, we copy from C5 to C6:C12 the formula *COUNTIF(Singer,B5)*. In cell C5, this formula now displays the number of cells in the range Singer that match the value in B5 (Eminem). The database contains 114 songs sung by Eminem. Similarly, Cher sang 112 songs, and so on, as you can see in Figure 18-2. I could have also found the number of songs sung by Eminem with the formula *COUNTIF(Singer,"Eminem")*. Note that you must enclose text such as Eminem in quotation marks (" ") and that criteria are not case sensitive.

	B	C
2	count	9
3	counta	18
4	countblank	2
5	Eminem	114
6	Cher	112
7	Moore	131
8	Spears	129
9	Mellencamp	115
10	Madonna	133
11	Springsteen	103
12	Manilow	114
13	Total	951

Figure 18-2   Using COUNTIF to determine how many songs were sung by each singer.

How many songs were not sung by Eminem?

To solve this problem, you need to know that Excel interprets the character combination <> as "not equal to." The formula *COUNTIF(Singer,"<>Eminem")*, entered in cell C15, tells us that 837 songs in the database were not sung by Eminem, as you can see in Figure 18-3. I need to enclose *<>Eminem* in quotation marks because Excel treats the not equal to (<>) character combination as text and *Eminem* is, of course, text. You could obtain the same result by using the formula *COUNTIF(Singer,"<>"&B5)*, which uses the ampersand (&) symbol to concatenate the reference to cell B5 and the <> operator.

	B	C
15	Not by Eminem	837
16	Songs >= 4 minutes	477
17	Songs longer than average	477
18	Singer begins with S	232
19	Singer has six letters in name	243
20	Songs after 6/15/2005	98
21	Songs Before 2009	951
22	Songs exactly 4 minutes	247
23	Songs exactly 5 minutes	230
24	Springsteen songs 4 minutes	24
25	Madonna songs 3 or 4 minutes	70

Figure 18-3   You can combine the COUNTIF function with the not-equal-to operator (<>).

How many songs were at least four minutes long?

In cell C16, I've computed the number of songs played that lasted at least four minutes by using the formula *COUNTIF(Minutes,">=4")*. You need to enclose >=4 in quotation marks because the greater than or equal to (>=) character combination, like <>, is treated as text. We find that 477 songs lasted at least four minutes.

How many songs were longer than the average length of all songs on the list?

To answer this question, I first computed in cell G5 the average length of a song with the formula *AVERAGE(Minutes)*. Then, in cell C17, I computed the number of songs that last longer than the average with the formula *COUNTIF(Minutes,">"&G5)*. I can refer to another cell (in this case G5) in the criteria by using the & character. You can see that 477 songs lasted longer than average, which matches the number of songs lasting at least 4 minutes. The reason these numbers match is that I assumed the length of each song was an integer. For a song to last at least 3.48 minutes, it has to last at least 4 minutes.

How many songs were sung by singers whose last names begin with S?

To answer this question, I use a wildcard character, the asterisk (*), in the criteria. An asterisk represents any sequence of characters. Thus the formula *COUNTIF(Singer,"S*")* in cell C18 picks up any song sung by a singer whose last name begins with S. (The criteria are not case sensitive.) Two hundred thirty-two songs were sung by singers with last names that begin with S. This number is simply the total of the songs sung by either Bruce Springsteen or Britney Spears (*103+129=232*).

How many songs were sung by singers whose last names contain exactly six letters?

In this example, I used the question mark (?) wildcard character. The question mark matches any character. Therefore, entering the formula *COUNTIF(Singer,"??????")* in cell C19 counts the number of songs sung by singers having six letters in their last name. The result is 243. (Two singers have last names of six characters, Britney Spears and Eminem, who together sang a total of 243 songs—*129+114=243*.)

How many songs were played after June 15, 2005?

The criteria you use with COUNTIF functions handle dates on the basis of a date's serial number. (A later date is considered larger than an earlier date.) The formula *COUNTIF(Date,">6/15/2005")* in cell C20 tells us that 98 songs were sung after June 15, 2005.

How many songs were played before 2009?

We want our criteria to pick up all dates on or before December 31, 2008. I've entered in cell C21 the formula *COUNTIF(Date,"<=12/31/2008")*. We find that 951 songs (which turns out to be all the songs) were sung before the start of 2009.

How many songs were exactly four minutes long?

In cell C22, I compute the number of songs lasting exactly four minutes with the formula *COUNTIF(Minutes,4)*. This formula counts the number of cells in the range G7:G957 containing a 4. We find that 247 songs lasted exactly four minutes. In a similar fashion, we found in cell C23 that 230 songs lasted exactly five minutes.

How many songs were sung by Bruce Springsteen and were exactly four minutes long?

We want to count each row where an entry in the Singer column is *Springsteen* and an entry in the Minutes column is *4*. This is a job for the wonderful new COUNTIFS function. Simply enter in cell C24 the formula *=COUNTIFS(Singer,"Springsteen",Minutes,4)*.

This formula counts any row in which Singer is *Springsteen* and Minutes equals 4. We find that Bruce Springsteen sang 24 songs that were exactly four minutes long. My favorite Springsteen song is "Thunder Road," but that song is more than four minutes long.

How many songs were sung by Madonna and were three to four minutes long?

Because we are dealing with multiple criteria, this is again a job for COUNTIFS. Entering in cell C25 the formula *=COUNTIFS(Singer,"Madonna",Minutes,"<=4",Minutes,">=3")* counts all rows in which Madonna sang a song that was from three to four minutes long. These are exactly the rows we wish to count. We find that Madonna sang 70 songs that were from three to four minutes long (my favorite one is "Crazy for You!").

How do I count the number of cells in a range containing numbers?

The COUNT function counts the number of cells in a range containing a numeric value. For example, the formula *COUNT(B5:C14)* in cell C2 displays 9 because nine cells (the cells in C5:C13) in the range B5:C14 contain numbers. (See Figure 18-2.)

How do I count the number of blank cells in a range?

The COUNTBLANK function counts the number of blank cells in a range. For example, the formula *COUNTBLANK(B5:C14)* entered in cell C4 returns a value of 2 because two cells (B14 and C14) in the range B5:C14 contain blanks.

How do I count the number of nonblank cells in a range?

The COUNTA function returns the number of nonblank cells in a range. For example, the formula *COUNTA(B5:C14)* in cell C3 returns 18 because 18 cells in the range B5:C14 are not blank.

Remarks

In the remainder of the book we discuss alternative methods to answer questions involving two or more criteria, (such as how many Britney Spears songs were played before June 10, 2005).

- Database statistical functions are discussed in Chapter 39.

- Array formulas are discussed in Chapter 74, "Array Formulas and Functions."

Problems

The following questions refer to the file Rock.xlsx.

1. How many songs were not sung by Britney Spears?

2. How many songs were played before June 15, 2004?

3. How many songs were played between June 1, 2004, and July 4, 2006? Hint: Take the difference between two COUNTIF functions.

4. How many songs were sung by singers whose last names begin with *M*?

5. How many songs were sung by singers whose names contain an *e*?

6. Create a formula that will always yield the number of songs played today. Hint: Use the TODAY() function.

7. For the cell range D4:G15, count the cells containing a numeric value. Count the number of blank cells. Count the number of nonblank cells.

8. How many songs sung by Barry Manilow were played in 2004?

9. How many songs at least four minutes long and sung by Mandy Moore were played in 2007 or earlier?

10. How many songs exactly three minutes long and sung by Britney Spears were played later than 2004?

11. The file NBA.xlsx contains the following information:

- ❑ Columns A and B contain the name of each NBA team and a code number for each team. For example, Team 1 is Atlanta.
- ❑ Column C contains the home team for each game.
- ❑ Column D contains the visiting team for each game.
- ❑ Column E contains points scored by the home team.
- ❑ Column F contains points scored by the visiting team.

From this data, compute the number of games played by each team.

12. The file Matchthesecond.xlsx gives a list of names. Note that some names occur more than once. We want to be able to determine the row in which, for example, the second occurrence of the name "Dave" occurs. Set up a worksheet that allows us to enter a person's name and a positive integer (such as *n*), and returns the row in which the name occurs for the *n*'th time.

Chapter 19

The SUMIF, AVERAGEIF, SUMIFS, and AVERAGEIFS Functions

I'm a sales manager for a makeup company and have summarized for each sales transaction the following information: salesperson, date of sale, units sold (or returned), total price received (or paid out for returns). How can I answer the following questions?

- What was the total dollar amount of merchandise sold by each salesperson?

- How many units were returned?

- What was the total dollar amount of sales in or after 2005?

- How many units of lip gloss were sold? How much revenue did lip gloss sales bring in?

- What was the total dollar amount of sales made by someone other than a specific salesperson?

- What was the average number of units sold in each transaction made by a specific salesperson?

- What was the total dollar amount of lipstick sold by a specific salesperson?

- What was the average quantity (in units) of lipstick in each sale made by a specific salesperson?

- Among transactions involving at least 50 units, what was the average quantity of lipstick in each sale made by a specific salesperson?

- Among transactions of more than $100, what was the total dollar amount of lipstick sold by a specific salesperson? What about transactions of less than $100?

If you want to sum all the entries in one column (or row) matching criteria that depend on another column (or row), the SUMIF function gets the job done. The syntax of the SUMIF function is *SUMIF(range,criterion,[sum range])*.

- *Range* is the range of cells that you want to evaluate with a criterion.

- *Criterion* is a number, date, or expression that determines whether a given cell in the sum range is added.

- *Sum range* is the range of cells that are added. If *sum range* is omitted, it is assumed to be the same as *range*.

The rules for criteria you can use with the SUMIF function are identical to the rules used for the COUNTIF function. For information about the COUNTIF function, see Chapter 18, "The COUNTIF, COUNTIFS, COUNT, COUNTA, and COUNTBLANK Functions."

The new AVERAGEIF function has the syntax *AVERAGEIF(range,criterion,[average_range])*. AVERAGEIF will average the range of cells meeting a criterion.

Microsoft Office Excel 2007 includes three new functions you can use to flag rows that involve multiple criteria: COUNTIFS (discussed in Chapter 18), SUMIFS, and AVERAGEIFS. Other functions that you can use to do calculations involving multiple criteria are discussed in our chapter on database statistical functions (see Chapter 39, "Summarizing Data with Database Statistical Functions"). Array functions (see Chapter 74, "Array Functions and Formulas") can also be used to handle calculations involving multiple criteria.

The syntax of SUMIFS is *SUMIFS(sumrange,range1,criterion1,range2,criterion2,...,rangeN, criterionN)*. Then SUMIFS will sum up every entry in the *sumrange* for which *criterion1* (based on *range1*), *criterion2* (based on *range2*),...,*criterionN* (based on *rangeN*) are all satisfied. In a similar fashion the new AVERAGEIF function has the syntax *AVERAGEIFS(sumrange, range1,criterion1,range2,criterion2,...,rangeN,criterionN)*. Then AVERAGEIFS will average every entry in the *sumrange* for which *criterion1* (based on *range1*), *criterion2* (based on *range2*),..., *criterionN* (based on *rangeN*) are all satisfied.

What was the total dollar amount of merchandise sold by each salesperson?

Our work for the problems in this chapter is in the file Makeup2007.xlsx. Figure 19-1 shows a subset of the data.

As usual, we begin by labeling the data in columns G through L with the corresponding names in cells G4:L4. For example, the range name *Product* corresponds to the range J5:J1904. To compute the total amount sold by each salesperson (see Figure 19-2), I simply copy from cell B5 to B6:B13 the formula *SUMIF(Name,A5,Dollars)*. This formula adds up every entry in the Dollars column that contains the name *Emilee* in the Name column. We find that Emilee sold $25,258.87 worth of makeup. Of course, the formula =*SUMIF(Name,"Emilee",Dollars)* would yield the same result.

	G	H	I	J	K	L
4	Trans Number	Name	Date	Product	Units	Dollars
5	1	Betsy	4/1/2004	lip gloss	45	$ 137.20
6	2	Hallagan	3/10/2004	foundatio	50	$ 152.01
7	3	Ashley	2/25/2005	lipstick	9	$ 28.72
8	4	Hallagan	5/22/2006	lip gloss	55	$ 167.08
9	5	Zaret	6/17/2004	lip gloss	43	$ 130.60
10	6	Colleen	11/27/2005	eye liner	58	$ 175.99
11	7	Cristina	3/21/2004	eye liner	8	$ 25.80
12	8	Colleen	12/17/2006	lip gloss	72	$ 217.84
13	9	Ashley	7/5/2006	eye liner	75	$ 226.64
14	10	Betsy	8/7/2006	lip gloss	24	$ 73.50
15	11	Ashley	11/29/2004	mascara	43	$ 130.84
16	12	Ashley	11/18/2004	lip gloss	23	$ 71.03
17	13	Emilee	8/31/2005	lip gloss	49	$ 149.59
18	14	Hallagan	1/1/2005	eye liner	18	$ 56.47
19	15	Zaret	9/20/2006	foundatio	-8	$ (21.99)
20	16	Emilee	4/12/2004	mascara	45	$ 137.39
21	17	Colleen	4/30/2006	mascara	66	$ 199.65
22	18	Jen	8/31/2005	lip gloss	88	$ 265.19
23	19	Jen	10/27/2004	eye liner	78	$ 236.15
24	20	Zaret	11/27/2005	lip gloss	57	$ 173.12
25	21	Zaret	6/2/2006	mascara	12	$ 38.08
26	22	Betsy	9/24/2004	eye liner	28	$ 86.51
27	23	Colleen	2/1/2006	mascara	25	$ 77.31
28	24	Hallagan	5/2/2005	foundatio	29	$ 88.22
29	25	Jen	11/7/2004	mascara	-4	$ (9.94)
30	26	Emilee	12/6/2006	lip gloss	24	$ 74.62

Figure 19-1   Data we'll use for SUMIF examples

	A	B	C
4	Name	Dollar Volume	
5	Emilee	$ 25,258.87	
6	Hallagan	$ 28,705.16	
7	Ashley	$ 25,947.24	
8	Zaret	$ 26,741.31	
9	Colleen	$ 24,890.66	
10	Cristina	$ 23,849.56	
11	Betsy	$ 28,803.15	
12	Jen	$ 29,050.53	
13	Cici	$ 27,590.57	
14			
15			
16	Units returned	922	
17	Total dollars sold 2005 or later	$ 157,854.32	
18	Units of lip gloss sold	16333	
19	$s of lip gloss sold	$ 49,834.64	
20	$s sold not by Jen	$ 211,786.51	
21	Lipstick $s by Jen	3953	
22	avg units lipstick by Zaret	33	
23	avg units lipstick Zaretunits >=50	68	
24	Lipstick $s >=$100 Jen	3583	
25	Lipstick $s <$100 Jen	370	check
26	average units by Jen	43.548	43.548

Figure 19-2   Results of SUMIF computations

How many units were returned?

In cell B16, the formula *SUMIF(Units,"<0",Units)* totals every number less than 0 in the Units column (column K). The result is −922. After inserting a minus sign in front of the *SUMIF* formula, we see that 922 units were returned. (Recall that when the *sum range* argument is omitted from a SUMIF function, Excel assumes that *sum range* equals *range*. Therefore, the formula *−SUMIF(Units,"<0")* would also yield 922.)

What was the total dollar amount of sales in or after 2005?

In cell B17, the formula *SUMIF(Date,">=1/1/2005",Dollars)* totals every entry in the Dollar column (column L) that contains a date on or after 1/1/2005 in the Date column. We find that $157,854.32 worth of makeup was sold in 2005 or later.

How many units of lip gloss were sold? How much revenue did lip gloss sales bring in?

In cell B18, the formula *SUMIF(Product,"lip gloss",Units)* totals every cell in the Units column that contains the text *lip gloss* in the Product column (column J). You can see that 16,333 units of lip gloss were sold. This is the net sales amount; transactions in which units of lip gloss were returned are counted as negative sales.

In a similar fashion, in cell B19 the formula *SUMIF(Product,"lip gloss",Dollars)* tells us that a net amount of $49,834.64 worth of lip gloss was sold. This calculation counts refunds associated with returns as negative revenue.

What was the total dollar amount of sales made by someone other than Jen?

In cell B20, the formula *SUMIF(Name,"<>Jen",Dollars)* sums the dollar amount of all transactions that do not have *Jen* in the Name column. We find that salespeople other than Jen sold $211,786.51 worth of makeup.

What was the average number of units sold in each transaction made by a specific salesperson?

This is a job for the AVERAGEIF function. Entering in cell B26 the formula *=AVERAGEIF(Name,"Jen",Units)* averages every entry in the Units column that contains *Jen* in the Name column. We find that Jen's average transaction size was 43.548 units. We verified this in cell C25 with the formula *=SUMIF(Name,"Jen",Units)/COUNTIF(Name,"Jen")*.

What was the total dollar amount of lipstick sold by Jen?

This calculation involves two criteria (*Name="Jen"* and *Product="lipstick"*). Therefore we compute the desired quantity in cell B21 with the formula *=SUMIFS(Dollars,Name, "Jen",Product,"lipstick")*.

We find that the total dollar amount of all transactions in which Jen sold lipstick was $3,953.

What was the average quantity (in units) of lipstick in each sale made by Zaret?

This calculation requires the AVERAGEIFS function. We compute the desired quantity in cell B22 with the formula *=AVERAGEIFS(Units,Name,"Zaret",Product,"lipstick")*. We find that for the sales transactions in which Zaret sold lipstick, the average number of units sold was 33.

Among transactions involving at least 50 units, what was the average quantity of lipstick in each sale made by Zaret?

Again we use AVERAGEIFS, but we add a criterion to ensure units sold in transaction was at least 50. In cell B23, we compute the desired quantity with the formula *=AVERAGEIF(Units,Name,"Zaret",Product,"lipstick",Units,">=50")*. We find that in all transactions in which Zaret sold at least 50 units of lipstick, the average transaction size was 68 units.

Among transactions of more than $100, what was the total dollar amount of lipstick sold by Jen? What about transactions of less than $100?

Because our criteria is *Name=Jen, Product=lipstick*, and some statement about the dollar size of each order, we need to use the SUMIFS function. In cell B24 we compute the total amount in transactions in which Jen sold lipstick and the dollar amount was at least $100 with the formula *=SUMIFS(Dollars,Name,"Jen",Product,"lipstick",Dollars">=100")*. We find that Jen sold $3,583 worth of lipstick in such transactions. In lipstick transactions involving less than $100, we find in cell B25 (formula is *=SUMIFS(Dollars,Name, "Jen",Product,"lipstick",Dollars,"<100")* the answer is $370. Note that $370+$3,583 equals the total revenue Jen generated from lipstick sales (computed in cell B21).

Problems

1. For each product, determine the total number of units and dollar volume sold.

2. Determine the total revenue earned before December 10, 2005.

3. Determine the total units sold by salespeople whose last names begin with C.

4. Determine the total revenue earned by people who have five letters in their names.

5. How many units were sold by people other than Colleen?

6. How many units of makeup were sold from January 15, 2004, through February 15, 2005?

7. The file NBA.xlsx contains the following information:

   ❑ Columns A and B list the name of each NBA team and a code number for each team. For example, team 1 is Atlanta, and so on.

   ❑ Column C lists the home team for each game.

   ❑ Column D lists the visiting team for each game.

   ❑ Column E lists points scored by the home team.

   ❑ Column F lists points scored by the visiting team.

   From this data, compute for each team the average number of points the team scored per game and the average number of points the team gave up.

8. The file Toysrus.xlsx contains sales revenue (in millions of dollars) during each quarter for the years 1997–2001 and the first two quarters of 2002. Use this data to compute a *seasonal index* for each quarter of the year. For example, if average sales during the first quarter were 80 percent of the overall average sales per quarter, the first quarter would have a seasonal index of 0.8.

9. How much revenue was made on sales transactions involving at least 50 units of makeup?

10. The file Sumifrows.xlsx contains sales data during several winter, spring, summer, and fall quarters. Determine average sales during the winter, spring, summer, and fall quarters.

11. How many units of lip gloss did Cici sell in 2004?

12. What was the average number of units of foundation sold by Emilee?

13. What was the average dollar size of a foundation sale made by Betsy after the end of 2004?

14. In transactions in which Ashley sold at least 40 units of lipstick, what was the total dollar amount?

15. Create a table that contains sales of each product made by each person.

16. Create a table that, when you enter a year in your worksheet, contains sales of each product by person during that year.

Chapter 20
The OFFSET Function

- How can I create a reference to a range of cells that is a specified number of rows and columns from a cell or another range of cells?

- How can I perform a lookup operation based on the right-most column in a table range instead of the left-most column?

- I often download software product sales information listed by country. I need to track revenues from Iran as well as costs and units sold, but the data about Iran isn't always in the same location in the worksheet. Can I create a formula that will always pick out Iran's revenues, costs, and units sold?

- Each drug developed by my company goes through three stages of development. I have a list of the cost by month for each drug, and I also know the length in months of each development stage. Can I create formulas that compute for each drug the total cost incurred during each stage of development?

- I run a small video store. In a worksheet, my accountant has listed the name of each movie and the number of copies in stock. Unfortunately, he combined this information in one cell for each movie. How can I extract the number of copies of each movie in stock to a separate cell?

- How can I write a formula that always returns the last number in a column?

- How can I set up a range name that automatically includes new data?

- I am charting my company's monthly unit sales. Each month, I download the most recent month's unit sales. I would like my chart to update automatically. Is there an easy way to accomplish this?

The OFFSET function is used to create a reference to a range that is a specified number of rows and columns away from a cell or range of cells. Basically, to create a reference to a range of cells, you first specify a reference cell. You then indicate the number of rows and columns away from the reference cell that you want to create your range. For example, by using the OFFSET function, I can create a reference to a cell range that contains two rows and three columns and begins two columns to the right and one row above the current cell. You can calculate the specified number of rows and columns you move from a reference cell by using other Excel functions.

The syntax of the OFFSET function is *OFFSET(reference,rows moved,columns moved, height,width)* where:

- *Reference* is a cell or range of cells from which the offset begins. If you specify a range of cells, the cells must be adjacent to each other.
- *Rows moved* is the number of rows away from the reference cell or range that you want the range reference to start (the upper-left cell in the offset range). A negative number of rows moves you up from the reference; a positive number of rows moves you down. For example, if *reference* equals C5 and *rows moved* equals −1, you move to row 4. If *rows moved* equals +1, you move to row 6. If *rows moved* equals 0, you stay at row 5.
- *Columns moved* is the number of columns away from the reference cell or range that you want the range reference to start. A negative number of columns moves you left from the reference; a positive number of columns moves you right. For example, if *reference* equals C5 and *columns moved* equals −1, you move to column B. If *columns moved* equals +1, you move to column D. If *columns moved* equals 0, you stay at column C.
- *Height* and *Width* are optional arguments that give the number of rows and columns in the offset range. If *height* or *width* is omitted, the OFFSET function creates a range for which the value of *height* or *width* equals the height or width of the reference cell or range.

How can I create a reference to a range of cells that is a specified number of rows and columns from a cell or another range of cells?

The file Offsetexample.xlsx, shown in Figure 20-1, provides some examples of the OFFSET function in action.

	A	B	C	D	E	F	G	H	I	J	K
1											
2											
3		Offset examples									
4											
5											
6		1	2	3	4			1	2	3	4
7		5	6	7	8			5	6	7	8
8		9	10	11	12			9	10	11	12
9											
10	=SUM(OFFSET(B7,-1,1,2,1))	8					=SUM(OFFSET(H6,0,1,3,2))	39			
11											
12											
13											
14		1	2	3	4						
15		5	6	7	8						
16		9	10	11	12						
17											
18	=SUM(OFFSET(E16,-2,-3,2,3))	24									

Figure 20-1 Using the OFFSET function

For example, in cell B10, I entered the formula (shown in cell A10) *SUM(OFFSET(B7,−1,1,2,1))*. This formula begins in cell B7. We move one row up and one column to the right, which brings us to cell C6. We now select a range consisting of two rows and one column, which yields the range C6:C7. The SUM function adds the numbers in this range, which yields 2+6=8. The other two examples shown in Figure 20-1 work the same way. In the following sections, we'll apply the OFFSET function to solve some problems that were sent to me by former students working at major U.S. companies.

How can I perform a lookup operation based on the right-most column in a table range instead of the left-most column?

In Figure 20-2 (see workbook Lefthandlookup.xlsx), I've listed the members of the Dallas Mavericks NBA basketball team and their field goal percentages. If I'm asked to find the player with a specific field goal percentage, I could easily solve that problem by using a VLOOKUP function. But what I really want to do is a "left-hand lookup," which involves finding the field goal percentage for a player by using his name. A VLOOKUP function can't perform a left-hand lookup, but a left-hand lookup is simple if you combine the MATCH and OFFSET functions.

	B	C	D	E
5		Left-hand lookup		
6			Name	FG %age
7	FG%	Player	Walt Williams	0.397
8	45.8%	Dirk Nowitzki		
9	41.8%	Michael Finley		
10	46.3%	Steve Nash		
11	39.5%	Nick Van Exel		
12	53.5%	Raef LaFrentz		
13	60.2%	Eduardo Najera		
14	51.2%	Shawn Bradley		
15	39.7%	Walt Williams		
16	44.4%	Adrian Griffin		
17	48.4%	Avery Johnson		
18	47.6%	Raja Bell		
19	66.7%	Evan Eschmeyer		
20	41.0%	Popeye Jones		
21	40.0%	Mark Strickland		
22	23.5%	Adam Harrington		

Figure 20-2   You can do a left-hand lookup by using the MATCH and OFFSET functions.

First, I enter the player's name in cell D7. Then I use a reference cell of B7 (the field goal percentage column header) in the OFFSET function. To find the player's field goal percentage, we need to move down to the row below row 7 where the player's name appears. This is a job for the MATCH function. The MATCH function portion of the formula *OFFSET(B7,MATCH(D7,$C$8:$C$22,0),0)* moves down to the row containing the specified player's name and then moves over 0 columns. Because the reference consists of one cell, omitting the *height* and *width* arguments of the OFFSET function ensures that the range returned by this formula is also one cell. Thus, we pick up the player's field goal percentage.

I often download software product sales information listed by country. I need to track revenues from Iran as well as costs and units sold, but the data about Iran isn't always in the same location in the worksheet. Can I create a formula that will always pick out Iran's revenues, costs, and units sold?

The file Asiansales.xlsx (see Figure 20-3) contains data for the units sold, sales revenue, and variable cost for software sold to several countries in Asia and the Middle East. Each month, when we download the monthly financial reports, the location of each country in the worksheet changes, so we want formulas that will always return (for a given country) the correct units sold, revenue, and variable cost.

	C	D	E	F
6	Country/Region	Units sold	Revenue	Variable Cost
7	India	541	$ 4,328	$ 1,623
8	China	1000	$ 5,000	$ 3,000
9	Iran	577	$ 2,308	$ 1,731
10	Israel	454	$ 3,632	$ 1,362
11	Japan	141	$ 705	$ 423
12	Taiwan	221	$ 1,105	$ 663
13	Thailand	223	$ 1,115	$ 669
14	Indonesia	524	$ 2,620	$ 1,572
15	Malaysia	328	$ 1,968	$ 984
16	Vietnam	469	$ 2,814	$ 1,407
17	Cambodia	398	$ 1,990	$ 1,194
18				
19		Units sold	Revenue	Variable Cost
20	Country/Region	1	2	3
21	Iran	577	2308	1731

Figure 20-3   You can use the OFFSET function in calculations when you're working with data that isn't always in the same location in a worksheet.

By copying from D21 to E21:F21 the formula *OFFSET($C$6,MATCH ($C21,$C$7:$C$17, 0),D20)*, we compute the result we want. This formula sets *reference* equal to cell C6 (which contains the word *Country*). Then it moves over one column (to cell D20) to find units sold and down to the row containing the country listed in C21. In cell E21, the reference to D20 now refers to E20 and becomes a 2, so we move over two columns to the right of column C to find revenue. In cell E21, the reference to D20 now refers to F20 and becomes a 3, so we move three columns to the right of column C to find variable cost.

Each drug developed by my company goes through three stages of development. I have a list of the cost by month for each drug, and I also know how many months each development stage took for each drug. Can I create formulas that compute for each drug the total cost incurred during each stage of development?

The file Offsetcost.xlsx contains the monthly costs incurred to develop five drugs and, for each drug, the number of months required to complete each phase. A subset of the data is shown in Figure 20-4.

⊿	B	C	D	E	F	G	H
1		Dur Phase 1	2	3	9	12	6
2		Dur Phase 2	2	8	5	4	12
3		Dur Phase 3	2	11	4	11	15
4		Phase 1 Cost	110	313	795	1167	615
5		Phase 2 Cost	142	789	465	397	1096
6		Phase 3 Cost	234	876	401	1135	1588
7							
8							
9	Code	Month	Drug 1	Drug 2	Drug 3	Drug 4	Drug 5
10	1	Jan-98	52	135	131	121	69
11	2	Feb-98	58	120	77	60	68
12	3	Mar-98	80	58	66	52	113
13	4	Apr-98	62	56	78	61	146
14	5	May-98	130	126	98	118	94
15	6	Jun-98	104	102	64	117	125
16	7	Jul-98	121	59	115	112	137
17	8	Aug-98	107	123	56	102	77
18	9	Sep-98	80	88	110	85	93
19	10	Oct-98	51	111	72	118	89
20	11	Nov-98	74	124	82	143	66
21	12	Dec-98	76	107	99	78	66
22	13	Jan-99	97	97	129	77	142

Figure 20-4   Using the OFFSET function to compute development costs for Phases 1–3.

The goal is to determine for each drug the total cost incurred during each development phase. In cells D4:D6, I compute the total development costs for Phases 1–3 for Drug 1. I compute Phase 1 costs for Drug 1 by using a cell reference of D10, with *rows moved* and *columns moved* equal to 0. Setting *height* equal to the number of months in Phase 1 and *width* equal to 1 captures all Phase 1 costs. I compute Phase 1 costs for Drug 1 in cell D4 with the formula *SUM(OFFSET(D10,0,0,D1,1))*. Next, in cell D5, I compute Phase 2 total costs for Drug 1 by using the formula *SUM(OFFSET(D10,D1,0,D2,1))*. Note that I start with a cell reference of D10 (the first month of costs) and move down the number of rows equal to the length of Phase 1. This brings me to the beginning of Phase 2. Setting *height* equal to the value in cell D2 ensures that we include all Phase 2 costs. Finally, in cell D6, I find the Phase 3 development costs for Drug 1 by using the formula *SUM(OFFSET(D10,D1+D2,0,D3,1))*. In this formula, I start from the first month of sales and move down the number of rows equal to the total time needed for Phases 1 and 2. This brings us to the beginning of Phase 3, where in cell D3, we total the number of rows to capture Phase 3 costs. Then, by copying the formulas in D4:D6 to E4:H6, I can compute total costs for Phases 1–3 for Drugs 2 through 5. For example, we find that for Drug 2, total Phase 1 costs equal \$313, total Phase 2 costs equal \$789, and total Phase 3 costs equal \$876.

I run a small video store. In a worksheet, my accountant has listed the name of each movie and the number of copies in stock. Unfortunately, he combined this information into one cell for each movie. How can I extract the number of copies of each movie in stock to a separate cell?

The file Movies.xlsx, shown in Figure 20-5, contains the name of each movie and the number of copies in stock.

	A	B	C	D	E	F	G	H	I
1	count words	Number	Movie and Number of Copies						
2	2	40	Seabiscuit 40	Seabiscuit	40				
3	4	12	Laura Croft Tombraider 12	Laura	Croft	Tombraid	12		
4	6	36	Raiders of the Lost Ark 36	Raiders	of	the	Lost	Ark	36
5	3	5	Annie Hall 5	Annie	Hall	5			
6	2	4	Manhattan 4	Manhattan	4				
7	3	112	Star Wars 112	Star	Wars	112			
8	4	128	How to Deal 128	How	to	Deal	128		
9	4	1	The Matrix Reloaded 1	The	Matrix	Reloaded	1		
10	3	1040	Johnny English 1040	Johnny	English	1040			
11	3	12	Rosemary's Baby 12	Rosemary's	Baby	12			
12	3	1002	High Noon 1002	High	Noon	1002			

Figure 20-5 Movie example using the OFFSET function

We want to extract the number of copies owned of each movie to a separate cell. If the number of copies were listed to the left of a movie's title, this problem would be easy. We could use the FIND function to locate the first space and then use the LEFT function to return all the data to the left of the first space. (See Chapter 5, "Text Functions," for a discussion of how to use the LEFT and FIND functions, as well as other functions you can use to work with text.) Unfortunately, this technique doesn't work when the number of copies is listed to the right of the movie title. For a one-word movie title, for example, the number of copies is to the right of the first space, but for a four-word movie title, the number of copies is to the right of the fourth space.

One way to solve this problem is to click the Data tab on the Ribbon, and in the Data Tools group, click Text To Columns to place each word in a title and the number of copies in separate columns. We can use the COUNTA function to count the total number of words in a title, including the number of items as a word, for each movie. We can then use the OFFSET function to locate the number of items.

To begin, insert enough columns to the right of the data to allow each word in the movies' titles and the number of items to be extracted to a separate column. I used six columns (*Raiders of the Lost Ark* requires six columns), as you can see in Figure 20-5. Then I select the cell range C2:C12 and on the Data tab, in the Data Tools group, click Text To Columns. I select Delimited in the Convert Text To Columns Wizard and use the space character as the delimiting character. After selecting cell D2 as the destination cell, I have the results shown in columns D through I of Figure 20-5.

Now we count the number of words in each movie's cell (counting the number of items as a word), by copying from A2 to A3:A12 the formula *COUNTA(D2:I2)*. The results are shown in Figure 20-5.

Finally, copying from B2 to B3:B12 the formula *OFFSET(C2,0,A2)*, I can locate the number of copies of each movie in stock. This formula begins at the reference cell containing the movie title and moves over the number of columns equal to the number of "words" in the title cell. Because the reference cell contains only one cell, we can omit the *height* and *width* arguments of the OFFSET function so that the function uses only the cell containing the last "word" (the number of copies) of the title cell.

If you select any portion of a cell formula and then press F9, Excel displays the value created by that portion of the formula. You must press Esc or you will lose the formula. This trick makes it easier to debug and understand complex formulas. Thus, it might be easier to understand what the OFFSET portion of the formula does if you apply this trick to any of our formulas. For example, in file Offsetcost.xlsx cell E4 generates total Phase 1 cost with the formula =*SUM(OFFSET(E10,0,0,E1,1))*. If we move the cursor over *OFFSET(E10,0,0,E1,1)* and select F9, you will see =*SUM({135,120,58})*, which indicates that the OFFSET portion of the formula in cell D4 used the correct cells (D10:D12).

Another way to see how a complex formula works is to use the Evaluate Formula command. Move the cursor to E4 and click the Formulas tab on the Ribbon. In the Formula Auditing group, click Evaluate Formula. (See Figure 20-6.) Click the Evaluate button (it looks like a magnifying glass), and Excel simplifies the formula step by step until you see the formula's final result. After clicking Evaluate twice, the formula appears as =*SUM($E$10:E$12)*, so we know that in cell E4 we have selected the Phase 1 cells for Drug 2, which is what we wanted.

Figure 20-6   Evaluate Formula dialog box

How can I write a formula that always returns the last number in a column?

We often download new data into a worksheet. Can we write a formula that will always return sales during the most recent month? (See the file Mostrecent.xlsx and Figure 20-7 on the next page.)

	B	C	D	E
3			Most recent	
4			110	
5				
6	Sales			
7	20			
8	3			
9	40			
10	50			
11	60			
12	90			
13	110			

Figure 20-7   Finding the last number in a column

Simply enter in cell D4 the formula *OFFSET(B6,COUNT(B:B),0,1,1)*.

This formula begins in cell B6 and moves down a number of rows equal to the number of numerical entries in column B. This takes us to the most recent month of sales, which is selected because *1,1* returns only one cell.

How can I set up a range name that automatically includes new data?

We often add rows or columns of data to a range of data that is used to create a Pivot-Table or to perform another type of analysis. Usually, we simply update the range of cells referred to in our formula and then rerun our analysis. If we used dynamic range names, we will never have to update the range of data referred to in a formula or PivotTable. The range will automatically update. Here is an example.

In the file Dynamicrange.xlsx, we have an HR database. (See Figure 20-8.)

	A	B	C	D	E	F	G
1	Name	Salary	Exp	Gender			
2	John	35500	3	M			
3	Jack	42300	4	M			
4	Jill	53426	5	F	Example of dynamic range		
5	Erica	56000	6	F			
6	JR	62000	8	M			
7	Bianca	49000	10	F			
8	Francis	52000	5	M			
9	Roger	56000	7	M			
10	Maggie	42000	4				
11							448278

Figure 20-8   Example of a dynamic range

Currently, our data contains nine rows and four columns of data. Wouldn't it be nice if we could create a range name that would automatically include more rows and/or columns when we add people or fields of information to our database?

To create a dynamic range, click the Formulas tab on the Ribbon, and in the Defined Names group, click Name Manager. Then define a range as shown in Figure 20-9.

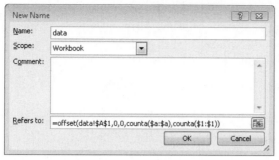

Figure 20-9   Creating a dynamic range

Our range starts in cell A1 (we move 0 rows and columns from cell A1). Our selected range has *number of rows=number of nonblank entries in column A* and *number of columns=number of nonblank entries in row 1*. Thus, if we add people or data fields, the formula will automatically expand to include them. The dollar signs ($) are needed so the defined range will not shift if we move around the worksheet.

To try this out, enter the formula *=SUM(data)* in cell G14. At present, this formula totals all numbers in the range A1:D9 and yields $448,278.

Now add to row 10 the name *Meredith*, enter in B10 a salary of $10,000, enter in E1 a variable for Mistakes (add the word *Mistakes*), and in E10 enter 1000. The formula *=SUM(data)* now includes the 10,000 and 1000, and automatically updates to $459,278.

I am charting my company's monthly unit sales. Each month I download the most recent month's unit sales. I would like my chart to update automatically. Is there an easy way to accomplish this?

The workbook Chartdynamicrange.xlsx (see Figure 20-10) contains units sold of our company's product. As you can see, the units sold have been charted using an XY (Scatter) chart.

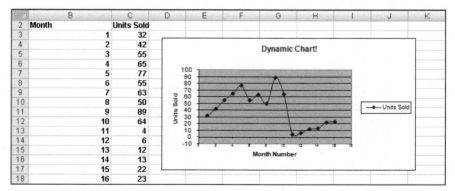

Figure 20-10   We can use the OFFSET function to update this chart dynamically.

Beginning in row 19, we will download new sales data. Is there an easy way to ensure that the chart automatically includes the new data?

The key to updating the chart is to use the OFFSET function to create dynamic range names for both the Months column and the Units Sold column. As new data is entered, the dynamic range for unit sales will automatically include all sales data, and the dynamic range for months will include each month number. After creating these ranges, I modify the chart, replacing the data ranges used in the chart with the dynamic ranges. The chart will now be updated as new data is entered.

To begin, click Define Names on the Formulas tab of the Ribbon to display the New Name dialog box. Create a range named Units by filling in the dialog box as shown in Figure 20-11.

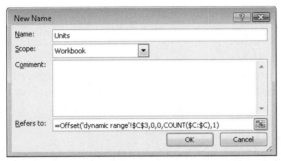

Figure 20-11   Creating a dynamic range name for the units sold

Entering =OFFSET('dynamic range'!$C$3,0,0,COUNT(!$C:$C),1) in the Refers To area of the dialog box creates a range one column wide beginning in cell C3, which contains the first unit sales data point. The range will contain as many numbers as there are in column C, which is derived by the portion of the formula that reads COUNT('dynamic range'!$C:$C). As new data is entered into column C, the data is automatically included in the range named Units.

Next, we create a dynamic range named Month for the months entered in column B. The formula is shown in Figure 20-12.

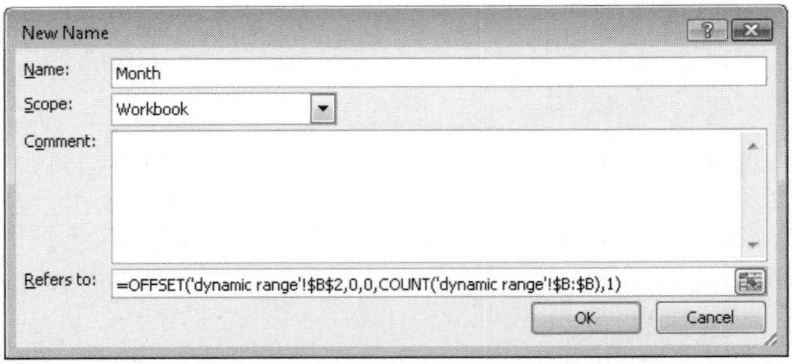

Figure 20-12   The formula used to define a dynamic range named Month

Now we go to our chart and click any point. In the formula box, you'll see the formula SERIES('dynamic range'!$C$2,'dynamic range'!$B$3:$B$18,'dynamic range'!$C$3:$C$18,1). This formula is Excel's version of the data originally used to set up the chart. Replace the ranges $B$3:$B$18 and $C$3:$C$18 with our dynamic range names as follows: SERIES('dynamic range'!$C$2,dynamicrange.xlsx!Month,dynamicrange.xlsx!Units,1). Of course, if a blank space is listed above any new data, this method won't work. Enter some new data and you'll see that it is included in the chart.

Remark

The Table feature in Excel 2007 makes it easy to set things up so that charts and formulas automatically incorporate new data. See Chapter 24, "Tables," for a discussion of this new feature.

Problems

1. The file C20p1.xlsx contains data about unit sales for 11 products during the years 1999–2003. Write a formula using the MATCH and OFFSET functions that determines the sales of a given product during a given year. Can you think of another way to solve this problem without using the MATCH and OFFSET functions?

2. A commonly suggested moving average trading rule is to buy a stock when its price moves above the average of the last D months and to sell it when its price moves below the average of the last D months. In Chapter 11, "IF Statements," we showed that for D=15, this trading rule outperformed the Standard &Poor's 500 by a substantial amount. By combining a one-way data table with the OFFSET function, determine the value of D that maximizes trading profit (excluding transactions costs). You can find pertinent data in the file Matradingrule.xlsx.

3. A commonly suggested moving average trading rule is to buy a stock when its price moves above the average of the last B months and to sell it when its price moves below the average of the last S months. In Chapter 12, "Time and Time Functions," we showed that for B=S=15, this trading rule outperformed the Standard & Poor's 500 by a substantial amount. By combining a two-way data table with the OFFSET function, determine the values of B and S that maximize trading profit (excluding transactions costs). You'll find data for this problem in the file Matradingrule.xlsx.

4. The file Lagged.xlsx contains data about the number of magazine ads placed by U.S. Army Recruiting during each of 60 consecutive months. For each month, we define the k-month lagged number of ads to equal the number of ads placed k months ago. For months 7–60, we would like to compute the 1-month lagged, 2-month lagged through 6-month lagged values of the number of ads. Use the OFFSET function to efficiently compute these lagged values.

5. The file Verizondata.xlsx gives sales of 4 different Verizon phones in 5 regions. Determine an efficient method to enter for each of the 20 region-product combinations the region, type of phone, and sales of each phone into one row.

6. This is a difficult one!! The file Agingdata.xlsx gives the number of insurance claims projected to be received daily and the number of insurance company workers available. Each day, a worker can process up to 30 claims. Workers process the oldest claims in the system first. Cells H6:AL6 contain the number of claims already in the system on January 1, before new claims arrive. Set up a worksheet to track the "aging" of the claims. That is, for each day, how many 1-day old , 2-day old, ... 30-day old and over 30-day old claims will be in the system.

7. Each row of the file Tapesales.xlsx contains monthly sales of a video tape. Write a formula to determine sales for each tape during its first six months on the market.

8. To obtain a golfer's handicap, we average the 10 lowest of the golfer's last 20 rounds. Then we subtract 80 and round to the nearest integer to obtain the handicap. Thus, if the 10 lowest of last 20 rounds added up to 864, the handicap would be 6. The file Golfdata.xlsx contains a golfer's scores. Beginning in row 24, compute the golfer's handicap after each round. We will assume that if the 10th best score in the last 20 rounds occurs more than once, then all rounds including that score will be included in the handicap calculation. Note that the Excel function =ROUND(x,0) will round x to the nearest integer.

9. Each row of the file Carsumdata.xlsx contains sales data for a product (car, train, or plane) from January thru July. Suppose we enter a month and a product into our worksheet. Write a formula that will give the total sales of that product during the given month.

10. The file Verizon.xlsx contains monthly returns on Verizon stock. Use the OFFSET function to extract all the January returns to one column, all the February returns to one column, and so on.

11. The file Casesensitive.xlsx contains product codes and product prices. Note that the product codes are case sensitive. For example, DAG32 is not the same product as dag32. Write a formula that gives the product price for any product code. Hint: You might need to use the EXACT function. The formula EXACT(cell1,cell2) yields TRUE if cell1 and cell2 have exactly the same contents. EXACT differentiates between uppercase and lowercase letters.

Chapter 21

The INDIRECT Function

- My worksheet formulas often contain references to cells, ranges, or both. Rather than change these references in my formulas, I'd like to know how I can place the references in their own cells so that I can easily change my cell or range references without changing my underlying formulas.

- Each worksheet in a workbook lists monthly sales of a product in cell D1. Is there an easy way to write and copy a formula that lists each month's product sales in one worksheet?

- Suppose I total the values in the range A5:A10 with the formula *SUM(A5:A10)*. If I insert a blank row somewhere between rows 5 and 10, my formula updates automatically to *SUM(A5:A11)*. How can I write a formula so that when I insert a blank row between rows 5 and 10, my formula still totals the values in the original range A5:A10?

- How can I use the INDIRECT function in a formula to "read" the range name portion of a formula in a worksheet?

The INDIRECT function is probably one of the most difficult Microsoft Office Excel functions to master. Knowing how to use the INDIRECT function, however, enables you to solve many seemingly unsolvable problems. Essentially, any reference to a cell within the INDIRECT portion of a formula results in the cell reference being immediately evaluated to equal the content of the cell. To illustrate the use of INDIRECT, look at the file Indirectsimpleex.xlsx, which is shown in Figure 21-1.

	A	B	C
3		Value	Indirect Reference
4	B4	6	6
5	B5	9	9

Figure 21-1 A simple example of the INDIRECT function

In cell C4, I've entered the formula *=INDIRECT(A4)*. Excel returns a value of 6, because the reference to A4 is immediately replaced by the text string *B4*. Therefore, the formula is evaluated as *=B4*, which yields a value of 6. Similarly, entering in cell C5 the formula *=INDIRECT(A5)* returns the value in cell B5, which is 9.

My worksheet formulas often contain references to cells, ranges, or both. Rather than change these references in my formulas, I'd like to know how I can place the references in their own cells so that I can easily change my cell or range references without changing my underlying formulas.

In this example, the data we'll use is contained in the file Sumindirect.xlsx, shown in Figure 21-2. The cell range B4:H16 lists monthly sales data for six products during a 12-month period.

I currently calculate total sales of each product during months 2–12. An easy way to make this calculation is to copy from C18 to D18:H18 the formula *SUM(C6:C16)*. Suppose, however, that you want to be able to change which months are totaled. For example, you might want total sales for months 3–12. You could change the formula in cell C18 to *SUM(C7:C16)* and then copy this formula to D18:H18, but using this approach is problematic because you have to copy the formula in C18 to D18:H18 and, without looking at the formulas, nobody knows which rows are being added.

	B	C	D	E	F	G	H
1			Lower	Upper			
2			6	16			
3		C	D	E	F	G	H
4	Month	Prod 1	Prod 2	Prod 3	Prod 4	Prod 5	Prod 6
5	1	28	86	79	31	84	58
6	2	38	7	61	1	20	2
7	3	91	48	73	8	80	14
8	4	33	32	24	77	29	80
9	5	82	70	41	29	57	90
10	6	75	40	15	92	55	91
11	7	52	21	26	45	59	21
12	8	19	6	35	67	40	81
13	9	11	18	68	11	52	78
14	10	90	30	52	32	30	1
15	11	47	86	46	0	38	55
16	12	69	71	75	65	53	52
17							
18	Total	607	429	516	427	513	565

Figure 21-2   You can use the INDIRECT function to change cell references in formulas without changing the formulas themselves.

The INDIRECT function provides another approach. I've placed in cells D2 and E2 the starting and ending rows of our summation. Then, by using the INDIRECT function, all I need to do is change the starting and ending row references in D2 and E2, and the sums are updated to include the rows we want. Also, by looking at the values in D2 and E2, it is obvious which rows (months) are being added! All I need to do is copy from C18 to D18:H18 the formula *SUM(INDIRECT(C$3&$D$2&":"&C$3&$E$2))*. If you want to see how Excel evaluates a reference to the INDIRECT function, use the following trick. Place the cursor over part of the formula (for example, C$3) and then press F9. Excel will show you the value of the selected portion of the formula. For example, C$3 will evaluate to C. Make sure to press Esc to return to Excel. Every cell reference within the INDIRECT portion of this formula is evaluated to equal the contents of the cell. C$3 is evaluated as C, $D$2 is evaluated as 6, and $E$2 is evaluated as 16. Using an ampersand (&) as the concatenation symbol Excel evaluates this formula as *SUM(C6:C16)*, which is exactly want we want. The formula in C18 returns the value *38+91+...69=607*. In cell D18, our formula evaluates as *SUM(D6:D16)*, which is the result we want. Of course, if we want to add up sales during, months 4 through 6, we simply enter 8 in D2 and 10 in E2. Then the formula in C18 returns *33+82+75=190*. (For information about using the ampersand to concatenate values, see Chapter 6, "Dates and Date Functions.")

Each worksheet in a workbook lists monthly sales of a product in cell D1. Is there an easy way to write and copy a formula that lists each month's product sales in one worksheet?

The file Indirectmultisheet.xlsx (see Figure 21-3) contains seven worksheets. In each worksheet, cell D1 contains data about the sales of a product during a particular month. Let's suppose Sheet1 contains month 1 sales, Sheet 2 contains month 2 sales, and so on. For example, sales in month 1 equals 1, in month 2 equals 4, and so on.

	C	D	E
1		1	
2			
3			
4			
5			
6			
7			
8			
9		Sheet#	Cell D1 entry
10	Sheet	1	1
11		2	4
12		3	0
13		4	12
14		5	15
15		6	3
16		7	4

Figure 21-3   Monthly sales (months 1–7) of a product listed by using the INDIRECT function

Suppose you want to compile a list of each month's sales into one worksheet. A tedious approach would be to list month 1 sales with the formula *=Sheet1!D1*, list month 2 sales with the formula *=Sheet2!D1*, and so on until you've listed month 7 sales with the formula *=Sheet7!D1*. If you have 100 months of data, this approach would be very time consuming! A much more elegant approach is to list month 1 sales in cell E10 of Sheet1 with the formula *INDIRECT($C$10&D10&"!D1")*. Excel evaluates C10 as *Sheet*, D10 as *1*, and *"!D1"* as the text string *!D1*. The whole formula is evaluated as *=Sheet1!D1*, which, of course, yields month 1 sales, located in cell D1 of Sheet1. Copying this formula to the range E11:E16 lists the entries in cell D1 of sheets 2 through 7. Note that when the formula in cell E10 is copied to cell E11, the reference to D10 changes to D11, and cell E11 returns the value located at Sheet2!D1.

Suppose I total the values in the range A5:A10 with the formula *SUM(A5:A10)*. If I insert a blank row somewhere between rows 5 and 10, my formula updates automatically to *SUM(A5:A11)*. How can I write a formula so that when I insert a blank row between rows 5 and 10, my formula still totals the values in the original range A5:A10?

The worksheet named *Sum(A5A10)* in the file Indirectinsertrow.xlsx (shown in Figure 21-4) illustrates several ways to total the numbers in cell range A5:A10. In cell A12, I've entered the traditional formula *SUM(A5:A10)*, which yields 6+7+8+9+1+2=33.

Similarly, the formula *SUM($A$5:$A$10)* in cell E9 yields a value of 33. As you'll soon see, however, if we insert a row between rows 5 and 10, both formulas will attempt to total the cells in the range A5:A11.

	A	B	C	D	E	F	G
1							
2							
3			Begin	End			
4			5	10			
5	6		Indirect Way				
6	7		33				
7	8						
8	9				Absolute Reference	Indirect Reference	Insert a blank row and see what happens?
9	1				33	33	
10	2						
11	Old way						
12	33						

Figure 21-4   Several ways to sum the values in the cell range A5:A10

With the INDIRECT function, you have at least two ways to total the values in the range A5:A10. In cell F9, I've entered the formula *SUM(INDIRECT("A5:A10"))*. Because Excel treats *INDIRECT("A5:A10")* as the text string "A5:A10", if I insert a row in the worksheet, this formula still totals the entries in the cell range A5:A10!

Another way to use the INDIRECT function to total the entries in the range A5:A10 is the formula *SUM(INDIRECT("A"&C4&":A"&D4))*, which is the formula entered in cell C6. Excel treats the reference to C4 as a 5 and the reference to D4 as a 10, so this formula becomes *SUM(A5:A10)*. Inserting a blank row between row 5 and row 10 has no effect on this formula because the reference to C4 will still be treated as a 5 and the reference to D4 will still be treated as a 10. In Figure 21-5, you can see the sums calculated by our four formulas after a blank row is inserted below row 7. You can find this data on the worksheet *Row Inserted* in the file Indirectinsertrow.xlsx.

Note that the classic SUM formulas that do not use the INDIRECT function have changed to add up the entries in the range A5:A11, so these formulas still yield a value of 33. The two SUM formulas that do use the INDIRECT function continue to add up the entries in the range A5:A10, so we lose the value of 2 (now in cell A11) when we calculate our sum. The SUM formulas that use the INDIRECT function yield a value of 31.

	A	B	C	D	E	F
1						
2						
3			Begin	End		
4			5	10		
5	6		Indirect Way			
6	7		31			
7	8					
8						
9	9				Absolute Reference	Indirect Reference
10	1				33	31
11	2					
12	Old way					
13	33					

Figure 21-5 Results of SUM formulas after inserting a blank row in the original range

How can I use the INDIRECT function in a formula to "read" the range name portion of a formula in a worksheet?

Suppose we have named several ranges in our worksheet to correspond to quarterly product sales. (See Figure 21-6 and the file Indirectrange.xlsx.) For example, the range D4:E6 (named Quarter1) contains fictitious first-quarter sales of various Microsoft products.

	D	E	F	G	H	I	J
3	Quarter1						
4	Office	63					
5	Windows	66					
6	Xbox	70					
7							
8	Quarter2						
9	Office	93					
10	Windows	90					
11	Xbox	99					
12							
13	Quarter3						
14	Office	77					
15	Windows	58					
16	Xbox	60			Office	Windows	Xbox
17				Quarter1	63	66	70
18	Quarter4			Quarter2	93	90	99
19	Office	97		quarter3	77	58	60
20	Windows	56		quarter4	97	56	95
21	Xbox	95					

Figure 21-6 Use the INDIRECT function to create reference to range name within a formula

We would like to write a formula that can easily be copied and that will then yield the sales of each product in each quarter in a single rectangular range of the worksheet, as shown in H17:J20. You would think you could enter in cell H17 the formula *=VLOOKUP(H$16,$G17,2,FALSE)* and then copy this formula to the range H17:J20. Unfortunately, Excel does not recognize $G17 as referring to the range name Quarter1. Rather, Excel just thinks $G17 is the text string Quarter1. The formula, therefore, returns an #NA error. To remedy this problem, simply enter in cell H17 the formula *=VLOOKUP(H$16,INDIRECT($G17),2,FALSE)* and then copy this formula to range H17:J20. This works perfectly! *INDIRECT($G17)* is evaluated as Quarter1, and is now recognized as a range name. We now have easily generated sales of all products during all four quarters!

Problems

1. The ADDRESS function yields the actual cell address associated with a row and column. For example, the formula *ADDRESS(3,4)* yields $D$3. What result would be obtained if you entered the formula *=INDIRECT(ADDRESS(3,4))*?

2. The workbook P21_2.xlsx contains data for the sales of five products in four regions (East, West, North, and South). Use the INDIRECT function to create formulas that enable you to easily calculate the total sales of any combination of consecutively numbered products, such as Products 1–3, Products 2–5, and so on.

3. The file P21_3.xlsx contains six worksheets. Sheet i contains month i sales for Products 1–4. These sales are always listed in the range E5:H5. Use the INDIRECT function to efficiently tabulate the sales of each product by month in a separate worksheet.

4. Write a formula that will total the entries in the cell range G2:K2 even if you insert one or more columns between columns G and K.

5. The file Marketbasketdata.xlsx contains sales of various items. For each row, a 1 in columns B through K indicates a purchased item, whereas a 0 marks an item that was not purchased. In the day week column, a 1 means the transactions was on a Monday, a 2 means the transaction was on a Tuesday, and so on. For each item listed in K9:K14, calculate the percentage of transactions for which the item was purchased. Also calculate the fraction of transactions taking place on each day.

6. The file Verizonindirectdata.xlsx contains each employee's hours of work and employee rating for January–May. Set up a consolidation sheet that enables us to choose any person, and then reports their hours of work during each month along with their overall rating for the month.

Chapter 22
Conditional Formatting

- How can I visually indicate whether recent temperature data is consistent with global warming?
- How does the Highlights Cells conditional formatting feature work?
- How do I check or customize my rules?
- What are the great new data bars, color scales, and icon sets included with Excel 2007 conditional formatting?
- How can I color-code monthly stock returns so that every good month is indicated in one color, and every bad month in another?
- Given quarterly corporate revenues, how can I indicate quarters in which revenues increased over the previous quarter in one color, and quarters in which revenues decreased from the previous quarter in another?
- Given a list of dates, how can I indicate weekend dates in a specific color?
- Our basketball coach has given each player a rating between 1 and 10 based on the player's ability to play Guard, Forward, or Center. Can I set up a worksheet that visually indicates the ability of each player to play the position to which she's assigned?
- What does the Stop If True option in the Manage Rules dialog box do?

Conditional formatting lets you specify formatting for a cell range depending on the contents of the cell range. For example, given exam scores for students, you can use conditional formatting to display in red the names of students who have a final average of at least 90. Basically, when you set up conditions to format a range of cells, Microsoft Office Excel checks each cell in the range to determine whether any of the conditions you specified (such as *exam score>90*) is satisfied. Then Excel applies the format you choose for that condition to all the cells that satisfy the condition. If the content of a cell does not satisfy any of the conditions, the formatting of the cell remains unchanged. Conditional formatting in Excel 2007 has been completely revised and expanded. Let's show you how to use these exciting new conditional formatting features.

To view your conditional formatting options, select the range you want to format. Then, on the Home tab of the Ribbon, in the Styles group, click the Conditional Formatting arrow. (See Figure 22-1.)

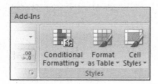

Figure 22-1   Conditional formatting commands

A submenu of conditional formatting options appears, as shown in Figure 22-2.

Figure 22-2   Conditional formatting options

- **Highlight Cells Rules** allows you to assign a format to cells whose contents meet one of the following criteria:

  1. Within a specific numerical range

  2. Match a specific text string

  3. Within a specific range of dates (relative to the current date)

  4. Occur more than once (or only once) in the selected range

- **Top/Bottom Rules** allows you to assign a format to any of the following:

  1. *N* largest or smallest values in a range

  2. Top or bottom *n* percent of numbers in a range

  3. Numbers above or below the average of all the numbers in a range

- **Data Bars, Color Scales, and Icon Sets** allow you to easily identify large, small, or intermediate values in a selected range. Larger data bars are associated with larger numbers. With Color Scales you might, for example, have smaller values appear in red and larger values in blue, with a smooth transition applied as values in the range change from small to large. With Icon Sets, you can use sets of up to five symbols to identify different ranges of values. For example, you might display an arrow pointing up to indicate a large value, pointing to the right to indicate an intermediate value, and pointing down to indicate a small value.

- **New Rule** allows you to create your own formula to determine whether a cell should have a specific format. For example, if a cell exceeds the value of the cell above it, you could apply the color green to the cell. If the cell is the fifth largest value in its column, you could apply the color red to the cell, etc.

- **Clear Rules** allows you to delete all conditional formats you have created for a selected range or for the entire worksheet.

- **Manage Rules** allows you to view, edit, or delete existing conditional formatting rules, create new rules, or change the order in which Excel applies the conditional formatting rules you have set.

How can I visually indicate whether recent temperature data is consistent with global warming?

This is a perfect job for applying the Excel 2007 Top/Bottom conditional formatting rules. The file Globalwarming.xlsx (see Figure 22-4 on the next page), contains the average world temperatures for the years 1856–2005 (we have hidden the years 1866–1989). These temperatures are deviations from a base level of 15 degrees Centigrade. If there has been global warming, we would expect the numbers in recent years to be larger than the numbers in earlier years. To determine if recent years are warmer, we first select the range B3:B152 containing the temperatures. On the Home tab, in the Styles group, click Conditional Formatting, and then on the submenu, click Top/Bottom Rules. Next, we select Top 10 Items and fill in the dialog box as shown In Figure 22-3.

Figure 22-3   Highlighting the ten highest temperatures in red

Next, we again selected the range B3:B152 and went back to set the Top/Bottom rules. This time, we selected Bottom 10 Items, and chose to highlight the 10 smallest numbers in orange. Note that the 10 highest temperatures occurred since 1990, whereas three of the 10 lowest temperatures occurred before 1865. In a similar fashion, in column C we highlighted the top 10 percent of the temperatures in red, and the bottom 10 percent in green. Finally, in column D we highlighted above-average temperatures in green and below-average temperatures in red. Note that all years earlier than 1865 had below average temperatures, whereas all years from 1990 or later had above average temperatures.

Conditional formatting is a powerful visual tool that can be used to demonstrate that the Earth (for whatever reason) seems to have become warmer in the recent past.

Note that clicking the arrow shown on the right side of Figure 22-3 displays a list of options, including Custom Format. Selecting this option displays the Format Cells dialog box, which allows you to create a custom format that is applied when the conditional formatting condition is satisfied.

	A	B	C	D
2	Year	Temp(relative to 15 degrees)		
3	1856	-0.36	-0.36	-0.36
4	1857	-0.47	-0.47	-0.47
5	1858	-0.42	-0.42	-0.42
6	1859	-0.23	-0.23	-0.23
7	1860	-0.4	-0.4	-0.4
8	1861	-0.41	-0.41	-0.41
9	1862	-0.53	-0.53	-0.53
10	1863	-0.26	-0.26	-0.26
11	1864	-0.46	-0.46	-0.46
12	1865	-0.25	-0.25	-0.25
136	1989	0.17	0.17	0.17
137	1990	0.34	0.34	0.34
138	1991	0.29	0.29	0.29
139	1992	0.15	0.15	0.15
140	1993	0.19	0.19	0.19
141	1994	0.26	0.26	0.26
142	1995	0.38	0.38	0.38
143	1996	0.22	0.22	0.22
144	1997	0.43	0.43	0.43
145	1998	0.57	0.57	0.57
146	1999	0.33	0.33	0.33
147	2000	0.26	0.26	0.26
148	2001	0.48	0.48	0.48
149	2002	0.52	0.52	0.52
150	2003	0.46	0.46	0.46
151	2004	0.58	0.58	0.58
152	2005	0.65	0.65	0.65

Figure 22-4 Conditional formatting using Top/Bottom rules

How does the Highlights Cells conditional formatting feature work?

The file Highlightcells.xlsx (see Figure 22-5) demonstrates how the Excel Highlight Cells features are used. For example, suppose we want to highlight all duplicate names in C2:C11 in red. Simply select the cell range C2:C11. Then click Conditional Formatting in the Styles group, click Highlight Cells Rules, click Duplicate Values, and then choose Light Red Fill With Dark Red Text. Click OK to apply the rule so that all names occurring more than once (John and Josh) are highlighted in red.

Now suppose that we want to highlight in red all cells in the range D2:D11 that contain the text *Eric*. We simply select the cell range D2:D11. Click Conditional Formatting, click Highlight Cells Rules, and then click Text That Contains. Enter Eric in the left box, and choose Light Red Fill With Dark Red Text on the right. As shown in Figure 22-5, we see that both Eric and Erica are highlighted (Erica, of course, contains the text string Eric).

Suppose we have a list of dates (such as E2:E11), and we want to highlight any cell that contains yesterday's date and any date during the last seven days in red. See the worksheet *Rightway* in the file Highlightcells.xlsx. Assume as shown in Figure 22-5 that the current date is March 16, 2007. Note that cell E3 contains the formula =*TODAY()−1*, so cell E3 will always contain yesterday's date. Cell E4 contains the formula =*TODAY()−5*. We began by selecting the cell range we want to format (E2:E11). Then we clicked Conditional Formatting, Highlight Cell Rules, and then A Date Occurring. In the A Date Occurring dialog box, we selected Yesterday and Green Fill With Dark Green Text and clicked OK. Next, we selected the A Date Occurring option again, and this time selected the In The Last Seven Days option with Light Red Fill With Dark Red Text. Note that formats created earlier have precedence over formats created later (unless you later reverse the order of precedence, as explained below). This explains why 3/16/2007 is formatted in green rather than red.

	C	D	E	F
1	duplicates red fill	text containing Eric red fill red text	yesterday green then last 7 days red	
2	John	John	6/1/2006	
3	Eric	Eric	3/16/2007	today()-1
4	James	James	3/12/2007	today()-5
5	John	John	5/15/2007	
6	Erica	Erica	6/14/2006	
7	JR	JR	2/3/2003	
8	Adam	Adam	5/12/2006	
9	Josh	Josh	6/17/2005	
10	Babe	Babe	8/1/2006	
11	Josh	Josh	9/2/2005	

Figure 22-5   Using the Highlight Cells rules

How do I check or customize my rules?

After creating conditional formatting rules, you can view your rules by clicking Manage Rules on the Conditional Formatting submenu. For example, select the dates in E2:E11, click Conditional Formatting, click Manage Rules, and you will see the rules displayed in Figure 22-6. You can see that our Yesterday formatting rule will be applied before our Last 7 Days formatting rule.

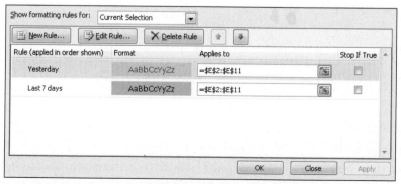

Figure 22-6   Conditional Formatting Rules Manager dialog box

From the Manage Rules dialog box, we can do the following:

- ❑ Create a rule by clicking the New Rule button.
- ❑ Edit or change a rule by clicking the Edit Rule button.
- ❑ Delete a rule by selecting it and then clicking the Delete Rule button.
- ❑ Change the order of precedence by selecting a rule and then clicking the up arrow or down arrow.

To illustrate the use of the Manage Rules dialog box, we copied the previous worksheet (simply right-click the worksheet tab, click Move Or Copy, and then check the Create A Copy box) to the *Wrongway* worksheet of the Highlightcells.xlsx file. We selected the Last 7 Days rule and clicked the up arrow. The Last 7 Days rule now has higher precedence than the Yesterday rule, so E3 will be formatted red and not green. Figure 22-7 shows how the Conditional Formatting Rules Manager dialog box looks, and Figure 22-8 shows that no cells in column E are formatted in green.

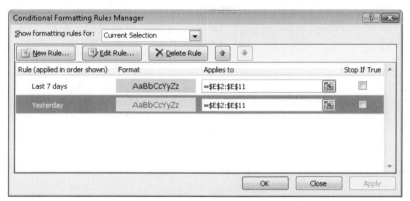

Figure 22-7   The result of giving the Last 7 Days rule higher precedence than the Yesterday rule

	C	D	E	F
1	duplicates red fill	text containing Eric red fill red text	last 7 days red then yesterday green	
2	John	John	6/1/2006	
3	Eric	Eric	3/16/2007	today()-1
4	James	James	3/12/2007	today()-5
5	John	John	5/15/2007	
6	Erica	Erica	6/14/2006	
7	JR	JR	2/3/2003	
8	Adam	Adam	5/12/2006	
9	Josh	Josh	6/17/2005	
10	Babe	Babe	8/1/2006	
11	Josh	Josh	9/2/2005	

Figure 22-8   After changing the precedence of rules, the Yesterday format will never be applied.

What are the great new data bars, color scales, and icon sets included with Excel 2007 conditional formatting?

When you have a long list of numbers, it would be nice to have a visual indicator that enables you to easily identify large and small numbers. Data bars, color scales, and icon sets (all new in Excel 2007) are perfect tools to display differences in a list of numbers. The file Scalesiconsdatabars.xlsx illustrates the use of these exciting new tools.

Figure 22-9 shows the use of data bars. We begin by applying the default data bars to the data in D6:D15. We first select the data in D6:D15, click Conditional Formatting, and then click Data Bars. Then we select blue data bars to automatically create the format shown in column D of Figure 22-9. Cells containing bigger numbers also contain longer blue bars. The default option is to have the shortest data bar associated with the smallest number in the selected range, and the longest data bar associated with the largest number.

	C	D	E	F	G
1					
2					
3		Data Bars			
4	shortest	lowest value	<=3	bottom 20 percent	20th percentile
5	longest	highest value	>=8	top 20 percent	90th percentile
6		1	1	1	1
7		2	2	2	1
8		3	3	3	1
9		4	4	4	3
10		5	5	5	4
11		6	6	6	7
12		7	7	7	6
13		8	8	8	8
14		9	9	9	9
15		10	10	10	10

Figure 22-9   Visually distinguishing numeric values by using data bars

If, after clicking Data Bars, we click More Rules, then the New Formatting Rule dialog box shown in Figure 22-10 on the next page is displayed. (You can also display this dialog box by clicking Manage Rules, and then either clicking Edit Rule or double-clicking on the rule.) From this dialog box, you can change the criteria used to assign the shortest and longest data bars to cells. In E6:E15, we chose to assign the shortest bar to the number 3 and the longest bar to the number 8. As shown in Figure 22-9, all numbers in column E that are less than or equal to 3 have the shortest bar, all numbers that are greater than or equal to 8 have the longest bar, and the numbers between 3 and 8 have the graduated bars. Note that in the Edit Formatting Rule dialog box, you can check the Show Bar Only box to display only the color bar and not the cell value in the conditionally formatted cells.

Next, in column F we chose to assign the shortest bar to numbers in the bottom 20 percent of the range F6:F15, and the longest bar to numbers in the top 20 percent. In other words, all numbers $<=1+.2(10-1)=2.8$ will have the shortest data bar, and all numbers $>=1+.8(10-1)=8.2$ will have the longest data bar. Figure 22-9 shows that in column F, the numbers 1 and 2 have the shortest data bar and the numbers 9 and 10 have the longest data bar.

Figure 22-10   Customizing your data bars

In cell range G6:G13, we associated the shortest data bar with all numbers on or below the 20th percentile of the data (1), and we associate the longest data bar with all numbers on or above the 90th percentile of the data (9).

Now let's use color scales to summarize some data sets. Like the Highlight Cells rule, a color scale uses cell shading to visually display the difference in cell values. Let's look at an example of a three-color scale. (The Colorscaleinvestment.xlsx file and Figure 22-11 illustrate the use of a three-color scale. Note that we have hidden rows 19-75; to unhide them, select rows 18 and 76, right-click the selection, and then click Unhide.) We selected the annual returns on Stocks, T-Bills, and T-Bonds in cells B8:D81 (). We clicked Conditional Formatting, Color Scales, and then More Rules to display the Edit Formatting Rule dialog box, which we filled in as shown in Figure 22-12.

Note that we chose the color red to indicate the lowest return, green to indicate the highest return, and orange to indicate the return at the midpoint. Amazingly, Excel 2007 makes small changes to the color shading of each cell based on the value in the cell. In column B of Figure 22-11, the lowest return is shaded red. As the returns approach the 50th percentile, the cell color gradually changes to yellow. Then, as the returns increase from the 50th percentile toward the largest return, the cell color changes from yellow to green. Note that most of your green and red cells are associated with stocks. This is because annual stock returns are more variable than bond or T-Bill returns. This causes large or small stock returns to occur quite frequently. Virtually all annual returns for T-Bills or T-Bonds are yellow, because the low variability of annual returns on these investments means that intermediate returns occur most of the time.

	A	B	C	D	E
3		red bad			
4		orange medium			
5		green great			
6		Annual Returns on Investments in			
7	Year	Stocks	T.Bills	T.Bonds	
8	1928	43.81%	3.08%	0.84%	
9	1929	-8.30%	3.16%	4.20%	
10	1930	-25.12%	4.55%	4.54%	
11	1931	-43.84%	2.31%	-2.56%	
12	1932	-8.64%	1.07%	8.79%	
13	1933	49.98%	0.96%	1.86%	
14	1934	-1.19%	0.30%	7.96%	
15	1935	46.74%	0.23%	4.47%	
16	1936	31.94%	0.15%	5.02%	
17	1937	-35.34%	0.12%	1.38%	
18	1938	29.28%	0.11%	4.21%	
76	1996	23.82%	5.14%	1.43%	
77	1997	31.86%	4.91%	9.94%	
78	1998	28.34%	5.16%	14.92%	
79	1999	20.89%	4.39%	-8.25%	
80	2000	-9.03%	5.37%	16.66%	
81	2001	-11.85%	5.73%	5.57%	

Figure 22-11   Three-color scales

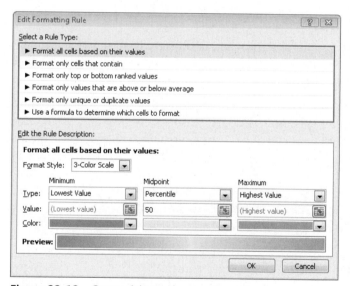

Figure 22-12   Customizing a three-color scale

We created some two-color scales in the Scalesiconsdatabars.xlsx file (shown in Figure 22-13 on the next page). We selected the range of cells and then clicked Conditional Formatting and Color Scales. You can select the color combination you want from the given list or create your own by clicking More Rules.

We chose a two-color scale indicating lower values in white and higher values in dark blue.

❑   In cell range D19:D28, we chose to make the lowest value white and the highest value blue. Note that as numbers increase, the cell shading becomes darker.

❏ In cell range E19:E28, we chose to make values less than or equal to 3 white and values greater than or equal to 8 blue. Note that for numbers between 3 and 8, as numbers increase, the cell shading becomes darker.

❏ In cell range F19:F28, we chose to make values in the bottom 20 percent of the range white and numbers in top 20 percent blue. For numbers in the middle 60 percent, cell shading becomes darker as numbers increase.

❏ In cell range G19:G28, we chose to make values on or below the 20th percentile of data white, and values on or above the 80th percentile blue. For all other numbers, cell shading becomes darker as numbers increase.

We can also display numerical differences by using icon sets. (See Figure 22-14 and the Scalesiconsdatabars.xlsx file.) An icon set consists of three to five symbols. The user defines criteria to associate an icon with each value in a cell range. For example, we may use a down arrow for small numbers, an up arrow for large numbers, and a horizontal arrow for intermediate values. The cell range E32:G41 contains three illustrations of the use of icons. For each column, we used the red down arrow, the yellow horizontal arrow, and the green up arrow.

	C	D	E	F	G
16		Color Scales			
17	shortest	lowest value	<=3	bottom 20 percent	20th percentile
18	longest	highest value	>=8	top 20 percent	80th percentile
19		1	1	1	1
20		2	2	1	1
21		3	3	1	2
22		4	4	2	2
23		5	5	4	4
24		6	6	5	5
25		7	7	5	5
26		8	8	8	7
27		9	9	9	9
28		10	10	10	10

Figure 22-13   Two-color scales

	D	E	F	G
30	down arrow	<=3	bottom 20 percent	20th percentile
31	up arrow	>=8	top 20 percent	80th percentile
32	⬇	1 ⬇	1 ⇨	1
33	⬇	2 ⬇	1 ⇨	1
34	⬇	3 ⬇	1 ⇨	1
35	⇨	4 ⬇	2 ⇨	2
36	⇨	5 ⇨	3 ⇨	3
37	⇨	6 ⇨	5 ⇨	5
38	⇨	7 ⇨	5 ⇨	5
39	⬆	8 ⇨	8 ⇨	7
40	⬆	9 ⇨	8 ⬆	8
41	⬆	10 ⬆	10 ⬆	10

Figure 22-14   Icon sets

Here is how we assigned icons to different range of numerical values.

- ❑ After selecting the numbers in E32:E41, we clicked Conditional Formatting, and clicked Icon Sets, and then, we clicked More Rules, and chose the 3 Arrows (Colored) icon set. In column E, we want numbers less than 4 to display a down arrow, from 4 to 8 to display a horizontal arrow, and 8 or larger to display an up arrow. To accomplish this goal, we set the options in the Edit Formatting Rule dialog box as shown in Figure 22-15.

- ❑ After selecting the numbers in F32:F41, we clicked Conditional Formatting, and then clicked Icon Sets. Then we clicked More Rules, and selected the 3 Arrows icon set. In column F, we want numbers in the top 20 percent of the range from smallest to largest (numbers greater than or equal to $1+0.8(10-1) = 8.2$) to have an up arrow, numbers in the bottom 20 percent of range (numbers $<= 1+0.2(10-1) = 2.8$) to have a down arrow, and all other numbers to have a horizontal arrow. To accomplish this goal, we set up the dialog box as shown in Figure 22-16 on the next page.

- ❑ In a similar fashion, we set up our formatting rule for G31:G42 so that up arrows are placed in cells containing numbers in the top 20 percent of all values, ($>=8$), and down arrows are placed in cells containing numbers in the bottom 20 percent of all values (<1).

Optional settings include Reverse Icon Order, which associates the icons on the left with small numbers and the icons on the right with larger numbers, and Show Icon Only, which hides the contents of the cell.

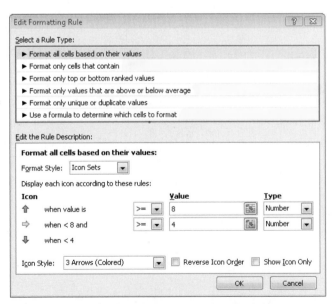

Figure 22-15   Assigning icons to numerical values

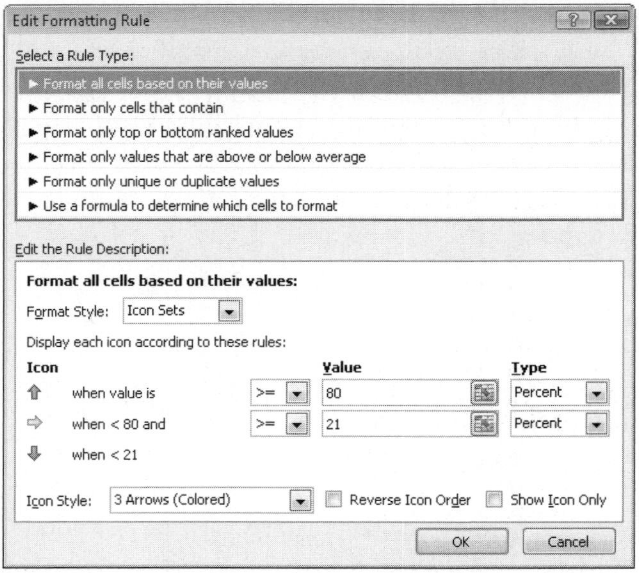

Figure 22-16 Assigning icons to percentage values

How can I color-code monthly stock returns so that every good month is indicated in one color, and every bad month in another?

The file Sandp.xlsx, shown in Figure 22-17, contains monthly values and returns on the Standard & Poor's stock index. Suppose that you want to highlight in green each month in which the S&P index went up by more than 3 percent, and to highlight in red each month in which it went down more than 3 percent.

I begin by moving to cell C10 (the first month containing an S&P return), and selecting all monthly returns by pressing Ctrl+Shift+Down Arrow. Next, I click Conditional Formatting, Manage Rules, New Rule, and select Format Only Cells That Contain. Then I fill in the dialog box as shown in Figure 22-18. We tell Excel to format cells in the selected range that are >0.03 and, after clicking Format, we select the desired Format (green fill).

Notice that the lists for fonts and font size aren't available, so your choice of formatting can't change the font or font size. The Fill tab provides the option to shade cells in a color you choose, whereas the Borders tab lets you create a border for cells that satisfy your conditional criteria. After clicking OK in the Format Cells dialog box, you're returned to the Conditional Formatting dialog box. We now select New Rule again, and in a similar fashion set things up so that all cells containing numbers that are less than −0.03 have a red fill. (See Figure 22-19.)

When you now click OK, all months with an S&P return that's greater than 3 percent (see cell C223, for example) are displayed in green, and all months with an S&P return of less than −3 percent (see cell C18) are displayed in red. Cells in which the monthly returns don't meet either of our conditions maintain their original formatting.

	A	B	C
6		S&P	
7		Comp.	
8	Date	P	Change
9	1871.01	4.44	
10	1871.02	4.5	0.01351
11	1871.03	4.61	0.02444
12	1871.04	4.74	0.0282
13	1871.05	4.86	0.02532
14	1871.06	4.82	−0.0082
15	1871.07	4.73	−0.0187
16	1871.08	4.79	0.01268
17	1871.09	4.84	0.01044
18	1871.1	4.59	−0.0517
19	1871.11	4.64	0.01089
20	1871.12	4.74	0.02155
21	1872.01	4.86	0.02532
22	1872.02	4.88	0.00412
23	1872.03	5.04	0.03279
24	1872.04	5.18	0.02778
25	1872.05	5.18	0
26	1872.06	5.13	−0.0097

Figure 22-17   Conditional formatting highlights returns in the S&P stock index

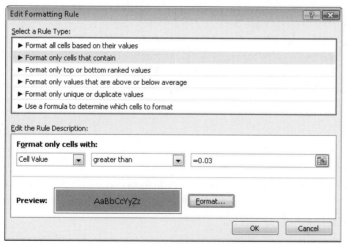

Figure 22-18   Applying special formatting to S&P returns greater than 3 percent

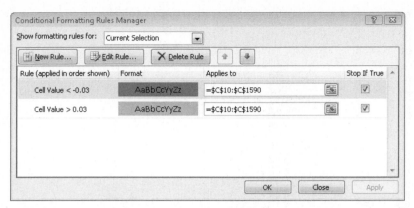

Figure 22-19 Coloring stock returns less than -3 percent in red and greater than 3 percent in green

Here are some useful tips concerning conditional formatting:

❑ To delete conditional formatting (or any format) applied to a range of cells, simply select the range of cells, click Conditional Formatting, click Clear Rules, and then click Clear Rules from Selected Cells.

❑ To select all the cells in a worksheet to which conditional formatting applies, press F5 to display the Go To dialog box. In the dialog box, click Special, select Conditional Formats, and then click OK.

❑ If you wish to edit a conditional formatting rule, click Manage Rules, and then either double-click the rule or click Edit Rules.

❑ You may delete a specific conditional formatting rule by clicking Manage Rules, clicking on the rule, and then clicking Delete Rule.

Note that after we have entered both rules, the red format rule is listed first (because it was created more recently than the green format rule). In the Conditional Formatting Rules Manager dialog box, rules are listed in order of precedence. In our example, it does not matter which rule is listed first because no cell could satisfy the criteria for both rules. If rules conflict, however, the rule listed first will take precedence. To change the order of conditional formatting rules, simply select a rule and click the up arrow to move the rule up in precedence, or the down arrow to move the rule down in precedence.

Given quarterly corporate revenues, how can I indicate quarters in which revenues increased over the previous quarter in one color, and quarters in which revenues decreased from the previous quarter in another?

The file Toysrusformat.xlsx contains quarterly revenues (in millions) for Toys "R" Us during the years 1997–2002. (See Figure 22-20.) We'd like to highlight quarters in which revenues increased over the previous quarter in green, and to highlight quarters in which revenues decreased over the previous quarter in red.

	C	D	E
1		Toys "R" US	
2			
3	Year	Quarter	Sales
4	1997	1	
5	1997	2	1738
6	1997	3	1883
7	1997	4	4868
8	1998	1	1924
9	1998	2	1989
10	1998	3	2142
11	1998	4	4383
12	1999	1	2043
13	1999	2	2020
14	1999	3	2171
15	1999	4	4338
16	2000	1	2186
17	2000	2	2204
18	2000	3	2465
19	2000	4	5027
20	2001	1	2319
21	2001	2	1994
22	2001	3	2220
23	2001	4	4799
24	2002	1	2061
25	2002	2	2021

Figure 22-20 HIghlighting increased sales in green and decreased sales in red

The Use A Formula option in the Conditional Formatting Rules Manager dialog box enables you to use a formula to define conditions that Excel checks before it applies formatting to a cell. We'll use this option in this example, but before we work with the Formula Is option, let's look at how Excel evaluates some logical functions.

What happens when we type a formula such as *=B3<2* in cell B4? If the value in B3 is a number smaller than 2, Excel returns the value TRUE in cell B4; otherwise, Excel returns FALSE. You can refer to the file Logicalexamples.xlsx, shown in Figure 22-21, for other examples like this. As you can see in Figure 22-21 on the next page, you can also use combinations of AND, OR, and NOT in formulas.

- In cell B6, the formula *=OR(B3<3, C3>5)* returns the value TRUE if either of the conditions *B3<3 or C3>5* is true. Because the value of C3 is greater than 5, Excel returns TRUE.
- In cell B7, the formula *=AND(B3=3,C3>5)* returns TRUE if *B3=3* and *C3>5*. Because B3 is not equal to 3, Excel returns FALSE. In cell B8, however, the formula *=AND(B3>3,C3>5)* returns TRUE because *B3>3* and *C3>5* are both true.
- In cell B9, the formula *=NOT(B3<2)* returns TRUE because *B3<2* would return FALSE, and a not false value becomes TRUE.

	A	B	C
2		**Logical functions**	
3		4	6
4	B3<2	FALSE	
5	B3>3	TRUE	
6	OR(B3<3,C3>5)	TRUE	
7	AND(B3=3,C3>5)	FALSE	
8	AND(B3>3,C3>5)	TRUE	
9	NOT(B3<2)	TRUE	

Figure 22-21   Logical functions

Now let's look at how the Use A Formula feature allows us to create a conditional format in a range of cells. Begin by selecting the range of cells to which you want to apply a conditional format. Then, click Conditional Formatting, followed by Manage Rules, to display the Conditional Formatting Rules Manager dialog box. Click New Rule, and then select Use A Formula To Determine Which Cells To Format option (the last option). To use the Formula option, we enter a formula (the formula must start with an equals sign) that is TRUE if and only if we want the cell in the upper-left corner to be assigned the chosen format. Our logical formula will copy like an ordinary formula to the remainder of the selected range, so judicious use of dollar signs ($) is needed to ensure that for each cell of the selected range, the formula will be TRUE if and only if we want our format to apply to the cell. Click Format, and then enter the formatting you want. Click OK. After clicking OK in the Conditional Formatting dialog box, your formula and formatting are copied to the whole cell range. The format will be applied to any cell in the selected range that satisfies the condition defined in the formula.

Returning to the file Toysrusformat.xlsx, let's focus on highlighting in green the quarters in which revenues increase. Basically, what we want to do is select the range E5:E25 (there is no prior quarter to which we can compare the revenue figure in cell E4), and then instruct Excel that if a cell's value is larger than the cell above it, highlight the cell in green. Figure 22-22 shows how to set up the desired rule.

If you enter =E5>E4 by pointing to the appropriate cells, be sure you remove the $ signs from the formula in the Conditional Formatting dialog box or the formula won't be copied. Probably the easiest way to insert or delete dollar signs is to use the F4 key. When you highlight a cell reference such as A3, pressing F4 cycles dollars signs in the following order: A3, $A$3, A$3, $A3. Thus, if we start with $A$3, pressing F4 changes cell reference to A$3. The formula in this example ensures that cell E5 is colored green if, and only if, sales in that quarter exceed the previous quarter. After clicking OK, you'll find that all quarters in which revenue increased are colored green. Notice that in cell E6, for example, the formula was copied in the usual way, becoming =E6>E5.

To add the condition for formatting cells in which revenue decreased, select the range E5:E25 again, open the Conditional Formatting Rules Manager dialog box, click New Rule, and then select Use A Formula To Determine Which Cells To Format. Enter the formula =E5<E4, and then click Format. On the Fill tab, change the fill color to red, and then click OK twice. The Conditional Formatting Rules Manager dialog box will now appear as shown in Figure 22-23.

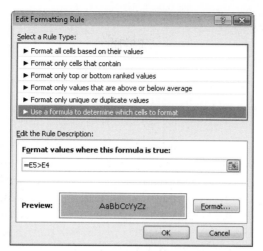

Figure 22-22 Conditional formatting settings that will display in green the quarters in which revenue increased

You can use the Formula option with Color Scales, Data Bars, and Icon Sets. Simply select the 'Use a formula to determine which cells to format' option (which we will simply call the Formula option) when setting the criteria for your scale, bar, or icons.

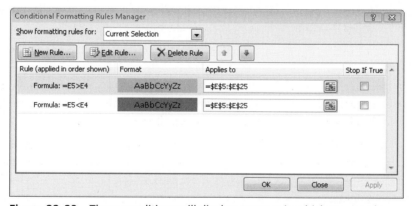

Figure 22-23 These conditions will display quarters in which revenue increased in green, and quarters in which revenue decreased in red.

Given a list of dates, how can I indicate weekend dates in a specific color?

The file Weekendformatting.xlsx (see Figure 22-24 on the next page), contains several dates. We want to highlight all Saturdays and Sundays in red. To do this, I first copied the formula *WEEKDAY(C6,2)* from cell D6 to D7:D69. Choosing *Type*=2 for the WEEKDAY function returns a 1 for each Monday, a 2 for each Tuesday, and so on, so that the function returns a 6 for each Saturday and a 7 for each Sunday.

	C	D	E	F
3		Monday = 1 Tuesday = 2 ,etc.		
4				
5	Date	Weekday		
6	2/8/2003	6		
7	1/2/2007	2		
8	1/2/2005	7		
9	10/25/2005	2		
10	10/10/2004	7		
11	10/13/2006	5		
12	9/26/2006	2		
13	9/25/2006	1		
14	11/1/2005	2		
15	11/29/2006	3		
16	2/16/2005	3		
17	7/27/2007	5		
18	3/24/2004	3		
19	10/6/2008	1		
20	4/11/2007	3		
21	2/3/2004	2		
22	1/22/2009	4		
23	10/29/2006	7		
24	6/9/2005	4		
25	8/16/2008	6		
26	12/13/2006	3		
27	3/5/2007	1		
28	8/8/2008	5		
29	9/1/2007	6		
30	9/5/2004	7		

Figure 22-24   Using the WEEKDAY function to highlight weekend days in red

I now select the range D6:D69, click Conditional Formatting, and then click Manage Rules. After clicking New Rule and the Formula option from the Rules Manager, I fill in the dialog box as shown in Figure 22-25.

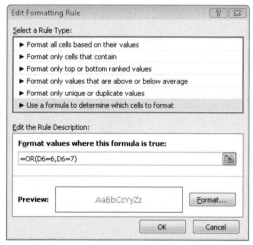

Figure 22-25   The Edit Formatting Rule dialog box set up to display weekend days in red font

After clicking OK, each date having its weekday equal to 6 (for Saturday) or 7 (for Sunday) is colored red. Note the formula =OR(D6=6,D6=7) implies that a cell entry of 6 or 7 will activate the red font color. Of course, we could have used Format Only Cells That Contain and used >=6 or >5 to obtain the same formatting .

Our basketball coach has given each player a rating between 1 and 10 based on the player's ability to play Guard, Forward, or Center. Can I set up a worksheet that visually indicates the ability of each player to play the position to which she's assigned?

The file Basketball.xlsx, shown in Figure 22-26, contains ratings given to 20 players for each position and the position (*1=Guard, 2=Forward, 3=Center*) played by each player. We would like to fill with red the cell containing the rating for each player for the position to which she's assigned.

	A	B	C	D	E	F
1			1	2	3	
2	Position played	Player	Guard rating	Forward rating	Center rating	
3	1	1	1	9	2	1=Guard
4	1	2	4	3	9	2=Forward
5	2	3	7	3	7	3=Center
6	2	4	9	8	8	
7	2	5	5	8	9	
8	3	6	2	7	2	
9	3	7	7	6	6	
10	3	8	4	4	3	
11	3	9	3	8	10	
12	3	10	6	1	4	
13	2	11	6	7	5	
14	2	12	2	6	5	
15	2	13	8	6	9	
16	1	14	1	1	3	
17	1	15	3	6	8	
18	2	16	4	10	1	
19	2	17	8	5	1	
20	2	18	1	7	7	
21	3	19	9	2	7	
22	3	20	10	3	10	

Figure 22-26   This worksheet rates each player's ability to play a position.

Begin by selecting the range C3:E22, which contains the players' ratings. Click Conditional Formatting, and then Manage Rules. Then click New Rule, and choose the Formula option. Now fill in the dialog box as shown Figure 22-27.

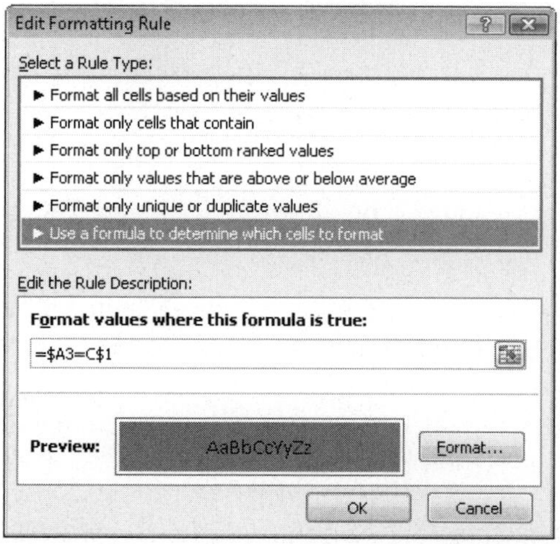

Figure 22-27   The Edit Formatting Rule dialog box set up to show player ratings in red fill.

The formula =$A3=C$1 compares the player's assigned position to the column heading (1, 2, or 3) in row 1. If the player's assigned position is set to 1 (Guard), her rating in column C, which is her Guard rating, appears in red. Similarly, if the player's assigned position is set to 2, her Forward rating in column D appears in red. Finally, if the assigned position is set to 3, her Center rating in column E appears in red.

What does the Stop If True option in the Manage Rules dialog box do?

Suppose the Stop If True option is checked for a rule. If a cell satisfied this rule, all lower precedent rules are ignored. To illustrate the use of Stop If True, suppose you have created a data bar format, but you don't want data bars to appear in cells having values greater than or equal to 50. Simply use Manage Rules to add a first format to the cell range which takes effect only if the value of the cell is >=50. Make the first format use an automatic (black) font and check Stop If True for the first format. Now, for all cells having values greater than or equal to 50, Excel will stop and not use the data bar format.

Problems

Using the data in the file Sandp.xlsx, use conditional formatting in the following situations:

1. Format in bold each month in which the value of the S&P index increased, and underline each month in which the value of the S&P index decreased.

2. Highlight in green each month in which the S&P index changed by a maximum of 2 percent.

3. Highlight the largest S&P index value in red, and the smallest in purple.

4. Using the data in the file Toysrusformat.xlsx, highlight in red all quarters for which revenue has increased over at least the last two quarters. Highlight all fourth-quarter revenues in blue, and first-quarter revenues in red.

5. The file Test.xlsx contains exam scores for students. The top 10 students receive an A, the next 20 students receive a B, and all other students receive a C. Highlight the A grades in red, the B grades in green, and the C grades in blue. Hint: The function LARGE(D4:D63,10) gives you the tenth highest grade on the test.

6. In the file Weekendformatting.xlsx, highlight all weekdays in red. Highlight in blue all days that occur in the first 10 days of the month.

7. Suppose each worker in Microsoft's finance department has been assigned to one of four groups. The supervisor of each group has rated each worker on a 0–10 scale, and each worker has rated his satisfaction with each of the four groups. (See the file Satissuper.xlsx.) Based on the group to which each worker is assigned, highlight the supervisor rating and the worker satisfaction rating for each worker.

8. The file Varianceanalysis.xlsx contains monthly profit forecasts and monthly actual sales. The sales variance for a month equals:

$$\frac{actualsales - predictedsales}{predictedsales}$$

Highlight in red all months with a favorable variance of at least 20 percent, and highlight in green all months with an unfavorable variance of more than 20 percent.

9. For our drug cost example from Chapter 20, "The OFFSET Function," format the worksheet so that all Phase 1 costs are displayed in red, all Phase 2 costs are displayed in green, and all Phase 3 costs are displayed in purple.

10. The file Names.xlsx contains a list of names. Highlight all duplicates in green, and all names containing *Ja* in red.

11. The file Duedates.xlsx contains due dates for various invoices. Highlight in red all invoices due by the end of the next month.

12. In the file Historicalinvest.xlsx, set up conditional formatting with three icons so that 10 percent of returns have an up arrow, 10 percent have a down arrow, and 80 percent have a horizontal arrow.

13. The file Nbasalaries.xlsx contains salaries of NBA players in millions of dollars. Set up data bars to summarize this data. Players making less than $1 million should have the shortest data bar, and players making more than $15 million should have largest data bar.

14. Set up a three-color scale to summarize the NBA salary data. Change the color of the bottom 10 percent of all salaries to green, and the top 10 percent to red.

15. Use five icons to summarize the NBA player data. Create break points for icons at $3 million, $6 million, $9 million, and $12 million.

16. The file Fractiondefective.xlsx contains the percentage of defective units produced daily. A day's production is considered acceptable if 2 percent or fewer items produced are defective. Highlight all acceptable days with a green flag. In another worksheet, highlight all acceptable days with a red flag. Hint: Use the Stop If True option to make sure that no icon occurs in any cell containing a number less than 2.

17. How could you set things up so no icons are shown for players who had salaries between $7 million and $8 million? Hint: Use the Stop If True option.

18. Summarize global warming data with a three-color scale. Lower temperatures should be blue, intermediate temperatures should be yellow, and higher temperatures should be red.

19. Suppose you are saving for your child's college fund. You are going to contribute the same amount of money to the fund at the end of each year. Your goal is to end up with $100,000. For annual investment returns ranging from 4 percent to 15 percent, and number of years investing varying from 5–15 years, determine your required annual contribution. Suppose you are able to save $10,000 per year. Use conditional formatting to highlight for each annual return rate the minimum number of years needed to accumulate $100,000.

20. The file Amazon.xlsx contains quarterly revenues for Amazon.com. Use conditional formatting to ensure that sales during each quarter are highlighted in a different color.

21. Set up conditional formatting which colors the cell range A1:H8 like a checkerboard, with alternating white and black coloring. Hint: The ROW() function gives the row number of a cell, and the COLUMN() function gives the column number of a cell.

Chapter 23
Sorting in Excel

- How can I sort sales transaction data so that transactions are sorted first by salesperson, then by product, then by units sold, and finally in chronological order from oldest to most recent?

- I have always wanted to sort my data based on cell color or font color. Is this possible in Excel 2007?

- I love the great icons described in Chapter 22, "Conditional Formatting." Can I sort my data based on the icon in the cell?

- My worksheet includes a column containing the month in which each sale occurred. When I sort by this column, I get either April (first month alphabetically) or October (last month alphabetically) on top. How can I sort by this column so that January transactions are on top, followed by February, and so on?

- Can I sort data without using the Sort dialog box?

Almost every user of Microsoft Office Excel has at one time or another sorted columns of data either alphabetically or by numerical value. Let's look at some examples of how wonderful and powerful sorting is in Excel 2007.

How can I sort sales transaction data so that transactions are sorted first by salesperson, then by product, then by units sold, and finally in chronological order from oldest to most recent?

JAC is a small company that sells makeup. The *Makeup* worksheet in the Makeupsort-temp.xlsx file (see Figure 23-1 on the next page) contains the following sales transaction information:

- ❏ Transaction Number
- ❏ Name of salesperson
- ❏ Date of transaction
- ❏ Product sold
- ❏ Units sold
- ❏ Dollars received
- ❏ Location of transaction

	Trans Nun	Name	Date	Product	Units	Dollars	Location
3	**Trans Nun**	**Name**	**Date**	**Product**	**Units**	**Dollars**	**Location**
4	785	Ashley	4/10/2005	eye liner	92	$ 278.34	east
5	1879	Ashley	8/18/2006	eye liner	90	$ 271.85	midwest
6	1685	Ashley	11/5/2005	eye liner	88	$ 265.96	south
7	1737	Ashley	3/28/2006	eye liner	88	$ 265.53	east
8	1579	Ashley	6/6/2004	eye liner	87	$ 262.85	east
9	1748	Ashley	5/4/2004	eye liner	85	$ 256.45	east
10	999	Ashley	10/14/2005	eye liner	82	$ 248.12	west
11	449	Ashley	6/6/2004	eye liner	81	$ 244.97	east
12	503	Ashley	7/7/2005	eye liner	81	$ 245.19	west
13	356	Ashley	8/29/2006	eye liner	76	$ 229.58	east
14	9	Ashley	7/5/2006	eye liner	75	$ 226.64	south
15	84	Ashley	10/1/2006	eye liner	73	$ 221.48	west
16	1552	Ashley	1/26/2004	eye liner	72	$ 218.33	south
17	1201	Ashley	12/17/2006	eye liner	66	$ 199.89	south
18	465	Ashley	6/13/2006	eye liner	58	$ 176.27	south
19	124	Ashley	1/10/2006	eye liner	57	$ 173.36	west
20	1653	Ashley	5/4/2004	eye liner	56	$ 170.25	east
21	1428	Ashley	12/6/2006	eye liner	53	$ 160.85	midwest
22	1470	Ashley	10/3/2005	eye liner	51	$ 155.05	west
23	1008	Ashley	12/8/2005	eye liner	51	$ 154.87	east
24	1541	Ashley	7/7/2005	eye liner	46	$ 139.34	west

Figure 23-1   Sales transaction data before sorting

We would like to sort the data so that:

❑ Transactions are listed alphabetically by salesperson. We want to sort in the usual A to Z order, so that all of Ashley's transactions are first and all of Zaret's transactions are last.

❑ Each person's transactions are sorted by product. Thus, Ashley's eye liner transactions will be followed by Ashley's foundation transactions, and so on.

❑ For each salesperson and product, transactions are listed by number of units sold (in descending order).

❑ If a salesperson sells makes two or more sales of the same product for the same number of units, transactions are listed in chronological order.

In older versions of Excel, it was difficult to sort on more than 3 criteria. Excel 2007 allows the user to involve up to 64 criteria in one sort. To sort our sales data, we first select the data (cell range E3:K1894). Two easy ways to select this data are as follows:

❑ Position the cursor in the upper-left corner of the data (cell E3), and press Ctrl+Shift+Right Arrow followed by Ctrl+Shift+Down Arrow.

❑ Position the cursor anywhere in the cell range and press Ctrl+*.

Next, on the Data tab, in the Sort & Filter group, click Sort to display the Sort dialog box shown in Figure 23-2.

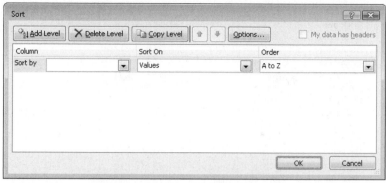

Figure 23-2   Sort dialog box not yet filled in

Because row 3 contains headings for our data columns, we check the My Data Has Headers box. We will now select the following four criteria in the order shown:

1. Sort by the Name column so that Values (this means cell contents) are in A to Z order.

2. Sort by the Product column so that Values are in A to Z order.

3. Sort by the Units column so that Values are in order from largest to smallest.

4. Sort by the Date column so that Values are in chronological order from oldest to newest.

Our dialog box now looks like Figure 23-3.

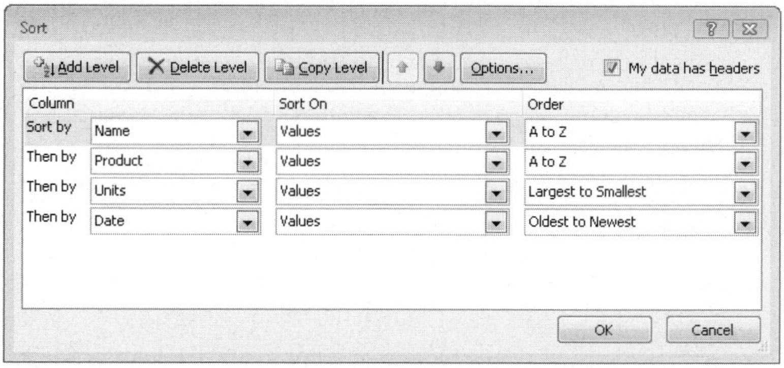

Figure 23-3   Sort dialog box set up for sales sorting example

The final result of our sort is shown in Figure 23-4 on the next page.

	E	F	G	H	I	J	K
3	Trans Numbi	Name	Date	Product	Units	Dollars	Location
4	785	Ashley	4/10/2005	eye liner	92	$ 278.34	east
5	1879	Ashley	8/18/2006	eye liner	90	$ 271.85	midwest
6	1685	Ashley	11/5/2005	eye liner	88	$ 265.96	south
7	1737	Ashley	3/28/2006	eye liner	88	$ 265.53	east
8	1579	Ashley	6/6/2004	eye liner	87	$ 262.85	east
45	1858	Ashley	7/7/2005	foundation	95	$ 286.83	south
46	1491	Ashley	7/18/2005	foundation	93	$ 281.34	south
199	555	Ashley	11/14/2006	mascara	-1	$ (1.28)	south
200	1245	Ashley	11/16/2005	mascara	-10	$ (27.09)	south
201	1290	Betsy	7/7/2005	eye liner	95	$ 286.61	east
202	1777	Betsy	12/19/2005	eye liner	95	$ 286.41	midwest
203	855	Betsy	1/23/2005	eye liner	94	$ 284.42	south
204	1609	Betsy	4/10/2005	eye liner	94	$ 283.46	east
205	1483	Betsy	7/29/2005	eye liner	94	$ 284.31	midwest
206	735	Betsy	5/2/2005	eye liner	91	$ 274.96	west
207	1509	Betsy	4/30/2006	eye liner	83	$ 251.40	midwest
208	91	Betsy	8/18/2006	eye liner	83	$ 251.18	south
209	872	Betsy	9/20/2006	eye liner	79	$ 239.06	south
210	487	Betsy	1/23/2005	eye liner	75	$ 227.10	west
211	100	Betsy	10/3/2005	eye liner	74	$ 224.23	west
212	176	Betsy	11/27/2005	eye liner	70	$ 211.76	south
213	1656	Betsy	1/1/2005	eye liner	67	$ 203.00	east
214	1095	Betsy	4/1/2004	eye liner	66	$ 199.92	west
215	741	Betsy	4/12/2004	eye liner	63	$ 191.25	west
216	1023	Betsy	9/22/2005	eye liner	56	$ 169.67	south

Figure 23-4 Sorted sales transaction data

Note that all of Ashley's transactions are listed first, with eye liner followed by foundation, and so on. Eye liner transactions are listed from largest number of units sold to smallest. In the case of a tie (see rows 6 and 7), the transactions are listed in chronological order.

Using the Sort dialog box, you can easily add sort criteria (Add Level), delete sort criteria (Delete Level), copy the settings that define a level of the sort, or specify whether your data has headers. By selecting Options, you can make the sort operation case sensitive or even sort data for which each case is listed in a different column (instead of the more common situation where each case is in a different row).

I have always wanted to sort my data based on cell color or font color. Is this possible in Excel 2007?

In Excel 2007, sorting on cell or font color is simple. Consider the *Makeup* worksheet in the Makeupsorttemp.xlsx file. Several names in column F are highlighted in different colors. For example, Cici in cell F620 is highlighted in red, and Colleen in cell F833 is highlighted in yellow. Suppose we want names with green fill on top, followed by yellow, and then by red, with the rest of the rows on the bottom. To sort the Name column by color, simply select the range you want to sort (E3:K1894), click Sort, and click Add Level. After selecting the Name column, click the Sort On setting, and select Cell Color (selecting Font Color sorts by font color). For the first level, select green from the Order list, select yellow for the second level, and select red for the third level. The completed dialog box is shown in Figure 23-5. The resulting sort is shown in *Colors* worksheet of the Makeupsort.xlsx file (see Figure 23-6).

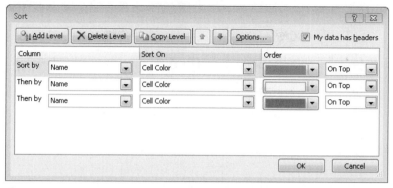

Figure 23-5   Sort dialog box set up to sort by color

	E	F	G	H	I	J	K
3	Trans Num	Name	Date	Product	Units	Dollars	Location
4	105	Cristina	9/13/2004	lipstick	51	$ 155.30	midwest
5	165	Hallagan	12/19/2005	foundatio	25	$ 76.99	east
6	86	Jen	8/9/2005	eye liner	-2	$ (4.24)	east
7	23	Colleen	2/1/2006	mascara	25	$ 77.31	midwest
8	14	Hallagan	1/1/2005	eye liner	18	$ 56.47	south
9	33	Cici	6/17/2004	mascara	41	$ 125.27	west
10	785	Ashley	4/10/2005	eye liner	92	$ 278.34	east
11	1879	Ashley	8/18/2006	eye liner	90	$ 271.85	midwest
12	1685	Ashley	11/5/2005	eye liner	88	$ 265.96	south
13	1737	Ashley	3/28/2006	eye liner	88	$ 265.53	east
14	1579	Ashley	6/6/2004	eye liner	87	$ 262.85	east
15	1748	Ashley	5/4/2004	eye liner	85	$ 256.45	east
16	999	Ashley	10/14/2005	eye liner	82	$ 248.12	west
17	449	Ashley	6/6/2004	eye liner	81	$ 244.97	east
18	503	Ashley	7/7/2005	eye liner	81	$ 245.19	west
19	356	Ashley	8/29/2006	eye liner	76	$ 229.58	east
20	9	Ashley	7/5/2006	eye liner	75	$ 226.64	south
21	84	Ashley	10/1/2006	eye liner	73	$ 221.48	west
22	1552	Ashley	1/26/2004	eye liner	72	$ 218.33	south
23	1201	Ashley	12/17/2006	eye liner	66	$ 199.89	south
24	465	Ashley	6/13/2006	eye liner	58	$ 176.27	south
25	124	Ashley	1/10/2006	eye liner	57	$ 173.36	west
26	1653	Ashley	5/4/2004	eye liner	56	$ 170.25	east

Figure 23-6   Results of sorting by color

I love the great icons described in Chapter 22, "Conditional Formatting." Can I sort my data based on the icon in the cell?

To sort by icon, simply select Cell Icon from the Sort On area list in the Sort dialog box. Then, in the Order list, choose the icon you want on top for the first level, and so on.

My worksheet includes a column containing the month in which each sale occurred. When I sort by this column, I get either April (first month alphabetically) or October (last month alphabetically) on top. How can I sort by this column so that January transactions are on top, followed by February, and so on?

The *Dates* worksheet in the Makeupsorttemp.xlsx file contains a list of months (see Figure 23-7). We would like to sort the months so they appear in chronological order beginning with January. We begin by selecting the range D6:D15 and sorting column D by values. When selecting the order, we select Custom List and then select the option beginning with *January, February, March.* Note that we could also have sorted by the day of the week. The completed dialog box is shown in Figure 23-8, with the resulting sort shown in Figure 23-9.

Note that from the Custom Lists box you can create a custom sort order list. Simply select NEW LIST, and under List Entries, type the entries in the order you want to sort by, and then click Add. Your new list will now be included as a menu selection. For example, if you entered Jack John Alan in List Entries (on different lines or separated by commas), all entries with Jack would be listed first, followed by John listings, with Alan listings on the bottom.

Figure 23-7 Months to be sorted

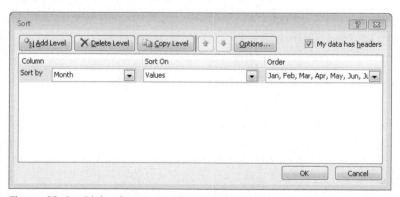

Figure 23-8 Dialog box to sort by month

	D
6	**Month**
7	Jan
8	Jan
9	Feb
10	Feb
11	Feb
12	Feb
13	**Mar**
14	**Apr**
15	**May**
16	**Aug**

Figure 23-9   Months sorted in chronological order

Can I sort data without using the Sort dialog box?

Sometimes it is more convenient to sort data without using the Sort dialog box. To illustrate how this is done, suppose again that we want to sort the sales transaction data in the *Makeup* worksheet in the Makeupsorttemp.xlsx file, so that transactions are sorted first by salesperson, then by product, then by units sold, and finally in chronological order from the oldest to the most recent. To begin, we select the least important column to sort on first, which is the date column (G3:G1894). Next, in the Sort & Filter group on the Data tab, we click the Sort A To Z button (see Figure 23-10), and with the Expand The Selection option selected, click Sort so all our columns are sorted. The Sort A To Z button will sort numerical data so the smallest numbers or oldest dates are on top and will sort text so that A precedes B, and so on.

Figure 23-10   Sorting

The Sort Z To A button, of course, sorts numerical data so that the largest numbers or most recent dates are on top and sorts text data so that Z precedes Y.

Next, we sort by the second least important column (Units) and click Sort Z To A because we want larger sales on top. We then sort from A to Z by Product, and finally from A to Z by salesperson. This achieves the same results as shown in Figure 23-4.

Problems

1. In the Makeupsort.xlsx file, sort the sales data alphabetically by location, then by product type, then by name, then by date of sale, and finally, by units sold.

2. The Sortday.xlsx file contains hours worked on different days of the week. Sort the data so that Monday data is followed by Tuesday data and so on.

3. The Sorticons.xlsx file contains annual investment returns with an up arrow used to indicate good years, a horizontal arrow used to indicate average years, and a red arrow used to indicate bad years. Sort the data by the icons in the Stock column with up arrows on top, followed by horizontal arrows and then red arrows.

4. The Makeupsortfont.xlsx vcontains our makeup data with certain dates shown in blue, red, or brown font. Sort the data so that brown dates are on top, followed by red dates and then blue dates.

Chapter 24
Tables

- I have entered into a worksheet the number of units sold and total revenue for each salesperson, and can easily compute average price for each salesperson. I have created a nice format for my data. However, when I add new data, it is really annoying to have to copy the formula down and extend the format. Is there an easy way to have my format and formulas automatically copy down when new data is added?

- I have entered into my worksheet several years of natural gas prices, and have created a nice line chart displaying the monthly variation in prices. Can I set things up so that when I add new gas price data, my chart automatically updates?

- For each sales transaction, I have the salesperson, date, product, location, and size of the transaction. Can I easily summarize, for example, total lipstick sales in the east made by Jen or Colleen?

- How can I easily refer to portions of a table in other parts of my workbook?

- Do conditional formats automatically apply to new data added to a table?

When most of us use Microsoft Office Excel, we often enter new data. Then we manually update our formulas, formats, and charts. What a drag! But the Excel 2007 table capabilities can make this drudgery a thing of the past.

I have entered into a worksheet the number of units sold and total revenue for each salesperson, and can easily compute average price for each salesperson. I have created a nice format for my data. However, when I add new data, it is really annoying to have to copy the formula down and extend the format. Is there an easy way to have my format and formulas automatically copy down when new data is added?

The file Tableexampletemp.xlsx (see Figure 24-1 on the next page) contains units sold and revenue data for each of six salespersons. We know that new data will be added (beginning in row 12). Also, in column H, we would like to calculate the average price (*Units/Revenue*) earned by each salesperson. We would like to create an attractive format for the data, and have our formula for average price copy down automatically as new data is added.

E	F	G
5 Name	Units	Revenue
6 John	814	39886
7 Adam	594	26136
8 Dixie	528	13200
9 Tad	806	20956
10 Erica	826	27258
11 Gabrielle	779	28044

Figure 24-1   Data for creating a table

Creating a table will allow our analysis and formatting to automatically update as new data is added. Begin by selecting the current range of data (E5:G11), including headers. Next, either click Table from the Insert tab, or press Ctrl+T. After checking the My Table Has Headers box, you will see that the table range (E5:G11) is formatted beautifully. This formatting will continue automatically whenever new data is entered into the table. Note that when you are working in a table, many styles and options are available on the Design tab (see Figure 24-2). You can then select a formatting style that will be continued as new data is added to the table.

Note that our column headings have arrows, or filters (see Figure 24-3), that can be used to sort or filter the table (more on filtering later in this chapter).

Figure 24-2   Table design options

E	F	G
5 Name ▼	Units ▼	Revenue ▼
6 John	814	39886
7 Adam	594	26136
8 Dixie	528	13200
9 Tad	806	20956
10 Erica	826	27258
11 Gabrielle	779	28044
12 Amanda	400	5000

Figure 24-3   Formatted table with filters

The cells in your selected table (excluding the headers) are given the name Table1 by default. We changed the name to Sales in the Properties group on the Design tab. If you click the Formulas tab, and then click Name Manager, you will see that range E6:G11 is named Sales. The beauty of this range name (and the table) is that the range dynamically expands to include new rows added to the bottom of the table, and new columns added to the right of the table. In Chapter 20, "The OFFSET Function," we used the OFFSET function to create a dynamic range, but the new table capabilities make creation of a dynamic range a snap.

Suppose that in D15 we want to compute total revenue. We begin by typing =SUM(S. Excel will offer us the option to automatically complete the entry with the table range Sales. We implemented Autocomplete by double clicking on the range name. You can also implement Autocomplete by moving the cursor to Sales and pressing the Tab key. Then, when we see =*SUM(Sales* and type [(an opening bracket), Formula AutoComplete offers the option to complete the formula with column headings from the Sales table (see Figure 24-4). We can complete our formula as =*SUM(Sales[Revenue])* and calculate total revenue as $155,480. (See Figure 24-5.) Note that we will select the entries in the AutoComplete box that begin with number signs (#) later in this chapter.

If new rows of data are added, then the data in these rows will automatically be added to the formula.

Figure 24-4   AutoComplete options for a table

	C	D	E	F	G
1					
2					
3					
4					
5			Name	Units	Revenue
6			John	814	39886
7			Adam	594	26136
8			Dixie	528	13200
9			Tad	806	20956
10			Erica	826	27258
11			Gabrielle	779	28044
12					
13					
14					
15	revenue	155480			

Figure 24-5   Total revenue for original data

To illustrate this idea, suppose we add new data in row 12: Amanda sold 400 units for $5,000. As shown in Figure 24-6 on the next page, our total revenue has increased by $5,000 to $160,480.

Our formatting has been extended to row 12, and our total units and total revenue formulas have automatically updated to include Amanda's data! Even if data is added within the table (instead of at the bottom), everything will be updated in a consistent fashion.

	C	D	E	F	G
1					
2					
3					
4					
5			Name ▼	Units ▼	Revenue ▼
6			John	814	39886
7			Adam	594	26136
8			Dixie	528	13200
9			Tad	806	20956
10			Erica	826	27258
11			Gabrielle	779	28044
12			Amanda	400	5000
13					
14					
15	revenue	160480			

Figure 24-6   New data added to table in row 12

Now suppose that we want to compute in column H the price per unit earned by each salesperson. We simply type Unit Price in H5 as the column heading, and then in cell H6 type =SALES[. In the AutoComplete list, click Revenue. The formula is now =SALES[Revenue]. Type / and use Formula AutoComplete to complete the formula as =SALES[Revenue]}/Sales[Units]. An amazing thing happens. Excel automatically copies the formula down to the bottom of the table in cell H12 (see Figure 24-7). If you go to any cell in column H, the formula will show up as =[Revenue]/[Units]. Of course, =[Revenue]/[Units] is a lot easier to understand than =G6/F6. This formula can be interpreted as taking whatever is in the current row in the Revenue column and divided it by whatever is in the current row in the Units column.

	C	D	E	F	G	H
5			Name ▼	Units ▼	Revenue ▼	Unit pr ▼
6			John	814	39886	49
7			Adam	594	26136	44
8			Dixie	528	13200	25
9			Tad	806	20956	26
10			Erica	826	27258	33
11			Gabrielle	779	28044	36
12			Amanda	400	5000	12.5
13						
14						
15	revenue	160480				

Figure 24-7   Unit price formula autocopy

If we click anywhere in a table, the Table Tools contextual tab appears on the Ribbon, and offers choices including the following:

❑ Change Table Name–(we changed our name from Table1 (the default) to Sales).

❑ Convert to Range–Converts the table range to normal cells and removes the table structure.

❑ Resize Table–Adds or subtracts rows and/or columns to the defined table range.

- ❏ Remove Duplicates—Removes rows which contain duplicates. For example, selecting only the Name column in the Remove Duplicates dialog box will ensure that a Name will not occur more than once. Checking both the Names and Units columns will ensure that no rows in the table will match both Name and Units, and so on.

- ❏ Header Row—If checked, the header row is displayed. If unchecked, the header row is not displayed.

- ❏ Total Row—We will discuss the Total Row later in this chapter.

- ❏ First Column—If checked, a special format can be applied to the first column of the table.

- ❏ Last Column—If checked, the last column of the table will be assigned a special format.

- ❏ Banded Rows—If checked, even-numbered rows in the table are given a different format than odd-numbered rows.

- ❏ Banded Columns—If checked, odd-numbered columns in the table are given a different format than even-numbered columns.

- ❏ Table Styles—Select from any of the table formats shown in this group. Of course, if the table expands or contracts, the format will adjust appropriately.

I have entered into my worksheet several years of natural gas prices, and have created a nice line chart displaying the monthly variation in prices. Can I set things up so that when I add new gas price data, my chart automatically updates?

In the file Gasprices507.xlsx, the worksheet *Original* contains natural gas prices per thousand feet from July 2002 through December 2004 (see Figure 24-8 on the next page). As previously described, we selected B5:C34 (containing months and prices) and pressed Ctrl+T to create a table from this range. Then we created a line graph to display this data by clicking Line in the Charts group on the Insert tab, and selecting the fourth type of line graph. The line graph we created is shown in Figure 24-9 on the next page.

	B	C
4	month	gas price
5	Jul-02	3.278
6	Aug-02	2.976
7	Sep-02	3.288
8	Oct-02	3.686
9	Nov-02	4.126
10	Dec-02	4.140
11	Jan-03	4.988
12	Feb-03	5.660
13	Mar-03	9.133
14	Apr-03	5.146
15	May-03	5.123
16	Jun-03	5.945
17	Jul-03	5.291
18	Aug-03	4.693
19	Sep-03	4.927
20	Oct-03	4.430
21	Nov-03	4.459
22	Dec-03	4.860
23	Jan-04	6.150
24	Feb-04	5.775
25	Mar-04	5.150
26	Apr-04	5.365
27	May-04	5.935
28	Jun-04	6.680
29	Jul-04	6.141
30	Aug-04	6.048
31	Sep-04	5.082
32	Oct-04	5.723
33	Nov-04	7.626
34	Dec-04	7.976

Figure 24-8   Gas price data: 2002–2004

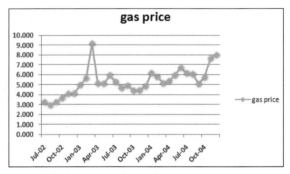

Figure 24-9   Gas price line graph: 2002–2004 data

Next, we copied this worksheet (by right-clicking the worksheet name, clicking Move Or Copy Sheet, and then clicking Make A Copy) and added gas prices through July 2006 (the data now extends to row 53). We named the new worksheet *New Data*. Note the line graph in this worksheet automatically updated to include the new data! (See Figure 24-10.)

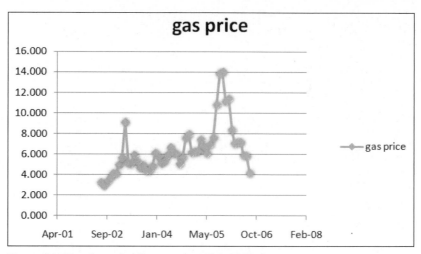

Figure 24-10   Gas price line graph: 2002–2006 data

This example illustrates that if you create a table of your data before creating a chart, new data will automatically be included in the chart.

For each sales transaction I have the salesperson, date, product, location, and size of the transaction. Can I easily summarize, for example, total lipstick sales in the east made by Jen or Colleen?

The file Tablemakeuptemp.xlsx contains sales transactions (see Figure 24-11 on the next page). For each transaction, we have the following information: Transaction Number, Name, Date, Product, Location, Dollars, and Units sold. If we format this data as a table, we can add a Total row to the Units and Dollars columns, and then use the filter arrows to make the Total rows include the desired subset of transactions. To begin, we place our cursor anywhere within our data and create a table by pressing Ctrl+T. Note that if we scroll through the table, our header rows remain visible. With your cursor in the table, check the Total Row box in the Table Style Options group on the Design tab. By default, Excel will enter the total number of rows in the table in cell K1895, which we will delete. Click the arrow to the right of cells I1895 and J1895, and then click Sum. This totals all entries in columns I and J of our table. Thus, currently the total revenue is $239,012.67, and 78,707 units were sold (see Figure 24-12 on the next page and file Tablemakeup-totals.xlsx).

Trans Number	Name	Date	Product	Units	Dollars	Location
1	Betsy	38078	lip gloss	45	137.2045583	south
2	Hallagan	38056	foundation	50	152.0073031	midwest
3	Ashley	38408	lipstick	9	28.71948312	midwest
4	Hallagan	38859	lip gloss	55	167.0753225	west
5	Zaret	38155	lip gloss	43	130.6028724	midwest
6	Colleen	38683	eye liner	58	175.9909741	midwest
7	Cristina	38067	eye liner	8	25.80069218	midwest
8	Colleen	39068	lip gloss	72	217.8396539	midwest
9	Ashley	38903	eye liner	75	226.6423269	south
10	Betsy	38936	lip gloss	24	73.50234217	east
11	Ashley	38320	mascara	43	130.8353684	east
12	Ashley	38309	lip gloss	23	71.03436769	west
13	Emilee	38595	lip gloss	49	149.5927969	west
14	Hallagan	38353	eye liner	18	56.47199923	south
15	Zaret	38980	foundation	-8	-21.99304472	east
16	Emilee	38089	mascara	45	137.3903759	east
17	Colleen	38837	mascara	66	199.6543347	south
18	Jen	38595	lip gloss	88	265.1875515	midwest
19	Jen	38287	eye liner	78	236.1469779	south
20	Zaret	38683	lip gloss	57	173.1152946	midwest
21	Zaret	38870	mascara	12	38.08143571	west
22	Betsy	38254	eye liner	28	86.5127757	midwest

Figure 24-11 Makeup sales data

Trans Number	Name	Date	Product	Units	Dollars	Location
1889	Emilee	39046	eye liner	76	229.9178081	west
1890	Cici	38518	foundation	16	49.7539874	east
1891	Betsy	38452	foundation	39	119.1888319	east
1892	Cici	38771	mascara	92	278.4349111	west
1893	Cici	38199	foundation	20	61.92385747	midwest
1894	Colleen	38122	lip gloss	60	181.8703479	east
1895	Emilee	38683	eye liner	15	47.16102233	east
1896	Ashley	38397	foundation	36	109.8425992	east
1897	Colleen	38661	lip gloss	46	140.4088994	west
1898	Zaret	38001	lipstick	72	217.8358862	west
1899	Hallagan	39024	eye liner	28	85.65682953	south
1900	Cristina	38881	eye liner	54	164.4873342	midwest
Total				78707	239912.6741	

Figure 24-12 Total revenue and units sold

To make our totals reflect only lipstick sales in the East made by either Jen or Colleen, click the arrow in F3 (to right of the Name header). Clear the Select All box, so that no names are selected. Then check the Colleen and the Jen boxes (see Figure 24-13), and then click OK. Next, click the Product arrow and check the lipstick box, and then click the Location arrow and check the East box. Use the same approach to show only lipstick in the Product column and only East in the location column. We now see all the data fitting our filtering criteria in Figure 24-14 and in the file Tablemakeupfinal.xlsx. We find that Colleen and Jennifer sold 497 units of lipstick in the East for a total of $1,515.89. This table filtering feature makes it a snap to easily compute totals for any subset of rows in an Excel worksheet!

Figure 24-13   Selecting names from the table

Trans Number	Name	Date	Product	Units	Dollars	Location
180	Colleen	38133	lipstick	60	182.0222938	east
343	Colleen	38397	lipstick	15	46.63789886	east
509	Jen	38430	lipstick	6	20.04283816	east
515	Jen	38034	lipstick	67	202.6222612	east
539	Colleen	38078	lipstick	7	22.95994806	east
697	Jen	38782	lipstick	36	110.2585155	east
769	Jen	38375	lipstick	12	37.85449636	east
770	Colleen	38067	lipstick	25	76.80845834	east
852	Jen	38925	lipstick	34	103.3986361	east
1232	Colleen	38738	lipstick	52	157.8620126	east
1238	Jen	38254	lipstick	92	277.6301019	east
1787	Jen	38595	lipstick	24	74.61122832	east
1821	Jen	38859	lipstick	67	203.1815597	east
Total				497	1515.890249	

Figure 24-14   Filtered subtotals for units and revenue

How can I easily refer to portions of a table in other parts of my workbook?

The file Tablestructure.xlsx shows many examples of how we can refer to parts of a table when we are outside of the table. These references are often called *structured references* (see Figure 24-15 on the next page). When you enter a table name into a formula, Auto-Complete will make the column names and the following table specifiers available for selection:

❑ Table Name—All cells in the table, excluding the header and total rows.

❑ #All—All cells in the table, including the total row (if any).

❑ #Data—All cells in the table except for the first row and the total row.

❑ #Headers—Just the header row.

❑ #Totals—Just the total row. If there is no total row, this returns an empty cell range.

- ❑ #This Row—All table entries in the current row.

- ❑ A column reference includes all cells in a table column, excluding the header and total row entry (if any).

Here are some examples of how table specifiers can be used in formulas:

- ❑ In cell C15, the formula =COUNTA(Table1[All#]) yields 55 because the table contains 55 entries.

- ❑ In cell C16, the formula =COUNTA([Table1]) yields 45 because the headers and total row are not counted.

- ❑ In cell C17, the formula =COUNTA(Table[#data]) yields 45 because the cell range D5:H13 is referenced.

- ❑ In cell C18, the formula =COUNTA(Table1[#Headers]) yields 5 because only the header row (D4:H4) is referenced.

- ❑ In cell C19, the formula =SUM(Table1[Q1]) yields 367 because the formula sums the entries in E5:E13.

- ❑ In cell C20, the formula =SUM(Table1[#Totals]) sums up all entries in the total row and yields 1,340, which is the total sum of all table entries.

- ❑ In cell C21, the formula =SUM(Table1[[Data#],[Q1]:[Q3]]) sums up all data entries that are in columns Q1:Q3, inclusive (cells E5:G13). Thus, column names separated by a colon include all data entries between and including the column name before the colon and the column name after the colon.

- ❑ In cell B8, the formula =SUM(Table1[#This Row]) sums the entries in row 8 (41+28+49+40).

Of course, all of these formulas will automatically update if new data is added to the table.

	A	B	C	D	E	F	G	H
4				Product	Q1	Q2	Q3	Q4
5				food1	37	42	24	32
6				mag1	20	23	24	41
7				drug1	47	34	41	28
8		158		drug2	41	28	49	40
9				food2	44	22	46	50
10	=SUM(Table1[#This Row])			drug1	39	25	38	29
11				mag2	26	35	31	30
12				food4	48	49	50	50
13				mag3	65	34	35	43
14				Total	367	292	338	343
15			55	=COUNTA(Table1[#All])				
16			45	=COUNTA(Table1[])				
17			45	=COUNTA(Table1[#Data])				
18			5	=COUNTA(Table1[#Headers])				
19			367	=SUM(Table1[Q1])				
20			1340	=SUM(Table1[#Totals])				
21			997	=SUM(Table1[[#Data],[Q1]:[Q3]])				

Figure 24-15   Structured references

Do conditional formats automatically apply to new data added to a table?

Yes, conditional formats will automatically include new table data. (See Figure 24-16.) To illustrate, we placed in worksheet *Original* of file Tablestructure.xlsx a conditional format to highlight the three largest Q1 sales in column E. Then entries in rows 7, 12, and 13 are highlighted. In worksheet *Add Biggersale*, we added in cell E14 the entry 90. This becomes the largest entry in the column and is immediately highlighted. Cell E7 is no longer highlighted because it is no longer one of the three largest numbers in column E of the table.

	D	E	F	G	H
4	Product	Q1	Q2	Q3	Q4
5	food1	37	42	24	32
6	mag1	20	23	24	41
7	drug1	47	34	41	28
8	drug2	41	28	49	40
9	food2	44	22	46	50
10	drug1	39	25	38	29
11	mag2	26	35	31	30
12	food4	48	49	50	50
13	mag3	65	34	35	43
14	drug3	90	45	34	23

Figure 24-16   Conditional formatting extends automatically to new table data

Problems

1. The file Singers.xlsx contains a list of songs sung by different singers, as well as the length of each song. Set up your worksheet to compute the total number of songs sung by Eminem and the average length of each song. Of course, if new data is added, your formulas should automatically update.

2. In file Tableexample.xlsx, set things up so that each salesperson's rank in regards to total revenue and units sold is included in the worksheet. Of course, if new data is included, your ranks should automatically update. You might find it convenient to use the RANK function. The syntax of the rank function is =RANK(number,array,0). This function yields the rank of number in range array, with *rank=1* being largest number.

3. The file Lookupdata.xlsx contains product codes and prices. Set up the worksheet so that a product code can be entered and your worksheet will return the product price. Of course, when new products are introduced, your formula should still work.

4. The file Productlookup.xlsx contains the product sales made each day of the week. Set up a formula that returns the sale of any product on any given day. Of course, if new products are added to the data, your formula should be able to include sales for those products.

5. The file Tablepie.xlsx contains sales information for different products sold in a small general store. We want to set up a pie chart to summarize this data. Of course, if new product categories are added, the pie chart should automatically include the new data.

6. The file Tablexnvdata.xlsx lists cash flows received by a small business. Set up a formula to compute (as of January 5, 2007) the NPV of all cash flows. Assume an annual discount rate of 10 percent. Of course, if new cash flows are entered, your formula should automatically include them.

7. The file Nikedata.xlsx contains quarterly sales revenues for Nike. Create a graph of Nike sales that automatically includes new sales revenue data.

8. For the data in file Tablemakeuptemp.xlsx, determine total units and revenue for all lip gloss or lipstick sold by Jen or Ashley in the south or east.

9. The file Closest.xlsx contains people's names and salaries. Set up a worksheet that takes any number and finds the person whose salary is closest to that number. Your worksheet should accomplish this goal even if new names are added or existing names are deleted from the list.

Chapter 25

Spin Buttons, Scroll Bars, Option Buttons, Check Boxes, Combo Boxes, and Group List Boxes

- I need to run a sensitivity analysis that has many key inputs, such as sales, annual sales growth, price, and unit cost. Is there a way I can quickly vary these inputs and see the effect of the variation on the calculation of net present value, for example?

- How do I set up a simple check box that toggles conditional formatting on and off?

- How can I set up my worksheet so that my supply chain personnel can click a button to choose whether we charge a high, low, or medium price for a product?

- How can I create an easy way for a user of my worksheet to enter a day of the week without having to type any text?

User forms enable the Microsoft Office Excel user to add a variety of cool, useful controls to a worksheet. In this chapter, we will show you how easy it is to use spin buttons, scroll bars, check boxes, option buttons, combo boxes, and list boxes. To access Excel user forms, on the Developer tab of the Ribbon, click Insert from the Controls group to display the Forms Controls (not to be confused with the ActiveX Controls, which are usually used within the Microsoft Visual Basic for Applications (VBA) programming language.)

 Note To display the Developer tab, click the Microsoft Office Button, and then click Excel Options. On the Popular tab, check the Show Developer Tab In The Ribbon box, and then click OK.

The user forms we will discuss are shown in Figures 25-1 through 25-7 on the next page.

Figure 25-1   Spin button

Figure 25-2   Scroll bar

Figure 25-3   Check box

Figure 25-4   Option button

Figure 25-5   Group box

Figure 25-6   Combo box

Figure 25-7   List box

We begin by showing you how to use spin buttons and scroll bars.

Spin Buttons and Scroll Bars

As discussed in Chapter 17, "Using the Scenario Manager for Sensitivity Analysis," the Scenario Manager lets you change a group of input cells to see how various outputs change. Unfortunately, the Scenario Manager requires you to enter each scenario individually, which makes it difficult to create more than a few. For example, suppose you believe that four key inputs to our car net present value (NPV) model are Year1 sales, Sales growth, Year1 price, and

Year1 cost. (See the file NPVspinners.xlsx.) We'd like to see how NPV changes as the inputs change in the following ranges:

Input	Low value	High value
Year 1 sales	5,000	30,000
Annual sales growth	0%	50%
Year 1 price	$6	$20
Year 1 cost	$2	$15

Using the Scenario Manager to generate the scenarios in which the input cells vary within the given ranges would be very time consuming. By using *spin buttons*, however, a user can quickly generate a host of scenarios that vary each input between its low and high value. A spin button is a button control that is linked to a specific cell. As you click the up or down arrow on the spin button, the value of the linked cell changes. You can see how formulas of interest (such as a car's NPV) change in response to changes in the inputs.

I need to run a sensitivity analysis that has many key inputs, such as year 1 sales, annual sales growth, year 1 price, and year 1 unit cost. Is there a way I can quickly vary these inputs and see the effect of the variation on the calculation of net present value, for example?

Here's how to create spin buttons that allow us to vary Year1 sales, Sales growth, Year1 price, and Year1 cost within the ranges we want. Our original worksheet (see the file NPVspinners.xlsx) is shown in Figure 25-8.

	A	B	C	D	E	F
1		taxrate	0.4			
2		Year1sales	10000			
3		Sales growth	0			
4		Year1price	$ 9.00			
5		Year1cost	$ 6.00			
6		intrate	0.15			
7		costgrowth	0.05			
8		pricegrowth	0.03			
9	Year	1	2	3	4	5
10	Unit Sales	10000	10000	10000	10000	10000
11	unit price	$ 9.00	$ 9.27	$ 9.55	$ 9.83	$ 10.13
12	unit cost	$ 6.00	$ 6.30	$ 6.62	$ 6.95	$ 7.29
13	Revenues	$ 90,000.00	$ 92,700.00	$ 95,481.00	$ 98,345.43	$ 101,295.79
14	Costs	$ 60,000.00	$ 63,000.00	$ 66,150.00	$ 69,457.50	$ 72,930.38
15	Before Tax Profit	$ 30,000.00	$ 29,700.00	$ 29,331.00	$ 28,887.93	$ 28,365.42
16	Tax	$ 12,000.00	$ 11,880.00	$ 11,732.40	$ 11,555.17	$ 11,346.17
17	Aftertax Profits	$ 18,000.00	$ 17,820.00	$ 17,598.60	$ 17,332.76	$ 17,019.25
18						
19	NPV	$59,069.66				

Figure 25-8   The automobile sales data worksheet without any spin buttons

To create the spin buttons, select the rows (I used rows 2–5 in this example) in which you want to insert spin buttons, and then increase the height of the rows by right-clicking and selecting Format, Row, and then Height. A row height of 25 is usually enough to accommodate the spin button arrows. Alternatively, holding down the Alt key while you draw the control in the cell fits it to the cell.

Display the User Forms toolbar by clicking Insert in the Controls group on the Developer tab. Click the spin button form control (shown in Figure 25-1), and drag it to where you want it to appear in your worksheet (cell D2). You will see a plus sign (+). Clicking the mouse button will anchor the spin button where you want it, and allows you to draw the desired shape for the spin button. To change the shape of a user form control or to move the control, place the cursor on the control and hold down the Ctrl key. When the four-headed arrow appears, drag it to move the form. When the two-headed arrow appears, drag it to resize the form.

A spin button now appears in cell D2. We'll use this spin button to change the value of Year1 sales. Right-click the spin button, and on the shortcut menu, click Copy. Right-click cell D3, and then click Paste. Also paste the spin button into cells D4 and D5. You should now see four spin buttons as shown in Figure 25-9.

	A	B	C	D
1		taxrate	0.4	
2		Year1sales	10000	
3		Sales growth	0	
4		Year1price	$ 9.00	
5		Year1cost	$ 6.00	

Figure 25-9   Spin buttons placed in worksheet cells

Now we need to link each spin button to an input cell. To link the spin button in D2 to cell C2, right-click the spin button in cell D2 and then click Format Control. Fill in the Format Control dialog box as shown in Figure 25-10.

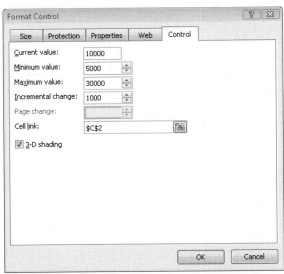

Figure 25-10   Use the Format Control dialog box to link Year1 sales to a spin button.

The current value is not important. The rest of the settings tell Excel that this spin button is linked to the values in cell C2 (Year1 sales), that each click on the up arrow will increase the value in C2 by 1000, and that each click on the down arrow will decrease the value in C2 by 1000. When the value in C2 reaches 30,000, clicking the up arrow will not increase it; when the value in C2 reaches 5,000, clicking the down arrow will not decrease the value in cell C2.

Next, we use the Format Control dialog box to link the spin button in D4 to Year1 price (cell C4). For current value, I used 9. The minimum value is 6, the maximum value is 20, and the incremental change is 1. Clicking the spin button arrows in cell D4 will vary the Year1 price between $6 and $20, in $1 increments.

To link the spin button in cell D5 to Year1 cost (cell D5), I used 6 for the current value, 2 for the minimum value, 15 for the maximum value, and 1 as the incremental change. Clicking the spin button arrows in cell D5 will change Year1 cost from $2 to $15, in $1 increments.

Linking the spin button in cell D3 to Sales growth is trickier. We would like the spin button control to change Sales growth to 0 percent, 1 percent, ... 50 percent. The problem is that the minimum increment a spin button value can change is 1. Therefore, we link our spin button to a dummy value in cell E3 and place the formula $E3/100$ in cell C3. Now, as cell E3 varies from 1 to 50, our Sales growth varies between 1 percent and 50 percent. Figure 25-11 shows how to link our spin button to cell E3. Remember that Sales growth in cell C3 is simply the number in cell E3 divided by 100.

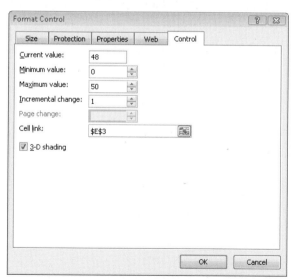

Figure 25-11   The Format Control dialog box settings that link the spin button in cell D3 to cell E3.

By clicking a spin button arrow, we can easily see how changing a single input cell—given the values for the other inputs listed in the worksheet—will change the car's NPV. To see the effect of the changes, you can select cell F9, and on the View menu click Freeze Panes, and then click Freeze Panes again. This command freezes the data above row 9 and to left of column F. You can now use the scroll bars on the right of your screen to arrange the window as you see it in Figure 25-12.

	A	B	C	D	E
1		taxrate	0.4		
2		Year1sales	10000		
3		Sales growth	0.48		48
4		Year1price	$ 9.00		
5		Year1cost	$ 6.00		
6		intrate	0.15		
7		costgrowth	0.05		
8		pricegrowth	0.03		
19	NPV	$133,664.07			

Figure 25-12   You can freeze panes to see the results of calculations in other parts of a worksheet.

Given the values of our other inputs, clicking the Sales growth spin button arrows shows us that a 1 percent increase in Sales growth is worth about $2,000! (To return the worksheet to its normal state, click Freeze Panes on the View menu, followed by Unfreeze Panes.)

The scroll bar control is very similar to the spin button. The main difference is that by moving the cursor over the gray area in the middle of the scroll bar, you can cause the linked cell to continuously change in value. By selecting Format Control on the shortcut menu and changing the value under Page Change in the Format Control dialog box, you can control the speed with which the linked cell changes.

How do I set up a simple check box that toggles conditional formatting on and off?

A check box is a form control that enables us to check a box. When the box is checked, a TRUE is placed in a cell. When the box is unchecked, a FALSE is entered into the cell. Check boxes can be used to enable "toggle switches" which turn a particular feature on or off. As an example of the use of a check box, we show how a check box can be used to turn the conditional formatting feature on or off.

Suppose our worksheet contains monthly sales and we want to color the five largest sales in green and the five smallest sales in red (see the file Checkbox.xlsx). We enter in cell G4 the formula =LARGE(Sales,5), which computes the fifth-largest sales value. Then, in cell H4, we compute the fifth-smallest sales value with the formula =SMALL(Sales,5). (See Figure 25-13.)

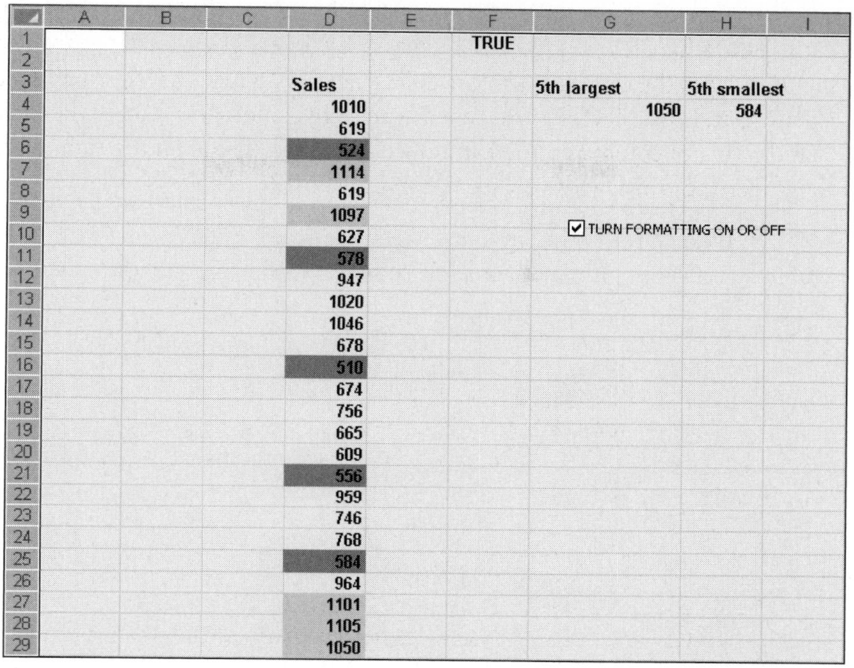

	A	B	C	D	E	F	G	H	I
1						TRUE			
2									
3				Sales			5th largest	5th smallest	
4				1010			1050	584	
5				619					
6				524					
7				1114					
8				619					
9				1097					
10				627			☑ TURN FORMATTING ON OR OFF		
11				578					
12				947					
13				1020					
14				1046					
15				678					
16				510					
17				674					
18				756					
19				665					
20				609					
21				556					
22				959					
23				746					
24				768					
25				584					
26				964					
27				1101					
28				1105					
29				1050					

Figure 25-13   Use of a check box to turn conditional formatting on and off

Next, we will create a check box and cause it to enter a TRUE or FALSE in cell F1. On the Developer tab, click Insert and select the check box (see Figure 25-3) from the Forms palette. Drag the check box to cell G9, and change its text to read *TURN FORMATTING ON OR OFF*. Then right-click the check box, click Format Control, and fill in the dialog box as shown in Figure 25-14.

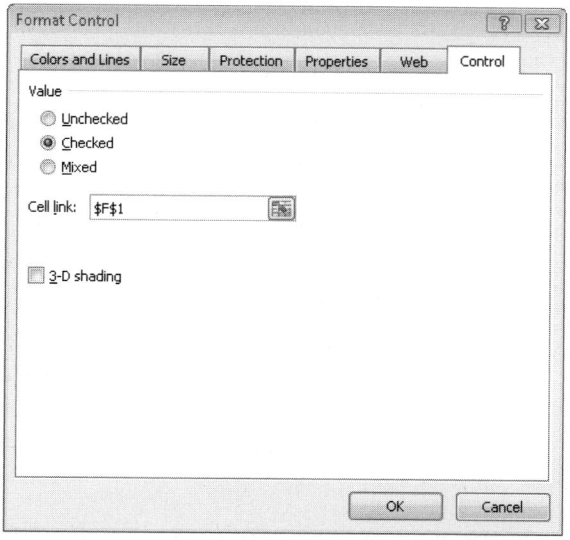

Figure 25-14   Format Control for a check box

Now, whenever we place a check in the check box, a TRUE is placed in F1, and whenever we do not have a check in the check box, a FALSE is placed in cell F1.

After selecting the cell range D4:D29, click Conditional Formatting in the Styles group on the Home tab, and then click New Rule. Enter the formulas shown in Figures 25-15 and 25-16 to color the top five sales green and the bottom five sales red. Note that the *AND($F$1)* portion of the formula ensures that our format can be applied if cell F1 is TRUE. Of course, our check box determines whether cell F1 is TRUE or FALSE, so if the check box is not checked, then our cells will not turn green or red.

Figure 25-15   Format to turn five largest cells green

Figure 25-16   Format to turn five smallest cells red

If desired, we can select cell F1 and change the Font Color to white so that TRUE or FALSE is hidden.

How can I set up my worksheet so that my supply chain personel can check a button to choose whether we charge a high, low, or medium price for a product?

Let's suppose that there are three prices we can charge for a product: High, Medium, or Low. These prices are listed in cells B7:B9 of the file Optionbuttons.xlsx. We could easily use a lookup table to print out the price if the user typed in High, Medium, or Low. It's a better design, however, if the user can select an option button that says High Price, Medium Price, or Low Price, and then have a formula automatically compute the price (see Figure 25-17). To use option buttons, you first draw a Group Box (see Figure 25-5) from the User Forms toolbar. Then you drag an option button for each choice into the group box. Because we have three price levels, we drag three option buttons into the group box. Right-click any option button. Then using Format Control, we can link any one of the option buttons to a cell. We chose to link the first option button to cell E4. All of the option buttons in the group box are now linked to the same cell. Selecting the first option button will enter a 1 in cell E4, selecting the second option button will enter a 2 in cell E4, and selecting the third option button will enter a 3 in cell E4.

Entering the formula =INDEX(A7:A9,E4,1) in cell E7 will return the price description corresponding to the selected option button. In cell F7, the formula =VLOOKUP(E7, A7:B9,2,FALSE) computes the price corresponding to the selected option button.

	A	B	C	D	E	F
4					3	
5			2			
6					Price level	Price
7	High	$ 8.00			Low	$ 3.00
8	Medium	$ 6.00				
9	Low	$ 3.00				
10						
11						
12						
13						
14	┌ Select price					
15						
16	○ High price					
17						
18	○ Medium price					
19	⦿ Low price					
20						
21						

Figure 25-17   Using option buttons to select product price

How can I create an easy way for a user of my spreadsheet to select a day of the week without having to type any text?

The file Combobox.xlsx shows how to use a combo box or a list box to allow the user to easily select an item from a list (data validation also makes it easy to create drop-down boxes; see Chapter 35, "Validating Data"). (See Figure 25-18 on the next page.) Our goal is to compute the number of hours an employee worked on a given day. The hours worked each day are listed in cells G9:G15. A combo or list box allows you select an entry from a list. If the combo or list box is linked to a cell (via Format Controls), then if the first entry in the box is selected, a 1 is placed in the linked cell; if the second entry in the list is selected, a 2 is entered in the linked cell, and so on. After selecting the Developer and Forms toolbar, and selecting Insert, we drag a combo box from the Form Controls to C5 and a list box to B14. After right-clicking the combo box and clicking Format Control, we selected the input range F9:F15 (this contains days of the week) and cell link A8. After right-clicking the list box and selecting format control, we selected input range F9:F15 and cell link A13. If, for example, we select Tuesday from the combo box and Friday from the list box, we see a 2 in A8 and 5 in A13.

In cell F3, the formula =INDEX(F9:F15,A8,1) lists the day of the week corresponding to our combo box selection. In cell G3, the formula =VLOOKUP(F3,$F$9:$G$15,2,False) locates the number of hours worked for the day selected in the combo box. In a similar fashion, the formulas in F4 and G4 list the day of the week and hours worked for the day selected in the list box.

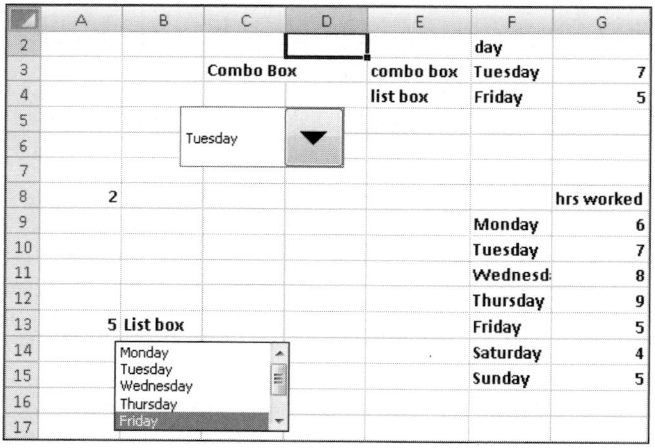

Figure 25-18   Combo and list boxes

Problems

1. Add a spin button for the car NPV example that allows the tax rate to vary between 30 percent and 50 percent.

2. Add a spin button for the car NPV example that allows the interest rate to vary between 5 percent and 20 percent.

3. The Format Control dialog box allows a minimum value of 0. Despite this limitation, can you figure out a way to use a spin button to vary sales growth between −10 percent and 20 percent?

4. Using our lemonade example in Chapter 15, "Sensitivity Analysis with Data Tables," create spin buttons that allow our inputs to vary within the following ranges:

Input	Low value	High value
Price	$2.00	$5.00
Unit cost	$0.20	$1.00
Fixed cost	$20,000.00	$100,000.00

5. Using the mortgage payment example in Chapter 15, create spin buttons that allow our inputs to vary within the following ranges:

Input	Low value	High value
Amount borrowed	$250,000	$800,000
Number of months of payments	120	360
Annual interest rate	4%	10%

6. For the weekend example used in Chapter 22, "Conditional Formatting," set up a check box that will turn conditional formatting on or off.

7. In the financial formulas described in Chapter 9, "More Excel Financial Functions," we use a last argument of 1 to indicate end of month cash flows and and 0 to indicate beginning of month cash flows. Excel recognizes a TRUE as equivalent to a 1 and a FALSE as equivalent to 0. Set up a worksheet where a user can enter the number of months in a loan, principal, and annual interest rate to find the monthly payment. Then use a check box to select whether the payments are at the beginning or end of the month.

8. The file Quarterly.xlsx contains quarterly sales at different department stores. Use option buttons to select the quarter and a list box to select the product. Your worksheet should then compute sales at a specified store during a specific quarter.

Chapter 26
An Introduction to Optimization with Excel Solver

- How can a large drug company determine the monthly product mix at their Indianapolis plant that maximizes corporate profitability?

- If Microsoft produces Xbox consoles at three different locations, how can they minimize the cost of meeting demand for them?

- What price for Xbox consoles and games will maximize Microsoft's profit from Xbox sales?

- Microsoft would like to undertake 20 strategic initiatives that will tie up money and skilled programmers for the next five years. They do not have enough resources for all 20 projects; which ones should they undertake?

- How do bookmakers find the best set of "ratings" for NFL teams, in order to set accurate point spreads?

- How should I allocate my retirement portfolio among high-tech stocks, value stocks, bonds, cash, and gold?

In all these situations, we want to find the best way to do something. More formally, we want to find the values of certain cells in a worksheet that *optimize* (maximize or minimize) a certain objective. Microsoft Office Excel Solver tool helps you answer optimization problems.

An optimization model has three parts: the target cell, the changing cells, and the constraints. The *target cell* represents the objective or goal. We want to either minimize or maximize the amount in the target cell. In the example of a drug company's product mix given above, the plant manager would presumably want to maximize the profitability of the plant during each month. The cell that measures profitability would be the target cell. The target cells for each situation described at the beginning of the chapter are listed in Table 26-1 on the next page.

Keep in mind, however, that in some situations you might have multiple target cells. For example, Microsoft might have a secondary goal to maximize Xbox market share.

Table 26-1   List of Target Cells

Model	Maximize or minimize	Target cell
Drug company product mix	Maximize	Monthly profit
Xbox shipping	Minimize	Distribution costs
Xbox pricing	Maximize	Profit from Xbox consoles and games
Microsoft project initiatives	Maximize	Net present value (NPV) contributed by selected projects
NFL ratings	Minimize	Difference between scores predicted by ratings and actual game scores
Retirement portfolio	Minimize	Risk factor of portfolio

Changing cells are the worksheet cells that we can change or adjust to optimize the target cell. In the drug company example, the plant manager can adjust the amount produced for each product during a month. The cells in which these amounts are recorded are the changing cells in this model. Table 26-2 lists the appropriate changing cell definitions for the models described at the beginning of the chapter.

Table 26-2   List of Changing Cells

Model	Changing cells
Drug company product mix	Amount of each product produced during the month
Xbox shipping	Amount produced at each plant each month that is shipped to each customer
Xbox pricing	Console and game prices
Microsoft program initiatives	Which projects are selected
NFL ratings	Team ratings
Retirement portfolio	Fraction of money invested in each asset class

Table 26-3   List of Problem Constraints

Model	Constraints
Drug company product mix	Product mix uses no more resources than are available
	Do not produce more of a product than can be sold
Xbox shipping	Do not ship more units each month from a plant than plant capacity
	Make sure that each customer receives the number of Xbox consoles that they need
Xbox pricing	Prices can't be too far out of line with competitors' prices
Microsoft project initiatives	Projects selected can't use more money or skilled programmers than are available

Table 26-3   List of Problem Constraints

Model	Constraints
NFL ratings	None
Retirement portfolio	Invest all our money somewhere (cash is a possibility)
	Obtain an expected return of at least 10 percent on our investments

The best way to understand how to use Solver is by looking at some detailed examples. In later chapters, you'll learn how to use Solver to address each of the problems presented in this chapter, as well as several other important business problems.

To install Solver, click the Microsoft Office Button, click Excel Options, and click Add-Ins. In the Manage box at the bottom of the window, select Excel Add-ins, and click Go. Check the Solver Add-in box in the Add-Ins dialog box, and click OK. After Solver is installed, you can run Solver by clicking Solver in the Analysis group on the Data tab. Figure 26-1 shows the Solver Parameters dialog box. In the next few chapters, you'll see how to use this dialog box to input the target cell, changing cells, and constraints for a Solver model.

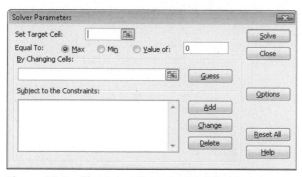

Figure 26-1   The Solver Parameters dialog box

After you have input the target cell, changing cells, and constraints, what does Solver do? To answer this question, you need some background in Solver terminology. Any specification of the changing cells that satisfies the model's constraints is known as a *feasible solution*. For instance, in our example, any product mix that satisfies the following three conditions would be a feasible solution:

- Does not use more raw material or labor than is available.

- Does not produce more of each product than is demanded.

- Does not produce a negative amount of any product.

Essentially, Solver searches all feasible solutions and finds the one that has the "best" target cell value (the largest value for maximum optimization, the smallest for minimum optimization). Such a solution is called an *optimal solution*. As you'll see in Chapter 27, "Using Solver to Determine the Optimal Product Mix," some Solver models have no optimal solution and some have a unique solution. Other Solver models have multiple (actually, an infinite number of) optimal solutions. In the next chapter, we'll begin our study of Solver examples by examining the drug company product mix problem.

Problems

For each situation described below, identify the target cell, changing cells, and constraints.

1. I am borrowing $100,000 for a 15-year mortgage. The annual rate of interest is 8 percent. How can I determine my monthly mortgage payment?

2. How should an auto company allocate its advertising budget between different advertising formats?

3. How should cities transport students to more distant schools to obtain racial balance?

4. If a city has only one hospital, where should it be located?

5. How should a drug company allocate its sales-force efforts among their products?

6. A drug company has $2 billion allocated to purchasing bio-tech companies. Which companies should they buy?

7. The tax rate charged to a drug company depends on the country in which a product is produced. How can a drug company determine where each drug should be made?

Chapter 27
Using Solver to Determine the Optimal Product Mix

- How can I determine the monthly product mix that maximizes profitability?
- Does a Solver model always have a solution?
- What does it mean if a Solver model yields the result Set Values Do Not Converge?

How can I determine the monthly product mix that maximizes profitability?

Companies often need to determine the quantity of each product to produce on a monthly basis. In its simplest form, the *product mix* problem involves how to determine the amount of each product that should be produced during a month to maximize profits. Product mix must usually adhere to the following constraints:

❑ Product mix can't use more resources than are available.

❑ There is a limited demand for each product. We can't produce more of a product during a month than demand dictates, because the excess production is wasted (for example, a perishable drug).

Let's now solve the following example of the product mix problem. You can find the solution to this problem in the file Prodmix.xlsx, shown in Figure 27-1.

	B	C	D	E	F	G	H	I
2		Pounds made	150	160	170	180	190	200
3	Available	Product	1	2	3	4	5	6
4	4500	Labor	6	5	4	3	2.5	1.5
5	1600	Raw Material	3.2	2.6	1.5	0.8	0.7	0.3
6		Unit price	$ 12.50	$ 11.00	$ 9.00	$ 7.00	$ 6.00	$ 3.00
7		Variable cost	$ 6.50	$ 5.70	$ 3.60	$ 2.80	$ 2.20	$ 1.20
8		Demand	960	928	1041	977	1084	1055
9		Unit profit cont.	$ 6.00	$ 5.30	$ 5.40	$ 4.20	$ 3.80	$ 1.80
10								
11								
12		Profit	$ 4,504.00					
13					Available			
14		Labor Used	3695 <=		4500			
15		Raw Material Used	1488 <=		1600			

Figure 27-1 The product mix

Let's say we work for a drug company that produces six different products at their plant. Production of each product requires labor and raw material. Row 4 in Figure 27-1 shows the hours of labor needed to produce a pound of each product, and row 5 shows the pounds of raw material needed to produce a pound of each product. For example, producing a pound of Product 1 requires six hours of labor and 3.2 pounds of raw material. For each drug, the price per pound is given in row 6, the unit cost per pound is given in row 7, and the profit contribution per pound is given in row 9. For example, Product 2 sells for $11.00 per pound, incurs a unit cost of $5.70 per pound, and contributes $5.30 profit per pound. The month's demand for each drug is given in row 8. For example, demand for Product 3 is 1041 pounds. This month, 4500 hours of labor and 1600 pounds of raw material are available. How can this company maximize its monthly profit?

If we knew nothing about Excel Solver, we would attack this problem by constructing a worksheet to track profit and resource usage associated with the product mix. Then we would use trial and error to vary the product mix to optimize profit without using more labor or raw material than is available, and without producing any drug in excess of demand. We use Solver in this process only at the trial-and-error stage. Essentially, Solver is an optimization engine that flawlessly performs the trial-and-error search.

A key to solving the product mix problem is to efficiently compute the resource usage and profit associated with any given product mix. An important tool that we can use to make this computation is the SUMPRODUCT function. The SUMPRODUCT function multiplies corresponding values in cell ranges and returns the sum of those values. Each cell range used in a SUMPRODUCT evaluation must have the same dimensions, which implies that you can use SUMPRODUCT with two rows or two columns, but not with one column and one row.

As an example of how we can use the SUMPRODUCT function in our product mix example, let's try to compute our resource usage. Our labor usage is calculated by

```
(Labor used per pound of drug 1)*(Drug 1 pounds produced)+
(Labor used per pound of drug 2)*(Drug 2 pounds produced) + ...
(Labor used per pound of drug 6)*(Drug 6 pounds produced)
```

We could compute labor usage in a more tedious fashion as $D2*D4+E2*E4+F2*F4+G2*G4+H2*H4+I2*I4$. Similarly, raw material usage could be computed as $D2*D5+E2*E5+F2*F5+G2*G5+H2*H5+I2*I5$. However, entering these formulas in a worksheet for six products is time-consuming. Imagine how long it would take if you were working with a company that produced, for example, 50 products at their plant. A much easier way to compute labor and raw material usage is to copy from D14 to D15 the formula $SUMPRODUCT(\$D\$2:\$I\$2,D4:I4)$. This formula computes $D2*D4+E2*E4+F2*F4+G2*G4+H2*H4+I2*I4$ (which is our labor usage) but is much easier to enter! Notice that I use the $ sign with the range D2:I2 so that when I copy the formula I still capture the product mix from row 2. The formula in cell D15 computes raw material usage.

In a similar fashion, our profit is determined by

```
(Drug 1 profit per pound)*(Drug 1 pounds produced) +
(Drug 2 profit per pound)*(Drug 2 pounds produced) + ...
(Drug 6 profit per pound)*(Drug 6 pounds produced)
```

Profit is easily computed in cell D12 with the formula *SUMPRODUCT(D9:I9,$D$2:$I$2)*.

We now can identify the three components of our product mix Solver model.

❑ **Target cell.** Our goal is to maximize profit (computed in cell D12).

❑ **Changing cells.** The number of pounds produced of each product (listed in the cell range D2:I2)

❑ **Constraints.** We have the following constraints:

● Do not use more labor or raw material than is available. That is, the values in cells D14:D15 (the resources used) must be less than or equal to the values in cells F14:F15 (the available resources).

● Do not produce more of a drug than is in demand. That is, the values in the cells D2:I2 (pounds produced of each drug) must be less than or equal to the demand for each drug (listed in cells D8:I8).

● We can't produce a negative amount of any drug.

I'll show you how to enter the target cell, changing cells, and constraints into Solver. Then all you need to do is click the Solve button to find a profit-maximizing product mix!

To begin, click the Data tab, and in the Analysis group, click Solver.

> **Note** As explained in Chapter 26, "An Introduction to Optimization with Excel Solver," Solver is installed by clicking the Microsoft Office Button, then Excel Options, followed by Add-Ins. In the Manage list, click Excel Add-ins, check the Solver Add-in box, and then click OK.

The Solver Parameters dialog box will appear, as shown in Figure 27-2.

Figure 27-2 The Solver Parameters dialog box

Click the Set Target Cell box and then select our profit cell (cell D12). Click the By Changing Cells box and then point to the range D2:I2, which contains the pounds produced of each drug. The dialog box should now look Figure 27-3.

Figure 27-3 The Solver Parameters dialog box with the target cell and changing cells defined

We're now ready to add constraints to the model. Click the Add button. You'll see the Add Constraint dialog box, shown in Figure 27-4.

Figure 27-4 The Add Constraint dialog box

To add the resource usage constraints, click the Cell Reference box, and then select the range D14:D15. Select <= from the middle list. Click the Constraint box, and then select the cell range F14:F15. The Add Constraint dialog box should now look like Figure 27-5.

Figure 27-5 The Add Constraint dialog box with the resource usage constraints entered

We have now ensured that when Solver tries different values for the changing cells, only combinations that satisfy both *D14<=F14* (labor used is less than or equal to labor available) and *D15<=F15* (raw material used is less than or equal to raw material available) will be considered. Click Add to enter the demand constraints. Fill in the Add Constraint dialog box as shown in Figure 27-6.

Figure 27-6   The Add Constraint dialog box with the demand constraints entered

Adding these constraints ensures that when Solver tries different combinations for the changing cell values, only combinations that satisfy the following parameters will be considered:

❑ *D2<=D8* (the amount produced of Drug 1 is less than or equal to the demand for Drug 1)

❑ *E2<=E8* (the amount of produced of Drug 2 is less than or equal to the demand for Drug 2)

❑ *F2<=F8* (the amount produced of Drug 3 made is less than or equal to the demand for Drug 3)

❑ *G2<=G8* (the amount produced of Drug 4 made is less than or equal to the demand for Drug 4)

❑ *H2<=H8* (the amount produced of Drug 5 made is less than or equal to the demand for Drug 5)

❑ *I2<=I8* (the amount produced of Drug 6 made is less than or equal to the demand for Drug 6)

Click OK in the Add Constraint dialog box. The Solver window should look like Figure 27-7.

Figure 27-7   The final Solver Parameters dialog box for the product mix problem

We enter the constraint that changing cells must be non-negative in the Solver Options dialog box. Click the Options button in the Solver Parameters dialog box. Check the Assume Linear Model box and the Assume Non-Negative box, as shown in Figure 27-8 on the next page. Click OK.

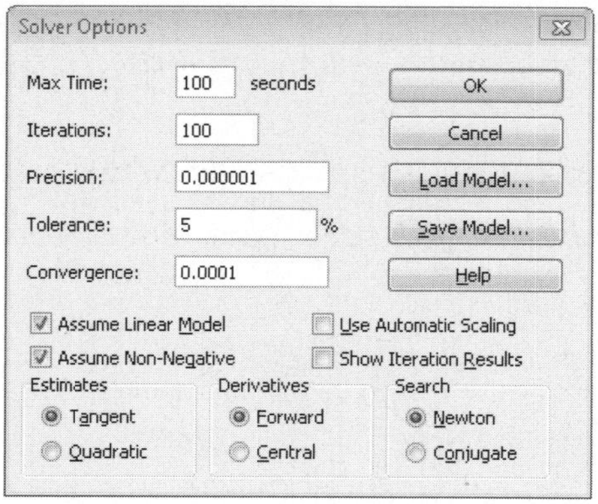

Figure 27-8   Solver options settings

Checking the Assume Non-Negative box ensures that Solver considers only combinations of changing cells in which each changing cell assumes a non-negative value. We checked the Assume Linear Model box because the product mix problem is a special type of Solver problem called a *linear model*. Essentially, a Solver model is linear under the following conditions:

❑ The target cell is computed by adding together the terms of the form *(changing cell)*(constant)*.

❑ Each constraint satisfies the "linear model requirement." This means that each constraint is evaluated by adding together the terms of the form *(changing cell)*(constant)* and comparing the sums to a constant.

Why is this Solver problem linear? Our target cell (profit) is computed as

```
(Drug 1 profit per pound)*(Drug 1 pounds produced) +
(Drug 2 profit per pound)*(Drug 2 pounds produced) + ...
(Drug 6 profit per pound)*(Drug 6 pounds produced)
```

This computation follows a pattern in which the target cell's value is derived by adding together terms of the form *(changing cell)*(constant)*.

Our labor constraint is evaluated by comparing the value derived from *(Labor used per pound of Drug 1)*(Drug 1 pounds produced) + (Labor used per pound of Drug 2)*(Drug 2 pounds produced)+...(Labor used per pound of Drug 6)*(Drug 6 pounds produced)* to the labor available.

Therefore, the labor constraint is evaluated by adding together the terms of the form *(changing cell)*(constant)* and comparing the sums to a constant. Both the labor constraint and the raw material constraint satisfy the linear model requirement.

Our demand constraints take the form

```
(Drug 1 produced)<=(Drug 1 Demand)
(Drug 2 produced)<=(Drug 2 Demand)
§
(Drug 6 produced)<=(Drug 6 Demand)
```

Each demand constraint also satisfies the linear model requirement, because each is evaluated by adding together the terms of the form *(changing cell)*(constant)* and comparing the sums to a constant.

Having shown that our product mix model is a linear model, why should we care?

❑ If a Solver model is linear and we select Assume Linear Model, Solver is guaranteed to find the optimal solution to the Solver model. If a Solver model is not linear, Solver may or may not find the optimal solution.

❑ If a Solver model is linear and we select Assume Linear Model, Solver uses a very efficient algorithm (the simplex method) to find the model's optimal solution. If a Solver model is linear and we do not select Assume Linear Model, Solver uses a very inefficient algorithm (the GRG2 method) and might have difficulty finding the model's optimal solution.

After clicking OK in the Solver Options dialog box, we return to the main Solver dialog box, shown earlier in Figure 27-7. When we click Solve, Solver calculates an optimal solution (if one exists) for our product mix model. As I stated in Chapter 26, an optimal solution to the product mix model would be a set of changing cell values (pounds produced of each drug) that maximizes profit over the set of all feasible solutions. Again, a feasible solution is a set of changing cell values satisfying all constraints. The changing cell values shown in Figure 27-9 are a feasible solution because all production levels are non-negative, production levels do not exceed demand, and resource usage does not exceed available resources.

	B	C	D	E	F	G	H	I
2		Pounds made	150	160	170	180	190	200
3	Available	Product	1	2	3	4	5	6
4	4500	Labor	6	5	4	3	2.5	1.5
5	1600	Raw Material	3.2	2.6	1.5	0.8	0.7	0.3
6		Unit price	$ 12.50	$ 11.00	$ 9.00	$ 7.00	$ 6.00	$ 3.00
7		Variable cost	$ 6.50	$ 5.70	$ 3.60	$ 2.80	$ 2.20	$ 1.20
8		Demand	960	928	1041	977	1084	1055
9		Unit profit cont.	$ 6.00	$ 5.30	$ 5.40	$ 4.20	$ 3.80	$ 1.80
10								
11								
12		Profit	$ 4,504.00					
13					Available			
14		Labor Used	3695 <=		4500			
15		Raw Material Used	1488 <=		1600			

Figure 27-9   A feasible solution to the product mix problem fits within constraints.

The changing cell values shown in Figure 27-10 on the next page represent an *infeasible solution* for the following reasons:

❑ We produce more of Drug 5 than the demand for it.

❑ We use more labor than what is available.

❑ We use more raw material than what is available.

	B	C	D	E	F	G	H	I
2		Pounds made	300	0	0	0	1085	1000
3	Available	Product	1	2	3	4	5	6
4	4500	Labor	6	5	4	3	2.5	1.5
5	1600	Raw Material	3.2	2.6	1.5	0.8	0.7	0.3
6		Unit price	$ 12.50	$ 11.00	$ 9.00	$ 7.00	$ 6.00	$ 3.00
7		Variable cost	$ 6.50	$ 5.70	$ 3.60	$ 2.80	$ 2.20	$ 1.20
8		Demand	960	928	1041	977	1084	1055
9		Unit profit cont.	$ 6.00	$ 5.30	$ 5.40	$ 4.20	$ 3.80	$ 1.80
10								
11								
12		Profit	$ 7,723.00					
13					Available			
14		Labor Used	6012.5 <=		4500			
15		Raw Material Used	2019.5 <=		1600			

Figure 27-10 An infeasible solution to the product mix problem doesn't fit within the defined constraints.

After clicking Solve, Solver quickly finds the optimal solution shown in Figure 27-11. You need to select Keep Solver Solution to preserve the optimal solution values in the worksheet.

	B	C	D	E	F	G	H	I
3	Available	Product	1	2	3	4	5	6
4	4500	Labor	6	5	4	3	2.5	1.5
5	1600	Raw Material	3.2	2.6	1.5	0.8	0.7	0.3
6		Unit price	$ 12.50	$ 11.00	$ 9.00	$ 7.00	$ 6.00	$ 3.00
7		Variable cost	$ 6.50	$ 5.70	$ 3.60	$ 2.80	$ 2.20	$ 1.20
8		Demand	960	928	1041	977	1084	1055
9		Unit profit cont.	$ 6.00	$ 5.30	$ 5.40	$ 4.20	$ 3.80	$ 1.80
10								
11								
12		Profit	$6,625.20					
13					Available			
14		Labor Used	4500 <=		4500			
15		Raw Material Used	1236.1333 <=		1600			

Figure 27-11 The optimal solution to the product mix problem

Our drug company can maximize its monthly profit at a level of $6,625.20 by producing 596.67 pounds of Drug 4, 1084 pounds of Drug 5, and none of the other drugs! We can't determine if we can achieve the maximum profit of $6,625.20 in other ways. All we can be sure of is that with our limited resources and demand, there is no way to make more than $6,627.20 this month.

Does a Solver model always have a solution?

Suppose that demand for each product *must* be met. (See the *No Feasible Solution* worksheet in the file Prodmix.xlsx.) We then have to change our demand constraints from D2:I2<=D8:I8 to D2:I2>=D8:I8. To do this, open Solver, select the D2:I2<=D8:I8 constraint, and then click Change. The Change Constraint dialog box, shown in Figure 27-12, appears.

Figure 27-12 The Change Constraint dialog box

Select >=, and then click OK. We've now ensured that Solver will consider changing only cell values that meet all demands. When you click Solve, you'll see the message "Solver could not find a feasible solution." This message does not mean that we made a mistake in our model, but rather that with our limited resources, we can't meet demand for all products. Solver is simply telling us that if we want to meet demand for each product, we need to add more labor, more raw materials, or more of both.

What does is mean if a Solver model yields the result Set Values Do Not Converge?

Let's see what happens if we allow unlimited demand for each product and we allow negative quantities to be produced of each drug. (You can see this Solver problem on the *Set Values Do Not Converge* worksheet in the file Prodmix.xlsx.) To find the optimal solution for this situation, open Solver, click the Options button, and clear the Assume Non-Negative box. In the Solver Parameters dialog box, select the demand constraint D2:I2<=D8:I8 and then click Delete to remove the constraint. When you click Solve, Solver returns the message "Set Cell Values Do Not Converge." This message means that if the target cell is to be maximized (as in our example), there are feasible solutions with arbitrarily large target cell values. (If the target cell is to be minimized, the message "Set Cell Values Do Not Converge" means there are feasible solutions with arbitrarily small target cell values.) In our situation, by allowing negative production of a drug, we in effect "create" resources that can be used to produce arbitrarily large amounts of other drugs. Given our unlimited demand, this allows us to make unlimited profits. In a real situation, we can't make an infinite amount of money. In short, if you see "Set Values Do Not Converge," your model does have an error.

Problems

1. Suppose our drug company can purchase up to 500 hours of labor at $1 more per hour than current labor costs. How can we maximize profit?

2. At a chip manufacturing plant, four technicians (A, B, C, and D) produce three products (Products 1, 2, and 3). This month, the chip manufacturer can sell 80 units of Product 1, 50 units of Product 2, and at most 50 units of Product 3. Technician A can make only Products 1 and 3. Technician B can make only Products 1 and 2. Technician C can make only Product 3. Technician D can make only Product 2. For each unit produced, the products contribute the following profit: Product 1, $6; Product 2, $7; and Product 3, $10. The time (in hours) each technician needs to manufacture a product is as follows:

Product	Technician A	Technician B	Technician C	Technician D
1	2	2.5	Cannot do	Cannot do
2	Cannot do	3	Cannot do	3.5
3	3	Cannot do	4	Cannot do

Each technician can work up to 120 hours per month. How can the chip manufacturer maximize its monthly profit? Assume a fractional number of units can be produced.

3. A computer manufacturing plant produces mice, keyboards, and video game joysticks. The per-unit profit, per-unit labor usage, monthly demand, and per-unit machine-time usage are given in the following table:

	Mice	Keyboards	Joysticks
Profit/unit	$8	$11	$9
Labor usage/unit	.2 hour	.3 hour	.24 hour
Machine time/unit	.04 hour	.055 hour	.04 hour
Monthly demand	15,000	27,000	11,000

Each month, a total of 13,000 labor hours and 3000 hours of machine time are available. How can the manufacturer maximize its monthly profit contribution from the plant?

4. Resolve our drug example assuming that a minimum demand of 200 units for each drug must be met.

5. Jason makes diamond bracelets, necklaces, and earrings. He wants to work a maximum of 160 hours per month. He has 800 ounces of diamonds. The profit, labor time, and ounces of diamonds required to produce each product are given below. If demand for each product is unlimited, how can Jason maximize his profit?

Product	Unit profit	Labor hours per unit	Ounces of diamonds per unit
Bracelet	$300	.35	1.2
Necklace	$200	.15	.75
Earrings	$100	.05	.5

Chapter 28

Using Solver to Schedule Your Workforce

Many organizations (such as banks, restaurants, and postal service companies) know what their labor requirements will be at different times of the day, and need a method to efficiently schedule their workforce. You can use Microsoft Office Excel Solver to easily solve workforce scheduling problems.

- How can I efficiently schedule my workforce to meet labor demands?

How can I efficiently schedule my workforce to meet labor demands?

Bank 24 processes checks 7 days a week. The number of workers needed each day to process checks is shown in row 14 of the file Bank24.xlsx, which is shown in Figure 28-1. For example, 13 workers are needed on Tuesday, 15 workers are needed on Wednesday, and so on. All bank employees work 5 consecutive days. What is the minimum number of employees Bank 24 can have and still meet its labor requirements?

	A	B	C	D	E	F	G	H	I	J
2	Total					There are multiple solutions all of which use 20 workers.				
3	20		Working?							
4	Number starting	Day worker starts	Monday	Tuesday	Wednesday	Thursday	Friday	Saturday	Sunday	
5	1	Monday	1	1	1	1	1	0	0	
6	3	Tuesday	0	1	1	1	1	1	0	
7	0	Wednesday	0	0	1	1	1	1	1	
8	4	Thursday	1	0	0	1	1	1	1	
9	1	Friday	1	1	0	0	1	1	1	
10	2	Saturday	1	1	1	0	0	1	1	
11	9	Sunday	1	1	1	1	0	0	1	
12		Number working	17	16	15	17	9	10	16	
13			>=	>=	>=	>=	>=	>=	>=	
14		Number needed	17	13	15	17	9	9	12	

Figure 28-1 The data we'll use to work through the bank workforce scheduling problem.

We begin by identifying the target cell, changing cells, and constraints for our Solver model.

❑ **Target cell.** Minimize total number of employees.

❑ **Changing cells.** Number of employees who start work (the first of five consecutive days) each day of the week. Each changing cell must be a non-negative integer.

❏ **Constraints.** For each day of the week, the number of employees who are working must be greater than or equal to the number of employees required. (*Number of employees working*)>=(*Needed employees*)

To set up our model, we need to track the number of employees working each day. I began by entering in the cell range A5:A11 trial values for the number of employees who start their five-day shift each day. For example, in A5, I entered 1, indicating that 1 employee begins work on Monday and works Monday through Friday. I entered each day's required workers in the range C14:I14.

To track the number of employees working each day, I entered a 1 or a 0 in each cell in the range C5:I11. The value 1 in a cell indicates that the employees who started working on the day designated in the cell's row are working on the day associated with the cell's column. For example, the 1 in cell G5 indicates that employees who started working on Monday are working on Friday; the 0 in cell H5 indicates that the employees who started working on Monday are not working on Saturday.

By copying from C12 to D12:I12 the formula =SUMPRODUCT($A$5:$A$11,C5:C11), I compute the number of employees working each day. For example, in cell C12, this formula evaluates to =A5+A8+A9+A10+A11, which equals (*Number starting on Monday*)+ (*Number starting on Thursday*)+(*Number starting on Friday*)+(*Number starting on Saturday*)+ (*Number starting on Sunday*). This total is indeed the number of people working on Monday.

After computing the total number of employees in cell A3 with the formula =SUM(A5:A11), I can enter our model in Solver as shown in Figure 28-2.

Figure 28-2 The Solver Parameters dialog box filled in to solve the bank workforce problem

In the target cell (A3), we want to minimize the number of total employees. The constraint C12:I12>=C14:I14 ensures that the number of employees working each day is at least as large as the number needed each day. The constraint A5:A11=integer ensures that the number of employees beginning work each day is an integer. To add this constraint, I clicked Add in the Solver Parameters dialog box and filled in the Add Constraint dialog box as shown in Figure 28-3.

Figure 28-3   This constraint defines as an integer the number of workers who start each day.

I also selected the options Assume Linear Model and Assume Non-Negative for the changing cells by clicking Options in the Solver Parameters dialog box and then checking these boxes in the Solver Options dialog box. After clicking Solve, we find the optimal solution that's shown earlier in Figure 28-1.

A total of 20 employees is needed. One employee starts on Monday, three start on Tuesday, four start on Thursday, one starts on Friday, two start on Saturday, and nine start on Sunday.

Note that this model is linear because the target cell is created by adding together changing cells, and the constraint is created by comparing the result obtained by adding together the product of each changing cell times a constant (either 1 or 0) to the required number of workers.

Problems

1. Suppose Bank 24 had 22 employees and that the goal was to schedule employees so that they would have the maximum number of weekend days off. How should the workers be scheduled?

2. Suppose Bank 24 employees are paid $150 per day the first five days they work and can work a day of overtime at a cost of $350. How should the bank schedule its employees?

3. The number of telephone reservation operators needed by an airline during each time of day is as follows:

Time	Operators needed
Midnight–4 A.M.	12
4 A.M.–8 A.M.	16
8 A.M.–Noon	22
Noon–4 P.M.	28
4 P.M.–8 P.M.	31
8 P.M.–Midnight	22

Each operator works one of the following six-hour shifts: midnight–6:00 A.M., 6:00 A.M.–noon, noon–6:00 P.M., 6:00 P.M.–midnight. What is the minimum number of operators needed?

4. Shown below are the number of people in different demographic groups who watch various TV shows and the cost (in thousands of dollars) of placing a 30-second ad with each show. For example, it costs $160,000 to place a 30-second ad on *Friends*. The show is watched by 6 million males between the ages 18 and 35, 3 million males between 36 and 55, 1 million males over 55, 9 million females between 18 and 35, 4 million females between 36 and 55, and 2 million females over 55. The data also includes the number of people in each group (in millions) that we want to see the ad. For example, the advertiser wants at least 60 million 18 to 35 year old males to see its ads. What is the cheapest way to meet our goals?

	C	D	E	F	G	H	I	J
4	000s	needed	60	60	28	60	60	28
5	Cost	Show	M 18-35	M 36-55	M >55	W 18-35	W 36-55	W >55
6	180	Friends	6	3	1	9	4	2
7	100	MNF	6	5	3	1	1	1
8	80	Malcolm	5	2	0	4	2	0
9	9	Sports Center	0.5	0.5	0.3	0.1	0.1	0
10	13	MTV	0.7	0.2	0	0.9	0.1	0
11	16	Lifetime	0.1	0.1	0	0.6	1.3	0.4
12	8	CNN	0.1	0.2	0.3	0.1	0.2	0.3
13	85	Jag	1	2	4	1	3	4
14	Solution uses							
15	Mostly cable ads							
16	This is why the networks are having a hard time.							
17	Cable enables you to better target (per dollar spent)							
18	the demographic groups you are trying to watch.							

Figure 28-4   Data for Problem 4

95
317
32 853
2873
962 75
853
31
365

Chapter 29

Using Solver to Solve Transportation or Distribution Problems

- How can a drug company determine at which location they should produce drugs, and from which they should ship drugs to customers?

Many companies manufacture products at different locations (often called *supply points*), and ship their products to customers (often called *demand points*). A natural question then is, what is the least expensive way to produce and ship products to customers and still meet demand? This type of problem is called a *transportation problem*. A transportation problem can be set up as a linear Solver model with the following specifications:

- **Target cell.** Minimize total production and shipping cost.

- **Changing cells.** The amount produced at each supply point that is shipped to each demand point.

- **Constraints.** The amount shipped from each supply point can't exceed plant capacity. Each demand point must receive its required demand. Also, each changing cell must be non-negative.

How can a drug company determine at which location they should produce drugs, and from which they should ship drugs to customers?

You can follow along with this problem by looking at the file Transport.xlsx. Let's suppose a company produces a certain drug at its Los Angeles, Atlanta, and New York facilities. Each month, the Los Angeles plant can produce up to 10,000 pounds of the drug. Atlanta can produce up to 12,000 pounds, and New York can produce up to 14,000 pounds. The company must make monthly shipments to the four regions of the United States—East, Midwest, South, and West—the number of pounds listed in cells B2:E2, as shown in Figure 29-1 on the next page. For example, the West region must receive at least 13,000 pounds of the drug each month. The cost per pound of producing a drug at each plant and shipping the drug to each region of the country is given in cells B4:E6.

For example, it costs $3.50 to produce one pound of the drug in Los Angeles and ship it to the Midwest region. What is the cheapest way to get each region the quantity of the drug they need?

	A	B	C	D	E	F	G	H
2	DEMAND	9000	6000	6000	13000			
3		EAST	MIDWEST	SOUTH	WEST	CAPACITY		
4	LA	$ 5.00	$ 3.50	$ 4.20	$ 2.20	10000		
5	ATLANTA	$ 3.20	$ 2.60	$ 1.80	$ 4.80	12000		
6	NEW YORK CITY	$ 2.50	$ 3.10	$ 3.30	$ 5.40	14000		
7								
8	Shipments							
9		EAST	MIDWEST	SOUTH	WEST	Sent		Capacity
10	LA	0	0	0	10000	10000 <=		10000
11	ATLANTA	0	3000	6000	3000	12000 <=		12000
12	NEW YORK CITY	9000	3000	0	0	12000 <=		14000
13	Received	9000	6000	6000	13000			
14		>=	>=	>=	>=			
15	Demand	9000	6000	6000	13000			
16								
17								
18	Total Cost	$ 86,800.00						

Figure 29-1   Data for a transportation problem

To express our target cell, we need to track total shipping cost. After entering in the cell range B10:E12 trial values for our shipments from each supply point to each region, we can compute total shipping cost as follows:

```
(Amount sent from LA to East)*(Cost per pound of sending drug from LA to East)+
(Amount sent from LA to Midwest)*(Cost per pound of sending drug from LA to Midwest)+
(Amount sent from LA to South)*(Cost per pound of sending drug from LA to South)+
(Amount sent from LA to West)*(Cost per pound of sending drug from LA to West)+...
(Amount sent from New York City to West)*(Cost per pound of sending drug from New
York City to West)
```

The SUMPRODUCT function can multiply corresponding elements in two separate rectangles (as long as the rectangles are the same size) and add together the products. I've named the cell range B4:E6 as *costs* and the changing-cells range (B10:E12) as *shipped*. Therefore, our total shipping and production cost is computed in cell B18 with the formula *SUMPRODUCT(costs,shipped)*.

To express our constraints, we first compute the total shipped from each supply point. By entering the formula *SUM(B10:E10)* in cell F10, we compute the total number of pounds shipped from Los Angeles as *(LA shipped to East)+(LA shipped to Midwest)+ (LA shipped to South)+(LA shipped to West)*. Copying this formula to F11:F12 computes the total shipped from Atlanta and New York City. Later I'll add constraints (called *supply constraints*) that ensure the amount shipped from each location does not exceed the plant's capacity.

Next, I compute the total received by each demand point. I begin by entering in cell B13 the formula *SUM(B10:B12)*. This formula computes the total number of pounds received in the East as *(Pounds shipped from LA to East)+(Pounds shipped from Atlanta to East)+ (Pounds shipped from New York City to East)*. By copying this formula from B13 to C13:E13, I compute the pounds of the drug received by the Midwest, South, and West regions. Later, I'll add constraints (called *demand constraints*) that ensure that each region receives the amount of the drug it requires.

We now open the Solver Parameters dialog box (click Solver in the Analysis group, on the Data tab) and fill it in as shown in Figure 29-2.

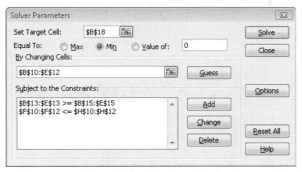

Figure 29-2   The Solver set up to solve our transportation problem.

We want to minimize total shipping cost (computed in cell B18). Our changing cells are the number of pounds shipped from each plant to each region of the country. (These amounts are listed in the range named *shipped*, consisting of cells B10:E12.) The constraint *F10:F12<=H10:H12* (the supply constraint) ensures that the amount sent from each plant does not exceed its capacity. The constraint *B13:E13>=B15:E15* (the demand constraint) ensures that each region receives at least the amount of the drug it needs.

Our model is a linear Solver model because our target cell is created by adding together the terms of the form *(changing cell)*(constant),* and both our supply and demand constraints are created by comparing the sum of changing cells to a constant.

I now click Options in the Solver Parameters dialog box and check the Assume Linear Model and Assume Non-Negative boxes. After clicking Solve in the Solver Parameters dialog box, we're presented with the optimal solution shown earlier in Figure 29-1. The minimum cost of meeting customer demand is $86,800. This minimum cost can be achieved if the company uses the following production and shipping schedule:

❑   Ship 10,000 pounds from Los Angeles to the West region.

❑   Ship 3000 pounds from Atlanta to the West region, and the same amount from Atlanta to the Midwest region. Ship 6000 pounds from Atlanta to the South region.

❑   Ship 9000 pounds from New York City to the East region, and 3000 pounds from New York City to the Midwest region.

Problems

1. The following table gives the distances between Boston, Chicago, Dallas, Los Angeles, and Miami. Each city requires 40,000 kilowatt hours (kWh) of power, and Chicago, Dallas, and Miami are capable of producing 70,000 kWh. Assume that shipping 1000 kWh over 100 miles costs $4. From where should power be sent to minimize the cost of meeting each city's demand?

	Boston	Chicago	Dallas	Los Angeles	Miami
Chicago	983	0	1205	2112	1390
Dallas	1815	1205	0	801	1332
Miami	1539	1390	1332	2757	0

2. We produce and sell drugs at several different locations. The decision of where to produce goods for each sales location can have a huge impact on profitability. Our model is similar to the model used in this chapter to determine where drugs should be produced. We're using the following assumptions:

   We produce drugs at six locations and sell to customers in six different areas.

   - Tax rate and variable production cost depend on the location where the drug is produced. For example, any units produced at Location 3 cost $6 per unit to produce; profits from these goods are taxed at 20 percent.

   - The sales price of each drug depends on where the drug is sold. For example, each product sold in Location 2 is sold for $40.

Production location	1	2	3	4	5	6
Sales price	$45	$40	$38	$36	$39	$34
Tax rate	29%	40%	20%	40%	35%	18%
Variable production cost	$8	$7	$6	$9	$7	$7

   - Each of our six plants can produce up to 6 million units per year.
   - The annual demand (in millions) for our product in each location is as follows:

Sales location	1	2	3	4	5	6
Demand	1	2	3	4	5	6

❏ The unit shipping cost depends on the plant where the product is produced and the location where the product is sold.

	Sold 1	Sold 2	Sold 3	Sold 4	Sold 5	Sold 6
Plant 1	$3	$4	$5	$6	$7	$8
Plant 2	$5	$2	$6	$9	$10	$11
Plant 3	$4	$3	$1	$6	$8	$6
Plant 4	$5	$5	$7	$2	$5	$5
Plant 5	$6	$9	$6	$5	$3	$7
Plant 6	$7	$7	$8	$9	$10	$4

For example, if we produce a unit at Plant 1 and sell it in Location 3, it costs $5 to ship it.

3. How can we maximize after-tax profit with our limited production capacity?

Suppose that each day, northern, central, and southern California each use 100 billion gallons of water. Also assume that northern California and central California have available 120 billion gallons of water, whereas southern California has 40 billion gallons of water available. The cost of shipping one billion gallons of water between the three regions is as follows:

	Northern	Central	Southern
Northern	$5,000	$7,000	$10,000
Central	$7,000	$5,000	$6,000
Southern	$10,0000	$6,000	$5,000

We will not be able to meet all demand for water, so we assume that each billion gallons of unmet demand incurs the following shortage costs:

	Northern	Central	Southern
Shortage cost/billion gallons short	$6,000	$5,500	$9,000

How should California's water be distributed to minimize the sum of shipping and shortage costs?

Chapter 30
Using Solver for Capital Budgeting

■ How can a company use Solver to determine which projects it should undertake?

Each year, a company like Eli Lilly needs to determine which drugs to develop; a company like Microsoft, which software programs to develop; a company like Proctor & Gamble, which new consumer products to develop. The Solver feature in Microsoft Office Excel 2007 can help a company make these decisions.

■ **How can a company use Solver to determine which projects it should undertake?**

Most corporations want to undertake projects that contribute the greatest net present value (NPV), subject to limited resources (usually capital and labor). Let's say that a software development company is trying to determine which of 20 software projects it should undertake. The NPV (in millions of dollars) contributed by each project as well as the capital (in millions of dollars) and the number of programmers needed during each of the next three years is given on the *Basic Model* worksheet in the file Capbudget.xlsx, which is shown in Figure 30-1 on the next page. For example, Project 2 yields $908 million. It requires $151 million during Year 1, $269 million during Year 2, and $248 million during Year 3. Project 2 requires 139 programmers during Year 1, 86 programmers during Year 2, and 83 programmers during Year 3. Cells E4:G4 show the capital (in millions of dollars) available during each of the three years, and cells H4:J4 indicate how many programmers are available. For example, during Year 1 up to $2.5 billion in capital and 900 programmers are available.

The company must decide whether it should undertake each project. Let's assume that we can't undertake a fraction of a software project; if we allocate 0.5 of the needed resources, for example, we would have a nonworking program that would bring us $0 revenue!

The trick in modeling situations in which you either do or don't do something is to use *binary changing cells*. A binary changing cell always equals 0 or 1. When a binary changing cell that corresponds to a project equals 1, we do the project. If a binary changing cell that corresponds to a project equals 0, we don't do the project. You set up Solver to use a range of binary changing cells by adding a constraint—select the changing cells you want to use and then choose Bin from the list in the Add Constraint dialog box.

	A	B	C	D	E	F	G	H	I	J
1		Total NPV								
2		9293		Used	2460	2684	2742	876	895	702
3					<=	<=	<=	<=	<=	<=
4				Available	2500	2800	2900	900	900	900
5	Do IT?		NPV		Cost Year 1	Cost Year 2	Cost Year 3	Labor Year 1	Labor Year 2	Labor Year 3
6	0	Project 1	928		398	180	368	111	108	123
7	1	Project 2	908		151	269	248	139	86	83
8	1	Project 3	801		129	189	308	56	61	23
9	0	Project 4	543		275	218	220	54	70	59
10	0	Project 5	944		291	252	228	123	141	70
11	1	Project 6	848		80	283	285	119	84	37
12	1	Project 7	545		203	220	77	54	44	42
13	1	Project 8	808		150	113	143	67	101	43
14	1	Project 9	638		282	141	160	37	55	64
15	1	Project 10	841		214	254	355	130	72	62
16	0	Project 11	664		224	271	130	51	79	58
17	0	Project 12	546		225	150	33	35	107	63
18	0	Project 13	699		101	218	272	43	90	71
19	1	Project 14	599		255	202	70	3	75	83
20	1	Project 15	903		228	351	240	60	93	80
21	1	Project 16	859		303	173	431	60	90	41
22	0	Project 17	748		133	427	220	59	40	39
23	0	Project 18	668		197	98	214	95	96	74
24	1	Project 19	888		313	278	291	66	75	74
25	1	Project 20	655		152	211	134	85	59	70

Figure 30-1   Data we will use with Solver to determine which projects to undertake

With this background, we're ready to solve the software project selection problem. As always with a Solver model, we begin by identifying our target cell, the changing cells, and the constraints.

- **Target cell.** We maximize the NPV generated by selected projects.

- **Changing cells.** We look for a 0 or 1 binary changing cell for each project. I've located these cells in the range A6:A25 (and named the range *doit*). For example, a 1 in cell A6 indicates that we undertake Project 1; a 0 in cell C6 indicates that we don't undertake Project 1.

- **Constraints.** We need to ensure that for each Year t ($t=1, 2, 3$), Year t capital used is less than or equal to Year t capital available, and Year t labor used is less than or equal to Year t labor available.

As you can see, our worksheet must compute for any selection of projects the NPV, the capital used annually, and the programmers used each year. In cell B2, I use the formula *SUMPRODUCT(doit,NPV)* to compute the total NPV generated by selected projects. (The range name *NPV* refers to the range C6:C25.) For every project with a 1 in column A, this formula picks up the NPV of the project, and for every project with a 0 in column A, this formula does not pick up the NPV of the project. Therefore, we're able to compute the NPV of all projects, and our target cell is linear because it is computed by summing terms that follow the form *(changing cell)*(constant)*. In a similar fashion, I compute the capital used each year and the labor used each year by copying from E2 to F2:J2 the formula *SUMPRODUCT(doit,E6:E25)*.

I now fill in the Solver Parameters dialog box as shown in Figure 30-2.

Figure 30-2   Solver Parameters dialog box set up for the project selection model

Our goal is to maximize NPV of selected projects (cell B2). Our changing cells (the range named *doit*) are the binary changing cells for each project. The constraint *E2:J2<=E4:J4* ensures that during each year the capital and labor used are less than or equal to the capital and labor available. To add the constraint that makes the changing cells binary, I click Add in the Solver Parameters dialog box and then select Bin from the list in the middle of the dialog box. The Add Constraint dialog box should appear as shown in Figure 30-3.

Figure 30-3   Use the Bin option in the Add Constraint dialog box to set up binary changing cells—cells that will display either a 0 or a 1.

Our model is linear because the target cell is computed as the sum of terms that have the form *(changing cell)*(constant)* and because the resource usage constraints are computed by comparing the sum of *(changing cells)*(constants)* to a constant.

With the Solver Parameters dialog box filled in, click Solve and we have the results shown earlier in Figure 30-1. The company can obtain a maximum NPV of $9,293 million ($9.293 billion) by choosing Projects 2, 3, 6–10, 14–16, 19, and 20.

Handling Other Constraints

Sometimes project-selection models have other constraints. For example, suppose that if we select Project 3, we must also select Project 4. Because our current optimal solution selects Project 3 but not Project 4, we know that our current solution can't remain optimal. To solve this problem, simply add the constraint that the binary changing cell for Project 3 is less than or equal to the binary changing cell for Project 4.

You can find this example on the *If 3 then 4* worksheet in the file Capbudget.xlsx, which is shown in Figure 30-4. Cell L9 refers to the binary value related to Project 3, and cell L12 to the binary value related to Project 4. By adding the constraint *L9<=L12*, if we choose Project 3, L9 equals 1 and our constraint forces L12 (the Project 4 binary) to equal 1. Our constraint must also leave the binary value in the changing cell of Project 4 unrestricted if we do not select Project 3. If we do not select Project 3, L9 equals 0 and our constraint allows the Project 4 binary to equal 0 or 1, which is what we want. The new optimal solution is shown in Figure 30-4.

	A	B	C	D	E	F	G	H	I	J	K	L
1		Total NPV										
2		9157		Used	2444	2760	2837	866	895	659		
3					<=	<=	<=	<=	<=	<=		
4				Available	2500	2800	2900	900	900	900		
5	Do IT?		NPV		Cost Year 1	Cost Year 2	Cost Year 3	Labor Year 1	Labor Year 2	Labor Year 3		
6	0	Project 1	928		398	180	368	111	108	123		
7	1	Project 2	908		151	269	248	139	86	83		
8	1	Project 3	801		129	189	308	56	61	23		Proj 3
9	1	Project 4	543		275	218	220	54	70	59		1
10	0	Project 5	944		291	252	228	123	141	70		<=
11	1	Project 6	848		80	283	285	119	84	37		Proj 4
12	1	Project 7	545		203	220	77	54	44	42		1
13	1	Project 8	808		150	113	143	67	101	43		
14	1	Project 9	638		282	141	160	37	55	64		
15	0	Project 10	841		214	254	355	130	72	62		
16	0	Project 11	664		224	271	130	51	79	58		
17	0	Project 12	546		225	150	33	35	107	63		
18	0	Project 13	699		101	218	272	43	90	71		
19	0	Project 14	599		255	202	70	3	75	83		
20	1	Project 15	903		228	351	240	60	93	80		
21	1	Project 16	859		303	173	431	60	90	41		
22	1	Project 17	748		133	427	220	59	40	39		
23	1	Project 18	668		197	98	214	95	96	74		
24	1	Project 19	888		313	278	291	66	75	74		
25	0	Project 20	655		152	211	134	85	59	70		

Figure 30-4   New optimal solution for *if not Project 3 then Project 4*

A new optimal solution is calculated if selecting Project 3 means we must also select Project 4. Now suppose that we can do only four projects from among Projects 1 through 10. (See the *At Most 4 Of P1–P10* worksheet, shown in Figure 30-5.) In cell L8, we compute the sum of the binary values associated with Projects 1 through 10 with the formula *SUM(A6:A15)*. Then we add the constraint *L8<=L10*, which ensures that, at most, 4 of the first 10 projects are selected. The new optimal solution is shown in Figure 30-5. The NPV has dropped to $9.014 billion.

	A	B	C	D	E	F	G	H	I	J	K	L
1		Total NPV										
2		9014		Used	2378	2734	2755	778	896	702		
3					<=	<=	<=	<=	<=	<=		
4				Available	2500	2800	2900	900	900	900		
5	Do IT?		NPV		Cost Year 1	Cost Year 2	Cost Year 3	Labor Year 1	Labor Year 2	Labor Year 3		
6	0	Project 1	928		398	180	368	111	108	123		
												At most 4 of Projects 1-10
7	0	Project 2	908		151	269	248	139	86	83		4
8	1	Project 3	801		129	189	308	56	61	23		
9	0	Project 4	543		275	218	220	54	70	59		<=
10	0	Project 5	944		291	252	228	123	141	70		4
11	0	Project 6	848		80	283	285	119	84	37		
12	1	Project 7	545		203	220	77	54	44	42		
13	1	Project 8	808		150	113	143	67	101	43		
14	0	Project 9	638		282	141	160	37	55	64		
15	1	Project 10	841		214	254	355	130	72	62		
21	1	Project 16	859		303	173	431	60	90	41		
22	1	Project 17	748		133	427	220	59	40	39		
23	1	Project 18	668		197	98	214	95	96	74		
24	1	Project 19	888		313	278	291	66	75	74		
25	1	Project 20	655		152	211	134	85	59	70		

Figure 30-5   Optimal solution when we can select only 4 of 10 projects

Solving Binary and Integer Programming Problems

Linear Solver models in which some or all changing cells are required to be binary or integer are usually harder to solve than linear models in which all changing cells are allowed to be fractions. For this reason, we often are satisfied with a near-optimal solution to a binary or integer programming problem. If your Solver model runs for a long time, you may want to consider adjusting the Tolerance setting in the Solver Options dialog box. (See Figure 30-6.) For example, a Tolerance setting of 0.5% means that Solver will stop the first time it finds a feasible solution that is within 0.5 percent of the theoretical optimal target cell value (the theoretical optimal target cell value is the optimal target value found when the binary and integer constraints are omitted). Often we are faced with a choice between finding an answer within 10 percent of optimal in 10 minutes or finding an optimal solution in two weeks of computer time! The default Tolerance value is 0.05%, which means that Solver stops when it finds a Target cell value within 0.05 percent of the theoretical optimal target cell value.

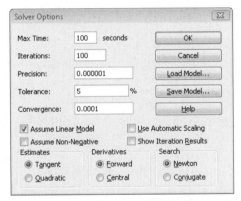

Figure 30-6   Adjusting the Tolerance option

Problems

1. A company has nine projects under consideration. The NPV added by each project and the capital required by each project during the next two years is shown in the following table. (All numbers are in millions.) For example, Project 1 will add $14 million in NPV and require expenditures of $12 million during Year 1 and $3 million during Year 2. During Year 1, $50 million in capital is available for projects, and $20 million is available during Year 2.

	NPV	Year 1 expenditure	Year 2 expenditure
Project 1	14	12	3
Project 2	17	54	7
Project 3	17	6	6
Project 4	15	6	2

	NPV	Year 1 expenditure	Year 2 expenditure
Project 5	40	30	35
Project 6	12	6	6
Project 7	14	48	4
Project 8	10	36	3
Project 9	12	18	3

- ❑ If we can't undertake a fraction of a project but must undertake either all or none of a project, how can we maximize NPV?

- ❑ Suppose that if Project 4 is undertaken, Project 5 must be undertaken. How can we maximize NPV?

2. A publishing company is trying to determine which of 36 books it should publish this year. The file Pressdata.xlsx gives the following information about each book:

- ❑ Projected revenue and development costs (in thousands of dollars)

- ❑ Pages in each book

- ❑ Whether the book is geared toward an audience of software developers (indicated by a 1 in column E)

A publishing company can publish books totaling up to 8500 pages this year and must publish at least four books geared toward software developers. How can the company maximize its profit?

Chapter 31
Using Solver for Financial Planning

- Can I use Solver to verify the accuracy of the Excel PMT function or to determine mortgage payments for a variable interest rate?

- Can I use Solver to determine how much money I need to save for retirement?

The Solver feature in Microsoft Office Excel 2007 can be a powerful tool for analyzing financial planning problems. In many financial planning problems, a quantity such as the unpaid balance on a loan or the amount of money needed for retirement changes over time. For example, consider a situation in which you borrow money. Because only the non-interest portion of each monthly payment reduces the unpaid loan balance, we know that the following equation (which I'll refer to as Equation 1) is true.

```
(Unpaid loan balance at end of period t)=(Unpaid loan balance at beginning of period t)-
[(Month t payment)-(Month t interest paid)]
```

Now suppose that you are saving for retirement. Until you retire, you deposit at the beginning of each period (let's say *periods* equal *years*) an amount of money in your retirement account, and during the year, your retirement fund is invested and receives a return of some percentage. During retirement, you withdraw money at the beginning of each year and your retirement fund still receives an investment return. We know that the following equation (Equation 2) describes the relationship between contributions, withdrawals, and return.

```
(Retirement savings at end of Year t+1)=(Retirement savings at end of Year t+
retirement contribution at beginning of Year t+1- Year t+1 retirement withdrawal)*
(Investment return earned during Year t+1)
```

Combining basic relationships such as these with Solver enables you to answer a myriad of interesting financial planning problems.

Can I use Solver to verify the accuracy of the Excel PMT function or to determine mortgage payments for a variable interest rate?

Recall that in Chapter 10, "Circular References," we found the monthly payment (assuming payments occur at the end of a month) on a 10-month loan for $8,000.00 at an

annual interest rate of 10 percent to be $1,037.03. Could we have used Solver to deter-
mine our monthly payment? You'll find the answer in the *PMT By Solver* worksheet in the
file Finmathsolver.xlsx, which is shown in Figure 31-1.

	A	B	C	D	E
1			rate	0.006667	
2					
3		From PMT function	$1,037.03		
4	Month	Beginning Balance	Payment	Interest Owed	Ending Balance
5	1	$ 10,000.00	$ 1,037.03	$ 66.67	$ 9,029.63
6	2	$ 9,029.63	$ 1,037.03	$ 60.20	$ 8,052.80
7	3	$ 8,052.80	$ 1,037.03	$ 53.69	$ 7,069.45
8	4	$ 7,069.45	$ 1,037.03	$ 47.13	$ 6,079.55
9	5	$ 6,079.55	$ 1,037.03	$ 40.53	$ 5,083.05
10	6	$ 5,083.05	$ 1,037.03	$ 33.89	$ 4,079.90
11	7	$ 4,079.90	$ 1,037.03	$ 27.20	$ 3,070.07
12	8	$ 3,070.07	$ 1,037.03	$ 20.47	$ 2,053.51
13	9	$ 2,053.51	$ 1,037.03	$ 13.69	$ 1,030.16
14	10	$ 1,030.16	$ 1,037.03	$ 6.87	$ 0.00

Figure 31-1   Solver model for calculating the monthly payment for a loan

The key to our model is to use Equation 1 to track the monthly beginning balance. Our
Solver target cell is to minimize our monthly payment. The changing cell is the monthly
payment. The only constraint is that the ending balance in month 10 equal 0.

I entered the beginning balance in cell B5. I entered a trial monthly payment in cell C5.
Then I copied the monthly payment to the range C6:C14. Because we've assumed that
the payments occur at the end of each month, interest is incurred on the balance at the
beginning of the month. Our monthly interest rate (I've named cell C1 *rate*) is computed
in D1 by dividing the annual rate of 0.08 by 12. The interest paid each month is computed by copying from cell D5 to D6:D14 the formula *rate*B5*. Each month, this formula
computes the interest as *.006666*(month's beginning balance)*. By copying the formula
(B5−(Payment−D5)) from cell E5 to E6:E14, we use Equation 1 to compute each month's
ending balance. Because *(Month t+1 beginning balance)=(Month t ending balance)*, we compute each month's beginning balance by copying from cell B6 to B7:B14 the formula *=E5*.

We are now ready to use Solver to determine our monthly payment. To see how I've set
up the Solver Parameters dialog box, take a look at Figure 31-2.

Our goal is to minimize the monthly payment (cell C5). Note that the changing cell is
the same as the target cell. The only constraint is that the ending balance for Month 10
must equal 0. Adding this constraint ensures that the loan is paid off. After we check the
Assume Linear Model option and the Assume Non-Negative changing cells option (both
located in the Solver Options dialog box; click Options in the Solver Parameters dialog

box to select these options), the Solver calculates a payment of $1,037.03, which matches the amount calculated by the Excel PMT function.

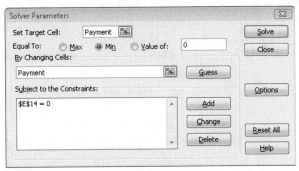

Figure 31-2   Solver Parameters dialog box set up to determine mortgage payments

This model is linear because the target cell equals the changing cell and the constraint is created by adding multiples of changing cells.

We should mention that when Solver models involve very large and/or very small numbers, the Solver sometimes thinks models that *are* linear are *not* linear. To avoid this problem, it is good practice to check the Use Automatic Scaling option in the Options dialog box. This should ensure that Solver properly recognizes linear models as being linear.

Can I use Solver to determine how much money I need to save for retirement?

By using Equation 2 (shown earlier in the chapter), we can easily determine how much money a person needs to save for retirement. Here's an example.

I am planning for my retirement, and at the beginning of this year and each of the next 39 years, I'm going to contribute some money to my retirement fund. Each year, I plan to increase my retirement contribution by $500. When I retire in 40 years, I plan to withdraw (at the beginning of each year) $100,000 per year for 20 years. I've made the following assumptions about the yields for my retirement investment portfolio:

❑ During the first 20 years of my investing, the investments will earn 10 percent per year.

❑ During all other years, my investments will earn 5 percent per year.

I've assumed that all contributions and withdrawals occur at the beginning of the year. Given these assumptions, what is the least amount of money I can contribute this year and still have enough to make my retirement withdrawals?

You can find the solution to this question on the *Retire* worksheet in the file Finmath-solver.xlsx, shown in Figure 31-3 on the next page. Note that I've hidden many rows in the model.

This worksheet simply tracks my retirement balance during each of the next 60 years. Each year, I earn the indicated interest rate on the retirement balance. I begin by entering a trial value for my Year 1 payment in cell C6. Copying the formula *C6+500* from cell C7 to C8:C45 ensures that the retirement contribution increases by $500 per year during years 2–40. I've entered in column D the assumed return on my investments for each of the next 60 years. In cells E46:E65, I've entered the annual $100,000 withdrawal for years 41–60. Copying the formula *(B6+C6−E6)*(1+D6)* from F6 to F7:F65 uses Equation 2 to compute each year's ending retirement account balance. Copying the formula *=F6* from cell B7 to B8:B65 computes the beginning balance for years 2–60. Of course, the Year 1 initial balance is 0. We note that the 6.8704E-07 in cell F65 is approximately 0, with the difference due to roundoff error.

	A	B	C	D	E	F
		Initial				Ending
5	Year	balance	Contribution	Return	Withdrawal	Balance
6	1	0	1387.86809	10%	0	1526.6549
7	2	1526.6549	1887.86809	10%	0	3755.9753
8	3	3755.9753	2387.86809	10%	0	6758.22773
44	39	1146596.1	20387.8681	5%	0	1225333.17
45	40	1225333.17	20887.8681	5%	0	1308532.09
46	41	1308532.09		5%	100000	1268958.69
47	42	1268958.69		5%	100000	1227406.62
62	57	372324.803		5%	100000	285941.043
63	58	285941.043		5%	100000	195238.095
64	59	195238.095		5%	100000	100000
65	60	100000		5%	100000	6.8704E-07

Figure 31-3   Retirement planning data that can be set up for analysis with Solver

The Solver Parameters dialog box for this model is shown in Figure 31-4. We want to minimize our Year 1 contribution (cell C6). The changing cell is also our Year 1 contribution (cell C6). We ensure that we never run out of money during retirement by adding the constraint *F46:F65>=0*. This formula ensures that the ending balance for Years 41–60 is non-negative.

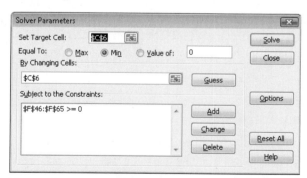

Figure 31-4   Solver Parameters dialog box set up for the retirement problem

After checking the Assume Linear Model and Assume Non-Negative options in the Solver Options dialog box and clicking Solve in the Solver Parameters dialog box, we find that our first year's contribution should equal $1,387.87.

This model is linear because the target cell equals the changing cell and our constraint is created by adding multiples of changing cells. Note that because the return on the investments is not the same each year, there is no easy way to use Excel financial functions to solve this problem. Solver provides a general framework that can be used to analyze financial planning problems when mortgage rates or investment returns are not constant.

Problems

1. I am borrowing $15,000 to buy a new car. I am going to make 60 end-of-month payments. The annual interest rate on the loan is 10 percent. The car dealer is a friend of mine, and he will allow me to make the monthly payment for Months 1–30 equal to one-half the payment for Months 31–60. What is the payment during each month?

2. Solve the retirement planning problem assuming that withdrawals occur at the end of each year and contributions occur at the beginning of each year.

3. Solve our mortgage example assuming that payments are made at the beginning of each month.

4. In the retirement-planning example, suppose that during Year 1, our salary is $40,000 and our salary increases 5 percent per year until retirement. We want to save the same percentage of our salary each year we work. What percentage of our salary should we save?

5. In the mortgage example, suppose that we want our monthly payment to increase by $50 each month. What should each month's payment be?

6. Assume we want to take out a $300,000 loan on a 20-year mortgage with end-of-month payments. The annual rate of interest is 6 percent. Twenty years from now, we need to make an ending balloon payment of $40,000. Because we expect our income to increase, we want to structure our loan so at the beginning of each year our monthly payments increase by 2 percent. Determine the amount of each year's monthly payment.

Chapter 32
Using Solver to Rate Sports Teams

- Can I use Excel to set NFL point spreads?

Many of us follow basketball, football, hockey, and baseball. Bookmakers set point spreads on games in all these sports and others. For example, the bookmakers' best guess was that the Pittsburgh Steelers would win the 2006 Super Bowl by three points. (Boy, did the Colts choke in the divisional round! Of course, the Colts redeemed themselves by winning the 2007 Super Bowl.) How can you use Microsoft Office Excel 2007 to come up with team "ratings" that generate reasonable point spreads?

Using a simple Solver model, you can generate reasonable point spreads for teams based on the scores of the 2005 season. (Playoff games for this season occurred in 2006). Our work is in file Nfl2005.xlsx (see Figure 32-1). We simply use the score of each game of the NFL 2005 season as input data. The changing cells for the Solver model will be a rating for each team and the size of the home field advantage. For example, if the Indianapolis Colts have a rating of +5 and the New York Jets have a rating of +7, the Jets are considered two points better than the Colts.

With regard to the home-field edge, in most years, college and professional football teams, as well as professional basketball teams, tend to win by an average of three points (whereas home college basketball teams tend to win by an average of five points). In our model, however, we will define the home edge as a changing cell and have our Solver model estimate the home edge. We can define the outcome of an NFL game to be the number of points by which the home team outscores the visitors. We can predict the outcome of each game by using the following equation (which I'll refer to as Equation 1):

(1)(Predicted points by which home team outscores visitors)=(Home edge)+(Home team rating)−(Away Team rating)

For example, if the home field edge equals three points, when the Colts host the Jets, the Colts will be a one-point favorite (3+5−7). If the Jets host the Colts, the Jets will be a five-point favorite (3+7-5). A complication that arose in the 2005 season is that Hurricane Katrina caused the New Orleans Saints (Team 20) to play games at a nearby site (San Antonio, Texas or Baton

Rouge, Louisiana). (This is indicated by a C in column A.) We assigned 0.5 home-field advantage for the Saints in these games. Also Game 59 (San Francisco 49ers against Arizona Cardinals) was played in Mexico City (a neutral site) so no home-field advantage should be assigned for this game.

What target cell will yield "good" ratings? Our goal is to find the set of values for team ratings and home-field advantage that best predict the outcome of all games. In short, we want the prediction for each game to be as close as possible to the outcome of each game. This suggests that we want to minimize the sum over all games of *(Actual outcome)–(Predicted outcome)*. The problem with using this target is that positive and negative prediction errors cancel each other out. For example, if we overpredict the home-team margin by 50 points in one game and underpredict the home-team margin by 50 points in another game, our target cell would yield a value of 0, indicating perfect accuracy, when in fact we were off by 50 points a game. We can remedy this problem by minimizing the sum over all games by using *[(Actual Outcome)–(Predicted Outcome)]*^{2}. Now positive and negative errors will not cancel each other out.

Can I use Excel to set NFL point spreads?

Let's now see how to determine accurate ratings for NFL teams by using the scores from the 2005 regular season. You can find the data for this problem in the file Nfl2005.xlsx, which is shown in Figure 32-1. Note that I've hidden the ratings of teams 8–18 so that the ratings and model would fit on one screen.

	A	B	C	D	E	F	G	H	I	J
1					-1E-06		home			
2					RATING		3.53439			
3			1	1 Arizona Cardinals	-5.033249556					
4			2	2 Atlanta Falcons	-0.795553378					
5			3	3 Baltimore	-1.718927465					
6			4	4 Buffalo Bills	-5.722553688					
7			5	5 Carolina	6.490681014					
8			6	6 Chicago Bears	1.296790636					
9			7	7 Cincinnati	3.379044852					
21			19	19 New England	4.351248755					
22			20	20 New Orleans	-9.618987859					
23			21	21 New York	5.247799897					
24			22	22 New York	-6.207312776					
25			23	23 Oakland	-3.15719757					
26			24	24 Philadelphia	-2.800546577					
27			25	25 Pittsburgh	10.126106					
28			26	26 St. Louis Rams	-5.393274714					
29			27	27 San Diego	9.689603191					
30			28	28 San Francisco	-11.6834945					
31			29	29 Seattle	9.6831805					
32			30	30 Tampa Bay	-0.85884563					
33			31	31 Tennessee	-7.699293234					
34			32	32 Washington	5.551217573					
35										
36										
37										36454.44896
38		game#	home	away	homescore	awayscore	margin	predict	error	squared error
39		1	19	23	30	20	10	11.0428	-1.04284	1.087510231
40		2	32	6	9	7	2	7.78882	-5.78882	33.51041612
41		3	8	7	13	27	-14	-3.90319	-10.0968	101.9455206
42		4	17	10	34	10	24	-6.62866	30.6287	938.1147431
43		5	4	13	22	7	15	7.97425	7.02575	49.36116317
44		6	5	20	20	23	-3	19.6441	-22.6441	512.7534594
45		7	16	22	27	7	20	16.3609	3.63914	13.24330582
46		8	15	29	26	14	12	-2.70609	14.7061	216.2689494

Figure 32-1 Data rating NFL teams that we'll use with Solver

To begin, I named the range E3:E34, which contains each team's rating, *rating*. I also named (for reasons that will soon become apparent) the range C3:E34 *lookup2*. I placed a trial home-field advantage value in cell G2.

Starting in row 39, columns C and D contain the team code number (listed in C3:C34) for the home and away team for each game. For example, the first game (listed in row 39) is the Oakland Raiders (Team 23) playing at the New England Patriots (Team 19). Column E contains the home team's score, and column F contains the visiting team's score. As you can see, the Patriots beat the Raiders 30-20. I can now compute the outcome of each game (the number of points by which the home team beats the visiting team) by entering the formula *=E39−F39* in cell G39. By pointing to the lower-right portion of this cell and double-clicking the left mouse button, you can copy this formula down to the last game, which appears in row 304. (By the way, an easy way to select all the data is to press Ctrl+Shift+Down Arrow key. This key combination takes you to the last row filled with data—row 304 in this case.)

In column H, I use Equation 1 to generate the prediction for each game. The prediction for the first game is computed in cell H39:

=IF(A39="c",0.5*$G$2,IF(A39="n",0,$G$2))+VLOOKUP(C39,lookup2,3)− VLOOKUP(D39,lookup2,3)

This formula creates a prediction for the first game by adding the home edge to the home-team rating and then subtracting the visiting-team rating. Note that *VLOOKUP(C39,lookup2,3)* locates the home-team rating by using the home-team code number in column C, whereas *VLOOKUP(D39,lookup,3)* looks up the visiting team's rating by using the visiting team's code number in column D. (For more information about using lookup functions, see Chapter 3, "Lookup Functions.") The IF statement picks up the full home advantage in most games, *0.5*Home edge* in Saints home games, and no home advantage for the Mexico City game.

In column I, I compute the error (*actual score−predicted score*) for each game. Our error for the first game is computed in cell I36 with the formula *=G39−H39*. In column J, I compute the squared error for each game. The squared error for the first game is computed in cell J39 with the formula *=I39^2*. After selecting the cell range H36:J36, I copied the formulas down to the bottom of our spreadsheet (H304:J304).

In cell J37, I've computed our target cell by summing all the squared errors with the formula *SUM(J36:J304)*. (You can enter a formula for a large column of numbers such as this by typing *=SUM(* and then selecting the first cell in the range you want to add together. Press Ctrl+Shift+Down Arrow key to enter the range from the cell you've selected to the bottom row in the column and then add the closing parenthesis.)

It is convenient to make our average team rating equal to 0. A team with a positive rating is better than average and a team with a negative rating is worse than average. I've computed the average team rating in cell E1 with the formula *AVERAGE(E3:E34)*.

I can now fill in the Solver Parameters dialog box as shown in Figure 32-2.

Figure 32-2   Solver Parameters dialog box set up for NFL ratings

We minimize the sum of our squared prediction errors for all games (computed in cell J37) by changing each team's rating (listed in cells E3:E34) and the home advantage (cell G2). The constraint *E1=0* ensures that the average team rating is 0. From Figure 32-1, we find that the home team has an advantage of 3.5 points over the visiting team. Our 10 highest-rated teams are shown in Figure 32-3. Remember that the ratings listed in cell range E3:E34 were computed by Solver. In our template file we could start with any numbers in these cells and Solver would still find the "best" ratings.

	M	N
38	Team	RATING
39	14 Indianapolis Colts	10.3586
40	25 Pittsburgh Steelers	10.1261
41	27 San Diego Chargers	9.6896
42	29 Seattle Seahawks	9.68318
43	10 Denver Broncos	9.55303
44	16 Kansas City Chiefs	6.61916
45	5 Carolina Panthers	6.49068
46	32 Washington Redskins	5.55122
47	21 New York Giants	5.2478
48	19 New England Patriots	4.35125

Figure 32-3   Top 10 teams for the NFL 2005 season

Because the Colts are the highest rated AFC team and the Seahawks are the highest rated NFC team, we would have predicted that the Colts would play the Seattle Seahawks in the Super Bowl. Unfortunately, our Colts did not make it. Our data includes all playoff games for the 2005 season, so our prediction for the Super Bowl would have been the Pittsburgh Steelers over the Seattle Seahawks by *10.13–9.68=.45*. There is no home advantage because the Super Bowl field was not a home field for either team.

Our model is not linear because the target cell adds together terms of the form *(Home Team Rating+Home Field Edge–Visiting Team Rating)*^{2}. Recall that for a Solver model to be linear, the target cell must be created by adding together terms with the form *(changing cell)*(constant)*. This relationship doesn't exist in this case, so our model is not linear. Solver does obtain the correct answer, however, for any sports-rating model in which the target cell minimizes the sum of squared errors.

Problems

1. The file Nfl01.xlsx contains scores for every regular season game during the 2001 NFL season. Rate the teams. Who would you have forecast to make the Super Bowl?

2. The file Nfl02.xlsx contains scores for every regular season game during the 2002 NFL season. Rate the teams. Who would you have forecast to make the Super Bowl?

3. The file Nfl03.xlsx contains scores for every regular season game during the 2003 NFL season. Rate the teams. Who would you have forecast to make the Super Bowl?

4. The file Nfl04.xlsx contains scores for every regular season game during the 2004 NFL season. Rate the teams. Who would you have forecast to make the Super Bowl?

5. For the 2004 season, devise a method to predict the actual score of each game. Hint: Give each team an offensive rating and a defensive rating. Who had the best offense? Who had the best defense?

6. True or False? An NFL team could lose every game and be an above average team.

7. The file Nba01_02.xlsx contains scores for every game during the 2001–2002 NBA season. Rate the teams.

8. The file Nba02_03.xlsx contains scores for every regular season game during the 2002–2003 NBA season. Rate the teams.

9. The file Worldball.xlsx contains all scores from the 2006 World Basketball Championships. Rate the teams. Who were the best three teams?

10. Our method of rating teams works fine for football and basketball. What problems arise if we apply our method to hockey or baseball?

Chapter 33

Importing Data from a Text File or Document

■ How can I import data from a text file into Excel so that I can analyze it?

Jeff Sagarin, the creator of the *USA Today* basketball and football ratings, and I have developed a system to rate NBA players for the Dallas Mavericks team and its owner Mark Cuban. Every day during the season, Jeff's FORTRAN program produces a multitude of information, including ratings for each Dallas Maverick lineup during each game. Jeff's program produces this information in the form of a text file.

How can I import data from a text file into Excel so that I can analyze it?

We often receive data in a Microsoft Office Word document or in a text (.txt) file that we need to import into Microsoft Office Excel for numerical analysis. To import a Word document into Excel 2007, you should first save it as a text file. You can then use the Text Import Wizard to import the text file into Excel. With the Text Import Wizard you can break data in a text file into columns by using one of the following approaches.

❑ If you choose the *fixed-width* option, Excel guesses where the data should be broken into columns. You can easily modify Excel's assumptions.

❑ If you choose the *delimited* option, you pick a character (common choices are a comma, a space, or a plus sign), and Excel breaks the data into columns wherever it encounters the character you chose.

As an example, the file Lineupsch33.docx (a sample of the data is shown below) contains the length of time each lineup played for Dallas in several games during the 2002–2003 season. The file also contains the "rating" of the lineup. For example, the first two lines tell us that against Sacramento, the lineup of Bell, Finley, LaFrentz, Nash, and Nowitzki were on the court together for 9.05 minutes and that the lineup played at a level of 19.79 points (per 48 minutes), worse than an average NBA lineup.

```
Bell    Finley   LaFrentz  Nash     Nowitzki   - 19.79
695# 9.05m SAC DAL*
Finley   Nash    Nowitzki  Van Exel  Williams   - 11.63
```

```
695# 8.86m SAC DAL*
Finley   LaFrentz Nash     Nowitzki  Van Exel    102.98
695# 4.44m SAC DAL*
Bradley  Finley   Nash     Nowitzki  Van Exel   - 44.26
695# 4.38m SAC DAL*
Bradley  Nash     Nowitzki Van Exel  Williams     9.71
695# 3.05m SAC DAL*
Bell    Finley   LaFrentz  Nowitzki  Van Exel  - 121.50
695# 2.73m SAC DAL*
Bell    LaFrentz Nowitzki  Van Exel  Williams    39.35
695# 2.70m SAC DAL*
Bradley  Finley   Nowitzki Van Exel  Williams    86.87
695# 2.45m SAC DAL*
Bradley  Nash     Van Exel Williams  Rigaudeau  - 54.55
695# 2.32m SAC DAL*
```

We'd like to import this lineup information into Excel so that, for each lineup, we would have the following information listed in different columns.

❑ Each player's name

❑ Minutes played by the lineup

❑ Rating of the lineup

The player Van Exel (actually Nick Van Exel) raises a problem. If we choose the delimited option and use a space character to break the data into columns, Van Exel will occupy two columns. For lineups that include Van Exel, the numerical data will be located in a different column than the column in which the data is located for lineups that don't include Van Exel. To remedy this problem, I've used the Replace command in Word to change each occurrence of Van Exel to Exel. Now, when we break up the data where a space occurs, Van Exel will require only one column. The first few rows of our data now look like the following.

```
Bell    Finley   LaFrentz Nash     Nowitzki   - 19.79  695# 9.05m SAC DAL*
Finley   Nash     Nowitzki Exel    Williams   - 11.63  695# 8.86m SAC DAL*
Finley   LaFrentz Nash     Nowitzki Exel      102.98  69 5# 4.44m SAC DAL*
Bradley  Finley   Nash     Nowitzki Exel      - 44.26  695# 4.38m SAC DAL*
Bradley  Nash     Nowitzki Exel    Williams     9.71  69 5# 3.05m SAC DAL*
Bell    Finley   LaFrentz Nowitzki Exel     - 121.50  695# 2.73m SAC DAL*
Bell    LaFrentz Nowitzki Exel    Williams    39.35  69 5# 2.70m SAC DAL*
Bradley  Finley   Nowitzki Exel    Williams    86.87  69 5# 2.45m SAC DAL*
Bradley  Nash     Exel     Williams Rigaudeau  - 54.55  695# 2.32m SAC DAL*
```

The trick in importing data from a Word or text file into Excel is to use the Excel Text Import Wizard. As I mentioned earlier, you first need to save the Word file (Lineupsch33.docx in this example) as a text file. To do this, simply open the file in Word, click the Microsoft Office Button followed by File, Save As, and then select Plain Text in the Save As Type list. In the File Conversion dialog box, select the Windows (Default) option, and then click OK. Your file will now be saved with the name Lineupsch33.txt. Close the Word document. In Excel, open the file Lineupsch33.txt. You'll see Step 1 of the Text Import Wizard, which is shown in Figure 33-1.

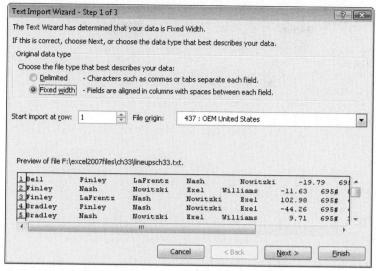

Figure 33-1   Step 1 of the Text Import Wizard

Clearly, we want to select the Delimited option and break the data at each space. However, let's suppose that we choose Fixed Width. Then Step 2 of the Text Import Wizard appears, shown in Figure 33-2. As you can see, you can create, move, or delete a break line. For many data import operations, changing column breaks can be a hit-or-miss adventure.

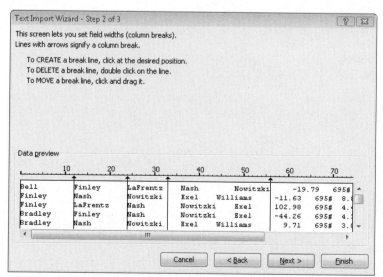

Figure 33-2   Step 2 of the Text Import Wizard after selecting the Fixed Width option

If we select Delimited in Step 1, you'll see the second step of the Text Import Wizard that's shown in Figure 33-3 on the next page. In this example, I've selected Space as the delimiter. Selecting the Treat Consecutive Delimiters As One option ensures that consecutive spaces will result in only a single column break. I recommend keeping Tab selected because many Excel add-ins do not work properly if Tab is deselected.

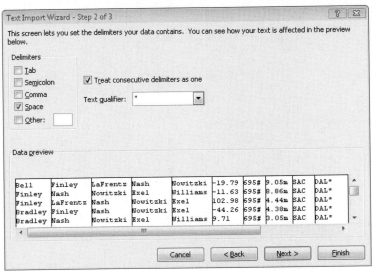

Figure 33-3   Step 2 of the Text Import Wizard after selecting Delimited Option

When you click Next, you're sent to the third step in the wizard, which is shown in Figure 33-4. By selecting the General option as the format, we have Excel treat numerical data as numbers and other values as text.

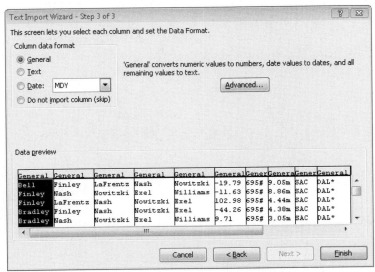

Figure 33-4   Step 3 of the wizard, in which you can select a format to apply to the data you're importing

When you click Finish, the wizard imports the data into Excel, as shown in Figure 33-5.

	A	B	C	D	E	F	G	H	I	J
1	Bell	Finley	LaFrentz	Nash	Nowitzki	-19.79	695#	9.05m	SAC	DAL*
2	Finley	Nash	Nowitzki	Exel	Williams	-11.63	695#	8.86m	SAC	DAL*
3	Finley	LaFrentz	Nash	Nowitzki	Exel	102.98	695#	4.44m	SAC	DAL*
4	Bradley	Finley	Nash	Nowitzki	Exel	-44.26	695#	4.38m	SAC	DAL*
5	Bradley	Nash	Nowitzki	Exel	Williams	9.71	695#	3.05m	SAC	DAL*
6	Bell	Finley	LaFrentz	Nowitzki	Exel	-121.5	695#	2.73m	SAC	DAL*
7	Bell	LaFrentz	Nowitzki	Exel	Williams	39.35	695#	2.70m	SAC	DAL*
8	Bradley	Finley	Nowitzki	Exel	Williams	86.87	695#	2.45m	SAC	DAL*
9	Bradley	Nash	Exel	Williams	Rigaudeau	-54.55	695#	2.32m	SAC	DAL*
10	Finley	LaFrentz	Exel	Williams	Rigaudeau	-26.4	695#	1.73m	SAC	DAL*
11	Bradley	Finley	Nash	Nowitzki	Williams	91.89	695#	1.70m	SAC	DAL*
12	Bell	Finley	Nash	Nowitzki	Exel	34.18	695#	1.05m	SAC	DAL*
13	LaFrentz	Nash	Nowitzki	Exel	Williams	-50.9	695#	1.02m	SAC	DAL*
14	Bell	Bradley	Finley	Nash	Nowitzki	1.42	695#	1.00m	SAC	DAL*
15	Bradley	Finley	Exel	Williams	Rigaudeau	46.75	695#	0.93m	SAC	DAL*
16	Bell	Bradley	Nowitzki	Exel	Williams	-314.43	695#	0.60m	SAC	DAL*
17	Bell	Finley	LaFrentz	Nash	Nowitzki	123.62	686#	6.05m	UTA	DAL*
18	Finley	LaFrentz	Nash	Nowitzki	Exel	62.3	686#	5.80m	UTA	DAL*
19	LaFrentz	Nash	Nowitzki	Exel	Williams	-10.09	686#	5.68m	UTA	DAL*
20	Bell	Bradley	Finley	Nash	Nowitzki	-30.32	686#	5.60m	UTA	DAL*
21	Bell	Finley	Nowitzki	Exel	Williams	-42.93	686#	4.75m	UTA	DAL*
22	Bell	Finley	LaFrentz	Nowitzki	Exel	40.09	686#	3.53m	UTA	DAL*

Figure 33-5   Excel file with lineup information

Each player is listed in a separate column (columns A–E); column F contains the rating of each lineup, column G contains the game number, column H contains the minutes played by each lineup, and columns I and J list the two teams playing in the game. After saving the file as an Excel workbook (.xlsx), you can use all of the analytic capabilities of Excel to analyze the performance of Dallas's lineups. For example, we could calculate the average performance of the team when Dirk Nowitzki is on or off the court.

Problems

1. The file Kingslineups.docx contains performance ratings for some of the Sacramento Kings lineups. Import this data into Excel.

2. In the example discussed in the chapter, the time each lineup played (column H) ends with an *m*. Modify the file so that the time played by each lineup is an actual number.

Chapter 34

Importing Data from the Internet

- The MSN Money Central Web site provides analyst ratings (buy, sell, and hold) for stocks. How can I import this information into Excel?

- Is there a way I can download current stock prices into Excel?

We all know that the World Wide Web contains useful data on just about everything. However, we can't really do any sort of analysis of this data while it's on the Web. We need to import the data into Microsoft Office Excel. Excel 2007 makes importing data from the Web very easy. After you find the URL where the data you want is located, copy the URL to the Windows Clipboard. Then open an Excel worksheet and on the Data tab, in the Get External Data group, click From Web. When the New Web Query dialog box appears, paste the URL into it, and then click Go. The Web page appears, and you can select the data you want to import into Excel. Our first example will show you how to implement this easy procedure.

The MSN Money Central Web site provides analyst ratings (buy, sell, and hold) for stocks. How can I import this information into Excel?

The URL *http://moneycentral.msn.com/investor/invsub/analyst/recomnd.asp?Symbol=MSFT* contains information about analysts' forecasts for the future price of Microsoft stock. For example, in Figure 34-1, we find that on March 27, 2007, 9 of 18 analysts rated Microsoft a strong buy, whereas a month before, 10 of 19 analysts rated Microsoft a strong buy. It would be useful to import this data into Excel so that we could better understand the data.

Analyst Ratings				
Recommendations	Current	1 Month Ago	2 Months Ago	3 Months Ago
Strong Buy	9	10	9	10
Moderate Buy	4	4	4	4
Hold	4	4	5	4
Moderate Sell	0	0	0	0
Strong Sell	1	1	1	1
Mean Rec.	1.89	1.84	1.95	1.84

Figure 34-1 Analyst forecast for Microsoft in March 2007. The Web contains a lot of useful data, but it isn't easy to analyze on a Web site.

To import the data into Excel, copy the URL and then open a blank worksheet. Now display the Data tab of the Ribbon, and in the Get External Data group, click From Web. When the New Web Query dialog box appears, press Ctrl+V to paste the URL into the Address box, and then click Go. The New Web Query dialog box displays the data shown in Figure 34-2.

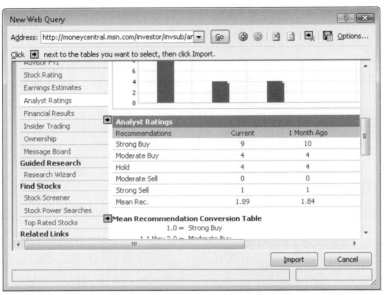

Figure 34-2   New Web Query dialog box after choosing a URL

You now click the arrow that points to the data you want to download and import. In our case, we would click the arrow directly to the left of Analyst Ratings. The arrow changes to a check mark. After clicking Import, you'll see the Import Data dialog box, in which you indicate to Excel where you want to place the data. I chose cell C2 of the current worksheet for this example. After clicking OK, the analysts' ratings are imported into the worksheet. (See Figure 34-3.) Note that the numbers are beautifully separated into different columns!

	B	C	D	E	F
4	Analyst Ratings				
5	Recommendations	Current	1 Month Ago	2 Months Ago	3 Months Ago
6	Strong Buy	9	10	9	10
7	Moderate Buy	4	4	4	4
8	Hold	4	4	5	4
9	Moderate Sell	0	0	0	0
10	Strong Sell	1	1	1	1
11	Mean Rec.	1.89	1.84	1.95	1.84

Figure 34-3   Analyst forecasts in March 2007 imported into Excel

You can easily set your query to refresh, or update in any desired fashion. Just right-click anywhere in the query results, select Data Range Properties, and change the Refresh Control settings. As shown in Figure 34-4, we selected our query to refresh every minute and automatically refresh when the file is reopened.

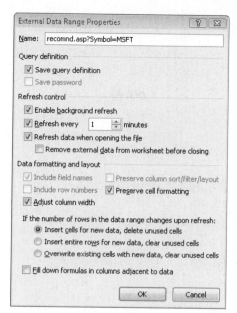

Figure 34-4   Refresh settings for Web query

To edit this query, simply right-click anywhere within the query output and select Edit Query. By clicking the options button, you can control the fomatting of your query results. Off course, when you run this Web query again, you'll probably see different information because analysts are constantly changing their views of future stock price for Microsoft.

Is there a way I can download current stock prices into Excel?

Excel comes with a built-in Web query that can be used to download current information about stocks. This Web query is a *dynamic Web query*, which means that you can set the query to update stock information as it changes in real time. All you have to do is select the data you want to update and on the Data tab, in the Connections group, click Refresh All. Let's see how to download real-time stock information about Microsoft (ticker symbol MSFT) and General Motors (ticker symbol GM) into Excel.

Open or create a worksheet in Excel. Display the Data tab of the Ribbon, and in the Get External Data group, double-click Existing Connections. Now select the Web query named *MSN MoneyCentral Investor Stock Quotes*. Click Open, and then use the Import Data dialog box to indicate where you want to place the data in the worksheet. Click OK, and then fill in the Enter Parameter Value dialog box as shown in Figure 34-5. The query downloads information about Microsoft and GM into Excel. Figure 34-6 (and the file Msftgmquotes.xlsx) shows a sample of the downloaded information. Checking the options shown in Figure 34-5 on the next page ensures that the worksheet changes to reflect the most current information.

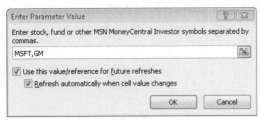

Figure 34-5 Use the Enter Parameter Value dialog box to designate the stocks for which you want the dynamic Web query to download information.

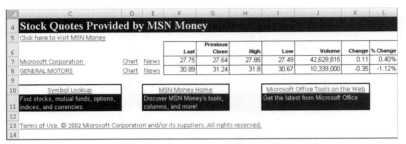

Figure 34-6 Downloaded information about Microsoft and General Motors stocks

Excel also ships with Web queries designed to download currency exchange rates and information about major stock indexes. These Web queries are static, however, and will not update information in real time unless you rerun the query.

Of course, you can create your own Web queries. Creating Web queries is beyond the scope of this book. See Chapter 4 of *Data Analysis for Managers with Microsoft Excel* by S. Christian Albright, Wayne L. Winston, and Christopher Zappe (Duxbury Press, 2004) for an introduction to creating Web queries.

Problems

1. Download real-time information about Disney (ticker symbol DIS) and the Gap (ticker symbol GPS) into Excel.

2. Use the built-in Web query designed to download current foreign exchange rate information into Excel.

3. Go to NBA.com and download the career statistics of your favorite player into Excel.

4. Go to MLB.com and download the career statistics of your favorite player into Excel.

5. Go to NFL.com and download the season statistics of your favorite player into Excel.

6. Go to *http://www.boxofficeguru.com/blockbusters.htm* and download data on the top moneymaking movies of all time into Excel.

7. Go to *http://money.cnn.com/magazines/fortune/fortune500/full_list/* and download information on the Fortune 500 into Excel.

Chapter 35
Validating Data

- I'm entering scores from professional basketball games into Excel. I know that a team scores from 50 through 200 points per game. I once entered 1000 points instead of 100 points, which messed up my analysis. Is there a way to have Excel prevent me from making this type of error?

- I'm entering the date and amount of my business expenses for a new year. Early in the year, I often enter the previous year in the Date field by mistake. Is there a way I can set up Excel to prevent me from making this type of error?

- I'm entering a long list of numbers. Can I have Excel warn me if I enter a nonnumeric value?

- My assistant needs to enter state abbreviations when she enters dozens and dozens of sales transactions. Can we set up a list of state abbreviations to minimize the chance that she'll enter an incorrect abbreviation?

Our work often involves mind-numbing data entry. When you're entering a lot of information into Microsoft Office Excel 2007, it's easy to make an error. The data validation feature of Excel can greatly lessen the chances that you'll commit a costly error. To set up data validation, you begin by selecting the cell range that you want to apply data validation to. Choose Data Validation from the Data tab and then specify the criteria (as you'll see in this chapter's examples) that Excel uses to flag any invalid data that's entered.

I'm entering scores from professional basketball games into Excel. I know that a team scores from 50 through 200 points per game. I once entered 1000 points instead of 100 points, which messed up my analysis. Is there a way to have Excel prevent me from making this type of error?

Let's suppose that you're going to enter into cells A2:A11 the number of points scored by the home team, and in cells B2:B11, you'll enter the number of points scored by the visiting team. (You'll find the work I did to solve this problem in the file Nbadvl.xlsx.) You want to ensure that each value entered in the range A2:B11 is a whole number from 50 through 200.

Begin by selecting the range A2:B11, and then choose Data Validation from the Data tab. Then select the Settings tab. Select Whole Number from the Allow list, and then fill in the Data Validation dialog box as shown in Figure 35-1. In response to invalid data, the default response (called an *Error Alert*) is a message stating "The value entered is not valid. A user has restricted values that can be entered into the cell."

Figure 35-1 Use the Settings tab in the Data Validation dialog box to set up data-validation criteria.

Figure 35-2 Error Alert tab options in the Data Validation dialog box

You can use the Error Alert tab in the Data Validation dialog box (see Figure 35-2) to change the nature of the error alert, including the icon, the title for the message box, and the text of the message itself. On the Input Message tab, you can create a prompt that informs a user about the type of data that can be safely entered. The message is displayed as a comment in the selected cell. For example, in cell E5, I created the prompt shown in Figure 35-3. To do this, I clicked the Input Message tab shown in Figure 35-2 and typed the input message shown in Figure 35-3.

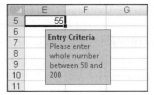

Figure 35-3   Add a data-validation input prompt so that users know what data they can enter.

I'm entering the date and amount of my business expenses for a new year. Early in the year, I often enter the previous year in the date field by mistake. Is there a way I can set up Excel to prevent me from making this type of error?

Suppose you're entering the year in the cell range A2:A20. (See the file Datedv.xlsx.) Simply select the A2:A20 range, and then choose Data Validation from the Data tab. Fill in the Settings tab of the Data Validation dialog box as shown in Figure 35-4.

Figure 35-4   Use settings such as these to ensure the validity of dates you enter.

If you enter a date in this range that occurs earlier than January 1, 2005, you'll be warned about the error. For example, entering 1/15/2004 in cell A3 will bring up the error alert shown earlier in Figure 35-2.

I'm entering a long list of numbers. Can I have Excel warn me if I enter a nonnumeric value?

To unleash the power of data validation, you need to use the Custom setting. When you select Custom in the Allow list on the Settings tab of the Data Validation dialog box (see Figure 35-1), you use a formula to define valid data. A formula you enter for data validation works the same as a formula used for conditional formatting, which is described in Chapter 22, "Conditional Formatting." You enter a formula that is true if and only if the content of the first cell in the selected range is valid. When you click OK in the Data Validation dialog box, the formula is copied to the remaining cells in the range. When you enter a value in a cell in the selected range, Excel displays an error alert if the formula you entered returns False for that value.

To illustrate the use of the Custom setting, let's suppose we want to ensure that each entry in the cell range B2:B20 is a number. (See the file Numberdv.xlsx.) The key to solving this problem is using the Excel ISNUMBER function. The ISNUMBER function returns True if the function refers to a cell that contains numeric data. The function returns False if the function refers to a cell that contains a nonnumeric value.

After selecting the cell range B2:B20 and placing the cursor in B2, display the Data tab of the Ribbon, click Data Validation in the Data Tools group, and then fill in the Settings tab of the Data Validation dialog box as shown in Figure 35-5.

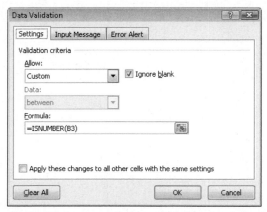

Figure 35-5   Use the ISNUMBER function to ensure that the data in a range is numeric.

After clicking OK, we'll receive an error prompt if we try to enter any nonnumeric value in B2:B20. For example, if we type John in cell B3, we receive an error prompt.

If you click Data Validation while in cell B3, the formula shown in Figure 35-5 is displayed as *=ISNUMBER(B3)*. This demonstrates that the formula entered in cell B2 is copied in the correct fashion. Entering John in cell B3 causes *=ISNUMBER(B3)* to return False, so we receive the error alert.

My assistant needs to enter state abbreviations when she enters dozens and dozens of sales transactions. Can we set up a list of state abbreviations to minimize the chance that she'll enter an incorrect abbreviation?

The key to this data validation problem is to use the List validation criteria. Begin by entering a list of state abbreviations. See the file Statedv.xlsx. In this example, I've used the range I6:I55 and named the range *abbrev*. Next, select the range in which you'll enter state abbreviations. (The example uses D5:D156.) After clicking Data Validation from the Data tab, fill in the Data Validation dialog box as shown in Figure 35-6.

Now, whenever you select a cell in the range D5:D156, clicking the drop-down arrow causes a list to appear, as shown in Figure 35-7. The list contains the state abbreviations. Only abbreviations that appear on the list are valid values in this range.

If you do not use the drop-down list and instead type in a state abbreviation, should you enter an incorrect abbreviation (such as ALK for Alaska), you'll receive an error message.

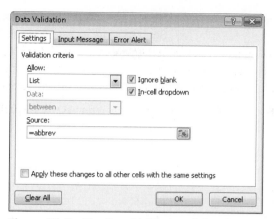

Figure 35-6   The Data Validation dialog box can be used to define a list of valid values.

Figure 35-7   Drop-down list of state abbreviations

Remarks

- If you select F5 Special and check Data Validation, Excel will select all cells containing Data Validation settings.

- If you want to use the Data Validation drop-down list and the data source list is in a different sheet than the drop-down list, then you must name the list (as we did in our example) or the drop-down list will not work.

- If you use the dynamic-range technique described in Chapter 20, "The OFFSET Function," then when you add new items (or delete items) from the data source list activating the drop-down list, the changes in the list will automatically be reflected in the drop-down box. See Problem 10. Also, if you name the data source list as an Excel Table (see Chapter 24, "Tables") then changes in the list will be reflected in the drop-down list. This will work as long as you point to the list range and do not try to type in the Table name.

- Suppose you want to use a drop-down list to select a company you sell candy bars to. Then you want another drop-down list that you can use to select the list of candy bars you sell at the selected store. The problem is that the same set of candy bars might not be sold at each store. How do you create such a nested list selection? For example, suppose the stores were Target and CVS. Suppose you assign a range name of *Target* to the list of candy bars sold at Target and a range name of *CVS* to the list of candy bars sold at

CVS. If the drop-down list for store selection is in, for example, A20, then you could create the appropriate drop-down list in cell B20 by clicking Data Validation and fill in for the list selected =INDIRECT(A20). As we discussed in Chapter 21, "The INDIRECT Function," if A20 contains CVS then the list will key off the range CVS that contains all candy bars sold at CVS, and so on. See Problem 11.

■ To clear Data Validations from a range, select the range containing the data validations. Then choose Data Validation from the Data tab and select Clear All.

Problems

1. You are entering nonnegative whole numbers into the cell range C1:C20. Enter a data validation setting that ensures that each entry is a nonnegative whole number.

2. You are entering in the cell range C1:C15 the dates of transactions that occured during July 2004. Enter a data validation setting that ensures that each date entered occurs in July 2004.

3. With the List option in the group of data validation settings, you can generate an error message if a value that is not included in a list is entered in the cell range you're validating. Suppose you're entering employee first names in the cell range A1:A10. The only employees of the company are Jen, Greg, Vivian, Jon, and John. Use the List option to ensure that no one misspells a first name.

4. With the Text Length option in the group of data validation settings, you can generate an error message when the number of characters in a cell does not match the number you define. Use the Text Length option to ensure that each cell in the range C1:C10 will contain, at most, five characters (including blanks).

5. You are entering employee names in the cell range A1:A10. Use data validation to ensure that no employee's name is entered more than twice. (Hint: Use the Custom setting and the COUNTIF function.)

6. You are entering product ID codes in the cell range A1:A15. Product ID codes must always end with the characters *xyz*. Use data validation to ensure that each product ID code entered ends with *xyz*. (Hint: Use the Custom setting and the RIGHT function.)

7. Suppose you want every entry in the cell range B2:B15 to contain text and not a numerical value. Use data validation to ensure that entering a numerical value will return an error. (Hint: Use the ISTEXT function.)

8. Set up a data validation procedure that will ensure that all numbers typed in column E will contain exactly two decimal places. Hint: Use the LEN and FIND functions.

9. The file Latitude.xlsx contains a formula to compute distance between two cities from their latitude and longitude. The file also contains the latitude and longitude of various US cities. Set up a drop-down list so that when you select a city in cell P2 and another city in cell Q2, the distance between the cities is computed in Q10.

10. Ensure that if new cities are added to the list of cities in Problem 9, the drop-down list will include the new cities.

11. The file Candybardata.xlsx contains a list of stores where we sell candy bars. The worksheet also contains the types of candy bars we sell at each store and the price charged for each candy bar. Set up your worksheet so that users can enter or select both store and candy bar from a drop-down list, and then your price shows up in D19.

   ❑ Enable users to select a store from the drop-down box in B19.

   ❑ Set up a drop-down list in C13 to let users choose a type of candy from a list containing only those candies sold at a selected store. (Hint: Use the INDIRECT function when defining the list.)

   ❑ If we change the store in B19, then temporarily C19 may not list a candy sold at the newly selected store. Ensure that in C19 your worksheet says *Make selection above* if this is the case. For example, if B19 says *CVS* and C13 says *gumballs* then C19 should say *Make selection above*.

12. We have a $100,000 expense budget. In column A, we will enter expenses as the year incurred. Set up a data validation criterion that ensures that the total expenses listed in column E do not exceed our budget.

13. Set up a data validation criterion that ensures that a column of numbers is entered in descending order.

Chapter 36

Summarizing Data by Using Histograms

- People often say that a picture is worth a thousand words. Can I use Excel to create a picture (called a *histogram*) that summarizes the values in a data set?

- What are some common shapes of histograms?

- What can I learn by comparing histograms from different data sets?

The ability to summarize a large data set is important. The three tools used most often to summarize data in Microsoft Office Excel 2007 are *histograms*, *descriptive statistics*, and *PivotTables*. In this chapter, I'll discuss the use of histograms for summarizing data. I cover descriptive statistics in Chapter 37, "Summarizing Data by Using Descriptive Statistics," and PivotTables in Chapter 38, "Using PivotTables to Describe Data."

People often say that a picture is worth a thousand words. Can I use Excel to create a picture (called a histogram) that summarizes the values in a data set?

A histogram is a commonly used tool to summarize data. Essentially, a histogram tells us how many observations (another term for *data points*) fall in various ranges of values. For example, a histogram created from monthly Cisco stock returns might show how many monthly returns Cisco had from 0 percent through 10 percent, 11 percent through 20 percent, and so on. The ranges in which you group data are referred to as *bin ranges*.

Let's look at how to construct and interpret histograms that summarize the values of monthly returns for Cisco and GM stock in the years 1990–2000. You'll find this data (and returns for other stocks) in the file Stock.xlsx. Figure 36-1 on the next page shows a subset of the data (in the *Stockprices* worksheet). During March 1990, for example, Cisco stock increased in value by 1.075 percent.

	A	B	C	D	E	F
49				min	-0.24032043	-0.2025
50				max	0.276619107	0.33898
51	Date	Microsoft	GE	Intel	GM	CSCO
52	30-Mar-90	0.121518984	0.040485829	0.037267081	0.022284122	0.01075
53	30-Apr-90	0.047404062	-0.00389105	-0.05389221	-0.03542234	0.01064
54	31-May-90	0.258620679	0.083515622	0.221518993	0.115819208	0.04211
55	29-Jun-90	0.04109589	0.005444646	-0.02590674	-0.02056555	0.07071
56	31-Jul-90	-0.125	0.034296028	-0.05319149	-0.02099738	-0.0377
57	31-Aug-90	-0.07518797	-0.13438046	-0.25	-0.1313673	-0.0294
58	28-Sep-90	0.024390243	-0.11338709	-0.00374532	-0.08805031	-0.0909
59	31-Oct-90	0.011904762	-0.04587156	0.007518797	0.013793103	0.31111
60	30-Nov-90	0.13333334	0.052884616	0.119402982	0.013605442	0.33898
61	31-Dec-90	0.041522492	0.057260275	0.026666667	-0.05821918	0.13608
62	31-Jan-91	0.303986698	0.115468413	0.188311681	0.054545455	0.30362
63	28-Feb-91	0.057324842	0.070468754	0.043715846	0.100689657	-0.0427
64	28-Mar-91	0.022891566	0.023897059	-0.02094241	-0.0443038	-0.1295
65	30-Apr-91	-0.06713781	0.016157989	0.053475935	-0.05298013	0.22051
66	31-May-91	0.108585857	0.09908127	0.131979689	0.217482507	0.08403
67	28-Jun-91	-0.06890661	-0.0420712	-0.16591929	-0.05507246	-0.0543
68	31-Jul-91	0.078899086	-0.01013514	0.010752688	-0.02453988	0.28689
69	30-Aug-91	0.159863949	0.022184301	0.053191491	-0.03396227	0.15605
70	30-Sep-91	0.043988269	-0.06664441	-0.14646465	-0.01644737	-0.0964
71	31-Oct-91	0.054775283	-0.00540541	-0.03846154	-0.06020067	0.18902
72	29-Nov-91	0.035952065	-0.0615942	0.009230769	-0.11316726	0.01538
73	31-Dec-91	0.143958867	0.189961389	0.195121944	-0.06097561	0.33838
74	31-Jan-92	0.080898874	-0.01633987	0.221938774	0.121212125	0.13396

Figure 36-1   Monthly stock returns

When constructing histograms with Excel, you can let Excel define the bin ranges or you can define the bin ranges yourself. If Excel defines the bin ranges, you could end up with weird-looking bin ranges, such as –12.53 percent to 4.52 percent. For this reason, I prefer to define the ranges myself.

A good way to start defining bin ranges for a histogram (you can think of defining bin ranges as setting boundaries) is to divide the range of values (between the smallest and largest) into 8 to 15 equally spaced categories. All the monthly returns for Cisco are from –30 percent through 40 percent, so I chose bin range boundaries of –30 percent, –20 percent, –10 percent, 0 percent, and so on up to 40 percent.

To create our bin ranges, I first enter CSCO, .4, .3, .2,..., –.2, –.3 (the boundaries of the bin ranges) in cells H54:H62. Next, on the Data tab of the Ribbon, in the Analysis group, I click Data Analysis to open the Data Analysis dialog box. The dialog box lists the functions of the Analysis Toolpak, which contains many of the statistical capabilities of Excel.

> **Note**   If the Data Analysis command doesn't appear on the Data tab, click the Microsoft Office Button followed by Excel Options. In the Manage box, click Excel Add-Ins and click Go. In the Add-Ins dialog box, check the Analysis ToolPak box, and then click OK. Now you can access the Analysis ToolPak functions by clicking Data Analysis in the Analysis group on the Data tab.

By clicking Histogram in the Data Analysis dialog box, we open the Histogram dialog box shown in Figure 36-2.

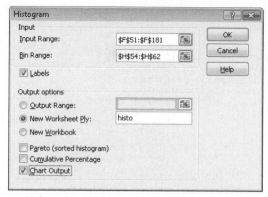

Figure 36-2   Histogram dialog box for the Cisco histogram

Here's how to fill in the dialog box as it's shown:

❑ Select the Input Range (F51:F181). (To select the range F51:F181, you can select cell F51 and then press Ctrl+Shift+Down Arrow key. This takes you to the bottom of the column.) This range includes all the data we want to use to create our histogram. I included the label CSCO from cell F51 because when you do not include a label in the first row, the x-axis of the histogram is often labeled with a number, which can be confusing.

❑ The Bin Range (H54:H62) includes the boundaries of our bin ranges. Excel will create bins of –30 percent through –20 percent, –20 percent through –10 percent, and so on up to 30–40 percent.

❑ I checked the Labels option because the first rows of both our bin range and input range contain labels.

❑ I chose to create the histogram in a new worksheet (named *histo*).

❑ Select Chart Output, or Excel will not create a histogram.

Click OK in the Histogram dialog box. Our Cisco histogram will look like the one shown in Figure 36-3.

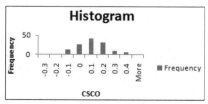

Figure 36-3   Cisco histogram created by using an Excel Analysis ToolPak function

When you create the histogram, you'll see gaps between the bars. To remove these gaps, right-click any bar on the graph and choose Format, Data Series. On the Series Options tab, drag Gap Width to 0%. You will also see that a label does not appear for each bar. If all the labels do not appear, you can make all labels appear. Select the graph and drag any handle that has two arrows to widen the graph. You can also reduce the font size to make a label appear. To reduce the font size, right-click the graph axis, and then right-click Font. Change the font size to 5. You can also change the title of the chart by selecting the text and entering the title you want. After making these changes, the histogram appears as its shown in Figure 36-4.

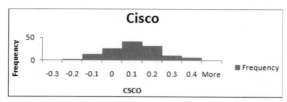

Figure 36-4   You can change the format of different elements in the chart.

Notice that Cisco returns are most likely between 0 and 10 percent per month, and the height of the bars drops off as the graph moves away from the tallest bar. When we create the histogram, we also obtain the bin-range frequency summary shown in Figure 36-5.

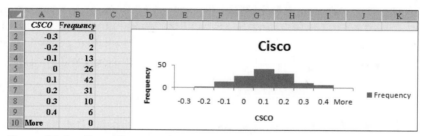

Figure 36-5   Cisco bin-range frequencies

From the bin-range frequencies, we learn, for example, that for two months, Cisco's return was greater than −30 percent and less than or equal to −20 percent; in 13 months, the monthly return was greater than −20 percent and less than or equal to −10 percent.

What are some common shapes of histograms?

For most data sets, a histogram created from the data will be classified as one of the following:

- ❏ Symmetric
- ❏ Skewed right (positively skewed)
- ❏ Skewed left (negatively skewed)
- ❏ Multiple peaks

Let's look at each type in more detail. See the file Skewexamples.xlsx.

- ❏ **Symmetric distribution.** A histogram is symmetric if it has a single peak and looks approximately the same to the left of the peak as to the right of the peak. Test scores (such as IQ tests) are often symmetric. For example, the histograms of IQs (see cell W42) might look like Figure 36-6. Notice that the height of the bars one bar away from the peak bar are approximately the same, the height of the bars two bars away from the peak bar are approximately the same, and so on. The bar labeled 105 represents all people with an IQ greater than 95 and less than or equal to 105, the bar labeled 65 represents all people having an IQ less than or equal to 65, and so on. Also note that Cisco monthly returns are approximately symmetric.

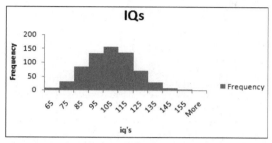

Figure 36-6   Symmetric histogram

❑ **Skewed right (positively skewed).** A histogram is skewed right (positively skewed) if it has a single peak and the values of the data set extend much farther to the right of the peak than to the left of the peak. Many economic data sets (such as family or individual income) exhibit a positive skew. Figure 36-7 (see cell T24) shows an example of a positively skewed histogram created from a sample of family incomes.

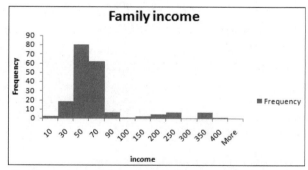

Figure 36-7   A positively skewed histogram created from data about family income.

❑ **Skewed left (negatively skewed).** A histogram is skewed left (negatively skewed) if it has a single peak and the values of the data set extend much farther to the left of the peak than to the right of the peak. Days from conception to birth are negatively skewed. An example is shown in cell Q7 of Figure 36-8 on the next page. The height of each bar represents the number of women whose time from conception to birth fell in the given bin range. For example, two women gave birth fewer than 180 days after conception.

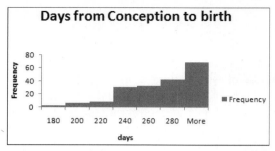

Figure 36-8   A negatively skewed histogram of data plotting days from conception to birth.

❑ **Multiple peaks.** When a histogram exhibits multiple peaks, it usually means that data from two or more populations are being graphed together. For example, suppose the diameter of elevator rails produced by two machines yields the histogram shown in Figure 36-9. See cell Q11 of the file Twinpeaks.xlsx.

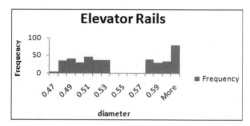

Figure 36-9   A multiple-peak histogram

In this histogram, the data clusters into two separate groups. In all likelihood, each group of data corresponds to the elevator rails produced by one of the machines. If we assume that the diameter we want for an elevator rail is .55 inches, we can conclude that one machine is producing elevator rails that are too short, whereas the other machine is producing elevator rails that are too long. We should follow up with our interpretation of this histogram by constructing a histogram charting the elevator rails produced by each machine. This example shows why histograms are a powerful tool in quality control.

What can I learn by comparing histograms from different data sets?

We're often asked to compare different data sets. For example, we might wonder how the monthly returns on GM and Cisco stock differ. To answer a question such as this, you can construct a histogram for GM by using the same bin ranges as for Cisco, and then place one histograms above the other, as shown in Figure 36-10. See the *Histograms* worksheet of file Stock.xlsx.

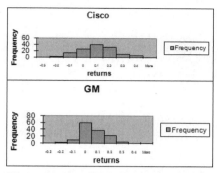

Figure 36-10 Using histograms that include the same bin ranges to compare different data sets

By comparing these two histograms, we can draw two important conclusions:

❑ Typically, Cisco performed better than GM. We know this because the highest bar for Cisco is one bar to the right of the highest bar for GM. Also, the Cisco bars extend farther to the right than the GM bars.

❑ Cisco had more variability, or spread about the mean, than GM. Note that GM's peak bar contains 59 months, whereas Cisco's peak bar contains only 41 months. This shows that for Cisco, more of the returns are outside the bin that represents the most likely Cisco return. Cisco returns are more "spread out" than GM returns.

In Chapter 37, we'll look at more details about the differences between the monthly returns on Cisco and GM.

Problems

1. Use the data in Stock.xlsx to construct histograms for monthly returns on GE and Intel.

2. Use the data in Historicalinvest.xlsx to create histograms for annual returns on stocks and bonds. Then compare the annual returns on these stocks and bonds.

3. You are given (in the file Deming.xlsx) the measured diameter (in inches) for 500 rods produced by Rodco, as reported by the production foreman. A rod is considered acceptable if it is at least 1 inch in diameter. In the past, the diameter of the rods produced by Rodco has followed a symmetric histogram.

   ❑ Construct a histogram of these measurements.

   ❑ Comment on any unusual aspects of the histogram.

   Can you guess what might have caused any unusual aspects of the histogram? (Hint: One of quality-guru Deming's 14 points is to "Drive Out Fear.")

Chapter 37

Summarizing Data by Using Descriptive Statistics

- What defines a typical value for a data set?
- How can I measure how much a data set spreads from its typical value?
- Together, what do the mean and standard deviation of a data set tell me about the data?
- How can I use descriptive statistics to compare data sets?
- For a given data point, can I easily find its percentile ranking within the data set? For example, how can I find the 90th percentile of a data set?
- How can I easily find the second largest or second smallest number in a data set?
- How can I rank numbers in a data set?
- What is the trimmed mean of a data set?
- When I select a range of cells, is there an easy way to get a variety of statistics that describe the data in those cells?
- Why do financial analysts often use the geometric mean to summarize the average return on a stock?

In Chapter 36, "Summarizing Data by Using Histograms," I showed how you can describe data sets by using histograms. In this chapter, I'll show how to describe a data set by using particular characteristics of the data, such as the mean, median, standard deviation, and variance—measures that Microsoft Office Excel 2007 groups together as *descriptive statistics*. You can obtain the descriptive statistics for a set of data by clicking Data Analysis on the Analysis tab of the Ribbon, and then selecting the Descriptive Statistics option. After you enter the relevant data and click OK, all the descriptive statistics of your data are displayed.

What defines a typical value for a data set?

To illustrate the use of descriptive statistics, let's return to the Cisco and GM monthly stock return data in the file Stock.xlsx. To create a set of descriptive statistics for this data, click Data Analysis on the Analysis tab, and then select Descriptive Statistics. Fill in the Descriptive Statistics dialog box as shown in Figure 37-1.

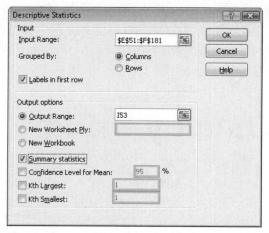

Figure 37-1   Descriptive Statistics dialog box

The Input Range is the monthly Cisco and GM returns, located in the range E51:F181 (including the labels in row 51). I filled in the remainder of the Descriptive Statistics dialog box as shown in Figure 37-1 for the following reasons:

❑ I selected Columns in the Grouped By options because each data set is listed in a different column.

❑ I checked the Labels In First Row box because the first row of the data range contains labels and not data.

❑ I selected cell I53 of the current worksheet as the first cell in the output range.

❑ By selecting Summary Statistics, I ensure that we get the most commonly used descriptive-statistics measures for both GM and Cisco monthly returns.

When you click OK, Excel calculates the descriptive statistics, as shown in Figure 37-2.

55	0.4	Mean	0.009276966 Mean
56	0.3	Standard Error	0.007864031 Standard Error
57	0.2	Median	-0.005420048 Median
58	0.1	Mode	#N/A Mode
59	0	Standard Deviatio	0.089663746 Standard Deviat
60	-0.1	Sample Variance	0.008039587 Sample Variance
61	-0.2	Kurtosis	0.474825023 Kurtosis
62	-0.3	Skewness	0.223940162 Skewness
63		Range	0.516939536 Range
64		Minimum	-0.240320429 Minimum
65		Maximum	0.276619107 Maximum
66		Sum	1.20600562 Sum
67		Count	130 Count
68			
69		mean-2s	-0.19
70		mean+2s	0.30

Figure 37-2   Descriptive statistics results for Cisco and GM stocks

Let's interpret the descriptive statistics that define a typical value (or a central location) for Cisco's monthly stock returns. The Descriptive Statistics output contains three measures of central location: mean (or average), median, and mode.

Mean   The mean of a data set is written as $\bar{x}$ and is simply the average of all observations in the sample. Thus, if the data values were $x_1, x_2,..., x_n$, then the following equation calculates the mean.

$$\bar{x} = \frac{1}{n} \sum_{i=1}^{i=n} x_i$$

Here, n equals the number of observations in the sample, and x_i is the ith observation in the sample. We find that Cisco's mean monthly return was 5.6 percent per month.

It is always true that the sum of the deviations of all values from the mean equals 0. Thus, you can think of a data set's mean as a "balancing point" for the data. Of course, without using the Descriptive Statistics option, we can obtain a sample's mean in Excel by applying the AVERAGE function to the appropriate cell range.

Median   The median of a sample is the "middle" observation, when the data is listed from smallest to largest. If a sample contains an odd number of observations, the median is the observation that has as many observations below it as above it. Thus, for a sample of 9, the median would be the fifth smallest (or fifth largest) observation. When a sample includes an even number of observations, you can simply average the two middle observations. Essentially, the median is the 50th percentile of the data. For example, the median monthly return on Cisco was 5 percent. We could also obtain this information by using the MEDIAN function.

Mode   The mode is the most frequently occurring value in the sample. If no value occurs more than once, the mode does not exist. For GM, no monthly return occurred more than once for the years 1990–2000, so the mode does not exist. For Cisco, the mode was approximately 5.14 percent. You can also use the MODE function to compute the mode. If no data value occurs more than once, the MODE function returns #NA.

The mode is rarely used as a measure of central location. It is interesting to note, however, that for a symmetric data set, the mean, median, and mode are equal.

A natural question is whether the mean or median is a better measure of central location. Essentially, we use the mean as the best measure of central location if the data set does not exhibit an excessive skew. Otherwise, we use the median as the measure of central location. If a data set is highly skewed, extreme values distort the mean. In this case, the median is a better measure of a typical data set value. For example, the U.S. government reports median family income instead of mean family income because family income is highly positively skewed.

The skewness measure reported by the Descriptive Statistics output informs us whether a data set is highly skewed.

- A skew greater than +1 indicates a high degree of positive skew.
- A skew less than −1 indicates a high degree of negative skew.
- A skew between −1 and +1 inclusive indicates a relatively symmetric data set.

Thus, monthly returns of GM and Cisco exhibit a slight degree of positive skewness. Because the skewness measure for each data set is less than +1, the mean is a better measure of a typical return than the median. You can also use the SKEW function to compute the skew of a data set.

Kurtosis   Kurtosis, which sounds like a disease, is not a very important measure. Kurtosis near 0 means a data set exhibits "peakedness" close to the normal (or standard Bell-shaped) curve. (I'll discuss the normal curve in Chapter 58, "The Normal Random Variable.") Positive kurtosis means that a data set is more peaked than a normal random variable, whereas negative kurtosis means that data is less peaked than a normal random variable. GM monthly returns are more peaked than a normal curve, whereas Cisco monthly returns are less peaked than a normal curve.

How can I measure how much a data set spreads from its typical value?

Let's consider two investments that each yield an average of 20 percent per year. Before deciding which investment we prefer, we'd like to know about the spread, or riskiness, of the investment. The most important measures of the spread (or dispersion) of a data set from its mean are sample variance, sample standard deviation, and range.

Sample variance and sample standard deviation   The sample variance s^2 is defined by the following formula.

$$s^2 = \frac{1}{n-1} \sum_{i=1}^{i=n} (x_i - \bar{x})^2$$

You can think of the sample variance as the average squared deviation of the data from its mean. Intuitively, it seems like we should divide by n to compute a true average squared deviation, but technical reasons require us to divide by $n-1$.

Dividing the sum of the squared deviations by $n-1$ ensures that our sample variance will be an unbiased measure of the true variance of the population from which the sampled data was drawn.

The sample standard deviation s is just the square root of s^2.

Here is an example of these computations for the three numbers 1, 3, and 5.

$$s^2 = \frac{1}{(3-1)} [(1-3)^2 + (3-3)^2 + (5-3)^2] = 4$$

Then we find that

$$s = \sqrt{4} = 2$$

We find that the sample standard deviation of monthly returns for Cisco is 12.2% with a sample variance of 0.015%^{2}. Naturally, %^{2} is hard to interpret, so we usually look at the sample standard deviation. For GM, the sample standard deviation is 8.97%.

Range   The range of a data set is the largest number in the data set minus the smallest number. We find that the range in the monthly Cisco returns is equal to 54 percent and the range for GM monthly returns is 52 percent.

Together, what do the mean and standard deviation of a data set tell me about the data?

Assuming that a histogram is symmetric, the rule of thumb tells us the following:

❑ Approximately 68 percent of all observations are between $\bar{x}-s$ and $\bar{x}+s$.

❑ Approximately 95 percent of all observations are between $\bar{x}-2s$ and $\bar{x}+2s$.

❑ Approximately 99.7 percent of all observations are between $\bar{x}-3s$ and $\bar{x}+3s$.

For example, we would expect approximately 95 percent of all Cisco monthly returns to be from −19 percent through 30 percent.

Mean−2s=.056−2*(.122)=−19% and Mean+2s=.056+2*(.122)=30%

Any observation more than two standard deviations away from the mean is called an *outlier*. For the Cisco data, 9 of 130 observations (or roughly 7 percent of all returns) are outliers. In general, the rule of thumb is less accurate for highly skewed data sets than it is for relatively symmetric data sets.

Many valuable insights can be obtained by finding causes of outliers. Companies should try to ensure that the causes of "good outliers" occur more frequently and the causes of "bad" outliers occur less frequently.

Using Conditional Formatting to Highlight Outliers

Figure 37-3   Outliers for Cisco highlighted with conditional formatting

Date	MSFT	GE	INTC	GM	CSCO
30-Mar-90	0.121519	0.0404858	0.0372671	0.0222841	0.01075
30-Apr-90	0.0474041	-0.003891	-0.053892	-0.035422	0.01064
31-May-90	0.2586207	0.0835156	0.221519	0.1158192	0.04211
29-Jun-90	0.0410959	0.0054446	-0.025907	-0.020566	0.07071
31-Jul-90	-0.125	0.034296	-0.053191	-0.020997	-0.03774
31-Aug-90	-0.075188	-0.13438	-0.25	-0.131367	-0.02941
28-Sep-90	0.0243902	-0.113387	-0.003745	-0.08805	-0.09091
31-Oct-90	0.0119048	-0.045872	0.0075188	0.0137931	0.31111
30-Nov-90	0.1333333	0.0528846	0.119403	0.0136054	0.33896
31-Dec-90	0.0415225	0.0572603	0.0266667	-0.058219	0.13608
31-Jan-91	0.3039867	0.1154684	0.1883117	0.0545455	0.30962
28-Feb-91	0.0573248	0.0704688	0.0437158	0.1006897	-0.04274
28-Mar-91	0.0228916	0.0238971	-0.020942	-0.044304	-0.12946
30-Apr-91	-0.067138	0.016158	0.0534759	-0.05298	0.22051
31-May-91	0.1085859	0.0990813	0.1319797	0.2174825	0.08403
28-Jun-91	-0.068907	-0.042071	-0.165919	-0.055072	-0.05426
31-Jul-91	0.0789991	-0.010135	0.0107527	-0.02454	0.26689
30-Aug-91	0.1598639	0.0221843	0.0531915	-0.033962	0.15605
30-Sep-91	0.0439883	-0.066644	-0.146465	-0.016447	-0.09642
31-Oct-91	0.0547753	-0.005405	-0.038462	-0.060201	0.18902
29-Nov-91	0.0359521	-0.061594	0.0092308	-0.113167	0.01538
31-Dec-91	0.1439589	0.1899614	0.1951219	-0.060976	0.33938

Additional summary values shown in the figure:

	value		
min	-0.24032	-0.203	90ile	0.20543201
max	0.2766191	0.339	Rank of Aug-98	0.038

CSCO statistics:

	CSCO		CSCO
Mean	0.055572635	Mean	0.055
Standard Error	0.010701017	Standard Error	0.01
Median	0.050069587	Median	0.050
Mode	0.051428571	Mode	0.05
Standard Deviation	0.122010367	Standard Deviation	0.12
Sample Variance	0.01488653	Sample Variance	0.014
Kurtosis	-0.319515017	Kurtosis	-0.70
Skewness	0.10465029	Skewness	0.104
Range	0.54149205	Range	0.541
Minimum	-0.202508956	Minimum	-0.20
Maximum	0.338983059	Maximum	0.338
Sum	7.224442489	Sum	7.224
Count	130	Count	130

mean−2s	-0.19
mean+2s	0.30

To begin, I computed the lower cutoff for an outlier (*mean–2s*) in cell J69 and the upper cutoff for an outlier (*mean+2s*) in cell J70. Next, I selected the entire range of Cisco returns (cells F52:F181). I then go to the first cell in the range (F52), select Conditional Formatting on the Home tab, and select New Rule. Then in the New Formatting Rule dialog box, select Use A Formula To Determine Which Cells To Format and fill in the rest of the dialog box as shown in Figure 37-4.

Figure 37-4   Conditional formatting rules to select outliers, as shown in the New Formatting Rule dialog box

This condition ensures that if cell F52 is either more than 2s above or below the mean monthly Cisco return, the format we select (a red font color in this case) will be applied to cell F52. This formatting condition is automatically copied to our selected range. Note that all outliers show up in red.

How can I use descriptive statistics to compare data sets?

As an example, you can use descriptive statistics to summarize the differences between Cisco and GM monthly returns. Looking at the shape and the measures and spread of a typical value, we can conclude the following:

- ❑ Typically (looking at either mean or median), Cisco monthly returns are higher than GM.

- ❑ Cisco monthly returns are more variable (looking at standard deviation, variance, and range) than monthly GM returns.

- ❑ Both Cisco and GM monthly returns exhibit slightly positive skews. GM monthly returns are more peaked than a normal curve, whereas Cisco monthly returns are less peaked than a normal curve.

For a given data point, can I easily find its percentile ranking within the data set? For example, how can I find the 90th percentile of a data set?

The PERCENTILE and PERCENTRANK functions are useful when you want to determine an observation's relative position in a data set.

The PERCENTILE function returns the percentile of a data set that you specify. The syntax of the PERCENTILE function is *PERCENTILE(data,k)*, which returns the *k*th percentile of the information in the cell range specified by *data*. For example, *k=.9* returns a value such that 90 percent of all data points are below the returned value, and *k=.10* returns a value such that 10 percent of all data points are below the returned value. To find the 90th percentile of the monthly Cisco returns, I entered in cell J49 the formula *PERCENTILE(CSCO,0.9)*. (The range F52:F181, where Cisco returns are recorded, is named *CSCO*.) As you can see in Figure 37-3, during 10 percent of all months, monthly returns on Cisco exceeded 20.5 percent.

The PERCENTILE function will yield the exact kth percentile only if k is an exact multiple of 1/(n−1). Thus, we would obtain the exact percentile for 1/129, 2/129,...,128/129. Otherwise, Excel interpolates in a complex fashion to obtain an approximation for the percentile specified.

The PERCENTRANK function returns the ranking of an observation relative to all values in a data set. The syntax of this function is *PERCENTRANK(data,value)*. For example, in cell J50, we calculate the percentage rank for August 1998 with the formula *PERCENTRANK(CSCO,F153)*. As shown in Figure 37-3, only 3.8 percent of all months yielded a return lower than August 1998.

> **Note** The PERCENTILE and PERCENTRANK functions are easily confused. To simplify, PERCENTILE yields a value of the data, whereas PERCENTRANK yields a percentage.

How can I easily find the second largest or second smallest number in a data set?

The formula *=LARGE(range,k)* returns the *k*th largest number in a cell range. The formula *=SMALL(range,k)* returns the *k*th smallest number in a cell range. For example, in the file Trimmean.xlsx, in cell F1 the formula *=LARGE(C4:C62,2)* returns the second largest number in the cell range C4:C62 (99), whereas in cell F2 the formula *=SMALL (C4:C62,2)* returns the second smallest number in the cell range C4:C62 (80). (See Figure 37-5 on the next page.)

	Scores	Rank			
1			2nd highest score	99	
2			2nd lowest score	80	
3	Scores	Rank	10% trimmed mean	90.03636	
4	93	20	5% trimmed mean	90.01754	
5	84	48			
6	88	38			
7	100	1			
8	86	45			
9	86	45			
10	95	12			
11	92	24			
12	88	38			
13	94	17			
14	97	5			
15	91	26			
16	92	24			
17	95	12			
18	93	20			
19	80	56			
20	89	32			
21	98	3			
22	98	3			
23	90	29			
24	89	32			
25	96	9			
26	91	26			
27	90	29			
28	84	48			

Figure 37-5   LARGE and SMALL functions and trimmed mean

How can I rank numbers in a data set?

With the RANK function, we can rank numbers in a data set. The syntax of the rank function is =RANK(number,array,0). This formula yields the rank of a number in a given array, where the largest number in the array is assigned rank 1, the second largest number is rank 2, and so on. The syntax =RANK(number,array,1) results in assigning a rank of 1 to the smallest number in the array, a rank of 2 to the second smallest number, and so on. In the file Trimmean.xlsx (see Figure 37-5), copying the formula =RANK(C4,$C$4, c62,0) from cell D4 to D5:D62 returns the rank of each test score. For example, the score of 100 in cell C7 was the highest score, whereas the scores of 98 in cells C21 and C22 tied for third highest.

What is the trimmed mean of a data set?

Extreme skew in a data set can distort the mean of the data set. In these situations, people usually use median as a measure of the data set's typical value. The median, how-ever, is unaffected by many changes in the data. For example, compare the following two data sets:

Set 1: −5, −3, 0, 1,3, 5, 7, 9,11,13,15

Set 2: −20, −18, −15, −10, −8, 5, 6, 7, 8, 9, 10

These have the same median (5), but the second data set should have a lower "typical" value than the first. The Excel TRIMMEAN function is less distorted by extreme values than the AVERAGE function, but is more influenced by extreme values than the median. The formula =TRIMMEAN(range,percent) computes the mean of a data set after deleting the top percent divided by 2 and bottom percent divided by 2 data points. For example, applying the TRIMMEAN function with *percent=10%* converts the mean after deleting the top 5% and bottom 5% of the data. For example, in cell F3 of the file Trimmean.xlsx the formula =TRIMMEAN(C4:C62,.10) in cell F3 computes the mean of the golf scores in C4:C62 after deleting the three highest and three lowest scores (result is 90.06). In cell F4, the formula =TRIMMEAN(C4:C62,.05) computes the mean of the golf scores in C4:C62 after deleting the top and bottom scores. This is because .05*59=2.95 would indicate the deletion of 1.48 of the largest observations and 1.48 of the smallest. Rounding off 1.48 results in deleting only the top and bottom observations. (See Figure 37-5.)

When I select a range of cells, is there an easy way to get a variety of statistics that describes the data in those cells?

As an example, select the cell range C4:C36 in the file Trimmean.xlsx. In the lower-right corner of your screen, the Excel status bar displays a cornucopia of statistics describing the numbers in the selected cell range. (See Figure 37-6.) For example, for the cell range C4:C36, the mean is 90.39, there are 33 numbers, the smallest value is 80, and the largest value is 100. If you right-click the status bar, you can change the displayed set of statistics.

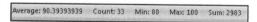

Average: 90.39393939   Count: 33   Min: 80   Max: 100   Sum: 2983

Figure 37-6   Status bar

Why do financial analysts often use the geometric mean to summarize the average return on a stock?

The file Geommean.xlsx contains the annual returns on two fictitious stocks. (See Figure 37-7.)

	B	C	D	E	F	G
1					Geometric mean	
2					example	
3						
4		Stock 1	Stock 2			
5	Year 1	0.05	-0.5			
6	Year 2	0.05	0.7			
7	Year 3	0.05	-0.5			
8	Year 4	0.05	0.7			
9	Average	0.05	0.1			
10						
11		1+return				
12		1.05	0.5			
13		1.05	1.7			
14		1.05	0.5			
15		1.05	1.7			
16	geometric means	0.05	-0.07805			

Figure 37-7   Geometric mean

Cell C9 indicates the average annual return on Stock 1 is 5 percent and the average annual return on Stock 2 is 10 percent. This would seem to indicate that Stock 2 is a better investment. If you think about it, however, what will probably happen with Stock 2 is that one year, you will lose 50 percent, and the next, gain 70 percent. This means that every two years $1.00 will become $1(1.7)(.5)=.85$. Because Stock 1 never loses money, we know that it is clearly the better investment. Using the geometric mean as a measure of average annual return helps us to correctly conclude that Stock 1 is the better investment. The geometric mean of n numbers is simply the nth root of the product of the numbers. For example, the geometric mean of 1 and 4 is the square root of 4 (2), whereas the geometric mean of 1, 2, and 4 is the cube root of 8 (also 2). To use the geometric mean to calculate an average annual return on an investment, we add 1 to each annual return and take the geometric mean of the resulting numbers. Then subtract 1 from this result to obtain an estimate of the stock's average annual return.

The formula *=GEOMMEAN(range)* finds the geometric mean of numbers in a range. Thus to estimate the average annual return on each stock, we proceed as follows:

- Compute *1+each annual return* by copying from C12 to C12:D15 the formula *=1+C5*.

- Copy from C16 to D16 the formula *=GEOMEAN(C12:C15)−1*.

We estimate that the annual average return on Stock 1 is 5 percent and the annual average return on Stock 2 is −7.8 percent. Note that if Stock 2 yields our mean return of −7.8 percent during two consecutive years, $1 will become $1(1-.078)^2=.85$, which agrees with common sense.

Problems

1. Use the data in the file Stock.xlsx to generate descriptive statistics for Intel and GE stock.

2. Use your answer to Problem 1 to compare the monthly returns on Intel and GE stock.

3. City Power & Light produces voltage-regulating equipment in New York and ships the equipment to Chicago. A voltage regulator is considered acceptable if it can hold a voltage of 25–75 volts. The voltage held by each unit is measured in New York before each unit is shipped. The voltage is measured again when the unit arrives in Chicago. A sample of voltage measurements from each city is given in the file Powercity.xlsx.

   - Using descriptive statistics, comment on what you have learned about the voltage held by units before and after shipment.

   - What percentage of units are acceptable before and after shipping?

   - Do you have any suggestions about how to improve the quality of City Power & Light's regulators?

   - Ten percent of all New York regulators have a voltage exceeding what value?

   - Five percent of all New York regulators have a voltage less than or equal to what value?

4. In the file Decadeincome.xlsx, you are given a sample of family incomes (in thousands of 1980 dollars) for a set of families sampled in 1980 and 1990. Assume that these families are representative of the whole United States. Republicans claim that the country was better off in 1990 than in 1980 because average income increased. Do you agree?

5. Use descriptive statistics to compare the annual returns on stocks, T-Bills, and corporate bonds. Use the data contained in the file Historicalinvest.xlsx.

6. In 1970 and 1971, eligibility for the Vietnam draft was determined on the basis of a draft lottery number. The number was determined by birth date. A total of 366 balls, one for each possible birth date, were placed in a container and shaken. The first ball selected was given the number *1* in the lottery, and so on. Men whose birthdays corresponded to the lowest numbers were drafted first. The file Draftlottery.xlsx contains the actual results of the 1970 and 1971 drawings. For example, in the 1970 drawing, January 1 received the number 305. Use descriptive statistics to demonstrate that the 1970 draft lottery was not random and the 1971 lottery was random (Hint: Use the AVERAGE and MEDIAN functions to compute the mean and median lottery number for each month.)

7. The file Jordan.xlsx gives the starting salaries (hypothetical) of all 1984 geography graduates from the University of North Carolina (UNC). What is your best estimate of a "typical" starting salary for a geography major? In reality, the major at UNC having the highest average starting salary in 1984 was actually geography. This was because Michael Jordan was a geography major!

8. Use the LARGE or SMALL function to sort the annual stock returns in the file Historicalinvest.xlsx. What advantage does this method of sorting have over clicking the Sort button?

9. Compare the mean, median, and trimmed mean (trimming 10 percent of the data) of the annual returns on stocks, T-Bills, and corporate bonds given in the file Historicalinvest.xlsx.

10. Use the geometric mean to estimate the mean annual return on stocks, bonds, and T-Bills in the file Historicalinvest.xlsx.

11. The file Dow.xlsx contains monthly returns on the 30 Dow stocks during the last 20 years. Use this data to determine the three stocks with largest mean monthly returns.

12. Using the Dow.xlsx data again, determine the three stocks with the most risk or variability.

13. Using the Dow.xlsx data again, determine the three stocks with the highest skew.

14. Using the Dow.xlsx data again, how do the trimmed mean returns (trim off 10 percent of the returns) differ from the overall mean returns?

Chapter 38
Using PivotTables to Describe Data

- What is a PivotTable?

- How can I use a PivotTable to summarize grocery sales at several grocery stores?

- What are the different PivotTable layouts available in Excel 2007?

- Why is a PivotTable called a PivotTable?

- How can I easily change the format in a PivotTable?

- How can I collapse and expand fields?

- How do I sort and filter PivotTable fields?

- How do I summarize a PivotTable by using a PivotChart?

- How do I use the Report Filter section of the PivotTable?

- How do I add blank rows or hide subtotals in a PivotTable?

- How do I apply conditional formatting to a PivotTable?

- How can I update my calculations when I add new data?

- I work for a small travel agency for which I need to mass-mail a travel brochure. My funds are limited, so I want to mail the brochure to people who spend the most money on travel. From information in a random sample of 925 people, I know the gender, the age, and the amount these people spent on travel last year. How can I use this data to determine how gender and age influence a person's travel expenditures? What can I conclude about the type of person to whom I should mail the brochure?

- I'm doing market research about Volvo Cross Country Wagons. I need to determine what factors influence the likelihood that a family will purchase a station wagon. From information in a large sample of families, I know the family size (large or small) and the family income (high or low). How can I determine how family size and income influence the likelihood that a family will purchase a station wagon?

- I work for a manufacturer that sells microchips globally. I'm given monthly actual and predicted sales for Canada, France, and the United States for Chip 1, Chip 2, and

Chip 3. I'm also given the variance, or *difference*, between actual and budgeted revenues. For each month and each combination of country and product, I'd like to display the following data: actual revenue, budgeted revenue, actual variance, actual revenue as a percentage of annual revenue, and variance as a percentage of budgeted revenue. How can I display this information?

- What is a calculated field?

- How do you use the Report Filter?

- How do you group items in a PivotTable?

- What is a calculated item?

- What is "drilling down"?

- I often have to use specific data in a PivotTable to determine profit, such as the April sales in France of Chip 1. Unfortunately, this data moves around when new fields are added to my PivotTable. Does Excel have a function that enables me to always extract April's Chip 1 sales in France from the PivotTable?

What is a PivotTable?

In numerous business situations, you need to analyze, or "slice and dice," your data to gain important business insights. Imagine that we sell different grocery products in different stores at different points in time. We might have hundreds of thousands of data points to track. PivotTables let us quickly summarize our data in almost any way imaginable. I call this "slicing and dicing data." For example, for our grocery store data, we could use a PivotTable to quickly determine the following:

- Amount spent per year in each store on each product

- Total spending at each store

- Total spending for each year

In the travel agency example, for instance, you would like to slice the data so that you can determine whether the average amount spent on travel is influenced by age or gender or by both factors. In the station wagon example, we'd like to compare the fraction of large families that buy a station wagon to the fraction of small families that purchase a station wagon. In the microchip example, we'd like to determine our total Chip 1 sales in France during April, and so on. A PivotTable is an incredibly powerful tool that can be used to slice and dice data. The easiest way to understand how a PivotTable works is to walk through some carefully constructed examples, so let's get started! We begin with an introductory example and then illustrate many advanced PivotTable features through subsequent examples.

How can I use a PivotTable to summarize grocery sales at several grocery stores?

The *Data* worksheet in the file Groceriespt.xlsx contains more than 900 rows of sales data. (See Figure 38-1.) Each row contains the number of units and revenue sold of a product at a store, as well as the month and year of the sale. The product group (either fruit, milk, cereal, or ice cream) is also included. We would like to see a breakdown of sales during each year of each product group and product at each store. We would also like to be able to show this breakdown during any subset of months in a given year (for example, what the sales were during January–June).

	C	D	E	F	G	H	I
2	Year	Month	Store	Group	Product	Units	Revenue
3	2007	August	south	milk	low fat	805	$ 3,187.80
4	2007	March	south	ice cream	Edies	992	$ 3,412.48
5	2007	January	east	milk	skim	712	$ 1,808.48
6	2006	March	north	ice cream	Edies	904	$ 2,260.00
7	2006	January	south	ice cream	Edies	647	$ 2,076.87
8	2005	September	west	fruit	plums	739	$ 1,707.09
9	2006	March	east	milk	low fat	974	$ 2,181.76
10	2007	June	north	fruit	apples	615	$ 1,894.20
11	2007	July	west	fruit	cherries	714	$ 1,856.40
12	2006	May	south	cereal	Special K	703	$ 1,553.63
13	2005	June	west	ice cream	Edies	528	$ 2,064.48
14	2006	October	east	cereal	Raisin Bran	644	$ 1,809.64
15	2005	June	south	fruit	grapes	919	$ 2,196.41
16	2007	May	west	milk	skim	767	$ 1,932.84
17	2007	June	west	cereal	Raisin Bran	984	$ 1,987.68
18	2005	March	south	cereal	Raisin Bran	744	$ 2,217.12
19	2007	September	east	ice cream	Edies	693	$ 2,189.88
20	2006	October	east	milk	chocolate	658	$ 1,895.04
21	2005	November	east	ice cream	Breyers	878	$ 3,274.94
22	2005	May	south	ice cream	Breyers	848	$ 3,281.76

Figure 38-1   Data for the grocery PivotTable example

Before creating a PivotTable, we must have headings in the first row of our data. Notice that our data contains headings (Year, Month, Store, Group, Product, Units, and Revenue) in row 2. Place your cursor anywhere in your data and on the Insert tab, in the Tables group, click PivotTable. Microsoft Office Excel will open the Create PivotTable dialog box and try to guess your data range. (In our case, Excel correctly guessed that our data range was C2:I924.) (See Figure 38-2.) By selecting Use An External Data Source, you can also refer to a database as a source for your PivotTable.

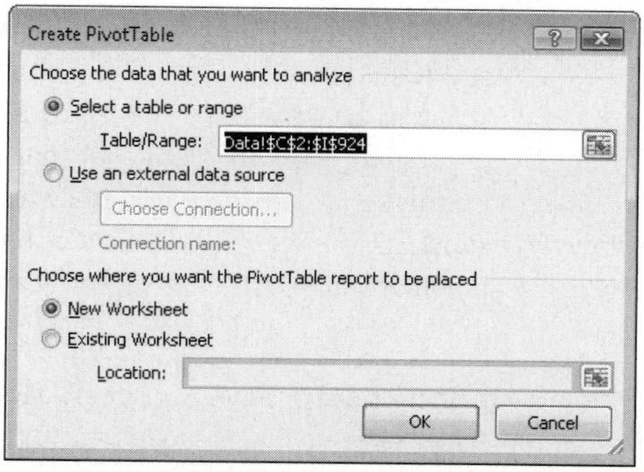

Figure 38-2   The Create PivotTable dialog box

After clicking OK, you will see the PivotTable Field List dialog box shown in Figure 38-3.

Figure 38-3   The PivotTable Field List dialog box

You fill in the PivotTable Field List dialog box by dragging PivotTable headings or fields into the desired boxes, or *zones*. This step is critical to ensuring that the PivotTable will summarize and display the data in the manner you wish. The four zones are as follows:

❑ **Row Labels.** Fields dragged here will be listed on the left side of the table in the order they are dragged. For example, we dragged to the Row Labels box the fields Year, Group, Product, and Store, in that order. This will cause Excel to summarize data first by Year; then for each product Group within a given a year; then by Product within each group, and finally break down each product by Store. You can at any time drag a field to a different zone or reorder the fields within a zone by dragging a field up or down in a zone or by clicking the arrow to the right of the field label.

❑ **Column Labels.** Fields dragged here will have their values listed across the top row of the PivotTable. To begin, we will have no fields in the Column Labels zone.

❑ **∑ Values.** Fields dragged here will be summarized mathematically in the table. We will drag Units and Revenue (in that order) to this zone. Excel tries to guess what kind of calculation you want to perform on a field. In our example, Excel guesses that we want to sum Revenue and Units, which happens to be correct. If you want to change the method of calculation for a data field to average, count, or something else, simply click the data field and choose Value Field Settings. I will give an example of how to use Value Field Settings later in the chapter.

❑ **Report Filter.** In Excel 2007, *Report Filter* is the new name for the old Page Field area. For fields dragged to the Report Filter area, we can easily pick any subset of the field values so the PivotTable will show calculations based only on that subset of field values. In our example, we dragged Month to the Report Filter area. Then we can easily select any subset of months, for example January–June, and our calculations are based on only those months.

Our completed PivotTable Field List dialog box is shown in Figure 38-4. The resulting PivotTable is shown in Figure 38-5 and in the *All Row Fields* worksheet of the workbook Groceriespt.xlsx. Before discussing the PivotTable, I'll give some advice on navigating worksheets (like this one) containing many worksheets. In the lower-right corner (to the left of the worksheet names) of your screen, you will see four arrows. Clicking the left-most arrow takes you to the first worksheet; clicking the right-most arrow shows the last worksheet; and clicking the other arrows moves you one worksheet to the left or right.

To see the Field list, you need to be in a field in the PivotTable. If you do not see the Field list, right-click any cell in the PivotTable and select Show Field List.

Figure 38-4   Completed PivotTable Field List dialog box

Our resulting PivotTable is in the *All Row Fields* worksheet. (See Figure 38-5.) In row 6, we see that 233,161 units were sold for $702,395.82 in 2007. In row 30, we find that 2719 units of Ben and Jerry's ice cream were sold in the west store for $9,627.41 in 2007.

	A	B	C
6	⊟2007	233161	702395.82
7	⊟milk	56981	170623.06
8	⊟chocolate	10430	30567.38
9	west	4379	12668.95
10	south	1545	4528.31
11	north	2322	7579.02
12	east	2184	5791.1
13	⊟low fat	17573	53902.15
14	west	4668	15042.24
15	south	2431	7606.76
16	north	7957	23490.32
17	east	2517	7762.83
18	⊟skim	14782	44234.18
19	west	3571	9951.37
20	south	2778	8881.2
21	north	3594	10792.09
22	east	4839	14609.52
23	⊟whole	14196	41919.35
24	west	3252	8311.84
25	south	1562	4495.15
26	north	2621	7640.88
27	east	6761	21471.48
28	⊟ice cream	55693	169327.53
29	⊟Ben and Jerry's	7542	24011.45
30	west	2719	9627.41

Figure 38-5   The Grocery PivotTable in compact form

What are the different PivotTable layouts available in Excel 2007?

The PivotTable layout shown in Figure 38-5 is called the *compact form*. In the compact form, the Row fields are shown one on top of another. To change the layout, place your cursor anywhere within the table, and on the Design tab, in the Layout Group, click Report Layout. and choose one of the following: Show In Compact Form (see Figure 38-5), Show In Outline Form (see Figure 38-6 and the *Outline Form* worksheet), or Show In Tabular Form (Figure 38-7 and the *Tabular Form* worksheet).

	A	B	C	D	E	F
2	Month	(All) ▾		Outline form		
3						
4					Values	
5	Year ▾	Group ▾	Product ▾	Store ▾	Sum of Units	Sum of Revenue
6		⊟2007			233161	702395.82
7		⊟milk			56981	170623.06
8			⊟chocolate		10430	30567.38
9				west	4379	12668.95
10				south	1545	4528.31
11				north	2322	7579.02
12				east	2184	5791.1
13			⊟low fat		17573	53902.15
14				west	4668	15042.24
15				south	2431	7606.76
16				north	7957	23490.32
17				east	2517	7762.83
18			⊟skim		14782	44234.18
19				west	3571	9951.37
20				south	2778	8881.2
21				north	3594	10792.09
22				east	4839	14609.52
23			⊟whole		14196	41919.35
24				west	3252	8311.84
25				south	1562	4495.15
26				north	2621	7640.88

Figure 38-6   The outline form

	A	B	C	D	E	F
2	Month	(All) ▾		Tabular form		
3						
4					Values	
5	Year ▾	Group ▾	Product ▾	Store ▾	Sum of Units	Sum of Revenue
6		⊟2007	⊟milk	⊟chocolate	west	4379	12668.95
7					south	1545	4528.31
8					north	2322	7579.02
9					east	2184	5791.1
10				chocolate Total		10430	30567.38
11				⊟low fat	west	4668	15042.24
12					south	2431	7606.76
13					north	7957	23490.32
14					east	2517	7762.83
15				low fat Total		17573	53902.15
16				⊟skim	west	3571	9951.37
17					south	2778	8881.2
18					north	3594	10792.09
19					east	4839	14609.52
20				skim Total		14782	44234.18
21				⊟whole	west	3252	8311.84
22					south	1562	4495.15
23					north	2621	7640.88
24					east	6761	21471.48
25				whole Total		14196	41919.35
26			milk Total			56981	170623.06

Figure 38-7   The tabular form

Why is a PivotTable called a PivotTable?

We can easily "pivot" fields from a row to a column and vice versa to create a different layout. For example, by dragging the Year field to the column field, we find the PivotTable layout shown in Figure 38-8 (see the *Years Column* worksheet).

	A	B	C	D	E	F	G
2	Month	(All)					
3							
4		**Column Labels**					
5		**2007**		**2006**		**2005**	
6	**Row Labels**	**Sum of Units**	**Sum of Revenue**	**Sum of Units**	**Sum of Revenue**	**Sum of Units**	**Sum of Revenue**
7	⊟milk	56981	170623.06	54117	162606.44	62974	178853.28
8	⊟chocolate	10430	30567.38	8056	24960.9	18063	53011.54
9	west	4379	12668.95			6326	17483.25
10	south	1545	4528.31	3732	10691.19	5237	15688.3
11	north	2322	7579.02	1505	5857.06	2200	5261.65
12	east	2184	5791.1	2819	8412.65	4300	14578.34
13	⊟low fat	17573	53902.15	17421	54380.63	20698	56663.71
14	west	4668	15042.24	6091	19667.95	6183	17261.35
15	south	2431	7606.76	2929	9482.11	3648	10197.44
16	north	7957	23490.32	4489	14235.35	4034	11723.98
17	east	2517	7762.83	3912	10995.22	6833	17480.94
18	⊟skim	14782	44234.18	11102	32314.84	12662	38446.44
19	west	3571	9951.37	3572	11213.49	2809	8413.33
20	south	2778	8881.2	4732	13021.17	3569	9872.84
21	north	3594	10792.09	1880	4610.14	1922	7268.71
22	east	4839	14609.52	918	3470.04	4362	12891.56
23	⊟whole	14196	41919.35	17538	50950.07	11551	30731.59
24	west	3252	8311.84	5866	15763.65		
25	south	1562	4495.15	3313	11038.24	3156	8323.8
26	north	2621	7640.88	2358	6608.96	3502	9231.37

Figure 38-8 The Years field pivoted to the column field

How can I easily change the format in a PivotTable?

If you want to change the format of an entire column field, simply double-click the column heading and select Number Format from the Value Field Settings dialog box. Then apply the desired format. For example, in the *Formatted $s* worksheet, we formatted the Revenue field as currency by double-clicking the Sum of Revenue heading and applying a currency format. You can also change the format of a value field by clicking the arrow to the right of the Value field in the PivotTable Field List dialog box. Then select Value Field Settings followed by Number Format, and you can reformat the column as desired.

From any cell in the PivotTable, you can select the Design tab on the Ribbon. Then many PivotTable styles become available.

How can I collapse and expand fields?

Expanding and collapsing fields is a great new Excel 2007 feature. In Figure 38-5, you see minus (–) signs by each year, group, and product. Clicking the minus sign will collapse a field and change the sign to a plus (+) sign. Clicking the plus sign will expand the field. For example, if you click the minus sign by *cereal* in A6, you will find that in each year, cereal is contracted to one row, and the various cereals are no longer listed. See Figure 38-9 and the *Cerealcollapse* worksheet. Clicking the plus sign in cell A6 will bring back the detailed or expanded view including all the cereals.

	A	B	C
1	Month	(All)	
2			
3		**Values**	
4	**Row Labels**	**Sum of Units**	**Sum of Revenue**
5	⊟2005	243228	728218.68
6	⊞cereal	63689	192172.93
7	⊟fruit	60047	182813.88
8	⊟apples	14535	48127.74
9	east	1229	3972.44
10	north	3734	13631.83
11	south	4317	14763.88
12	west	5255	15759.59
13	⊟cherries	11083	32042.39
14	east	1646	4051.22
15	north	3701	11087.14
16	south	3277	9092.92
17	west	2459	7811.11
18	⊟grapes	20005	60126.15
19	east	4811	13052.68
20	north	4865	14698.63
21	south	6268	20474.65
22	west	4061	11900.19

Figure 38-9   The cereal field collapsed

We can also expand or contract an entire field! To expand or contract an entire field, go to any row containing a member of that field and select PivotTable Tools Options on the Ribbon. Then click either the green Expand Entire Field button (labeled with a plus sign) or the red Contract Entire Field button (labeled with a minus sign) from the Active Field group on the Ribbon. (See Figure 38-10.)

Figure 38-10   The Expand Entire Field and Contract Entire Field buttons

For example, suppose you simply want to see for each year the sales by product group. Pick any cell containing a group's name (for example, A6), select PivotTable Tools Options on the Ribbon, and click the Collapse Entire Field button. You will see the result shown in Figure 38-11 on the next page (*Groups* worksheet collapsed). Selecting the Expand Entire Field button would bring us back to our original view.

	A	B	C
1	Month	(All)	
2			
3		**Values**	
4	Row Labels ▼	Sum of Units	Sum of Revenue
5	⊟2005	243228	728218.68
6	⊞cereal	63689	192172.93
7	⊞fruit	60047	182813.88
8	⊞ice cream	56518	174378.59
9	⊞milk	62974	178853.28
10	⊟2006	216738	637719.85
11	⊞cereal	52489	150710
12	⊞fruit	53910	157192.37
13	⊞ice cream	56222	167211.04
14	⊞milk	54117	162606.44
15	⊟2007	233161	702395.82
16	⊞cereal	58671	172828.96
17	⊞fruit	61816	189616.27
18	⊞ice cream	55693	169327.53
19	⊞milk	56981	170623.06
20	**Grand Total**	693127	2068334.35

Figure 38-11   The Group field collapsed

How do I sort and filter PivotTable fields?

In Figure 38-5, the products are listed alphabetically within each group. For example, *chocolate* is the first type of milk listed. If we want the products to be listed in reverse alphabetical order, simply move the cursor to any cell containing a product (for example, A7 of the *All Row Fields* worksheet) and click the drop-down arrow to the right of the Row Labels entry in A5. You will see the list of filtering options shown in Figure 38-12. Selecting Sort Z To A would ensure that *whole milk* is listed first for milk, *plums* is listed first for fruit, and so on. Our current table displays results first from 2007, then 2006, then 2005. If we wanted to see the Year 2005 first, simply move the cursor to any cell containing a year (for example, A5) and choose Sort Smallest To Largest from the available options.

Note that from the bottom of the filtering options dialog box, we can also select any subset of products to be visible. You may want to first clear Select All and then select the products you want to show.

Figure 38-12   PivotTable filtering options for the Product field

For another example of filtering, look at the file Ptcustomers.xlsx, shown in Figure 38-13 on the next page. The worksheet data contains for each customer transaction the customer number, amount paid, and the quarter of the year in which payment was received. After dragging Customer to the Row Labels box, Quarter to the Column Labels box, and Paid to the Σ Values box, the PivotTable shown in Figure 38-14 on the next page is displayed (see the *Ptable* worksheet in the Pcustomers.xlsx file).

	F	G	H
4	**Customer**	**Paid**	**Quarter**
5	20	8048	4
6	6	7398	4
7	10	5280	2
8	28	3412	3
9	8	3316	1
10	17	821	2
11	4	7024	3
12	20	1379	1
13	27	1924	2
14	23	631	3
15	28	9743	4
16	8	8192	2
17	19	875	1
18	3	9803	4
19	24	7344	3
20	13	6114	1
21	9	6728	4
22	2	4554	1
23	16	8230	4
24	25	1296	1
25	30	4179	1
26	8	7801	2
27	3	1803	1
28	18	1166	4

Figure 38-13   The Customer PivotTable data

	A	B	C	D	E	F
3	**Sum of Paid**	**Column Labels**				
4	**Row Labels**	**1**	**2**	**3**	**4**	**Grand Total**
5	1	30965	42039	57790	43417	174211
6	2	96038	121118	59089	45355	321600
7	3	57419	33589	61960	97548	250516
8	4	48947	79352	63052	59520	250871
9	5	57270	86555	69517	33471	246813
10	6	75639	71976	55212	78644	281471
11	7	53130	65768	49064	89018	256980
12	8	33289	74001	45219	43512	196021
13	9	61611	99009	61075	50945	272640
14	10	31785	71213	60417	63835	227250
15	11	59127	35567	62130	107832	264656
16	12	71862	21670	67312	63558	224402
17	13	100626	56058	39500	75109	271293
18	14	74240	63023	36217	77218	250698
19	15	30612	62277	45561	52567	191017
20	16	41870	71490	64909	57120	235389
21	17	61811	85706	46978	40802	235297
22	18	24456	44916	55519	81421	206312
23	19	89591	53157	37558	38247	218553
24	20	68349	104140	35083	69424	276996
25	21	77336	37476	51815	57065	223692
26	22	31149	77333	104364	65664	278510
27	23	87124	56387	63290	71953	278754

Figure 38-14   The Customer PivotTable

Naturally, we might like to show a list of just our top 10 customers. To obtain this layout, simply click the Row Labels arrow and select Value Filters. Then choose Top 10 items to obtain the resulting layout shown in Figure 38-15 (see the *Top 10 cus* worksheet). Of course, by selecting Clear Filter, you can return to the original layout.

	A	B	C	D	E	F
3	Sum of Paid	Column Labels				
4	Row Labels	1	2	3	4	Grand Total
5	2	96038	121118	59089	45355	321600
6	6	75639	71976	55212	78644	281471
7	9	61611	99009	61075	50945	272640
8	11	59127	35567	62130	107832	264656
9	13	100626	56058	39500	75109	271293
10	20	68349	104140	35083	69424	276996
11	22	31149	77333	104364	65664	278510
12	23	87124	56387	63290	71953	278754
13	27	45214	89826	56302	71285	262627
14	28	53737	69938	73471	69135	266281
15	Grand Total	678614	781352	609516	705346	2774828

Figure 38-15   Top 10 customers

Suppose you simply want to see the top customers that generate 50 percent of your revenue. Select the Row Labels filtering icon, select Value Filters, Top 10, and fill in the dialog box as shown in Figure 38-16.

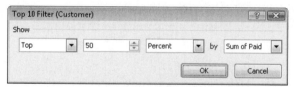

Figure 38-16   Configuring the Top 10 Filter dialog box to show customers generating 50 percent of revenue

The resulting PivotTable is in the *Top half* worksheet. (See Figure 38-17.) Thus, our top 14 customers generate a little more than half our revenue.

	A	B	C	D	E	F
3	Sum of Paid	Column Labels				
4	Row Labels	1	2	3	4	Grand Total
5	2	96038	121118	59089	45355	321600
6	3	57419	33589	61960	97548	250516
7	4	48947	79352	63052	59520	250871
8	6	75639	71976	55212	78644	281471
9	7	53130	65768	49064	89018	256980
10	9	61611	99009	61075	50945	272640
11	11	59127	35567	62130	107832	264656
12	13	100626	56058	39500	75109	271293
13	14	74240	63023	36217	77218	250698
14	20	68349	104140	35083	69424	276996
15	22	31149	77333	104364	65664	278510
16	23	87124	56387	63290	71953	278754
17	27	45214	89826	56302	71285	262627
18	28	53737	69938	73471	69135	266281
19	Grand Total	912350	1023084	819809	1028650	3783893

Figure 38-17   The top customers generating half of the revenues

Now let's suppose we want to sort our customers by their Quarter 1 revenue (see the *Sorted q1* worksheet). We right-click anywhere in the Quarter 1 column, point to Sort, and then click Sort Largest To Smallest. (See Figure 38-18.) The resulting PivotTable is shown in Figure 38-19. Note that Customer 13 paid us the most in Quarter 1, Customer 2 paid us the second most, and so on.

Figure 38-18   Sorting on the Quarter 1 column

	A	B	C	D	E	F
3	**Sum of Paid**	**Column Labels**				
4	**Row Labels**	**1**	**2**	**3**	**4**	**Grand Total**
5	13	100626	56058	39500	75109	271293
6	2	96038	121118	59089	45355	321600
7	19	89591	53157	37558	38247	218553
8	23	87124	56387	63290	71953	278754
9	21	77336	37476	51815	57065	223692
10	6	75639	71976	55212	78644	281471
11	14	74240	63023	36217	77218	250698
12	12	71862	21670	67312	63558	224402
13	20	68349	104140	35083	69424	276996
14	17	61811	85706	46978	40802	235297
15	9	61611	99009	61075	50945	272640
16	26	59994	70594	50446	44050	225084
17	30	59599	64192	44335	42944	211070
18	11	59127	35567	62130	107832	264656
19	3	57419	33589	61960	97548	250516
20	5	57270	86555	69517	33471	246813
21	28	53737	69938	73471	69135	266281
22	7	53130	65768	49064	89018	256980
23	4	48947	79352	63052	59520	250871

Figure 38-19   Customers sorted on Quarter 1 revenue

How do I summarize a PivotTable by using a PivotChart?

Excel makes it easy to visually summarize PivotTables by using PivotCharts. The key to laying out the data the way you want it charted in a PivotChart is to use methods such as sorting data and collapsing or expanding fields. In our grocery example, suppose we want to summarize the trend over time of each food group's unit sales. See the *Chart 1* worksheet in the file Groceriespt.xlsx. Then we should move the Year field to a Column field and delete Revenue as a ∑ Values field. We also need to collapse the entire Group field in the Row Labels zone. Now we are ready to create our first PivotChart. Simply click anywhere inside the table and select Options, PivotChart. You can now pick the chart type you want created. We chose the fourth Line Graph option, which displays the chart in Figure 38-20. For example, the chart shows us that milk sales were highest in 2005 and lowest in 2006.

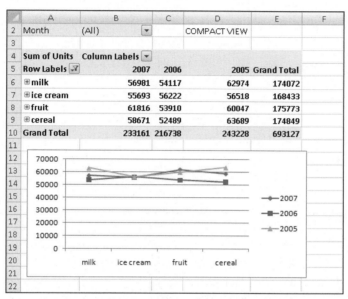

Figure 38-20   PivotChart for unit group sales trend

How do I use the Report Filter section of the PivotTable?

Recall that we placed Months in the Report Filter section of the table. To see how we use the Report Filter, suppose that we want to summarize sales for the months January–June. By clicking the Filter icon in cell B2 of the *First 6 months* worksheet, we can select January–June. This results in the PivotTable shown in the *First 6 Months* worksheet, which summarizes the number of units sold by product, group, and year for the months January–June. (See Figure 38-21 on the next page.)

	A	B	C
2	Month	(Multiple Items) ⬇	
3			
4		**Values**	
5	**Row Labels** ⬇	**Sum of Units**	**Sum of Revenue**
6	⊟2007	115258	346295.58
7	⊟milk	30069	89222.68
8	⊟chocolate	4875	14077.99
9	west	2014	5839.06
10	south	736	2141.76
11	north	1437	4136.37
12	east	688	1960.8
13	⊟low fat	9447	27341.25
14	west	3285	10732.35
15	south	531	1062
16	north	3905	10212.44
17	east	1726	5334.46
18	⊟skim	10182	30450.57
19	west	2156	6169.53
20	south	2778	8881.2
21	north	2521	7726.56
22	east	2727	7673.28
23	⊟whole	5565	17352.87
24	west	735	1764

Figure 38-21   A PivotTable summarizing January–June sales

How do I add blank rows or hide subtotals in a PivotTable?

If you want to add a blank row between each grouped item, simply select PivotTable Tools Design on the Ribbon, click Blank Rows, and then click Insert Blank Line after Each Item. If you want to hide subtotals or grand totals, select PivotTable Tools Design on the Ribbon and then select Subtotals or Grand Totals. After adding blank rows and hiding all totals, we obtain the table in the *Blank rows no totals* worksheet. (See Figure 38-22.) After right clicking when in any PivotTable cell, you may select PivotTable Options, thereby bringing up the PivotTable Options dialog box. From this dialog box, you can replace empty cells by using any character, such as an underscore (_), or by using a 0.

	A	B	C
2	Month	(All)	
3			
4		**Values**	
5	**Row Labels**	**Sum of Units**	**Sum of Revenue**
6	⊟2007		
7	⊟milk		
8	⊟chocolate		
9	west	4379	12668.95
10	south	1545	4528.31
11	north	2322	7579.02
12	east	2184	5791.1
13			
14	⊟low fat		
15	west	4668	15042.24
16	south	2431	7606.76
17	north	7957	23490.32
18	east	2517	7762.83
19			
20	⊟skim		
21	west	3571	9951.37
22	south	2778	8881.2
23	north	3594	10792.09
24	east	4839	14609.52
25			
26	⊟whole		
27	west	3252	8311.84
28	south	1562	4495.15
29	north	2621	7640.88
30	east	6761	21471.48

Figure 38-22   Grocery PivotTable without totals

How do I apply conditional formatting to a PivotTable?

Suppose we want to apply data bars to the Units column of our PivotTable. The problem is that our subtotals and grand totals will have large data bars and also make the other data bars smaller than they should be. We want the data bars to apply to all product sales, not the subtotals and grand totals. See the *Cond form* worksheet of workbook Groceriespt.xlsx. To apply the data bars to only the unit sales by product, begin by placing the cursor in a cell containing a product (for example, chocolate milk in B8) and then select the Sum Of Units column data (cell range B7:B227). Now, on the Home tab of the Ribbon, click Conditional Formatting, followed by Data Bars, and choose More Rules. You will see the New Formatting Rule dialog box shown in Figure 38-23 on the next page.

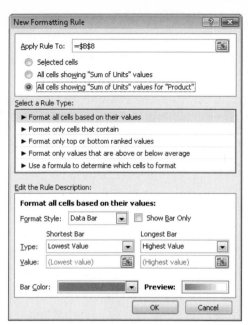

Figure 38-23 New Formatting Rule dialog box for using conditional formatting with PivotTables

By selecting All Cells Showing "Sum of Units" Values For "Product" we ensure that our data bars will apply to only cells listing unit sales for products. This results in the data bars shown in the *Cond form* worksheet and Figure 38-24.

	A	B	C
2	Month	(All)	
3			
4		**Values**	
5	**Row Labels**	**Sum of Units**	**Sum of Revenue**
6	⊟2007	233161	702395.82
7	⊟milk	56981	170623.06
8	⊟chocolate	10430	30567.38
9	west	4379	12668.95
10	south	1545	4528.31
11	north	2322	7579.02
12	east	2184	5791.1
13	⊟low fat	17573	53902.15
14	west	4668	15042.24
15	south	2431	7606.76
16	north	7957	23490.32
17	east	2517	7762.83
18	⊟skim	14782	44234.18
19	west	3571	9951.37
20	south	2778	8881.2
21	north	3594	10792.09
22	east	4839	14609.52
23	⊟whole	14196	41919.35
24	west	3252	8311.84
25	south	1562	4495.15
26	north	2621	7640.88
27	east	6761	21471.48
28	⊟ice cream	55693	169327.53
29	⊟Ben and Jerry's	7542	24011.45

Figure 38-24 Data bars for a PivotTable

How can I update my calculations when I add new data?

If the data in your original set of rows changes, you can update your PivotTable to include the data changes by simply right-clicking the table and selecting Refresh. You can also select Refresh after choosing options.

If you want new data to be automatically included in your PivotTable calculations when you refresh, then you should name your original data set as a table (see Chapter 24, "Tables") by selecting Ctrl+T. Then when you add new data and refresh, your new data will automatically be included in the PivotTable calculations!

If you want to change the range of data used to create a PivotTable, you can always select Change Data Source from the Options tab. You can also move the table to a different location by selecting Move PivotTable.

I work for a small travel agency for which I'm about to mass-mail a travel brochure. My funds are limited, so I want to mail the brochure to people who spend the most money on travel. From information in a random sample of 925 people, I know the gender, the age, and the amount these people spent on travel last year. How can I use this data to determine how gender and age influence a person's travel expenditures? What can I conclude about the type of person to whom I should mail the brochure?

To understand this data, we need to break it down into the following:

❑ Average amount spent on travel by gender

❑ Average amount spent on travel for each age group

❑ Average amount spent on travel by gender for each age group

Our data is included on the *Data* worksheet in the file Traveldata.xlsx. A sample of the data is shown in Figure 38-25 on the next page. For example, our first person is a 44-year-old male who spent $997 on travel.

Let's first get a breakdown of spending by gender. To obtain this breakdown, we begin by selecting Insert PivotTable. Excel extracts the range A2:D927. After clicking OK, we put the cursor in the table so the field list appears. Next, we drag the Gender column to the Row Labels zone and drag Amount Spent On Travel to the Σ Values zone. This results in the PivotTable shown in Figure 38-26 on the next page.

We can tell from the heading Sum Of Amount Spent On Travel that we are summarizing the total amount spent on travel, but we actually want the average amount spent on travel by men and women. To calculate these quantities, we double-click Sum Of Amount Spent On Travel and then select Average from the Value Field Settings dialog box, shown in Figure 38-27 on the next page.

	A	B	C
2	**Amount Spent on Travel**	**Age**	**Gender**
3	997	44	M
4	850	39	F
5	997	43	M
6	951	41	M
7	993	50	F
8	781	39	F
9	912	45	F
10	649	59	M
11	1265	25	M
12	680	38	F
13	800	41	F
14	613	32	F
15	993	46	F
16	1059	38	M
17	939	42	F
18	841	44	F
19	828	38	F
20	1004	50	F
21	983	48	F
22	837	46	M
23	924	42	M
24	852	48	M
25	963	39	M
26	1046	36	M

Figure 38-25 Travel agency data showing amount spent on travel, age, and gender

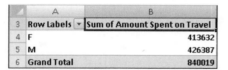

	A	B
3	**Row Labels** ▼	**Sum of Amount Spent on Travel**
4	F	413632
5	M	426387
6	**Grand Total**	840019

Figure 38-26 PivotTable summarizing the total travel expenditures by gender

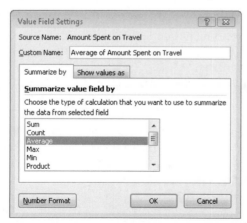

Figure 38-27 You can select a different summary function in the Value Field Settings dialog box.

We now obtain the results shown in Figure 38-28.

	A	B
3	Row Labels ▾	Average of Amount Spent on Travel
4	F	901.1590414
5	M	914.9935622
6	Grand Total	908.1286486

Figure 38-28   Average travel expenditures by gender

We find that, on average, people spend $908.13 on travel. Women spend an average of $901.16, whereas men spend $914.99. This PivotTable indicates that gender has little influence on the propensity to travel. By clicking the Row Labels arrow, you can show just male or female results.

Now we want to see how age influences travel spending. To remove Gender from the PivotTable, simply click Gender in the Row Labels portion of the PivotTable Field List and remove it from the Row Labels area. Then, to break down spending by age, drag Age to the row area. The PivotTable now appears as it's shown in Figure 38-29.

	A	B
3	Row Labels ▾	Average of Amount Spent on Travel
4	25	948.9666667
5	26	889.04
6	27	1061.16
7	28	960.952381
8	29	814
9	30	877.3333333
10	31	1038.904762
11	32	876.875
12	33	913.2592593
13	34	920.2916667
14	35	886.1176471
15	36	859.173913
16	37	904.1666667
17	38	913.8
18	39	887.6551724
19	40	925.3529412
20	41	906.7142857
21	42	900.8947368
22	43	869.5652174
23	44	907.8275862
24	45	897.56
25	46	904.2
26	47	901.7727273
27	48	897.7083333
28	49	887.9473684
29	50	922.68
30	51	878.9259259
31	52	907.1111111
32	53	895.1666667
33	54	876.4166667

Figure 38-29   PivotTable showing the average travel expenditures by age

We find that age seems to have little effect on travel expenditures. In fact, this PivotTable is pretty useless in its present state. We need to group data by age to see any trends. To group our results by age, right-click anywhere in the Age column and choose Group. In the Grouping dialog box, you can designate the interval by which to define an age group. Using 10-year increments, we obtain the PivotTable shown in Figure 38-30 on the next page.

We now find that 25–34 year olds on average spend $935.84 on travel, 55–64 year olds spend $903.57 on travel, and so on. This information is more useful, but it still indicates that people of all ages tend to spend about the same amount on travel. This view of our data does not help determine who we should mail our brochure to.

	A	B
3	Row Labels	Average of Amount Spent on Travel
4	25-34	935.8355556
5	35-44	895.7180617
6	45-54	897.9955752
7	55-64	903.5668016
8	Grand Total	908.1286486

Figure 38-30   Use the Group And Show Detail command to group detailed records.

Finally, let's get a breakdown of average travel spending by age, for men and women separately. All we have to do is drag Gender to the Column Labels zone of the Field List resulting in the PivotTable shown in Figure 38-31.

	A	B	C	D
3	Average of Amount Spent on Travel	Column Labels		
4	Row Labels	F	M	Grand Total
5	25-34	585.4752475	1221.209677	935.8355556
6	35-44	790.1652174	1004.098214	895.7180617
7	45-54	979.4782609	813.5765766	897.9955752
8	55-64	1179.609375	606.6470588	903.5668016
9	Grand Total	901.1590414	914.9935622	908.1286486

Figure 38-31   Age/gender breakdown of travel spending

Now we're cooking! We see that as age increases, women spend more on travel and men spend less. Now we know who should get the brochure: older women and younger men. As one of my students said, "That would be some kind of cruise!"

A graph provides a nice summary of our analysis. After moving the cursor inside the PivotTable and choosing PivotChart, we select the fourth option from Column Graphs. The result is the chart shown in Figure 38-32. If you want to edit the chart further, select PivotChart Tools. Then, for example, if you choose Layout, you can add titles to the chart and axis and make other changes.

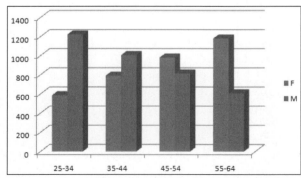

Figure 38-32   PivotChart for the age/gender travel expenditure breakdown

We see that each age group spends approximately the same on travel, but as age increases, women spend more than men. If you want to use a different type of chart, you can change the chart type by right-clicking the PivotChart and then choosing Chart Type.

Notice that the bars showing expenditures by males decrease with age, and the bars representing the amount spent by women increase with age. We can see why the Pivot-Tables that showed only gender and age data failed to unmask this pattern. Because half our sample population are men and half are women, we found that the average amount spent by people does not depend on the age. (Notice that the average height of the two bars for each age is approximately the same.) We also found that the average amount spent for men and women was approximately the same. We can see this because, averaged over all ages, the blue and red bars have approximately equal heights. Slicing and dicing our data simultaneously across age and gender does a much better job of showing us the real information.

I'm doing market research about Volvo Cross Country Wagons. I need to determine what factors influence the likelihood that a family will purchase a station wagon. From information in a large sample of families, I know the family size (large or small) and the family income (high or low). How can I determine how family size and income influence the likelihood that a family will purchase a station wagon?

In the file Station.xlsx, you can find the following information:

- ❑   Is the family size large or small?

- ❑   Is the family's income high or low?

- ❑   Did the family buy a station wagon? Yes or No.

A sample of the data is shown in Figure 38-33. For example, the first family listed is a small, high-income family that did not buy a station wagon.

	B	C	D
2	Station Wagon?	Family Size	Salary
3	No	Small	High
4	Yes	Large	High
5	Yes	Large	High
6	Yes	Large	High
7	Yes	Large	High
8	No	Small	High
9	Yes	Large	High
10	Yes	Large	High
11	Yes	Large	Low
12	Yes	Large	High
13	Yes	Large	Low
14	No	Small	Low
15	No	Small	Low
16	No	Small	High
17	Yes	Large	High
18	Yes	Large	High
19	No	Small	High
20	Yes	Large	High
21	No	Small	High
22	No	Large	Low
23	Yes	Large	High
24	No	Small	High
25	No	Small	Low
26	No	Small	Low

Figure 38-33   Data collected about income, family size, and the purchase of a station wagon

We want to determine how family size and income influence the likelihood that a family will purchase a station wagon. The trick is to look at how income affects purchases for each family size and how family size affects purchases for each income level.

To begin, we choose Insert Pivot Table, and then select our data (the cell range B2:D345). Using the PivotTable field list, we drag Family Size to the Row Labels area, Station Wagon to the Column Labels area, and any of the three fields to the Σ Values area. The result is the PivotTable shown in Figure 38-34. Notice that Excel has chosen to summarize the data appropriately by counting the number of observations in each category. For example, 34 high-salary, large families did not buy a station wagon, whereas 100 high-salary, large families did buy one.

	A	B	C	D
3	Count of Station Wagon?	Column Labels		
4	Row Labels	No	Yes	Grand Total
5	⊟ Large	48	138	186
6	High	34	100	134
7	Low	14	38	52
8	⊟ Small	147	10	157
9	High	104	8	112
10	Low	43	2	45
11	Grand Total	195	148	343

Figure 38-34   Summary of station wagon ownership by family size and salary

We would like to know, for each row in the PivotTable, the percentage of families that purchased a station wagon. To display the data in this format, we right-click anywhere in the PivotTable data and then choose Value Field Settings, which displays the Value Field Settings dialog box. In the dialog box, click Show Values As, and then select % Of Row in the Show Data As list. We now obtain the PivotTable shown in Figure 38-35.

	A	B	C	D
3	Count of Station Wagon?	Column Labels		
4	Row Labels	No	Yes	Grand Total
5	⊟ Large	25.81%	74.19%	100.00%
6	High	25.37%	74.63%	100.00%
7	Low	26.92%	73.08%	100.00%
8	⊟ Small	93.63%	6.37%	100.00%
9	High	92.86%	7.14%	100.00%
10	Low	95.56%	4.44%	100.00%
11	Grand Total	56.85%	43.15%	100.00%

Figure 38-35   Percentage breakdown of station wagon ownership by income for large and small families

From Figure 38-35, we learn that for both large and small families, income has little effect on whether the family purchases a station wagon. Now we try to determine how family size affects the propensity to buy a station wagon for high-income and low-income families. To do this, we move Salary above Family Size in the Row Labels zone, resulting in the PivotTable shown in Figure 38-36.

	A	B	C	D
3	Count of Station Wagon?	Column Labels		
4	Row Labels	No	Yes	Grand Total
5	⊟High	56.10%	43.90%	100.00%
6	Large	25.37%	74.63%	100.00%
7	Small	92.86%	7.14%	100.00%
8	⊟Low	58.76%	41.24%	100.00%
9	Large	26.92%	73.08%	100.00%
10	Small	95.56%	4.44%	100.00%
11	Grand Total	56.85%	43.15%	100.00%

Figure 38-36 Breakdown of station wagon ownership by family size for high and low salaries

From this table, we learn that for high-income families, a large family is much more likely to buy a station wagon than a small family. Similarly, for low-income families, a large family is also more likely to purchase a wagon than a small family. The bottom line is that family size has a much greater effect on the likelihood that a family will purchase a station wagon than does income.

I work for a manufacturer that sells microchips globally. I'm given monthly actual and predicted sales for Canada, France, and the United States for Chip 1, Chip 2, and Chip 3. I'm also given the variance, or *difference*, between actual and budgeted revenues. For each month and each combination of country and product, I'd like to display the following data: actual revenue, budgeted revenue, actual variance, actual revenue as a percentage of annual revenue, and variance as a percentage of budgeted revenue. How can I display this information?

In this scenario, you are a finance manager for a microchip manufacturer. You sell your products in different countries and at different times. PivotTables can help you summarize your data in a format that's easily understood.

The file Ptableexample.xlsx includes monthly actual and predicted sales during 1997 of Chip 1, Chip 2, and Chip 3 in Canada, France, and the United States. The file also contains the variance, or difference, between actual revenues and budgeted revenues. A sample of the data is shown in Figure 38-37 on the next page. For example, in the U.S. in January, sales of Chip 1 totaled $4,000, although sales of $5,454 were predicted. This yielded a variance of −$1,454.

	A	B	C	D	E	F
1	Month	Product	Country	Revenue	Budget	Var
2	January	Chip 1	US	4000	5454	-1454
3	January	Chip 1	Canada	3424	5341	-1917
4	January	Chip 1	US	8324	1232	7092
5	January	Chip 1	France	5555	3424	2131
6	January	Chip 1	Canada	5341	8324	-2983
7	January	Chip 1	US	1232	5555	-4323
8	January	Chip 1	France	3424	5341	-1917
9	January	Chip 1	Canada	8324	1232	7092
10	January	Chip 1	US	5555	3424	2131
11	January	Chip 1	France	5341	8324	-2983
12	January	Chip 1	Canada	1232	5555	-4323
13	January	Chip 1	US	3424	5341	-1917
14	January	Chip 1	Canada	8383	5454	2929
15	January	Chip 1	France	8324	1232	7092
16	January	Chip 1	Canada	5555	3424	2131
17	January	Chip 1	US	5341	8324	-2983
18	January	Chip 1	France	1232	5555	-4323
19	January	Chip 1	France	3523	9295	-5772
20	February	Chip 2	Canada	5555	3424	2131
21	February	Chip 2	US	5454	4000	1454
22	February	Chip 2	US	5341	8324	-2983

Figure 38-37 Chip data from different countries for different months showing actual, budget, and variance revenues

For each month and each combination of country and product, we would like to display the following data:

❑ Actual revenue

❑ Budgeted revenue

❑ Actual variance

❑ Actual revenue as a percentage of annual revenue

❑ Variance as a percentage of budgeted revenue

To begin, select a cell within the range of data we're working with (remember that the first row must include headings) and then choose Insert PivotTable. Excel automatically determines that our data is in the range A1:F208.

If we drag Month to the Row Labels area, Country to the Column Labels area, and Revenue to the Values area, for example, we obtain the total revenue each month by country. A field you add to the Report Filter area (Product, for example) lets you filter your Pivot-Table by using values in that field. By adding Product to the Report Filter area, we can view sales of only Chip 1 by month for each country. Given that we want to be able to show data for any combination of country and product, we should add Month to the Row Labels area of the PivotTable and both Country and Product to the Report Filter area. Next, we drag Var, Revenue, and Budget to the Σ Values zone. We have now created the PivotTable that is shown in Figure 38-38.

	A	B	C	D
1	Product	(All)		
2	Country	(All)		
3				
4		Values		
5	Row Labels	Sum of Var	Sum of Revenue	Sum of Budget
6	January	-4297	87534	91831
7	February	2843	90377	87534
8	March	-1389	88988	90377
9	April	-2774	84982	87756
10	May	-423	84559	84982
11	June	-548	84011	84559
12	July	2366	86377	84011
13	August	-2843	83534	86377
14	September	1389	84923	83534
15	October	-4318	80605	84923
16	November	3406	84011	80605
17	December	2366	86377	84011
18	Grand Total	-4222	1026278	1030500

Figure 38-38   Monthly summary of revenue, budget, and variances

For example, in January, total revenue was $87,534 and total budgeted sales were $91,831, so our actual sales fell $4,297 short of the forecast.

We want to determine the percentage of revenue earned during each month. We again drag Revenue from the field list to the ∑ Values area of the PivotTable. Right-click in this data column, and then choose Value Field Settings. In the Value Field Settings dialog box, click Show Values As. In the Show Values As list, select % Of Column and rename this field as Sum Of Revenue2, as shown in Figure 38-39.

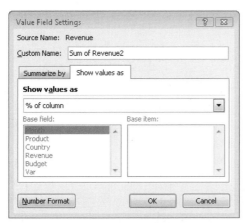

Figure 38-39   Creating each month's percentage of annual revenue

We now obtain the PivotTable shown in Figure 38-40 on the next page. January sales provided 8.53 percent of revenue. Total revenue for the year was $1,026,278.

	A	B	C	D	E
1	Product	(All)			
2	Country	(All)			
3					
4		Values			
5	Row Labels	Sum of Var	Sum of Revenue	Sum of Budget	Sum of Revenue2
6	January	-4297	87534	91831	8.53%
7	February	2843	90377	87534	8.81%
8	March	-1389	88988	90377	8.67%
9	April	-2774	84982	87756	8.28%
10	May	-423	84559	84982	8.24%
11	June	-548	84011	84559	8.19%
12	July	2366	86377	84011	8.42%
13	August	-2843	83534	86377	8.14%
14	September	1389	84923	83534	8.27%
15	October	-4318	80605	84923	7.85%
16	November	3406	84011	80605	8.19%
17	December	2366	86377	84011	8.42%
18	Grand Total	-4222	1026278	1030500	100.00%

Figure 38-40 Monthly revenue breakdown

What is a calculated field?

Now we want to determine for each month the variance as a percentage of total sales. To do this, we will create a *calculated field*. Select a cell anywhere within the data area of the PivotTable, and then choose Formulas from the Option tab. Next choose Calculated Field to display the Insert Calculated Field dialog box. As shown in Figure 38-41, enter a name for your field, and then enter your formula. The formula we're using in this example is *=Var/Budget*. You can enter the formula yourself or use the list of fields and the Insert Field button to add a field to the formula. After clicking Add and then OK, we obtain the PivotTable shown in Figure 38-42.

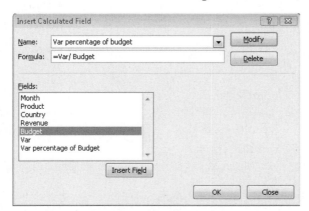

Figure 38-41 Creating a calculated field

	A	B	C	D	E	F
1	Product	(All) ▼				
2	Country	(All) ▼				
3						
4		Values				
5	Row Labels ▼	Sum of Var	Sum of Budget	Sum of Revenue	Sum of Revenue2	Sum of Var percentage of Budget
6	January	-4297	91831	87534	8.53%	-0.046792477
7	February	2843	87534	90377	8.81%	0.032478808
8	March	-1389	90377	88988	8.67%	-0.015368954
9	April	-2774	87756	84982	8.28%	-0.031610374
10	May	-423	84982	84559	8.24%	-0.004977525
11	June	-548	84559	84011	8.19%	-0.006480682
12	July	2366	84011	86377	8.42%	0.028162979
13	August	-2843	86377	83534	8.14%	-0.032913854
14	September	1389	83534	84923	8.27%	0.01662796
15	October	-4318	84923	80605	7.85%	-0.050846061
16	November	3406	80605	84011	8.19%	0.042255443
17	December	2366	84011	86377	8.42%	0.028162979
18	Grand Total	-4222	1030500	1026278	100.00%	-0.00409704

Figure 38-42   The PivotTable with calculated field for variance percentage

Thus, in January, our sales were 4.7 percent lower than budgeted. By displaying the Insert Calculated Field dialog box again, you can modify or delete a calculated field.

How do you use the Report Filter?

To see sales of Chip 2 in France, for example, you can select the appropriate values from the Product and Country fields in the Page Fields area. With Chip 2 and France selected, we would see the PivotTable shown in Figure 38-43.

	A	B	C	D	E	F
1	Product	Chip 2 ▼				
2	Country	France ▼				
3						
4		Values				
5	Row Labels ▼	Sum of Var	Sum of Budget	Sum of Revenue	Sum of Revenue2	Sum of Var percentage of Budget
6	February	-3846	32954	29108	23.90%	-0.116708139
7	May	3318	32045	35363	29.04%	0.103541894
8	August	2769	30663	33432	27.45%	0.090304276
9	November	0	23876	23876	19.61%	0
10	Grand Total	2241	119538	121779	100.00%	0.018747177

Figure 38-43   Sales of Chip 2 in France

How do you group items in a PivotTable?

Often, we want to group headings in a PivotTable. For example, we might want to combine sales for January–March. To create a group, select the items you want to group, right-click the selection, and then choose Group And Show Detail, Group. After changing the name Group 1 to Jan-March, we obtain the PivotTable shown in Figure 38-44 on the next page.

	A	B	C	D	E
1	Product	(All) ▼			
2	Country	(All) ▼			
3					
4		Values			
5	Row Labels ▼	Sum of Var	Sum of Revenue	Sum of Budget	Sum of Revenue2
6	⊞ Jan-March	-2843	266899	269742	26.01%
7	⊟ April				
8	April	-2774	84982	87756	8.28%
9	⊟ May				
10	May	-423	84559	84982	8.24%
11	⊟ June				
12	June	-548	84011	84559	8.19%
13	⊟ July				
14	July	2366	86377	84011	8.42%
15	⊟ August				
16	August	-2843	83534	86377	8.14%
17	⊟ September				
18	September	1389	84923	83534	8.27%
19	⊟ October				
20	October	-4318	80605	84923	7.85%
21	⊟ November				
22	November	3406	84011	80605	8.19%
23	⊟ December				
24	December	2366	86377	84011	8.42%
25	Grand Total	-4222	1026278	1030500	100.00%

Figure 38-44   Grouping items together for January, February, and March

Remarks About Grouping

- You can disband a group by selecting Group And Show Detail and then Ungroup.

- You can group nonadjacent selections by holding down the Ctrl key while you select nonadjacent rows or columns.

- With numerical values or dates in a row field, you can group by number or dates in arbitrary intervals. For example, you can create groups for age ranges and then find the average income for all 25–34 year olds.

What is a calculated item?

A calculated item works just like a calculated field except that you are creating one row rather than a column. To create a calculated item, you should select an item in the row area of the PivotTable, not an item in the body of the PivotTable. Then from the Options tab, select Formulas, followed by Calculated Item. See Problem 11 in the "Problems" section of this chapter for an example of creating a calculated item. In our chip PivotTable example we could not create a calculated item because we had multiple copies of the Revenue field.

What is "drilling down"?

"Drilling down" is when you double-click a cell in a PivotTable to display all the detailed data that's summarized in that field. For example, double-clicking any March entry in the microchip scenario will display the data that's related to March sales.

I often have to use specfic data in a PivotTable to determine profit, such as the April sales of Chip 1 in France. Unfortunately, this data moves around when new fields are added to my PivotTable. Does Excel have a function that enables me to always pull April's Chip 1 sales in France from the PivotTable?

Yes, there is such a function. The GETPIVOTDATA function fills the bill. Suppose that you want to extract sales of Chip 1 in France during April from the PivotTable contained in the file Getpivotdata.xlsx. (See Figure 38-45.) Entering in cell E2 the formula *GET-PIVOTDATA(A4,"April France Chip 1 Sum of Revenue")* yields the correct value ($37,600) even if additional products, countries, and months are added to the PivotTable later. We can also obtain the resulting revenue by simply pointing to the cell containing Chip 2 April sales in France (cell D24).

The first argument for this function is in the upper-left corner of the PivotTable (cell A4). We enclose in quotation marks (separated by spaces) the PivotTable headings that define the entry we want. The last entry must specify the data field, but other headings can be listed in any order. Thus, our formula means "For the PivotTable whose upper-left corner is in cell A4, find the Sum of Revenue for Chip 1 in France during April." This formula will return the correct answer even if the sales data for Chip 1 in France in April moves to a different location in the PivotTable.

	A	B	C	D	E	F
1					april chip 1 France revenue	total revenue
2					37600	1026278
3						
4		**Values**				
5	**Row Labels** ▼	**Sum of Var**	**Sum of Budget**	**Sum of Revenue**	**Sum of Revenue2**	**Sum of Var percentage of Budget**
6	⊟January	-4297	91831	87534	8.53%	-0.046792477
7	⊟Chip 1	-4297	91831	87534	8.53%	-0.046792477
8	Canada	2929	29330	32259	3.14%	0.099863621
9	France	-5772	33171	27399	2.67%	-0.174007416
10	US	-1454	29330	27876	2.72%	-0.049573815
11	⊟February	2843	87534	90377	8.81%	0.032478808
12	⊟Chip 2	2843	87534	90377	8.81%	0.032478808
13	Canada	3318	32045	35363	3.45%	0.103541894
14	France	-3846	32954	29108	2.84%	-0.116708139
15	US	3371	22535	25906	2.52%	0.149589527
16	⊟March	-1389	90377	88988	8.67%	-0.015368954
17	⊟Chip 3	-1389	90377	88988	8.67%	-0.015368954
18	Canada	-10733	35363	24630	2.40%	-0.303509318
19	France	11529	20784	32313	3.15%	0.554705543
20	US	-2185	34230	32045	3.12%	-0.063832895
21	⊟April	-2774	87756	84982	8.28%	-0.031610374
22	⊟Chip 1	-2774	87756	84982	8.28%	-0.031610374
23	Canada	1054	19289	20343	1.98%	0.054642542
24	France	-54	37654	37600	3.66%	-0.001434111
25	US	-3774	30813	27039	2.63%	-0.122480771

Figure 38-45   Use the GETPIVOTDATA function to locate April Chip 1 Sales in France.

If you want to simply return total revenue ($1,026,278), you could enter the formula (see cell F2) *GETPIVOTDATA(A4,"Sum of Revenue")*.

Often, the *GETPIVOTDATA* function is a nuisance. Suppose you want to refer to data in cells B5:B11 from a PivotTable elsewhere in your workbook. You would probably use the formula =B5 and copy it to the range B6:B11. Hopefully, this would extract B6, B7,..., B11 to desired cells. Unfortunately, if the GETPIVOTDATA option is active, you will get a bunch of GETPIVOTDATA functions that refer to the same cell. If you want to turn off GETPIVOTDATA, you can click the Microsoft Office Button and click Excel Options. Then select Formulas, and under Working With Formulas, clear the GetPivotdata Function For PivotTable References. This will ensure that clicking inside a PivotTable yields a formula like =B5 rather than a GETPIVOTDATA function.

Finally, we note that you can also combine the MATCH and OFFSET functions (explained in Chapter 4, "The MATCH Function," and Chapter 20, "The OFFSET Function," respectively) to extract various PivotTable entries.

Problems

1. Contoso, Ltd. produces microchips. Five types of defects (labeled 1–5) have been known to occur. Chips are manufactured by two operators (A and B) using four machines (1–4). You are given data about a sample of defective chips, including the type of defect, the operator, machine number, and day of the week the defect occurred. Use this data to chart a course of action that would lead, as quickly as possible, to improved product quality. You should use the PivotTable Wizard to "stratify" the defects with respect to type of defect, day of the week, machine used, and operator working. You might even want to break down the data by machine, operator, and so on. Assume that each operator and machine made an equal number of products. You'll find this data in the file Contoso.xlsx.

2. You own a fast food restaurant and have done some market research in an attempt to better understand your customers. For a random sample of customers, you are given the income, gender, and number of days per week that residents go out for fast food. Use this information to determine how gender and income influence the frequency with which a person goes out to eat fast food. The data is in the file Macdonalds.xlsx.

3. Students at the School of Fine Art apply to study either English or Science. You have been assigned to determine whether the School of Fine Art discriminates against women in admitting students to the school of their choice. You are given the following data on the School of Fine Art's students:

   ❑ Female or male

   ❑ Major applied for: English (Eng) or Science (Sci)

   ❑ Admit? Yes or No

Assuming that women are as equally qualified for each major as the men, does this data indicate that the college discriminated against women? Ensure you use all available information! The data is in the file Finearts.xlsx.

4. You have been assigned to evaluate the quality of care given to heart attack patients at Emergency Room (ER) and Chicago Hope (CH). For the last month you are given the following patient data:

   ❑ Hospital (ER or CH).

   ❑ Risk category (high or low). High-risk people are less likely to survive than low-risk people.

   ❑ Patient outcome (live or die).

   Use this data to determine which hospital is doing a better job of caring for heart attack patients. Hint: Use all the data! The data is in the file Hospital.xlsx.

5. You are given the monthly level of the Dow Jones Index for the years 1947–1992. Does this data indicate any unusual seasonal patterns in stock returns? Hint: You can extract the month (January, February, and so on) by using the formula *TEXT(A4,"mmm")* copied to any column. The data is in the file Dow.xlsx.

6. The file Makeupdb.xlsx contains information about the sales of makeup products. For each transaction, you are given the following information:

   ❑ Name of salesperson

   ❑ Date of sale

   ❑ Product sold

   ❑ Units sold

   ❑ Transaction revenue

   Create a PivotTable to compile the following information:

   ❑ The number of sales transactions for each salesperson.

   ❑ For each salesperson, the total revenue by product.

   ❑ Using your answer to the previous question, create a function that always yields Jen's lipstick sales.

   ❑ Total revenue generated by each salesperson broken down by location.

   ❑ Total revenue by salesperson and year. (Hint: You will need to group the data by year.)

7. For the years 1985–1992, you are given monthly interest rates on bonds that pay money one year after the day they're bought. It's often suggested that interest rates are more volatile—tend to change more—when interest rates are high. Does the data in the file

Intratevol-volatility.xlsx support this statement? Hint: PivotTables can display standard deviations.

8. For our grocery example, prepare a chart that summarizes the trend over time of the sales at each store.

9. For our grocery example, create a calculate field that computes an average per unit price received for each product.

10. For our grocery example, create a PivotChart that summarizes the sales of each product at each store for the years 2005 and 2006.

11. For the data in the file Calcitemdata.xlsx, create calculated fields that summarize sales of dessert (*cakes+puddings*) and fruits (*apples+grapes*).

12. In the chip PivotTable example, create a PivotTable that summarizes monthly sales of Chips 1 and 3 in France and the U.S.

13. In the customer PivotTable example, show the top 15 customers in one table and the bottom 5 customers in another table.

14. The file Ptablepartsdata.xlsx contains sales of various parts. Each part code begins with either Part (for *computer part*) or Comp (for *computer*). Create a PivotTable that only shows sales of Parts. (Hint: Use a Labels Filter.)

15. For the data in Problem 14, summarize the total sales of parts and computers.

Chapter 39

Summarizing Data with Database Statistical Functions

Joolas is a small makeup company. In a Microsoft Office Excel 2007 worksheet, they track each sales transaction. Often, they want to answer questions such as:

- How many dollars worth of lip gloss did Jen sell?

- What was the average number of lipstick units sold each time Jen made a sale in the East region?

- What was the total dollar amount of all makeup sold by Emilee or in the East region?

- How many dollars worth of lipstick were sold by Colleen or Zaret in the East region?

- How many lipstick transactions were not in the East region?

- How many dollars worth of lipstick did Jen sell during 2004?

- How many units of makeup were sold for a price of at least $3.20?

- What is the total dollar amount each salesperson sold of each makeup product?

- What helpful tricks can I use to set up criteria ranges?

- I have a database that lists for each sales transaction the revenue, the date sold, and the product ID code. Given the date sold and the ID code for a transaction, is there an easy way to extract the transaction's revenue?

As you saw in Chapter 38, "Using PivotTables to Describe Data," Microsoft PivotTables are a great tool for summarizing data. Often, however, a PivotTable gives us much more information than we need. *Database statistical functions* make it easy to answer any "reporting" question without having to create a PivotTable.

You are already familiar with functions such as SUM, AVERAGE, COUNT, MAX, and MIN. By prefixing a *D* (which stands for *database*) to these (and other functions), you create database statistical functions. But what does the DSUM function do, for example, that the SUM function can't? Whereas the SUM function adds up every cell in a cell range, the DSUM function enables you to specify (by using criteria) a subset of rows to add together in a cell range. For example, suppose we have a sales database for a small makeup company that contains the following information about each sales transaction:

- Name of salesperson
- Transaction date
- Product sold
- Units sold
- Dollars of revenue generated per transaction
- Region of country where the transaction took place

You can find this data in the file Makeupdb.xlsx, which is shown in Figure 39-1.

Trans Number	Name	Date	Product	Units	Dollars	Location
1	Betsy	4/1/2004	lip gloss	45	$137.20	south
2	Hallagan	3/10/2004	foundatic	50	$152.01	midwest
3	Ashley	2/25/2005	lipstick	9	$ 28.72	midwest
4	Hallagan	5/22/2006	lip gloss	55	$167.08	west
5	Zaret	6/17/2004	lip gloss	43	$130.60	midwest
6	Colleen	11/27/2005	eye liner	58	$175.99	midwest
7	Cristina	3/21/2004	eye liner	8	$ 25.80	midwest
8	Colleen	12/17/2006	lip gloss	72	$217.84	midwest
9	Ashley	7/5/2006	eye liner	75	$226.64	south
10	Betsy	8/7/2006	lip gloss	24	$ 73.50	east
11	Ashley	11/29/2004	mascara	43	$130.84	east
12	Ashley	11/18/2004	lip gloss	23	$ 71.03	west
13	Emilee	8/31/2005	lip gloss	49	$149.59	west
14	Hallagan	1/1/2005	eye liner	18	$ 56.47	south
15	Zaret	9/20/2006	foundatic	-8	$(21.99)	east
16	Emilee	4/12/2004	mascara	45	$137.39	east
17	Colleen	4/30/2006	mascara	66	$199.65	south
18	Jen	8/31/2005	lip gloss	88	$265.19	midwest
19	Jen	10/27/2004	eye liner	78	$236.15	south
20	Zaret	11/27/2005	lip gloss	57	$173.12	midwest
21	Zaret	6/2/2006	mascara	12	$ 38.08	west
22	Betsy	9/24/2004	eye liner	28	$ 86.51	midwest
23	Colleen	2/1/2006	mascara	25	$ 77.31	midwest
26	Emilee	12/6/2006	lip gloss	24	$ 74.62	west
27	Jen	4/12/2004	lipstick	38	$115.99	midwest
28	Cristina	9/22/2005	foundatic	77	$233.05	midwest
32	Cristina	3/28/2006	lip gloss	53	$161.46	midwest
33	Cici	6/17/2004	mascara	41	$125.27	west
34	Zaret	9/9/2006	mascara	19	$ 59.15	west
39	Cici	2/23/2006	foundatic	-9	$(24.63)	west
40	Hallagan	6/24/2006	foundatic	38	$115.58	south
41	Emilee	2/6/2004	eye liner	25	$ 76.56	south
42	Emilee	4/10/2005	mascara	19	$ 59.38	midwest
43	Betsy	4/1/2004	foundatic	86	$259.86	west

Figure 39-1 We'll use this data to describe how to work with database statistical functions.

Using the DSUM function with appropriate criteria, we could, for example, add up the revenue generated only by transactions involving lip gloss sales in the East during 2004. Essentially, the criteria we set up flags those rows that we want to include in the total sum. Within these rows, the DSUM function acts like the ordinary SUM function.

The syntax of the DSUM function is:

```
DSUM(database,field,criteria)
```

■ *Database* is the cell range that makes up the database. The first row of the list contains labels for each column.

■ *Field* is the column containing the values you want the function to add. You can define the field by enclosing the column label in quotation marks. (For example, we would designate the Dollars column by entering "Dollars".) The field can also be specified by using the position of the column in the database, measured from left to right. For example, our database will use columns H through M. (We did not include the Transactions column as part of our database.) We could specify column H as *field 1* and column M as *field 6*.

■ *Criteria* refers to a cell range that specifies the rows on which the function should operate. The first row of a criteria range must include one or more column labels. (The only exception to this rule is *computed criteria*, which I'll discuss in the last two examples in this chapter.) As our examples illustrate, the key to creating a criteria range is to understand that multiple criteria in the same row are joined by AND, whereas criteria in different rows are joined by OR.

Now let's go on to some examples that illustrate the power and versatility of database statistical functions.

How many dollars worth of lip gloss did Jen sell?

In this example, we want to apply DSUM to column 5 of the database. Column 5 contains the dollar volume for each transaction. (I gave the name *data* to our database, which consists of the range H4:M1895.) Our criteria range in O4:P5 flags all rows in the database in which Name equals Jen *and* Product equals lip gloss. Thus, entering in cell N5 (see Figure 39-2) the formula *DSUM(data,5,O4:P5)* calculates the total dollar amount of lip gloss sold by Jen. We could have also entered the formula as *DSUM (data,"Dollars",O4:P5)*. We find that Jen sold $5,461.61 worth of lip gloss. In cell N6 we found the same answer by using the SUMIFS function (see Chapter 19, "The SUMIF, AVERAGEIF, SUMIFS, and AVERAGEIFS Functions") with the formula *=SUMIFS(Dollars,Name,"Jen",Product,"lip gloss")*.

	N	O	P	Q	R
4	Jen lip gloss $	Name	Product		
5	$ 5,461.61	Jen	lip gloss		
6	5461.61479				
7	Jen avg.units lipstick in east	Name	Product	Location	
8	42.25	Jen	lipstick	east	
9	42.25				
10	$s Emilee or east	Name	Location		
11	$ 76,156.48	Emilee			
12			east		
13	$s lipstick by Colleen or Zaret in east	Name	Location	Product	
14	$ 1,073.20	Colleen	east	lipstick	
15	1073.203709	Zaret	east	lipstick	
16	Number of lipstick transactions not in	Product	Location		
17	164	lipstick	<>east	164	
18	total $s jen lipstick in 2004	Name	Product	Date	Date
19	$ 1,690.79	Jen	lipstick	>=1/1/2004	<1/1/2005
20	1690.793115				

Figure 39-2   Database statistical functions

What was the average number of lipstick units sold each time Jen had a sale in the East region?

We can compute this number by entering in cell N8 the formula *DAVERAGE (data,4,O7:Q8)*. Using 4 as the value for *field* specifies the Units column, and the criteria range O7:Q8 flags all rows in the database in which Name equals Jen, Product equals lipstick, and Location equals East. Using DAVERAGE ensures that we average the units sold for the flagged rows. We find that, on average, Jen sold 42.25 units of lipstick in transactions in the East region. In cell N9, we found the same answer by using the formula =AVERAGEIFS(Units,Name,"Jen",Product,"lipstick",Location,"east").

What was the total dollar amount of all makeup sold by Emilee or in the East region?

In cell N11, we can compute the total dollars ($76,156.48) of sales made by Emilee or in the East by using the formula *DSUM(data,5,O10:P12)*. The criteria in O10:P12 flags sales in the East *or* by Emilee. This is because criteria in different rows are treated as "OR." The great programmers at Microsoft have ensured that this formula will not double-count Emilee's sales in the East. Here, we cannot use SUMIFS to easily find the answer.

How many dollars worth of lipstick were sold by Colleen or Zaret in the East region?

The formula *DSUM(data,5,O13:Q15)* in cell N14 computes the total lipstick revenue generated through Colleen and Zaret's sales ($1,073.20) in the East. Notice that O14:Q14 specifies criteria that selects Colleen's lipstick sales in the East, and O15:Q15 specifies criteria that selects by Zaret's lipstick sales in the East. Remember that criteria in different rows are treated as "or." In cell N15, we also found the answer with the formula =SUMIFS(Dollars,Name,"Colleen",Product,"lipstick",Location,"east")+SUMIFS(Dollars, Name,"Zaret",Product,"lipstick",Location,"east").

How many lipstick transactions were not in the East region?

In cell N17, we compute the total number of lipstick transactions (164) outside the East region with the formula *DCOUNT(data,4,O16:P17)*. I use DCOUNT in this problem because we want to specify criteria by which the function will count the number of rows involving lipstick sales and regions other than the East. Excel treats the expression <>*East* in the criteria range as "not East." For this problem, using SUMIFS would require that we have a SUMIFS function for each region.

Because the COUNT function counts numbers, we need to refer to a column containing numerical values. Column 4, the Units column, contains numbers, so I designated that column in the formula. The formula *DCOUNT(data,3,O16:P17)* would return 0 because there are no numbers in the database's third column (which is column J in the worksheet). Of course, the formula *DCOUNTA(data,3,O16:P17)* would return the correct answer because COUNTA counts text as well as numbers.

How many dollars worth of lipstick did Jen sell during 2004?

The trick here is how to flag only sales that occurred in 2004. By including in one row of our criteria range a reference to the Date field, using the expressions >=1/1/2004 and

<1/1/2005, we capture only the 2004 sales. Thus, entering in cell N19 the formula *DSUM(data,5,O18:R19)* computes the total lipstick sales by Jen ($1,690.79) after January 1, 2004, and before January 1, 2005. In cell N20, we found the answer to this problem with the formula *=SUMIFS(Dollars,Date,">=1/1/2004",Date,"<=12/31/2004",Product,"lipstick",Name,"Jen")*.

How many units of makeup were sold for a price of at least $3.20?

This example involves *computed criteria*. Basically, computed criteria flags rows of the database on the basis of whether a computed condition is true or false for that row. For this question, we want to flag each row that contains *Dollars/Units>=$3.20*. When setting up a computed criteria (see Figure 39-3), the label in the first row above the computed criteria *must not* be a column label. For example, you can't use Name, Product, or another label from row 4 of this worksheet. The computed criteria is set up to be a formula that returns *True* based on the first row of information in the database. Thus, to specify rows in which the average price is greater than or equal to $3.20, we need to enter *=(L5/K5)>=3.2* in our criteria range below a heading that is not a column label. If the first row of data does not satisfy this condition, you will see FALSE in the worksheet, but Excel will still flag all rows having a unit price that's greater than or equal to $3.20. Entering in N22 the formula *DSUM(data,4,O21:O22)* computes the total number of units of makeup sold (1127) in orders for which the unit price was greater than or equal to $3.20. Note that cell O22 contains the formula *=(L5/K5)>=3.2*.

	N	O
21	**Units sold for >=$3.20**	**Big price**
22		1127 FALSE

← criteria formula

Figure 39-3   Computed criteria

What is the total dollar amount each salesperson sold of each makeup product?

For this problem, I'd like to use a DSUM function whose criteria range is based on both the Name and Product columns. Using a data table, I can easily "loop through" all possible combinations of Name and Product in the criteria range and compute the total revenue for each Name and Product combination.

I begin by entering any name in cell X26 and any product in cell Y26. Then I enter in cell Q25 the formula *DSUM(data,5,X25:Y26)*, which computes total sales revenue for (in this case) Betsy and eye liner. Next, I enter each salesperson's name in the cell range Q26:Q33 and each product in the cell range R25:V25. Now select the data table range (Q25:V33). On the Data tab, in the Data Tools group, click What-If Analysis, and then click Data Table. Choose cell X26 as the Column Input Cell and Y26 as the Row Input Cell. We then obtain the results shown in Figure 39-4 on the next page. Each entry in the data table computes the revenue generated for a different name/product combination because the data table causes the names to be placed in cell X26 and the products to be placed in cell Y26. For example, we find that Ashley sold $3,245.44 worth of lipstick.

(handwritten: DSUM ... ignore)

	O	P	Q	R	S	T	U	V	W	X	Y
25	dbase functions		6046.5343	lip gloss	foundatic	lipstick	mascara	eye liner		Name	Product
26			Betsy	5675.65	8043.49	3968.61	4827.25	6046.53		Betsy	eye liner
27			Hallagan	5603.1194	6985.73	3177.87	5703.35	6964.62			
28			Zaret	5670.3293	6451.65	2448.71	3879.95	8166.75			
29			Colleen	5573.3237	6834.77	2346.41	6746.53	3389.63			
30			Cristina	5297.9798	5290.99	2401.67	5461.65	5397.27			
31			Jen	5461.6148	5628.65	3953.3	6887.17	7010.44			
32			Ashley	6053.6846	4186.06	3245.44	6617.1	5844.95			
33			Emilee	5270.2503	5313.79	2189.14	4719.3	7587.39			
34											
35											
36	sumifs			lip gloss	foundatic	lipstick	mascara	eye liner			
37			Betsy	5675.65	8043.49	3968.61	4827.25	6046.53			
38			Hallagan	5603.1194	6985.73	3177.87	5703.35	6964.62			
39			Zaret	5670.3293	6451.65	2448.71	3879.95	8166.75			
40			Colleen	5573.3237	6834.77	2346.41	6746.53	3389.63			
41			Cristina	5297.9798	5290.99	2401.67	5461.65	5397.27			
42			Jen	5461.6148	5628.65	3953.3	6887.17	7010.44			
43			Ashley	6053.6846	4186.06	3245.44	6617.1	5844.95			
44			Emilee	5270.2503	5313.79	2189.14	4719.3	7587.39			

Figure 39-4   Combining data tables with a DSUM function

This example shows how combining data tables with database statistical functions can quickly generate many statistics of interest.

We also solved this problem by copying from cell R37 to R37:V44 the formula =SUMIFS(Dollars,Name,$Q37,Product,R$36).

What helpful tricks can I use to set up criteria ranges?

Here are some examples of little tricks that might help you set up an appropriate criteria range. Suppose the column label in the first row of the criteria range refers to a column containing text (for example, column H).

❑ *Allie* will flag records containing the text string Allie in column H.

❑ A?X will flag a record if the record's column H entry begins with A and contains the character X as its third character. (The second character can be anything!)

❑ <>*B* will flag a record if column H's entry does not contain any Bs.

If a column (for example, column I) contains numerical values,

❑ >100 will flag a record if column I contains a value greater than 100.

❑ <>100 will flag a record if column I contains a value not equal to 100.

❑ >=1000 will flag a record if column I contains a value greater than or equal to 1000.

I have a database that lists for each sales transaction the revenue, the date sold, and the product ID code. Given the date sold and the ID code for a transaction, is there an easy way to capture the transaction's revenue?

The file Dget.xlsx (see Figure 39-5) contains a database that lists revenues, dates, and product ID codes for a series of sales transactions. If you know the date and the product ID code for a transaction, how can you find the transaction's revenue? With the DGET function, it's simple. The syntax of the DGET function is DGET(database,field#,criteria). Given a database (a cell range) and a field# in the database (counting columns from left to right across the range) the DGET function returns the entry in column field# from the database record satisfying the criteria. If no record satisfies the criteria, the DGET function returns the #VALUE error message. If more than one record satisfies the criteria, the DGET function returns the #NUM! error message.

Suppose that we want to know the revenue for a transaction involving product ID code 62426 that occurred on 1/9/2006. Assuming that the transaction involving this product on the given date is unique, the formula (entered in cell G9) *DGET(B7:28,G5:H6)* yields the transaction's revenue of $992. Note that we used *1* for the *field#* argument because Revenue is listed in the first column of the database. (Our database is contained in the cell range B7:D28). The criteria range G5:H6 ensures we find a transaction involving product 62426 on 1/9/2006.

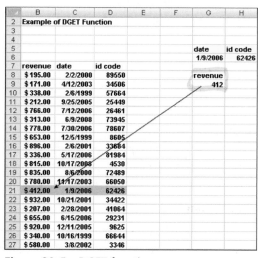

Figure 39-5 DGET function

Problems

1. How many units of lip gloss did Zaret sell during 2004 and 2005?

2. Create a data table that contains each person's total revenue and units sold.

3. How many units of lip gloss did Colleen sell outside the West region?

4. Using the data in file Makeupdb.xlsx, create a data table that shows the average per-unit revenue generated by each person for sales in which the average per-unit price exceeded $3.30.

5. Use the data in the file Sales.xlsx to determine the following:

   ❑ Total dollar sales in the Midwest

   ❑ Total dollars that Heather sold in the East

   ❑ Total dollars that Heather sold or that were sold in the East

- ❏ Total dollars sold in the East by Heather or John

- ❏ Number of transactions in the East region

- ❏ Number of transactions with greater than average sales

- ❏ Total sales not in the Midwest

6. The file Housepricedata.xlsx contains the following information for selected homes:

   - ❏ Square footage

   - ❏ Price

   - ❏ Number of bathrooms

   - ❏ Number of bedrooms

   Use this information to answer the following questions:

   - ❏ What is the average price of all homes having a total number of bathrooms and bedrooms greater than or equal to 6?

   - ❏ How many homes sell for more than $300,000 and have a total number of bedrooms and bathrooms less than or equal to 5?

   - ❏ How many homes have at least 3 bathrooms but the total number of bedrooms and bathrooms is less than or equal to 6?

   - ❏ What is the highest price of a home having at most 3000 square feet and a total number of bedrooms and bathroom less than or equal to 6? (Hint: Use the DMAX function to solve this problem.)

7. The file Deciles.xlsx contains the unpaid balance for 20 accounts. Use DBASE functions to compute the total unpaid balances in each decile.

Chapter 40
Filtering Data and Removing Duplicates

Joolas is a small company that manufactures makeup. They track each sales transaction in a Microsoft Office Excel spreadsheet. There are times when they want to extract, or "filter out," a subset of their sales data. For example, they might want to identify sales transactions that answer the following questions:

- How can I identify all transactions in which Jen sold lipstick in the East region?

- How can I identify all transactions in which Cici or Colleen sold lipstick or mascara in the East or South region?

- How can I copy all transactions in which Cici or Colleen sold lipstick or mascara in the East or South region to a different worksheet?

- How do I clear filters from a column or database?

- How can I identify all transactions which involved sales of >$280 and >90 units?

- How can I identify all sales occurring in 2005 or 2006?

- How can I identify all transactions in the last three months of 2005 or the first three months of 2006?

- How can I identify all transactions where the salesperson's first name starts with C?

- How can I identify all transactions where the cell containing the product name was colored in red?

- How can I identify all transactions in the Top 30 revenue values where Hallagan or Jen was the salesperson?

- How can I easily obtain a complete list of salespeople?

- How can I view every combination of salesperson, product, and location that occurs in the database?

■ If my data changes, how can I reapply the same filter?

■ How can I extract all foundation transactions in the first six months of 2005 for which Emilee or Jen was the salesperson and the average per-unit price was more than $3.20?

Microsoft Office Excel 2007 has filtering capabilities that make identifying any subset of data a snap. Excel also makes it easy to remove duplicate records from a list. Our work for this chapter is in the file Makeupfilter.xlsx. For the 1891 sales transactions listed in this file, we have the following information. (Figure 40-1 shows a subset of the data.)

■ Transaction number

■ Name of the salesperson

■ Date of the transaction

■ Product sold

■ Units sold

■ Dollar amount of the transaction

■ Transaction location

	C	D	E	F	G	H	I
3	Transaction number	Name	Date	Product	Units	Dollars	Location
4	1	Betsy	4/1/2004	lip gloss	45	$ 137.20	south
5	2	Hallagan	3/10/2004	foundatio	50	$ 152.01	midwest
6	3	Ashley	2/25/2005	lipstick	9	$ 28.72	midwest
7	4	Hallagan	5/22/2006	lip gloss	55	$ 167.08	west
8	5	Zaret	6/17/2004	lip gloss	43	$ 130.60	midwest
9	6	Colleen	11/27/2005	eye liner	58	$ 175.99	midwest
10	7	Cristina	3/21/2004	eye liner	8	$ 25.80	midwest
11	8	Colleen	12/17/2006	lip gloss	72	$ 217.84	midwest
12	9	Ashley	7/5/2006	eye liner	75	$ 226.64	south
13	10	Betsy	8/7/2006	lip gloss	24	$ 73.50	east
14	11	Ashley	11/29/2004	mascara	43	$ 130.84	east
15	12	Ashley	11/18/2004	lip gloss	23	$ 71.03	west
16	13	Emilee	8/31/2005	lip gloss	49	$ 149.59	west
17	14	Hallagan	1/1/2005	eye liner	18	$ 56.47	south
18	15	Zaret	9/20/2006	foundatio	-8	$ (21.99)	east
19	16	Emilee	4/12/2004	mascara	45	$ 137.39	east
20	17	Colleen	4/30/2006	mascara	66	$ 199.65	south
21	18	Jen	8/31/2005	lip gloss	88	$ 265.19	midwest
22	19	Jen	10/27/2004	eye liner	78	$ 236.15	south
23	20	Zaret	11/27/2005	lip gloss	57	$ 173.12	midwest
24	21	Zaret	6/2/2006	mascara	12	$ 38.08	west
25	22	Betsy	9/24/2004	eye liner	28	$ 86.51	midwest
26	23	Colleen	2/1/2006	mascara	25	$ 77.31	midwest

Figure 40-1 Makeup sales data

Each column (C through I) of our "database" (cell range C4:I1894) is called a *field*. Each row of the database that contains data is called a *record*. (Thus, the records in our database are contained in the cell range C5:I1894.) The first row of each field must contain a field name. For example, the name of the field in column F is Product. By using the Excel AutoFilter, you can "query" a database using AND criteria to identify a subset of records. This means that you can use queries of the form "Find all records where Field 1 satisfies certain conditions, *and* Field 2 satisfies certain conditions, *and* Field 3 satisfies certain conditions." Our examples illustrate the capabilities of the Excel AutoFilter.

How can I identify all transactions in which Jen sold lipstick in the East region?

To begin, we place our cursor anywhere in the database and select Filter in the Sort & Filter group on the Data tab of the Ribbon. As shown in Figure 40-2, each column of the database now has an arrow in the heading row.

	C	D	E	F	G	H	I
3	Transaction number ▼	Name ▼	Date ▼	Product ▼	Units ▼	Dollars ▼	Location ▼
4	1	Betsy	4/1/2004	lip gloss	45	$137.20	south
5	2	Hallagan	3/10/2004	foundatio	50	$152.01	midwest
6	3	Ashley	2/25/2005	lipstick	9	$ 28.72	midwest
7	4	Hallagan	5/22/2006	lip gloss	55	$167.08	west
8	5	Zaret	6/17/2004	lip gloss	43	$130.60	midwest
9	6	Colleen	11/27/2005	eye liner	58	$175.99	midwest
10	7	Cristina	3/21/2004	eye liner	8	$ 25.80	midwest
11	8	Colleen	12/17/2006	lip gloss	72	$217.84	midwest
12	9	Ashley	7/5/2006	eye liner	75	$226.64	south
13	10	Betsy	8/7/2006	lip gloss	24	$ 73.50	east
14	11	Ashley	11/29/2004	mascara	43	$130.84	east
15	12	Ashley	11/18/2006	lip gloss	23	$ 71.03	west
16	13	Emilee	8/31/2005	lip gloss	49	$149.59	west
17	14	Hallagan	1/1/2005	eye liner	18	$ 56.47	south
18	15	Zaret	9/20/2006	foundatio	-8	$ (21.99)	east
19	16	Emilee	4/12/2004	mascara	45	$137.39	east
20	17	Colleen	4/30/2006	mascara	66	$199.65	south
21	18	Jen	8/31/2005	lip gloss	88	$265.19	midwest
22	19	Jen	10/27/2004	eye liner	78	$236.15	south
23	20	Zaret	11/27/2005	lip gloss	57	$173.12	midwest
24	21	Zaret	6/2/2006	mascara	12	$ 38.08	west

Figure 40-2   AutoFilter heading arrows

After clicking the arrow for the Name column, you will see the choices shown in Figure 40-3 on the next page.

We see that we could choose Text Filters which allow us to filter based on characteristics of the person's name (more on this later). For now, we just want to work with data for Jen, so we first clear the Select All box, then check the Jen box and click OK. We now see only those records where Jen was the salesperson. Next, we go to the Product column and check the lipstick box, and then to the Location column and check the East box. We now see only those transactions where Jen sold lipstick in the East region (see Figure 40-4 on the next page). Note the arrow has changed to a cone in the columns where we have set up filtering criteria.

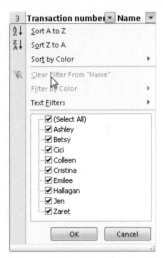

Figure 40-3   Choices for filtering or sorting the Name column

	C	D	E	F	G	H	I
3	Transaction number	Name	Date	Product	Units	Dollars	Location
503	500	Jen	3/19/2005	lipstick	6	$ 20.04	east
509	506	Jen	2/17/2004	lipstick	67	$ 202.62	east
691	688	Jen	3/6/2006	lipstick	36	$ 110.26	east
763	760	Jen	1/23/2005	lipstick	12	$ 37.85	east
846	843	Jen	7/27/2006	lipstick	34	$ 103.40	east
1232	1229	Jen	9/24/2004	lipstick	92	$ 277.63	east
1781	1778	Jen	8/31/2005	lipstick	24	$ 74.61	east
1815	1812	Jen	5/22/2006	lipstick	67	$ 203.18	east

Figure 40-4   Jen sells lipstick in the East region.

How can I identify all transactions in which Cici or Colleen sold lipstick or mascara in the East or South region?

We simply select Cici and Colleen from the Name column list, lipstick and mascara from the Product column list, and East and South from the Location column list. The records meeting our filtering criteria are shown in Figure 40-5.

Transaction number	Name	Date	Product	Units	Dollars	Location
17	Colleen	4/30/2006	mascara	66	$ 199.65	south
81	Cici	6/13/2006	lipstick	-3	$ (7.62)	south
103	Cici	11/18/2004	mascara	38	$ 115.86	south
136	Cici	9/24/2004	mascara	89	$ 269.40	east
140	Cici	3/8/2005	lipstick	37	$ 113.65	east
171	Colleen	5/26/2004	lipstick	60	$ 182.02	east
188	Colleen	2/6/2004	mascara	-5	$ (12.90)	east
198	Colleen	2/6/2004	mascara	60	$ 181.94	east
234	Colleen	7/9/2004	lipstick	-3	$ (7.40)	south
236	Cici	7/9/2004	mascara	5	$ 17.20	east
241	Colleen	11/3/2006	mascara	64	$ 194.25	east
250	Colleen	2/14/2005	lipstick	65	$ 196.49	south
252	Cici	7/16/2006	mascara	-1	$ (1.93)	south
314	Colleen	3/17/2006	lipstick	43	$ 130.95	south
334	Colleen	2/14/2005	lipstick	15	$ 46.64	east
336	Cici	7/18/2004	mascara	85	$ 257.29	south
397	Colleen	2/17/2004	mascara	91	$ 274.81	south
432	Cici	3/19/2005	mascara	27	$ 83.00	south
439	Cici	1/15/2004	mascara	4	$ 14.17	east
450	Colleen	4/10/2005	mascara	71	$ 214.77	south
451	Colleen	4/23/2004	mascara	74	$ 224.18	east
459	Cici	6/26/2005	mascara	22	$ 68.36	east

Figure 40-5   Transactions where Cici or Colleen sold lipstick or mascara in the East or South region

How can I copy all transactions in which Cici or Colleen sold lipstick or mascara in the East or South region to a different worksheet?

The trick here is to first press F5, click Special, and then select the Visible Cells Only option. Now when you copy, Excel will only include the visible rows (in this case, the rows selected by the filtering criteria). Now we select all the filtered cells in the worksheet (Cici, Colleen, lipstick, and mascara) and paste them into a blank worksheet. We can create a new blank worksheet in our workbook by right-clicking any worksheet tab, clicking Insert, selecting Worksheet, then clicking OK. The worksheet Visible Cells Copied contains the records where Cici or Colleen sold lipstick or mascara in the East.

How do I clear filters from a column or database?

Clicking Filter on the Data tab will remove all filters. Clicking the cone for any column where you have created a filter displays an option to clear the filter from that column.

How can I identify all transactions which involved sales of >$280 and >90 units?

After clicking Filter on the Data tab, we first click the Units column arrow to display the options shown in Figure 40-6 on the next page.

Figure 40-6 Filtering options for a numerical column

We can check any subset of numerical unit values (for example, all transactions where sales were −10 or −8 units). We click Number Filters to display the choices in Figure 40-7.

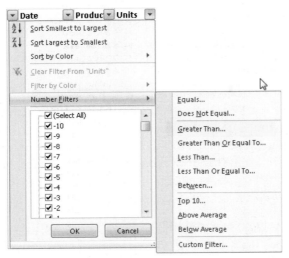

Figure 40-7 Number Filters options

Most of these are self-explanatory. We choose the Greater Than option and then fill in the dialog box as shown in Figure 40-8.

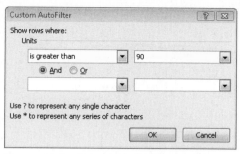

Figure 40-8   Selecting all records where units sold >90.

Next, we go to the Dollars column and click to include only records where *$ amount is >$280.* We obtain the records shown in Figure 40-9.

	C	D	E	F	G	H	I
3	Transaction number	Name	Date	Product	Units	Dollars	Location
40	37	Ashley	8/9/2005	mascara	93	$ 280.69	east
57	54	Cici	6/17/2004	eye liner	95	$ 287.76	midwest
64	61	Emilee	12/21/2004	eye liner	95	$ 287.05	midwest
65	62	Ashley	11/16/2005	lipstick	93	$ 280.77	west
165	162	Betsy	10/14/2005	foundatio	93	$ 280.17	west
217	214	Betsy	9/13/2004	foundatio	94	$ 283.74	west
284	281	Emilee	11/16/2005	foundatio	94	$ 283.85	midwest
289	286	Betsy	7/27/2006	mascara	94	$ 284.14	west
314	311	Jen	5/15/2004	eye liner	94	$ 283.88	east
338	335	Ashley	5/26/2004	mascara	94	$ 283.62	midwest
340	337	Colleen	11/18/2004	lip gloss	95	$ 286.86	west
406	403	Jen	6/4/2005	mascara	93	$ 281.17	south
450	447	Cici	10/1/2006	mascara	94	$ 283.45	west
545	542	Ashley	4/19/2006	foundatio	93	$ 281.17	midwest
579	576	Emilee	4/10/2005	lipstick	93	$ 280.80	midwest
587	584	Emilee	1/15/2004	foundatio	94	$ 284.61	east
599	596	Colleen	10/3/2005	mascara	94	$ 284.25	east
632	629	Hallagan	7/31/2004	mascara	94	$ 283.88	east
676	673	Emilee	11/7/2004	foundatio	94	$ 284.33	midwest
680	677	Hallagan	10/1/2006	foundatio	94	$ 283.77	south
722	719	Hallagan	6/13/2006	lip gloss	95	$ 286.68	midwest
780	777	Cici	4/21/2005	eye liner	93	$ 280.86	midwest

Figure 40-9   Transactions where >90 units were sold for a total of >$280.

How can I identify all sales occurring in 2005 or 2006?

After clicking Filter on the Ribbon, we click the arrow for the Date column and see the choices in Figure 40-10 on the next page.

Figure 40-10 Possible filtering options for the Date column

After selecting 2005 and 2006, we obtain only those records involving sales in 2005 or 2006, as shown in Figure 40-11.

	C	D	E	F	G	H	I
3	Transaction number	Name	Date	Product	Units	Dollars	Location
6	3	Ashley	2/25/2005	lipstick	9	$ 28.72	midwest
7	4	Hallagan	5/22/2006	lip gloss	55	$ 167.08	west
9	6	Colleen	11/27/2005	eye liner	58	$ 175.99	midwest
11	8	Colleen	12/17/2006	lip gloss	72	$ 217.84	midwest
12	9	Ashley	7/5/2006	eye liner	75	$ 226.64	south
13	10	Betsy	8/7/2006	lip gloss	24	$ 73.50	east
16	13	Emilee	8/31/2005	lip gloss	49	$ 149.59	west
17	14	Hallagan	1/1/2005	eye liner	18	$ 56.47	south
18	15	Zaret	9/20/2006	foundatio	-8	$ (21.99)	east
20	17	Colleen	4/30/2006	mascara	66	$ 199.65	south
21	18	Jen	8/31/2005	lip gloss	88	$ 265.19	midwest
23	20	Zaret	11/27/2005	lip gloss	57	$ 173.12	midwest
24	21	Zaret	6/2/2006	mascara	12	$ 38.08	west
26	23	Colleen	2/1/2006	mascara	25	$ 77.31	midwest
27	24	Emilee	12/6/2006	lip gloss	24	$ 74.62	west
29	26	Cristina	9/22/2005	foundatio	77	$ 233.05	midwest
30	27	Cristina	3/28/2006	lip gloss	53	$ 161.46	midwest
32	29	Zaret	9/9/2006	mascara	19	$ 59.15	west
33	30	Cici	2/23/2006	foundatio	-9	$ (24.63)	west
34	31	Hallagan	6/24/2006	foundatio	38	$ 115.58	south
36	33	Emilee	4/10/2005	mascara	19	$ 59.38	midwest
39	36	Emilee	9/20/2006	lip gloss	2	$ 7.85	east

Figure 40-11 Sales during 2005 and 2006

Note we could also have selected Date Filters to display the options shown in Figure 40-12.

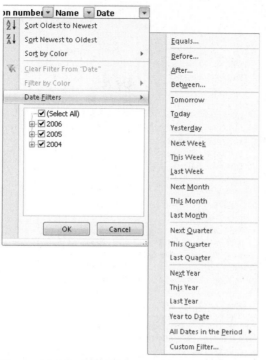

Figure 40-12   Date Filters options

Most of these are self-explanatory. The Custom Filter option allows you to select any range of dates as your filtering criteria.

How can I identify all transactions in the last three months of 2005 or the first three months of 2006?

After clicking the arrow for the Date column, we see the list of years shown in Figure 40-10. Clicking the + sign to the left of the year displays a list of months. We checked October-December of 2005 and then January-March of 2006 to show all sales during those months (see Figure 40-13 on the next page).

	C	D	E	F	G	H	I
1			last 3 months 05 and first 3 months 06				
2							
3	Transaction number	Name	Date	Product	Units	Dollars	Location
9	6	Colleen	11/27/2005	eye liner	58	$175.99	midwest
23	20	Zaret	11/27/2005	lip gloss	57	$173.12	midwest
26	23	Colleen	2/1/2006	mascara	25	$ 77.31	midwest
30	27	Cristina	3/28/2006	lip gloss	53	$161.46	midwest
33	30	Cici	2/23/2006	foundatio	-9	$ (24.63)	west
53	50	Cristina	12/8/2005	lip gloss	8	$ 26.24	midwest
55	52	Colleen	11/16/2005	foundatio	62	$189.25	midwest
61	58	Hallagan	11/5/2005	foundatio	63	$191.37	south
65	62	Ashley	11/16/2005	lipstick	93	$280.77	west
70	67	Colleen	3/6/2006	foundatio	-2	$ (3.94)	west
75	72	Jen	1/10/2006	lip gloss	69	$208.69	east
82	79	Zaret	12/19/2005	eye liner	26	$ 80.30	south
93	90	Colleen	1/21/2006	lip gloss	75	$226.74	south
94	91	Betsy	10/3/2005	eye liner	74	$224.23	west
98	95	Jen	3/17/2006	lipstick	-8	$ (22.11)	west
109	106	Emilee	1/21/2006	foundatio	39	$118.63	south
114	111	Hallagan	10/25/2005	mascara	61	$184.56	south
115	112	Zaret	3/6/2006	foundatio	30	$ 92.43	south
118	115	Ashley	1/10/2006	eye liner	57	$173.36	west
119	116	Hallagan	11/16/2005	lip gloss	41	$124.39	midwest
123	120	Zaret	2/12/2006	mascara	-10	$ (28.89)	west

Figure 40-13   All sales during October 2005–March 2006

How can I identify all transactions where the salesperson's first name starts with C?

Simply click the Name column arrow and choose Text Filters. Next, select Begins With, and from the dialog box shown in Figure 40-14, choose begins with C.

Figure 40-14   Custom AutoFilter dialog box to select all records where salesperson's name begins with C

How can I identify all transactions where the cell containing the product name was colored in red?

Simply click the Product column arrow and choose Filter By Color. You can now select the Color on which to filter. As shown in Figure 40-15, we chose to include only the rows where the Product is colored in red. Figure 40-16 shows the resulting records.

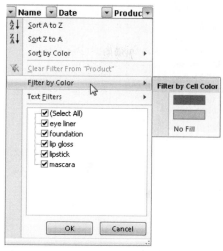

Figure 40-15   Dialog box for filtering by cell color

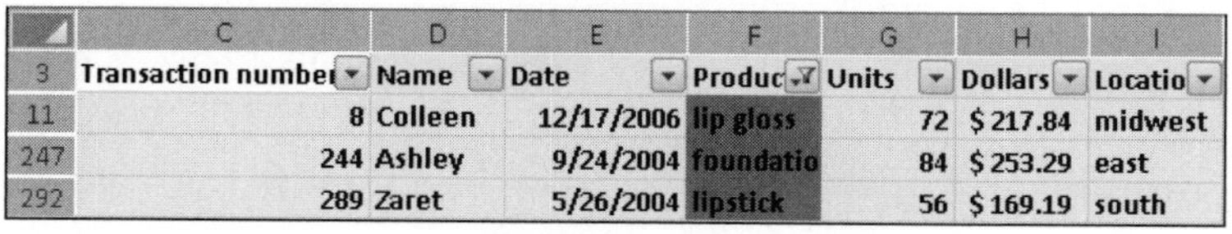

	C	D	E	F	G	H	I
3	Transaction number	Name	Date	Product	Units	Dollars	Location
11	8	Colleen	12/17/2006	lip gloss	72	$ 217.84	midwest
247	244	Ashley	9/24/2004	foundatio	84	$ 253.29	east
292	289	Zaret	5/26/2004	lipstick	56	$ 169.19	south

Figure 40-16   All records where the product cell color is red

How can I identify all transactions in the Top 30 revenue values where Hallagan or Jen was the salesperson?

After clicking Filter on the Ribbon, we click the Name column arrow and then check the boxes for Hallagan and Jen. Then we click the Dollar arrow and choose Number Filters. From the Number Filters list, we select the Top 10 option and fill in the dialog box as shown in Figure 40-17. We have now filtered all records in the Top 30 revenue values where Jen or Hallagan was the salesperson. See the results in Figure 40-18 on the next page. Note only 5 of the Top 30 $ sales had Hallagan or Jen as the salesperson. Note we may also select Top 5 percent, Bottom 20 percent, and so on, for any numerical column.

Figure 40-17   Dialog box to select the Top 30 records by $ value

	D	E	F	G	H	I
3	Name	Date	Produc	Units	Dollars	Locatio
314	Jen	5/15/2004	eye liner	94	$ 283.88	east
722	Hallagan	6/13/2006	lip gloss	95	$ 286.68	midwest
797	Hallagan	8/18/2006	foundatio	95	$ 287.80	midwest
1259	Hallagan	4/8/2006	lip gloss	95	$ 286.76	midwest
1619	Hallagan	7/29/2005	eye liner	95	$ 287.15	west

Figure 40-18 Top 30 records by $ value

How can I easily obtain a complete list of salespeople?

We want a list of all the salespeople, without anybody's name repeated. We begin by selecting Remove Duplicates on the Data tab of the Ribbon. This displays the Remove Duplicates dialog box shown in Figure 40-19. We check only the Name box and click OK. This will filter out the first record involving each salesperson's name. See the results in Figure 40-20.

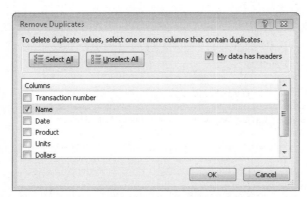

Figure 40-19 Remove Duplicates dialog box

	C	D	E	F	G	H	I
3	Transaction numb	Name	Date	Product	Units	Dollars	Location
4	1	Betsy	4/1/2004	lip gloss	45	$ 137.20	south
5	2	Hallagan	3/10/2004	foundatio	50	$ 152.01	midwest
6	3	Ashley	2/25/2005	lipstick	9	$ 28.72	midwest
7	5	Zaret	6/17/2004	lip gloss	43	$ 130.60	midwest
8	6	Colleen	11/27/2005	eye liner	58	$ 175.99	midwest
9	7	Cristina	3/21/2004	eye liner	8	$ 25.80	midwest
10	13	Emilee	8/31/2005	lip gloss	49	$ 149.59	west
11	18	Jen	8/31/2005	lip gloss	88	$ 265.19	midwest
12	28	Cici	6/17/2004	mascara	41	$ 125.27	west

Figure 40-20 List of salespersons' names

How can I view every combination of salesperson, product, and location that occurs in the database?

Again, we click Remove Duplicates on the Data tab of the Ribbon. Then we fill in the Remove Duplicates dialog box as shown in Figure 40-21.

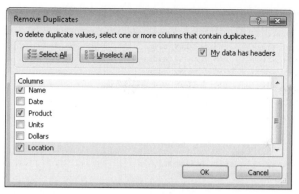

Figure 40-21   Finding unique salesperson, product, and location combinations

Figure 40-22 lists the first record for each combination of person, product, and location occurring in the database. We find that 180 unique combinations occurred.

	C	D	E	F	G	H	I
3	Transaction number	Name	Date	Product	Units	Dollars	Location
4	1	Betsy	4/1/2004	lip gloss	45	$ 137.20	south
5	2	Hallagan	3/10/2004	foundatio	50	$ 152.01	midwest
6	3	Ashley	2/25/2005	lipstick	9	$ 28.72	midwest
7	4	Hallagan	5/22/2006	lip gloss	55	$ 167.08	west
8	5	Zaret	6/17/2004	lip gloss	43	$ 130.60	midwest
9	6	Colleen	11/27/2005	eye liner	58	$ 175.99	midwest
10	7	Cristina	3/21/2004	eye liner	8	$ 25.80	midwest
11	8	Colleen	12/17/2006	lip gloss	72	$ 217.84	midwest
12	9	Ashley	7/5/2006	eye liner	75	$ 226.64	south
13	10	Betsy	8/7/2006	lip gloss	24	$ 73.50	east
14	11	Ashley	11/29/2004	mascara	43	$ 130.84	east
15	12	Ashley	11/18/2004	lip gloss	23	$ 71.03	west
16	13	Emilee	8/31/2005	lip gloss	49	$ 149.59	west
17	14	Hallagan	1/1/2005	eye liner	18	$ 56.47	south
18	15	Zaret	9/20/2006	foundatio	-8	$ (21.99)	east
19	16	Emilee	4/12/2004	mascara	45	$ 137.39	east
20	17	Colleen	4/30/2006	mascara	66	$ 199.65	south
21	18	Jen	8/31/2005	lip gloss	88	$ 265.19	midwest
22	19	Jen	10/27/2004	eye liner	78	$ 236.15	south
23	21	Zaret	6/2/2006	mascara	12	$ 38.08	west

Figure 40-22   List of unique salesperson, product, and location combinations

If my data changes, how can I reapply the same filter?

Simply right-click any cell in your filtered results, point to Filter, and then click Reapply. Any changes to your data will now be reflected in the filtered data.

How can I extract all foundation transactions in the first six months of 2005 for which Emilee or Jen was the salesperson and the average per-unit price was more than $3.20?

The AutoFilter feature (even with the Custom option) is limited to AND queries across columns. This means, for example, that we cannot find all transactions for lipstick sales by Jen during 2005 *OR* foundation sales by Zaret during 2004. To perform more complex queries such as this one, we need to use the Advanced Filter feature. To use

Advanced Filter, we set up a criteria range that specifies the records we want to extract. (This process is described in detail in Chapter 37, "Summarizing Data with Descriptive Statistics.") After specifying the criteria range, we tell Excel whether we want the records extracted to the current location or to a different location. To identify all foundation transactions in the first six months of 2005 for which Emilee or Jen was the salesperson and for which the average per-unit price was more than $3.20, we use the criteria range shown in cell range O4:S6 in Figure 40-23. See the file Advancedfilter.xlsx.

	O	P	Q	R	S	T	U
4	Name	Date	Date	Price	Product		
5	Jen	>=1/1/2005	<=6/30/2005	FALSE	Foundation		
6	Emilee	>=1/1/2005	<=6/30/2005	FALSE	Foundation		
7							
8							
9							
10							
11							
12							
13							
14	Trans Numbe	Name	Date	Product	Units	Dollars	Location
15	392	Jen	2/25/2005	foundation	8	$ 26.31	south
16	479	Emilee	5/24/2005	foundation	2	$ 7.68	east
17	1035	Emilee	4/10/2005	foundation	8	$ 26.40	east
18	1067	Jen	3/19/2005	foundation	1	$ 4.86	east

Figure 40-23 Setting up a criteria range to use with an advanced filter

In cells R5 and R6, I entered the formula $=(L5/K5)>3.2$. Recall from Chapter 39, "Summarizing Data with Database Statistical Functions," that this formula creates computed criteria that flags each row in which the per-unit price is more than $3.20. Also remember that our heading for a computed criteria must not be a field name, so I used Price as the field heading. Our criteria in O5:S5 flags all records in which Jen is the salesperson, the date is between 1/1/2005 and 6/30/2005, the product sold is foundation, and the per-unit price is more than $3.20. Our criteria in O6:S6 flags all records in which Emilee is the salesperson, the date is between 1/1/2005 and 6/30/2005, the product sold is foundation, and the per-unit price is more than $3.20. The criteria range of O4:S6 flags exactly the records we want. Remember that criteria in different rows are joined by OR.

We can now select any cell within the database range and, on the Data tab of the Ribbon, select Advanced from the Sort & Filter group. We fill in the dialog box as shown in Figure 40-24.

Figure 40-24 Advanced Filter dialog box settings

With these settings, we are telling Excel to extract all records in the database (cell range G4:M1895) that satisfy the criteria specified in O4:S6. These records should be copied to a range whose upper-left corner is cell O14. The records extracted are shown in the cell range O14:U18. Only four records meet the criteria we defined.

If we check the Unique Records Only box in the Advanced Filter dialog box, no duplicate records are returned. For example, if Jen had another foundation transaction in the East region on 3/19/2005 for one unit for $4.88, only one of these transactions would be extracted.

Problems

1.   Find all transactions in which Hallagan sold eye liner in the West region.

2.   Find all transactions that rank in the top five percent with regards to units sold.

3.   Find the top 20 revenue-generating transactions that involve foundation sales.

4.   Find all transactions involving sales of at least 60 units during 2004 for which the per-unit price was a maximum of $3.10.

5.   Find all foundation transactions during the first three months of 2004 for which the per-unit price was larger than the average price received for foundation during the entire time period.

6.   Find all transactions in which Zaret or Betsy sold either lipstick or foundation.

7.   Find all unique combinations of product and salesperson's name.

8.   Find all of the top 30 sales (by units) occurring in 2005 which involved lip gloss or mascara.

9.   Find all sales by Jen between August 10 and September 15, 2005.

10.   Find all sales of lipstick sold by Colleen where the number of units sold is higher than the average number of units in a lipstick transaction.

11.   Find all unique combinations of name, product, and location occurring during the first three months of 2006.

12.   Find all records in which the product cell is colored in yellow.

Chapter 41
Consolidating Data

Suppose your company sells products in several regions of the United States. Each region keeps records of the number of units of each product sold during the months of January, February, and March. You might have a question like the following: Is there an easy way to create a "master workbook" that always combines each region's sales and gives a tally of the total amount of each product sold in the U.S. during each month?

A business analyst often receives worksheets that tally the same information (such as monthly product sales) from different affiliates or regions. To determine the company's overall profitability, the analyst usually needs to combine or consolidate this information into a single Microsoft Office Excel 2007 workbook. PivotTables built from multiple consolidation ranges can be used to accomplish this goal, but the little known Consolidate command (on the Data tab of the Ribbon) is another way to accomplish this goal. With Consolidate, you can ensure that changes in the individual worksheets will be automatically reflected in the consolidated worksheet.

Is there an easy way to create a "master workbook" that always combines each region's sales and gives a tally of the total amount of each product sold in the U.S. during each month?

The file East.xlsx (shown in Figure 41-1 on the next page) displays monthly unit sales of Products A–H in the eastern U.S. during January, February, and March. Similarly, the file West.xlsx (shown in Figure 41-2 on the next page) displays monthly unit sales of Products A–H in the western U.S. from January through March. We want to create a consolidated worksheet that tabulates each product's total sales by month.

	A	B	C	D	E	F
1	Product	January	February	March		East Sales
2	A	205	263	20		
3	B	164	-17	146		
4	C	278	177	179		
5	D	156	214	240		
6	D	72	134	48		
7	D	7	256	104		
8	A	141	87	148		
9	A	2	-15	135		
10	A	-44	47	72		
11	B	7	-81	2		
12	E	25	120	171		
13	E	197	90	124		
14	E	221	121	48		
15	A	84	103	134		
16	G	-13	250	51		
17	D	-5	159	70		
18	E	136	152	28		

Figure 41-1   East region sales during January–March

	A	B	C	D	E	F
1	Product	January	February	March		West sales
2	A	173	1	256		
3	A	208	201	224		
4	B	176	33	350		
5	B	190	249	215		
6	D	162	74	156		
7	D	90	150	170		
8	D	112	284	141		
9	G	154	217	113		
10	G	152	200	275		
11	G	277	183	372		
12	H	131	71	266		
13	F	294	211	249		
14	F	146	125	5		
15	A	115	214	141		
16	F	157	241	73		
17	A	125	227	135		
18	A	314	189	180		
19	C	189	154	101		
20	C	313	182	68		
21	C	389	247	257		
22	B	353	151	99		
23	C	62	162	238		
24	D	173	153	270		

Figure 41-2   West region sales during January–March

Before using the Consolidate command, it's helpful to see both spreadsheets together on the same screen. To do this, open both workbooks, click Arrange All in the Window group on the View tab, and select the Tiled option. Your screen should look like Figure 41-3.

Now open a blank worksheet in a new workbook and click Arrange All and Tiled again. In the blank worksheet, click Consolidate in the Data Tools group on the Data tab, and you'll see the Consolidate dialog box, shown in Figure 41-4.

To consolidate the data from the East and West regions into our new, blank worksheet, we enter the ranges we want to consolidate in the Reference box of the Consolidate dialog box, clicking Add after selecting each range. By checking the Top Row and Left Column boxes in the Use Labels In area, we ensure that Excel will consolidate the selected ranges by looking at labels in the top row and left column of the ranges we select. The Create Links To Source Data option enables changes in our selected ranges to be reflected in the consolidated worksheet. We select Sum in the Function box because we want Excel to add up the total sales of each product by month. Selecting Count, for instance, would count the number of transactions for each product during each month; selecting Max would compute the largest sales transaction for each product during each month. The Consolidate dialog box should be filled out as shown in Figure 41-5 on the next page.

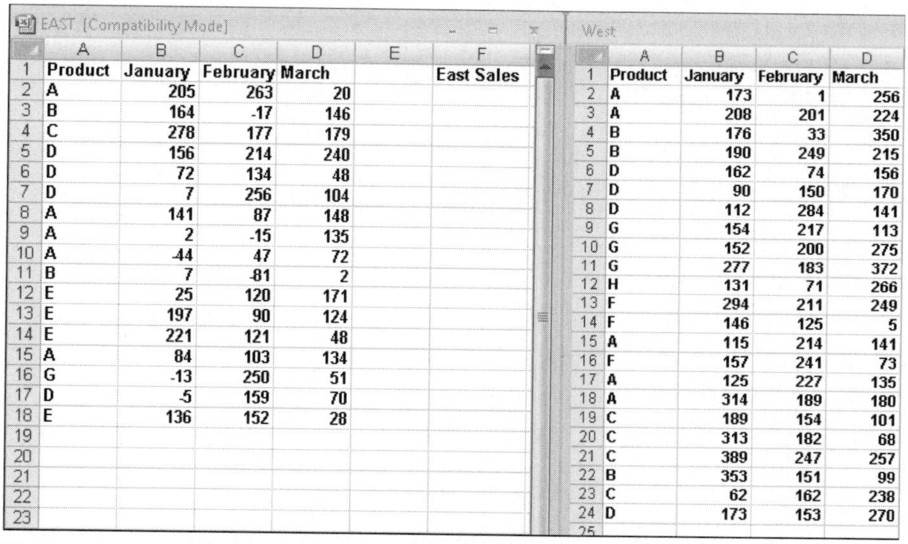

EAST [Compatibility Mode]

	A	B	C	D	E	F
1	Product	January	February	March		East Sales
2	A	205	263	20		
3	B	164	-17	146		
4	C	278	177	179		
5	D	156	214	240		
6	D	72	134	48		
7	D	7	256	104		
8	A	141	87	148		
9	A	2	-15	135		
10	A	-44	47	72		
11	B	7	-81	2		
12	E	25	120	171		
13	E	197	90	124		
14	E	221	121	48		
15	A	84	103	134		
16	G	-13	250	51		
17	D	-5	159	70		
18	E	136	152	28		
19						
20						
21						
22						
23						

West

	A	B	C	D
1	Product	January	February	March
2	A	173	1	256
3	A	208	201	224
4	B	176	33	350
5	B	190	249	215
6	D	162	74	156
7	D	90	150	170
8	D	112	284	141
9	G	154	217	113
10	G	152	200	275
11	G	277	183	372
12	H	131	71	266
13	F	294	211	249
14	F	146	125	5
15	A	115	214	141
16	F	157	241	73
17	A	125	227	135
18	A	314	189	180
19	C	189	154	101
20	C	313	182	68
21	C	389	247	257
22	B	353	151	99
23	C	62	162	238
24	D	173	153	270
25				

Figure 41-3   East and West sales arranged on the same screen

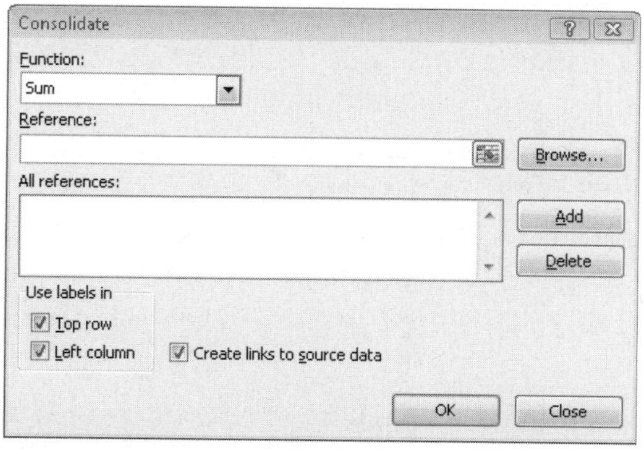

Figure 41-4   Consolidate dialog box

After clicking OK, our new worksheet looks like the one shown in Figure 41-6 on the next page. See file Eastandwestconsolidated.xlsx.

We find, for example, that 1317 units of Product A were sold in February, 597 units of Product F were sold in January, and so on.

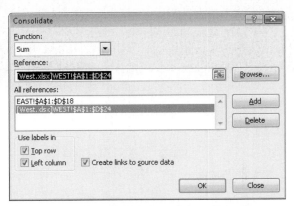

Figure 41-5 Completed Consolidate dialog box

1 2		A	B	C	D	E
	1			January	February	March
+	3	H		131	71	266
+	7	F		597	577	327
+	18	A		1323	1317	1445
+	24	B		890	335	812
+	30	C		1231	922	843
+	39	D		767	1424	1199
+	44	E		579	483	371
+	49	G		570	850	811
	50					

Figure 41-6 Total sales after consolidation

Now go to the cell C2 of East.xlsx and change the February Product A sales from 263 to 363. Note that in the consolidated worksheet, our entry for February Product A sales has also increased by 100 (from 1317 to 1417). This change occurs because we checked the Create Links To Source Data box in the Consolidate dialog box. (By the way, if you click the 2 right below the workbook name in the consolidated worksheet, you'll see how Excel grouped the data to perform the consolidation.) Our final result is contained in the file Eastandwestconsolidated.xlsx.

If you frequently download new data to your source workbooks (in this case, East.xlsx and West.xlsx), it's a good idea to name the ranges including your data as a table. Then new data will automatically be included in the consolidation.

Problems

The following problems refer to the data in files Jancon.xlsx and Febcon.xlsx. Each file contains the unit sales, dollar revenues, and product sold for each transaction during the month.

1. Create a consolidated worksheet that gives the total unit sales and dollar revenue for each product by region.

2. Create a consolidated worksheet that gives the largest first-quarter transaction for each product by region from the standpoint of revenue and units sold.

Chapter 42
Creating Subtotals

Joolas is a small company that manufactures makeup. For each transaction, they track the name of the salesperson, the location of the transaction, the product sold, the units sold, and the revenue. They want answers to the following questions:

- Is there an easy way to set up a worksheet to calculate total revenue and units sold by region?

- Can I also obtain a breakdown by salesperson of sales in each region?

We know that PivotTables can be used to "slice and dice" data in Microsoft Office Excel 2007. Often, however, we'd like an easier way to summarize a list or a database within a list. In a sales database, for example, we might want to create a summary of sales revenue by region, a summary of sales revenue by product, and a summary of sales revenue by salesperson. If we sort a list by the column in which specific data is listed, the Subtotal command allows us to create a subtotal in a list on the basis of the values in the column. For example, if we sort our makeup database by location, we can calculate total revenue and units sold for each region and place the totals just below the last row for that region. As another example, after sorting our database by product, we can use the Subtotal command to calculate total revenue and units sold for each product and display the totals below the row in which the product changes. In the next section, we'll look at some specific examples.

Is there an easy way to set up a worksheet to calculate total revenue and units sold by region?

Our data is in the file Makeupsubtotals.xlsx. In Figure 42-1 on the next page, you can see a subset of the data as it appears after sorting the list by the Location column.

To calculate revenue and units sold by region, place the cursor anywhere in the database and then click Subtotal in the Outline group on the Data tab of the Ribbon. In the Subtotal dialog box, we fill in the values as shown in Figure 42-2 on the next page.

By selecting Location from the At Each Change In list, we ensure that subtotals are created at each point in which the value in the Location column changes. This corresponds to the different regions. Selecting Sum from the Use Function box tells Excel to total the units and dollars for each different region. By checking the Units and Dollars boxes in the Add Subtotal To area, we indicate that subtotals should be created on the basis of the values in these columns. The Replace Current Subtotals option causes Excel to remove any previously computed subtotals. Because we haven't created any subtotals, it doesn't matter whether or not this option is checked for this example. If the Page Break Between Groups box is checked, Excel inserts a page break after each subtotal. Checking the Summary Below Data box causes Excel to place subtotals below the data. If this box is not checked, the subtotals are created above the data used for the computation. Clicking Remove All removes subtotals from the list.

	A	B	C	D	E	F	G
4	Trans Number	Name	Date	Product	Units	Dollars	Location
5	10	Betsy	8/7/2006	lip gloss	24	$ 73.50	east
6	11	Ashley	11/29/2004	mascara	43	$ 130.84	east
7	15	Zaret	9/20/2006	foundatio	-8	$ (21.99)	east
8	16	Emilee	4/12/2004	mascara	45	$ 137.39	east
9	45	Emilee	9/20/2006	lip gloss	2	$ 7.85	east
10	46	Ashley	8/9/2005	mascara	93	$ 280.69	east
11	58	Cristina	4/12/2004	foundatio	34	$ 104.09	east
12	60	Jen	10/27/2004	mascara	89	$ 269.09	east
13	69	Cristina	1/23/2005	eye liner	73	$ 221.41	east
14	77	Cristina	1/15/2004	mascara	27	$ 83.29	east
15	81	Jen	1/10/2006	lip gloss	69	$ 208.69	east
16	86	Jen	8/9/2005	eye liner	-2	$ (4.24)	east
17	87	Emilee	8/31/2005	eye liner	5	$ 17.03	east
18	98	Jen	4/12/2004	lip gloss	92	$ 277.54	east
19	108	Cici	8/31/2005	lip gloss	-10	$ (28.41)	east
20	114	Betsy	9/22/2005	lipstick	77	$ 233.33	east
21	116	Zaret	6/24/2006	eye liner	22	$ 68.07	east
22	119	Colleen	5/22/2006	eye liner	20	$ 62.37	east
23	131	Jen	11/29/2004	mascara	56	$ 168.87	east
24	133	Betsy	7/9/2004	mascara	11	$ 34.42	east
25	140	Jen	6/28/2004	eye liner	80	$ 242.50	east
26	145	Cici	9/24/2004	mascara	89	$ 269.40	east
27	147	Emilee	3/8/2005	lipstick	90	$ 271.75	east
28	149	Cici	3/8/2005	lipstick	37	$ 113.65	east
29	164	Hallagan	10/12/2006	eye liner	16	$ 49.92	east
30	165	Hallagan	12/19/2005	foundatio	25	$ 76.99	east
31	169	Ashley	2/17/2004	lip gloss	63	$ 191.11	east

Figure 42-1   After sorting a list by the values in a specific column, you can easily create subtotals for that data.

Figure 42-2   Subtotal dialog box

A sample of our subtotals results is shown in Figure 42-3. We find that 18,818 units were sold in the East region, earning revenue of $57,372.09.

	A	B	C	D	E	F	G
451	1867	Cristina	8/18/2006	mascara	73	$ 220.77	east
452	1869	Betsy	10/3/2005	lipstick	18	$ 56.08	east
453	1877	Cici	9/13/2004	eye liner	66	$ 199.36	east
454	1881	Emilee	10/3/2005	foundatio	0	$ 2.66	east
455	1883	Betsy	7/20/2004	lip gloss	-6	$ (15.74)	east
456	1890	Cici	6/15/2005	foundatio	16	$ 49.75	east
457	1891	Betsy	4/10/2005	foundatio	39	$ 119.19	east
458	1894	Colleen	5/15/2004	lip gloss	60	$ 181.87	east
459	1895	Emilee	11/27/2005	eye liner	15	$ 47.16	east
460	1896	Ashley	2/14/2005	foundatio	36	$ 109.84	east
461					18818	$ 57,372.09	east Total
462	2	Hallagan	3/10/2004	foundatio	50	$ 152.01	midwest
463	3	Ashley	2/25/2005	lipstick	9	$ 28.72	midwest
464	5	Zaret	6/17/2004	lip gloss	43	$ 130.60	midwest
465	6	Colleen	11/27/2005	eye liner	58	$ 175.99	midwest
466	7	Cristina	3/21/2004	eye liner	8	$ 25.80	midwest
467	8	Colleen	12/17/2006	lip gloss	72	$ 217.84	midwest
468	18	Jen	8/31/2005	lip gloss	88	$ 265.19	midwest
469	20	Zaret	11/27/2005	lip gloss	57	$ 173.12	midwest
470	22	Betsy	9/24/2004	eye liner	28	$ 86.51	midwest
471	23	Colleen	2/1/2006	mascara	25	$ 77.31	midwest
472	27	Jen	4/12/2004	lipstick	38	$ 115.99	midwest
473	28	Cristina	9/22/2005	foundatio	77	$ 233.05	midwest
474	32	Cristina	3/28/2006	lip gloss	53	$ 161.46	midwest
475	42	Emilee	4/10/2005	mascara	19	$ 59.38	midwest
476	44	Colleen	6/6/2004	lip gloss	55	$ 167.12	midwest
477	51	Zaret	6/15/2005	eye liner	24	$ 73.60	midwest

Figure 42-3   Subtotals for each region

Notice that in the left corner of the screen below the Name Box, buttons with the numbers 1, 2, and 3 appear. Clicking the largest number (in this case, 3) yields the data and subtotals. If we click the 2 button, we see just the subtotals by region, as shown in Figure 42-4. Clicking the 1 button yields the Grand Total, as shown in Figure 42-5. In short, clicking a lower number reduces the level of detail shown.

4	E Units	F Dollars	G Location
461	18818	$ 57,372.09	east Total
886	17985	$ 54,805.41	midwest Total
1408	21083	$ 64,296.35	south Total
1899	20821	$ 63,438.82	west Total
1900	78707	$ 239,912.67	Grand Total

Figure 42-4   When you create subtotals, Excel adds buttons that, when clicked, display only subtotals or both subtotals and details.

4	E Units	F Dollars	G Location
1900	78707	$ 239,912.67	Grand Total

Figure 42-5   Displaying the overall total without any detail

Can I also obtain a breakdown by salesperson of sales in each region?

If you wish, you can nest subtotals. In other words, you can obtain a breakdown of sales by each salesperson in each region, or you can even get a breakdown of how much each salesperson sold of each product in each region. See the file Nestedsubtotals.xlsx. To demonstrate the creation of nested subtotals, we will create a breakdown of sales by each salesperson in each region.

To begin, you must sort your data first by Location and then by Name. This will give a breakdown for each salesperson of units sold and revenue within each region. If we sorted first by Name and then by Location, we would get a breakdown of units sold and revenue for each salesperson by region. After sorting the data, we proceed as before and create the subtotals by region. Then we click Subtotal again and fill in the dialog box as shown in Figure 42-6.

Figure 42-6   Creating nested subtotals

We now want a breakdown by Name. Clearing the Replace Current Subtotals box ensures that we will not replace our regional breakdown. We now see the breakdown of sales by each salesperson in each region as shown in Figure 42-7.

	A	B	C	D	E	F	G
4	Trans Number	Name	Date	Product	Units	Dollars	Location
56		Ashley Total			2558	$ 7,772.70	
122		Betsy Total			2879	$ 8,767.43	
173		Cici Total			1951	$ 5,956.32	
220		Colleen Total			1874	$ 5,713.07	
261		Cristina Total			1348	$ 4,126.27	
312		Emilee Total			2064	$ 6,295.47	
355		Hallagan Total			1626	$ 4,965.62	
409		Jen Total			2282	$ 6,949.21	
469		Zaret Total			2236	$ 6,826.00	
470					18818	$ 57,372.09	east Total
511		Ashley Total			1635	$ 4,985.90	
555		Betsy Total			1598	$ 4,878.09	
616		Cici Total			2671	$ 8,129.62	
670		Colleen Total			2159	$ 6,586.14	
721		Cristina Total			1923	$ 5,870.03	
766		Emilee Total			1852	$ 5,642.20	
809		Hallagan Total			2431	$ 7,378.32	
862		Jen Total			2092	$ 6,381.32	
903		Zaret Total			1624	$ 4,953.80	
904					17985	$ 54,805.41	midwest Total
963		Ashley Total			2425	$ 7,398.57	
1019		Betsy Total			2541	$ 7,732.06	
1088		Cici Total			2347	$ 7,174.45	
1150		Colleen Total			2556	$ 7,785.63	
1210		Cristina Total			1947	$ 5,964.16	
1266		Emilee Total			1981	$ 6,050.59	
1328		Hallagan Total			2697	$ 8,210.81	
1379		Jen Total			2338	$ 7,116.02	
1434		Zaret Total			2251	$ 6,864.07	
1435					21083	$ 64,296.35	south Total

Figure 42-7   Nested subtotals

Problems

You can find the data for this chapter's problems in the file Makeupsubtotals.xlsx. Use the Subtotal command for the following computations:

1. Find the units sold and revenue for each salesperson.
2. Find the number of sales transactions for each product.
3. Find the largest transaction (in terms of revenue) for each product.
4. Find the average dollar amount per transaction by region.
5. Display a breakdown of units sold and revenue for each salesperson that shows the results for each product by region.

Chapter 43
Estimating Straight Line Relationships

Suppose you manage a plant that manufactures small refrigerators. National headquarters tells you how many refrigerators to produce each month. For budgeting purposes, you want to forecast your monthly operating costs. You have the following questions:

- How can I determine the relationship between monthly production and monthly operating costs?

- How accurately does this relationship explain the monthly variation in plant operating cost?

- How accurate are my predictions likely to be?

- When estimating a straight line relationship, which functions can I use to get the slope and intercept of the line that best fits the data?

Every business analyst should have the ability to estimate the relationship between important business variables. In Microsoft Office Excel 2007, the trend curve, which we'll discuss in this chapter as well as in Chapter 44, "Modeling Exponential Growth," and in Chapter 45, "The Power Curve," is often helpful in determining the relationship between two variables. The variable we're trying to predict is called the *dependent variable*. The variable we use for prediction is called the *independent variable*. Here are some examples of business relationships we might want to estimate.

Independent variable	Dependent variable
Units produced by plant in a month	Monthly cost of operating plant
Dollars spent on advertising in a month	Monthly sales
Number of employees	Annual travel expenses
Company revenue	Number of employees (headcount)
Monthly return on the stock market	Monthly return on a stock (for example, Dell)
Square feet in home	Value of home

The first step in determining how two variables are related is to graph the data points (by using the Scatter Chart option) so that the independent variable is on the x-axis and the dependent variable is on the y-axis. With the chart selected, you click a data point (they are then all displayed in blue), click Trendline in the Analysis group on the Chart Tools Layout tab, and then click More Trendline Options (or right-click and select Add Trendline). You'll see the Format Trendline dialog box, which is shown in Figure 43-1.

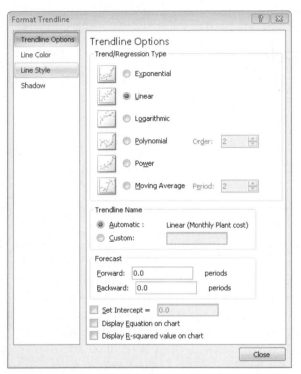

Figure 43-1   Format Trendline options

If your graph indicates that a straight line is a reasonable fit to the points, choose the Linear option. If the graph indicates that the dependent variable increases at an increasing rate, the Exponential (and perhaps Power) option probably fits the relationship. If the graph shows that the dependent variable increases at a decreasing rate, or that the dependent variable decreases at a decreasing rate, the Power option is probably the most relevant.

In this chapter, I'll focus on the Linear option. In Chapter 44, I'll discuss the Exponential option. In Chapter 45, I'll cover the Power option. In Chapter 52, "Using Moving Averages to Understand Time Series," I'll discuss the moving average curve, and in Chapter 71, "Pricing Products by Using Tie-Ins," I'll discuss the polynomial curve. (The logarithmic curve is of little value in this discussion, so I won't address it.)

How can I determine the relationship between monthly production and monthly operating costs?

The file Costestimate.xlsx, shown in Figure 43-2, contains data about the units produced and the monthly plant operating cost for a 14-month period. We are interested in predicting monthly operating costs from units produced, which will help the plant manager determine the operating budget and better understand the cost to produce refrigerators.

	C	D	E	F
1			sum errors	-0.0304
2	Units Produced	Monthly Plant cos	Predicted cost	Error
3	1260	123118	118872.66	4245.342
4	1007	99601	102612.68	-3011.68
5	1296	132000	121186.33	10813.67
6	873	80000	94000.671	-14000.7
7	532	52000	72085.044	-20085
8	476	58625	68485.997	-9861
9	482	74624	68871.609	5752.391
10	1273	110000	119708.15	-9708.15
11	692	81000	82368.036	-1368.04
12	690	73507	82239.499	-8732.5
13	564	95024	74141.642	20882.36
14	470	88004	68100.385	19903.62
15	675	70000	81275.468	-11275.5
16	870	110253	93807.865	16445.14
17	1100		108589.67	

Figure 43-2   Plant operating data

We begin by creating an XY chart (or a scatter plot) that displays our independent variable (units produced) on the x-axis and our dependent variable (monthly plant cost) on the y-axis. The column of data that you want to display on the x-axis must be located to the left of the column of data you want to display on the y-axis. To create the graph, we select the data in the range C2:D16 (including the labels in cells C2 and D2). We then click Scatter in the Charts group on the Insert tab of the Ribbon, and select the first option (Scatter With Only Markers) as the chart type. You'll see the graph shown in Figure 43-3.

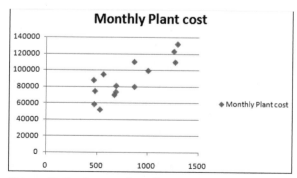

Figure 43-3   Scatter plot of operating cost vs. units produced

If you want to modify this chart, you can click anywhere inside the chart to display the Chart Tools contextual tab. Using the commands on the Chart Tools Design tab, you can:

❑ Change the chart type.

❑ Change the source data.

❑ Change the style of the chart.

❑ Move the chart.

Using the commands on the Chart Tools Layout tab, you can:

❑ Add a chart title.

❑ Add axis labels.

❑ Add labels to each point that give the x and y coordinate of each point.

❑ Add gridlines to the chart.

Looking at our scatter plot, it seems reasonable that there is a straight line (or linear relationship) between units produced and monthly operating costs. We can see the straight line that "best fits" the points by adding a trendline to the chart. Click within the chart to select it, and then click a data point. All the data points are displayed in blue with an X covering each point. Right-click, and then click Add Trendline. In the Format Trendline dialog box, select the Linear option, and then check the Display Equation On Chart and the Display R-Squared Value On Chart boxes, as shown in Figure 43-4.

Figure 43-4   Selecting trendline options.

After clicking Close, you'll see the results shown in Figure 43-5. Notice that I added a title to the chart and labels for the x-and y-axes by selecting Chart Tools and clicking Chart Title and then Axis Titles in the Labels group on the Layout tab.

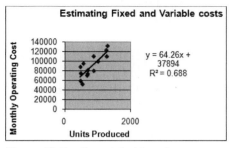

Figure 43-5 Completed trend curve

To add more decimal points to the equation, I right-clicked the trendline equation, clicked Format Trendline Label, and set the number of decimal points to four.

How does Excel determine the "best fitting" line? Excel chooses the line that minimizes (over all lines that could be drawn) the sum of the squared vertical distance from each point to the line. The vertical distance from each point to the line is called an *error*, or *residual*. The line created by Excel is called the *least-squares line*. We minimize the sum of squared errors rather than the sum of the errors because in simply summing the errors, positive and negative errors can cancel each other out. For example, a point 100 units above the line and a point 100 units below the line will cancel each other if we add errors. If we square errors, however, the fact that our predictions for each point are wrong will be used by Excel to find the best fitting line.

Thus, Excel calculates that the best fitting straight line for predicting monthly operating cost from monthly units produced as

```
(Monthly operating cost)=37,894.0956+64.2687(Units produced)
```

By copying from cell E3 to the cell range E4:E16 the formula *64.2687*C3+37894.0956*, we compute the predicted cost for each observed data point. For example, when 1260 units are produced, the predicted cost is $123,118 (see Figure 43-2).

You should not use a least-squares line to predict values of an independent variable that lie outside the range for which you have data. Our line should be used only to predict monthly plant operating costs during months in which production is between approximately 450 and 1300 units.

The intercept of this line is $37,894.10, which can be interpreted as the *monthly fixed cost.* So, even if the plant does not produce any refrigerators during a month, we estimate the plant will still incur costs of $37,894.10. The slope of this line (64.2687) indicates that each extra refrigerator we produce increases monthly cost by $64.27. Thus we estimate the *variable cost* of producing a refrigerator is $64.27.

In cells F3:F16, I've computed the errors (or residuals) for each data point. We define the error for each data point as the amount by which the point varies from the least-squares line. For each month, error equals the observed cost minus the predicted cost. Copying from F3 to F4:F16 the formula *D3-E3* computes the error for each data point. A positive error indicates a point is above the least-squares line, and a negative error indicates that the point is below the least-squares line. In cell F1, I computed the sum of the errors and obtained −0.03. In reality, for any least-squares line, the sum of the errors should equal 0. (I obtained −0.03 because I rounded the equation to four decimal points.) The fact that errors sum to 0 implies that the least-squares line has the intuitively satisfying property of splitting the points in half.

How accurately does this relationship explain the monthly variation in plant operating cost?

Clearly, each month both the operating cost and the units produced vary. A natural question is, what percentage of the monthly variation in operating cost is explained by the monthly variation in units produced? The answer to this question is the R^2 value (0.688) shown in Figure 43-5. We can state that our linear relationship explains 68.82 percent of the variation in monthly operating costs. This implies that 31.8 percent of the variation in monthly operating costs is explained by other factors. Using *multiple regression* (see Chapters 46 through 48), we can try to determine other factors that influence operating costs.

People always ask, what is a good R^2 value? There is really no definitive answer to this question. With one independent variable, of course, a larger R^2 value indicates a better fit of the data than a smaller R^2 value. A better measure of the accuracy of your predictions is the *standard error of the regression*, which I'll describe in the next section.

How accurate are my predictions likely to be?

When we fit a line to points, we obtain a standard error of the regression that measures the "spread" of the points around the least-squares line. The standard error associated with a least-squares line can be computed with the STEYX function. The syntax of this function is STEYX(*yrange,xrange*), where *yrange* contains the values of the dependent variable, and *xrange* contains the values of the independent variable. In cell K1, I computed the standard error of our cost estimate line with the formula *STEYX(D3:D16,C3:C16)*. The result is shown in Figure 43-6.

Approximately 68 percent of our points should be within one standard error of regression (SER) of the least-squares line, and about 95 percent of our points should be within two SER of the least-squares line. These measures are reminiscent of the descriptive statistics rule of thumb that I described in Chapter 37, "Summarizing Data by Using Descriptive Statistics." In our example, the absolute value of around 68 percent of the errors should be $13,772 or smaller, and the absolute value of around 95 percent of the errors should be $27,544, or 2*13,772, or smaller. Looking at the errors in column F, we find that 10 out of 14, or 71 percent, of our points are within one SER of the least-squares line and all (100 percent) of our points are within two standard SER of the least-squares line. Any point that is more than two SER from the least-squares line is called an *outlier*. Looking for causes of outliers can often help you to improve the operation of your business. For example, a month in which actual operating costs were $30,000 higher than anticipated would be a cost outlier on the high side. If we could ascertain the cause of this high cost outlier and prevent it from recurring, we would clearly improve plant efficiency. Similarly, consider a month in which actual costs are $30,000 less than expected. If we could ascertain the cause of this low cost outlier and ensure it occurred more often, we would improve plant efficiency.

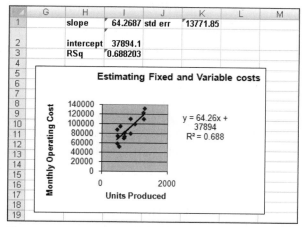

Figure 43-6   Computation of slope, intercept, RSQ, and standard error of regression

When estimating a straight line relationship, which functions can I use to get the slope and intercept of the line that best fits the data?

The Excel SLOPE(*yrange,xrange*) and INTERCEPT(*yrange,xrange*) functions return the slope and intercept, respectively, of the least-squares line. Thus, entering in cell I1 the formula SLOPE(*D3:D16,C3:C16*) (see Figure 43-6) returns the slope (64.27) of the least-squares line. Entering in cell I2 the formula INTERCEPT(*D3:D16,C3:C16*) returns the intercept (37,894.1) of the least-squares line. By the way, the RSQ(*yrange,xrange*) function returns the R^2 value associated with a least-squares line. So, entering in cell I3 the formula RSQ(*D3:D16,C3:C16*) returns the R^2 value of 0.6882 for our least-squares line.

Problems

The file Delldata.xlsx contains monthly returns for the Standard & Poor's stock index and for Dell stock. The *beta* of a stock is defined as the slope of the least-squares line used to predict the monthly return for a stock from the monthly return for the market.

1. Estimate the beta of Dell.

2. Interpret the meaning of Dell's beta.

3. If you believe a recession is coming, would you rather invest in a high beta or low beta stock?

4. During a month in which the market goes up 5 percent, you are 95 percent sure that Dell's stock price will increase between which range of values?

The file Housedata.xlsx gives the square footage and sales prices for several houses in Bellevue, Washington.

1. You are going to build a 500-square-foot addition to your house. How much do you think your home value will increase as a result?

2. What percentage of the variation in home value is explained by variation in house size?

3. A 3000-square-foot house is selling for $500,000. Is this price out of line with typical real estate values in Bellevue? What might cause this discrepancy?

4. We know that 32 degrees Fahrenheit is equivalent to 0 degrees Celsius, and that 212 degrees Fahrenheit is equivalent to 100 degrees Celsius. Use the trend curve to determine the relationship between Fahrenheit and Celsius temperatures. When you create your initial chart, before clicking Finish, you must indicate that data is in columns and not rows, because with only two data points, Excel assumes different variables are in different rows.

5. The file Betadata.xlsx contains the monthly returns on the Standard & Poor's index as well as the monthly returns on Cinergy, Dell, Intel, Microsoft, Nortel, and Pfizer. Estimate the beta of each stock.

6. The file Electiondata.xlsx contains, for several elections, the percentage of votes Republicans gained from voting machines (counted on election day) and the percentage Republicans gained from absentee ballots (counted after election day). Suppose that during an election, Republicans obtained 49 percent of the votes on election day and 62 percent of the absentee ballot votes. The Democratic candidate cried "fraud." What do you think?

Chapter 44

Modeling Exponential Growth

- How can I model the growth of a company's revenue over time?

If you want to value a company, it's important to have some idea about its future revenues. Although the future may not be like the past, we often begin a valuation analysis of a corporation by studying the company's revenue growth during the recent past. Many analysts like to fit a trend curve to recent revenue growth. To fit a trend curve, you plot the year on the x-axis. (For example, the first year of data is year 1, the second year of data is year 2, and so on.) On the y-axis, you plot the company's revenue.

Usually, the relationship between time and revenue will not be a straight line. Recall that a straight line always has the same slope, which implies that when the independent variable (in this case, year) is increased by 1, our prediction for the dependent variable (revenue) increases by the same amount. For most companies, revenue grows by a fairly constant percentage each year. If this is the case, as revenue increases, the annual increase in revenue will also increase. After all, revenue growth of 10 percent of $1 million means revenue grows by $100,000. Revenue growth of 10 percent of $100 million means revenue grows by $10 million. This analysis implies that a trend curve for forecasting revenue should grow more steeply and have an increasing slope. The *exponential function* has the property that as the independent variable increases by 1, the dependent variable increases by the same percentage. This relationship is exactly what we need to model revenue growth.

The equation for the exponential function is $y=ae^{bx}$. Here, x is the value of the independent variable (in this example, the year), whereas y is the value of the dependent variable (in this case, annual revenue). The value e (approximately 2.7182) is the base of natural logarithms. If we select Exponential from the Microsoft Office Excel 2007 trendline options, Excel calculates the values of a and b that best fit the data. Let's look at an example.

How can I model the growth of a company's revenue over time?

The file Ciscoexpo.xlsx, shown in Figure 44-1 on the next page, contains the revenues for Cisco for the years 1990 through 1999. All revenues are in millions of dollars. In 1990, for example, Cisco's revenues were $103.47 million.

	A	B	C	D
3	Year	Sales	Prediction	Ratio
4	1	70	103.471229	
5	2	183	182.848984	1.767148
6	3	340	323.121233	1.767148
7	4	649	571.003071	1.767148
8	5	1243	1009.04699	1.767148
9	6	1979	1783.13546	1.767148
10	7	4096	3151.06443	1.767148
11	8	6440	5568.39749	1.767148
12	9	8459	9840.18301	1.767148
13	10	12154	17389.0606	1.767148
14				
15	16		529558.325	

Figure 44-1   Cisco's annual revenues for the years 1990 through 1999

To fit an exponential curve to this data, begin by selecting the cell range A3:B13. Next, on the Insert tab in the Charts group, click Scatter. Selecting the first chart option (Scatter With Only Markers) creates the chart shown in Figure 44-2.

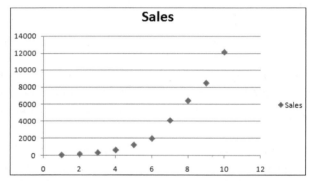

Figure 44-2   Scatter plot for the Cisco trend curve

Fitting a straight line to this data would be ridiculous. When a graph's slope is rapidly increasing as in this example, an exponential growth will usually provide a good fit to the data.

To obtain the exponential curve that best fits this data, right-click a data point (all the points turn blue), and then click Add Trendline. In the Format Trendline dialog box, select the Exponential option in the Trendline Options section, and check the Display Equation On Chart and Display R-Squared Value On Chart boxes. After you click Close, you'll see the trend curve shown in Figure 44-3.

Our estimate of Cisco's revenue in year x (remember that $x=1$ is the year 1990) is computed from the formula

$$\text{Estimated Revenue} = 58.552664 * e^{.569367x}$$

I computed estimated revenue in the cell range C4:C13 by copying from C4 to C5:C13 the formula =58.552664*EXP(0.569367*A4). For example, our estimate of Cisco's revenue in 1999 (year 10) is $17.389 billion.

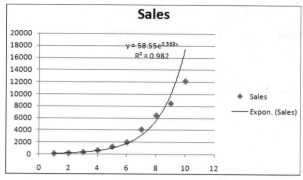

Figure 44-3   Exponential trend curve for Cisco revenues

Notice that most of the data points are very close to the fitted exponential curve. This pattern indicates that exponential growth does a good job of explaining Cisco's revenue growth during the 1990s. The fact that the R^2 value (0.98) is very close to 1 is also consistent with the visual evidence of a good fit.

Remember that whenever x increases by 1, the estimate from an exponential curve increases by the same percentage. We can verify this fact by computing the ratio of each year's estimated revenue to the previous year's estimated revenue. To compute this ratio, copy from D5 to D6:D13 the formula=*C5/C4*. We find that our estimate of Cisco's growth rate is 76.7 percent per year, which is the best estimate of Cisco's annual growth rate for the years 1990 through 1999.

Of course, to use this estimated annual revenue growth rate in a valuation analysis, we need to ask ourselves whether it's likely that this growth rate can be maintained. Be forewarned that exponential growth cannot continue forever. For example, if we use our exponential trend curve to forecast revenues for 2005 (year 16), we would predict Cisco's 2005 revenues to be $530 billion. If this estimate were realized, Cisco's revenues would be triple the 2002 revenues of the world's largest company (Wal-Mart). This seems highly unrealistic. The moral is that during its early years, the revenue growth for a technology company follows exponential growth. After a while, however, the growth rate slows down. If Wall Street analysts had understood this fact during the late 1990s, the Internet stock bubble might have been avoided.

Note that during 1999, Cisco's actual revenue fell well short of the trend curve's estimated revenue. This fact may well have indicated the start of the technology slowdown, which began during late 2000.

By the way, why must we use $x=1$ instead of $x=1990$? If we used $x=1990$, Excel would have to juggle numbers around the size of e^{1990}. A number this large causes Excel a great deal of difficulty.

Problems

The file Exponentialdata.xlsx contains annual sales revenue for Staples, Wal-Mart, and Intel. Use this data to work through the following problems.

1. For each company, fit an exponential trend curve to its sales data.

2. For which company does exponential growth have the best fit with its revenue growth?

3. For which company does exponential growth have the worst fit with its revenue growth?

4. For each company, estimate the annual percentage growth rate for revenues.

5. For each company, use your trend curve to predict 2003 revenues.

Chapter 45
The Power Curve

- As my company produces more of a product, it learns how to make the product more efficiently. Can I model the relationship between units produced and the time needed to produce a unit?

A power curve is calculated with the equation $y = ax^b$. In the equation, a and b are constants. Using a trend curve, we can determine the values of a and b that make the power curve best fit a scatter plot diagram. In most situations, a is greater than 0. When this is the case, the slope of the power curve depends on the value of b, as follows:

- For $b>1$, y increases as x increases, and the slope of the power curve increases as x increases.

- For $0<b<1$, y increases as x increases, and the slope of the power curve decreases as x increases.

- For $b=1$, the power curve is a straight line.

- For $b<0$, y decreases as x increases, and the power curve flattens out as x increases.

Here are examples of different relationships that can be modeled by the power curve. These examples are contained in the file Powerexamples.xlsx.

If we are trying to predict total production cost as a function of units produced, we might find a relationship similar to that shown in Figure 45-1 on the next page.

Notice that b equals 2. As I mentioned previously, with this value of b, the cost of production increases with the number of units produced. The slope becomes steeper, which indicates that each additional unit costs more to produce. This relationship might occur because increased production requires more overtime labor, which costs more than regular labor.

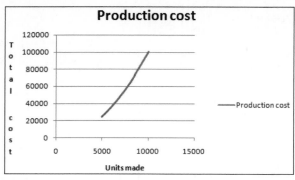

Figure 45-1 Predicting cost as a function of the number of units produced

If we are trying to predict sales as a function of advertising expenditures, we might find a curve similar to that shown in Figure 45-2.

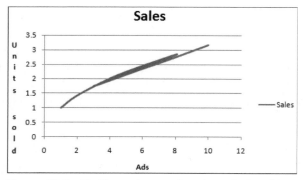

Figure 45-2 Plotting sales as a function of advertising

Here, b equals 0.5, which is between 0 and 1. When b has a value in this range, sales increase with increased advertising but at a decreasing rate. Thus, the power curve allows us to model the idea of diminishing return—that each additional dollar spent on advertising will provide less benefit.

If we are trying to predict the time needed to produce the last unit of a product based on the number of units produced to date, we often find a scatter plot similar to that shown in Figure 45-3.

Here we find that b equals -0.1. Because b is less than 0, the time needed to produce each unit decreases, but the rate of decrease—that is, the rate of "learning"—slows down. This relationship means that during the early stages of a product's life cycle, huge savings in labor time occur. As we make more of a product, however, savings in labor time occur at a slower rate. The relationship between cumulative units produced and time needed to produce the last unit is called the *learning* or *experience* curve.

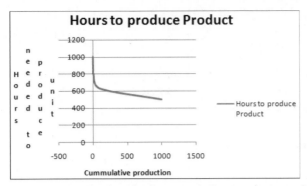

Figure 45-3   Plotting the time needed to produce a unit based on cumulative production

A power curve has the following properties:

- Property 1   If x increases by 1 percent, y increases by approximately b percent.

- Property 2   Whenever x doubles, y increases by the same percentage.

Suppose that demand for a product as a function of price can be modeled as $1000(Price)^{-2}$. Property 1 then implies that a 1 percent increase in price will lower demand (regardless of price) by 2 percent. In this case, the exponent b (without the negative sign) is called the *elasticity*. We will discuss elasticity further in Chapter 70, "Estimating a Demand Curve." With this background, let's take a look at how to fit a power curve to data.

As my company produces more of a product, it learns how to make the product more efficiently. Can I model the relationship between units produced and the time needed to produce a unit?

The file Fax.xlsx contains data about the number of fax machines produced and the unit cost (in 1982 dollars) of producing the "last" fax machine made during each year. In 1983, for example, 70,000 fax machines were produced, and the cost of producing the last fax machine was $3,416. The data is shown in Figure 45-4.

	A	B	C	D	E	F	G
1	Learning curve FAX data						
2							
3	Year	Production	Cumulative Production	Unit Cost	Forecast		
4	1982	64000	64000	$3,700.00	3955.81		
5	1983	70000	134000	$3,416.00	3280.54		
6	1984	100000	234000	$3,125.00	2848.51		
7	1985	150000	384000	$2,583.00	2512.63		
8	1986	175000	559000	$2,166.00	2284.66		
9	1987	400000	959000	$1,833.00	1992.72		
10	1988	785000	1744000	$1,788.00	1712.60		
11	1989	1000000	2744000		1526.85		learning
12		double	3488000		1436.83		percentage
13		cumulative production					0.838975

Figure 45-4   Data used to plot the learning curve for producing fax machines

Because a learning curve tries to predict either cost or the time needed to produce a unit from data about cumulative production, I've calculated in column C the cumulative number of fax machines produced by the end of each year. In cell C4, I refer to cell B4 to show the number of fax machines produced in 1982. By copying from C5 to C6:C10 the formula *C4+B5*, I compute cumulative fax machine production for the end of each year.

We can now create a scatter plot that shows cumulative units produced on the x-axis and unit cost on the y-axis. After creating the chart, click one of the data points (the data points will be displayed in blue), then right-click and click Add Trendline. In the Format Trendline dialog box, select the Power option, and check the Display Equation On Chart and the Display R-Squared Value On Chart boxes. With these settings, we obtain the chart shown in Figure 45-5. The curve drawn represents the power curve that best fits the data.

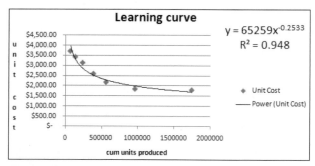

Figure 45-5 Learning curve for producing fax machines

Our power curve predicts the cost of producing a fax machine as follows:

```
Cost of producing fax machine=65,259(cumulative units produced)⁻²⁵³³
```

Notice that most data points are near the fitted power curve and that the R^2 value is nearly 1, indicating that the power curve fits the data well.

By copying from cell E4 to E5:E10 the formula *65259*C4^–0.2533*, we compute the predicted cost for the last fax machine produced during each year. (The carat symbol [^], which is located over the 6 key, is used to raise a number to a power.)

If we estimated that 1,000,000 fax machines were produced in 1989, after computing the total 1989 production (2,744,000) in cell C11 we can copy our forecast equation to cell E11 to predict that the last fax machine produced in 1989 cost $1,526.85.

Remember that Property 2 of the power curve states that whenever *x* doubles, *y* increases by the same percentage. By entering twice cumulative 1988 production in cell C12 and copying our forecast formula in E10 to cell E12, we find that doubling cumulative units produced reduces our predicted cost to 83.8 percent of its previous value (*1,456.83/1,712.60*). For this reason, the current learning curve is known as an 84 percent learning curve. Each time we double units produced, the labor required to make a fax machine drops by 16.2 percent.

If a curve gets steeper, the exponential curve might fit the data as well as the power curve does. A natural question is, which curve fits the data better? In most cases, this question can be answered simply by eyeballing the curves and choosing the one that looks like it's a better fit.

The learning curve was discovered in 1936 at Wright-Patterson Air Force Base in Dayton, Ohio, when it was found that whenever the cumulative number of airplanes produced doubled, the time required to make each airplane dropped by around 15 percent.

Wikipedia gives the following learning curve estimates for various industries:

❏ Aerospace: 85 percent

❏ Shipbuilding: 80–85 percent

❏ Complex machine tools for new models: 75–85 percent

❏ Repetitive electronics manufacturing: 90–95 percent

❏ Repetitive machining or punch-press operations: 90–95 percent

❏ Repetitive electrical operations: 75–85 percent

❏ Repetitive welding operations: 90 percent

❏ Raw materials: 93–96 percent

❏ Purchased parts: 85–88 percent

Problems

1. Use the fax machine data to model the relationship between cumulative fax machines produced and total production cost.

2. Use the fax machine data to model the relationship between cumulative fax machines produced and average production cost per machine.

3. A marketing director estimates that total sales of a product as a function of price will be as shown in the table below. Estimate the relationship between price and demand, and predict demand for a $46 price. A 1 percent increase in price will reduce demand by what percentage?

Price	Demand
$30.00	300
$40.00	200
$50.00	110
$60.00	60

4. The brand manager for a new drug believes that the annual sales of the drug as a function of the number of sales calls on doctors will be as shown in the table below. Estimate sales of the drug if 80,000 sales calls are made on doctors.

Sales calls	Units sold
50,000	25,000
100,000	52,000
150,000	68,000
200,000	77,000

5. The time needed to produce each of the first ten airplanes produced is as follows:

Unit	Hours
1	1000
2	800
3	730
4	630
5	600
6	560
7	560
8	500
9	510
10	450

Estimate the total number of hours needed to produce the next ten airplanes.

Chapter 46

Using Correlations to Summarize Relationships

- How are monthly stock returns for Microsoft, GE, Intel, GM, and Cisco related?

Trend curves are a great help in understanding how two variables are related. Often, however, we need to understand how more than two variables are related. Looking at the correlation between any pair of variables can provide insights into how multiple variables move up and down in value together.

The correlation (usually denoted by r) between two variables (call them x and y) is a unit-free measure of the strength of the linear relationship between x and y. The correlation between any two variables is always between -1 and $+1$. Although the exact formula used to compute the correlation between two variables isn't very important, being able to interpret the correlation between the variables is.

A correlation near $+1$ means that x and y have a strong positive linear relationship. That is, when x is larger than average, y tends to be larger than average, and when x is smaller than average, y also tends to be smaller than average. When a straight line is applied to the data, there will be a straight line with a positive slope that does a good job of fitting the points. As an example, for the data shown in Figure 46-1 (*x=units produced* and *y=monthly production cost*), x and y have a correlation of $+0.90$.

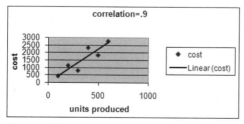

Figure 46-1   Correlation near +1, indicating that two variables have a strong positive linear relationship

On the other hand, a correlation near −1 means that there is a strong negative linear relationship between x and y. That is, when x is larger than average, y tends to be smaller than average, and when x is smaller than average, y tends to be larger than average. When a straight line is applied to the data, the line will have a negative slope that does a good job of fitting the points. As an example, for the data shown in Figure 46-2 ($x=$ *the price charged for a product* and $y=$ *product demand*), x and y have a correlation of −0.94.

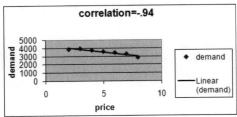

Figure 46-2 Correlation near −1, indicating that two variables have a strong negative linear relationship

A correlation near 0 means that x and y have a weak linear relationship. That is, knowing whether x is larger or smaller than its mean tells you little about whether y will be larger or smaller than its mean. Figure 46-3 shows a graph of the dependence of unit sales (y) on years of sales experience (x). Years of experience and unit sales have a correlation of 0.003. In our data set, the average experience is 10 years. We see that when a person has more than 10 years of sales experience, his or her sales can be either low or high. We also see that when a person has fewer than 10 years of sales experience, sales can be low or high. Although experience and sales have little or no linear relationship, there is a strong non-linear relationship (see the fitted curve) between years of experience and sales. Correlation does not measure the strength of non-linear relationships.

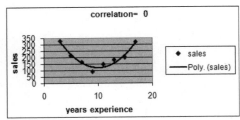

Figure 46-3 Correlation near 0, indicating a weak linear relationship between two variables

How are monthly stock returns for Microsoft, GE, Intel, GM, and Cisco related?

The file Stockcorrel.xlsx (see Figure 46-4) shows monthly stock returns for Microsoft, GE, Intel, GM, and Cisco during the 1990s. We can use correlations to try to understand how movements in these stocks are related.

To find the correlations between each pair of stocks, click Data Analysis in the Analysis group on the Data tab, and then select the Correlation option. You must install the Analysis ToolPak (as described in Chapter 36) before you can use this feature. Click OK, and then fill in the Correlation dialog box as shown in Figure 46-5.

	A	B	C	D	E	F
51	Date	MSFT	GE	INTC	GM	CSCO
52	3/30/1990	0.121518984	0.040485829	0.037267081	0.022284122	0.01075
53	4/30/1990	0.047404062	-0.00389105	-0.05389221	-0.03542234	0.01064
54	5/31/1990	0.258620679	0.083515622	0.221518993	0.115819208	0.04211
55	6/29/1990	0.04109589	0.005444646	-0.02590674	-0.02056555	0.07071
56	7/31/1990	-0.125	0.034296028	-0.05319149	-0.02099738	-0.0377
57	8/31/1990	-0.07518797	-0.13438046	-0.25	-0.1313673	-0.0294
58	9/28/1990	0.024390243	-0.11338709	-0.00374532	-0.08805031	-0.0909
59	10/31/1990	0.011904762	-0.04587156	0.007518797	0.013793103	0.31111
60	11/30/1990	0.13333334	0.052884616	0.119402982	0.013605442	0.33898
61	12/31/1990	0.041522492	0.057260275	0.026666667	-0.05821918	0.13608
62	1/31/1991	0.303986698	0.115468413	0.188311681	0.054545455	0.30362
63	2/28/1991	0.057324842	0.070468754	0.043715846	0.100689657	-0.0427
64	3/28/1991	0.022891566	0.023897059	-0.02094241	-0.0443038	-0.1295
65	4/30/1991	-0.06713781	0.016157989	0.053475935	-0.05298013	0.22051
66	5/31/1991	0.108585857	0.09908127	0.131979689	0.217482507	0.08403
67	6/28/1991	-0.06890661	-0.0420712	-0.16591929	-0.05507246	-0.0543
68	7/31/1991	0.078899086	-0.01013514	0.010752688	-0.02453988	0.28689
69	8/30/1991	0.159863949	0.022184301	0.053191491	-0.03396227	0.15605
70	9/30/1991	0.043988269	-0.06664441	-0.14646465	-0.01644737	-0.0964
71	10/31/1991	0.054775283	-0.00540541	-0.03846154	-0.06020067	0.18902
72	11/29/1991	0.035952065	-0.0615942	0.009230769	-0.11316726	0.01538
73	12/31/1991	0.143958867	0.189961389	0.195121944	-0.06097561	0.33838
74	1/31/1992	0.080898874	-0.01633987	0.221938774	0.121212125	0.13396
75	2/28/1992	0.027027028	0.044850498	0.060542796	0.170656368	0.08486

Figure 46-4   Monthly stock returns during the 1990s

Figure 46-5   Correlation dialog box

The easiest way to enter the input range is to select the upper-left cell of the data range (B51) and then press Ctrl+Shift+Right Arrow, followed by Ctrl+Shift+Down Arrow. Check the Labels In First Row box if the first row of the input range contains labels. I entered cell H52 as the upper-left cell of our output range. After clicking OK, we see the results shown in Figure 46-6.

	H	I	J	K	L	M	N
52		*Date*	*MSFT*	*GE*	*INTC*	*GM*	*CSCO*
53	Date	1					
54	MSFT	-0.101320176	1				
55	GE	0.072919508	0.445043012	1			
56	INTC	-0.018500648	0.516508463	0.323540548	1		
57	GM	0.011200429	0.068831361	0.379625186	0.31739	1	
58	CSCO	-0.126124686	0.512801711	0.375512888	0.48845	0.15934815	1

Figure 46-6   Stock return correlations

We find, for example, that the correlation between Cisco and Microsoft is 0.513, whereas the correlation between GM and Microsoft is 0.07. The analysis shows that returns on

Cisco, Intel, and Microsoft are most closely tied together. Because the correlation between each pair of these stocks is around 0.5, these stocks exhibit a moderate positive relationship. In other words, if one stock does better than average, it is likely (but not certain) that the other stocks will do better than average. Because Cisco, Intel, and Microsoft stock returns are closely tied to technology spending, their fairly strong correlation is not surprising. We find also that the monthly returns on Microsoft and GM are virtually uncorrelated. This relationship indicates that when Microsoft stock does better than average, we really can't tell whether GM stock will do better or worse than average. Again, this trend is not surprising because GM is not really a high-tech company and is more susceptible to the vagaries of the business cycle.

Filling in the correlation matrix   As you can see in this example, Microsoft Office Excel 2007 left some entries in the correlation matrix blank. For example, the correlation between Microsoft and GE (which is equal to the correlation between GE and Microsoft) is omitted. If you want to fill in the entire correlation matrix, right-click the matrix, and then click Copy. Right-click a blank portion of the worksheet, and then click Paste Special. In the Paste Special dialog box, select Transpose. This flips the data on its side. Now right-click the flipped data, and click Copy. Right-click the original correlation matrix, and click Paste Special again. In the Paste Special dialog box, check the Skip Blanks box, and then click OK. The transposed data is copied to the original matrix, but does not copy the blanks from the transposed data. The full correlation matrix is shown in Figure 46-7.

	H	I	J	K	L	M	N
48		correl function					
49		0.159348153					
50							
51			Full correlation matrix				
52		*Date*	*MSFT*	*GE*	*INTC*	*GM*	*CSCO*
53	Date	1	-0.101320176	0.072919508	-0.0185	0.01120043	-0.1261
54	MSFT	-0.101320176	1	0.445043012	0.51651	0.06883136	0.5128
55	GE	0.072919508	0.445043012	1	0.32354	0.37962519	0.37551
56	INTC	-0.018500648	0.516508463	0.323540548	1	0.31738567	0.48845
57	GM	0.011200429	0.068831361	0.379625186	0.31739	1	0.15935
58	CSCO	-0.126124686	0.512801711	0.375512888	0.48845	0.15934815	1
59							
60							
61		1	-0.101320176	0.072919508	-0.0185	0.01120043	-0.1261
62			1	0.445043012	0.51651	0.06883136	0.5128
63				1	0.32354	0.37962519	0.37551
64					1	0.31738567	0.48845
65						1	0.15935
66							1
67							
68			Transposed correlations				

Figure 46-7   Complete correlation matrix

Using the CORREL function   As an alternative to using the Correlation option of the Analysis Toolpak, you can use the CORREL function. For example, entering in cell I49 the formula *CORREL(E52:E181,F52:F181)* confirms that the correlation between monthly returns on Cisco (shown in column F) and GM (shown in column E) is 0.159.

Relationship between correlation and R²   In Chapter 45, "Estimating Straight Line Relationships," we found an R2 value for units produced and monthly operating cost of 0.688. How is this value related to the correlation between units produced and monthly operating costs? The correlation between two sets of data is simply

$$\sqrt{R^2\,value}$$

for the trendline, where we choose the sign for the square root to be the same as the sign of the slope of the trendline. Thus the correlation between units produced and monthly operating cost for our Chapter 41, "Consolidating Data," data is

$$+\sqrt{.688} = +\,.829$$

Correlation and regression towards the mean   You have probably heard the phrase "regression towards the mean." Essentially, this means that the predicted value of a dependent variable will be in some sense closer to its average value than the independent variable. More precisely, suppose we try to predict a dependent variable y from an independent variable x. If x is k standard deviations above average, then our prediction for y will be $r{\times}k$ standard deviations above average (here, $r{=}correlation$ between x and y). Because r is between -1 and +1 this means that y is fewer standard deviations away from the mean than x. This is the real definition of "regression towards the mean." See Problem 5 for an interesting application of the concept of regression towards the mean.

Problems

The data for the following problems is in file Ch46data.xlsx.

1. The *Problem 1* worksheet contains the number of cars parked each day both in the outdoor lot and in the parking garage near the Indiana University Kelley School of Business. Find and interpret the correlation between the number of cars parked in the outdoor lot and in the parking garage.

2. The *Problem 2* worksheet contains daily sales volume (in dollars) of laser printers, printer cartridges, and school supplies. Find and interpret the correlations between these quantities.

3. The *Problem 3* worksheet contains annual returns on stocks, T-Bills, and T-Bonds. Find and interpret the correlations between the annual returns on these three classes of investments.

    Here are a few more problems:

4. The file Dow.xlsx contains the monthly returns between the 30 stocks comprising the Dow Jones Index. Find the correlations between all stocks. Then, for each stock, use conditional formatting to highlight the three stocks most correlated with that stock. (Of course, you should not highlight a stock as correlated with itself.)

5. NFL teams play 16 games during the regular season. Suppose the standard deviation of the number of games won by all teams is 2, and the correlation between the number of games a team wins in two consecutive seasons is 0.5. If a team goes 12 and 4 during a season, what is your best prediction for how many games they will win next season?

Chapter 47

Introduction to Multiple Regression

- Our factory manufactures three products. How can I predict the cost of running the factory based on the number of units produced?

- How accurate are my forecasts for predicting monthly cost based on units produced?

- I know how to use the Data Analysis command to run a multiple regression. Is there a way to run the regression without using this command and place the regression's results in the same worksheet as the data?

Our factory manufactures three products. How can I predict the cost of running the factory based on the number of units produced?

In Chapters 43 through 45, I described how to use the trend curve in Microsoft Office Excel 2007 to predict one variable (called y, or the *dependent* variable) from another variable (called x, or the *independent* variable). However, we often want to use more than one independent variable (called the independent variables $x1$, $x2$, ... xn) to predict the value of a dependent variable. In these cases, we can use either the multiple regression option in the Excel Data Analysis feature or the LINEST function to estimate the relationship we want.

Multiple regression assumes that the relationship between y and $x1$, $x2$, ... xn has the form

```
Y=Constant+B1X1+B2X2+...BnXn
```

Excel calculates the values of *Constant*, *B1*, *B2*, ... *Bn* to make the predictions from this equation as accurate (in the sense of minimizing the sum of squared errors) as possible. The following example illustrates how multiple regression works.

The *Data* worksheet in in the file Mrcostest.xlsx (see Figure 47-1 on the next page) contains the cost of running a plant over 19 months as well as the number of units of Product A, Product B, and Product C produced during each month.

	A	B	C	D	E
3	Month	Cost	A Made	B Made	C Made
4	1	44439	515	541	928
5	2	43936	929	692	711
6	3	44464	800	710	824
7	4	41533	979	675	758
8	5	46343	1165	1147	635
9	6	44922	651	939	901
10	7	43203	847	755	580
11	8	43000	942	908	589
12	9	40967	630	738	682
13	10	48582	1113	1175	1050
14	11	45003	1086	1075	984
15	12	44303	843	640	828
16	13	42070	500	752	708
17	14	44353	813	989	804
18	15	45968	1190	823	904
19	16	47781	1200	1108	1120
20	17	43202	731	590	1065
21	18	44074	1089	607	1132
22	19	44610	786	513	839

Figure 47-1   Data for predicting monthly operating costs

We would like to find the best forecast for monthly operating cost that has the form (which I'll refer to as Form 1)

```
Monthly operating cost=Constant+B1*(Units A produced)+B2*(Units B produced)+B3*(Units C produced)
```

The Excel Data Analysis feature can find the equation for this form that best fits our data. Click Data Analysis in the Analysis group on the Data tab, and then select Regression. Fill in the Regression dialog box as shown in Figure 47-2.

> **Note**   If you haven't previously installed the Analysis Toolpak, click the Microsoft Office Button, click the Excel Options button, and select Add-Ins. With Excel Add-ins in the Manage box, click Go, check the Analysis ToolPak box, and click OK.

Figure 47-2   Regression dialog box

❑ The Input Y range, B3:B22, contains the dependent variable or data (including the Cost label) that we want to predict.

❑ The Input X range, C3:E22, contains the data or independent variables (including the labels A Made, B Made, and C Made) that we want to use in the prediction. Excel has a limit of 15 independent variables, which must be in adjacent columns.

❑ Because both the Input X and Input Y ranges include labels, I've checked the Labels box.

❑ I chose to place the output in a new worksheet titled *Regression*.

❑ Checking the Residuals box causes Excel to list, for each observation, the prediction from Form 1 and the residual, which equals the observed cost minus the predicted cost.

After clicking OK in the Regression dialog box, we obtain the output shown in Figures 47-3 and 47-4.

	A	B	C	D	E	F	G	H	I
1	SUMMARY OUTPUT								
2									
3	*Regression Statistics*								
4	Multiple R	0.803398744							
5	R Square	0.645449542							
6	Adjusted R Square	0.57453945							
7	Standard Error	1252.763898							
8	Observations	19							
9									
10	ANOVA								
11		*df*	*SS*	*MS*	*F*	*Significance F*			
12	Regression	3	42856229.89	14285409.96	9.102365067	0.001126532			
13	Residual	15	23541260.74	1569417.383					
14	Total	18	66397490.63						
15									
16		*Coefficients*	*Standard Error*	*t Stat*	*P-value*	*Lower 95%*	*Upper 95%*	*Lower 95.0%*	*Upper 95.0%*
17	Intercept	35102.90045	1837.226911	19.10645889	6.11198E-12	31186.94158	39018.85932	31186.94158	39018.85932
18	A Made	2.065953296	1.664981779	1.240826369	0.23372682	-1.482873542	5.614780134	-1.482873542	5.614780134
19	B Made	4.176355531	1.681252566	2.484073849	0.025287785	0.592848311	7.759862751	0.592848311	7.759862751
20	C Made	4.790641037	1.789316107	2.677358695	0.017222643	0.97680169	8.604480385	0.97680169	8.604480385

Figure 47-3   Original multiple regression output

	A	B	C
24	RESIDUAL OUTPUT		
25			
26	*Observation*	*Predicted Cost*	*Residuals*
27	1	42871.98962	1567.010379
28	2	43318.35487	617.6451343
29	3	43668.36373	795.6362727
30	4	43575.81462	-2042.814615
31	5	45342.07289	1000.927109
32	6	44685.80146	236.1985373
33	7	42784.48312	418.516882
34	8	43662.84685	-662.8468468
35	9	42753.81859	-1786.818595
36	10	47339.69731	1242.302695
37	11	46550.0987	-1547.098705
38	12	43484.0174	818.982604
39	13	42668.27031	-598.2703105
40	14	44764.61149	-411.6114926
41	15	45329.26497	638.7350292
42	16	47574.96429	206.0357059
43	17	44179.19478	-977.1947761
44	18	45310.77705	-1236.77705
45	19	42888.55796	1721.442043

Figure 47-4   Original multiple regression residual output

What is the best prediction equation?   We find in the Coefficients column (column B of the summary output) that the best equation of Form 1 that can be used to predict monthly cost is

```
Predicted monthly cost=35,102.90+2.07(AMade)+4.18(BMade)+4.79(CMade)
```

A natural question is, which of our independent variables are useful for predicting monthly cost? After all, if we had chosen the number of games won by the Seattle Mariners during a one month period as an independent variable, we would expect that this variable would have little effect on predicting monthly operating cost. When you run a regression, each independent variable has a *p-value* between 0 and 1. Any independent variable with a p-value (see column E) of less than or equal to 0.15 is considered to be useful for predicting the dependent variable. Thus, the smaller the p-value, the higher the predictive power of the independent variable. Our three independent variables have p-values of 0.23 (for A Made), 0.025 (for B Made), and 0.017 (for C Made). These p-values may be interpreted as follows:

- When we use B Made and C Made to predict monthly operating cost, we have a 77 percent chance (1−0.23) that A Made adds predictive power.

- When we use A Made and C Made to predict monthly operating cost, there is a 97.5 percent chance (1−0.025) that B Made adds predictive power.

- When we use A Made and B Made to predict monthly operating cost, there is a 98.3 percent chance (1−0.017) that C Made adds predictive power.

Our p-values indicate that A Made does not add much predictive power to B Made and C Made, which means that if we know B Made and C Made, we can predict monthly operating cost about as well as we can if we include A Made as an independent variable. Therefore, we can opt to delete A Made as an independent variable and use just B Made and C Made for our prediction. I copied our data to the worksheet titled *A Removed* and deleted the A Made column (column C). I then adjusted the Input X range to be C3:D22. In the worksheet titled *NoA*, you can see the regression output shown in Figure 47-5 and Figure 47-6.

	A	B	C	D	E	F	G	H	I
1	SUMMARY OUTPUT								
2									
3	*Regression Statistics*								
4	Multiple R	0.78042							
5	R Square	0.60906							
6	Adjusted R Squa	0.56019							
7	Standard Error	1273.72							
8	Observations	19							
9									
10	ANOVA								
11		df	SS	MS	F	gnificance F			
12	Regression	2	4E+07	2E+07	12.4634	0.00055			
13	Residual	16	2.6E+07	1622351					
14	Total	18	6.6E+07						
15									
16		Coefficient	andard Err	t Stat	P-value	ower 95%	Jpper 95%	ower 95.0%	pper 95.0%
17	Intercept	35475.3	1842.86	19.2501	1.7E-12	31568.6	39382	31568.6	39382
18	B Made	5.32097	1.4291	3.72331	0.00185	2.29142	8.35051	2.29142	8.35051
19	C Made	5.41714	1.74531	3.10382	0.00683	1.71724	9.11703	1.71724	9.11703

Figure 47-5   Multiple regression output with A Made data removed as an independent variable

	A	B	C
23	RESIDUAL OUTPUT		
24			
25	Observation	Predicted Cost	Residuals
26	1	43381.05021	1057.95
27	2	43008.99747	927.003
28	3	43716.91148	747.089
29	4	43173.14649	-1640.15
30	5	45018.33547	1324.66
31	6	45352.53278	-430.533
32	7	42634.5734	568.427
33	8	43497.43576	-497.436
34	9	43096.66501	-2129.67
35	10	47415.43478	1166.57
36	11	46525.80688	-1522.81
37	12	43366.11226	936.888
38	13	43312.00414	-1242
39	14	45093.11881	-740.119
40	15	44751.5519	1216.45
41	16	47438.12957	342.87
42	17	44383.92553	-1181.93
43	18	44837.33022	-763.33
44	19	42749.93783	1860.06

Figure 47-6   Residual output calculated when A Made data is removed as an independent variable

We see that A Made and B Made each have very low p-values (0.002 and 0.007, respectively). These values indicate that both these independent variables have useful predictive power. Using the new coefficients in column B, we can now predict monthly operating cost using the equation

```
Predicted monthly operating cost=35,475.3+5.32(BMade)+5.42(CMade)
```

How accurate are my forecasts for predicting monthly cost based on units produced?

In the regression output in cell B5 of the *NoA* worksheet (see Figure 47-5), we find that R^2 equals 0.61. An R^2 value such as this one means that together, B Made and C Made explain 61 percent of the variation in monthly operating costs. Notice that in our original regression, which included A Made as an independent variable, R2 equals 0.65. This indicates that the addition of A Made as an independent variable explains only 4 percent more variation in monthly operating costs. Having such a minor difference is consistent with the decision to delete A Made as an independent variable.

In the regression output in cell B7 in the *NoA* worksheet, we find that the standard error for the regression with B Made and C Made as independent variables is 1274. We expect about 68 percent of our multiple regression forecasts to be accurate within one standard error, and 95 percent of our multiple regression forecasts to be accurate within two standard errors. Any forecast that differs from the actual value by more than two standard errors is considered an outlier. Thus, if our forecasted operating cost is in error by more than $2,548 (*2*1274*), we consider that observation to be an outlier.

In the Residual portion of our output, shown earlier in Figure 47-6, we are given for each observation the predicted cost and the residual, which equals the actual cost less the predicted cost. For the first observation, for example, we predict a cost of $43,381.10. Our residual of $1,057.95 indicates that our prediction of actual cost was too low by $1,057.95.

I know how to use the Data Analysis command to run a multiple regression. Is there a way to run the regression without using this command and place the regression's results in the same worksheet as the data?

The Excel LINEST function can be used to insert the results of a regression analysis directly into a workbook. To use the LINEST function when there are *m* independent variables, begin by selecting a blank cell range consisting of five rows and *m+1* columns, where you want LINEST to deposit the results. In the *A Removed* worksheet, I used the range F5:H9. The syntax of the LINEST function is

LINEST(KnownYs,KnownXs,True,True)

If the third argument is changed to False, Excel will estimate the equation without a constant term. Changing the fourth argument to False causes the LINEST function to omit many regression computations and return only the multiple regression equation.

With the upper-left cell of the target range selected (F5 in this example), select the range of desired size (in our case, the cell range F5:H9), and then enter the formula =LINEST(B4:B22,C4:D22,True,True). At this point, *do not* press Enter! LINEST is an array function (see Chapter 74, "Array Functions and Formulas," for further discussion of array functions), so you must hold down Ctrl+Shift and then press Enter for the function to work correctly. After using this key combination, we obtain the results shown in Figure 47-7.

	F	G	H	I	J
4				LINEST OUTPUT	
5	5.417137848	5.320968077	35475.30255		
6	1.745311646	1.429095476	1842.860853		
7	0.609057299	1273.715391	#N/A		
8	12.46335684	16	#N/A		
9	40439876.29	25957614.34	#N/A		
10					
11	Cmadecoef	Bmadecoef	Const		
12	Std err C	Std Err B	Std err const		
13	rsq	std err est			
14	F	df			
15	ssreg	ssresid			
16					

Figure 47-7 Using the LINEST function to calculate a multiple regression

In row 5, we find our prediction equation (coefficients read right to left, starting with the intercept) of *Predicted monthly cost*=35,475.3+5.32(*B Made*)+5.43(*C Made*). Row 6 contains standard errors for each coefficient estimate, but these are not too relevant. Cell F7 contains our R^2 value of 0.61, and cell G7 contains the regression standard error of 1274. Rows 8 and 9 contain information (F statistic, degrees of freedom, sum of squares regression, and sum of squares residual) that is also not very relevant.

Note Problems that you can work with to learn more about multiple regression are available at the end of Chapter 49.

Chapter 48

Incorporating Qualitative Factors into Multiple Regression

- How can I predict quarterly U.S. auto sales?

- How can I predict U.S. presidential elections?

- Is there an Excel function I can use to easily make forecasts from a multiple regression equation?

In our first example of multiple regression in Chapter 47, "Incorporating Qualitative Factors into Multiple Regression," we forecasted the monthly cost of plant operations by using the number of units of each product manufactured at the plant. Because we can quantify exactly the amount of a product produced at the plant, we can refer to the units produced of Product A, Product B, and Product C as *quantitative independent variables*. In many situations, however, independent variables can't be easily quantified. In this chapter, we'll look at ways to incorporate qualitative factors such as seasonality, gender, or the party of a presidential candidate into a multiple regression analysis.

How can I predict quarterly U.S. auto sales?

Suppose we want to predict quarterly U.S. auto sales to determine whether the quarter of the year impacts auto sales. We'll use the data in the file Auto.xlsx, shown in Figure 48-1 on the next page. Sales are listed in thousands of cars, and GNP is in billions of dollars.)

	A	B	C	D	E	F
10	Year	Quarter	Sales	GNP	Unemp	Int
11	79	1	Sales	2541	5.9	9.4
12	79	2	2910	2640	5.7	9.4
13	79	3	2562	2595	5.9	9.7
14	79	4	2385	2701	6	11.9
15	80	1	2520	2785	6.2	13.4
16	80	2	2142	2509	7.3	9.6
17	80	3	2130	2570	7.7	9.2
18	80	4	2190	2667	7.4	13.6
19	81	1	2370	2878	7.4	14.4
20	81	2	2208	2835	7.4	15.3
21	81	3	2196	2897	7.4	15.1
22	81	4	1758	2744	8.3	11.8
23	82	1	1944	2582	8.8	12.8
24	82	2	2094	2613	9.4	12.4
25	82	3	1911	2529	10	9.3
26	82	4	2031	2544	10.7	7.9
27	83	1	2046	2633	10.4	7.8
28	83	2	2502	2878	10.1	8.4
29	83	3	2238	3051	9.4	9.1
30	83	4	2394	3274	8.5	8.8
31	84	1	2586	3594	7.9	9.2
32	84	2	2898	3774	7.5	9.8
33	84	3	2448	3861	7.5	10.3
34	84	4	2460	3919	7.2	8.8
35	85	1	2646	4040	7.4	8.2
36	85	2	2988	4133	7.3	7.5
37	85	3	2967	4303	7.1	7.1
38	85	4	2439	4393	7	7.2
39	86	1	2598	4560	7.1	8.9
40	86	2	3045	4587	7.1	7.7
41	86	3	3213	4716	6.9	7.4
42	86	4	2685	4796	6.8	7.4

Figure 48-1 Auto sales data

You might be tempted to define an independent variable that equals 1 during the first quarter, 2 during the second quarter, and so on. Unfortunately, this approach would force the fourth quarter to have four times the effect of the first quarter, which might not be true. The quarter of the year is a *qualitative independent variable*. To model a qualitative independent variable, we create an independent variable (called a *dummy variable*) for all but one of the qualitative variable's possible values. (It is arbitrary which value you leave out. In this example, I chose to omit Quarter 4.) The dummy variables tell you which value of the qualitative variable occurs. Thus, we'll have a dummy variable for Quarter 1, Quarter 2, and Quarter 3 with the following properties:

❑ Quarter 1 dummy variable equals 1 if the quarter is Quarter 1, and 0 if otherwise.

❑ Quarter 2 dummy variable equals 1 if the quarter is Quarter 2, and 0 if otherwise.

❑ Quarter 3 dummy variable equals 1 if the quarter is Quarter 3, and 0 if otherwise.

A Quarter 4 observation will be identified by the fact that the dummy variables for Quarter 1 through Quarter 3 equal 0. You can see why we don't need a dummy variable for Quarter 4. In fact, if we include a dummy variable for Quarter 4 as an independent variable in our regression, Microsoft Office Excel 2007 returns an error message. The reason we get an error is that if an exact linear relationship exists between any set of independent variables, Excel must perform the mathematical equivalent of dividing by 0 (an impossibility) when running a multiple regression. In our situation, if we include a Quarter 4 dummy variable, every data point satisfies the following exact linear relationship:

(Quarter 1 Dummy)+(Quarter 2 Dummy)+(Quarter 3 Dummy)+(Quarter 4 Dummy)=1

> **Note**   An exact linear relationship occurs if there exists constants $c0$, $c1$, ... cN, such that for each data point $c0 + c1x1 + c2x2 + ... cNxN = 0$. Here $x1$, ... xN are the values of the independent variables.

To create our dummy variable for Quarter 1, I copied from G12 to G13:G42 the formula *IF(B12=1,1,0)*. This formula places a 1 in column G whenever a quarter is the first quarter, and places a 0 in column G whenever the quarter is not the first quarter. In a similar fashion, I created dummy variables for Quarter 2 (in H12:H42) and Quarter 3 (in I12:I42). You can see the results of the formulas in Figure 48-2.

	G	H	I	J	K	L
10	Q1	Q2	Q3	LagGNP	LagUnemp	LagInt
11	Q1	Q2	Q3	LagGNP	LagUnemp	LagInt
12	0	1	0	2541	5.9	9.4
13	0	0	1	2640	5.7	9.4
14	0	0	0	2595	5.9	9.7
15	1	0	0	2701	6	11.9
16	0	1	0	2785	6.2	13.4
17	0	0	1	2509	7.3	9.6
18	0	0	0	2570	7.7	9.2
19	1	0	0	2667	7.4	13.6
20	0	1	0	2878	7.4	14.4
21	0	0	1	2835	7.4	15.3
22	0	0	0	2897	7.4	15.1
23	1	0	0	2744	8.3	11.8
24	0	1	0	2582	8.8	12.8
25	0	0	1	2613	9.4	12.4
26	0	0	0	2529	10	9.3
27	1	0	0	2544	10.7	7.9
28	0	1	0	2633	10.4	7.8
29	0	0	1	2878	10.1	8.4
30	0	0	0	3051	9.4	9.1
31	1	0	0	3274	8.5	8.8
32	0	1	0	3594	7.9	9.2
33	0	0	1	3774	7.5	9.8
34	0	0	0	3861	7.5	10.3
35	1	0	0	3919	7.2	8.8
36	0	1	0	4040	7.4	8.2
37	0	0	1	4133	7.3	7.5
38	0	0	0	4303	7.1	7.1
39	1	0	0	4393	7	7.2
40	0	1	0	4560	7.1	8.9
41	0	0	1	4587	7.1	7.7
42	0	0	0	4716	6.9	7.4

Figure 48-2   Using dummy variables to track the quarter in which a sale occurs

In addition to seasonality, we'd like to use macroeconomic variables such as gross national product (GNP, in billions of 1986 dollars), interest rates, and unemployment rates to predict car sales. Suppose, for example, that we are trying to estimate sales for the second quarter of 1979. Because values for GNP, interest rate, and unemployment rate aren't known at the beginning of the second quarter 1979, we can't use second quarter 1979 GNP, interest rate, and unemployment rate to predict Quarter 2 1979 auto sales. Instead, we'll use the values for GNP, interest rate, and unemployment rate *lagged one quarter* to forecast auto sales. By copying from J12 to J12:L42 the formula =D11, we create the lagged value for GNP, the first of our macroeconomic independent variables. For example, the range J12:L12 contains GNP, unemployment rate, and interest rate for the first quarter of 1979.

We can now run our multiple regression by clicking Data Analysis on the Data tab, and then selecting Regression in the Data Analysis dialog box. We use C11:C42 as the Input Y Range, G11:L42 as the Input X Range, check the Labels box (row 11 contains labels), and also check the Residuals box. After clicking OK, we obtain the output, which you can see in the *Regression* worksheet and in Figures 48-3 through 48-5.

	A	B	C	D	E	F
1	SUMMARY OUTPUT					
2						
3	*Regression Statistics*					
4	Multiple R	0.884139126				
5	R Square	0.781701994				
6	Adjusted R Square	0.727127492				
7	Standard Error	190.5240756				
8	Observations	31				
9						
10	ANOVA					
11		*df*	*SS*	*MS*	*F*	*Significance F*
12	Regression	6	3119625	519937.5	14.32358	6.79746E-07
13	Residual	24	871186.2	36299.42		
14	Total	30	3990811			

Figure 48-3   Summary output and ANOVA table for auto sales data

In Figure 48-4, we can see that the equation (equation 1) used to predict quarterly auto sales is as follows:

```
Predicted quarterly sales=3154.7+156.833Q1+379.784Q2+203.03
6Q3+.174(LAGGNP in billions)-93.83(LAGUNEMP)-73.91(LAGINT)
```

Also in Figure 48-4, we see that each independent variable has a p-value less than or equal to 0.15. We can conclude that all independent variables have a significant effect on quarterly auto sales. We interpret all coefficients in our regression equation *ceteris paribus* (which means that each coefficient gives the effect of the independent variable after adjusting for the effects of all other variables in the regression).

	A	B	C	D	E	F	G	H	I
16		*Coefficients*	*andard Err*	*t Stat*	*P-value*	*Lower 95%*	*Upper 95%*	*Lower 95.0%*	*Upper 95.0%*
17	Intercept	3154.700285	462.6531	6.818717	4.72E-07	2199.83143	4109.56914	2199.83143	4109.56914
18	Q1	156.833091	98.87111	1.586238	0.125775	-47.22680256	360.8929846	-47.22680256	360.8929846
19	Q2	379.7835116	96.08922	3.952405	0.000594	181.4651595	578.1018637	181.4651595	578.1018637
20	Q3	203.035501	95.40892	2.128056	0.043801	6.12121161	399.9497905	6.12121161	399.9497905
21	LagGNP	0.174156906	0.05842	2.981118	0.00649	0.053583977	0.294729835	0.053583977	0.294729835
22	LagUnemp	-93.83233214	28.32329	-3.3129	0.002918	-152.2887117	-35.37595254	-152.2887117	-35.37595254
23	LagInt	-73.9167147	17.78852	-4.15531	0.000356	-110.6303992	-37.20303022	-110.6303992	-37.20303022

Figure 48-4   Coefficient information for auto sales regression

Here's an interpretation of each coefficient:

- ❑ A $1 billion increase in last quarter's GNP increases quarterly car sales by 174.

- ❑ An increase of 1 percent in last quarter's unemployment rate decreases quarterly car sales by 93,832.

- ❑ An increase of 1 percent in last quarter's interest rate decreases quarterly car sales by 73,917.

To interpret the coefficients of the dummy variables, we must realize that they tell us the effect of seasonality relative to the value left out of the qualitative variables. Therefore:

- ❑ In Quarter 1, car sales exceed Quarter 4 car sales by 156,833.

- ❑ In Quarter 2, car sales exceed Quarter 4 car sales by 379,784.

- ❑ In Quarter 3, car sales exceed Quarter 4 car sales by 203,036.

We find that car sales are highest during the second quarter (April through June; tax refunds and summer are coming) and lowest during the third quarter (October through December; why buy a new car when winter salting will ruin it?).

From the Summary output shown in Figure 48-3, we can learn the following:

- ❑ The variation in our independent variables (macroeconomic factors and seasonality) explains 78 percent of the variation in our dependent variable (quarterly car sales).

- ❑ The standard error of our regression is 190,524 cars. We can expect around 68 percent of our forecasts to be accurate within 190,524 cars and about 95 percent of our forecasts to be accurate within 381,048 cars (*2*190,524*).

- ❑ There are 31 observations used to fit the regression.

The only quantity of interest to us in the ANOVA table in Figure 48-3 is the significance (0.00000068). This measure implies that there are only 6.8 chances in 10,000,000 that, taken together, all of our independent variables are useless in forecasting car sales. Thus, we can be quite sure that our independent variables are useful in predicting quarterly auto sales.

Figure 48-5, on the next page, shows, for each observation, the predicted sales and residual. For example, for the second quarter of 1979 (observation 1), predicted sales from equation 1 are 2728.6 thousand and our residual is 181,400 cars (*2910–2728.6*). Note that no residual exceeds 381,000 in absolute value, so we have no outliers.

Observation	Predicted Sales	Residuals
	RESIDUAL OUTPUT	
1	2728.588616	181.4114
2	2587.848606	-25.8486
3	2336.034563	48.96544
4	2339.328281	180.6717
5	2447.266343	-305.266
6	2400.118977	-270.119
7	2199.7408	-9.7408
8	2076.383266	293.6167
9	2276.947422	-68.9474
10	2026.185621	169.8144
11	1848.731191	-90.7312
12	2138.394335	-194.394
13	2212.298456	-118.298
14	2014.216596	-103.217
15	1969.394332	61.60567
16	2166.640544	-120.641
17	2440.632301	61.3677
18	2290.352403	-52.3524
19	2131.386979	262.613
20	2433.681173	152.3188
21	2739.094517	158.9055
22	2586.877653	-138.878
23	2362.035446	97.96455
24	2667.994409	-21.9944
25	2937.601377	50.39862
26	2838.174893	128.8251
27	2713.079218	-274.079
28	2887.577992	-289.578
29	3004.570968	40.42903
30	2921.225251	291.7747
31	2781.597472	-96.5975

Figure 48-5   Residuals for the auto sales data

How can I predict U.S. presidential elections?

When asked which factors drive presidential elections, presidential advisor James Carville said, "It's the economy, stupid." Yale economist Roy Fair showed that Carville was correct in thinking that the state of the economy has a large influence on the results of presidential elections. Fair's dependent variable (see the file President.xlsx, shown in Figure 48-6) for each election (1916 through 2004) was the percentage of the two party vote (ignoring votes received by third party candidates) that went to the incumbent party. He tried to predict the incumbent party's percentage of the two-party vote by using independent variables such as:

- Party in power. In our data, we use 1 to denote when the Republican party was in power and 0 to denote when the Democratic party was in power.
- Percentage growth in GNP during the first nine months of the election year.
- Absolute value of the inflation rate during the first nine months of the election year. We use the absolute value because either a positive or a negative inflation rate is bad.
- Number of quarters during the last four years in which economic growth was strong. Strong economic growth is defined as growth at an annual level of 3.2 percent or more.
- Length of time an incumbent party had been in office. Fair used 0 to denote one term in office, 1 for two terms, 1.25 for three terms, 1.5 for four terms, and 1.75 for five terms or more. This definition implies that each term after the first term in office has less influence on the election results than the first term in office.

❏ Elections during wartime. The elections in 1920 (World War I), 1944 (World War II), and 1948 (World War II was still underway in 1945) were defined as wartime elections. (Elections held during the Vietnam war were not considered to be wartime elections.) During wartime years, the variables related to quarters of good growth and inflation were deemed irrelevant and were set to 0.

❏ The current president running for re-election. If this is the case, this variable is set to 1; otherwise, this variable is set to 0. In 1976, Gerald Ford was not considered a president running for re-election because he was not elected either as president or as vice-president.

							1=2 terms				
							1.25=3 terms				
							1.5=4 terms				
							1.75=5 terms				
				Growth rate in election year	Abs. Value Inflation rate in election year	Quarters Growth>3.2 %	Time Incumbent in Office	Incumbent Party 1 = Republican	War	President Running?	Prediction
Candidates	Year	Incumbent Share	Party in Power								
Wilson-Hughes	1916	51.7	D	2.2	4.3	3	0	0	0	1	50.78742
Harding-Cox	1920	36.1	D	-11.5	0	0	1	0	1	0	39.00437
Coolidge-Davis	1924	58.2	R	-3.9	5.2	10	0	1	0	1	57.74766
Hoover-Smith	1928	58.8	R	4.6	0.2	7	1	1	0	0	57.41967
Hoover-FDR	1932	40.8	R	-14.9	7.1	4	1.25	1	0	1	39.0912
FDR-Landon	1936	62.5	D	11.9	2.4	9	0	0	0	1	64.37954
FDR-Wilkie	1940	55	D	3.7	0	8	1	0	0	1	56.15866
FDR-Dewey	1944	53.8	D	4.1	0	0	1.25	0	1	1	52.86561
Truman-Dewey	1948	52.4	D	1.8	0	0	1.5	0	1	1	50.43002
Ike-Stevenson	1952	44.6	D	0.6	2.3	6	1.75	0	0	0	44.20949
Ike-Stevenson	1956	57.8	R	-1.5	1.9	5	0	1	0	1	57.25875
Kennedy-Nixon	1960	49.9	R	0.1	1.9	5	1	1	0	0	51.23525
Johnson-Goldwate	1964	61.3	D	5.1	1.2	10	0	0	0	1	61.41295
Nixon-Humphrey	1968	49.6	D	4.8	3.2	7	1	0	0	0	49.89246
Nixon-McGovern	1972	61.8	R	6.3	4.8	4	0	1	0	1	59.69504
Ford-Carter	1976	48.9	R	3.7	7.7	4	1	1	0	0	48.64809
Carter-Reagan	1980	44.7	D	-3.8	8.1	5	0	0	0	1	45.67703
Reagan-Mondale	1984	59.2	R	5.4	5.4	7	0	1	0	1	61.3616
Bush-Dukakis	1988	53.9	R	2.1	3.3	6	1	1	0	0	52.5282
Bush-Clinton	1992	46.5	R	2.3	3.7	1	1.25	1	0	1	50.81454
Clinton-Dole	1996	54.7	D	2.9	2.3	3	0	0	0	1	52.71998
Gore Bush	2000	50.3	D	2.2	1.7	7	1	0	0	0	49.16247
Kerry Bush	2004	51.2	R	2.9	2	2	0	1	0	1	57.52759

Figure 48-6 Presidential election data

> **Note** Our data comes from Roy Fair's excellent book *Predicting Presidential Elections and Other Things* (Stanford University Press, 2002).

I've attempted to use the data from the elections from 1916 through 2000 to develop a multiple regression equation that can be used to forecast future presidential elections. I saved the 2004 election as a "validation point." When fitting a regression to data, it's always a good idea to hold back some of your data for use in validating your regression equation. Holding back data allows you to determine whether your regression equation can do a good job of forecasting data it hasn't seen. Any forecasting tool that poorly forecasts data it hasn't seen should not be used to predict the future.

To run the regression, click Data Analysis in the Analysis group on the Data tab, and then select the Regression tool in the Data Analysis dialog box. I used C6:C28 as the Input Y Range and E6:K28 as the Input X Range. I also checked the Labels box (row 6 contains labels) and the Residuals box. I've placed the output in the *Results* worksheet, which you can see in Figures 48-7 and 48-8 on the next page.

		A	B	C	D	E	F	G	H	I
3		*Regression Statistics*								
4	Multiple R		0.969157143							
5	R Square		0.939265567							
6	Adjusted R Square		0.90889835							
7	Standard Error		2.10588869							
8	Observations		22							
9										
10	ANOVA									
11				*df*	*SS*	*MS*	*F*	*Significance F*		
12	Regression			7	960.1791686	137.1684527	30.93024893	1.7994E-07		
13	Residual			14	62.08674044	4.434767174				
14	Total			21	1022.265909					
15										
16			*Coefficients*	*Standard Error*	*t Stat*	*P-value*	*Lower 95%*	*Upper 95%*	*Lower 95.0%*	*Upper 95.0%*
17	Intercept		45.81778401	2.533611426	18.08398223	4.19198E-11	40.38372797	51.25184005	40.38372797	51.25184005
18	Growth rate in election year		0.697410487	0.091570567	7.616098858	2.41594E-06	0.501011156	0.893809819	0.501011156	0.893809819
19	Abs. Value Inflation rate in election year		-0.722182995	0.252755816	-2.857235912	0.012667807	-1.264290303	-0.180075687	-1.264290303	-0.180075687
20	Quarters Growth>3.2%		0.909180849	0.229881824	3.954992316	0.001437591	0.416133374	1.402228324	0.416133374	1.402228324
21	Time Incumbent in Office		-3.326172244	1.063226594	-3.128375704	0.00740306	-5.606566482	-1.045778006	-5.606566482	-1.045778006
22	Incumbent Party 1 = Republican		5.500142106	1.036606237	5.305912612	0.000110972	3.276842855	7.723441357	3.276842855	7.723441357
23	War		4.532976564	2.307896408	1.964116131	0.069688579	-0.416968913	9.482922042	-0.416968913	9.482922042
24	President Running?		3.813181464	1.169872938	3.259483436	0.005704062	1.304053567	6.322309361	1.304053567	6.322309361

Figure 48-7   Regression output for predicting presidential elections

	A	B	C
28	RESIDUAL OUTPUT		
29			
30	*Observation*	*Predicted Incumbent Share*	*Residuals*
31	1	50.78742421	0.912575787
32	2	39.00436772	-2.904367724
33	3	57.7476636	0.452336404
34	4	57.41967146	1.380328544
35	5	39.09120015	1.708799855
36	6	64.37953873	-1.879538725
37	7	56.15865882	-1.158658824
38	8	52.86560973	0.934390271
39	9	50.43002255	1.969977453
40	10	44.20949308	0.39050692
41	11	57.2587484	0.541251598
42	12	51.23525147	-1.335251474
43	13	61.41294785	-0.112947855
44	14	49.89246246	-0.292462463
45	15	59.69503867	2.104961331
46	16	48.64808701	0.251912991
47	17	45.67702761	-0.977027607
48	18	61.36160198	-2.161601981
49	19	52.5281971	1.371802895
50	20	50.81454016	-4.314540162
51	21	52.71997754	1.980022456
52	22	49.16246969	1.137530311

Figure 48-8   Presidential election residuals

In Figure 48-7, you can see that the p-value for each independent variable is much less than 0.15, which indicates that each of our independent variables is helpful in predicting presidential elections. We can predict elections using an equation such as the following (equation 2):

```
Predicted presidential election percentage=45.813+.70GROWTH-.72ABSINF+.91GOODQUARTERS-
3.33TIMEINCUMB+5.5REP+4.53WAR+3.81PRESRUNNING
```

The coefficients of the independent variables can be interpreted as follows (after adjusting for all other independent variables used in equation 2):

- A 1 percent increase in the annual GNP growth rate during an election year is worth 0.7 percent to the incumbent party.

- A 1 percent deviation from the ideal (0 percent inflation) costs the incumbent party 0.72 percent of the vote.

- Every good quarter of growth during an incumbent's term increases his (maybe her someday soon!) vote by 0.91 percent.

- Relative to having one term in office, the second term in office decreases the incumbent's vote by 3.33 percent, and each later term decreases the incumbent's vote by *0.25*(3.33 percent)=0.83 percent.*

- A Republican has a 5.5 percent edge over a Democrat.

- A wartime incumbent president has a 4.53 percent edge over his opponent.

- A sitting president running for re-election has a 3.81 percent edge over his opponent.

We find that 94 percent of the variation in the percentage received by an incumbent in a presidential election is explained by our independent variables. This is amazing! We have not mentioned whether the candidates are "good" or "bad" candidates. Our standard error of 2.10 percent indicates that about 95 percent of our forecasts will be accurate within 4.2 percent. From our residuals, shown in Figure 48-8, we find the only election outlier to be the 1992 Clinton-Bush election. George Bush Sr. received 4.31 percent less than our model predicted, which probably indicates that Bill Clinton was a great campaigner!

Is there an Excel function I can use to easily make forecasts from a multiple regression equation?

It's tedious to make forecasts using an equation such as equation 2, but the Excel TREND function makes it easy to generate forecasts from a multiple regression. You don't even have to run a regression with the Data Analysis command.

To illustrate the use of the TREND function, I'll describe how to generate forecasts for the 1916 through 2004 elections using data from only the 1916 through 2000 elections. Begin by selecting the cell range (in our example, L7:L29 in the *Data* worksheet) where you want your forecasts to go. With the pointer in the first cell of this range (cell L7 in our example), enter the formula *TREND(C7:C28,E7:K28,E7:K29)*. Next, press Ctrl+Shift+Enter. You'll now see the forecast for each election, generated in cells L7:L29. Note that the forecast for the 2004 election (using data only through 2000) was that Bush would receive 57.5 percent of the vote. Thus, Bush's share of the popular vote was an outlier on the low side. Maybe this was due to the unpopularity of the Iraq War.

The TREND function is an example of an *array function*. I'll provide a more complete discussion of array functions in Chapter 74, "Array Functions and Formulas." For now, here is some background about array functions:

- Before entering an array function, you must always select the cell range in which you want the results of the array function to be located.

- Instead of pressing Enter to perform the calculation, you must press Ctrl+Shift+Enter to complete the entry of an array function.

❑ After entering an array function, you'll see a curly bracket in the formula bar when you select a cell in which the array function's results are located. This bracket indicates that the results in the cell were computed with an array function.

❑ You can't modify data in any part of a range created by an array function.

Note Problems that you can work with to learn more about multiple regression are available at the end of Chapter 49.

Chapter 49
Modeling Nonlinearities and Interactions

- What does it mean when we say that an independent variable has a nonlinear effect on a dependent variable?

- What does it mean when we say that the effects of two independent variables on a dependent variable interact?

- How can I test for the presence of nonlinearity and interaction in a regression?

What does it mean when we say that an independent variable has a nonlinear effect on a dependent variable?

An independent variable will often influence a dependent variable through a nonlinear relationship. For example, if we try to predict product sales using an equation such as *Sales=500−10*Price,* price influences sales linearly. This equation indicates that a unit increase in price will (at any price level) reduce sales by 10 units. If the relationship between sales and price were governed by an equation such as *Sales=500+4*Price−.40*Price^2,* price and sales would be related nonlinearly. As shown in Figure 49-1, larger increases in price result in larger decreases in demand. In short, if the change in the dependent variable caused by a unit change in the independent variable is not constant, there is a nonlinear relationship between the independent and dependent variables.

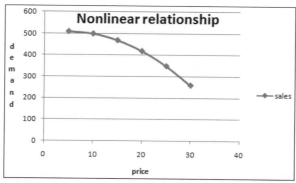

Figure 49-1 Nonlinear relationship between demand and price

What does it mean when we say that the effects of two independent variables on a dependent variable interact?

If the effect of one independent variable on a dependent variable depends on the value of another independent variable, we say that the two independent variables exhibit *interaction*. For example, suppose we try to predict sales using price and the amount spent on advertising. If the effect of changing the level of advertising dollars is large when the price is small and small when the price is high, price and advertising exhibit interaction. If the effect of changing the level of advertising dollars is the same for any price level, sales and price do not exhibit any interaction.

How can I test for the presence of nonlinearity and interaction in a regression?

To see whether an independent variable has a nonlinear effect on a dependent variable, we simply add an independent variable to the regression that equals the square of the independent variable. If the squared term has a low p-value (less than 0.15), we have evidence of a nonlinear relationship.

To check whether two independent variables exhibit interaction, we simply add a term to the regression that equals the product of the independent variables. If the term has a low p-value (less than 0.15), we have evidence of interaction.

To illustrate, let's try to determine how gender and experience influence salaries at a small manufacturing company. For each employee, we are given the following set of data. You can find the information in the *Data* worksheet in the file Interactions.xlsx, shown in Figure 49-2.

- ❑ Annual salary (in thousands of dollars)
- ❑ Years of experience working in the manufacturing business
- ❑ Gender (1=female, 0=male)

We'll use this data to predict salary (the dependent variable) based on years of experience and gender. To test whether years of experience has a nonlinear effect on salary, I added the term Experience Squared by copying from D2 to D3:D98 the formula $B2\char94 2$. To test whether experience and gender have a significant interaction, I added the term Experience*Gender by copying from E2 to E3:E98 the formula $B2*C2$. I ran a regression with an Input Y Range of A1:A98 and an Input X Range of B1:E98. After checking the Labels box in the Regression dialog box and clicking OK, I got the results shown in Figure 49-3.

	A	B	C	D	E
1	Salary	Exp	Gender	Exp^2	Exp*Gender
2	55.922	5	1	25	5
3	62.3987	15	0	225	0
4	67.8475	12	0	144	0
5	64.8081	19	0	361	0
6	58.2963	9	0	81	0
7	51.9397	3	0	9	0
8	36.3427	12	1	144	12
9	28.3883	15	1	225	15
10	73.5763	8	0	64	0
11	44.1673	12	1	144	12
12	57.0322	1	1	1	1
13	61.588	5	0	25	0
14	63.2191	14	0	196	0
15	58.1555	1	1	1	1
16	47.4811	3	1	9	3
17	44.4308	6	1	36	6
18	59.1071	4	0	16	0
19	64.555	9	0	81	0
20	64.6575	18	0	324	0
21	49.0959	7	1	49	7
22	69.0104	14	0	196	0
23	64.9956	16	0	256	0
24	37.5633	11	1	121	11
25	56.34	18	0	324	0
26	60.826	16	0	256	0
27	56.986	16	0	256	0
28	65.9592	5	0	25	0
29	72.1265	13	0	169	0
30	57.4413	3	1	9	3
31	64.0981	11	0	121	0
32	71.3074	18	0	324	0

Figure 49-2   Data for predicting salary based on gender and experience

	H	I	J	K	L	M	N	O	P
2	SUMMARY OUTPUT								
4	Regression Statistics								
5	Multiple R	0.930645916							
6	R Square	0.866101822							
7	Adjusted R Square	0.860280162							
8	Standard Error	4.530277908							
9	Observations	97							
11	ANOVA								
12		df	SS	MS	F	Significance F			
13	Regression	4	12213.26555	3053.32	148.7723146	2.77158E-39			
14	Residual	92	1888.154449	20.5234					
15	Total	96	14101.42						
17		Coefficients	Standard Error	t Stat	P-value	Lower 95%	Upper 95%	Lower 95.0%	Upper 95.0%
18	Intercept	58.30311924	1.960660525	29.7365	5.6775E-49	54.40907819	62.19716028	54.40907819	62.19716028
19	Exp	0.860472831	0.381574828	2.25506	0.02650141	0.102632286	1.618313377	0.102632286	1.618313377
20	Gender	1.119399728	1.94092596	0.57673	0.565527049	-2.735446764	4.974246221	-2.735446764	4.974246221
21	Exp^2	-0.035148705	0.017761027	-1.97898	0.050808362	-0.070423637	0.000126228	-0.070423637	0.000126228
22	Exp*Gender	-2.164501713	0.180872223	-11.967	1.86636E-20	-2.523729559	-1.805273866	-2.523729559	-1.805273866

Figure 49-3   Regression results that test for nonlinearity and interaction

We find that gender is insignificant (its p-value is greater than 0.15). All other independent variables are significant (meaning they have a p-value less than or equal to 0.15). We can delete the insignificant gender variable as an independent variable. To do this, I copied the data into a new worksheet called *FinalRegression* (right-click any worksheet tab, click Move Or Copy, and check the Create A Copy box.) After deleting the Gender column, we obtain the regression results included in the *FinalRegression* worksheet and shown in Figure 49-4 on the next page.

	H	I	J	K	L	M	N	O	P
2	SUMMARY OUTPUT								
3									
4	*Regression Statistics*								
5	Multiple R	0.93039							
6	R Square	0.86562							
7	Adjusted R Squ	0.86128							
8	Standard Error	4.51399							
9	Observations	97							
10									
11	ANOVA								
12		df	SS	MS	F	gnificance F			
13	Regression	3	12206.4	4068.81	199.685	2.1E-40			
14	Residual	93	1894.98	20.3761					
15	Total	96	14101.4						
16									
17		Coefficient	andard Err	t Stat	P-value	ower 95%	Jpper 95%	ower 95.0%	Upper 95.0%
18	Intercept	59.0574	1.45541	40.5778	6.1E-61	56.1673	61.9476	56.1673	61.94759951
19	Exp	0.78112	0.35462	2.20266	0.03009	0.07691	1.48533	0.07691	1.485329146
20	Exp^2	-0.03359	0.01749	-1.92052	0.05786	-0.06833	0.00114	-0.06833	0.001141843
21	Exp*Gender	-2.07339	0.08777	-23.6219	4.5E-41	-2.2477	-1.89909	-2.2477	-1.899092079

Figure 49-4 Regression results after deleting insignificant gender variable

All independent variables are now significant (have a p-value less than or equal to 0.15). Therefore, we can predict salary (in thousands of dollars) by using the following equation (equation 1):

```
Predicted salary=59.06+.78(EXP)-.033EXP² - 2.07(EXP*GENDER)
```

The negative EXP^2 term indicates that each additional year of experience has less impact on salary, which means that experience has a nonlinear effect on salary. In fact, our model shows that after 13 years of experience, each additional year of experience actually reduces salary.

Remember that gender equals 1 for a woman and 0 for a man. After substituting 1 for gender in equation 1, we find that for a woman:

```
Predicted salary=59.06+78EXP-.03EXP² - 2.07(EXP*1)=59.06-.033EXP2 - 1.29EXP
```

For a man (substituting *gender=0*), we find that:

```
Predicted salary=59.06+.78EXP-.03EXP² - 2.07(EXP*0)=59.06+.78EXP-.033EXP²
```

Thus, the interaction between gender and experience shows that each additional year of experience benefits a woman an average of $0.78-(-1.29)=\$2,070$ less than a man. This indicates that women are not being treated fairly.

Problems for Chapters 47 Through 49

Fizzy Drugs wants to optimize the yield from an important chemical process. The company thinks that the number of pounds produced each time the process is run depends on the size of the container used, the pressure, and the temperature. The scientists involved believe the effect of changing one variable might depend on the values of other variables. The size of the process container must be between 1.3 and 1.5 cubic meters, pressure must be between 4 and 4.5 mm, and temperature must be between 22 and 30 degrees Celsius. The scientists patiently set up experiments at the lower and upper levels of the three control variables and obtain the data shown in the file Fizzy.xlsx.

1. Determine the relationship between yield, size, temperature, and pressure.

2. Discuss the interactions between pressure, size, and temperature.

3. What settings for temperature, size, and pressure would you recommend?

   Here are additional multiple regression problems:

4. For 12 straight weeks, you have observed the sales (in number of cases) of canned tomatoes at Mr. D's Supermarket. (See the file Grocery.xlsx.) Each week, you keep track of the following:

   ❑ Was a promotional notice for canned tomatoes placed in all shopping carts?

   ❑ Was a coupon for canned tomatoes given to each customer?

   ❑ Was a price reduction (none, 1, or 2 cents off) given?

   Use this data to determine how the above factors influence sales. Predict sales of canned tomatoes during a week in which we use a shopping cart notice, a coupon, and reduce price by 1 cent.

5. The file Countryregion.xlsx contains the following data for several underdeveloped countries:

   ❑ Infant mortality rate

   ❑ Adult literacy rate

   ❑ Percentage of students finishing primary school

   ❑ Per capita GNP

   Use this data to develop an equation that can be used to predict infant mortality. Are there any outliers in this set of data? Interpret the coefficients in your equation. Within what value should 95 percent of our predictions for infant mortality be accurate?

6. The file Baseball96.xlsx gives runs scored, singles, doubles, triples, home runs, and bases stolen for each major league baseball team during the 1996 season. Use this data to determine the effects of singles, doubles, and other activities on run production.

7. The file Cardata.xlsx provides the following information for 392 different car models:

   ❑ Cylinders

   ❑ Displacement

   ❑ Horsepower

   ❑ Weight

   ❑ Acceleration

   ❑ Miles per gallon (MPG)

   Determine an equation that can be used to predict MPG. Why do you think all the independent variables are not significant?

Chapter 50

Analysis of Variance: One-Way ANOVA

- The owner of my company, which publishes computer books, wants to know whether the position of our books in the computer book section of bookstores influences sales. More specifically, does it really matter whether the books are placed in the front, back, or middle of the computer book section?

- If I am determining whether populations have significantly different means, why is the technique called *analysis of variance*?

- How can I use the results of one-way ANOVA for forecasting?

We often have several different groups of people or items and want to determine whether data about the groups differs significantly. Here are some examples:

- Is there a significant difference in the length of time that four doctors keep mothers in the hospital after they give birth?

- Does the production yield for a new drug depend on whether the size of the container in which the drug is produced is large, small, or medium?

- Does the drop in blood pressure attained after taking one of four drugs depend on the drug taken?

When you're trying to determine whether the means in several sets of data that depend on one factor are significantly different, one-way analysis of variance, or ANOVA, is the correct tool to use. In the examples given above, the factors are the doctors, the container size, and the drug, respectively. In analyzing the data, we can choose between two hypotheses:

- *Null hypothesis*, which indicates that the means of all groups are identical.

- *Alternative hypothesis*, which indicates that there is a statistically significant difference between the groups' means.

To test these hypotheses in Microsoft Office Excel 2007, we can use the Anova: Single Factor option in the Data Analysis dialog box. If the p-value computed by Excel is small (usually less than or equal to 0.15), we can conclude that the alternative hypothesis is true (the means are significantly different). If the p-value is greater than 0.15, the null hypothesis is true (the populations have identical means). Let's look at an example.

The owner of my company, which publishes computer books, wants to know whether the position of our books in the computer book section of bookstores influences sales. More specifically, does it really matter whether the books are placed in the front, back, or middle of the computer book section?

The publishing company wants to know whether its books sell better when a display is set up in the front, back, or middle of the computer book section. Weekly sales (in hundreds) were monitored at 12 different stores. At 5 stores, the books were placed in the front; at 4 stores, in the back; and at 3 stores, in the middle. Resulting sales are contained in the *Signif* worksheet in the file Onewayanova.xlsx, which is shown in Figure 50-1. Does the data indicate that the location of the books has a significant effect on sales?

	A	B	C	D
1	One-Way ANOVA			
2				
3	Front	Back		Middle
4	7		12	10
5	10		13	11
6	8		15	12
7	9		16	
8	11			

Figure 50-1 Book sales data

We assume that the 12 stores have similar sales patterns and are approximately the same size. This assumption allows us to use one-way ANOVA because we believe that at most one factor (the position of the display in the computer book section) is affecting sales. (If the stores were different sizes, we would need to analyze our data with two-way ANOVA, which I'll discuss in Chapter 51, "Randomized Blocks and Two-Way ANOVA.")

To analyze the data, on the Data tab, click Data Analysis, and then select Anova: Single Factor. Fill in the dialog box as shown in Figure 50-2.

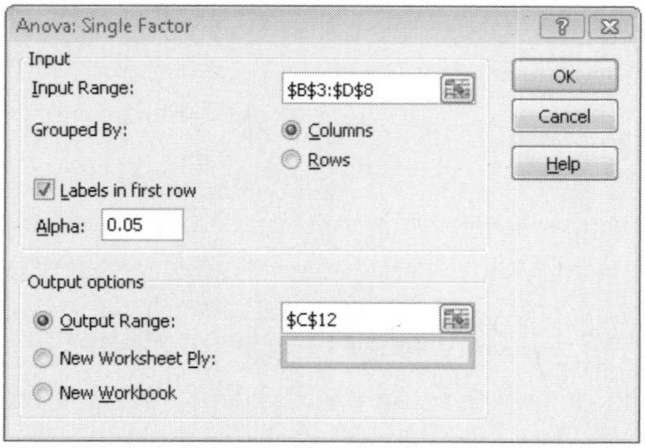

Figure 50-2 Anova: Single Factor dialog box

We use the following configurations:

❑ The data for our input range, including labels, is in cells B3:D8.

❑ Select the Labels option because the first row of our input range contains labels.

❑ I've selected the Columns option because the data is organized in columns.

❑ I've selected C12 as the upper-left cell of the output range.

❑ The selected alpha value is not important. You can use the default value.

After clicking OK, we obtain the results shown in Figure 50-3.

	C	D	E	F	G	H	I
12	Anova: Single Factor						
13							
14	SUMMARY						
15	*Groups*	*Count*	*Sum*	*Average*	*Variance*		
16	Front	5	45	9	2.5		
17	Back	4	56	14	3.333333		
18	Middle	3	33	11	1		
19							
20							
21	ANOVA						
22	*Source of Variation*	*SS*	*df*	*MS*	*F*	*P-value*	*F crit*
23	Between Groups	55.66666667	2	27.83333	11.38636	0.003426	4.256495
24	Within Groups	22	9	2.444444			
25							
26	Total	77.66666667	11				
27							
28	est std error	1.56347192					

Figure 50-3   One-way ANOVA results

In cells F16:F18, we see average sales depending on the location of the display. When the display is at the front of the computer book section, average sales are 900; when the display is at the back of the section, sales average 1400; and when the display is in the middle, sales average 1100. Because our p-value of 0.003 (in cell H23) is less than 0.15, we can conclude that these means are significantly different.

If I am determining whether populations have significantly different means, why is the technique called *analysis of variance*?

Suppose that the data in our book sales study is the data shown in the worksheet named *Insig*, shown in Figure 50-4 on the next page (also in the file Onewayanova.xlsx). If we run a one-way ANOVA on this data, we obtain the results shown in Figure 50-5 on the next page.

Note that the mean sales for each part of the store are exactly as before, yet our p-value of .66 indicates that we should accept the null hypothesis and conclude that the position of the display in the computer book section doesn't affect sales. The reason for this strange result is that in our second data set, we have much more variation in sales when the display is at each position in the computer book section. In our first data set, for example, the variation in sales when the display is at the front is between 700 and 1100, whereas in the second data set, the variation in sales is between 200 and 2000. The variation of sales within each store position is measured by the sum of the squares of data within a group. This measure is shown in cell D24 in the first data set and in cell F24 in the second. In our first data set, the sum of squares of data within groups is only 22, whereas in the second data set, the sum of squares within groups is 574! This large variation within the data points at each store position masks the variation between the groups (store positions) themselves and makes it impossible to conclude for the second data set that the difference between sales in different store positions is significant.

	E	F	G	H	I	J	K
12	Anova: Single Factor		Overall mean				
13			11.1666667				
14	SUMMARY						
15	Groups	Count	Sum	Average	Variance		
16	Front	5	45	9	44		
17	Back	4	56	14	90		
18	Middle	3	33	11	64		
19							
20							
21	ANOVA						
22	ource of Variatic	SS	df	MS	F	P-value	F crit
23	Between Group	55.66667	2	27.83333	0.436411	0.659334	4.256492
24	Within Groups	574	9	63.77778			
25							
26	Total	629.6667	11				
27							
28	est std err	3.316625					

Figure 50-4   Book store data for which the null hypothesis is accepted

	B	C	D
3	Front	Back	Middle
4	7	2	3
5	20	16	19
6	8	25	11
7	8	13	
8	2		

Figure 50-5   Anova results accepting the null hypothesis

How can I use the results of a one-way ANOVA for forecasting?

If there is a significant difference between group means, our best forecast for each group is simply the group's mean. Therefore, in the first data set, we predict the following:

- Sales when the display is at the front of the computer book section will be 900 books per week.

- Sales when the display is at the back will be 1400 books per week.

- Sales when the display is in the middle will be 1100 books per week.

If there is no significant difference between the group means, our best forecast for each observation is simply the overall mean. Thus, in the second data set, we predict weekly sales of 1117, independent of where the books are placed.

We can also estimate the accuracy of our forecasts. The square root of the Within Groups MS (mean square) is the standard deviation of our forecasts from a one-way ANOVA. As shown in Figure 50-6, our standard deviation of forecasts for the first data set is 156. By the rule of thumb, this means that we would expect, for example:

- During 68 percent of all the weeks in which books are placed at the front of the computer section, sales will be between *900–156=744* and *900+156=1056* books.

- During 95 percent of all weeks in which books are placed at the front of the computer book section, sales will be between *900–2(156)=588* books and *900+2(156) =1212* books.

	E	F	G	H	I	J	K
12	Anova: Single Factor		Overall mean				
13			11.1666667				
14	SUMMARY						
15	*Groups*	*Count*	*Sum*	*Average*	*Variance*		
16	Front	5	45	9	44		
17	Back	4	56	14	90		
18	Middle	3	33	11	64		
19							
20							
21	ANOVA						
22	*Source of Variation*	*SS*	*df*	*MS*	*F*	*P-value*	*F crit*
23	Between Groups	55.66667	2	27.83333	0.436411	0.659334	4.256492
24	Within Groups	574	9	63.77778			
25							
26	Total	629.6667	11				
27							
28	est std err	3.316625					

Figure 50-6   Computation of forecast standard deviation

Problems

You can find the data for the following problems in the file Chapter50data.xlsx.

1. For patients of four cardiologists, we are given the number of days the patients stayed in the hospital after open-heart surgery.
   - Is there evidence that the doctors have different discharge policies?
   - You are 95 percent sure that a patient of Doctor 1 will stay in the hospital between what range of days?

2. A drug can be produced by using a 400-degree, 300-degree, or 200-degree oven. You are given the pounds of the drug yielded when various batches are baked at different temperatures.
   - Does temperature appear to influence the process yield?
   - What is the range of pounds of the product that you are 95 percent sure will be produced with a 200-degree oven?
   - If you believe that pressure within the container also influences process yield, does this analysis remain valid?

Chapter 51

Randomized Blocks and Two-Way ANOVA

- I am trying to analyze the effectiveness of my sales force. The problem is that in addition to a sales representative's effectiveness, the amount that a representative sells depends on the district to which he or she is assigned. How can I incorporate the district assignments of my representatives into my analysis?

- Based on my knowledge of sales representatives and districts, how can I forecast sales? How accurate are my sales forecasts?

- How can I determine whether varying the price and the amount of advertising affects the sales of a video game? How can I determine whether price and advertising interact significantly?

- How can I interpret the effects of price and advertising on sales when there is the absence of significant interaction between price and advertising?

In many sets of data, two factors can influence a dependent variable. Here are some examples.

Factors	Dependent variable
Sales representative and district assignment	Sales
Product price and advertising expenditure	Sales
Temperature and pressure	Production yield
Surgeon and brand of stent used	Health of patient after open-heart surgery

When two factors might influence a dependent variable, randomized blocks or two-way analysis of variance (ANOVA) can easily be used to determine which, if any, of the factors have a significant influence on the dependent variable. With two-way ANOVA, you can also determine whether two factors exhibit a significant interaction. For example, suppose we are trying to predict sales by using product price and advertising budget. Price and advertising interact significantly if the effect of advertising depends on the product price.

In a randomized block model, we observe each possible combination of factors exactly once. You can't test for interactions in a randomized block design. In a two-way ANOVA model, we observe each combination of factors the same number of times (call it k). In this case, k must be greater than 1. In a two-way ANOVA model, you can easily test for interactions.

I am trying to analyze the effectiveness of my sales force. The problem is that in addition to a sales representative's effectiveness, the amount that a representative sells depends on the district to which he or she is assigned. How can I incorporate the district assignments of my representatives into my analysis?

Suppose we want to determine how a sales representative and the sales district to which the representative is assigned influence product sales. To answer the question in this example, we can have each of four sales reps spend a month selling in each of five sales districts. The resulting sales are given in the *Randomized Blocks* worksheet in the file Two-wayanova.xlsx, shown in Figure 51-1. For example, Rep 1 sold 20 units during the month she was assigned to District 4.

	C	D	E	F	G
5		Rep 1	Rep 2	Rep 3	Rep 4
6	Dist 1	1	3	10	12
7	Dist 2	17	12	16	14
8	Dist 3	17	21	22	25
9	Dist 4	20	10	17	23
10	Dist 5	22	21	37	32

Figure 51-1   Data for the randomized blocks example

This model is called a *two-way ANOVA without replication* because two factors (district and sales representative) can potentially influence sales, and we have only a single instance pairing each representative with each district. This model is also called a *randomized block* design because we'd like to randomize (chronologically) the assignment of representatives to districts. In other words, we'd like to ensure that the month during which Rep 1 is assigned to District 1 is equally likely to be the first, second, third, fourth, or fifth month. This randomization hopefully lessens the effect of time (a representative presumably becomes better over time) on our analysis; in a sense, we are "blocking" the effect of districts when we try to compare sales representatives.

To analyze this data in Microsoft Office Excel 2007, click Data Analysis on the Data tab, and then select the Anova: Two-Factor Without Replication option. Then fill in the dialog box as shown in Figure 51-2.

We use the following information to set up our analysis:

❑ Our input range data is in cells C5:G10.

❑ I've checked Labels because the first row of the input range contains labels.

❑ I entered B12 as the upper-left cell of our output range.

❑ The alpha value is not important. You can use the default value.

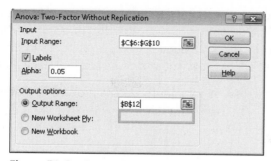

Figure 51-2   Anova: Two-Factor Without Replication dialog box for setting up a randomized blocks model

The output we obtain is shown in Figure 51-3. (The results in cells G12:G24 were not created by the Excel Data Analysis feature. I entered formulas in these cells, as I'll explain later in the chapter.)

	B	C	D	E	F	G	H
12	Anova: Two-Factor Without Replication					17.6	
13							
14	SUMMARY	Count	Sum	Average	Variance		
15	Dist 1	4	26	6.5	28.33333	-11.1	
16	Dist 2	4	59	14.75	4.916667	-2.85	
17	Dist 3	4	85	21.25	10.91667	3.65	
18	Dist 4	4	70	17.5	31	-0.1	
19	Dist 5	4	112	28	60.66667	10.4	
20						-17.6	
21	Rep 1	5	77	15.4	69.3	-2.2	
22	Rep 2	5	67	13.4	59.3	-4.2	
23	Rep 3	5	102	20.4	104.3	2.8	
24	Rep 4	5	106	21.2	67.7	3.6	
25							
26							
27	ANOVA						
28	Source of Variation	SS	df	MS	F	P-value	F crit
29	Rows	1011.3	4	252.825	15.87598	9.74E-05	3.259167
30	Columns	216.4	3	72.13333	4.529566	0.024095	3.490295
31	Error	191.1	12	15.925			
32			stdev	3.990614			
33	Total	1418.8	19				

Figure 51-3   Randomized blocks output

To determine whether the row factor (districts) or column factor (sales representatives) has a significant effect on sales, just look at the p-value. If the p-value for a factor is low (less than .15), the factor has a significant effect on sales. The row p-value (.0000974) and column p-value (.024) are both less than .15, so both the district and the representative have a significant effect on sales.

Based on my knowledge of sales representatives and districts, how can I forecast sales? How accurate are my sales forecasts?

How should we predict product sales? We can predict sales during a month by using equation 1, shown here:

```
Predicted sales=Overall average+(Rep effect)+(District effect)
```

In this equation, *Rep effect* equals 0 if the sales rep factor is not significant. If the sales rep factor is significant, *Rep effect* equals the mean for the given rep minus the overall average. Likewise, *District effect* equals 0 if the district factor is not significant. If the district factor is significant, *District effect* equals the mean for the given district minus the overall average.

I computed the overall average (17.6) in cell G12 by using the formula *AVERAGE(D6:G10)*. The representative and district effects are computed by copying from cell G15 to G16:G24 the formula *E15–$G$12*. As an example, you can compute predicted sales by Rep 4 in District 2 as *17.6–2.85+3.6=18.35*. This value is computed in cell D38 (see Figure 51-4) with the formula *G12+G16+G24*. If the district effect was significant and the sales representative effect was not, our predicted sales for Rep 4 in District 2 would be *17.6– 2.85=14.75.*

	C	D
36	District 2	
37	Rep 4 Forecast	
38	Mean	18.35
39	Lower	10.368772
40	Upper	26.331228

Figure 51-4 Forecast for sales in District 2 by sales Rep 4

As in one-way ANOVA, the standard deviation of our forecast errors is the square root of the mean square error shown in cell E31. I computed this standard deviation in cell E32 with the formula *SQRT(E31)*. Thus, we are 95 percent sure that if Rep 4 is assigned to District 2, monthly sales will be between *18.35–2(3.99)=10.37* and *18.35+2(3.99)=26.33*. These limits are computed in cell D39 and D40 with the formulas *D38–2*E32* and *D38+2*E32*, respectively.

How can I determine whether varying the price and the amount of advertising affects the sales of a video game? How can I determine whether price and advertising interact significantly?

When you have more than one observation for each combination of the row and column factors, you have a two-factor ANOVA *with* replication. To perform this sort of analysis, Excel requires that you have the same number of observations for each row-and-column combination.

In addition to testing for the significance of the row and column factors, we can also test for significant interaction between them. For example, if we want to understand how price and advertising affect sales, an interaction between price and advertising would indicate that the effect of an advertising change would depend on the price level (or equivalently, the effect of a price change would depend on the advertising level). A lack of interaction between price and advertising would mean that the effect of a price change would not depend on the level of advertising.

As an example of two-factor ANOVA with replication, suppose we want to determine how price and advertising level affect the monthly sales of a video game. In the *Two Way ANOVA No Interaction* worksheet in the file Twowayanova.xlsx, we have the data shown in Figure 51-5. During the three months in which we had low advertising and a medium price, for example, we sold 21, 20, and 16 units.

	B	C	D	E	F	G
1		Average	25.037037			
2		Price				
3			Low	Medium	High	Effect
4		Low	41	21	10	-5.59259
5	Adv		25	20	11	
6			23	16	8	
7		Medium	28	28	11	-1.81481
8			30	22	22	
9			32	18	18	
10		High	35	26	21	7.407407
11			45	40	26	
12			47	32	20	
13		Effect	8.962963	-0.25926	-8.7037	

Figure 51-5   Video game sales data; no interaction

Notice that for each price/advertising combination, we have exactly three observations. In cell D1, I've computed the overall average (25.037) of all observations with the formula *AVERAGE(D4:F12)*. In cells G4, G7, and G10, I computed the effect for each level of advertising. For example, the effect of having a low level of advertising equals the average for low advertising minus the overall average. In cell G4, I computed the low advertising effect of −5.59 with the formula *AVERAGE(D4:F6)−$D$1*. In a similar fashion, I computed the effect of each price level by copying from D13 to E13:F13 the formula *AVERAGE(D4:D12)−$D$1*.

To analyze this data, click Data Analysis on the Data tab, and then select Anova: Two-Factor With Replication in the Data Analysis dialog box. Fill in the dialog box as shown in Figure 51-6.

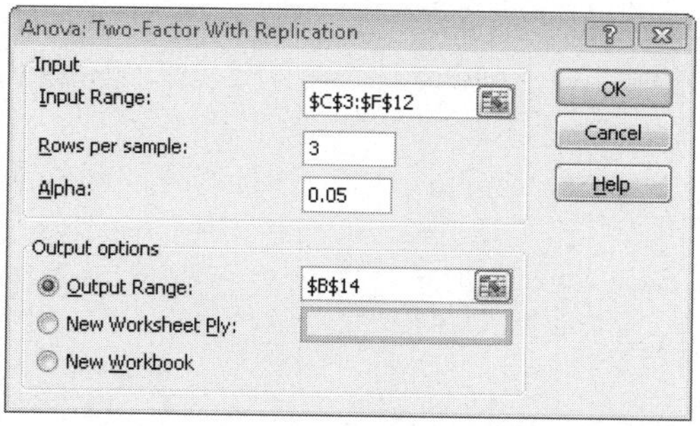

Figure 51-6   Anova: Two-Factor With Replication dialog box for running a two-factor ANOVA with replication

We use the following information to set up our analysis:

❑   Our input range data, including labels, is in C3:F12. In two-way ANOVA with replication, Excel requires a label for each level of the column effect in the first row of each column in the input range. Thus, we entered Low, Medium, and High in cells D3:F3 to indicate the possible price levels. Excel also requires a label for each level of the row effect in the first column of the input range. These labels must appear in the row that marks the beginning of the data for each level. Thus we placed labels corresponding to low, medium, and high levels of advertising in cells C4, C7, and C10.

❏ In the Rows Per Sample box, I've entered 3 because we have three replications for each combination of price and advertising level.

❏ The upper-left cell of our output range is B14.

The only important portion of the output is the ANOVA table, which is shown in Figure 51-7.

	B	C	D	E	F	G	H	I
42	ANOVA							
43	Source of Variation	SS	df	MS	F	P-value	F crit	F crit
44	Sample	804.962963	2	402.4815	13.51617	0.00026	3.554561	3.55456109
45	Columns	1405.40741	2	702.7037	23.59826	9.32E-06	3.554561	3.55456109
46	Interaction	50.5925926	4	12.64815	0.424751	0.788777	2.927749	2.92774871
47	Within	536	18	29.77778				
48								
49	Total	2796.96296	26					

Figure 51-7   Two-way ANOVA with replication output; no interaction

As with randomized blocks, an effect (including interactions) is significant if it has a p-value that's less than .15. We find that Sample (this is the row for advertising effect) and Price (shown in the row labeled Columns) are highly significant and also that there is no significant interaction. (The interaction p-value is .79!) Therefore, we can conclude that price and advertising influence sales and that the effect of advertising on sales does not depend on the price level. Figure 51-8 graphically demonstrates the fact that price and advertising do not exhibit a significant interaction.

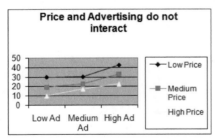

Figure 51-8   Price and advertising do not interact in this data set.

Notice that as advertising increases, sales increase at roughly the same rate, whether the price level is low, medium, or high.

How can I interpret the effects of price and advertising on sales when there is the absence of significant interaction between price and advertising?

In the absence of a significant interaction, we can forecast sales in a two-factor ANOVA with replication in the same way that we do in a two-factor ANOVA without replication. Here's the equation we use (equation 2):

```
Predicted sales=Overall average+[Row or advertising effect(if significant)]+[Column or
price effect(if significant)]
```

Our analysis assumes that price and advertising are the only factors that affect sales. If sales are highly seasonal, seasonality would need to be incorporated into the analysis. (Seasonality will be discussed in Chapter 53, "Winter's Method," and Chapter 54, "Forecasting in the Presence of Special Events." For example, when price is high and advertising is medium, our predicted sales are given by 25.04+(−1.814)+(−8.7)=14.52. (See cell E54 in Figure 51-9.) In Figure 51-5, shown earlier, you can see that we found the overall average is equal to 25.037, the medium advertising effect equals −1.814, and the high price effect=−8.704.

	B		C	D	E	F	G	H	I
42	ANOVA								
43		Source of Variation	SS	df	MS	F	P-value	F crit	F crit
44	Sample		804.962963	2	402.4815	13.51617	0.00026	3.554561	3.55456109
45	Columns		1405.40741	2	702.7037	23.59826	9.32E-06	3.554561	3.55456109
46	Interaction		50.5925926	4	12.64815	0.424751	0.788777	2.927749	2.92774871
47	Within		536	18	29.77778				
48									
49	Total		2796.96296	26					
50									
51				Stdev	5.456902				
52				Medium Ad					
53				High Price					
54				Mean	14.51852				
55				Lower	3.604715				
56				Upper	25.43232				

Figure 51-9   Forecasts for sales with high price and medium advertising

The standard deviation of our forecast errors equals the square root of our mean squared within error.

$$\sqrt{29.78} = 5.46$$

We are 95 percent sure that our forecast is accurate within 10.92 units. In other words, we are 95 percent sure that sales during a month with high price and medium advertising will be between 3.60 and 25.43 units.

In the *Two Way ANOVA with Interaction* worksheet, I've changed the data from the previous example to the data shown in Figure 51-10. After running our analysis for a two-factor ANOVA with replication, we obtain the results shown in Figure 51-11 on the next page.

	C	D	E	F	G
1					
2				Price	
3					
4			Low	Medium	High
5		Low	41	21	15
6	Adv		25	20	14
7			23	16	13
8		Medium	28	28	14
9			30	22	13
10			32	18	12
11		High	50	34	13
12			51	40	13
13			52	32	13

Figure 51-10   Sales data with interaction between price and advertising

	C	D	E	F	G	H	I
43	ANOVA						
44	*Source of Variation*	*SS*	*df*	*MS*	*F*	*P-value*	*F crit*
45	Sample	828.963	2	414.4815	24.22294	7.85669E-06	3.5545611
46	Columns	2498.741	2	1249.37	73.01515	2.30747E-09	3.5545611
47	Interaction	509.9259	4	127.4815	7.450216	0.001006454	2.9277487
48	Within	308	18	17.11111			
49							
50	Total	4145.63	26				
51		Std dev	4.136558				

Figure 51-11   Output for the two-factor ANOVA with interaction

In this data set, we find the p-value for interaction is .001. When we see a low p-value (less than .15) for interaction, *we do not even check p-values for row and column factors!* We simply forecast sales for any price and advertising combination to equal the mean of the three observations involving that price and advertising combination. For example, our best forecast for sales during a month with high advertising and medium price is:

$$\frac{34 + 40 + 32}{3} = \frac{106}{3} = 35.333 \; units$$

The standard deviation of our forecast errors is again the square root of the mean square within

$$(\sqrt{17.11} = 4.13)$$

Thus we are 95 percent sure that our sales forecast is accurate within 8.26 units.

Figure 51-12 illustrates why this data exhibits a significant interaction between price and advertising. For a low and medium price, increased advertising increases sales, but if price is high, increased advertising has no effect on sales. This explains why we cannot use equation 2 to forecast sales when a significant interaction is present. After all, how can we talk about an advertising effect when the effect of advertising depends on the price?

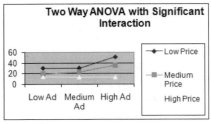

Figure 51-12   Price and advertising exhibit a significant interaction in this set of data.

Problems

The data for the following problems is in the file Ch51.xlsx.

1. We believe that pressure (high, medium, or low) and temperature (high, medium, or low) influence the yield of a production process. Given this theory, determine the answers to the following problems:

    ❑   Use the data in the *Problem 1* worksheet to determine how temperature and/or pressure influence the yield of the process.

    ❑   With high pressure and low temperature, we're 95 percent sure that process yield will be in what range?

2. We are trying to determine how the particular sales representative and the number of sales calls (either one, three, or five) made to a doctor influence the amount (in thousands of dollars) that each doctor prescribes of our drug. Use the data in the *Problem 2* worksheet to determine the answers to the following problems:

    ❑   How does the representative and number of sales calls influence our sales volume.

    ❑   If Rep 3 makes five sales calls to a doctor, we're 95 percent sure she will generate prescriptions within what range of dollars?

3. Answer the questions in Problem 2 by using the data in the *Problem 3* worksheet.

4. The file Coupondata.xlsx contains information on sales of peanut butter for weeks when a coupon was given out (or not) and advertising was done (or not) in the Sunday paper. Describe how the coupon and advertising influence peanut butter sales.

Chapter 52

Using Moving Averages to Understand Time Series

- I'm trying to analyze the upward trend in quarterly revenues of Amazon.com since 1996. Fourth quarter sales in the U.S. are usually larger (because of Christmas) than sales during the first quarter of the following year. This pattern obscures the upward trend in sales. Is there any way that I can graphically show the upward trend in revenues?

Time series data simply displays the same quantity measured at different points in time. For example, the *Data and Chart* worksheet in the file Amazon.xlsx, shown in Figure 52-1 on the next page, displays the time series for quarterly revenues in millions of dollars for Amazon.com. Our data covers the time interval from the first quarter of 1996 through the fourth quarter of 2005.

To graph this time series, select the range B5:B43, which contains the quarter number (the first quarter is Quarter 1, and the last is Quarter 38). Next, hold down the Ctrl key and select the range containing revenue (D5:D43). Then choose Chart on the Insert tab, and choose the second option under the Scatter chart type. (Scatter with Smooth Lines and Markers.) Then delete the blue points and line on the x-axis. The time series plot is shown in Figure 52-2 on the next page.

There is an upward trend in revenues, but the fact that fourth quarter revenues dwarf revenues during the first three quarters of each year makes it hard to spot the trend. Because there are four quarters per year, it would be nice to graph average revenues during the last four quarters. This is called a *4 period moving average*. Using a 4 quarter moving average smooths out the seasonal influence because each average will contain one data point for each quarter. Such a graph is called a *moving average graph* because the plotted average "moves" over time. Moving average graphs also "smooth out" random variation, which also helps us get a better idea of what is going on with our data.

Quarter	Quarter	Sales (in million $)
1	31-Mar-1996	0.9
2	30-Jun-1996	2.2
3	30-Sep-1996	4.2
4	31-Dec-1996	8.5
5	31-Mar-1997	16.0
6	30-Jun-1997	27.9
7	30-Sep-1997	37.9
8	31-Dec-1997	66.0
9	31-Mar-1998	87.4
10	30-Jun-1998	116.0
11	30-Sep-1998	153.7
12	31-Dec-1998	252.9
13	31-Mar-1999	293.6
14	30-Jun-1999	314.4
15	30-Sep-1999	355.8
16	31-Dec-1999	676.0
17	31-Mar-2000	573.9
18	30-Jun-2000	577.9
19	30-Sep-2000	637.9
20	31-Dec-2000	972.4
21	31-Mar-2001	701.0
22	30-Jun-2001	668.0
23	30-Sep-2001	639.0
24	31-Dec-2001	1115.0
25	31-Mar-2002	847.0
26	30-Jun-2002	806.0
27	30-Sep-2002	851.0
28	31-Dec-2002	1429.0
29	31-Mar-2003	1084.0
30	30-Jun-2003	1100.0
31	30-Sep-2003	1134.0
32	31-Dec-2003	1946.0
33	31-Mar-2004	1530.0
34	30-Jun-2004	1387.0
35	30-Sep-2004	1463.0
36	31-Dec-2004	2541.0
37	31-Mar-2005	1902.0
38	30-Jun-2005	1753.0

Figure 52-1   Quarterly revenues for Amazon sales

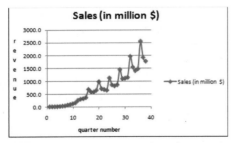

Figure 52-2   Time series plot of quarterly toy revenues

To create a moving average graph of quarterly revenues, we can modify our chart. Select the graph, and then click a data point until all the data points are displayed in blue. Right-click on any point and click Add Trendline, and then select the Moving Average option. Set the period equal to 4. Microsoft Office Excel 2007 now creates the 4 quarter moving average trend curve that's shown in Figure 52-3.

For each quarter, Excel plots the average of the current quarter and the last three quarters. Of course, for a four-quarter moving average, our moving average curve starts with the fourth data point. The moving average curve makes it clear that Amazon.com's revenues had a steady upward trend through Quarter 19. In Quarter 20 (the fourth quarter of 2000), the trend curve dips, indicating that revenue began to slow during late 2000, which was the start of the tech bubble bursting. This caused a recession in the entire world economy, thereby lessening the sharp upward trend in Amazon.com sales.

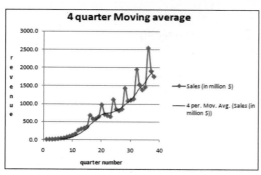

Figure 52-3   Four-quarter moving average trend curve

Problem

- The file Ch52data.xlsx contains quarterly revenues for GM, Ford, and GE. Construct a four-quarter moving average trend curve for each company's revenues. Describe what you learn from each trend curve.

Chapter 53
Winter's Method

Often, we must predict future values of a time series such as monthly costs or monthly product revenues. This is usually difficult because the characteristics of any time series are constantly changing. *Smoothing* or *adaptive* methods are usually best suited for forecasting future values of a time series. In this section, we describe the most powerful smoothing method: *Winter's method*. To help you understand how Winter's method works, we will use it to forecast monthly housing starts in the United States (U.S.). Housing starts are simply the number of new homes whose construction begins during a month. We begin by describing the three key characteristics of a time series.

Time Series Characteristics

The behavior of most time series can be explained by understanding the following three characteristics: base, trend, and seasonality.

- The *base* of a series describes the series' current level in the absence of any seasonality. For example, suppose the base level for U.S. housing starts is 160,000. In this case, we believe that if the current month were an "average" month relative to other months of the year, then 160,000 housing starts would occur.

- The *trend* of a time series is the percentage increase per period in the base. Thus a trend of 1.02 means that we estimate that housing starts are increasing by 2 percent each month.

- The *seasonality* (seasonal index) for a period tells us how far above or below a typical month we can expect housing starts to be. For example, if the December seasonal index is .8, then December housing starts are 20 percent below a typical month. If the June seasonal index is 1.3, then June housing starts are 30 percent higher than a typical month.

Parameter Definitions

After observing month t, we will have used all data observed through the end of month t to estimate the following quantities of interest:

- L_t=Level of series
- T_t=Trend of series
- S_t=Seasonal index for current month

The key to Winter's method is the following three equations, which are used to update L_t, T_t, and S_t. In the following formulas, *alp*, *bet*, and *gam* are called *smoothing parameters*. The values of these parameters will be chosen to optimize our forecasts. In the following formulas, c equals the number of periods in a seasonal cycle (c=12 months for example) and x_t equals the observed value of the time series at time t.

- Formula 1: $L_t=alp(x_t/s_{t-c})+(1-alp)(L_{t-1}*T_{t-1})$
- Formula 2: $T_t=bet(L_t/L_{t-1})+(1-bet)T_{t-1}$
- Formula 3: $S_t=gam(x_t/L_t)+(1-gam)s_{t-c}$

Formula 1 indicates that our new base estimate is a weighted average of the current observation (deseasonalized) and last period's base updated by our last trend estimate. Formula 2 indicates that our new trend estimate is a weighted average of the ratio of our current base to last period's base (this is a current estimate of trend) and last period's trend. Formula 3 indicates that we update our seasonal index estimate as a weighted average of the estimate of the seasonal index based on the current period and the previous estimate. Note that larger values of the smoothing parameters correspond to putting more weight on the current observation.

We define $F_{t,k}$ as our forecast (F) after period t for the period $t+k$. This results in the formula $F_{t,k}=L_t*(T_t)^k s_{t+k-c}$.

This formula first uses the current trend estimate to update the base k periods forward. Then the resulting base estimate for period $t+k$ is adjusted by the appropriate seasonal index.

Initializing Winter's Method

To start Winter's method, we must have initial estimates for the series base, trend, and seasonal indexes. We will use monthly housing starts for the years 1986 through 1987 to initialize Winter's method. Then we will choose our smoothing parameters to optimize our one-month-ahead forecasts for the years 1988 through 1996. See Figure 53-1 and the file House2.xlsx. We'll use the following process.

Step 1: We will estimate, for example, the January seasonal index as the average of January housing starts for 1986 through 1987 divided by the average monthly starts for 1986 through 1987. Therefore copying from G14 to G15:G25 the formula *=AVERAGE(B2,B14)/AVERAGE($B$2:$B$25)* will generate our estimates of seasonal indexes. For example, the January estimate is 0.75 and the June estimate is 1.17.

Step 2: To estimate the average monthly trend, we take the twelfth root of (1987 mean starts divided by the 1986 mean starts). We compute this in cell J3 (and copy it to cell D25) with the formula *=(J1/J2)^(1/12)*

	A	B	C	D	E	F	G	H	I	J
1	DATE	HS							1987 mean	150.45
2	Jan-86	105.4							1986 mean	145.142
3	Feb-86	95.4							Trend	1.003
4	Mar-86	145								
5	Apr-86	175.8								
6	May-86	170.2								
7	Jun-86	163.2								
8	Jul-86	160.7								
9	Aug-86	160.7								
10	Sep-86	147.7					alp	bet	gam	
11	Oct-86	173					0.493579053	0.01481	0.2724162	
12	Nov-86	124.1								
13		120.5					seasonal indices			
14	Jan-87	115.6					0.747653013			
15	Feb-87	107.2					0.685404974			
16	Mar-87	151					1.001381411			
17	Apr-87	188.2					1.231428491			
18	May-87	186.6					1.207070576			
19	Jun-87	183.6					1.173240122			
20	Jul-87	172					1.125539163			
21	Aug-87	163.8			MAPE	0.0731	1.097798202			
22	Sep-87	154					1.020664759			
23	Oct-87	154.8					1.108962262			
24	Nov-87	115.6	Base	Trend	Forecast	APE	0.81091595			
25	Dec-87	113	143.049	1.003			0.789941079			
26	Jan-88	105.1	142.044	1.00285	107.271	0.02066	0.745544111			
27	Feb-88	102.8	146.168	1.00324	97.6351	0.05024	0.690279755			
28	Mar-88	141.2	143.859	1.00296	146.844	0.03997	0.99596906			
29	Apr-88	159.3	136.919	1.0022	177.676	0.11536	1.212912968			
30	May-88	158	134.098	1.00186	165.634	0.04832	1.19921671			
31	Jun-88	162.9	136.568	1.0021	157.622	0.0324	1.178571717			
32	Jul-88	152.4	136.138	1.00203	154.036	0.01074	1.123881022			
33	Aug-88	143.6	133.647	1.00173	149.755	0.04286	1.091444695			

Figure 53-1   Initialization of Winter's method

Step 3: Going into January 1987, we estimate the base of the series as the deseasonalized December 1987 value. This is computed in C25 with the formula *=(B25/G25)*.

Estimating the Smoothing Constants

We are now ready to estimate our smoothing constants. In column C, we will update the series base; in column D, the series trend; and in column G, our seasonal indexes. In column E, we compute our forecast for next month, and in column F, we compute our absolute percentage error for each month. Finally, we will use solver to choose smoothing constant values that minimize the sum of our absolute percentage errors. We'll use the following process.

Step 1: In G11:I11, we enter trial values (between 0 and 1) for our smoothing constants.

Step 2: In C26:C119, we compute the updated series level with (1) by copying from C26 to C27:C119 the formula *=alp*(B26/G14)+(1–alp)*(C25*D25)*.

Step 3: In D26:D119, we use (2) to update the series trend. Copy from D26 to D27:D119 the formula *=bet*(C26/C25)+(1−bet)*D25*.

Step 4: In G26:G119, we use (3) to update the seasonal indexes. Copy from G26 to G27:G119 the formula *=gam*(B26/C26)+(1−gam)*G14*.

Step 5: In E26:E119, we use (4) to compute the forecast for the current month by copying from E26 to E27:E119 the formula *=(C25*D25)*G14*.

Step 6: In F26:F119, we compute the absolute percentage error for each month by copying from F26 to F27:F119 the formula *=ABS(B26-E26)/B26*.

Step 7: We compute the average absolute percentage error for the years 1988 through 1996 in F21 with the formula *=AVERAGE(F26:F119)*.

Step 8: We can now use the Microsoft Office Excel 2007 Solver feature to determine smoothing parameter values that minimize our average absolute percentage error. The Solver Parameters dialog box is shown in Figure 53-2.

Figure 53-2   Solver Parameters dialog box for Winter's model

We choose our smoothing parameters (G11:I11) to minimize the average absolute percentage error (cell F21). The Excel Solver ensures we will find the best combination of smoothing constants. Smoothing constants must be between 0 and 1. We find that *alp=.54*, *bet=.02*, and *gam=.29* minimizes our average absolute percentage error. You might find slightly different values of the smoothing constants, but you should obtain a MAPE close to 7.3 percent. In this example, there are many combinations of the smoothing constants that give forecasts having approximately the same MAPE. Our one-month-ahead forecasts are off by an average of 7.3 percent.

Remarks

- Instead of choosing our smoothing parameters to optimize one-period forecast errors, we could, for example, have chosen to optimize the average absolute percentage error incurred in forecasting total housing starts for the next six months.

- Suppose our time series is sales of a software product and we have conducted a major promotion during June 2000. Assume predicted sales for June 2000 were 20,000 units, but we sold 35,000 units. Then a good guess is that the promotion caused 15,000 extra sales during June. When updating the base, trend, and seasonal indexes, however, we should not put in June 2000 sales of 35,000. We should put in June 2000 sales of our forecast (20,000); otherwise, we will incorrectly bump up our forecasts of future sales. When making a forecast for a future month in which there is a promotion similar to the June promotion, we would just bump up the Winter's method forecast by using the formula $35,000/20,000 = 75\%$!

- If at the end of month t we wanted to forecast sales for the next four quarters, we would simply add $f_{t,1} + f_{t,2} + f_{t,3} + f_{t,4}$. If desired, we could choose our smoothing parameters to minimize the absolute percentage error incurred in estimating sales for the next year.

Problems

All the data for the following problems is in the file Quarterly.xlsx.

1. Use Winter's method to forecast one-quarter-ahead revenues for Apple.

2. Use Winter's method to forecast one-quarter-ahead revenues for Amazon.com.

3. Use Winter's method to forecast one-quarter-ahead revenues for Home Depot.

4. Use Winter's method to forecast total revenues for the next two quarters for Home Depot.

Chapter 54

Forecasting in the Presence of Special Events

- How can I determine whether specific factors influence customer traffic?

- How can I evaluate forecast accuracy?

- How can I check whether my forecast errors are random?

For a student project, we attempted to forecast the number of customers visiting the Eastland Plaza Branch of the Indiana University (IU) Credit Union each day. Interviews with the branch manager made it clear that the following factors affected the number of customers:

- Month of the year

- Day of the week

- Whether the day was a faculty or staff payday

- Whether the day before or the day after was a holiday

How can I determine whether specific factors influence customer traffic?

The data collected is contained in the *Original* worksheet in the file Creditunion.xlsx, shown in Figure 54-1 on the next page. If we try to run a regression on this data by using dummy variables (as described in Chapter 48, "Incorporating Qualitative Factors into Multiple Regression"), the dependent variable would be the number of customers arriving each day (the data in column E). We would need 19 independent variables:

- 11 to account for the month (12 months minus 1)

- 4 to account for the day of the week (5 business days minus 1)

- 2 to account for the types of paydays that occur each month

- 2 to account for whether a particular day follows or precedes a holiday

Microsoft Office Excel 2007 allows only 15 independent variables, so it appears that we're in trouble.

	B	C	D	E	F	G	H	I	J
3	MONTH	DAYMON	DAYWEEK	CUST	SPECIAL	SP	FAC	BH	AH
4	1	2	2	1825	SP,FAC,AF	1	1	0	1
5	1	3	3	1257	0	0	0	0	0
6	1	4	4	969	0	0	0	0	0
7	1	5	5	1672	SP	1	0	0	0
8	1	8	1	1098	0	0	0	0	0
9	1	9	2	691	0	0	0	0	0
10	1	10	3	672	0	0	0	0	0
11	1	11	4	754	0	0	0	0	0
12	1	12	5	972	0	0	0	0	0
13	1	15	1	816	0	0	0	0	0
14	1	16	2	717	0	0	0	0	0
15	1	17	3	728	0	0	0	0	0
16	1	18	4	711	0	0	0	0	0
17	1	19	5	1545	SP	1	0	0	0
18	1	22	1	873	0	0	0	0	0
19	1	23	2	713	0	0	0	0	0
20	1	24	3	626	0	0	0	0	0
21	1	25	4	653	0	0	0	0	0
22	1	26	5	1080	0	0	0	0	0
23	1	29	1	650	0	0	0	0	0
24	1	30	2	644	0	0	0	0	0
25	1	31	3	803	0	0	0	0	0
26	2	1	4	1282	FAC	0	1	0	0
27	2	2	5	2043	SP	1	0	0	0
28	2	5	1	1146	0	0	0	0	0

Figure 54-1   Data used to predict credit union customer traffic

When a regression forecasting model requires more than 15 independent variables, we can use the Excel Solver feature to estimate the coefficients of the independent variables. We can also use Excel to compute the R-squared values between forecasts and actual customer traffic and the standard deviation for the forecast errors. To analyze this data, I created a forecasting equation by using a lookup table to "look up" the day of the week, the month, and other factors. Then I used Solver to choose the coefficients for each level of each factor that yields the minimum sum of squared errors. (Each day's error equals actual customers minus forecasted customers.) Here are the particulars.

I began by creating indicator variables (in columns G through J) for whether the day is a staff payday (SP), faculty payday (FAC), before a holiday (BH), or after a holiday (AH). (See Figure 54-1.) For example, in cells G4, H4, and J4, I entered 1 to indicate that January 2 was a staff payday, faculty payday, and after a holiday. Cell I4 contains 0 to indicate that January 2 was not before a holiday.

Our forecast is defined by a constant (which helps to center the forecasts so that they will be more accurate), and effects for each day of the week, each month, a staff payday, a faculty payday, a day occurring before a holiday, and a day occurring after a holiday. I inserted trial values for all these parameters (the Solver changing cells) in the cell range O4:O26, shown in Figure 54-2. Solver will then choose values that make our model best fit the data. For each day, our forecast of customer count will be generated by the following equation:

```
Predicted customer count=Constant+(Month effect)+(Day of week effect)+(Staff payday
effect, if any)+(Faculty payday effect, if any)+(Before holiday effect, if any)+(After
holiday effect, if any)
```

Using this model, we compute a forecast for each day's customer count by copying from K4 to K5:K257 the formula

```
$O$26+VLOOKUP(B4,$N$14:$O$25,2)+VLOOKUP(D4,$N$4:$O$8,2)
+G4*$O$9+H4*$O$10+I4*$O$11+J4*$O$12
```

Cell O26 picks up the constant term. *VLOOKUP(B4,$N$14:$O$25,2)* picks up the month coefficient for the current month, and *VLOOKUP(D4,$N$4:$O$8,2)* picks up the day of the week coefficient for the current week. *G4*$O$9+H4*$O$10+I4*$O$11+ J4*$O$12* picks up the effects (if any) when the current day is SP, FAC, BH, or AH.

By copying from L4 to L5:L257 the formula *(E4-K4)^2*, I compute the squared error for each day. Then, in cell L2, I compute the sum of squared errors with the formula *SUM(L4:L257)*.

	I	J	K	L	M	N	O	P	Q	R
1	RSQ	0.771186		stdeverr	163.1772					
2			SSE	6736582						
3	BH	AH	Forecast	Sq Err	Error	Day of Week			average	
4	0	1	1766.78	3389.56	58.21993	1	103.357		dayweek	-3E-14
5	0	0	709.603	299643	547.3965	2	-139.19		month	-4E-09
6	0	0	745.698	49863.78	223.302	3	-150.34			
7	0	0	1557.22	13174.18	114.7788	4	-114.25			
8	0	0	963.303	18143.29	134.697	5	300.424			
9	0	0	720.753	885.2568	-29.7533	SP	396.851			
10	0	0	709.603	1414.02	-37.6035	FAC	394.894			
11	0	0	745.698	68.92317	8.301998	BH	205.293			
12	0	0	1160.37	35483.19	-188.37	AH	254.281			
13	0	0	963.303	21698.16	-147.303	Month				
14	0	0	720.753	14.08701	-3.75327	1	-110.69			
15	0	0	709.603	338.4326	18.39654	2	-75.715			
16	0	0	745.698	1203.951	-34.698	3	-40.341			
17	0	0	1557.22	149.3565	-12.2212	4	0.02839			
18	0	0	963.303	8154.623	-90.303	5	87.8157			
19	0	0	720.753	60.11313	-7.75327	6	133.341			
20	0	0	709.603	6989.539	-83.6035	7	115.803			
21	0	0	745.698	8592.92	-92.698	8	28.7743			
22	0	0	1160.37	6459.308	-80.3698	9	-87.563			
23	0	0	963.303	98158.74	-313.303	10	-53.002			
24	0	0	720.753	5891.064	-76.7533	11	-42.761			
25	0	0	709.603	8722.913	93.39654	12	44.3091			
26	0	0	1175.57	11328.02	106.4332	constant	970.635			

Figure 54-2   Changing cells and customer forecasts

In cell R4, I average the day of the week changing cells with the formula *AVERAGE (O4:O8)*, and in cell R5, I average the month changing cells with the formula *AVERAGE (O14:O25)*. Later, we'll constrain the average month and day of the week effects to equal 0, which ensures that a month or day of the week with a positive effect has a higher than average customer count, and a month or day of the week with a negative effect has a lower than average customer count.

We can use the Solver settings shown in Figure 54-3 on the next page to choose our forecast parameters to minimize the sum of squared errors.

Figure 54-3 Solver Parameters dialog box for determining forecast parameters

Our Solver model changes the coefficients for the month, day of the week, BH, AH, SP, FAC, and the constant to minimize the sum of square errors. We also constrain the average day of the week and month effect to equal 0. Using the Solver, we obtain the results shown in Figure 54-2. For example, we find that Friday is the busiest day of the week and June is the busiest month. A staff payday raises our forecast (all else being equal—in the Latin, *ceteris paribus*) by 397 customers.

How can I evaluate forecast accuracy?

To evaluate the accuracy of the forecast, we compute the R-squared value between the forecasts and the actual customer count in cell J1. The formula we use is *RSQ(E4:E257, K4:K257)*. This formula computes the percentage of the actual variation in customer count that is explained by our forecasting model. We find that our independent variables explain 77 percent of the daily variation in customer count.

We compute the error for each day in column M by copying from M4 to M5:M257 the formula *E4–K4*. A close approximation to the standard error of the forecast is given by the standard deviation of the errors. This value is computed in cell M1 by using the formula *STDEV(M4:M257)*. Thus, approximately 68 percent of our forecasts should be accurate within 163 customers, 95 percent accurate within 326 customers, and so on.

Let's try and spot any outliers. Recall that an observation is an outlier if the absolute value of our forecast error exceeds two times the standard error of the regression. Select the range M4:M257, and then click Conditional Formatting on the Home tab. Next, select New Rule and in the New Formatting Rule dialog box, choose Use A Formula To Determine Which Cells To Format. Fill in the rule description in the dialog box as shown in Figure 54-4. (For more information about conditional formatting, see Chapter 22, "Conditional Formatting.")

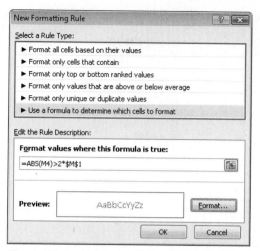

Figure 54-4   Using conditional formatting to spot forecast outliers

After choosing a format with a red font, our conditional formatting settings will display in red any error that exceeds 2*(*standard deviation of errors*) in absolute error. Looking at the outliers, we find that we often underforecast the customer count for the first three days of the month. Also, during the second week in March (spring break), we overforecast, and the day before spring break, we greatly underforecast.

To remedy this problem, in the *1st Three Days* worksheet, we added changing cells for each of the first three days of the month and for spring break and the day before spring break. We added trial values for these new effects in cells O26:O30. By copying from K4 to K5:K257 the formula

```
$O$25+VLOOKUP(B4,$N$13:$O$24,2)+VLOOKUP(D4,$N$4:$O$8,2)+G4*$O$9+H4*
$O$10+I4*$O$11+J4*$O$12+IF(C4=1,$O$26,IF(C4=2,$O$27,IF(C4=3,$O$28,0)))
```

we include the effects of the first three days of the month. (The term *IF(C4=1,$O$26, IF(C4=2,$O$27,IF(C4=3,$O$28,0)))* picks up the effect of the first three days of the month.) We manually entered the spring break coefficients in cells K54:K57. For example, in cell K52 we added +*O29* to the formula, and in cells K53:K57, we added +*O30*.

After including our new changing cells in the Solver dialog box, we find the results shown in Figure 54-5 on the next page. Notice that the first three days of the month greatly increase customer count (probably because of government support and Social Security checks) and that spring break reduces customer count. Figure 54-5 also shows the improvement in our forecasting accuracy. We have improved our R squared value (RSQ)t o 87 percent and reduced our standard error to 122 customers.

	H	I	J	K	L	M	N	O	P	Q	R
1		RSQ	0.8714979		stdeverr	122.285					
2				SSE	3783269						
3	FAC	BH	AH	Forecast	Sq Err	Error	Day of Week			average	
4	1	0	1	1879.63	2984.542	-54.631	1	107.706		dayweek	-2E-14
5	0	0	0	995.4	68434.54	261.6	2	-138.93		month	2.5E-14
6	0	0	0	722.934	60548.44	246.0659	3	-153.32			
7	0	0	0	1554.45	13818.16	117.5507	4	-115.08			
8	0	0	0	945.724	23188.13	152.2765	5	299.624			
9	0	0	0	699.086	65.38256	-8.08595	SP	416.808			
10	0	0	0	684.701	161.326	-12.7014	FAC	96.6442			
11	0	0	0	722.934	965.0912	31.06592	BH	196.457			
12	0	0	0	1137.64	27436.95	-165.641	AH	299.116			
13	0	0	0	945.724	16828.19	-129.724	1	-105.51			
14	0	0	0	699.086	320.9132	17.91405	2	-81.763			
15	0	0	0	684.701	1874.767	43.29858	3	-27.856			
16	0	0	0	722.934	142.4223	-11.9341	4	-7.2892			
17	0	0	0	1554.45	89.29022	-9.44935	5	83.8453			
18	0	0	0	945.724	5288.709	-72.7235	6	130.672			
19	0	0	0	699.086	193.6008	13.91405	7	106.616			
20	0	0	0	684.701	3445.857	-58.7014	8	13.2601			
21	0	0	0	722.934	4890.776	-69.9341	9	-64.687			
22	0	0	0	1137.64	3322.487	-57.641	10	-68.305			
23	0	0	0	945.724	87452.39	-295.724	11	-33.753			
24	0	0	0	699.086	3034.462	-55.0859	12	54.7719			
25	0	0	0	684.701	13994.55	118.2986	constant	943.528			
26	1	0	0	1396.77	13173.25	-114.775	d1	553.449			
27	0	0	0	1946.17	9375.367	96.82648	d2	367.977			
28	0	0	0	969.471	31162.46	176.5289	d3	310.699			
29	0	0	0	722.834	294.6881	17.16648	day before sp break	223.704			
30	0	0	0	708.449	109.1814	-10.449	sp break	-57.035			

Figure 54-5 Forecast parameters and forecasts including spring break and the first three days of the month

By looking at the forecast errors for the week 12/24 through 12/31 (see Figure 54-6), we see that we've greatly overforecasted the customer counts for the days in this week. We also underforecasted customer counts for the week before Christmas. Further examination of our forecast errors (often called residuals) also shows us the following:

❑ Thanksgiving is different than a normal holiday in that the credit union is far less busy than expected the day after Thanksgiving.

❑ The day before Good Friday is really busy because people leave town for Easter.

❑ Tax day (April 16) is also busier than expected.

❑ The week before Indiana University starts fall classes (last week in August) was not busy, probably because many staff and faculty take a "summer fling vacation" before the hectic onrush of the fall semester.

	B	C	D	K	L	M
1					stdeverr	122.285
2				SSE	3783269	
3	MONTH	DAYMON	DAYWEEl	Forecast	Sq Err	Error
249	12	18	2	859.369	39454.4	198.631
250	12	19	3	844.984	67089.1	259.016
251	12	20	4	883.217	18166.5	134.783
252	12	21	5	1714.73	57728.6	240.268
253	12	24	1	1302.46	130656	-361.463
254	12	26	3	1144.1	21054.1	-145.1
255	12	27	4	883.217	69810.6	-264.217
256	12	28	5	1297.92	130266	-360.924
257	12	31	1	1302.46	24480.7	-156.463

Figure 54-6 Errors for Christmas week

In the *Final mode* worksheet, I added changing cells to incorporate the effects of these factors. After adding the new parameters as changing cells, we ran Solver again. The results are shown in Figure 54-7. Our RSQ is up to 92 percent and our standard error is down to 98.61 customers! Note that the post-Christmas week reduced our daily customer count by 359; the day before Thanksgiving added 607 customers; the day after Thanksgiving reduced customer count by 161, and so on.

	F	G	H	I	J	K	L	M	N	O	P
1			RSQ		0.9164		stdeverr	98.615		cutoff	110.56262
2						SSE	2460390			actual	125
3	SPECIAL SP		FAC	BH	AH	Foreca	Sq Err	Error	Day of Week	sign change	average
4	SP,FAC,i	1	1	0	1	1981	24364	-156.1	1	108.1	daywee -0
5		0	0	0	0	976.1	78915	280.92	2	-155	1 month 1E-06
6		0	0	0	0	717.7	63163.6	251.32	3	-165	0
7	SP	1	0	0	0	1539	17578	132.58	4	-121	0
8		0	0	0	0	946.9	22839.2	151.13	5	332.3	0
9		0	0	0	0	684.2	46.5595	6.8235	SP	368.3	0
10		0	0	0	0	674	3.92566	-1.981	FAC	97.12	1
11		0	0	0	0	717.7	1319.41	36.324	BH	272.6	1
12		0	0	0	0	1171	39631.6	-199.1	AH	477.9	1
13		0	0	0	0	946.9	17127.9	-130.9	1	-111	0
14		0	0	0	0	684.2	1077.38	32.823	2	-82.1	1
15		0	0	0	0	674	2918.02	54.019	3	-26.4	0
16		0	0	0	0	717.7	44.5731	-6.676	4	-34.8	1
17	SP	1	0	0	0	1539	31.1588	5.582	5	71.04	1
18		0	0	0	0	946.9	5457.29	-73.87	6	127.4	1
19		0	0	0	0	684.2	830.792	28.823	7	93.99	1
20		0	0	0	0	674	2302.21	-47.98	8	60.87	1
21		0	0	0	0	717.7	4183.03	-64.68	9	-75.3	0
22		0	0	0	0	1171	8295.01	-91.08	10	-67.9	0
23		0	0	0	0	946.9	88133.9	-296.9	11	-35.9	0
24		0	0	0	0	684.2	1614.15	-40.18	12	80.33	0
25		0	0	0	0	674	16645.8	129.02	constant	949.9	1
26	FAC	0	1	0	0	1388	11207.1	-105.9	d1	544	1
27	SP	1	0	0	0	1922	14631.6	120.96	d2	353.6	1
28		0	0	0	0	975.9	28935.9	170.11	d3	302.1	0
29		0	0	0	0	713.2	718.37	26.802	day before sp b	183.2	0
30		0	0	0	0	703	25.0236	-5.002	sp break	-55.2	1
31		0	0	0	0	746.7	2672.61	-51.7	christmas week	-359	0
32		0	0	0	0	1200	1689.04	-41.1	before xmas we	182.9	0
33		0	0	0	0	975.9	9004.97	-94.89	before thanks	606.8	0
34		0	0	0	0	713.2	3003.31	54.802	after thanks	-161	1
35		0	0	0	0	703	2401.23	-49	good thurday	319.9	1
36		0	0	0	0	746.7	12388.3	111.3	summerfling	-165	1
37	SP	1	0	0	0	1568	6171.83	78.561	tax day	243.7	0

Figure 54-7   Final forecast parameters

Notice how we've improved our forecasting model by using outliers. If your outliers have something in common (like being the first three days of the month), include the common factor as an independent variable and your forecasting error will drop.

How can I check whether my forecast errors are random?

A good forecasting method should create forecast errors or residuals that are random. By random errors, I mean that our errors exhibit no discernible pattern. If forecast errors are random, the sign of your errors should change (from plus to minus or minus to plus) approximately half the time. Therefore, a commonly used test to evaluate the randomness of forecast errors is to look at the number of sign changes in the errors. If you have n observations, nonrandomness of the errors is indicated if you find either fewer than

$$\frac{n-1}{2} - \sqrt{n}$$

or more than

$$\frac{n-1}{2} + \sqrt{n}$$

changes in sign. In the *Final Model* worksheet, as shown in Figure 54-8, I determined the number of sign changes in our residuals by copying from cell P5 to P6:P257 the formula *IF(M5*M4<0,1,0)*. A sign change in the residuals occurs if and only if the product of two consecutive residuals is negative. Therefore, our formula yields 1 whenever a change in the sign of the residuals occurs. There were 125 changes in sign. In cell P1, I computed

$$\frac{254 - 1}{2} - \sqrt{254} = 110.6$$

changes in sign as the cutoff for nonrandom residuals. Therefore we have random residuals.

	M	N		O	P	Q	R
1	98.61471			cutoff	110.5626225		
2				actual	125		
3	Error	Day of Week			sign changes	average	
4	-156.09		1	108.117		dayweek	-9E-14
5	280.9181		2	-154.58	1	month	1E-06
6	251.3237		3	-164.78	0		
7	132.582		4	-121.08	0		
8	151.1265		5	332.32	0		
9	6.823454	SP		368.341	0		
10	-1.98133	FAC		97.1203	1		
11	36.32369	BH		272.64	1		
12	-199.077	AH		477.852	1		
13	-130.873		1	-111.15	0		
14	32.82345		2	-82.126	1		
15	54.01867		3	-26.374	0		
16	-6.67631		4	-34.814	1		
17	5.582005		5	71.042	1		
18	-73.8735		6	127.403	1		
19	28.82345		7	93.9867	1		
20	-47.9813		8	60.872	1		
21	-64.6763		9	-75.349	0		
22	-91.0769		10	-67.916	0		
23	-296.873		11	-35.91	0		
24	-40.1765		12	80.332	0		
25	129.0187	constant		949.904	1		
26	-105.864	d1		544.046	1		

Figure 54-8 Determing whether the residuals are random

A similar analysis was done to predict daily customer counts for dinner at a major restaurant chain. The special factors corresponded to holidays. We found Super Sunday (the day of the football Super Bowl) to be the least busy day and Valentine's Day and Mother's Day to be the busiest. Also, Saturday was the busiest day of the week for dinner and Friday was the busiest day of the week for lunch.

Problems

1. How can you use the techniques outlined in this chapter to predict the daily sales of pens at Staples?

2. If you had several years of data, how would you incorporate a trend in the analysis?

Chapter 55
An Introduction to Random Variables

- What is a random variable?

- What is a discrete random variable?

- What are the mean, variance, and standard deviation of a random variable?

- What is a continuous random variable?

- What is a probability density function?

- What are independent random variables?

In today's world, the only thing that's certain is that we face a great deal of uncertainty. In the next nine chapters, I'll give you some powerful techniques that you can use to incorporate uncertainty in business models. The key building block in modeling uncertainty is understanding how to use random variables.

What is a random variable?

Any situation whose outcome is uncertain is called an *experiment*. The value of a random variable is based on the (uncertain) outcome of an experiment. For example, tossing a pair of dice is an experiment, and a random variable might be defined as the sum of the values shown on each die. In this case, the random variable could assume any of the values 2, 3, and so on up to 12. As another example, consider the experiment of selling a new video game console, for which a random variable might be defined as the market share for this new product.

What is a discrete random variable?

A random variable is discrete if it can assume a finite number of possible values. Here are some examples of discrete random variables:

- ❑ Number of potential competitors for your product
- ❑ Number of aces drawn in a five-card poker hand

- ❑ Number of car accidents you have (hopefully zero!) in a year
- ❑ Number of dots showing on a die
- ❑ Number of free throws out of 12 that Steve Nash makes during a basketball game

What are the mean, variance, and standard deviation of a random variable?

In Chapter 37, "Summarizing Data with Descriptive Statistics," I discussed the mean, variance, and standard deviation for a data set. In essence, the mean of a random variable (often denoted by μ) is the average value of the random variable we would expect if we performed an experiment many times. The mean of a random variable is often referred to as the random variable's *expected* value. The variance of a random variable (often denoted by σ^2) is the average value of the squared deviation from the mean of a random variable that we would expect if we performed our experiment many times. The standard deviation of a random variable (often denoted by σ) is simply the square root of its variance. As with data sets, the mean of a random variable is a summary measure for a typical value of the random variable, whereas the variance and standard deviation measure the spread of the random variable about its mean.

As an example of how to compute the mean, variance, and standard deviation of a random variable, suppose we believe that the return on the stock market during the next year is governed by the following probabilities:

Probability	Market return
.40	+20 percent
.30	0 percent
.30	-20 percent

Hand calculations show the following:

μ=.40*(.20)+.30*(.00)+.30*(-.20)=.02 or 2 percent

σ^2=.4*(.20-.02)^2+.30*(.0-.02)^2+.30*(-.20-.02)^2=.0276

Then σ=.166 or 16.6 percent.

In the file Meanvariance.xlsx (shown in Figure 55-1), I've verified these computations.

	B	C	D
3	Value	Probability	Squared deviation
4	0.2	0.4	0.0324
5	0	0.3	0.0004
6	-0.2	0.3	0.0484
7			
8			
9	Mean	0.02	
10	Variance	0.0276	
11	Standard deviation	0.166132477	

Figure 55-1   Computing the mean, standard deviation, and variance of a random variable

I computed the mean of our market return in cell C9 with the formula =*SUMPRODUCT(B4:B6,C4:C6)*. This formula multiplies each value of the random variable by its probability and sums up the products.

To compute the variance of our market return, I determined the squared deviation of each value of the random variable from its mean by copying from D4 to D5:D6 the formula =*(B4−$C$9)^2*. Then, in cell C10, I computed the variance of the market return as the average squared deviation from the mean with the formula =*SUMPRODUCT (C4:C6,D4:D6)*. Finally, I computed the standard deviation of the market return in cell C11 with the formula =*SQRT(C10)*.

What is a continuous random variable?

A continuous random variable is a random variable that can assume a very large number or, to all intents and purposes, an infinite number of values. Here are some examples of continuous random variables:

❑ Price of Microsoft stock one year from now

❑ Market share for a new product

❑ Market size for a new product

❑ Cost of developing a new product

❑ Newborn baby's weight

❑ Person's IQ

❑ Dirk Nowitzki's three-point shooting percentage during next season

What is a probability density function?

A discrete random variable can be specified by a list of values and the probability of occurrence for each value of the random variable. Because a continuous random variable can assume an infinite number of values, we can't list the probability of occurrence for each value of a continuous random variable. A continuous random variable is completely described by its *probability density function*. For example, the probability density function for a randomly chosen person's IQ is shown in Figure 55-2.

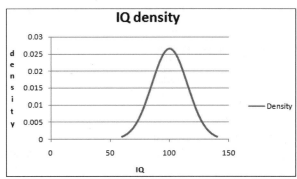

Figure 55-2   Probability density function for IQs

A probability density function (pdf) has the following properties:

❑ The value of the pdf is always greater than or equal to 0.

❑ The area under the pdf equals 1.

❑ The height of the density function for a value x of a random variable is proportional to the likelihood that the random variable assumes a value near x. For example, the height of the density for an IQ of 83 is roughly half the height of the density for an IQ of 100. This tells us that IQs near 83 are approximately half as likely as IQs around 100. Also, because the density peaks at 100, IQs around 100 are most likely.

❑ The probability that a continuous random variable assumes a range of values equals the corresponding area under the density function. For example, the fraction of people having IQs from 80 through 100 is simply the area under the density from 80 through 100.

What are independent random variables?

A set of random variables are independent if knowledge of the value of any of their subsets tells you nothing about the values of the other random variables. For example, the number of games won by the Indiana University football team during a year is independent of the percentage return on Microsoft during the same year. Knowing that Indiana did very well would not change your view of how Microsoft stock did during the year.

On the other hand, the returns on Microsoft stock and Intel stock are not independent. If we are told that Microsoft stock had a high return in one year, in all likelihood, computer sales were high, which tells us that Intel probably had a good year as well.

Problems

1. Identify the following random variables as discrete or continuous:

❑ Number of games Kerry Wood wins for the Chicago Cubs next season

❑ Number that comes up when spinning a roulette wheel

❑ Unit sales of Tablet PCs next year

❑ Length of time that a light bulb lasts before it burns out

2. Compute the mean, variance, and standard deviation of the number of dots showing when a die is tossed.

3. Determine whether the following random variables are independent:

❑ Daily temperature and sales at an ice cream store

❑ Suit and number of a card drawn from a deck of playing cards

❑ Inflation and return on the stock market

❑ Price charged for and the number of units sold of a car

4. The current price of a company's stock is $20. The company is a takeover target. If the takeover is successful, the company's stock price will increase to $30. If the takeover is unsuccessful, the stock price will drop to $12. Determine the range of values for the probability of a successful takeover that would make it worthwhile to purchase the stock today. Assume your goal is to maximize your expected profit. Hint: Use the Microsoft Office Excel 2007 Goal Seek command, which is discussed in detail in Chapter 16, "The Goal Seek Command."

Chapter 56

The Binomial, Hypergeometric, and Negative Binomial Random Variables

- What is a binomial random variable?

- How do I use the BINOMDIST function to compute binomial probabilities?

- If equal numbers of people prefer Coke to Pepsi and Pepsi to Coke and I ask 100 people whether they prefer Coke to Pepsi, what is the probability that exactly 60 people prefer Coke to Pepsi and the probability that between 40 and 60 people prefer Coke to Pepsi?

- Of all the elevator rails my company produces, 3 percent are considered defective. We are about to ship a batch of 10,000 elevator rails to a customer. To determine whether the batch is acceptable, the customer will randomly choose a sample of 100 rails and check whether each sampled rail is defective. If two or fewer sampled rails are defective, the customer will accept the batch. How can I determine the probability that the batch will be accepted?

- Airlines do not like flights with empty seats. Suppose that, on average, 95 percent of all ticket purchasers show up for a flight. If the airline sells 105 tickets for a 100-seat flight, what is the probability that the flight will be overbooked?

- What is the hypergeometric random variable?

- What is the negative binomial random variable?

What is a binomial random variable?

A *binomial random variable* is a discrete random variable used to calculate probabilities in a situation where all three of the following apply:

- ❑ n independent trials occur.

- ❑ Each trial results in one of two outcomes: success or failure.

- ❑ In each trial, the probability of success (p) remains constant.

In such a situation, the binomial random variable can be used to calculate probabilities related to the number of successes in a given number of trials. We let x be the random variable denoting the number of successes occurring in n independent trials when the probability of success on each trial is p. Here are some examples in which the binomial random variable is relevant.

Coke or Pepsi   Assume that equal numbers of people prefer Coke to Pepsi and Pepsi to Coke. We ask 100 people whether they prefer Coke to Pepsi. We're interested in the probability that exactly 60 people prefer Coke to Pepsi and the probability that from 40 through 60 people prefer Coke to Pepsi. In this situation, we have a binomial random variable defined by the following:

- Trial: survey individuals
- Success: prefer Coke
- p equals 0.50
- n equals 100

Let x equal the number of people sampled who prefer Coke. We want to determine the probability that $x=60$ and also the probability that $40 \leq x \leq 60$.

Elevator Rails   Of all the elevator rails we produce produce, 3 percent are considered defective. We are about to ship a batch of 10,000 elevator rails to a customer. To determine whether the batch is acceptable, the customer will randomly choose a sample of 100 rails and check whether each sampled rail is defective. If two or fewer sampled rails are defective, the customer will accept the batch. We want to determine the probability that the batch will be accepted.

We have a binomial random variable defined by the following:

- Trial: look at a sampled rail
- Success: rail is defective
- p equals 0.03
- n equals 100

Let x equal the number of defective rails in the sample. We want to find the probability that $x \leq 2$.

Airline Overbooking   Airlines don't like flights with empty seats. Suppose that, on average, 95 percent of all ticket purchasers show up for a flight. If the airline sells 105 tickets for a 100-seat flight, what is the probability that the flight will be overbooked?

We have a binomial random variable defined by the following:

- Trial: individual ticket holders
- Success: ticket holder shows up

- *p* equals 0.95
- *n* equals 105

Let *x* equal the number of ticket holders who show up. Then we want to find the probability that $x \geq 101$.

How do I use the BINOMDIST function to compute binomial probabilities?

Microsoft Office Excel 2007 includes the BINOMDIST function which you can use to compute binomial probabilities. If you want to compute the probability of *x* or fewer successes for a binomial random variable having *n* trials with probability of success *p*, simply enter BINOMDIST(*x,n, p,*1). If you want to compute the probability of exactly *x* successes for a binomial random variable having *n* trials with probability of success of *p*, enter BINOMDIST(*x,n,p,*0). Entering 1 as the last argument of BINOMDIST yields a "cumulative" probability; entering 0 yields the "probability mass function" for any particular value. Let's use the BINOMDIST function to calculate some probabilities of interest. Our work is in the file Binomialexamples.xlsx, which is shown in Figure 56-1.

	B	C
3	Coke vs. Pepsi	
4	Probability exactly 60 people prefer Coke to Pepsi	0.010844
5	Probability from 40 through 60 people prefer Coke to Pepsi	0.9648
6		
7	Elevator Rails	
8	Probability 2 or fewer of 100 rails are defective	0.419775
9	Airline Overbooking	
10	Probability flight is overbooked if 105 tickets are sold	0.392434

Figure 56-1   Using the binomial random variable

If equal numbers of people prefer Coke to Pepsi and Pepsi to Coke and I ask 100 people whether they prefer Coke to Pepsi, what is the probability that exactly 60 people prefer Coke to Pepsi and the probability that between 40 and 60 people prefer Coke to Pepsi?

We have *n*=100 and *p*=0.5. We seek the probability that *x*=60 and the probability that $40 \leq x \leq 60$ where *x* equals the number of people who prefer Coke to Pepsi. First, we find the probability that *x*=60 by entering the formula BINOMDIST(60,100,0.5,0). Excel returns the value 0.011.

To use the BINOMDIST function to compute the probability that $40 \leq x \leq 60$, we note that the probability that $40 \leq x \leq 60$ equals (*the probability that* $x \leq 60$)–(*the probability that* $x \leq 39$). Thus, we can obtain the probability that from 40 through 60 people prefer Coke by entering the formula BINOMDIST(60,100,0.5,1)–BINOMDIST(39,100,0.5,1). Excel returns the value 0.9648. So, if Coke and Pepsi are equally preferred, it is very unlikely that in a sample of 100 people, Coke or Pepsi would be more than 10 percent ahead. If a sample of 100 people shows Coke or Pepsi to be more than 10 percent ahead, we would probably doubt that Coke and Pepsi are equally preferred.

Of all the elevator rails my company produces, 3 percent are considered defective. We are about to ship a batch of 10,000 elevator rails to a customer. To determine whether the batch is acceptable, the customer will randomly choose a sample of 100 rails and check whether each sampled rail is defective. If two or fewer sampled rails are defective, the customer will accept the batch. How can I determine the probability that the batch will be accepted?

If we let x equal the number of defective rails in a batch, we have a binomial random variable with $n=100$ and $p=0.03$. We seek the probability that $x\leq2$. We simply enter the formula *BINOMDIST(2,100,0.03,1)*. Excel returns the value 0.42 Thus, the batch will be accepted 42 percent of the time.

Really, our chance of success is not exactly 3 percent on each trial. For example, if the first 10 rails are defective, the chance the next rail is defective has dropped to 290/9990; if the first 10 rails are not defective, the chance the next rail is defective is 300/9990. Therefore, the probability of success on the eleventh trial is not independent of the probability of success on one of the first 10 trials. Despite this fact, the binomial random variable is used as an approximation when a sample is drawn and the sample size is less than 10 percent of the total population. Here, our population size equals 10,000 and our sample size is 100. Exact probabilities involving sampling from a finite population can be calculated with the hypergeometric random variable, which I'll discuss later in this chapter.

Airlines do not like flights with empty seats. Suppose that, on average, 95 percent of all ticket purchasers show up for a flight. If the airline sells 105 tickets for a 100-seat flight, what is the probability that the flight will be overbooked?

Let x equal the number of ticket holders who show up for the flight. We have $n=105$ and $p=0.95$. We seek the probability that $x\geq101$. We note that *the probability that $x\geq101=1-$the probability that $x\leq100$*. So, to compute the probability that the flight is overbooked, we enter the formula *1–BINOMDIST(100,105,0.95,1)*. Excel yields 0.392, which means there is a 39.2 percent chance that the flight will be overbooked.

What is the hypergeometric random variable?

The *hypergeometric random variable* governs a situation such as the following:

❑ An urn contains N balls.

❑ Each ball is one of two types (called success or failure).

❑ There are s successes in the urn.

❑ A sample of size n is drawn from the urn.

Let's look at an example in the file Hypergeo.xlsx, which is shown in Figure 56-2. The Excel formula $HYPERGEOMDIST(x,n,s,N)$ gives the probability of x successes if n balls are drawn from an urn containing N balls, of which s are marked as "success."

For example, suppose that 40 of the Fortune 500 companies have a woman CEO. Then the 500 CEOs are analogous to the balls in the urn ($N=500$) and the 40 women are representative of the s successes in the urn. Then, copying from D8 to D9:D18 the formula $=HYPERGEOMDIST(C8,Sample\_size,Population\_women,Population\_size)$ gives the probability that a sample of 10 Fortune 500 companies will have 0, 1, 2,..., 10 women CEOs. Here *Sample_size*=10, *Population_women*=40, *Population_size*=500.

We consider finding a woman CEO a success. In our sample of 10, for example, we find a probability of 0.431 that no women CEOs will be in the sample. By the way, we could have approximated this probability with the formula $BINOMDIST(0,10,0.08,0)$, yielding 0.434, which is very close to the true probability of 0.431.

	C	D	E	F	G
3	Population size	500			
4	Sample Size	10			
5	Population women	40		Binomial approximation	
6				0.434388454	
7	Number of women	Probability			
8	0	0.430956908			
9	1	0.382223421			
10	2	0.148407545			
11	3	0.033197861			
12	4	0.004734717			
13	5	0.000449538			
14	6	2.87533E-05			
15	7	1.2224E-06			
16	8	3.30288E-08			
17	9	5.11702E-10			
18	10	3.44843E-12			

Figure 56-2   Using the hypergeometric random variable

What is the negative binomial random variable?

The *negative binomial random variable* applies to the same situation as the binomial random variable but the negative binomial random variable gives the probability of f failures occurring before the s'th success. Thus $=NEGBINOMDIST(f,s,p)$ gives the probability that exactly f failures will occur before the s'th success when the probability of success is p for each trial. For example, consider a baseball team that wins 40 percent of their games (see file Negbin.xlsx and Figure 56-3 on the next page). Copying from E9 to E34 the formula $=NEGBINOMDIST(D9,2,.4)$ gives the probability of 0, 1, 2,..., 25 losses occurring before the second win. Note here that success equals the game won. For example, there is a 19.2 percent chance the team will lose exactly one game before winning two games.

	D	E
8	Losses before 2nd win	prob
9	0	0.16
10	1	0.192
11	2	0.1728
12	3	0.13824
13	4	0.10368
14	5	0.07465
15	6	0.05225
16	7	0.03583
17	8	0.02419
18	9	0.01612
19	10	0.01064
20	11	0.00697
21	12	0.00453
22	13	0.00293
23	14	0.00188
24	15	0.0012
25	16	0.00077
26	17	0.00049
27	18	0.00031
28	19	0.00019
29	20	0.00012
30	21	7.7E-05
31	22	4.8E-05
32	23	3E-05
33	24	1.9E-05
34	25	1.2E-05

Figure 56-3   Using the negative binomial random variable

Problems

1. Suppose that, on average, 4 percent of all CD drives received by a computer company are defective. The company has adopted the following policy: Sample 50 CD drives in each shipment, and accept the shipment if none are defective. Using this information, determine the following:

   ❑ What fraction of shipments will be accepted?

   ❑ If the policy changes so that a shipment is accepted if only one CD drive in the sample is defective, what fraction of shipments will be accepted?

   ❑ What is the probability that a sample size of 50 will contain at least 10 defective CD drives?

2. Using the airline overbooking data:

   ❑ Determine how the probability of overbooking varies as the number of tickets sold varies from 100 through 115. Hint: Use a one-way data table.

   ❑ Show how the probability of overbooking varies as the number of tickets sold varies from 100 through 115, and the probability that a ticket holder shows up varies from 80 percent through 95 percent. Hint: Use a two-way data table.

3. Suppose that during each year, a given mutual fund has a 50 percent chance of beating the Standard & Poor's 500 Stock Index (S&P Index). In a group of 100 mutual funds, what is the probability that at least 10 funds will beat the S&P Index during at least 8 out of 10 years?

4. Professional basketball player Steve Nash is a 90-percent foul shooter.

    ❏ If he shoots 100 free throws, what is the probability that he will miss more than 15 shots?

    ❏ How good a foul shooter would Steve Nash be if he had only a 5 percent chance of making fewer than 90 free throws out of 100 attempts? Hint: Use Goal Seek.

5. When tested for extra sensory perception (ESP), participants are asked to identify the shape of a card from a 25-card deck. The deck consists of 5 cards of each of five shapes. If a person identifies 12 cards correctly, what would you conclude?

6. Suppose that in a group of 100 people, 20 have the flu and 80 do not. If we randomly select 30 people, what is the chance that at least 10 people have the flu?

7. A student is selling magazines for a school fundraiser. There is a 20 percent chance that a given house will buy a magazine. He needs to sell five magazines. Determine the probability that he will need to visit 5, 6, 7,..., 100 houses to sell five magazines.

Chapter 57

The Poisson and Exponential Random Variable

- What is the Poisson random variable?

- How do I compute probabilities for the Poisson random variable?

- If the number of customers arriving at a bank is governed by a Poisson random variable, what random variable governs the time between arrivals?

What is the Poisson random variable?

The *Poisson random variable* is a discrete random variable that is useful for describing probabilities for situations in which events (such as customer arrivals at a bank or orders placed for a product) have a small probability of occurring during a small time interval. More specifically, during a small time interval, denoted as t, either zero or one event will occur, and the probability of one event occurring during a small interval of length t is (for some λ) given by λt. Here, λ is the mean number of occurrences per time unit.

Situations in which the Poisson random variable can be applied include the following:

- ❑ Number of units of a product demanded during a month

- ❑ Number of deaths per year by horse kick in Prussian army

- ❑ Number of car accidents you have during a year

- ❑ Number of copies of *The Seat of the Soul* ordered today at Amazon.com

- ❑ Number of workers' compensation claims filed at a company this month

- ❑ Number of defects in 100 yards of string. (Here, 1 yard of string plays the role of time.)

How do I compute probabilities for the Poisson random variable?

You can use the Microsoft Office Excel 2007 POISSON function to compute probabilities involving the Poisson random variable. Just remember that in a length of time t, the mean of a Poisson random variable is t. The syntax of the POISSON function is as follows:

❑ POISSON(x,Lambda,True) calculates the probability that a Poisson random variable with a mean equal to Lambda is less than or equal to x.

❑ POISSON(x,Lambda,False) calculates the probability that a Poisson random variable with a mean equal to Lambda is equal to x.

Here are some examples of how to compute probabilities for Poisson random variables. You can find these examples in the file Poisson.xlsx, shown in Figure 57-1.

	B	C
1	Calls per hour	30
2	Mean	60
3		
4	Prob 60 calls in two hours	0.05143
5	Prob<= 60 calls in two hours	0.53426
6	Prob between 50 and 100 calls(inclusive) in two hours	0.91559

Figure 57-1 Using the Poisson random variable

Suppose that my consulting business receives an average of 30 phone calls per hour. During a two-hour period, I want to determine the following:

❑ Probability that exactly 60 calls will be received in the next two hours

❑ Probability that the number of calls received in the next two hours will be fewer than or equal to 60

❑ Probability that from 50 through 100 calls will be received in the next two hours

During a two-hour period, the mean number of calls is 60. In cell C4, we find the probability (0.05) that exactly 60 calls will be received in the next two hours by using the formula POISSON(60,C2,FALSE). In cell C5, we find the probability (0.53) that, at most, 60 calls will be received in two hours with the formula POISSON(60,C2,TRUE). In cell C6, we find the probability (0.915) that from 50 through 100 calls will be received in two hours with the formula POISSON(100,C2,TRUE)−POISSON(49,C2,TRUE). Note that we can always use a "1" instead of "TRUE" as an argument in any Excel function.

If the number of customers arriving at a bank is governed by a Poisson random variable, what random variable governs the time between arrivals?

The time between arrivals can be any value, which means that the time between arrivals is a continuous random variable. If an average of arrivals occur per time unit, the time between arrivals follows an exponential random variable having the probability density function (pdf) of $f(t)=\lambda e^{-\lambda t}, t\geq 0$. This random variable has a mean, or average, value equal to $1/\lambda$. For $\lambda=30$, a graph of the exponential pdf is shown in Figure 57-2. You can find this chart and the data for this example in the file Exponentialdist.xlsx.

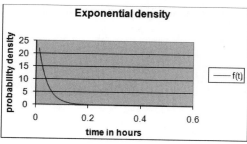

Figure 57-2   Exponential pdf

Recall from Chapter 55, "An Introduction to Random Variables," that for a continuous random variable, the height of the pdf for a number x reflects the likelihood that the random variable assumes a value near x. Thus, we see in Figure 57-2 that extremely short times between bank arrivals (for example, less than 0.05 hours) are very likely, but that for longer times, the pdf drops off sharply.

Even though the average time between arrivals is 1/30=0.033 hours, there's a reasonable chance that the time between arrivals will be as much as 0.20 hours. The Excel formula *EXPONDIST(x,1/mean,TRUE)* will give the probability that an exponential random variable with a given *mean* will assume a value less than or equal to x. Thus, the second argument to the EXPONDIST function is the rate per time unit at which events occur. For example, to compute the probability that the time between arrivals is at least 5, 10, or 15 minutes, I copied from cell D5 to D7 the formula *1−EXPONDIST(C5,$D$2,TRUE)*.

Note that I first converted minutes to hours (5 minutes equals 1/12 hour, and so on). Also, the mean time between arrivals is 0.033 hours, so I entered into our formula *1/Mean=1/.033=30*. In short, I entered the arrival rate per time unit, as you can see in Figure 57-3.

	B	C	D
1		mean	0.033333333
2		1/mean	30
3			
4		x = Time between arrivals	Prob time >=x
5	5 minutes	0.08333333	0.082084999
6	10 minutes	0.16666667	0.006737947
7	15 minutes	0.25	0.000553084

Figure 57-3   Computations of exponential probabilities

Problems

1. An average of 40 pitchers of beer are ordered per hour at Nick's Pub in Bloomington, Indiana.

    ❑ What is the probability that at least 100 pitchers are ordered in a two-hour period?

    ❑ What is the chance that the time between ordered pitchers will be 30 seconds or less?

2. Suppose that teenage drivers have an average of 0.3 accidents per year.

    ❑ What is the probability that a teenager will have no more than one accident during a year?

    ❑ What is the probability that the time between accidents will be six months or less?

Chapter 58

The Normal Random Variable

- What are the properties of the normal random variable?
- How do I use Excel to find probabilities for the normal random variable?
- Can I use Excel to find percentiles for normal random variables?
- Why is the normal random variable appropriate in many real-world situations?

What are the properties of the normal random variable?

In Chapter 55, "An Introduction to Random Variables," you learned that continuous random variables can be used to model quantities such as the following:

- ❏ Price of Microsoft stock one year from now
- ❏ Market share for a new product
- ❏ Market size for a new product
- ❏ Cost of developing a new product
- ❏ Newborn baby's weight
- ❏ Person's IQ

Remember that if a discrete random variable (such as sales of blazers during 2006) can assume many possible values, we can approximate the value by using a continuous random variable as well. As I described in Chapter 55, any continuous random variable X has a probability density function (pdf). The pdf for a continuous random variable is a nonnegative function with the following properties (a and b are arbitrary numbers).

- ❏ The area under the pdf is 1.
- ❏ The probability that $X<a$ equals the probability that $X \leq a$. This probability is represented by the area under the pdf to the left of a.
- ❏ The probability that $X>b$ equals the probability that $X \geq b$. This probability is shown in the area under the pdf to the right of b.

❏ The probability that $a<X<b$ equals the probability that $a \leq X \leq b$. This probability is the area under the pdf between a and b.

Thus, the area under a continuous random variable's pdf represents probability. Also, the larger the value of the density function at X, the more likely the random variable will take on a value near X. For example, if the density function of a random variable at 20 is twice the density function of the random variable at 5, then the random variable is twice as likely to take on a value near 20 than a value near 5. For a continuous random variable, the probability that X equals a will always equal 0. For example, some people are from 5.99999 feet through 6.00001 feet tall, but no person can be exactly 6 feet tall. This explains why we can replace the less than sign (<) with the less than or equal to sign (≤) in our probability statements.

Figure 58-1 displays the pdf for $X=IQ$ of a randomly chosen person. The area under this pdf is 1. If we want to find the probability that a person's IQ is less than or equal to 90, we simply find the area to the left of 90. If we want to find the probability that a person's IQ is from 95 through 120, we find the area under the pdf from 95 through 120. If we want to find the probability that a person's IQ is more than 130, we find the area under the density function to the right of 130.

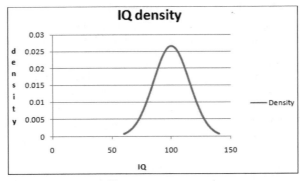

Figure 58-1   IQ pdf

Actually, the density sketched in Figure 58-1 is an example of the normal random variable. The normal random variable is specified by its mean and standard deviation. IQs follow a normal random variable with $\mu=100$ and $\sigma=15$. This is the pdf displayed in Figure 58-1. The normal random variable has the following properties:

❏ The most likely value of a normal random variable is μ (as indicated by the pdf peaking at 100 in Figure 58-1).

❏ As the value x of the random variable moves away from μ, the probability that the random variable is near x sharply decreases.

❏ The normal random variable is symmetric about its mean. For example, IQs near 80 are as likely as IQs near 120.

❑ A normal random variable has 68 percent of its probability within σ of its mean, 95 percent within 2σ of its mean, and 99.7 percent within 3σ of its mean. These measures should remind you of the rule of thumb I described in Chapter 37, "Summarizing Data by Using Descriptive Statistics." In fact, the rule of thumb is based on the assumption that data is "sampled" from a normal distribution, which explains why the rule of thumb does not work as well when the data fails to exhibit a symmetric histogram.

For a larger σ, a normal random variable is more spread out about its mean. This pattern is illustrated in Figures 58-2 and 58-3.

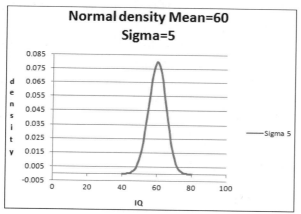

Figure 58-2   Normal random variable pdf with a mean equal to 60 and a standard deviation equal to 5

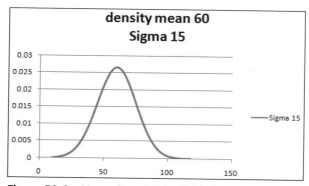

Figure 58-3   Normal random variable pdf with a mean equal to 60 and a standard deviation equal to 15

How do I use Excel to find probabilities for the normal random variable?

Consider a normal random variable X with a mean μ and standard deviation σ. Suppose for any number x, we want to find the probability that $X \leq x$, which is called the *normal cumulative function*. To find the probability in Microsoft Office Excel 2007 that $X \leq x$, simply enter the formula *NORMDIST(x,μ,σ,1)*. Of course the fourth argument of *1* could be replaced by *TRUE*.

The argument *1* tells Excel to compute the normal cumulative. If the last argument of the function is *0*, Excel returns the actual value of the normal random variable pdf.

We can use the NORMDIST function to answer many questions concerning normal probabilities. You can find examples in the file Normalexamples.xlsx, which is shown in Figure 58-4, and in the following three scenarios.

	B	C
2		Prob
3	IQ<90	0.25249254
4	95<IQ<120	0.53934744
5	IQ>130	0.02275013
6		
7	99 %ile Prozac	71.6317394
8	10% Bloomington income	19747.5875

Figure 58-4 Calculating normal probability

What fraction of people have an IQ of less than 90? Let *X* equal the IQ of a randomly chosen person. Then we seek the probability that *X*<90, which is equal to the probability that *X*≤90. Therefore, we can enter into cell C3 of the *Normal* worksheet the formula NORMDIST(90,100,15,1), and Excel returns 0.252. Thus, 25.2 percent of all people have an IQ less than 90.

What fraction of all people have IQs from 95 through 120? When finding the probability that *a*≤*X*≤*b*, we use the form (*area under the normal density function to the left of* b)–(*area under normal density function to the left of* a). Thus, we can find the probability that *a*≤*X*≤*b* by entering the formula NORMDIST(*b*,µ,σ,1)–NORMDIST(*a*,µ,σ,1). This fact is illustrated in Figure 58-5, where clearly the shaded area is (*area to left of* b)–(*area to left of* a). You can answer the question about IQs from 95 through 120 by entering into cell C4 of the worksheet Normal the formula NORMDIST(120,100,15,1)–NORMDIST(95,100,15,1). Excel returns the probability 0.539. So, 53.9 percent of all people have an IQ from 95 through 120.

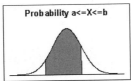

Figure 58-5 Calculating the probability that a random variable is between *a* and *b*

What fraction of all people have IQs of at least 130? To find the probability that *X*≥*b*, we note from Figure 58-6 that the probability that *X*≥*b* equals *1–probability X<b*. We can compute the probability that *X*≥*b* by entering the formula *1–NORMDIST(b,µ,σ,1)*. We seek the probability that *X*≥130. This equals *1–probability X<130*. We enter in cell C5 of the worksheet Normal the formula *1–NORMDIST(130,100,15,1)*. Excel returns 0.023, so we know that 2.3 percent of people have an IQ of at least 130.

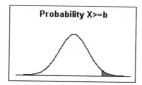

Figure 58-6   Calculating that the probability random variable is greater than or equal to *b*

Can I use Excel to find percentiles for normal random variables?

Consider a given normal random variable *X* with mean and standard deviation. In many situations, we want to answer questions such as the following:

- ❏ A drug manufacturer believes that next year's demand for its popular antidepressant will be normally distributed, with mean equal to 60 million days of therapy (DOT) and sigma equal to 5 million DOT. How many units of the drug should be produced this year if the company wants to have only a 1 percent chance of running out of the drug?

- ❏ Family income in Bloomington, Indiana, is normally distributed, with mean equal to $30,000 and sigma equal to $8,000. The poorest 10 percent of all families in Bloomington are eligible for federal aid. What should the aid cutoff be?

In our first example, we want to determine the 99th percentile of demand for the antidepressant. That is, we seek the number *x* such that there is only a 1 percent chance that demand will exceed *x* and a 99 percent chance that demand will be less than *x*. In our second example, we want the 10th percentile of family income in Bloomington. That is, we seek the number *x* such that there is only a 10 percent chance that family income will be less than *x* and a 90 percent chance that family income will exceed *x*.

Suppose we want to find the *p*th percentile (expressed as a decimal) of a normal random variable *X* with a mean and a standard deviation. Simply enter the formula *NORMINV(p,μ,σ)* into Excel. This formula returns the number *x* with the property that the probability that *X≤x* equals the percentile, as we want. We now can solve our examples. You'll find these exercises on the Normal worksheet in the file Normalexamples.xlsx.

For the drug manufacturing example, let *X* equal annual demand for the drug. We want a value *x* such that the probability that *X≥x* equals 0.01 or the probability that *X<x* equals 0.99. Again, we seek the 99th percentile of demand, which we find (in millions) by entering in cell C7 the formula *NORMINV(0.99,60,5)*. Excel returns 71.63, so the company must produce 71,630,000 DOT. This assumes, of course, that the company begins the year with no supply of the drug on hand. If, for example, they had a beginning inventory of 10 million DOT, they would need to produce 61,630,000 DOT during the current year.

To determine the cutoff for federal aid, if X equals the income of a Bloomington family, we seek a value of x such that the probability that $X \leq x$ equals 0.10, or the 10th percentile of Bloomington family income. We find this value with the formula *NORMINV(0.10, 30000,8000)*. Excel returns $19,747.59, so aid should be given to all families with incomes smaller than $19,749.59.

Why is the normal random variable appropriate in many real-world situations?

A well-known mathematical result called the *Central Limit Theorem* tells us that if we add together many (usually at least 30 is sufficient) independent random variables, their sum is normally distributed. This result holds true even if the individual random variables are not normally distributed. Many quantities (such as measurement errors) are created by adding together many independent random variables, which explains why the normal random variable occurs often in the real world. Here are some other situations in which we can use the Central Limit Theorem.

❑ The total demand for pizzas during a month at a supermarket is normally distributed, even if the daily demand for pizzas is not.

❑ The amount of money we win if we play craps 1000 times is normally distributed, even though the amount of money we win on each individual play is not.

Another important mathematical result tells us how to find the mean, variance, and standard deviations of sums of independent random variables. If we are adding together independent random variables $X_1, X_2,..., X_n$, where mean $X_i = \mu_i$, and standard deviation $X_i = \sigma_i$, then the following are true:

1. Mean $(X_1 + X_2 + ... X_n) = \mu_1 + \mu_2 + ... \mu_n$

2. Variance $(X_1 + X_2 + ... X_n) = \sigma_1^2 + \sigma_2^2 + ... \sigma_n^2$

3. Standard deviation $((X_1 + X_2 + ... X_n) = \sqrt{\sigma_1^2 + \sigma_2^2 + ... \sigma_n^2}$

We note that 1 is true even when the random variables are not independent. By combining 1 through 3 with the Central Limit Theorem, we can solve many complex probability problems, such as the demand for pizza. Our pizza solution is in the *Central Limit* worksheet in the file Normalexamples.xlsx, which is shown in Figure 58-7.

	C	D
2	Daily frozen pizza demand	
3	mean	45
4	sigma	12
5		
6	30 day	
7	mean	1350
8	variance	4320
9	sigma	65.72671
10		
11	Probability more than 1400 sol	0.225689
12	1% chance of running out	1502.903

Figure 58-7   Using the Central Limit Theorem

Even though the daily demand for frozen pizzas is not normally distributed, we know from the Central Limit Theorem that the 30-day demand for frozen pizzas is normally distributed. Given this, 1 through 3 above imply the following:

- From 1, the mean of a 30-day demand equals *30(45)=1350*.
- From 2, the variance of a 30-day demand equals *30(12)²=4320*.
- From 3, the standard deviation of a 30-day demand equals

$$\sqrt{4320} = 65.73$$

Thus, the 30-day demand for pizzas can be modeled following a normal random variable with a mean of 1350 and a standard deviation of 65.73. In cell D11, I compute the probability that at least 1400 pizzas are sold as the probability that our normal approximation is at least 1399.5 (note that a demand of 1399.6, for example, would round up to 1400) with the formula *1–NORMDIST(1399.5,D7,D9,TRUE)*. We find the probability that demand in a 30-day period for at least 1400 pizzas is 22.6 percent.

The number of pizzas that we must stock to have only a 1 percent chance of running out of pizzas is just the 99th percentile of our demand distribution. We determine the 99th percentile of our demand distribution (1503) in cell D12 with the formula *NORMINV (0.99,D7,D9)*. Therefore, at the beginning of a month, we should bring our stock of pizzas up to 1503 if we want to have only a 1 percent chance of running out of pizzas.

Problems

1. Suppose we can set the mean number of ounces of soda that is put into a can. The actual number of ounces has a standard deviation of 0.05 ounces.

   - If we set the mean at 12.03 ounces, and a soda can is acceptable if it contains at least 12 ounces, what fraction of cans is acceptable?
   - What fraction of cans have less than 12.1 ounces?
   - What should we set the mean to if we want, at most, 1 percent of our cans to contain, at most, 12 ounces? Hint: Use the Goal Seek command.

2. Annual demand for a drug is normally distributed with a mean of 40,000 units and a standard deviation of 10,000 units.

   - What is the probability that annual demand is from 35,000 through 49,000 units?
   - If we want to have only a 5 percent chance of running out of the drug, at what level should we set annual production?

3. The probability of winning a game of craps is 0.493. If I play 10,000 games of craps and bet the same amount on each game, what is the probability that I'm ahead? Begin by

determining the mean and standard deviation of the profit on one game of craps. Then use the Central Limit Theorem.

4. Weekly sales of Volvo's Cross Country station wagons are normally distributed with a mean of 1000 and standard deviation of 250.

   ❑ What is the probability that, during a week, from 400 through 1100 station wagons are sold?

   ❑ There is a 1 percent chance that fewer than what number of station wagons are sold during a week?

Chapter 59

Weibull and Beta Distributions: Modeling Machine Life and Duration of a Project

- How can I estimate the probability that a machine will work without failing for at least 20 hours?

- How can I estimate the probability that hanging drywall in a building will take more than 200 hours?

The *Weibull random variable* is a continuous random variable that is often used to model the lifetime of a machine. If we have data about how long similar machines have lasted in the past, we can estimate the two parameters (*alpha* and *beta*) that define a Weibull random variable. You can then use the WEIBULL function in Microsoft Office Excel 2007 to determine probabilities of interest, such as an estimate of how long a machine will run without failing.

The *Beta random variable* is a continuous random variable that's often used to model the duration of an activity. Given estimates of the minimum duration, maximum duration, mean duration, and the standard deviation of the duration, you can use the BETADIST function in Excel to determine probabilities of interest.

How can I estimate the probability that a machine will work without failing for at least 20 hours?

Suppose we have observed the lifetime of seven similar machines. The data we've collected about the machines is contained in the file Weibullest.xlsx, shown in Figure 59-1.

	B	C
16	Machine 1	8.5
17	Machine 2	12.54
18	Machine 3	13.75
19	Machine 4	19.75
20	Machine 5	21.46
21	Machine 6	26.34
22	Machine 7	28.45

Figure 59-1 Machine lifetime data

Reliability engineers have found that the Weibull random variable is usually appropriate for modeling machine lifetimes. The Weibull random variable is specified by two parameters: *alpha* and *beta*. Based on our data, we find (using the AVERAGE and STDEV functions in cells B13 and B14) that, on average, a machine lasts 18.68 hours, with a standard deviation of 7.40 hours. After copying these values into cells G6 and G11 and running the Solver, we find estimates of *alpha* and *beta* that ensure that the Weibull random variable will have a mean and standard deviation matching our data. In our case, we find that *alpha* equals 2.725 and *beta* equals 21.003, as you can see in Figure 59-2. Any value you enter for *alpha* and *beta* in cells E2 and E3 for a Weibull random variable yields a mean (computed in cell E6) and standard deviation (computed in cell E11). Our Solver model varies *alpha* and *beta* until the mean and standard deviation of the Weibull distribution equal the mean and standard deviation of machine lifetime computed from our data.

	A	B	C	D	E	F	G	H
5							assumed	Sq Err
6				mean	18.6843 =		18.6843	2.5E-12
7				variance part	441.156			
8					0.91549			
9					0.88957			
10				variance	54.7732			
11				sigma	7.40089 =		7.40088	3.6E-11
12								
13	mean	18.68429			SSE		3.8E-11	
14	sigma	7.400885						
15								
16		Machine 1	8.5		Prob>=20 hours			
17		Machine 2	12.54					
18		Machine 3	13.75		Prob between 15 and 30 hours			
19		Machine 4	19.75					
20		Machine 5	21.46					
21		Machine 6	26.34					
22		Machine 7	28.45					

Figure 59-2   Estimates of alpha and beta for a Weibull random variable

Here's the syntax of the WEIBULL function:

```
WEIBULL(x,alpha,beta,Cumulative)
```

When *Cumulative=True* this formula results in the probability that a Weibull random variable with parameters *alpha* and *beta* is less than or equal to *x*. Changing *True* to *False* yields the height of the Weibull probability density function (pdf). Remember from Chapter 55, "An Introduction to Random Variables," that the height of a pdf for any value *x* of a continuous random variable indicates the likelihood that the random variable assumes a value near *x*. Thus, if the Weibull density for 20 hours were twice the Weibull density for 10 hours, we would know that our machine is twice as likely to work for 20 hours before failing than to work for 10 hours before failing. We can now answer some questions involving probabilities of interest.

What is the probability that a machine will last at least 20 hours?   This probability (41.6 percent) is computed in cell G16 with the formula 1−WEIBULL(20,alpha,beta,1). Essentially, this formula computes the area under the Weibull pdf to the right of 20 hours by subtracting 1 from the area to the left of 20 hours.

What is the probability that a machine will last from 15 through 30 hours?   This probability (59.9 percent) is computed in cell G18 with the formula *WEIBULL(30,alpha,beta, TRUE)–WEIBULL(15,alpha,beta,TRUE)*. This formula finds the area under the Weibull pdf from 15 through 30 hours by computing the area to the left of 30 hours less the area to the left of 15 hours. After we subtract the probability of a machine working without failure for less than 15 hours from the probability of a machine working without failure for less than or equal to 30 hours, we are left with the probability that a machine will work without failure from 15 through 30 hours.

How can I estimate the probability that hanging drywall in a building will take more than 200 hours?

Since the development of the Polaris missile in the 1950s, project managers have modeled activity durations with the Beta random variable. To specify a Beta random variable, you need to specify a minimum value, a maximum value, and two parameters (*alpha* and *beta*). The data in the file Beta.xlsx (see Figure 59-3) can be used to estimate the parameters of a Beta distribution.

	B	C	D	E	F
3	Fit a beta				
4					
5	alpha	2.196262		mean	78.48647118
6	beta	14.59335		sigma	47.96749188
7	lower	0			Data
8	upper	600			26.25660896
9	mean	78.48647			91.84026718
10	sigma	47.96749			66.54324532
11	transformed mean	0.130811			53.89266014
12	transformed var	0.006391			222.4365234
13					72.0543623
14					75.35727024
15	Probability>=200 hours	0.020502			78.27422619
16	Probability <=80 hours	0.583238			99.04375076
17	Probability between 30 and 150 hours	0.771058			90.47598839
18					47.00031281
19					16.21513367
20					117.2774076
21					69.93505955
22					50.69425106

Figure 59-3   Determining probabilities with the Beta random variable

Let's estimate that the time needed to hang drywall in a building will be from 0 through 600 hours. These are our minimum and maximum values, entered in cells C7 and C8. The cell range F8:F22 contains the lengths of time needed to hang drywall in 15 buildings of a similar size. In cell F5, I used the AVERAGE function to compute the mean time (78.49 hours) needed to drywall these 15 buildings. In cell F6, I used the STDEV function to determine the standard deviation (47.97 hours) of the time needed to drywall these buildings. Any choice of values of *alpha* and *beta* determine the shape of the Beta distribution's pdf and the mean and standard deviation for the corresponding Beta random variable. If we can choose *alpha* and *beta* values to match the mean and standard deviation of the drywall installation times computed from our data, it seems reasonable that these *alpha* and *beta* values will yield probabilities consistent with the observed data. After entering the mean and standard deviation of the drywall installation from our data in cells C9 and C10, our worksheet computes values for *alpha* (2.20) in cell C5 and *beta* (14.59) in cell C6 that ensure that the mean and standard deviation of the Beta random variable match the mean and standard deviation of our data.

The function *BETADIST(x,alpha,beta,lower,upper)* determines the probability that a Beta random variable ranging from *lower* through *upper*, with parameters *alpha* and *beta*, assumes a value less than or equal to *x*. We can now use the BETADIST function to determine probabilities of interest.

To compute the probability that hanging drywall will take at least 200 hours, we can use the formula in cell C15, *1–BETADIST(200,alpha,beta,lower,upper)*. The result is 2.1 percent. This formula simply computes the probability that hanging drywall will take at least 200 hours as *1–probability drywalling takes less than or equal to 200 hours.*

The probability that hanging drywall will take, at most, 80 hours (58.3 percent) can be computed with the formula in cell C16, *BETADIST(80,alpha,beta,lower,upper)*. And to compute the probability that the task will take from 30 through 150 hours (77.1 percent), in cell C17 we use the formula *BETADIST(150,alpha,beta,lower,upper)–BETADIST(30,alpha,beta,lower,upper)*. This formula computes the probability that drywalling takes from 30 through 150 hours as the probability that drywalling takes less than or equal to 150 hours minus the probability that drywalling takes less than or equal to 30 hours. The difference between these probabilities counts only instances when drywalling takes from 30 through 150 hours.

Problems

The data for this chapter's problems is contained in the file Ch59data.xlsx.

1. In the *Problem 1* worksheet, you are given data about the duration of a machine's lifetime.

   ❑ What is the probability that the machine will last at least 10 hours?

   ❑ What is the probability that the machine will last from 1 through 5 hours?

   ❑ What is the probability that the machine will fail within 6 hours?

2. You need to clean your house today. In the *Problem 2* worksheet, you are given data about how long it has taken to clean your house in the past. If you start cleaning at noon, what are the chances that you'll be finished in time to leave at 7:00 P.M. for a movie?

Chapter 60

Introduction to Monte Carlo Simulation

- Who uses Monte Carlo simulation?

- What happens when I type =*RAND()* in a cell?

- How can I simulate values of a discrete random variable?

- How can I simulate values of a normal random variable?

- How can a greeting card company determine how many cards to produce?

We would like to accurately estimate the probabilities of uncertain events. For example, what is the probability that a new product's cash flows will have a positive net present value (NPV)? What is the risk factor of our investment portfolio? Monte Carlo simulation enables us to model situations that present uncertainty and then play them out on a computer thousands of times.

Note The name *Monte Carlo simulation* comes from the computer simulations performed during the 1930s and 1940s to estimate the probability that the chain reaction needed for an atom bomb to detonate would work successfully. The physicists involved in this work were big fans of gambling, so they gave the simulations the code name *Monte Carlo*.

In the next five chapters, I'll provide some examples of how you can use Microsoft Office Excel 2007 to perform Monte Carlo simulations.

Who uses Monte Carlo simulation?

Many companies use Monte Carlo simulation as an important part of their decision-making process. Here are some examples.

- ❑ General Motors, Proctor and Gamble, Pfizer, Bristol-Myers Squibb, and Eli Lilly use simulation to estimate both the average return and the risk factor of new products. At GM, this information is used by the CEO to determine which products come to market.

❏ GM uses simulation for activities such as forecasting net income for the corporation, predicting structural and purchasing costs, and determining its susceptibility to different kinds of risk (such as interest rate changes and exchange rate fluctuations).

❏ Lilly uses simulation to determine the optimal plant capacity for each drug.

❏ Proctor and Gamble uses simulation to model and optimally hedge foreign exchange risk.

❏ Sears uses simulation to determine how many units of each product line should be ordered from suppliers—for example, the number of pairs of Dockers trousers that should be ordered this year.

❏ Oil and drug companies use simulation to value "real options," such as the value of an option to expand, contract, or postpone a project.

❏ Financial planners use Monte Carlo simulation to determine optimal investment strategies for their clients' retirement.

What happens when I type =RAND() in a cell?

When you type the formula =RAND() in a cell, you get a number that is equally likely to assume any value between 0 and 1. Thus, around 25 percent of the time, you should get a number less than or equal to 0.25; around 10 percent of the time you should get a number that is at least 0.90, and so on. To demonstrate how the RAND function works, take a look at the file Randdemo.xlsx, shown in Figure 60-1.

	B	C	D	E	F
2	Trial			mean	0.495548
3	1	0.523853			
4	2	0.773927		Fraction	
5	3	0.688396		0-.25	0.275
6	4	0.370747		.25-.50	0.225
7	5	0.558396		.50-.75	0.26
8	6	0.971395		.75-1	0.24
9	7	0.577849			
10	8	0.820578			
11	9	0.144445			
12	10	0.836274			
13	11	0.989839			
14	12	0.833616			
15	13	0.952457			
16	14	0.634486			
17	15	0.19416			
18	16	0.238613			
19	17	0.947711			
20	18	0.965355			
21	19	0.265148			
22	20	0.378746			
23	21	0.111076			
24	22	0.506785			
25	23	0.556259			
26	24	0.589075			
27	25	0.16484			

Figure 60-1   Demonstrating the RAND function

> **Note**   When you open the file Randdemo.xlsx, you will not see the same random numbers shown in Figure 60-1. The RAND function always automatically recalculates the numbers it generates when a worksheet is opened or when new information is entered into the worksheet.

I copied from cell C3 to C4:C402 the formula =RAND(). I named the range C3:C402 *Data*. Then, in column F, I tracked the average of the 400 random numbers (cell F2) and used the COUNTIF function to determine the fractions that are between 0 and 0.25, 0.25 and 0.50, 0.50 and 0.75, and 0.75 and 1. When you press the F9 key, the random numbers are recalculated. Notice that the average of the 400 numbers is always approximately 0.5, and that around 25 percent of the results are in intervals of 0.25. These results are consistent with the definition of a random number. Also note that the values generated by RAND in different cells are independent. For example, if the random number generated in cell C3 is a large number (for example, 0.99), it tells us nothing about the values of the other random numbers generated.

How can I simulate values of a discrete random variable?

Suppose the demand for a calendar is governed by the following discrete random variable:

Demand	Probability
10,000	0.10
20,000	0.35
40,000	0.3
60,000	0.25

How can we have Excel play out, or simulate, this demand for calendars many times? The trick is to associate each possible value of the RAND function with a possible demand for calendars. The following assignment ensures that a demand of 10,000 will occur 10 percent of the time, and so on.

Demand	Random number assigned
10,000	Less than 0.10
20,000	Greater than or equal to 0.10, and less than 0.45
40,000	Greater than or equal to 0.45, and less than 0.75
60,000	Greater than or equal to 0.75

To demonstrate the simulation of demand, look at the file Discretesim.xlsx, shown in Figure 60-2 on the next page.

	A	B	C	D	E	F	G
1						Cutoffs	Demand
2	Trial		rand			0	10000
3	1	20000	0.288321			0.1	20000
4	2	20000	0.428983			0.45	40000
5	3	40000	0.560272			0.75	60000
6	4	20000	0.14788				
7	5	20000	0.354664			Fraction of time	
8	6	60000	0.815833		10000	0.1025	
9	7	60000	0.79892		20000	0.345	
10	8	40000	0.483586		40000	0.2925	
11	9	40000	0.616508		60000	0.26	
12	10	20000	0.287158				
13	11	10000	0.010866				
14	12	60000	0.76438				
15	13	60000	0.79811				
16	14	60000	0.896				
17	15	60000	0.846083				
18	16	40000	0.726104				
19	17	40000	0.55854				
20	18	10000	0.070515				
21	19	40000	0.474544				
22	20	40000	0.56721				
23	21	40000	0.717294				
24	22	60000	0.813545				
25	23	20000	0.34719				
26	24	10000	0.044306				

Figure 60-2 Simulating a discrete random variable

The key to our simulation is to use a random number to initiate a lookup from the table range F2:G5 (named *lookup*). Random numbers greater than or equal to 0 and less than 0.10 will yield a demand of 10,000; random numbers greater than or equal to 0.10 and less than 0.45 will yield a demand of 20,000; random numbers greater than or equal to 0.45 and less than 0.75 will yield a demand of 40,000; and random numbers greater than or equal to 0.75 will yield a demand of 60,000. I generated 400 random numbers by copying from C3 to C4:C402 the formula *RAND()*. I then generated 400 trials, or iterations, of calendar demand by copying from B3 to B4:B402 the formula *VLOOKUP(C3,lookup,2)*. This formula ensures that any random number less than 0.10 generates a demand of 10,000, any random number between 0.10 and 0.45 generates a demand of 20,000, and so on. In the cell range F8:F11, I used the COUNTIF function to determine the fraction of our 400 iterations yielding each demand. When we press F9 to recalculate the random numbers, the simulated probabilities are close to our assumed demand probabilities.

How can I simulate values of a normal random variable?

If you type in any cell the formula *NORMINV(rand(),mu,sigma)*, you will generate a simulated value of a normal random variable having a mean *mu* and standard deviation *sigma*. I've illustrated this procedure in the file Normalsim.xlsx, shown in Figure 60-3.

	A	B	C	D	E	F	G
1				mean	40000		
2				sigma	10000		
3	Trial	Normal Rv	Rand				
4	1	47223.49836	0.76496029			sim mean	40308.41493
5	2	26982.50442	0.096501006			sim sigma	11123.28607
6	3	44065.10192	0.657816115				
7	4	40869.95157	0.534662319				
8	5	27541.17553	0.106403778				
9	6	42876.8208	0.613204946				
10	7	55640.48693	0.941096933				
11	8	51802.56403	0.881050874				
12	9	27055.54228	0.097755745				
13	10	39160.2774	0.466539243				
14	11	30074.94364	0.160475466				
15	12	36130.46529	0.349395327				
16	13	27166.52463	0.099685173				
17	14	32210.17013	0.217994868				
18	15	40172.80201	0.50689346				
19	16	27315.06708	0.102310922				
20	17	39446.24758	0.47791976				
21	18	38533.71858	0.44171277				
22	19	32608.03551	0.229893858				

Figure 60-3   Simulating a normal random variable

Let's suppose we want to simulate 400 trials, or iterations, for a normal random variable with a mean of 40,000 and a standard deviation of 10,000. (I typed these values in cells E1 and E2, and named these cells *mean* and *sigma*, respectively.) Copying the formula =RAND() from C4 to C5:C403 generates 400 different random numbers. Copying from B4 to B5:B403 the formula NORMINV(C4,mean,sigma) generates 400 different trial values from a normal random variable with a mean of 40,000 and a standard deviation of 10,000. When we press the F9 key to recalculate the random numbers, the mean remains close to 40,000 and the standard deviation close to 10,000.

Essentially, for a random number x, the formula NORMINV(p,mu,sigma) generates the pth percentile of a normal random variable with a mean *mu* and a standard deviation *sigma*. For example, the random number 0.77 in cell C4 (see Figure 60-3) generates in cell B4 approximately the 77th percentile of a normal random variable with a mean of 40,000 and a standard deviation of 10,000.

How can a greeting card company determine how many cards to produce?

In this section, I'll demonstrate how Monte Carlo simulation can be used as a decision-making tool. Suppose that the demand for a Valentine's Day card is governed by the following discrete random variable:

Demand	Probability
10,000	0.10
20,000	0.35
40,000	0.3
60,000	0.25

The greeting card sells for $4.00, and the variable cost of producing each card is $1.50. Leftover cards must be disposed of at a cost of $0.20 per card. How many cards should be printed?

Basically, we simulate each possible production quantity (10,000, 20,000, 40,000, or 60,000) many times (for example, 1000 iterations). Then we determine which order quantity yields the maximum average profit over the 1000 iterations. You can find the data for this section in the file Valentine.xlsx, shown in Figure 60-4. I've assigned the range names in cells B1:B11 to cells C1:C11. I've assigned the cell range G3:H6 the name *lookup*. Our sales price and cost parameters are entered in cells C4:C6.

	B	C
1	produced	40000
2	rand#	0.875108533
3	demand	60000
4	unit prod cost	$ 1.50
5	unit price	$ 4.00
6	unit disp cost	$ 0.20
7		
8	revenue	$ 160,000.00
9	total var cost	$ 60,000.00
10	total disposing cost	$ -
11	profit	$ 100,000.00

Figure 60-4 Valentine's Day card simulation

I then enter a trial production quantity (40,000 in this example) in cell C1. Next I create a random number in cell C2 with the formula =RAND(). As previously described, I simulate demand for the card in cell C3 with the formula VLOOKUP(rand,lookup,2). (In the VLOOKUP formula, *rand* is the cell name assigned to cell C3, not the RAND function.)

The number of units sold is the smaller of our production quantity and demand. In cell C8, I compute our revenue with the formula MIN(produced,demand)*unit_price. In cell C9, I compute total production cost with the formula produced*unit_prod_cost.

If we produce more cards than are in demand, the number of units left over equals production minus demand; otherwise no units are left over. We compute our disposal cost in cell C10 with the formula unit_disp_cost*IF(produced>demand,produced−demand,0). Finally, in cell C11, we compute our profit as revenue− total_var_cost-total_disposing_cost.

We would like an efficient way to press F9 many times (for example, 1000) for each production quantity and tally our expected profit for each quantity. This situation is one in which a two-way data table comes to our rescue. (See Chapter 15, "Sensitivity Analysis with Data Tables," for details about data tables.) The data table I used in this example is shown in Figure 60-5.

	A	B	C	D	E	F
13	mean	25000	45044	58672	44580	
14	st dev	0	12550.0813	47605.9	73936.7	
15	100000	10000	20000	40000	60000	production quantity
16	1	25000	50000	100000	-18000	
17	2	25000	50000	16000	-18000	
18	3	25000	8000	16000	150000	
19	4	25000	50000	100000	66000	
20	5	25000	50000	-26000	-60000	
21	6	25000	8000	100000	-18000	
22	7	25000	8000	16000	150000	
23	8	25000	50000	100000	-18000	
24	9	25000	8000	100000	150000	
25	10	25000	50000	100000	66000	
26	11	25000	50000	100000	150000	
27	12	25000	50000	100000	-18000	
28	13	25000	50000	16000	-18000	
29	14	25000	8000	100000	150000	
30	15	25000	50000	100000	-18000	
31	16	25000	50000	16000	150000	
32	17	25000	50000	100000	-18000	
33	18	25000	50000	16000	-60000	
34	19	25000	50000	100000	150000	
35	20	25000	50000	100000	150000	
36	21	25000	50000	16000	150000	
37	22	25000	50000	-26000	66000	
38	23	25000	50000	100000	-18000	
39	24	25000	50000	100000	-60000	
40	25	25000	50000	100000	66000	
41	26	25000	50000	16000	-18000	

Figure 60-5   Two-way data table for greeting card simulation

In the cell range A16:A1015, I entered the numbers 1–1000 (corresponding to our 1000 trials). One easy way to create these values is to start by entering *1* in cell A16. Select the cell, and then on the Home tab in the Editing group, click Fill, and select Series to display the Series dialog box. In the Series dialog box, shown in Figure 60-6, enter a Step Value of 1 and a Stop Value of 1000. In the Series In area, select the Columns option, and then click OK. The numbers 1–1000 will be entered in column A starting in cell A16.

Figure 60-6   Using the Series dialog box to fill in the trial numbers 1 through 1000

Next we enter our possible production quantities (10,000, 20,000, 40,000, 60,000) in cells B15:E15. We want to calculate profit for each trial number (1 through 1000) and each production quantity. We refer to the formula for profit (calculated in cell C11) in the upper-left cell of our data table (A15) by entering *=C11*.

We are now ready to trick Excel into simulating 1000 iterations of demand for each production quantity. Select the table range (A15:E1014), and then in the Data Tools group on the Data tab, click What If Analysis, and then select Data Table. To set up a two-way data table, choose our production quantity (cell C1) as the Row Input Cell and select any blank cell (we chose cell I14) as the Column Input Cell. After clicking OK, Excel simulates 1000 demand values for each order quantity.

To understand why this works, consider the values placed by the data table in the cell range C16:C1015. For each of these cells, Excel will use a value of 20,000 in cell C1. In C16, the column input cell value of 1 is placed in a blank cell and the random number in cell C2 recalculates. The corresponding profit is then recorded in cell C16. Then the column cell input value of 2 is placed in a blank cell, and the random number in C2 again recalculates. The corresponding profit is entered in cell C17.

By copying from cell B13 to C13:E13 the formula *AVERAGE(B16:B1015)*, we compute average simulated profit for each production quantity. By copying from cell B14 to C14:E14 the formula *STDEV(B16:B1015)*, we compute the standard deviation of our simulated profits for each order quantity. Each time we press F9, 1000 iterations of demand are simulated for each order quantity. Producing 40,000 cards always yields the largest expected profit. Therefore, it appears that producing 40,000 cards is the proper decision.

- **The Impact of Risk on Our Decision**   If we produced 20,000 instead of 40,000 cards, our expected profit drops approximately 22 percent, but our risk (as measured by the standard deviation of profit) drops almost 73 percent. Therefore, if we are extremely averse to risk, producing 20,000 cards might be the right decision. Incidentally, producing 10,000 cards always has a standard deviation of 0 cards because if we produce 10,000 cards, we will always sell all of them without any leftovers.

> **Note**   In this workbook I set the Calculation option to Automatic Except For Tables. (Use the Calculation command in the Calculation group on the Formulas tab.) This setting ensures that our data table will not recalculate unless we press F9, which is a good idea because a large data table will slow down your work if it recalculates every time you type something into your worksheet. Note that in this example, whenever you press F9, the mean profit will change. This happens because each time you press F9, a different sequence of 1000 random numbers is used to generate demands for each order quantity.

- **Confidence Interval for Mean Profit**   A natural question to ask in this situation is, into what interval are we 95 percent sure the true mean profit will fall? This interval is called the *95 percent confidence interval for mean profit*. A 95 percent confidence interval for the mean of any simulation output is computed by the following formula:

$$\text{Mean Profit} \pm \frac{1.96 * \text{profitstd.dev.}}{\sqrt{\text{number iterations}}}$$

In cell J11, I computed the lower limit for the 95 percent confidence interval on mean profit when 40,000 calendars are produced with the formula *D13−1.96*D14/SQRT(1000)*.

In cell J12, I computed the upper limit for our 95 percent confidence interval with the formula *D13+1.96*D14/SQRT(1000)*. These calculations are shown in Figure 60-7.

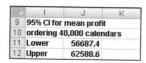

	I	J	K
9	95% CI for mean profit		
10	ordering 40,000 calendars		
11	Lower	56687.4	
12	Upper	62588.6	

Figure 60-7   95 percent confidence interval for mean profit when 40,000 calendars are ordered

We are 95 percent sure that our mean profit when 40,000 calendars are ordered is between $56,687 and $62,589.

Problems

1. A GMC dealer believes that demand for 2005 Envoys will be normally distributed with a mean of 200 and standard deviation of 30. His cost of receiving an Envoy is $25,000, and he sells an Envoy for $40,000. Half of all the Envoys not sold at full price can be sold for $30,000. He is considering ordering 200, 220, 240, 260, 280, or 300 Envoys. How many should he order?

2. A small supermarket is trying to determine how many copies of *People* magazine they should order each week. They believe their demand for *People* is governed by the following discrete random variable:

Demand	Probability
15	0.10
20	0.20
25	0.30
30	0.25
35	0.15

The supermarket pays $1.00 for each copy of *People* and sells it for $1.95. Each unsold copy can be returned for $0.50. How many copies of *People* should the store order?

Chapter 61
Calculating an Optimal Bid

- How do I simulate a binomial random variable?
- How can I determine whether a continuous random variable should be modeled as a normal random variable?
- How can I use simulation to determine the optimal bid for a construction project?

When bidding against competitors on a project, the two major sources of uncertainty are the number of competitors and the bid submitted by each competitor. If your bid is too high, you'll make a lot of money on each project, but you'll get very few projects. If your bid is too low, you'll work on lots of projects, but make very little money on each one. The optimal bid is somewhere in the middle. Monte Carlo simulation is a useful tool for determining the bid that maximizes expected profit.

How do I simulate a binomial random variable?

The formula $CRITBINOM(n,p,rand())$ simulates the number of successes in n trials, each of which has a probability of success equal to p. As shown in the file Binomialsim.xlsx (see Figure 61-1 on the next page), when you press F9, the formula $CRITBINOM(100,0.9,D3)$ entered in cell C3 simulates the number of free throws that Steve Nash (a 90 percent foul shooter in the NBA) makes in 100 attempts. The formula $CRITBINOM(100,0.5,D4)$ in cell C4 simulates the number of heads tossed in 100 tosses of a fair coin. In cell C5, the formula $CRITBINOM(3,0.4,D5)$ simulates the number of competitors entering the market during a year in which there are three possible entrants and each competitor is assumed to have a 40 percent chance of entering the market. Of course, in D3:D5, I've entered the formula $=RAND()$.

	B	C	D
2			Rand#
3	Number of free throws Steve Nash makes out of 100	90	0.443196
4	Number of heads in 100 tosses	48	0.349758
5	Number of competitors entering market; p =4 n= 3	2	0.82187

Figure 61-1   Simulating a binomial random variable

How can I determine whether a continuous random variable should be modeled as a normal random variable?

Let's suppose we think the most likely bid by a competitor is $50,000. Recall that the normal pdf is symmetric about its mean. Therefore, to determine whether a normal random variable can be used to model a competitor's bid, we need to test for symmetry about the bid's mean. If the competitor's bid exhibits symmetry about the mean of $50,000, bids of $40,000 and $60,000, $45,000 and $55,000, and so on should be approximately equally likely. If the symmetry assumption seems reasonable, we can then model each competitor's bid as a normal random variable with a mean of $50,000.

How can we estimate the standard deviation of each competitor's bid? Recall from the rule of thumb discussed in Chapter 37, "Summarizing Data by Using Descriptive Statistics," that data sets with symmetric histograms have roughly 95 percent of their data within two standard deviations of the mean. Similarly, a normal random variable has a 95 percent probability of being within two standard deviations of its mean. Suppose that we are 95 percent sure that a competitor's bid will be between $30,000 and $70,000. This implies that 2*(*standard deviation of competitor's bid*)=$20,000, or the standard deviation of a competitor's bid equals $10,000.

Assuming the symmetry assumption is reasonable, we could now simulate a competitor's bid with the formula *NORMINV(rand(),50000,10000)*. (See Chapter 60, "Introduction to Monte Carlo Simulation," for details about how to model normal random variables using the NORMINV function.)

How can I use simulation to determine the optimal bid for a construction project?

Let's assume that we're bidding on a construction project that will cost us $25,000 to complete. It costs us $1,000 to prepare our bid. There are six potential competitors, and we estimate that there is a 50 percent chance that each competitor will bid on the project. If a competitor places a bid, their bid is assumed to follow a normal random variable with a mean equal to $50,000 and a standard deviation equal to $10,000. Also suppose we are only considering bids that are exact multiples of $5,000. What should we bid to maximize expected profit? Remember, the low bid wins! Our work is in the file Bidsim.xlsx, shown in Figures 61-2 and 61-3.

	D	E	F	G
1	costproject	25000		
2	cost bid	1000	rand#	
3	Number bidders	1	0.066081	
4	mybid	40000		
5				
6				
7				
8	Bidder #	In	Bid	rand#
9	1	yes	53710.47	0.644699
10	2	no	100000	0.319042
11	3	no	100000	0.66172
12	4	no	100000	0.098727
13	5	no	100000	0.105095
14	6	no	100000	0.37622
15				
16	Do I win?			
17	yes			
18	Profit			
19	14000			

Figure 61-2   Bidding simulation model

	D	E	F	G	H	I	J	K
21	mean	3630	7290	8240	5680	3175	2120	225
22	14000	30000	35000	40000	45000	50000	55000	60000
23	1	4000	9000	-1000	19000	-1000	-1000	-1000
24	2	4000	9000	-1000	19000	-1000	-1000	-1000
25	3	-1000	9000	-1000	-1000	-1000	-1000	-1000
26	4	4000	9000	14000	-1000	24000	-1000	-1000
27	5	4000	9000	14000	19000	-1000	-1000	-1000
28	6	4000	-1000	-1000	-1000	24000	-1000	-1000
29	7	4000	9000	14000	-1000	-1000	-1000	-1000
30	8	4000	9000	-1000	-1000	-1000	-1000	-1000
31	9	4000	9000	14000	-1000	-1000	-1000	-1000
32	10	4000	9000	-1000	19000	24000	-1000	-1000
33	11	4000	9000	14000	-1000	-1000	-1000	-1000
34	12	4000	-1000	-1000	-1000	-1000	29000	-1000
35	13	4000	9000	-1000	-1000	24000	-1000	-1000
36	14	4000	9000	14000	-1000	-1000	-1000	-1000
37	15	4000	9000	14000	-1000	24000	-1000	-1000
38	16	4000	-1000	14000	-1000	-1000	-1000	-1000
39	17	4000	9000	14000	-1000	-1000	-1000	34000
40	18	4000	9000	14000	-1000	-1000	-1000	-1000
41	19	4000	9000	14000	-1000	24000	-1000	-1000
42	20	4000	9000	14000	-1000	-1000	-1000	-1000
43	21	4000	9000	-1000	-1000	24000	-1000	-1000
44	22	4000	9000	14000	19000	24000	-1000	-1000

Figure 61-3   Bidding simulation data table

Our strategy is as follows:

❑ Generate the number of bidders.

❑ For each potential bidder who actually bids, use the normal random variable to model the bid. If a potential bidder does not bid, we assign a large bid (for example, $100,000) to ensure that they do not win the bidding.

❑ Determine whether we are the low bidder.

❑ If we are the low bidder, we earn a profit equal to our bid, less project cost, less $1,000 (the cost of making the bid). If we are not the low bidder, we lose the $1,000 cost of the bid.

❏ Use a two-way data table to simulate each possible bid (for example, $30,000, $35,000, ... $60,000) 1000 times, and then choose the bid with the largest expected profit.

To begin, I've assigned the names in the cell range D1:D4 to the range E1:E4. We determine in cell E3 the number of bidders with the formula *CRITBINOM(6,0.5,F3)*. Cell F3 contains the *=RAND()* formula. Next we determine which of our potential bidders actually bid by copying from E9 to E10:E14 the formula *IF(D9<=Number_bidders,"yes","no")*.

We then generate a bid for each bidder (nonbidders are assigned a bid of $100,000) by copying from cell F9 to F10:F14 the formula *IF(E9="yes",NORMINV(G9,50000, 10000),100000)*. Each cell in the cell range G9:G14 contains the *=RAND()* function. In cell D17, I determine whether I am the low bidder and win the project with the formula *IF(mybid<=MIN(F9:F14),"yes","no")*. In cell D19, I compute my profit with the formula *IF(D17="yes",mybid−costproject−cost_bid,−cost_bid)*, recognizing that I only receive the amount of the bid and pay project costs if I win the bid.

Now we can use a two-way data table (shown in Figure 61-3) to simulate 1000 bids between $30,000 and $60,000. We copy our profit to cell D22 by entering the formula *=D19*. Then we select the table range D22:K1022. On the Data tab of the Ribbon, in the Data Tools group, click What-If Analysis and then click Data Table to specify the input values for the data table. Our column input cell is any blank cell in the worksheet, and our row input cell is E4 (the location of our bid). Clicking OK in the Data Table dialog box simulates the profit from each bid 1000 times.

Copying from E21 to F21:K21 the formula *AVERAGE(E23:E1022)* calculates the mean profit for each bid. Each time we press F9, we see that our mean profit for 1000 trials is maximized by bidding $40,000.

Problems

1. How would our optimal bid change if there were 12 competitors?

2. Suppose we are bidding for an oil well that we believe will yield $40 million (including the cost of developing and mining the oil) in profits. Three competitors are bidding against us, and each competitor's bid is assumed to follow a normal random variable with a mean of $30 million and a standard deviation of $4 million. What should we bid (within $1 million)?

3. A commonly used continuous random variable is the uniform random variable. A uniform random variable—written as $U(a,b)$—is equally likely to assume any value between two given numbers a and b. Explain why the formula $a+(b−a)*RAND()$ can be used to simulate $U(a,b)$.

4. Investor Peter Fischer is bidding to take over a biotech company. The company is equally likely to be worth any amount between $0 and $200 per share. Only the company itself

knows its true value. Peter is such a good investor that the market will immediately estimate the firm's value at 50 percent more than its true value. What should Peter bid per share for this company?

5. Ichiro is asking for salary arbitration on his baseball contract. Salary arbitration in Major League Baseball works as follows. The player submits a salary that he thinks he should be paid, as does the team. The arbitrator (without seeing the salaries submitted by the player or the team) estimates a fair salary. The player is then paid the submitted salary that is closer to the arbitrator's estimate. For example, suppose Ichiro submits a $12 million offer and the Seattle Mariners submit a $7 million offer. If the arbitrator says a fair salary is $10 million, then Ichiro will be paid $12 million, whereas if the arbitrator says a fair salary is $9 million, Ichiro will be paid $7 million. Assume that the arbitrator's estimate is equally likely to be anywhere between $8 and $11 million and the team's offer is equally likely to be anywhere between $6 million and $9 million. Within $1 million, what salary should Ichiro submit?

Chapter 62

Simulating Stock Prices and Asset Allocation Modeling

- I recently bought 100 shares of GE stock. What is the probability that during the next year this investment will return more than 10 percent?

- I'm trying to determine how to allocate my investment portfolio between stocks, T-Bills, and bonds. What asset allocation over a five-year planning horizon will yield an expected return of at least 10 percent and minimize risk?

The last few years have shown us that future returns on our investments are highly uncertain. In this chapter, I'll explain a relatively simple approach to assessing uncertainty in future investment returns. This approach is based on the idea of *bootstrapping*. Essentially, bootstrapping simulates future investment returns by assuming that the future will be similar to the past. For example, if we want to simulate the stock price of GE in one year, we can assume that each month's percentage change in price is equally likely to be one of, for example, the percentage changes for the previous 62 months. This method allows us to easily generate thousands of scenarios for the future value of our investments. In addition to scenarios that assume that future variability and average returns will be similar to the recent past, we can easily adjust bootstrapping to reflect a view that future returns on investments will be less or more favorable than in the recent past.

After we've generated future scenarios for investment returns, it's a simple matter to use Microsoft Office Excel 2007 Solver to work out the asset allocation problem—that is, how should we allocate our investments to attain the level of expected return we want but with minimum risk?

The following two examples will demonstrate the simplicity and power of the bootstrapping approach.

I recently bought 100 shares of GE stock. What is the probability that during the next year this investment will return more than 10 percent?

Let's suppose that GE stock is currently selling for $28.50 per share. We have data for the monthly returns on GE (as well as for Microsoft and Intel) for the months between August 1997 and July 2002. You can find this data in the file Gesim.xlsx, shown in Figure 62-1. For example, in the month ending on August 2, 2002 (basically, this is July 2002), GE lost 12.1 percent. These returns include dividends (if any) paid by each company.

	B	C	D	E	F
3		mean	0.014746	0.006237	0.008828
4	Code		MSFT	INTC	GE
5	1	8/2/2002	-0.08316	-0.15397	-0.12112
6	2	7/2/2002	-0.12285	0.028493	0.108434
7	3	6/2/2002	0.074445	-0.33853	-0.06139
8	4	5/2/2002	-0.02583	-0.03464	-0.01276
9	5	4/2/2002	-0.13348	-0.05894	-0.15658
10	6	3/2/2002	0.033768	0.064867	-0.02849
11	7	2/2/2002	-0.08429	-0.18514	0.041088
12	8	1/2/2002	-0.03834	0.114295	-0.07314
13	9	12/1/2001	0.031771	-0.03709	0.045898
14	10	11/1/2001	0.104213	0.337433	0.057167
15	11	10/1/2001	0.136408	0.194417	-0.02102
16	12	9/1/2001	-0.10307	-0.26889	-0.08653
17	13	8/1/2001	-0.13809	-0.06181	-0.05957
18	14	7/1/2001	-0.09329	0.019172	-0.10944
19	15	6/1/2001	0.055218	0.082654	0
20	16	5/1/2001	0.021107	-0.12601	0.009701
21	17	4/1/2001	0.238801	0.174658	0.159413
22	18	3/1/2001	-0.07305	-0.07886	-0.09653
23	19	2/1/2001	-0.03374	-0.22808	0.011168
24	20	1/1/2001	0.407561	0.231179	-0.04071
25	21	12/1/2000	-0.24399	-0.21021	-0.02973
26	22	11/1/2000	-0.16684	-0.15439	-0.09569
27	23	10/1/2000	0.141933	0.082872	-0.05204
28	24	9/1/2000	-0.13608	-0.44491	-0.01145

Figure 62-1   GE, Microsoft, and Intel stock data

The price of GE stock in one year is uncertain, so how can we get an idea about the range of variation in the price of GE stock one year from now? The bootstrapping approach simply estimates a return on GE during each of the next 12 months by assuming that the return during each month is equally likely to be any of the returns for the 60 months listed. In other words, the return on GE next month is equally likely to be any of the numbers in the cell range F5:F64. To implement this idea, we use the formula *RANDBE-TWEEN(1,60)* to choose a "scenario" for each of the next 12 months. For example, if this function returns 7 for next month, we use the GE return in cell F11 (4.1 percent), which is the seventh cell in the range, as next month's return. The results are shown in Figure 62-2. (You'll see different values because the RANDBETWEEN function automatically recalculates random values when you open the worksheet.)

To begin, we enter GE's current price per share ($28.50) in cell J6. Then we generate a scenario for each of the next 12 months by copying from K6 to K7:K17 the formula *RANDBETWEEN(1,60)*. Next we use a lookup table to obtain the GE return based on our scenario. To do this, we simply copy from L6 to L7:L17 the formula

VLOOKUP(K6,lookup,5). As the formula indicates, the range B5:F64 is named *Lookup*, with the returns for GE in the fifth column of the lookup range. In the scenarios shown in Figure 62-2, we see, for example, that the return for GE two months into the future is equal to our 8/1/1999 data point (a 3 percent return).

	I	J	K	L	M
4	GE				
5	Month	Start price	Scenario	Return	End price
6	1	28.5	38	-0.035371538	27.49191
7	2	27.49191	37	0.030415009	28.32808
8	3	28.32808	53	-0.01186197	27.99205
9	4	27.99205	37	0.030415009	28.84343
10	5	28.84343	52	-0.021098581	28.23487
11	6	28.23487	1	-0.121118012	24.81512
12	7	24.81512	23	-0.052040634	23.52373
13	8	23.52373	22	-0.095694679	21.27263
14	9	21.27263	12	-0.086533666	19.43183
15	10	19.43183	10	0.05716676	20.54269
16	11	20.54269	6	-0.028489284	19.95744
17	12	19.95744	19	0.011168193	20.18033

Figure 62-2   Simulating GE stock price in one year

Copying from M6 to M7:M17 the formula *(1+L6)*J6* determines each month's ending GE price. The formula takes the form *(1+ month's return)*(GE's beginning price)*. Finally, copying from J7 to J8:J17 the formula *=M6* computes the beginning price for each month as equal to the previous month's ending price.

We can now use a data table to generate 1000 scenarios for GE's price in one year and the one-year percentage return on our investment. The data table is shown in Figure 62-3. In cell J19, we copy our ending price with the formula *=M17*. In cell K19, we enter the formula *(M17–$J$6)/$J$6* to compute our one-year return as *(Ending GE price–Beginning GE price)/Beginning GE price*.

	J	K	L	M
18	End Price	End Return		
19	20.18033	-0.291918237	Mean	0.095537
20	25.62257	-0.100962286	Prob lose money	0.423
21	26.08858	-0.084611262	Prob make more than 10	0.439
22	31.2921	0.097968372	Make between 0 and 10%	0.138
23	42.92831	0.506256338	Lose between 0 and 10%	0.138
24	27.8614	-0.022407115	Lose More than 10%	0.285
25	35.60087	0.249153247		
26	31.41249	0.10219249		
27	30.04267	0.054128706		
28	25.83123	-0.093641212		
29	17.89813	-0.37199552		
30	23.50018	-0.175432256		
31	18.17147	-0.362404511		
32	34.08932	0.196116577		
33	22.941	-0.195052492		
34	18.65622	-0.345395692		
35	41.34783	0.450801148		
36	26.62092	-0.06593271		
37	29.91614	0.04968897		

Figure 62-3   Data table for GE simulation

Next we select our table range (J19:K1019), click What-If Analysis in the Data Tools group on the Data tab, and then select Data Table. We set up a one-way data table by selecting a blank cell as our Column Input Cell. After we click OK in the Data Table dialog box, we have generated 1000 scenarios for GE's stock price in one year. (The calculation option for this workbook has been set to Automatic Except For Tables on the Formulas tab in the Excel Options dialog box. You need to press F9 if you want to see the simulated prices change.)

In cells M20:M24, I used the COUNTIF function (see Chapter 18, "The COUNTIF, COUNTIFS, COUNT, COUNTA, and COUNTBLANK Functions") to summarize the range of returns that can occur in one year. For example, in cell M20, I computed the probability that we will lose money in one year with the formula *COUNTIF(returns,"<0")/ 1000*. (I named the range containing our 1000 simulated returns as *Returns*.) Our simulation indicates that, based on the data for 1997–2002, there is roughly a 42-percent chance that our GE investment will lose money during the next year. Similarly, we find the following results:

- There is a 44 percent probability that we will make more than 10 percent.
- There is a 14 percent probability that we will make between 0 and 10 percent.
- There is a 14 percent chance that we will lose between 0 and 10 percent.
- There is a 29 percent chance that we will lose more than 10 percent.
- The average return for the next year will be approximately 10 percent.

Many pundits believe that future stock returns will not be as good as in the recent past. Suppose we feel that in the next year, GE will perform 5 percent worse per year on average than it performed during the 1997–2002 period for which we have data. We can easily incorporate this assumption into our simulation by changing the final price formula for GE in cell M17 to *(1+L17)*J17−0.05*J6*. This simply reduces our ending GE price by 5 percent of its initial price, which will reduce our returns for the next year by 5 percent. You can see these results in the file Gesimless5.xlsx, shown in Figure 62-4.

	L	M
19	Mean	0.062461
20	Prob lose money	0.496
21	Prob make more than 10	0.391
22	Make between 0 and 10%	0.113
23	Lose between 0 and 10%	0.147
24	Lose More than 10%	0.349

Figure 62-4 Pessimistic view of the future

Note that we now estimate that there is a 42 percent chance that the price of GE stock will decrease during the next year. Our average is not exactly 5 percent lower than the previous simulation because each time we run 1000 iterations, the simulated values change.

I'm trying to determine how to allocate my investment portfolio between stocks, T-Bills, and bonds. What asset allocation over a five-year planning horizon will yield an expected return of at least 10 percent and minimize risk?

A key decision made by individuals, mutual fund managers, and other investors is how to allocate assets between different asset classes given the future uncertainty about returns for these asset classes. A reasonable approach to asset allocation is to use bootstrapping to generate 1000 simulated values for the future values of each asset class, and then use the Excel Solver to determine an asset allocation that yields an expected return yet minimizes risk. As an example, suppose we are given annual returns on stocks, T-Bills, and bonds during the 1972–2001 period. We are investing for a five-year planning horizon, and based on the historical data, we want to know which asset allocation yields a minimum risk (as measured by standard deviation) of annual returns and yields an annual expected return of at least 10 percent. You can see this data in the file Assetallsim.xlsx, shown in Figure 62-5. (Not all the data is shown.)

	A	B	C	D
6		**Annual Returns on Investments in**		
7	Year	Stocks	T.Bills	T.Bonds
8	1972	18.76%	4.01%	2.82%
9	1973	-14.31%	5.07%	3.66%
10	1974	-25.90%	7.45%	1.99%
11	1975	37.00%	7.15%	3.61%
12	1976	23.83%	5.44%	15.98%
13	1977	-6.98%	4.35%	1.29%
14	1978	6.51%	6.07%	-0.78%
15	1979	18.52%	9.08%	0.67%
16	1980	31.74%	12.04%	-2.99%
17	1981	-4.70%	15.49%	8.20%
18	1982	20.42%	10.85%	32.81%
19	1983	22.34%	7.94%	3.20%
20	1984	6.15%	9.00%	13.73%
21	1985	31.24%	8.06%	25.71%
22	1986	18.49%	7.10%	24.28%
23	1987	5.81%	5.53%	-4.96%
24	1988	16.54%	5.77%	8.22%
25	1989	31.48%	8.07%	17.69%
26	1990	-3.06%	7.63%	6.24%
27	1991	30.23%	6.74%	15.00%
28	1992	7.49%	4.07%	9.36%
29	1993	9.97%	3.22%	14.21%
30	1994	1.33%	3.06%	-8.04%
31	1995	37.20%	5.60%	23.48%
32	1996	23.82%	5.14%	1.43%
33	1997	31.86%	4.91%	9.94%
34	1998	28.34%	5.16%	14.92%

Figure 62-5   Historical returns on stocks, T-Bills, and bonds

To begin, we use bootstrapping to generate 1000 simulated values for stocks, T-Bills, and bonds in five years. We assume that each asset class has a current price of $1. (See Figure 62-6 on the next page.)

For each asset class, we enter an initial unit price of $1 in the cell range H10:J10. Next, by copying from K10 to K11:K14 the formula *RANDBETWEEN(1972,2001)*, we generate a "scenario" for each of the next five years. For example, for the data shown, next year will be similar to 1976, the following year will be similar to 1990, and so on. Copying from L10 to L10:N14 the formula *H10*(1+VLOOKUP($K10,lookup,L$8))* generates each year's ending value for each asset class. For stocks, for example, this formula computes the following:

```
(Ending year t stock value)=(Beginning year t stock value)*(1+Year t stock return)
```

	G	H	I	J	K	L	M	N
8						2	3	4
9	Year	Stock value	Bill value	Bond value	Scenario	End stock	End bill	End bond
10	1	1	1	1	1985	1.3124	1.0806	1.2571
11	2	1.3124	1.0806	1.2571	1985	1.72239	1.1677	1.5803
12	3	1.72239	1.16769636	1.5803	1978	1.83452	1.23858	1.56797
13	4	1.83452	1.23857553	1.56797	1997	2.419	1.29939	1.72383
14	5	2.419	1.29938959	1.72383	1995	3.31887	1.37216	2.12859
15			5 yr stock	5 year bill	5 yr bond			
16			3.31886824	1.37216	2.12859			
17		1	1.67360377	1.32943	1.69812			
18		2	1.95600394	1.46412	1.67342			
19		3	1.27982353	1.37578	1.4869			
20		4	3.55882722	1.35336	1.23763			
21		5	1.61100945	1.37211	1.281			
22		6	1.57671808	1.34	1.19834			
23		7	1.68869935	1.34234	1.27131			
24		8	1.39166657	1.29792	1.55144			
25		9	1.71538608	1.41724	1.20564			
26		10	2.23218752	1.41606	1.59484			
27		11	2.1384895	1.33944	1.19276			
28		12	2.16364065	1.33261	1.57672			
29		13	2.19687312	1.51345	2.07398			
30		14	1.33565445	1.38396	2.14179			
31		15	2.75297752	1.37628	1.41747			
32		16	1.70597614	1.28614	1.22799			
33		17	3.14304495	1.38294	1.71713			
34		18	1.09656978	1.32469	1.5498			

Figure 62-6 Simulating five-year returns on stocks, T-Bills, and bonds

Copying from H11 to H11:J14 the formula =*L10* computes the value for each asset class at the beginning of each successive year.

We can now use a one-way data table to generate 1000 scenarios of the value of stocks, T-Bills, and bonds in five years. Begin by copying the year 5 ending value for each asset class to cells I16:K16. Next select our table range (H16:K1015), click What If Analysis on the Data tab, and then click Data Table. Use any blank cell as the Column Input Cell to set up a one-way data table. After clicking OK in the Data Table dialog box, we obtain 1000 simulated values for the value of stocks, T-Bills, and bonds over five years. It is important to note that our approach models the fact that stock, T-Bills, and bonds do not move independently. In each of our five years, the stock, T-Bill, and bond returns are always chosen from the same row of data. This enables the bootstrapping approach to reflect the interdependence of returns on these asset classes that has been exhibited during the recent past. (See Problem 7 at the end of this chapter for concrete evidence that bootstrapping appropriately models the interdependence between the returns on our three asset classes.)

We are now ready to find the optimal asset allocation, which I've calculated in the file Assetallocationopt.xlsx, shown in Figure 62-7. To start, I copy the 1000 simulated five-year asset values to a blank worksheet and paste them into the cell range C4:E1003. In cells C2:E2, I enter trial fractions of our assets allocated to stocks, T-Bills, and bonds, respectively. In cell F2, I add these asset allocation fractions with the formula *SUM(C2:E2)*. Later, I'll add the constraint *F2=1* to our Solver model, which will ensure that we invest 100 percent of our money in one of the three asset classes.

	B	C	D	E	F	G	H	I	J
3	Iteration#	5 yr stock	5 yr bill	5 yr bond	final value	annual return		mean	0.1
4	1	2.415411	1.35984	1.108607	1.791653	0.12370102		stdev	0.040506
5	2	1.603314	1.33449	1.702971	1.524234	0.087953549			
6	3	1.03961	1.386724	1.087423	1.174277	0.032652262			
7	4	1.070247	1.442663	1.295489	1.246816	0.045106348			
8	5	1.984675	1.372362	1.504565	1.674116	0.108554718			
9	6	2.590193	1.35308	1.562307	1.952067	0.14313876			
10	7	2.182375	1.490447	1.915396	1.882267	0.134844236			
11	8	2.985769	1.399561	1.107142	2.064147	0.155974163			
12	9	1.461413	1.316099	1.734171	1.459044	0.078483862			
13	10	1.393477	1.524212	1.397079	1.44154	0.075883679			
14	11	1.72976	1.325904	1.344169	1.512213	0.086232064			
15	12	1.766351	1.466968	1.30982	1.573596	0.094910539			
16	13	1.709322	1.345	1.665987	1.569242	0.094304044			
17	14	1.588212	1.447162	1.180382	1.461844	0.078897558			
18	15	1.100759	1.347678	1.450658	1.254824	0.046445346			
19	16	2.090239	1.309887	1.559685	1.709453	0.113195452			
20	17	2.249205	1.427347	1.094926	1.738316	0.116929413			
21	18	2.18594	1.348865	2.084102	1.863671	0.132592993			
22	19	2.919315	1.416379	1.059493	2.031352	0.152277354			
23	20	1.367889	1.316715	1.459127	1.366166	0.06438978			
24	21	1.387159	1.451299	1.460458	1.423934	0.073242829			
25	22	1.977994	1.384595	2.027603	1.772008	0.121225879			
26	23	1.399248	1.383007	1.237254	1.363478	0.063970524			
27	24	1.778459	1.534788	1.330409	1.607466	0.09958392			
28	25	1.786845	1.362789	1.745657	1.625505	0.102040713			

Figure 62-7   Optimal asset allocation model

Next we want to determine our final portfolio value for each scenario. To make this calculation, we can use a formula such as *(Final portfolio value)=(Final value of stocks)+(Final value of T-bills)+(Final value of bonds)*. Copying from cell F4 to F5:F1003 the formula *SUMPRODUCT(C4:E4,$C$2:$E$2)* determines our final asset position for each scenario.

We now want to determine the annual return over the five-year simulated period for each scenario we generated. Note that $(1+ Annual\ return)^5=(Final\ portfolio\ value)/(Initial\ portfolio\ value)$. Because the initial portfolio value is just \$1, this tells us that *Annual return=(Final portfolio value)$^{1/5}$–1*.

Therefore, by copying from cell G4 to G5:G1003 the formula *(F4/1)^(1/5)–1*, we compute the annual return for each scenario during our five-year simulated period. After naming the range G4:G1003 (which contains the simulated annual returns) as *Returns*, I computed the average annual return in cell J3 with the formula *AVERAGE(returns)* and the standard deviation of our annual returns in cell J4 with the formula *STDEV(returns)*.

Now we're ready to use Solver to determine the set of allocation weights that yields an expected annual return of at least 10 percent yet minimizes the standard deviation of our annual returns. The Solver Parameters dialog box set up to perform this calculation is shown in Figure 62-8 on the next page.

Figure 62-8 Solver Parameters dialog box set up for our asset allocation model

❑ We try to minimize the standard deviation of our annual portfolio return (cell J4).

❑ Our changing cells are our asset allocation weights (cells C2:E2).

❑ We must allocate 100 percent of our money to the three asset classes (*F2=1*).

❑ Our expected annual return must be at least 10 percent (*J3>=0.1*).

❑ We assume that no short sales are allowed, which is modeled by forcing the fraction of our money in each asset class to be nonnegative (*C2:E2>=0*).

We find that the minimum risk asset allocation is 45.3 percent stocks, 36.3 percent T-Bills, and 18.4 percent bonds. This portfolio yields an expected annual return of 10 percent and an annual standard deviation of 4.1 percent. Deleting the constraint *C2:E2>=0* yields the same solution, so it appears there is no benefit to short selling.

Suppose we believe that the next 5 years will, on average, produce returns for stocks that are 5 percent worse than the last 30 years. It is easy to incorporate these expectations into our simulation (see Problem 4 at the end of the chapter).

Problems

The following problems utilize data in the file Gesim.xlsx.

1. Assume that the current price of Microsoft stock is $28 per share. What is the probability that in two years the price of Microsoft stock will be at least $35?

2. Solve Problem 1 again, but this time with the assumption that during the next two years, Microsoft will on average perform 6 percent better per year than it performed during the 1997–2002 period for which we have data.

3. Assume that the current price of Intel is $20 per share. What is the probability that during the next three years, we will earn at least a 30 percent return (for the three-year period) on a purchase of Intel stock?

Problems 1 through 3 utilize data in the file Asselallsim.xlsx.

4. Suppose you believe that over the next five years, stocks will produce returns that are 5 percent worse per year, on average, than our 1972–2001 data. Find an asset allocation between stocks, T-Bills, and bonds that yields an expected annual return of at least 6 percent yet minimizes risk.

5. Suppose you believe that it is two times more likely that investment returns for each of the next five years will be more like the period 1992–2001 than the period 1972–1991. For example, the chance that next year will be like 1993 has twice the probability that next year will be like 1980. This belief causes your bootstrapping analysis to give more weight to the recent past. How would you factor this belief into your portfolio optimization model?

6. Many mutual funds and investors hedge the risk that stocks will go down by purchasing put options. (See Chapter 63, "Fun and Games: Simulating Gambling and Sporting Event Probabilities," for more discussion of put options.) How could our asset allocation model be used to determine an optimal hedging strategy that uses puts?

7. Determine the correlations (based on our 1972–2001 data) between annual returns on stocks, T-Bills, and bonds. Then determine the correlation (based on our 1000 scenarios created by bootstrapping) between the final values for stocks, T-Bills, and assets. Does it appear that the bootstrapping approach picks up the interdependence between the returns on stocks, T-Bills, and bonds?

Chapter 63

Fun and Games: Simulating Gambling and Sporting Event Probabilities

- What is the probability of winning at craps?

- In five-card draw poker, what is the probability of getting three of a kind?

- Before the 2003 Super Bowl, Oakland was favored by 3 points. What was the probability that Tampa Bay would beat Oakland?

- Going into the 2003 NCAA men's basketball Final Four, what was the probability of each team winning the tournament?

Gambling and following sporting events are popular pastimes. I think gambling and sports are exciting because you never know what's going to happen. Monte Carlo simulation is a powerful tool that can be used to predict gambling and sporting event probabilities. Essentially, we predict probability by playing out our gambling or sporting event situation multiple times. If, for example, we have Microsoft Office Excel 2007 play out the game of craps 10,000 times and we win 4900 times, we would estimate the probability of winning at craps to equal 4900/10,000, or 49 percent. If we play out the 2003 NCAA men's Final Four 1000 times and Syracuse wins 300 of our iterations, we would estimate Syracuse's probability of winning the championship as 300/1000, or 30 percent.

What is the probability of winning at craps?

In the game of craps, a player rolls two dice. If the combination is 2, 3, or 12, the player loses. If the combination is 7 or 11, the player wins. If the combination is a different number, the player continues rolling the dice until he or she either matches the number thrown on the first roll (called the *point*) or rolls 7. If the player rolls the point before rolling 7, the player wins. If the player rolls 7 before rolling the point, the player loses. By complex calculations, we can show that the probability of a player winning at craps is 0.493. We can use Excel to simulate the game of craps many times (I chose 2000) to demonstrate this probability.

In this example, it is crucial to keep in mind that we don't know how many rolls the game will take. We can show that the chance of a game requiring more than 50 rolls of the dice is highly unlikely, so we'll play out 50 rolls of the dice. After each roll, we keep track of the game status as follows:

- ❏ 0 equals the game is lost.
- ❏ 1 equals the game is won.
- ❏ 2 equals the game continues.

Our output cell will keep track of the status of the game after the 50th roll by recording 1 to indicate a win and 0 to indicate a loss. You can review the work I did in the file Craps.xlsx, shown in Figure 63-1.

	A	B	C	D	E	F	G	H	AX	AY
1	TOSS#		1	2	3	4	5	6	7	49	50
2	Die Toss 1		2	1	4	2	5	3	4	2	6
3	Die Toss 2		6	1	2	2	1	2	5	6	5
4	Total		8	2	6	4	6	5	9	8	11
5	GAME STATUS		2	2	2	2	2	2	2	1	1
6		WIN??	1								
7											
8				prob win	0.4925						
9					1						
10				1	0						
11				2	0						
12				3	1						
13				4	1						
14				5	0						
15				6	0						
16				7	1						

Figure 63-1   Simulating a game of craps

In cell B2, I used the RANDBETWEEN function to generate the number on the first die on the first roll by using the formula RANDBETWEEN(1,6). The RANDBETWEEN function ensures that each of its arguments is equally likely, so each die has an equal (1/6) chance of yielding 1, 2, 3, 4, 5, or 6. Copying this formula to the range B2:AY3 generates 50 rolls of the dice. (In Figure 63-1, I've hidden rolls 8–48.)

In the cell range B4:AY4, I compute the total dice combination for each of the 50 rolls by copying from B4 to C4:AY4 the formula SUM(B2:B3). In cell B5, I determine the game status after the first roll with the formula IF(OR(B4=2,B4=3,B4=12),0,IF(OR(B4=7, B4=11),1,2)). Remember that a roll of 2, 3, or 12 results in a loss (entering 0 in the cell); a roll of 7 or 11 results in a win (1); and any other roll results in the game continuing (2).

In cell C5, I compute the status of the game after the second roll with the formula IF(OR(B5=0,B5=1),B5,IF(C4=$B4,1,IF(C4=7,0,2))). If the game ended on the first roll, we maintain the status of the game. If we make our point, we record a win with 1. If we roll a 7, we record a loss. Otherwise, the game continues. I added a dollar sign in the reference to column B ($B4) in this formula to ensure that with each roll, we try to match the point thrown on the first roll. Copying this formula from C5 to D5:AY5 records the game status after rolls 2 through 50.

The game result is in cell AY5, which is copied to C6 so that we can easily see it. I then use a one-way data table to play out the game of craps 2000 times. In cell E9 I enter the formula =C6, which tracks the final outcome of the game (0 if a loss or 1 if a win). Next I select the table range (D9:E2009), click What-If Analysis in the Data Tools group on the Data tab, and then click Data Table. I choose a one-way table with any blank cell as our Column Input Cell. After pressing F9, I've simulated the game of craps 2000 times.

In cell E8, I can compute the fraction of our simulations that result in wins with the formula *AVERAGE(E10:E2009)*. For our 2000 iterations, we won 49.25 percent of the time. If we had run more trials (for example, 10,000 iterations), we would have come closer to the true probability of winning at craps (49.3%). For information about using a one-way data table, see Chapter 15, "Sensitivity Analysis with Data Tables."

In five-card draw poker, what is the probability of getting three of a kind?

An ordinary deck of cards contains four cards of each type—four aces, four deuces, and so on, up to four kings. To estimate the probability of getting a particular poker hand, we'll assign the value 1 to an ace, 2 to a deuce, and on up through the deck so that a jack is assigned the value 11, a queen is assigned 12, and a king is assigned 13.

In five-card draw poker, you are dealt five cards. Many probabilities are of interest, but let's use simulation to estimate the probability of getting three of a kind, which requires that you have three of one type of card and no pairs. (If you have a pair and three of a kind, the hand is a full house.) To simulate the five cards drawn, we proceed as follows. (See the file Poker.xlsx, shown in Figure 63-2.)

❑ Associate a random number with each card in the deck.

❑ The five cards chosen will be the five cards associated with the five smallest random numbers, which gives each card an equal chance of being chosen.

❑ Count how many of each card (ace through king) are drawn.

Drawn hand	Rank			Rand#			How many	
1	10	31	1	0.71306			1	2
2	1	2	1	0.03766			2	0
3	1	3	1	0.17002			3	0
4	11	41	1	0.8892			4	0
5	13	24	2	0.62369			5	0
		47	2	0.93495			6	0
		25	2	0.62608			7	0
		7	2	0.21112			8	0
		36	3	0.83048			9	0
		29	3	0.66026			10	1
		50	3	0.98107			11	1
		39	3	0.85802			12	0
		45	4	0.92899			13	1
		33	4	0.78035				
		12	4	0.35047			three of kind?	0
		32	4	0.73819				
		49	5	0.96826				0
		51	5	0.99258	prob 3 of kind		1	0
		21	5	0.55513	0.019		2	0
		28	5	0.64091			3	0
		22	6	0.5785			4	0
		15	6	0.37902			5	0
		6	6	0.20446			6	0
		42	6	0.92167			7	0

Figure 63-2   Estimating the probability that we'll draw three of a kind in a poker game

To begin, we list in cells D3:D54 all the cards in the deck: four 1s, four 2s, and so on up to four 13s. Then we copy from cell E3 to E4:E54 the RAND() function to associate a random number with each card in the deck. Copying from C3 to C4:C54 the formula

RANK(E3,$E$3:$E$54,1) gives the rank (ordered from smallest to largest) of each random number. For example, in Figure 63-2, you can see that the first 3 in the deck (row 11) is associated with the 32nd smallest random number. (You will see different results in the worksheet because the random numbers are automatically recalculated when you open the worksheet.)

The syntax of the RANK function is *RANK(number,array,1 or 0)*. If the last argument of the RANK function is 1, the function returns the rank of the number in the array with the smallest number receiving a rank of 1, the second smallest number a rank of 2, and so on. If the last argument of the RANK function is 0, the function returns the rank of the number in the array with the largest number receiving a rank of 1, the second largest number receiving a rank of 2, and so on.

When ranking random numbers, no ties can occur (because the random numbers would have to match 16 digits).

Suppose, for example, we were ranking the numbers 1, 3, 3, and 4 and that the last argument of the RANK function was 1. Excel would return the following ranks:

Number	Rank (smallest number has rank of 1)
1	1
3	2
3	2
4	4

Because 3 is the second smallest number, 3 would be assigned a rank of 2. The other 3 would also be assigned a rank of 2. Because 4 is the fourth smallest number, it will be assigned a rank of 4. Understanding the treatment of ties by the RANK function will help you complete Problem 1 at the end of the chapter.

By copying from cell B3 to B4:B7 the formula *VLOOKUP(A3,lookup,2,FALSE)*, we can draw our five cards from the deck. This formula draws the five cards corresponding to the five smallest random numbers. (The lookup table range C3:D54 has been named *Lookup.*) We use *FALSE* in the VLOOKUP function because the ranks need not be in ascending order.

Having assigned the range name *Drawn* to our drawn cards (the range B3:B7), copying from J3 to J4:J15 the formula *COUNTIF(drawn,I3)* counts how many of each card are in our drawn hand. In cell J17, we determine whether we have three of a kind with the formula *IF(AND(MAX(J3:J15)=3,COUNTIF(J3:J15,2)=0),1,0)*. This formula returns a 1 if, and only if, our hand has three of one kind and no pairs.

We now use a one-way data table to simulate 4000 poker hands. In cell J19, we recopy the results of cell J17 with the formula *=J17*. Next we select our table range (I19:J4019). After clicking What-If Analysis in the Data Tools group on the Data tab, and then clicking Data Table, we set up a one-way data table by selecting any blank cell as our Column

Input Cell. After clicking OK, we have simulated 4000 poker hands. In cell G21, we record our estimated probability of three of a kind with the formula *AVERAGE(J20: J4019)*. We estimate the chance of three of a kind at 1.9 percent. (Using basic probability theory, we can show that the true probability of drawing three of a kind is 2.1 percent.)

Before the 2003 Super Bowl, Oakland was favored by 3 points. What was the probability that Tampa Bay would beat Oakland?

Extensive study by my friend, Jeff Sagarin (check out his sports ratings at *http:// www.usatoday.com/sports/sagarin.htm*), has shown that the number of points by which the favorite wins a college or professional football or basketball game follows a normal distribution with the mean equal to the bookies' forecast, with a standard deviation of 16 points for professional football, 14 points for college football, 12 points for professional basketball, and 10 points for college basketball. Therefore, the number of points by which Oakland wins the Super Bowl (Oakland winning by a negative number of points means they lose) is normally distributed with a mean of 3 and a standard deviation of 16 points. Again, for Oakland to lose, they must win by 0 points or less.

This problem can be computed with the formula *NORMDIST(0,3,16, True)*. (See Chapter 58, "The Normal Random Variable," for a discussion of the NORMDIST function.) This function yields a 42.6 percent chance for Oakland to lose. As we know, Tampa Bay won the game, but this was not a totally unexpected outcome.

Going into the 2003 NCAA men's basketball Final Four, what was the probability of each team winning the tournament?

Using a methodology similar to that described in Chapter 32, "Using Solver to Rate Sports Teams," where we used the Excel Solver to rate sports teams, you can use the scores of previous games to develop ratings for each college basketball team. On the eve of the 2003 men's Final Four, the ratings of the four teams were Syracuse, 91.03; Kansas, 92.76; Marquette, 89.01; and Texas, 90.66. Given this information, we can play out the Final Four several thousand times to estimate the chance that each team will win.

Our mean prediction for the number of points by which the home team wins equals *favorite rating–underdog rating*. In the Final Four, there is no home team, but if there was one, we would add 5 points to the home team's rating. (In professional basketball, the home edge is 4 points, and in college and pro football, the home edge is three points.) Then we can use the NORMINV function to simulate the outcome of each game. (See Chapter 58, "The Normal Random Variable," for a discussion of using the NORMINV function to simulate a normal random variable.)

We've calculated the likely outcome of the 2003 Final Four in the file Final4sim.xlsx, shown in Figure 63-3 on the next page. The semifinals pitted Kansas against Marquette and Syracuse against Texas.

	C	D	E	F	G	H	I	J	K	L	M
2			Semifinals								
3		Rating	Outcome	rand#							
4	KU	92.76	0.888992	0.3874	Final	rand#	Forecast	Outcome	Winner		
5	MARQ	89.01			KU	0.79265	92.76	9.88642	KU		
6					SYR		91.03				
7											
8	SYR	91.03	12.41063	0.88572							
9	TEX	90.66									
10											
11							odds		PROB WIN		KU
12							1.5641	KU	0.39	1	TEX
13							3.7619	TEX	0.21	2	TEX
14							3	SYR	0.25	3	MARQ
15							5.66667	MARQ	0.15	4	MARQ
16										5	KU
17										6	KU
18										7	TEX
19										8	KU
20										9	TEX
21										10	SYR
22										11	SYR
23										12	TEX
24										13	KU
25										14	TEX
26										15	KU
27										16	MARQ

Figure 63-3 Simulating the outcome of the NCAA 2003 Final Four

To begin, we enter each team's name and rating in the cell range C4:D5 and C8:D9. In cell F4, we use the RAND() function to enter a random number for the Marquette–Kansas game, and in cell F8, we enter a random number for the Syracuse–Texas game. Our simulated outcome is always relative to the top team listed.

In cell E4, we determine the outcome of the Kansas–Marquette game (from the standpoint of Kansas) with the formula *NORMINV(F4,D4–D5,10)*. Note that Kansas is favored by *D4–D5* points. In cell E8, we determine the outcome of the Texas–Syracuse game (from the standpoint of Syracuse) with the formula *NORMINV(F8,D8–D9,10)*. (Remember that the standard deviation for the winning margin of college basketball games is 10 points.)

In cells G5 and G6, we ensure that the winner of each semifinal game moves on to the finals. A semifinal outcome of greater than 0 causes the top-listed team to win; otherwise, the bottom-listed team wins. Thus, in cell G5, we enter the winner of the first game by using the formula *IF(E4>0,"KU", "MARQ")*. In cell G6, we enter the winner of the second game by using the formula *IF(E8>0,"SYR","TEX")*.

In cell H5, we enter a random number that will be used to simulate the outcome of the championship game. Copying from I5 to I6 the formula *VLOOKUP(G5,$C$4:$D$9, 2,FALSE)* obtains the rating for each team in the championship game. Next, in cell J5, we compute the outcome of the championship game (from the reference point of the top-listed team in cell G5) with the formula *NORMINV(H5,I5–I6,10)*. Finally, in cell K5, we determine the actual champion with the formula *IF(J5>0,G5,G6)*.

Now we can use a one-way data table in the usual fashion to play out the Final Four 2000 times. Our simulated winners are in the cell range M12:M2011. Copying from K12 to K13:K15 the formula *COUNTIF($M$12:$M$2011,J12)/2000* computes the predicted probability for each team winning: 39 percent for Kansas, 25 percent for Syracuse, 21 percent for Texas, and 15 percent for Marquette. These probabilities can be translated to odds using the following formula:

$$\text{Odds against team winning} = \frac{prob\ team\ loses}{prob\ team\ wins}$$

For example, the odds against Kansas are 1.56 to 1:

$$\frac{1 - .39}{.39} = 1.56$$

This means that if we placed $1 on Kansas to win and a bookmaker paid us $1.56 for a Kansas championship, the bet is fair. Of course, the bookie will lower these odds slightly to ensure that he makes money. (See Problem 6 at the end of this chapter for a related exercise.)

Our methodology can easily be extended to simulate the entire NCAA tournament. Just use IF statements to ensure that each winner advances, and use LOOKUP functions to find each team's rating. See the file Ncaa2003.xlsx for a simulation of the 2003 tournament. We gave Syracuse a 4-percent chance to win at the start of tournament.

In this worksheet, I used comments to explain my work, which you can see in Figure 63-4 on the next page. Here is some background about using comments:

❑ To insert a comment in a cell, select the cell, and on the Review tab, in the Comments group, click New Comment and then type your comment text. You will see a small red mark in the upper-right corner of any cell containing a comment.

❑ To edit a comment, right-click the cell containing the comment, and click Edit Comment.

❑ To make a comment always visible, right-click the cell, and click Show/Hide Comments. Clicking Hide Comment when the comment is displayed causes the comment to be hidden unless the pointer is in the cell containing the comment.

❑ If you want to print your comments, click the Page Setup dialog box launcher (the small arrow in the bottom right corner of the group) on the Page Layout tab to display the Page Setup dialog box. In the Comments box on the Sheet tab, you can indicate whether you want comments printed as displayed on the sheet or at the end of the sheet.

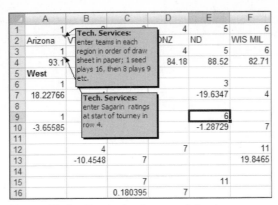

Figure 63-4 Comments in a worksheet

Problems

1. Suppose 30 people are in a room. What is the probability that at least two of them have the same birthday?

2. What is the probability of getting one pair in five-card draw poker?

3. What is the probability of getting two pairs in five-card draw poker?

4. In the game of keno, 80 balls (numbered 1–80) are mixed up, and then 20 balls are randomly drawn. Before the 20 balls are drawn, a player chooses 10 different numbers. If at least 5 of the numbers are drawn, the player wins. What is the probability of winning?

5. Going into the 2003 NBA finals, Jeff Sagarin rated San Antonio 3 points higher than New Jersey. The teams play until one team wins four games. The first two games were at San Antonio, the next three at New Jersey, and the final two games were scheduled for San Antonio. What is the probability that San Antonio will win the series?

6. What odds should the bookmaker give on Kansas winning the Final Four if the bookmaker wants to earn an average of 10 cents per dollar bet?

Chapter 64

Using Resampling to Analyze Data

- I've produced nine batches of a product by using a high temperature and seven batches by using a low temperature. What is the probability that the product yield is better at the high temperature?

In our work and personal lives, we often use data to answer questions such as these:

- What is the probability that a new teaching technique improves student learning?

- What is the probability that aspirin reduces the incidence of heart attacks?

- What is the probability that Machine 1 is the most productive of our three machines?

You can use a simple yet powerful technique known as *resampling* to make inferences from data. To make statistical inferences by using resampling, you regenerate data many times by sampling with replacement from your data. Sampling with replacement from data means that the same data point can be chosen more than once. You then make inferences based on the results of this repeated sampling. A key tool in implementing resampling is the RANDBE-TWEEN function. Entering the function *RANDBETWEEN(a,b)* yields with equal probability any integer between *a* and *b* (inclusive). For example, *RANDBETWEEN(1,9)* is equally likely to yield one of the numbers 1 through 9, inclusive.

I've produced nine batches of a product by using a high temperature and seven batches by using a low temperature. What is the probability that the product yield is better at the high temperature?

The file Resampleyield.xlsx, shown in Figure 64-1 on the next page, contains the product yield from nine batches of a product manufactured at a high temperature and seven batches manufactured at a low temperature.

The mean yield at a high temperature is 39.74, and the mean yield at a low temperature is 32.27. This difference does not prove, however, that mean yield at a high temperature is better than mean yield at a low temperature. We want to know, based on our sample data, the probability that yield at a high temperature is better than at a low temperature. To answer this question, we can randomly generate nine integers between 1 and 9, which creates a resampling of the high-temperature yields. For example, if we generate the random number 4, the resampled data for high-temperature yields will include a yield of 41.40, and so on. Next we randomly generate seven integers between 1 and 7, which creates our resampling of the low-temperature yields. We can then check the resampled data to see whether the high-temperature mean is larger than the low-temperature mean, and then use a data table to repeat this process several hundred times. (I repeated the process 400 times in this example.) In the resampled data, the fraction of the time that the high-temperature mean is larger than the low-temperature mean estimates the probability that the high-temperature process is superior to the low-temperature process.

	C	D	E
3	mean	39.74	32.27
4	Number	High Temp	Low Temp
5	1	17.55	37.37
6	2	39.93	43.20
7	3	48.98	34.85
8	4	41.40	31.22
9	5	35.70	26.59
10	6	42.24	42.67
11	7	54.75	10.00
12	8	46.96	
13	9	30.19	

Figure 64-1   Product yields at high and low temperature

To begin, we generate a resampling of the high-temperature data by copying from cell C16 to C17:C24 the formula *RANDBETWEEN(1,9)*, as shown in Figure 64-2. A given observation can be chosen more than once or not chosen at all. Copying from cell D16 to D17:D24 the formula *VLOOKUP(C16,lookup,2)*–the range C4:E13 has been named *Lookup*–generates the yields corresponding to our random resampling of the data. Next we generate a resampling from our low-temperature yields. Copying from E16 to E17:E22 the formula *RANDBETWEEN(1,7)* generates a resampling of seven observations from our original low-temperature data. Copying from F16 to F17:F22 the formula *VLOOKUP(E16,lookup,3)* generates the seven actual resampled low-temperature yields.

	C	D	E	F
15	Resampled	High Temp	Resampled	Low Temp
16	9	30.19	2	43.20
17	6	42.24	4	31.22
18	9	30.19	3	34.85
19	3	48.98	4	31.22
20	8	46.96	3	34.85
21	1	17.55	7	10.00
22	6	42.24	4	31.22
23	5	35.70		
24	3	48.98		
25				
26	Average	38.11		30.94
27				
28				
29	High better	1		
30				Prob high better
31		1		0.91
32	1	1		
33	2	1		
34	3	1		
35	4	0		
36	5	1		
37	6	1		
38	7	1		

Figure 64-2   Implementation of resampling

In cell D26, I compute the mean of our resampled high-temperature yields with the formula *AVERAGE(D16:D24)*. Similarly, in cell F26, I compute the mean of our resampled low-temperature yields with the formula *AVERAGE(F16:F22)*. In cell D29, I determine whether the resampled mean for high temperature is larger than the resampled mean for low temperature with the formula *IF(D26>F26,1,0)*.

To replay our resampling 400 times, we can use a one-way data table. I copy iteration numbers 1 through 400 to the cell range C32:431. (See Chapter 60, "Introduction to Monte Carlo Simulation," for an explanation of how to use the Fill Series command to easily create a list of iteration values.) By typing *=D29* in cell D31, I create the formula that records whether high-temperature mean is larger than low-temperature mean in the output cell for our data table. After selecting the table range (C31:D431) and then selecting Data Table from the What-If Analysis command in the Data Tools group on the Data tab, we can choose any blank cell in the worksheet as our Column Input Cell. We have now tricked Microsoft Office Excel 2007 into playing out our resampling 400 times. Each iteration with a value of 1 indicates a resampling in which high temperature has the larger mean. Each iteration with a value of 0 indicates a resampling for which low temperature has a larger mean. In cell F31, I determine the fraction of time that high-temperature yield has a larger mean by using the formula *=AVERAGE(D32:D431)*. In Figure 64-2, our resampling indicates a 91 percent chance that high temperature has a larger mean than low temperature. Of course, pressing F9 will generate a different set of 400 resamplings and will give us a slightly different estimate of the probability that high temperature yield is superior to low temperature yield.

Problems

1. We are testing a new flu drug. Out of 24 flu victims who were given the drug, 20 felt better and 4 felt worse. Out of 9 flu victims who were given a placebo, 6 felt better and 3 felt worse. What is the probability that the drug is more effective than the placebo?

2. A talk on the dangers of high cholesterol was given to eight workers. Each worker's cholesterol was tested both before and after the talk, with the results given below. What is the probability that the talk caused the workers to undertake lifestyle changes that reduced their cholesterol?

Cholesterol before	Cholesterol after
220	210
195	198
250	210
200	199
220	224
260	212
175	179
198	184

3. The *beta* of a stock is simply the slope of the best-fitting line used to predict the monthly return on the stock from the monthly return given in the Standard & Poor's (S&P) 500 index. A *beta* that is larger than 1 indicates that a stock is more cyclical than the market, whereas a *beta* of less than 1 indicates that a stock is less cyclical than the market. The file Betaresampling.xlsx contains more than 12 years of monthly returns on Microsoft (MSFT), Pfizer (PFE), other stocks and the S&P index. Use this data to determine the probability that Microsoft has a lower *beta* than Pfizer. You will need to use the Excel SLOPE function to estimate the *beta* for each iteration of resampling.

Chapter 65
Pricing Stock Options

- What are call and put options?

- What is the difference between an American and a European option?

- As a function of the stock price on the exercise date, what do the payoffs look like for European calls and puts?

- What parameters determine the value of an option?

- How can I estimate the volatility of a stock based on historical data?

- How can I use Excel to implement the Black-Scholes formula?

- How do changes in key parameters change the value of a call or put option?

- How can I use the Black-Scholes formula to estimate a stock's volatility?

- I don't want somebody changing my neat option-pricing formulas. How can I protect the formulas in my worksheet so that nobody can change them?

- How can I use option pricing to help my company make better investment decisions?

During the early 1970s, economists Fischer Black, Myron Scholes, and Robert Merton derived the Black-Scholes option-pricing formula, which enables us to derive a value for a European call or put option. Scholes and Merton were awarded the 1997 Nobel Prize in Economics for their efforts. (Black died before 1997; Nobel prizes are not awarded posthumously.) The work of these economists revolutionized corporate finance. In this chapter, I'll introduce you to their important work.

Note For an excellent technical discussion of options, see David G. Luenberger's book *Investment Science* (Oxford University Press, 1997).

What are call and put options?

A *call option* gives the owner of the option the right to buy a share of stock for a price called the *exercise price*. A *put option* gives the owner of the option the right to sell a share of stock for the exercise price.

What is the difference between an American and a European option?

An *American* option can be exercised on or before a date known as the *exercise date* (often referred to as the *expiration date*). A *European* option can be exercised only on the exercise date.

As a function of the stock price on the exercise date, what do the payoffs look like for European calls and puts?

Let's look at cash flows from a six-month European call option on shares of Microsoft with an exercise price of $110. Let P equal the price of Microsoft stock in six months. The payoff from a call option on these shares is $0 if $P{\leq}110$ and $P{-}110$ if $P{>}110$. With a value of P below $110, we would not exercise the option. If P is larger than $110, we would exercise the option to buy stock for $110 and immediately sell the stock for P, thereby earning a profit of $P{-}110$. Figure 65-1 shows the payoff from this call option. In short, a call option pays $1 for every dollar by which the stock price exceeds the exercise price. The payoff for this call option can be written as $Max(0,P{-}110)$. Notice that the call option graph in Figure 65-1 has a slope 0 for P smaller than the exercise price. Its slope is 1 for a value of P greater than the exercise price.

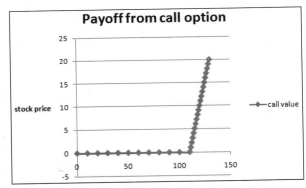

Figure 65-1   Cash flows from a call option

We can show that if a stock pays no dividends, it is never optimal to exercise an American call option early. Therefore, for a non-dividend-paying stock, an American and a European call option both have the same value.

Now let's look at cash flows from a six-month European put option on shares of Microsoft with an exercise price of $110. Let P equal the price of Microsoft in six months. The payoff from the put option is $0 if $P{\geq}110$ and $P{-}110$ if $P{<}110$. For a value of P below $110, we would buy a share of stock for P and immediately sell the stock for $110. This yields a profit of $110{-}P$. If P is larger than $110, it would not pay to buy the stock for P and sell it for $110, so we would not exercise our option to sell the stock for $110.

Figure 65-2 displays the payoff from this put option. In short, a put option pays us $1 for each dollar by which the stock price is below the exercise price. A put payoff can be written as $Max(0,110{-}P)$. Note that the slope of the put payoff is -1 for P less than the exercise price, and the slope of the put payoff is 0 for a value of P greater than the exercise price.

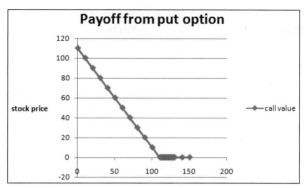

Figure 65-2   Cash flows from a put option

An American put option can be exercised early, so the cash flows from an American put option cannot be determined without knowledge of the stock price at the times before the expiration date.

What parameters determine the value of an option?

In their derivation of the Black-Scholes option-pricing model, Black, Scholes, and Merton showed that the value of a call or put option depends on the following parameters:

❑ Current stock price.

❑ Option's exercise price.

❑ Time (in years) until the option expires (referred to as the option's *duration*).

❑ Interest rate (per year on a compounded basis) on a risk-free investment (usually T-Bills) throughout the duration of the investment. This rate is called the *risk-free rate*. For example, if three-month T-Bills are paying 5 percent, the risk-free rate is computed as *LN(1+0.05)*. (Calculating the logarithm transforms a simple interest rate into a compounded rate.) Compound interest simply means that at every instant, you are earning interest on your interest.

❑ Annual rate (as a percentage of the stock price) at which dividends are paid. If a stock pays 2 percent of its value each year in dividends, the dividend rate is 0.02.

❑ Stock *volatility* (measured on an annual basis). An annual volatility of, for example, 30 percent means that (approximately) the standard deviation of the annual percentage changes in the stock's price is expected to be around 30 percent. During the Internet bubble of the late 1990s, the volatility of many Internet stocks exceeded 100 percent. I'll show you two ways to estimate this important parameter.

How can I estimate the volatility of a stock based on historical data?

To estimate the volatility of a stock based on data about the stock's monthly returns, we can proceed as follows:

❑ Determine the monthly return on the stock for a period of several years.

❑ Determine for each month *LN(1+monthly return)*.

❑ Determine the standard deviation of *LN(1+monthly return)*. This calculation gives us the monthly volatility.

❑ Multiply the monthly volatility by $\sqrt{12}$ to convert monthly volatility to an annual volatility.

This procedure is illustrated in the file Dellvol.xlsx, in which I estimate the annual volatility of Dell stock using monthly prices from the period August 1988 through May 2001. (See Figure 65-3, in which I've hidden several rows of data.)

	A	B	C	D	E	F	G	H
1	Date	Dell Price	Return	1+Return	ln(1+Return)			
2		5/1/01	24.36	-0.0716	0.92835	-0.074342521			
3		4/1/01	26.24	0.02151	1.02151	0.021280472		monthly vol	0.16688
4		3/1/01	25.6875	0.17429	1.17429	0.16066006		annual vol	0.57808
5		2/1/01	21.875	-0.1627	0.83732	-0.177548278			
148		3/1/89	0.0742	-0.0951	0.90488	-0.099955097			
149		2/1/89	0.082	-0.1717	0.82828	-0.188400603			
150		1/1/89	0.099	-0.0499	0.9501	-0.051192279			
151		12/1/88	0.1042	-0.0803	0.91968	-0.083727039			
152		11/1/88	0.1133	-0.0841	0.91593	-0.087820111			
153		10/1/88	0.1237	0.15824	1.15824	0.146901353			
154		9/1/88	0.1068	0.28211	1.28211	0.248509377			
155		8/1/88	0.0833						

Figure 65-3 Computing the historical volatility for Dell

Copying from cell C2 to C3:C154 the formula *(B2–B3)/B3* computes each month's return on Dell stock. Then copying from D2 to D3:D154 the formula *1+C2* computes for each month *1+month's return*. Next I compute *LN(1+ month's return)* for each month by copying from E2 to E3:E154 the formula *LN(D2)*, and I compute the monthly volatility in cell H3 with the formula *STDEV(E2:E154)*. Finally I compute an estimate of Dell's annual volatility with the formula *SQRT(12)*H3*. Dell's annual volatility is estimated to be 57.8 percent.

How can I use Excel to implement the Black-Scholes formula?

To apply the Black-Scholes formula in Microsoft Office Excel 2007, we need input values for the following parameters:

❑ *S*=Today's stock price

❑ *t*=Duration of the option (in years)

❑ *X*=Exercise price

❑ *r*=Annual risk-free rate (This rate is assumed to be continuously compounded.)

❑ σ=Annual volatility of stock

❑ *y*=Percentage of stock value paid annually in dividends

Given these input values, the Black-Scholes price for a European call option can be computed as follows:

Define

$$d_1 = \frac{Ln\left(\frac{S}{X}\right) + \left(r - y + \frac{\sigma^2}{2}\right)t}{\sigma\sqrt{t}}$$

and

$$d_2 = d_1 - \sigma\sqrt{t}$$

Then the call price C is given by

$$C = Se^{-yt}N(d_1) - Xe^{-rt}N(d_2)$$

Here, $N(x)$ is the probability that a normal random variable with a mean of 0 and a σ equal to 1 is less than or equal to x. For example, $N(-1)=.16, N(0)=.5, N(1)=.84$, and $N(1.96)=.975$. A normal random variable with a mean of 0 and a standard deviation of 1 is called a *standard normal*. The cumulative normal probability can be computed in Excel with the NORMSDIST function. Entering $NORMSDIST(x)$ returns the probability that a standard normal random variable is less than or equal to x. For example, entering the formula $NORMSDIST(-1)$ in a cell will yield 0.16, which indicates that a normal random variable with a mean of 0 and a standard deviation of 1 has a 16 percent chance of assuming a value less than −1.

The price of a European put P may be written as

$$P = Se^{-yt}(N(d_1) - 1) - Xe^{-rt}(N(d_2) - 1)$$

In the file named Bstemp.xlsx (see Figure 65-4), I've created a template that computes the value for a European call or put option. Enter the parameter values in B5:B10 and read the value of a European call in D13 and a European put in D14.

	A	B	C	D	E
4	Input data				
5	Stock price	20			
6	Exercise price	24			
7	Duration	7			
8	Interest rate	0.04879			
9	dividend rate	0			
10	volatility	0.5			
11					
12				Predicted	
13	Call price			$10.64	
14	put			$7.69	
15					
16					
17	Other quantities for option price				
18	d1	0.781789		N(d1)	0.782831
19	d2	-0.54109		N(d2)	0.294224

Figure 65-4   Valuing European calls and puts

> **Note**   Valuing American options is beyond the scope of this book. Interested readers should refer to Luenberger's excellent textbook.

As an example, suppose that Cisco stock sells for $20 today and that we've been issued a seven-year European call option. Assume that the annual volatility of Cisco stock is 50 percent, and the risk-free rate during the seven-year period is estimated at 5 percent per year. Compounded, this translates to *LN(1+.05)=.04879*. Cisco does not pay dividends, so the annual dividend rate is 0. We find the value of the call option to be $10.64. A seven-year put option with an exercise price of $24 would be worth $7.69.

How do changes in key parameters change the value of a call or put option?

In general, the effect of changing an input parameter on the value of a call or put is given in the following table:

Parameter	European call	European put	American call	American put
Stock price	+	-	+	-
Exercise price	-	+	-	+
Time to expiration	?	?	+	+
Volatility	+	+	+	+
Risk-free rate	+	-	+	-
Dividends	-	+	-	+

- An increase in today's stock price always increases the value of a call and decreases the value of a put.

- An increase in the exercise price always increases the value of a put and decreases the value of a call.

- An increase in the duration of an option always increases the value of an American option. In the presence of dividends, an increase in the duration of an option can either increase or decrease the value of a European option.

- An increase in volatility always increases option value.

- An increase in the risk-free rate increases the value of a call because higher rates tend to increase the growth rate of the stock price (which is good for the call). This situation more than cancels out the fact that the option payoff is worth less as a result of the higher interest rate. An increase in the risk-free rate always decreases the value of a put because the higher growth rate of the stock tends to hurt the put, as does the fact that future payoffs from the put are worth less. Again, this assumes that interest rates do not affect current stock prices, but they do.

- Dividends tend to reduce the growth rate of a stock price, so increased dividends reduce the value of a call and increase the value of a put.

Using one-way and two-way data tables (see Chapter 15, "Sensitivity Analysis with Data Tables," for details about how to work with data tables), we can, if we want, explore the specific effects of parameter changes on the value of calls and puts.

How can I use the Black-Scholes formula to estimate a stock's volatility?

Earlier in this chapter, I showed how to use historical data to estimate a stock's annual volatility. The problem with a historical volatility estimate is that the analysis looks backward. What we really want is an estimate of a stock's volatility looking forward. The *implied volatility* approach simply estimates a stock's volatility as the volatility value that will make the Black-Scholes price match the option's market price. In short, implied volatility extracts the volatility value implied by the option's market price.

We can easily use the Goal Seek command and our input parameters to compute an implied volatility. On July 22, 2003, Cisco was selling for $18.43. An October 2003 call option with a $17.50 exercise price was selling for $1.85. This option expires on October 18 (89 days in the future). Thus, the option has a duration of $89/365=0.2438$ years. Cisco does not expect to pay dividends, and we assume a T-Bill rate of 5 percent and a corresponding risk-free rate of $LN(1+.05)=0.04879$. To determine the volatility for Cisco implied by this option price, we enter the relevant parameters in cells B5:B10 of the file Ciscoimpvol.xlsx, which is shown in Figure 65-5.

	A	B	C	D	E
4	Input data				
5	Stock price	18.43			
6	Exercise price	17.5			
7	Duration	0.243836			
8	Interest rate	0.04879			
9	dividend rate	0			
10	volatility	0.340364			
11					
12				Predicted	
13	Call price			$1.85	
14	put			$0.71	
15					
16					
17	Other quantities for option price				
18	d1	0.462898		N(d1)	0.678281
19	d2	0.294827		N(d2)	0.615937

Figure 65-5   Using implied volatility to estimate Cisco's volatility.

Next we use Goal Seek (see Figure 65-6) to determine the volatility (the value in cell B10) that makes the call price (the formula in D13) hit a value of $1.85.

Figure 65-6   Goal Seek settings to find implied volatility

We find that this option implies an annual volatility for Cisco of 34 percent, as you can see in Figure 65-5.

> **Note**   The Web site at *http://www.lvolatility.com* provides an estimate of the volatility of any stock, either historical or implied.

I don't want somebody changing my neat option-pricing formulas. How can I protect the formulas in my worksheet so that nobody can change them?

I'm sure that you have often sent your worksheets to people who then change your carefully constructed formulas. Sometimes you want to protect your worksheets so that another user can only enter input data but not modify the worksheet's formulas. As an example, I'll show you how to protect all the formulas in our Black-Scholes template (see the file Bstemp.xlsx).

We begin by unlocking all of the cells in the worksheet. Then we will lock the cells we want to "protect." First click the gray box in the upper-left corner of the worksheet where the row and column headings intersect (next to the A and the 1). When you click this box, any format changes you make will affect the entire worksheet. For example, if you select a bold format after clicking this box, all of the cells in the worksheet will use the bold format.

After selecting the entire worksheet, click the Font dialog box launcher (the small arrow) on the Home tab. This displays the Format Cells dialog box, shown in Figure 65-7. On the Protection tab, clear the Locked box as shown in Figure 65-7, and then click OK. Now all cells in the worksheet are unlocked, which means that even if the worksheet is protected, we can still access these cells.

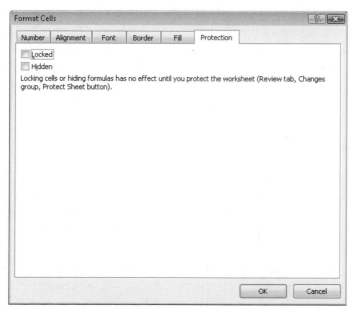

Figure 65-7   Format Cells dialog box

Next select all the formulas in the worksheet. To do this, press F5, which opens the Go To dialog box. Click Special, select Formulas, and click OK. Click the Font dialog box launcher again, and on the Protection tab, check the Locked box. Checking this box "locks" all our formulas.

Now we can protect our worksheet, which will prevent a user from changing our formulas. Click Protect Sheet in the Changes group on the Review tab. In the Protect Sheet dialog box, check the Select Unlocked Cells box, as shown in Figure 65-8. This option will allow users of our template to select unlocked cells, but our formulas will be off-limits.

Figure 65-8   Allowing user to access unlocked cells

Now, when you click any formula, you cannot see or change its contents. Go ahead and try to mess up a formula! The final result of protecting this workbook is saved in the file Bstempprotected.xlsx.

How can I use option pricing to help my company make better investment decisions?

Option pricing can be used to improve a company's capital budgeting or financial decision-making process. The use of option pricing to evaluate actual investment projects is called *real options*. The idea of real options is credited to Judy Lewent, the chief financial officer of Merck. Essentially, real options let you put an explicit value on managerial flexibility, which is often missed by traditional capital budgeting. The following two examples illustrate the concepts of real options.

Note   Refer to Luenberger's book for a more detailed discussion of real options.

Let's say that we own an oil well. Today, our best guess is that the oil in the well is worth $50 million. In five years (if we own the well), we will make a decision to develop the oil well, at a cost of $70 million. A wildcatter is willing to buy the well today for $10 million. Should we sell the well?

Traditional capital budgeting says that the well is worthless because the cost to develop it is more than the value of the oil in the well. But wait; in five years time, the value of the oil in the well will be different because many things (such as the global oil price) might change. There's a chance that the oil will be worth at least $70 million in five years. If the oil is worth $80 million in five years, developing the well in five years would return $10 million.

Essentially, we own a five-year European call option on this well, because our payoff from the well in five years is the same as the payoff on a European call option with a stock price of $50 million, an exercise price of $70 million, and a duration of five years. We can assume an annual volatility similar to the volatility of a typical oil company stock (for example, 30 percent). We will use a T-Bill rate of 5 percent, corresponding to a risk-free rate of 4.879 percent. In the file Oilwell.xlsx (see Figure 65-9), we find the value of this call option is $11.47 million, which means that we should not sell the well for $10 million.

Of course, we do not know the actual volatility for this oil well. Therefore, we can use a one-way data table to determine how the value of the option depends on our volatility estimate (see Figure 65-9). From the data table, we find that as long as the oil well's volatility is at least 27 percent, our oil well "option" is worth more than $10 million.

	A	B	C	D	E	F	G	H
1	**Call with dividends**							
2								
3								
4	Input data							
5	Stock price	50						
6	Exercise price	70						
7	Duration	5						
8	Interest rate	0.04879						
9	dividend rate	0					Volatility	$11.47
10	volatility	0.3					0.1	2.635253
11							0.11	3.064459
12				Predicted			0.12	3.498669
13	Call price			$11.47			0.13	3.936575
14	put			$16.32			0.14	4.377209
15							0.15	4.819841
16							0.16	5.263901
17	Other quantities for option price						0.17	5.708937
18	d1	0.197487		N(d1)	0.578277		0.18	6.154586
19	d2	-0.47333		N(d2)	0.317988		0.19	6.600545
20							0.2	7.046562
21							0.21	7.49242
22							0.22	7.937933
23							0.23	8.382938
24							0.24	8.827291
25							0.25	9.270864
26							0.26	9.713537
27							0.27	10.15521
28							0.28	10.59577
29							0.29	11.03514

Figure 65-9   Oil well real options

As a second example, consider a biotech drug company that is developing a drug for a major pharmaceutical firm. The biotech company currently believes the value of the drug is $50 million. Of course, the value of the drug might drop over time. To protect against a price drop, the biotech company wants to receive a guaranteed payment of $50 million in five years. If an insurance company wants to underwrite this liability, what is a fair price to charge?

Essentially, the biotech company is asking for a payment of $1 million in five years for each $1 million by which the value of the drug in five years is below $50 million. This is equivalent to a five-year put option on the value of the drug. Assuming a T-Bill rate is 5 percent and the annual volatility on comparable drug stocks is 40 percent (see the file Drugabandon.xlsx, shown in Figure 65-10), the value of this option is $10.51 million. This type of option is often referred to as an *abandonment option*, but it is equivalent to a put option. (We have also included a one-way data table to show how the value of the abandonment option depends on the assumed volatility, ranging from 30 to 45 percent of the drug's value.)

	A	B	C	D	E	F	G	H
1	Call with dividends							
2								
3								
4	Input data							
5	Stock price	50						
6	Exercise price	50						
7	Duration	5						
8	Interest rate	0.04879						
9	dividend rate	0					Volatility	$10.51
10	volatility	0.4					0.3	7.03399
11							0.31	7.383411
12				Predicted			0.32	7.732875
13	Call price			$21.34			0.33	8.082211
14	put			$10.51			0.34	8.431265
15							0.35	8.779894
16							0.36	9.127966
17	Other quantities for option price						0.37	9.475362
18	d1	0.719959		N(d1)	0.764225		0.38	9.821968
19	d2	-0.17447		N(d2)	0.430749		0.39	10.16768
20							0.4	10.51241
21							0.41	10.85605
22							0.42	11.19853
23							0.43	11.53976
24							0.44	11.87967
25							0.45	12.21819

Figure 65-10   Calculating an abandonment option

Problems

1. Use the monthly stock returns in the file Volatility.xlsx to determine estimates of annual volatility for Intel, Microsoft, and GE.

2. A stock is selling today for $42. The stock has an annual volatility of 40 percent and the annual risk-free rate is 10 percent.

   ❑ What is a fair price for a six-month European call option with an exercise price of $40?

   ❑ How much does the current stock price have to increase in order for the purchaser of the call option to break even in six months?

   ❑ What is a fair price for a six-month European put option with an exercise price of $40?

❑ How much does the current stock price have to decrease in order for the purchaser of the put option to break even in six months?

❑ What level of volatility would make the $40 call option sell for $6? (Hint: Use the Goal Seek command.)

3. On September 25, 2000, JDS Uniphase stock sold for $106.81 per share. On the same day, a $100 European put expiring on January 20, 2001, sold for $11.875. Compute an implied volatility for JDS Uniphase stock based on this information. Use a T-Bill rate of 5 percent.

4. On August 9, 2002, Microsoft stock was selling for $48.58 per share. A $35 European call option expiring on January 17, 2003, was selling for $13.85. Use this information to estimate the implied volatility for Microsoft stock. Use a T-Bill rate of 4 percent.

5. You have an option to buy a new plane in three years for $25 million. Your current estimate of the value of the plane is $21 million. The annual volatility for change in the plane's value is 25 percent, and the risk-free rate is 5 percent. What is the option to buy the plane worth?

6. The current price of copper is 95 cents per pound. The annual volatility for copper prices is 20 percent, and the risk-free rate is 5 percent. In one year, we have the option (if we desire) to spend $1.25 million to mine 8 million pounds of copper. The copper can be sold at whatever the copper price is in one year. It costs 85 cents to extract a pound of copper from the ground. What is the value of this situation to us?

7. We own the rights to a biotech drug. Our best estimate is that the current value of these rights is $50 million. Assuming that the annual volatility of biotech companies is 90 percent and the risk-free rate is 5 percent, what is the value of an option to sell the rights to the drug five years from now for $40 million?

8. Merck is debating whether to invest in a pioneer biotech project. They estimate that the worth of the project is –$56 million. Investing in the pioneer project gives Merck the option to own, if they want, a much bigger technology that will be available in four years. If Merck does not participate in the pioneer project, they cannot own the bigger project. The bigger project will require $1.5 billion in cash four years from now. Currently, Merck estimates the net present value (NPV) of the cash flows from the bigger project to be $597 million. Assuming a risk-free rate of 10 percent and that the annual volatility for the bigger project is 35 percent, what should Merck do? (This is the problem that started the whole field of real options!)

9. Develop a worksheet that uses the following inputs to compute annual profit:

❑ Annual fixed cost

❑ Unit cost

❑ Unit price

❑ Annual demand=10,000–100*(price)

Then protect the cells used to compute annual demand and annual profit.

Chapter 66

Determining Customer Value

- A credit-card company currently has an 80 percent retention rate. How will the company's profitability improve if the retention rate increases to 90 percent or higher?

- A long-distance phone company gives the competition's customers an incentive to switch. How large an incentive should they give?

Many companies undervalue their customers. When valuing a customer, a company should look at the net present value (NPV) of the long-term profits that the company earns from the customer. (For detailed information about net present value, see Chapter 7, "Evaluating Investments by Using Net Present Value Criteria.") Failure to look at the long-term value of a customer often causes a company to make poor decisions. For example, a company might cut its customer service staff by 10 percent to save $1 million, but the resulting decrease in service quality might cause them to lose much more than $1 million in "customer value," which would, of course, result in the company being less profitable. The following two examples show how to compute customer value.

A credit-card company currently has an 80 percent retention rate. How will the company's profitability improve if the retention rate increases to 90 percent or higher?

Our example is based on a discussion in Frederick Reichheld's excellent book *The Loyalty Effect* (Harvard Business School Press, 2001). You can find the sample data we'll use in the file Loyalty.xlsx, shown in Figure 66-1 on the next page. Reichheld estimates the profitability of a credit-card customer based on the number of years the customer has held a card. For example, during the first year a customer has the credit card, the cardholder generates –$40 profit, which is the result of customer acquisition costs and the cost of setting up the customer's account. During each successive year, the profit generated by the customer increases until a customer who has owned a card for 20 or more years generates $161 per year in profits.

The credit-card company wants to determine how the value of a customer depends on the company's retention rate. Currently, the company has an 80 percent retention rate, which means that at the end of each year, 20 percent (1–0.80) of all customers do not renew their card. (We refer to the 20 percent of customers who don't renew as the annual *churn rate.*) The credit-card company wants to determine the long-term value of a customer for retention rates of 80 percent, 85 percent, 90 percent, 95 percent, and 99 percent.

	A	B	C	D	E	F	G
4				npv per customer	141.718		
5							
6		retention rate	0.8				
7		Interest rate	0.15				
8	Year	Mean Profit(if :	Number	Profit		retention rate	141.718
9	1	($40.00)	100	($4,000.00)		0.8	141.718
10	2	$66.00	80	$5,280.00		0.85	193.15
11	3	$72.00	64	$4,608.00		0.9	269.347
12	4	$79.00	51.2	$4,044.80		0.95	390.713
13	5	$87.00	40.96	$3,563.52		0.99	548.577
14	6	$92.00	32.768	$3,014.66			
15	7	$96.00	26.2144	$2,516.58			
16	8	$99.00	20.9715	$2,076.18			
17	9	$103.00	16.7772	$1,728.05			
18	10	$106.00	13.4218	$1,422.71			
19	11	$111.00	10.7374	$1,191.85			
20	12	$116.00	8.58993	$996.43			
21	13	$120.00	6.87195	$824.63			
22	14	$124.00	5.49756	$681.70			
23	15	$130.00	4.39805	$571.75			
24	16	$137.00	3.51844	$482.03			
25	17	$142.00	2.81475	$399.69			
26	18	$148.00	2.2518	$333.27			
27	19	$155.00	1.80144	$279.22			
28	20	$161	1.44115	$232.03			
29	21	$161	1.15292	$185.62			
30	22	$161	0.92234	$148.50			
31	23	$161	0.73787	$118.80			
32	24	$161	0.5903	$95.04			
33	25	$161	0.47224	$76.03			
34	26	$161	0.37779	$60.82			
35	27	$161	0.30223	$48.66			
36	28	$161	0.24179	$38.93			
37	29	$161	0.19343	$31.14			
38	30	$161	0.15474	$24.91			

Figure 66-1 Value of a credit-card customer

To determine the long-term value of a customer, we start with a cohort of, for example, 100 customers. (A *cohort* is a group of individuals having a statistical factor in common. The size 100 is arbitrary here, but round numbers make it easier to follow the analysis.) Then we determine how many of these customers are still around each year with the formula (*Customers around for year t+1*)=(*Retention rate*)*(*Customers around for year t*). We assume that customers "quit" only at the end of each year. Then we use the NPV function to determine the total NPV (assuming a 15 percent discount rate) generated by our original cohort of 100 customers. The 15 percent discount rate implies that $1 earned one year from now is worth the same as $1.00/$1.15 of profit earned now. Dividing this number by the number of customers in our original cohort (100) gives us the value of an individual customer.

I first assign the names in the cell range B6:B7 to the cell range C6:C7. Then I enter our number of original customers (100) in cell C9. Copying from cell C10 to the range C11:C38 the formula *retention_rate*C9* generates the number of customers present for each year. For example, we will have 80 customers present in year 2.

I compute the profit earned each year by multiplying the number of remaining customers by each customer's profit. To make this calculation, copy from cell D9 to D10:D38 the formula *C9*B9*. In cell E4, I compute the average NPV generated by an individual customer with the formula *(1+Interest_rate)*NPV(Interest_rate,D9:D38)/100*. We are assuming cash flows at the beginning of the year and a 15 percent annual discount rate. The portion of the formula that reads *NPV(Interest_rate,D9:D38)* computes the average NPV generated by an individual customer assuming end-of-year cash flows. Multiplying by *(1+Interest_rate)* converts the end-of-year cash flow NPV to a beginning-of-year NPV.

With an 80 percent retention rate, we find that the average customer is worth $141.72. To determine how the value of an individual customer varies with a change in annual retention rate, I use a one-way data table. I enter the relevant annual retention rates in the cell range F9:F13. In cell G8, I enter the formula we want the data table to calculate (NPV per customer) with the formula *=E4*. Next, I select the table range (F8:G13) and then choose Data Table from the What-If Analysis command on the Data tab. After entering a Column Input Cell of C6, I obtain the profit calculations shown in Figure 66-1. Notice that increasing our retention rate from 80 percent to 90 percent nearly doubles the value of each customer, which strongly argues for being "nice" to these customers and against pinching pennies on activities related to customer service. Understanding the value of a customer gives most companies a crucial lever that can be used to increase their profitability.

A long-distance phone company gives the competition's customers an incentive to switch. How large an incentive should they give?

Let's say that we work for a phone company in which the average long-distance customer spends $400 per year and the company generates a 10 percent profit margin on each dollar spent. At the end of each year, 50 percent of our company's customers switch to the competition, and without any incentives, 30 percent of the competition's customers switch to our company. We're considering giving the competition's customers a one-time incentive to switch companies. How large an incentive can we give and still break even?

The key to analyzing this problem (which you can find in the file Phoneloyalty.xlsx, shown in Figure 66-2 on the next page) is to look at the NPV for two situations:

- Situation 1: 100 customers begin with the competition.
- Situation 2: We pay the 100 customers who are with the competition a certain amount to switch to us.

Following through each situation for a period of time (for example, 20 years), we can use the Excel Goal Seek command to determine the dollar amount *x* paid to a person switching to our company that makes us indifferent between the following two situations:

- Situation 1: We have just paid 100 non-loyal customers $*x* each to switch to us.
- Situation 2: The market consists of 100 non-loyal customers.

We assume that our analysis begins on June 30, 2004, and that customers switch companies, at most, once per year. I assigned the range names in cells A2:A6 to cells B2:B6. The key step in our analysis is to realize that *(year t+1 customers with us)=.3*(year t competitor customers)+.5*(year t our customers)*. Similarly *(year t+1 customers with competition)=.7*(year t competition customers)+.5*(year t our customers)*.

			Pay them			Do not pay them		
switch fee	34.222212			pay-no pay	0			
probleave	0.5							
probcome	0.3							
annrevenue	400	NPV	13676.01			13676.01		
profitmargin	0.1							
	Date	Year	Number with us	Number with them	Profit	Number with us	Number with them	Profit
	initial							
	6/30/2004	1	100	0	577.7788	30	70	1200
	6/30/2005	2	50	50	2000	36	64	1440
	6/30/2006	3	40	60	1600	37.2	62.8	1488
	6/30/2007	4	38	62	1520	37.44	62.56	1497.6
	6/30/2008	5	37.6	62.4	1504	37.488	62.512	1499.52
	6/30/2009	6	37.52	62.48	1500.8	37.4976	62.5024	1499.904
	6/30/2010	7	37.504	62.496	1500.16	37.49952	62.50048	1499.981
	6/30/2011	8	37.5008	62.4992	1500.032	37.4999	62.5001	1499.996
	6/30/2020	17	37.5	62.5	1500	37.5	62.5	1500
	6/30/2021	18	37.5	62.5	1500	37.5	62.5	1500
	6/30/2022	19	37.5	62.5	1500	37.5	62.5	1500
	6/30/2023	20	37.5	62.5	1500	37.5	62.5	1500

Figure 66-2   Phone incentive analysis

Next I enter 100 in cell D9 (customers with us) and 0 in cell E9 (customers with the competition). This customer alignment corresponds to the situation right after we offer our incentive to 100 customers. We're assuming that customers who receive the incentive must stay with us for at least one year. Copying from D10 to D11:D28 the formula (1–probleave)*D9+probcome*E9 generates the number of customers we have during each year (years 2012–2019 are hidden in Figure 66-2). Copying from E10 to E11:E28 the formula probleave*D9+(1–probcome)*E9 gives us the number of customers with the competition during each year.

In cell F9, I generate the profit earned during our first year with the formula D9* annrevenue*profitmargin–switch_fee*100. Note that I have subtracted the cost of paying the 100 customers with the competition to switch. Copying from F10 to F11:F28 the formula D10*annrevenue*profitmargin generates our profit during later years. In cell D5, I compute the NPV of the profits associated with the incentive by using the formula XNPV(0.1,F9:F28,B9:B28). (See Chapter 7 for a discussion of the XNPV function.)

In a similar fashion, in the cell range G8:I28 I generate the profits earned each year from 100 customers who were originally with the competition. On June 30, 2004, 30 of these 100 customers will have switched to us (even without incentives). In cell F2, I compute the difference between our NPV with the incentive and our NPV without the incentive.

Finally I use Goal Seek to vary the size of the incentive (cell B2) to set F2 equal to 0. The Goal Seek dialog box is shown in Figure 66-3. We find that an incentive of $34.22 makes the NPV of the two situations identical. Therefore, we could give incentives of up to $34.21 for a customer to switch and still have increased our profitability.

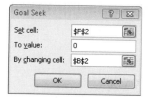

Figure 66-3   Goal Seek settings to determine the maximum incentive that increases profitability

Problems

1. Whirlswim Appliance is considering giving each of its customers free maintenance on each VCR purchased. They estimate that this proposal will require them to pay an average of $2.50 for each VCR sold today (the cost in today's dollars). Currently, the market consists of 72,000 consumers whose last purchase was from Whirlswim and 86,000 consumers whose last purchase was from a competitor. In a given year, 40 percent of all consumers purchase a VCR. If their last purchase was a Whirlswim, there is a 60 percent chance that their next purchase will be a Whirlswim. If their last purchase was not a Whirlswim, there is a 30 percent chance that their next purchase will be a Whirlswim. A purchase during the current year will lead to a $20 profit. The contribution to profit (and maintenance cost per purchaser) from a purchaser grows at 5 percent per year. Profits (over a 30-year horizon) are discounted at 10 percent per year.

    Suppose that we provide free maintenance. If the customer's last purchase was a Whirlswim, the probability that their next purchase will be a Whirlswim will increase by an unknown amount between 0 percent and 10 percent. Similarly, if we give free maintenance and the customer's last purchase was not a Whirlswim, the probability that their next purchase is a Whirlswim will increase by an unknown amount between 0 percent and 10 percent. Do you recommend that Whirlswim adopt the free maintenance policy?

2. Mr. D's Supermarket is determined to please its customers with a customer advantage card. Currently, 30 percent of all shoppers are loyal to Mr. D's. A loyal Mr. D's customer shops at Mr. D's 80 percent of the time. A non-loyal Mr. D's customer shops at Mr. D's 10 percent of the time. A typical customer spends $150 per week and Mr. D's is running on a 4 percent profit margin.

    The customer advantage card will cost Mr. D's an average of $0.01 per dollar spent. We believe Mr. D's share of loyal customers will increase by an unknown amount between 2 percent and 10 percent. We also believe that the fraction of the time a loyal customer shops at Mr. D's will increase by an unknown amount between 2 percent and 12 percent. Should Mr. D's adopt a customer advantage card? Should Mr. D's adopt the card if its profit margin is 8 percent instead of 4 percent?

Chapter 67

The Economic Order Quantity Inventory Model

- An electronics store sells 10,000 PDAs per year. Each time an order is placed for a supply of PDAs, the store incurs an order cost of $10. The store pays $100 for each PDA, and the cost of holding a PDA in inventory for a year is assumed to be $20. When the store orders PDAs, how large an order should it be?

- A manufacturing plant produces 10,000 computers per year. The cost to produce each computer is $2,000. The cost to set up a production run of computers is $200, and the cost to hold a computer in inventory for a year is $500. The plant can, if it wants, produce 25,000 computers per year. When the plant produces computers, how large a batch should it produce?

When a store orders an item repeatedly, a natural question is, what quantity should the store order each time? If the store orders too many items, it incurs excessive inventory or holding costs. If the store orders too few items, it incurs excessive re-ordering costs. Somewhere, there must be a happy medium that minimizes the sum of annual inventory and order costs.

Similarly, consider a manufacturing plant that produces batches of a product. What batch size minimizes the sum of annual inventory and setup costs? The two examples in this chapter show how to use the Economic Order Quantity formula (developed in 1913 by F. Harris of Westinghouse Corporation) to answer these questions.

An electronics store sells 10,000 PDAs per year. Each time an order is placed for a supply of PDAs, an order cost of $10 is incurred. The store pays $100 for each PDA, and the cost of holding a PDA in inventory for a year is assumed to be $20. When the store orders PDAs, how large an order should it be?

The size of an order that minimizes the sum of annual inventory and ordering costs can be determined after the following parameters are known:

- ❑ K=Cost per order

- ❑ h=Cost of holding one unit in inventory for a year

- ❑ D=Annual demand for product

You can follow an example of how to work with these parameters using the *EOQ* work-sheet in the file Eoq.xlsx, which is shown in Figure 67-1.

	A	B	C
2	cost/order	K	10
3	annual holding cost per unit	h	20
4	annual demand	D	10000
5	order quantity	EOQ	100
6	holding cost per year	annhc	$1,000.00
7	order cost per year	annoc	$1,000.00
8	total annual cost (excluding purchasin	anncost	$2,000.00
9	orders per year	annorders	100

Figure 67-1   EOQ template

If q equals order size, annual inventory cost equals $0.5qh$. (Throughout this example, I'll refer to this equation as Equation 1.) We derive Equation 1 because our average inventory level $(0.5q)$ will be half the maximum inventory level. To see why the average inventory level is $0.5q$, note that we can compute the average inventory level for a cycle (the time between the arrival of orders). At the beginning of a cycle, an order arrives, and our inventory level is q. At the end of the cycle, we are out of stock, and our inventory level is 0. Because demand occurs at a constant rate, the average inventory level during a cycle is simply the average of 0 and q or $0.5q$. Maximum inventory level will equal q because orders are assumed to arrive at the instant that the inventory level is reduced to 0.

Because D/q orders are placed per year, annual ordering cost equals $(D/q)*K$. (I'll refer to this equation as Equation 2.) Using calculus or the Microsoft Office Excel 2007 Solver, we can show that the annual sum of inventory and ordering costs is minimized for a value of q equal to the economic order quantity (EOQ), which is calculated using the following formula. (I'll refer to this equation as Equation 3.)

$$EOQ = \sqrt{\frac{2KD}{h}}$$

From this formula, we see the following:

❑   An increase in demand or ordering cost will increase the EOQ.

❑   An increase in holding cost will decrease the EOQ.

In the file Eoq.xlsx, I use Equation 3 to determine EOQ in cell C5. I determine annual holding cost in cell C6 by using Equation 1. I determine annual ordering cost in cell C7 with Equation 2. Notice that for EOQ, the annual ordering cost equals the annual holding cost, which will always be the case. In cell C8, I determine the total annual cost (ignoring the purchasing cost, which does not depend on our ordering strategy) with the formula *C6+C7*.

Of course, you can use one-way and two-way data tables to determine the sensitivity of the EOQ and various costs to variations in K, h, and D. For our example, we have K=$10,

$D=10,000$ PDAs per year, and $h=\$20$ per PDA. Inserting these values in cells C2:C4, we find the following:

- ❑ Each order should be for 100 PDAs.

- ❑ Annual holding and ordering costs each equal $1,000. The EOQ always sets annual holding costs equal to annual ordering costs.

- ❑ Total annual costs (exclusive of purchasing costs) equal $2,000.

When you are working with EOQ, keep the following in mind:

- ❑ The presence of quantity discounts invalidates the EOQ because the annual purchase cost then depends on the order size.

- ❑ The EOQ assumes that demand occurs at a relatively constant rate throughout the year. The EOQ should not be used for products for which there is seasonal demand.

- ❑ Annual holding cost is usually assumed to be between 10 percent and 40 percent of a product's unit purchasing cost.

- ❑ I've included (in the EOQ *Protected* worksheet in the file Eoq.xlsx) a version of the EOQ worksheet in which all formulas are protected. When the sheet is protected, nobody can change our formulas. See Chapter 65, "Pricing Stock Options," for instructions about how to protect a worksheet.

- ❑ For further discussion of inventory modeling, interested readers can refer to my book *Operations Research: Applications and Algorithms* (Duxbury Press, 2003).

A manufacturing plant produces 10,000 computers per year. The cost to produce each computer is $2,000. The cost to set up a production run of computers is $200, and the cost to hold a computer in inventory for a year is $500. The plant can, if it wants, produce 25,000 computers per year. When the plant produces computers, how large a batch should it produce?

With the EOQ model, we assume an order arrives the instant the order is placed. When a company manufactures a product instead of ordering it, an order must be produced and cannot arrive instantaneously. In such situations, instead of computing the cost-minimizing order quantity, we need to determine the cost-minimizing batch size. When a company produces a product internally instead of purchasing the product externally, the batch size that minimizes costs depends on the following parameters:

- ❑ K=Cost of setting up a batch for production

- ❑ h=Cost of holding each unit in inventory for a year

- ❑ D=Annual demand for product

- ❑ R=Annual rate at which the product can be produced. For example, IBM might have the capacity to produce 25,000 computers per year.

If q equals the size of each production batch, the annual holding cost equals $0.5*(q/R)*(R-D)*h$. (I'll refer to this equation as Equation 4.) Equation 4 follows because each batch takes q/R years to produce and, during a production cycle, inventory increases at a rate of $R-D$. Our maximum inventory level, which occurs at the completion of a batch, can be calculated as $(q/R)*(R-D)$. Our average inventory level will thus equal $0.5*(q/R)*(R-D)$.

Because D/q batches are produced per year, annual setup cost equals KD/q (which I'll refer to as Equation 5). Using calculus or the Excel Solver, we can show that the batch size that minimizes the sum of annual setup and production-run costs is given by the following (which I'll refer to as Equation 6). We call this model the economic order batch (EOB) size.

$$EOB = \sqrt{\frac{2KDR}{h(R-D)}}$$

From this formula, we find the following:

❑   An increase in K or D will increase the EOB.

❑   An increase in h or R will decrease the EOB.

In the *Cont Rate EOQ* worksheet in the file Contrateeoq.xlsx, I've constructed a template to determine the EOB, annual setup, and holding costs. The worksheet is shown in Figure 67-2.

	A	B	C
2	cost per batch	K	$ 200.00
3	annual holding cost per unit	h	$ 500.00
4	annual demand	D	10000
5	annual production rate	rate	25000
6	batch size	EOB	115.470054
7	holding cost per year	annhc	$17,320.51
8	order cost per year	annoc	$17,320.51
9	total annual cost (excluding purchasing)	anncost	$34,641.02
10	batches per year	annbatches	86.6025404

Figure 67-2   Template for computing EOB

For our example, $K=\$200$, $h=\$500$, $D=10,000$ units per year, and $R=25,000$ units per year. After entering these parameter values in the cell range C2:C5, we find the following:

❑   The batch size that minimizes costs is 115.47 computers. Thus, we should produce 115 or 116 computers in each batch.

❑   The annual holding cost and setup costs equal $17,320.51. Again, the EOB will always set annual holding cost equal to annual setup cost.

❑   Total annual cost (exclusive of variable production costs) is $34,641.02.

❑   86.6 batches per year will be produced.

When you are working with the EOB model, keep the following in mind:

- ❑ If the unit variable cost of producing a product depends on the batch size, the EOB model is invalid.

- ❑ The EOB assumes that demand occurs at a relatively constant rate throughout the year. The EOB should not be used for products for which there is seasonal demand.

- ❑ The annual holding cost is usually assumed to be between 10 percent and 40 percent of a product's unit purchasing cost.

- ❑ I've included (in the *Protected* worksheet in the file Contrateeoq.xlsx) a version of the EOB worksheet in which all formulas are protected. See Chapter 65 for instructions about how to protect a worksheet.

Problems

1. An appliance store sells plasma TVs. Annual demand is estimated at 1000 units. The cost to carry a TV in inventory for one year is $500, and the cost to place an order for plasma TVs is $400.

   - ❑ How many TVs should be ordered each time an order is placed?
   - ❑ How many orders per year should be placed?
   - ❑ What are the annual inventory and ordering costs?

2. Suppose that the Waterford Crystal company can produce up to 100 iced tea pitchers per day. Further suppose that the plant is open 250 days per year, and that annual demand is for 20,000 pitchers. The cost to hold a pitcher in inventory for a year might be $10, and the cost to set up the facility to produce iced tea pitchers might be $40.

   - ❑ What batch size would you recommend for iced tea pitchers?
   - ❑ How many batches per year should be produced?
   - ❑ What are the annual setup and inventory costs for iced tea pitchers?

Chapter 68

Inventory Modeling with Uncertain Demand

- At what inventory level should I place an order if my goal is to minimize annual holding, ordering, and shortage costs?

- What does the term *95 percent service level* mean?

In Chapter 67, "The Economic Order Quantity Inventory Model," we used the economic order quantity (EOQ) to determine an optimal order quantity and production batch size. We assumed that demand occurred at a constant rate. Thus, if annual demand occurred at a rate of, for example, 1200 units per year, then monthly demand would equal 100 units. As long as demand occurs at a relatively constant rate, the EOQ is a good approximation of the cost-minimizing order quantity.

In reality, demand during any time period is uncertain. When demand is uncertain, a natural question is how low to let the inventory level go before placing an order. We call the inventory level at which an order should be placed the *reorder point*. Clearly, a high reorder point will decrease shortage costs and increase holding costs. Similarly, a low reorder point will increase shortage costs and decrease holding costs. At some intermediate reorder point, the sum of shortage and holding costs is minimized. Our first example shows how to determine a reorder point that minimizes expected ordering, shortage, and holding costs based on the following two assumptions:

- Each unit we are short is back ordered by a customer, and we incur the shortage cost c_B. This cost is primarily a measure of the customer's dissatisfaction caused by late receipt of an ordered item.

- Each unit we are short results in a lost sale, and we incur the shortage cost $c_{LS} > c_B$. The lost sales cost includes the profit lost from the lost sale as well as the shortage cost included in c_B.

The second example shows how to determine the optimal reorder point based on a *service level* approach. For example, a 95 percent service level means that we set the reorder point at a level ensuring that, on average, 95 percent of all demand is met on time. It is usually difficult to determine the cost of a shortage in either the back-ordered case or the lost-sales case. For that reason, most companies set reorder points by using the service level approach.

> **Note** On this book's companion CD, for the back ordered and lost sales models, I've included a worksheet named *Protected* in which all formulas are protected for both the back-ordered and lost-sales cases. You can use these worksheets as templates.

At what inventory level should I place an order if my goal is to minimize annual holding, ordering, and shortage costs?

As I indicated in Chapter 67, the EOQ depends on the following parameters:

- ❑ K=Cost per order
- ❑ h=Cost of holding one unit in inventory for a year
- ❑ D=Annual demand for the product

Because demand is now uncertain, we will let D stand for the expected annual demand for the product.

The back-order case   See the file Reorderpoint_backorder.xlsx, shown in Figure 68-1, for the data I'm using in this example. Let's first suppose that each shortage results in the back-ordered units. In other words, a shortage does not result in any lost demand. We assume that each unit we are short incurs a cost c_B. In this case, the reorder point depends on the following quantities:

- ■ *EOQ* is the economic order quantity (the quantity ordered each time an order is placed)
- ■ *K* is the cost per order
- ■ *h* is the annual holding cost per unit
- ■ *D* is the mean annual demand
- ■ *SOC* is the cost per unit short
- ■ *annsig* is the standard deviation of annual demand
- ■ *meanLT* is the average *lead time*; that is, the average time between placing an order and the time the order is received
- ■ *sigmaLT* is the standard deviation of lead time

	A	B	C
2	cost/order	K	$ 50.00
3	annual holding cost per unit	h	$ 10.00
4	mean annual demand	D	1000
5	order quantity	EOQ	100
6	orders per year	annorders	10
7	unit stockout cost	SOC	$ 20.00
8	annual sigma	annsig	40.8
9	mean lead time	meanLT	0.0384615
10	sigma lead time	sigmaLT	0
11	mean lead time demand	meanLTD	38.461538
12	sigma lead time demand	sigmaLTD	8.0015383
13	probability of stockout	probout	0.05
14	reorder point	RP	51.622898
15	safety stock	SS	13.161359

Figure 68-1 Determining reorder point when shortages are back ordered

Let's suppose that a department store wants to determine an optimal inventory policy for ordering electric mixers. They have the following information:

- It costs $50 to place an order for mixers.

- It costs $10 to hold a mixer in inventory for a year.

- On average, the store sells 1000 mixers per year.

- All customers who try to purchase a mixer when the store is sold out of them return at a later date and buy a mixer when the mixer is in stock. The store incurs a penalty of $20 for each unit it is short.

- The annual demand for mixers (based on historical data) has a standard deviation of 40.8.

- Lead time is always two weeks (0.038 years), with a standard deviation of 0.

After we enter K, h, and D in cells C2:C4, our spreadsheet computes the EOQ (100 mixers) in C5. After we enter SOC, annsig, meanLT, and sigmaLT in cells C7:C10, our spreadsheet computes in cell C14 the reorder point that minimizes the sum of expected annual holding and shortage costs (51.63 mixers). Thus, our department store should order 100 mixers whenever their stock decreases to 51.62 (or 52) mixers.

The *safety stock level* associated with a given reorder point is *reorder point—mean lead time demand*. The department store maintains a safety stock level of *51.62–38.46=13.16* mixers, computed in cell C15. Essentially, the safety stock is always in inventory, resulting in extra holding costs. A higher level of safety stock will, of course, reduce shortages.

The lost-sales case   Now suppose that each shortage results in a lost sale. The cost associated with a lost sale is usually estimated as the back-order penalty plus the profit associated with a unit sold. Suppose that the department store earns a $20 profit on each mixer it sells. The unit shortage cost for the lost-sales case is then $40 (*$20 lost profit+$20 back-order penalty*).

In the file Reorderpoint_lostsales.xlsx, shown in Figure 68-2, you can see the work I did to estimate the reorder point for the lost-sales case. After entering in cell C7 of the spreadsheet the lost-sales cost of $40, we find the optimal inventory policy is to order 100 mixers and place an order when inventory is down to 54.23 mixers. Our safety stock level is 15.77 mixers, and 2.4 percent of the store's demand for mixers will be unmet. Notice that the assumption of a lost sale has increased our reorder point and reduced the probability of a shortage. This happens because the increased cost of a shortage (from $20 to $40) makes us more eager to avoid shortages.

	A	B	C
2	cost/order	K	$ 50.00
3	annual holding cost per unit	h	$ 10.00
4	mean annual demand	D	1000
5	order quantity	EOQ	100
6	orders per year	annorders	10
7	lost sales cost	LSC	$ 40.00
8	annual sigma	annsig	40.8
9	mean lead time	meanLT	0.038461538
10	sigma lead time	sigmaLT	0
11	mean lead time demand	meanLTD	38.46153846
12	sigma lead time demand	sigmaLTD	8.001538314
13	probability of stockout	probout	0.024390244
14	reorder point	RP	54.22861214
15	safety stock	SS	15.76707368

Figure 68-2   Determining reorder point when sales will be lost

Increased uncertainty greatly increases the reorder point. For example, in the lost-sales case, if the standard deviation for lead time is one week (0.019 years) rather than 0, the reorder point increases to 79.50 mixers and the safety stock more than doubles from the case in which our lead time was known with certainty.

What does the term 95 percent service level mean?

As stated earlier in this chapter, a *95 percent service level* simply means that we want 95 percent of our demand to be met on time. Because estimating the back-order penalty and/or the penalty that results from a lost sale is often difficult, many companies set safety stock levels for products by setting a service level. Using the file Servicelevelreorder.xlsx (shown in Figure 68-3), we can determine the reorder point corresponding to any service level we want.

	A	B	C	D	E	F	G
1	Service level	SL	0.95				
2	cost/order	K	$ 50.00				
3	annual holding cost per unit	h	$ 10.00				
4	mean annual demand	D	1000				
5	order quantity	EOQ	100				
6	orders per year	annorders	10				
7	annual sigma	annsig	69.28				
8	mean lead time	meanLT	0.083333				
9	sigma lead time	sigmaLT	0				
10	mean lead time demand	meanLTD	83.33333				
11	sigma lead time demand	sigmaLTD	19.99941				
12	reorder point	ROP	90.23008				
13	standardized reorder point	SROP	0.344847				DIFF
14	normal loss for stand. ROP	NLSTANDROP	0.250007 =		0.25001		6.43673E-08
15	safety stock	SS	6.896742				

Figure 68-3   Determination of reorder point using the service level approach

As an example, consider a pharmacy that is trying to determine an optimal inventory policy for a drug they stock. They would like to meet 95 percent of their demand on time. The following parameters are relevant.

- Each order for the drug costs $50.

- The cost to hold a unit of the drug in inventory for a year is $10.

- Average demand per year for the drug is 1000 units.

- The standard deviation of annual demand is 69.28 units.

- The time required to receive a shipment of the drug always takes exactly one month (0.083 years).

We enter the service level we want (0.95) in cell C1 and all other parameters in cells C2:C4 and C7:C9. To determine the reorder point yielding the desired service level, click Solver in the Data Analysis group on the Data tab of the Ribbon. Our Solver model adjusts the reorder point until the percentage of demand met on time matches the service level we want. We find that we should order 100 units of the drug whenever our inventory level drops to 90.23 units. This reorder point corresponds to a safety stock level of 6.90 units.

In the following table, I've listed the reorder point and safety stock levels corresponding to service levels between 80 percent and 99 percent.

Service level percentage	Reorder point	Safety stock
80%	65.34 units	-17.99 units
85%	71.85 units	-11.48 units
90%	79.57 units	-3.76 units
95%	90.23 units	6.90 units
99%	108.44 units	25.11 units

Notice that moving from an 80 percent service level to a 99 percent service level increases the reorder point by almost 67 percent! Also note that we can attain a 90 percent service level with a reorder point less than our mean lead time demand (refer back to cell C10 in Figure 68-3). A 90 percent service level results in a negative safety stock level, which is possible because shortages occur only during the lead time and our lead times usually cover a small portion of a year.

Problems

When working with Problems 1 and 2, assume that a restaurant serves an average of 5000 bottles of wine per year. The standard deviation of the annual demand for wine is 1000 bottles. The annual holding cost for a bottle of wine is $1. It costs $10 to place an order for wine, and it takes an average of three weeks (with a standard deviation of one week) for the wine to arrive.

1. Assume that when the restaurant is out of wine it incurs a penalty of $5 as the result of lost goodwill. Also, the restaurant earns a profit of $2 per bottle of wine. Determine an optimal ordering policy for the wine.

2. Determine an inventory policy for wine that yields a 99 percent service level.

3. A reorder point policy is often referred to as a *two-bin policy*. How can a reorder point policy be implemented in a situation in which two bins are used to store inventory?

Chapter 69

Queuing Theory: The Mathematics of Waiting in Line

- What factors affect the number of people and the time we spend waiting in line?

- What conditions should be met before analyzing the average number of people present or the average time spent in a queuing system?

- Why does variability degrade the performance of a queuing system?

- Can I easily determine the average time a person spends at airport security or waiting in line at a bank?

We have all spent a lot of time waiting in lines, and you'll soon see that a slight increase in service capacity can often greatly reduce the size of the lines we encounter. If you run a business, ensuring that your customers do not spend too much time waiting is important. Therefore, business people need to understand the mathematics of wait time, usually referred to as the *queuing theory*. In this chapter, I'll show you how to determine the service capacity needed to provide adequate service.

What factors affect the number of people and the time we spend waiting in line?

In this chapter, we will consider queuing problems in which all arriving customers wait in one line for the first available service person. (To keep things simple, we'll refer to service people as *servers*.) This model is a fairly accurate representation of the situations we face when we wait at a bank, at an airline ticket counter, or at the post office. By the way, the idea of having customers wait in one line started about 1970, when banks and Post Office branches realized that although waiting in one line does not reduce the average time spent waiting, it does reduce the variability of our time in line, thereby creating a "fairer" system.

Three main factors influence the time we spend in a queuing system:

- **The number of servers.** Clearly, the more servers, the less time on average we spend in line, and the fewer people on average will be present in the line.

❑ **The mean and the standard deviation of the time between arrivals.** (We call the time between arrivals *interarrival time*.) If the average interarrival time increases, the number of arrivals decreases, which results in shorter lines and less time spent in a queuing system. As you'll soon see, an increase in standard deviation of interarrival times increases the average time a customer spends in a queuing system and the average number of customers present.

❑ **The mean and the standard deviation of the time needed to complete service.** If the average service time increases, we will see an increase in the average time a customer spends in the system and the number of customers present. As you'll see, an increase in the standard deviation of service times increases the average time a customer spends in a queuing system and the average number of customers present.

What conditions should be met before analyzing the average number of people present or the average time spent in a queuing system?

When analyzing the time spent waiting in lines, mathematicians talk about *steady state* characteristics of a system. Essentially, steady state means that a system has operated for a long time. More specifically, we would like to know the value of the following quantities in the steady state:

❑ W=Average time a customer spends in the system

❑ W_q=Average time a customer spends waiting in line before the customer is served

❑ L=Average number of customers present in the system

❑ L_q=Average number of customers waiting in line

By the way, it is always true that $L=(1/mean\ interarrival\ time)*W$ and $L_q=(1/mean\ interarrival\ time)*W_q$.

To discuss the steady state of a queuing system meaningfully, the following must be the case:

❑ The mean and standard deviation of both the interarrival times and the service times changes little over time. The technical phrase is that the distribution of interarrival and service times is *stationary* over time.

❑ $(1/mean\ service\ time)*(number\ of\ servers)>(1/(mean\ interarrival\ time))$. I'll refer to this equation as Equation 1.

Essentially, if Equation 1 is true, we can serve more people per hour than are arriving. For example, if mean service time equals 2 minutes (or 1/30 of an hour), and mean interarrival time equals 1 minute (or 1/60 of an hour), Equation 1 tells us that *30*(number of servers)>60*, or that the number of servers must be greater than or equal to 3 for a steady state to exist. If you cannot serve customers faster than they arrive, eventually you fall behind and never catch up, resulting in an infinite line.

Why does variability degrade the performance of a queuing system?

To see why variability degrades the performance of a queuing system, consider a one-server system in which customers arrive every 2 minutes and service times always equal 2 minutes. There will never be more than one customer in the system. Now suppose that customers arrive every 2 minutes, but half of all service times are 0.5 minutes and half are 3.5 minutes. Even though arrivals are totally predictable, the uncertainty in service times means that eventually we will fall behind and a line will form. For example, if the first four customers have 3.5 minute service times, after 12 minutes, we will have four customers waiting, which is illustrated in the following table.

Time	Event	present after event
0 minutes	Arrival	1 person
2 minutes	Arrival	2 people
3.5 minutes	Service completed	1 person
4 minutes	Arrival	2 people
6 minutes	Arrival	3 people
7 minutes	Service completed	2 people
8 minutes	Arrival	3 people
10 minutes	Arrival	4 people
10.5 minutes	Service completed	3 people
12 minutes	Arrival	4 people

Can I easily determine the average time a person spends at airport security or waiting in line at a bank?

The *Model* worksheet of the file Queuingtemplate.xlsx contains a template that you can use to determine approximate values for L, W, L_q, and W_q (usually within 10 percent of their true value). The worksheet is shown in Figure 69-1.

	A	B
3	Arrival rate	0.077736
4	Service rate	0.01297
5	s(servers)	6
6	Mean interarrival time	12.864
7	Mean service time	77.102
8	Standard deviation of interarrival times	4.439
9	Standard deviation of service times	48.051
10	CV arrive	0.119074
11	CV service	0.388395
12	u	5.993626
13	ro	0.998938
14	R(s,mu)	0.735525
15	E_C(s,mu)	0.997054
16	W_q	3060.035
17	L_q	237.8758
18	W	3137.137
19	L	243.8694

Figure 69-1   Queuing template

After entering the following data, the template computes W_q, L_q, W, and L. The parameters in cells B6:B9 can easily be estimated by using past data:

❏ Number of servers (cell B5)

❏ Mean interarrival time (cell B6)

❏ Mean service time (cell B7)

❏ Standard deviation of interarrival times (cell B8)

❏ Standard deviation of service times (cell B9)

Here's an example of the template in action. We want to determine how the operating characteristics of an airline ticket counter during the 9:00 A.M. to 5:00 P.M. shift depend on the number of agents working. In the *Queuing Data* worksheet in the file Queuingtemplate.xlsx, shown in Figure 69-2, I've tabulated interarrival times and service times. (Some rows have been hidden.)

	A	B	C	D
1	mean	12.86440678	77.10169492	seconds!
2	sigma	4.43908047	48.05051039	
3		Interarrival time	Service Time	
4		5	95	
5		17	240	
6		12	71	
7		18	68	
8		9	90	
9		16	117	
10		15	291	
11		15	116	
12		10	107	
13		11	100	
14		9	28	
15		15	119	
16		19	98	
17		9	72	
18		16	127	
57		13	74	
58		11	27	
59		13	84	
60		19	90	
61		11	42	

Figure 69-2 Airline interarrival and service times

By copying from cell B1 to C1 the formula *AVERAGE(B4:B62)*, we find the mean interarrival time is 12.864 seconds and the mean service time is 77.102 seconds. Because mean service time is almost six times as large as mean interarrival time, we will need at least six agents to guarantee a steady state. Copying from cell B2 to C2 the formula *STDEV(B4:B62)* tells us that the standard deviation of the interarrival times is 4.439 seconds, and the standard deviation of the service times is 48.051 seconds.

Returning to the queuing template in the *Model* worksheet, if we enter these values in cells B6:B9 and enter 6 servers in cell B5, we find that disaster ensues. In the steady state, nearly 244 people will be in line (cell B19). You've probably been at the airport in this situation.

I used a one-way data table (shown in Figure 69-3) to determine how changing the number of agents affects the system's performance. In cells F10:F14, I entered the number of agents we want to consider (6 through 10). In cell G9, I enter the formula to compute $L(=B19)$ and in H9, I enter the formula to compute $W(=B18)$. Next, I select the table range (F8:H14) and then click Data Table from the What-If portion of the Data tab. After choosing cell B5 (the number of servers) as the Row Input Cell, we obtain the data table shown in Figure 69-3. Notice that adding just one ticket agent to our original six agents reduces the expected number of customers present in line from 244 to fewer than 7. Adding the seventh agent reduces a customer's average time in the system from 3137 seconds (53 minutes) to 90 seconds (1.5 minutes). This example shows that a small increase in service capacity can greatly improve the performance of a queuing system.

	E	F	G	H	I	J	K
8			L	W			
9		Servers	243.8694	3137.137			
10			6	243.8694	3137.137		
11			7	6.917954	88.99256		
12			8	6.263082	80.56828		
13			9	6.092279	78.37108		
14			10	6.03186	77.59385		
15						servers	
16		3137.137	6	7	8	9	10
17			40	2418.069	86.19844	79.75375	78.07286	77.47827
18			50	3330.979	89.74579	80.78786	78.45147	77.625
19	sigma		60	4446.757	94.08143	82.05177	78.91421	77.80435
20	service time		70	5765.405	99.20538	83.54548	79.46109	78.0163
21			80	7286.921	105.1176	85.26899	80.0921	78.26085
22			90	9011.305	111.8182	87.22231	80.80725	78.53802

Figure 69-3   Sensitivity analysis for an airline ticket counter

In cells F16:K22, I used a two-way data table to examine the sensitivity of the average time in the system (*W*) to changes in the number of servers and standard deviation of service times. The Row Input Cell is B5, and the Column Input Cell is B9. When seven agents are working, an increase in the standard deviation of service times from 40 seconds to 90 seconds results in a 29 percent increase in the mean time in the system (from 86.2 seconds to 111.8 seconds).

> **Note**   Readers who are interested in a more extensive discussion of the queuing theory should refer to my book *Operations Research: Applications and Algorithms* (Duxbury Press, 2003).

Problems

A bank has six tellers. Use the following information to answer Problems 1–4:

- Mean service time equals 1 minute.

- Mean interarrival time equals 25 seconds.

- Standard deviation of service times equals 1 minute.

- Standard deviation of interarrival times equals 10 seconds.

1. Determine the average time a customer waits in line.

2. On average, how many customers are present in the bank line?

3. Would you recommend adding more tellers?

4. Suppose it costs $20 per hour to have a teller working and we value a customer's time at $15 per hour. How many tellers should we have working?

Chapter 70

Estimating a Demand Curve

- What do I need to know to price a product?
- What is the meaning of *elasticity of demand*?
- Is there any easy way to estimate a demand curve?
- What does a demand curve tell us about a customer's willingness to pay for our product?

Every business must determine a price for each of its products. Pricing a product properly is difficult. In Chapter 71, "Pricing Products by Using Tie-Ins," and Chapter 72, "Pricing Products by Using Subjectively Determined Demand," I'll describe some simple models that might aid you in pricing a product to maximize profitability. For further insights into pricing, refer to the excellent book *Power Pricing*, by Robert J. Dolan and Hermann Simon (Free Press, 1996).

What do I need to know to price a product?

Let's consider a product such as a candy bar. In order to determine a profit-maximizing price, we need to know two things:

- ❑ The variable cost of producing each unit of the product (we'll call this *UC*).
- ❑ The product's demand curve. Simply put, a demand curve tells us the number of units of our product a customer will demand at each price. In short, if we charge a price of $\$p$ per unit, the demand curve gives us a number $D(p)$, which equals the number of units of our product that will be demanded at price $\$p$. Of course, a firm's demand curve is constantly changing and often depends on factors beyond the firm's control (such as the state of the economy and a competitor's price).

After we know *UC* and the demand curve, the profit corresponding to a price of $\$p$ is simply $(p-UC)*D(p)$. After we have an equation for $D(p)$, which gives the quantity of the product demanded for each price, we can use the Microsoft Office Excel Solver feature to find the profit-maximizing price, which we'll do in Chapters 71 and 72.

What is the meaning of *elasticity of demand*?

Given a demand curve, the *price elasticity* for demand is the percentage decrease in demand resulting from a 1 percent increase in price. When elasticity is larger than 1 percent, demand is price elastic. When demand is price elastic, a price cut will increase revenue. When elasticity is less than 1 percent, demand is price inelastic. When demand is price inelastic, a price cut will decrease revenue. Here are some observed estimates of elasticities:

- Salt, 0.1 (very inelastic)
- Coffee, 0.25 (inelastic)
- Legal fees, 0.4 (inelastic)
- TV sets, 1.2 (slightly elastic)
- Restaurant meals, 2.3 (elastic)
- Foreign travel, 4.0 (very elastic)

A 1 percent decrease in the cost of foreign travel, for example, will result in a 4 percent increase in demand for foreign travel.

Is there any easy way to estimate a demand curve?

Using q to represent the quantity demanded of a product, the two most commonly used forms for estimating demand curves are as follows:

Linear demand curve. In this case, demand follows a straight line relationship of the form $q=a-bp$. For example, $q=10-p$ is a linear demand curve. (Here a and b can be determined by using a method that I'll describe later in the chapter.) When the demand curve is linear, the elasticity is constantly changing.

Power Demand Curve. In this situation, the demand curve is described by a power curve of the form $q=ap^b$, $b<0$. (See Chapter 45, "The Power Curve," for a discussion of the power curve.) Again, a and b can be determined by the method I'll describe later in the chapter. The equation $q=100p^{-2}$ is an example of a power demand curve. If demand follows a power curve, for any price, the elasticity equals $-b$. Thus, for the demand curve $q=100p^{-2}$, the price elasticity of demand always equals 2.

Suppose that a product's demand curve follows a linear or power demand curve. Given the current price and demand for a product and the product's price elasticity of demand, determining the product's demand curve is a simple matter. Here are two examples.

A product is currently selling for $100 and demand equals 500 units. The product's price elasticity for demand is 2. Assuming the demand curve is linear, we want to determine the equation of the demand curve. Our solution is in the file Linearfit.xlsx, which is shown in Figure 70-1.

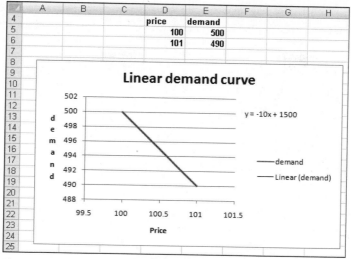

Figure 70-1   Fitting a linear demand curve

Given two points, we know that there is a unique straight line that passes through those two points. We actually know two points on our demand curve. One point is *p=100* and *q=500*. Because elasticity of demand equals 2, a 1 percent increase in price will result in a 2 percent decrease in demand. Thus, if *p=101* (a 1 percent increase), demand will drop by 2 percent of 500 (10 units), or 490. Thus *p=101* and *q=90* is a second point on our demand curve. We can now use the Excel trendline to find the straight line that passes through the points (100,500) and (101,490).

We begin by entering these points in our worksheet in the cell range D5:E6, as shown in Figure 70-1. Then we select the range D4:E6 and on the Ribbon, in the Charts group choose Scatter, Scatter With Straight Lines. After selecting this option for a Scatter chart we see the graph has a positive slope. This would imply that higher prices lead to higher demand, which cannot be correct. The problem is that with only two data points, Excel assumes that the data points we want to graph are in separate columns, not separate rows. To ensure Excel understands that the individual points are in separate rows, simply click inside the graph and on the Ribbon, click the Design tab in the Chart Tools section. Click Switch Row/Column in the Data section of the Design tab. Note that by clicking the Select Data button, you can change the source data that generates your chart. Now we right-click one of the points, click Add Trendline, and then click the Linear and the Display Equation On Chart options. After clicking OK in the Add Trendline dialog box, you will see the straight line plot, complete with the equation shown in Figure 70-1. Because *x* is price and *y* is demand, the equation for our demand curve is *q=1500−10p*. This equation means that each $1 increase in price costs us 10 units of demand. Of course, demand cannot be linear for all values of *p* because for large values of *p*, a linear demand curve will yield negative demand. For prices near the current price, however, the linear demand curve is usually a good approximation to the product's true demand curve.

As a second example, let's again assume that a product is currently selling for $100 and demand equals 500 units. The product's price elasticity for demand is 2. Now let's fit a power demand curve to this information. See the file Powerfit.xlsx, shown in Figure 70-2.

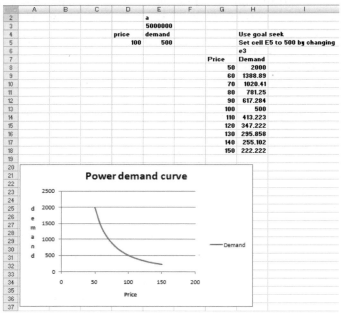

Figure 70-2   Power demand curve

In cell E3, we enter a trial value for a. Then, in cell D5, we enter the current price of $100. Because elasticity of demand equals 2, we know that the demand curve has the form $q=ap^{-2}$, where a is unknown. In cell E5, we enter the demand for a price of $100, corresponding to the value of a in cell E3, with the formula a*D5^-2. Now we use the Goal Seek command (for details, see Chapter 16, "The Goal Seek Command") to determine the value of a that makes our demand for price $100 equal to 500 units. I simply set cell E5 to the value of 500 by changing cell E3. I find that a value for a of 5 million yields a demand of 500 at a price of $100. Thus, our demand curve (graphed in Figure 70-2) is given by $q=5,000,000p^{-2}$. For any price, the price elasticity of demand on this demand curve equals 2.

What does a demand curve tell us about a customer's willingness to pay for our product?

Let's suppose we are trying to sell a software program to a Fortune 500 company. Let q equal the number of copies of the program the company demands, and let p equal the price charged for the software. Suppose we have estimated that the demand curve for software is given by $q=400-p$. Clearly, our customer is willing to pay less for each additional unit of our software program. Locked inside this demand curve is information about how much the company is willing to pay for each unit of our program. This information is crucial for maximizing profitability of sales.

Let's rewrite our demand curve as *p=400−q*. Thus, when *q=1*, *p=$399*, and so on. Now let's try and figure out the value our customer attaches to each of the first two units of our program. Assuming that our customer is rational, the customer will buy a unit if and only if the value of the unit exceeds our price. At a price of $400, demand equals 0, so the first unit cannot be worth $400. At a price of $399, however, demand equals 1 unit. Therefore, the first unit must be worth somewhere between $399 and $400. Similarly, at a price of $399, the customer does not purchase the second unit. At a price of $398, however, the customer is purchasing two units, so the customer does purchase the second unit. Therefore, the customer values the second unit somewhere between $399 and $398.

It can be shown that the best approximation to the value of the *i*th unit purchased by the customer is the price that makes demand equal to *i−0.5*. For example, by setting *q* equal to 0.5, we find that the value of the first unit is *400−0.5=$399.50*. Similarly, by setting *q=1.5*, we find that the value of the second unit is *400−1.5=$398.50*.

Problems

1. Suppose we are charging $60 for a board game we invented and have sold 3000 copies during the last year. Elasticity for board games is known to equal 3. Use this information to determine a linear and power demand curve.

2. For each of your answers in Problem 1, determine the value consumers place on the two thousandth unit purchased of your game.

Chapter 71

Pricing Products by Using Tie-Ins

- How does the fact that customers buy razor blades as well as razors affect the profit-maximizing price of razors?

Certain consumer product purchases frequently result in the purchase of related products, or *tie-ins*. Here are some examples:

Original purchase	Tie-in product
Razor	Razor blades
Men's suit	Shirt and/or tie
Personal computer	Software training manual
Video game console	Video game

Using the techniques I described in Chapter 70, "Estimating a Demand Curve," it's easy to determine a demand curve for the product that's originally purchased. We can then use Microsoft Office Excel Solver to determine the original product price that maximizes the sum of the profit earned from the original and the tie-in products. The following example shows how this analysis is done.

How does the fact that customers buy razor blades as well as razors affect the profit-maximizing price of razors?

Suppose that we're currently charging $5.00 for a razor and we're selling 6 million razors. Assume that the variable cost of producing a razor is $2.00. Finally, suppose that the price elasticity of demand for razors is 2. What price should we charge for razors?

Let's assume (incorrectly) that no purchasers of razors buy blades. We determine our demand curve (assuming a linear demand curve) as shown in Figure 71-1 on the next page. (You can find this data and the chart on the *No Blades* worksheet in the file Razors-andblades.xlsx.) Two points on the demand curve are *price=$5.00, demand=6 million razors* and *price=$5.05* (an increase of 1 percent), *demand=5.88 million* (2 percent less than 6 million). After drawing a chart and inserting a linear trend line as shown in Chapter 70, we find the demand curve equation is $y=18-2.4x$. Because x equals price and y equals demand, we can write the demand curve for razors as follows: *demand (in millions)=18–2.4(price)*.

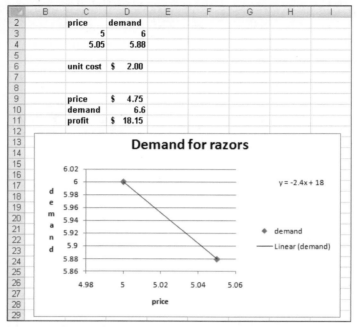

Figure 71-1 Determining the profit-maximizing price for razors

I associate the names in cell C6 and the range C9:C11 with cells D6 and D9:D11. Next, I enter a trial price in D9 and determine demand for that price in cell D10 with the formula *18-2.4*price*. Then I determine in cell D11 the profit for razors by using the formula *demand*(price–unit_cost)*.

Next, I use Solver to determine the profit-maximizing price. The Solver Parameters dialog box is shown in Figure 71-2.

Figure 71-2 Solver Parameters dialog box set up for maximizing razor profit

We choose to maximize our profit cell (cell D11) by changing our price (cell D9). The model is not linear because our target cell multiplies together two quantities—*demand*

and *(price–cost)*–each depending on our changing cell. Solver finds that by charging $4.75 for a razor, we can maximize our profit. (Maximum profit is $18.15 million.)

Now let's suppose that the average purchaser of a razor buys 50 blades and that we earn $0.15 of profit per blade purchased. How does this change the price we should charge for a razor? We assume that the price of a blade is fixed. (In Problem 3 at the end of the chapter, we will allow the blade price to change.) Our analysis is in the *Blades* worksheet, which is shown in Figure 71-3.

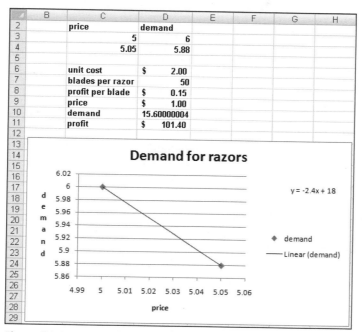

Figure 71-3   Price for razors with blade profit included

I used the Create From Selection command in the Defined Names group on the Formulas tab to associate the names in cells C6:C11 with cells D6:D11. (For example, cell D10 is named *Demand*.)

> **Note**   The astute reader will recall that I also named cell D10 of the *No Blades* worksheet *Demand*. What does Excel do when you use the range name *Demand* in a formula? Excel simply refers to the cell named *Demand* in the current worksheet. In other words, when we use the range name *Demand* in the *Blades* worksheet, Excel refers to cell D10 of that worksheet, and not to cell D10 in the *No Blades* worksheet.

In cells D7 and D8, I've entered the relevant information about blades. In D9, I entered a trial price for razors, and in D10, I computed our demand with the formula *18-2.4*price*. Next, in cell D11, I computed total profit from razors and blades with the formula *demand*(price–unit_cost)+demand*blades_per_razor*profit_per_blade*. Notice that *demand*blades_per_razor*profit_per_blade* is our profit from blades.

Our Solver setup is exactly as was shown earlier in Figure 71-2: change the price to max-imize the profit. Of course, now our profit formula includes the profit earned from blades. We find that profit is maximized by charging only $1.00 (half the variable cost!) for a razor. This price results from making so much money from the blades. We are much better off ensuring that many people have razors even though we lose $1.00 on each razor sold. Many companies do not understand the importance of the profit from tie-in products. This leads them to overprice their primary product and not maximize their total profit.

Problems

> **Note**   In all of the following problems, assume a linear demand curve.

1. We are trying to determine the profit-maximizing price for a video game console. Cur-rently we are charging $180 and selling 2 million consoles per year. It costs $150 to pro-duce a console, and price elasticity of demand for consoles is 3. What price should we charge for a console?

2. Now assume that, on average, a purchaser of our video game console buys 10 video games and we earn $10 profit on each video game. What is the correct price for consoles?

3. In our razor and blade example, suppose the cost to produce a blade is $0.20. If we charge $0.35 for a blade, a customer buys an average of 50 blades from us. Assume the price elas-ticity of demand for blades is 3. What price should we charge for a razor and for a blade?

4. You are managing a movie theater that can handle up to 8000 patrons per week. The cur-rent demand, price, and elasticity for ticket sales, popcorn, soda, and candy are given in Figure 71-4. The theater keeps 45 percent of ticket revenues. Unit cost per ticket, pop-corn sales, candy sales, and soda sales are also given. Assuming linear demand curves, how can the theater maximize profits? Demand for foods is the fraction of patrons who purchase the given food.

	A	B	C	D	E	F	G	H	I
2									
3				elasticity	current price	demand	cost	ticket percentage	
4		keep 45%	ticket	3	8	3000	0	0.45	
5			popcorn	1.3	3.5	0.5	0.35		
6			soda	1.5	3	0.6	0.6		
7			candy	2.5	2.5	0.2	1		

Figure 71-4   Movie problem data

5. A prescription drug is produced in the United States and sold internationally. Each unit of the drug costs $60 to produce. In the German market, we are selling the drug for 150 Euros per unit. The current exchange rate is 0.667 U.S. dollars per Euro. Current demand for the drug is 100 units, and the estimated elasticity is 2.5. Assuming a linear demand curve, determine the appropriate sales price (in Euros) for the drug.

Chapter 72

Pricing Products by Using Subjectively Determined Demand

- Sometimes I don't know the price elasticity for a product. In other situations, I don't believe a linear or power demand curve is relevant. Can I still estimate a demand curve and use Solver to determine a profit-maximizing price?

- How can a small drugstore determine the profit-maximizing price for lipstick?

Sometimes I don't know the price elasticity for a product. In other situations, I don't believe a linear or power demand curve is relevant. Can I still estimate a demand curve and use Solver to determine a profit-maximizing price?

In situations when you don't know the price elasticity for a product or don't think you can rely on a linear or power demand curve, a good way to determine a product's demand curve is to identify the lowest price and highest price that seem reasonable. You can then try to estimate the product's demand with the high price, the low price, and a price midway between the high and low prices. Given these three points on the product's demand curve, you can use the Microsoft Office Excel Trendline feature to fit a quadratic demand curve with the following formula (which I'll call Equation 1):

Demand=a(price)^2+b(price)+c

For any three specified points on the demand curve, values of a, b, and c exist that will make Equation 1 *exactly* fit the three specified points. Because Equation 1 fits three points on the demand curve, it seems reasonable to believe that the equation will give an accurate representation of demand for other prices. We can then use Equation 1 and Solver to maximize profit, which is given by the formula (*price−unit cost*)*demand*. The following example shows how this process works.

How can a small drugstore determine the profit-maximizing price for lipstick?

Let's suppose that a drugstore pays $0.90 for each unit of lipstick it orders. The store is considering charging from $1.50 through $2.50 for a unit of lipstick. They think that at a price of $1.50, they will sell 60 units per week. (See Figure 72-1 and the file

Lipstickprice.xlsx.) At a price of $2.00, they think they will sell 51 units per week, and at a price of $2.50, 20 units per week. What price should they charge for lipstick?

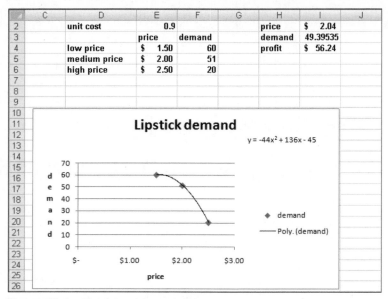

	C	D	E	F	G	H	I	J
2		unit cost	0.9			price	$ 2.04	
3			price	demand		demand	49.39535	
4		low price	$ 1.50	60		profit	$ 56.24	
5		medium price	$ 2.00	51				
6		high price	$ 2.50	20				

Figure 72-1   Lipstick pricing model

We begin by entering the three points with which we'll chart our demand curve in the cell range E3:F6. After selecting E3:F6, we click the Charts group on the Ribbon and then select the first option for a Scatter chart. We can then right-click a data point and select Add Trendline. In the Format Trendline dialog box, we choose Polynomial and select 2 in the Order box (to obtain a quadratic curve of the form of Equation 1). Then select the option Display Equation On Chart. See Figure 72-2.

You will see the chart shown in Figure 72-1. Our estimated demand curve (Equation 2) is *Demand=−44*Price^2+136*Price−45*.

Next, we insert a trial price in cell I2. We compute our product demand by using Equation 2 in cell I3 with the formula *−44*price^2+136*price−45*. (I've named cell I2 *Price*.) Then we compute our weekly profit from lipstick sales in cell I4 with the formula *demand*(price−unit_cost)*. (Cell E2 is named *Unit_Cost* and cell I3 is named *Demand*.) Then we use Solver to determine the price that maximizes profit. The Solver Parameters dialog box is shown in Figure 72-3. Note that we constrain our price to be from the lowest through the highest specified prices ($1.50 through $2.50). If we allow Solver to consider prices outside this range, the quadratic demand curve might slope upward, which implies that a higher price would result in larger demand. This result is unreasonable, which is why we constrain our price.

We find that our drugstore should charge $2.04 for a lipstick unit. This yields sales of 49.4 units per week and a weekly profit of $56.24.

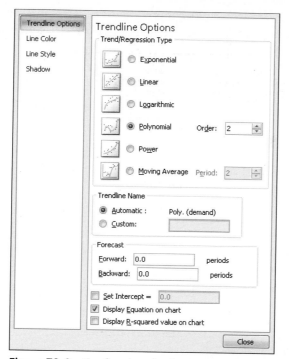

Figure 72-2   Configuring the Format Trendline dialog box for selecting polynomial demand curve

Figure 72-3   Configuring the Solver Parameters dialog box to calculate lipstick pricing

The approach to pricing outlined in this chapter requires no knowledge of the concept of price elasticity. Inherently, the Solver considers the elasticity for each price when it determines the profit-maximizing price. This approach can easily be applied by organizations that sell thousands of different products. The only data that needs to be specified for each product is its variable cost and the three given points on the demand curve.

Problems

1. Suppose it costs $250 to produce a video game console. A price from $200 through $400 is under consideration. Estimated demand for the game console is shown in the following table.

Price	Demand (in millions)
$200	2
$300	0.9
$400	0.2

What price should we charge for game console?

2. This problem uses the demand information given in Problem 1. Each game owner buys an average of 10 video games. We earn $10 profit per video game. What price should we charge for the game console?

3. We are trying to determine the correct price for a new weekly magazine. The variable cost of printing and distributing a copy of the magazine is $0.50. We are thinking of charging from $0.50 through $1.30 per copy. The estimated weekly sales of the magazine are shown in the following table.

Price	Demand (in millions)
$0.50	2
$0.90	1.2
$1.30	0.3

In addition to sales revenue from the magazine, we can charge $30 per 1000 copies sold for each of the 20 pages of advertising in each week's magazine. What price should we charge for the magazine?

Chapter 73
Nonlinear Pricing

- What is linear pricing?

- What is nonlinear pricing?

- What is bundling, and how can it increase profitability?

- How can I find a profit-maximizing nonlinear pricing plan?

What is linear pricing?

In Chapter 71, "Pricing Products by Using Tie-Ins," and Chapter 72, "Pricing Products by Using Subjectively Determined Demand," I showed how to determine a profit-maximizing price for a product. We made the implicit assumption, however, that no matter how many units a customer purchases, the customer is charged the same amount per unit. This model is known as *linear pricing* because the cost of buying x units is a straight line function of x (*cost of x units=(unit price)*x*). We will see in this chapter that *nonlinear pricing* can often greatly increase a company's profit.

What is nonlinear pricing?

A *nonlinear pricing* scheme simply means that the cost of buying x units is not a straight line function of x. We have all encountered nonlinear pricing strategies. Here are some examples:

- **Quantity discounts.** The first five units might cost $20 each and the remaining units $12 each. Quantity discounts are commonly used by companies selling software and computers. An example of the cost of purchasing x units is shown in the *Nonlinear Pricing Examples* worksheet in the file Nlp.xlsx, which is shown in Figure 73-1 on the next page. Notice that the graph has a slope of 20 for 5 or fewer units purchased and a slope of 12 for more than 5 units purchased.

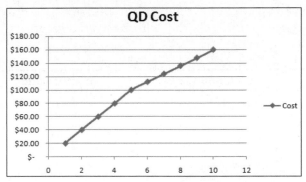

Figure 73-1 Cost of quantity discount plan

☐ **Two-part tariff.** When you join a country club, you usually pay a fixed fee for joining the club and then a fee for each round of golf you play. Suppose that your country club charges a membership fee of $500 per year and charges $20 per round of golf. This type of pricing strategy is called a *two-part tariff*. For this pricing policy, the cost of purchasing a given number of rounds of golf is shown in Figure 73-2. Again, look at the *Nonlinear Pricing Examples* worksheet in Nlp.xlsx. Note that the graph has a slope of 520 from 0 through 1 units purchased and a slope of 20 for more than 1 unit purchased. Because a straight line must always have the same slope, we can see that a two-part tariff is highly nonlinear.

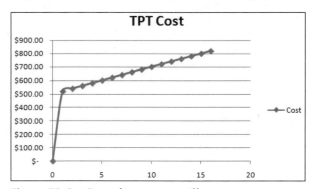

Figure 73-2 Cost of two-part tariff

What is bundling, and how can it increase profitability?

Price bundling involves offering a customer a set of products for a price less than the sum of the products' individual prices. To analyze why bundling works, we need to understand how a rational consumer makes decisions. For each product combination available, a rational consumer looks at the value of what we are selling and subtracts the cost to purchase it. This yields the *consumer surplus* of the purchase. A rational consumer buys nothing if the consumer surplus of each available option is negative. Otherwise, the consumer purchases the product combination having the largest consumer surplus.

So how can bundling increase our profitability? Suppose that we sell computers and printers and have two customers. The values each customer attaches to a computer and a printer are shown here:

Customer	Computer value	Printer value
1	$1,000	$500
2	$500	$1,000

We only offer the computer and printer for sale separately. By charging $1,000 for a printer and for a computer, we will sell one printer and one computer and receive $2,000 in revenue. Now suppose we offer the printer and computer in combination for $1,500. Each customer buys both the computer and the printer, and we receive $3,000 in revenue. By bundling the computer and printer, we can extract more of the consumer's total valuation. Bundling works best if customer valuations for the bundled products are negatively correlated. In our example, the negative correlation between the values for the bundled products is a consequence of the fact that the customer who places a high value on a printer places a low value on a computer, and the customer who places a low value on a printer places a high value on a computer.

We know that when you go to a theme park such as Disneyland, you don't buy a ticket for each ride. You either buy a ticket to enter the theme park or you don't go. This is an example of *pure bundling* because the consumer does not have the option of paying for a subset of the offered products. This approach reduces lines (imagine a line at *every* ride) and also results in more profit.

To see why this bundling approach increases profitability, suppose there is only one customer and that the number of rides the customer wants to go on is governed by a demand curve that is calculated as *(Number of rides)=20–2*(Price of ride)*. From the discussion of demand curves in Chapter 70, "Estimating a Demand Curve," we know that the value the consumer gives to the ith ride is the price that makes demand equal to $i-0.5$. Thus, we know that $i-0.5=20-2*(value of ride i)$ or, solving for the value of ride i, we find *(value of ride i)=10.25–(i/2)*. The first ride is worth $9.75, the second ride is worth $9.25...the twentieth ride is worth $0.25.

Assume we charge a constant price per ride and that it costs us $2 in variable costs per ride. We seek the profit-maximizing linear pricing scheme. In the *OnePrice* worksheet in the file Nlp.xlsx, shown in Figure 73-3, I show how to determine the profit-maximizing price per ride.

	B	C	D
6	Linear		
7	Pricing		
8		price	$ 6.00
9		Demand	$ 8.00
10		unit cost	$ 2.00
11			
12		profit	$ 32.00

Figure 73-3   Profit-maximizing linear pricing scheme

I've associated the range names in C8:C10 with cells D8:D10 I enter a trial price in cell D8 and compute the number of ride tickets purchased in cell D9 with the formula 20−(2*D8). Then I compute our profit in cell D12 with the formula *Demand*(price−unit_cost)*. I can now use the Microsoft Office Excel Solver feature to maximize the value in D12 (profit) by changing cell D8 (price). We find that a price of $6 results in eight ride tickets being purchased. We earn a maximum profit of $32.

Now let's pretend we're like Disneyland and offer only a bundle of 20 rides to the customer. We set a price equal to the sum of the customer's valuations for each ride ($9.75+$9.25+...$0.75+$0.25=$100.00). The customer values all 20 rides at $100.00, so the customer will buy a park entry ticket for $100.00. We earn a profit of *$100.00−$2.00(20)=$60.00*, which almost doubles our profit from linear pricing.

How can I find a profit-maximizing nonlinear pricing plan?

In this section, I'll show how you can determine a profit-maximizing, two-part-tariff pricing plan for our amusement park example. We'll proceed as follows:

- ❏ Hypothesize trial values for the fixed fee and the price per ride.
- ❏ Determine the value the customer associates with each ride (*Value of ride i= 10.5−0.5i*).
- ❏ Determine the cumulative value associated with buying *i* rides.
- ❏ Determine the price charged for *i* rides, *Fixed fee + i*(price per ride)*.
- ❏ Determine the consumer surplus for buying *i* rides, *Value of i rides−price of i rides*.
- ❏ Determine the maximum consumer surplus.
- ❏ Determine the number of units purchased. If the maximum consumer surplus is negative, no units are purchased. Otherwise, we'll use the MATCH function to find the number of units yielding the maximum surplus.
- ❏ Use a VLOOKUP function to look up our revenue corresponding to the number of units purchased.
- ❏ Compute our profit as *revenue−costs*.
- ❏ Use a two-way data table to determine a profit-maximizing fixed fee and price per ride.

Our work is in the *Two-Part Tariff* worksheet in the file Nlp.xlsx, which is shown in Figure 73-4.

To begin, I named call *F2.Fixed* and call F3 *LP*. I entered trial values for the fixed fee and the price per ride in cells F2 and F3. Next, I determine the value the consumer places on each ride by copying from cell E6 to E7:E25 the formula *10.25−(D6/2)*. We find that the customer places a value of $9.75 on the first ride, $9.25 on the second ride, and so on.

	C	D	E	F	G	H	I	J
1								
2	cost		fixed fee	$ 56.00		Units bought	15	
3	$ 2.00		price per ride	$ 2.50		Revenue	$ 93.50	
4					Max surplus	Prod Cost	$ 30.00	
5		Unit	Value	Cum Value	Price paid	0.25		
6		1	9.75	9.75	58.5	Surplus		Profit
7		2	9.25	19	61	-48.75		$ 63.50
8		3	8.75	27.75	63.5	-42		
9		4	8.25	36	66	-35.75		
10		5	7.75	43.75	68.5	-30		
11		6	7.25	51	71	-24.75		
12		7	6.75	57.75	73.5	-20		Fixed
13		8	6.25	64	76	-15.75		
14		9	5.75	69.75	78.5	-12		
15		10	5.25	75	81	-8.75		
16		11	4.75	79.75	83.5	-6		
17		12	4.25	84	86	-3.75		
18		13	3.75	87.75	88.5	-2		
19		14	3.25	91	91	-0.75		
20		15	2.75	93.75	93.5	0		
21		16	2.25	96	96	0.25		
22		17	1.75	97.75	98.5	0		
23		18	1.25	99	101	-0.75		
24		19	0.75	99.75	103.5	-2		
25		20	0.25	100	106	-3.75		
						-6		

Figure 73-4   Determination of optimal two-part tariff

To compute the cumulative value of the first *i* rides, I copy from F6 to F7:F25 the formula *SUM($E$6:E6)*. This formula adds up all values in column E that are in or above the current row. By copying from G6 to G7:G25 the formula *fixed_fee+price_per_ride*D6*, I compute the cost of *i* rides. For example, the cost of five rides is $68.50.

Recall that the consumer surplus for *i* rides equals *(Value of i rides)−(Cost of i rides)*. By copying from cell H6 to the range H7:H25 the formula *F6−G6*, I compute the consumer's surplus for purchasing any number of rides. For example, the consumer surplus for purchasing five rides is −$24.75, which is the result of the large fixed fee.

In cell H4, I compute the maximum consumer surplus with the formula *MAX(H6:H25)*. Remember that if the maximum consumer surplus is negative, no units are purchased. Otherwise, the consumer will purchase the number of units yielding the maximum consumer surplus. Therefore, entering in cell I1 the formula *IF(H4>=0,MATCH(H4,H6:H25,0),0)* determines the number of units purchased (in our case, 15). Notice that the MATCH function finds the number of rows we need to move down in the range H6:H24 to find the first match to the maximum surplus.

We now name the range D5:G25 as *Lookup*. We can then look up our total revenue in the fourth column of this range based on the number of units purchased (which is already computed in cell I1). Our total revenue is computed in cell I2 with the formula *IF(I1=0,0, VLOOKUP(I1,lookup,4))*. Notice that if no rides are purchased, we earn no revenue. We compute our total production cost for rides purchased in cell I3 with the formula *I1*C3*. In cell J6, I compute our profit as revenues less costs with the formula *I2−I3*.

Now we can use a two-way data table to determine the profit-maximizing combination of fixed fee and price per ride. The data table is shown in Figure 73-5 on the next page. (Many rows and columns are hidden.) In setting up the data table, we vary the fixed fee between $10.00 and $60.00 (the values in the range K10:K60) and vary the price per ride between $0.50 and $5.00 (the values in L9:BE9). We recompute profit in cell K9 with the formula =J6.

We now select the table range (cells K9:BE60), and then on the Data tab of the Ribbon, in the Data Tools group, click What-If Analysis, and then select Data Table. Our column input cell is F2 (the fixed fee) and row input cell is F3 (the price per ride). After clicking OK in the Table dialog box, we've computed our profit for each fixed fee and price per ride combination represented in the data table.

	J	K	L	M	N	AE	AF	BB	BC	BD	BE
8			Unit	cost							
9		$ 63.50	0.5	0.6	0.7	2.4	2.5	4.7	4.8	4.9	5
10		10	-18.5	-16.6	-14.7	16	17.5	39.7	38	39	40
11	Fixed	11	-17.5	-15.6	-13.7	17	18.5	40.7	39	40	41
12	cost	12	-16.5	-14.6	-12.7	18	19.5	41.7	40	41	42
13		13	-15.5	-13.6	-11.7	19	20.5	42.7	41	42	43
14		14	-14.5	-12.6	-10.7	20	21.5	43.7	42	43	44
15		15	-13.5	-11.6	-9.7	21	22.5	44.7	43	44	45
16		16	-12.5	-10.6	-8.7	22	23.5	45.7	44	45	46
17		17	-11.5	-9.6	-7.7	23	24.5	46.7	45	46	47
18		18	-10.5	-8.6	-6.7	24	25.5	47.7	46	47	48
19		19	-9.5	-7.6	-5.7	25	26.5	48.7	47	48	49
20		20	-8.5	-6.6	-4.7	26	27.5	49.7	48	49	50
21		21	-7.5	-5.6	-3.7	27	28.5	50.7	49	50	51
22		22	-6.5	-4.6	-2.7	28	29.5	51.7	50	51	52
23		23	-5.5	-3.6	-1.7	29	30.5	52.7	51	52	53
24		24	-4.5	-2.6	-0.7	30	31.5	53.7	52	53	54
48		48	19.5	21.4	23.3	54	55.5	0	0	0	0
49		49	20.5	22.4	24.3	55	56.5	0	0	0	0
50		50	21.5	23.4	25.3	56	57.5	0	0	0	0
51		51	22.5	24.4	26.3	57	58.5	0	0	0	0
52		52	23.5	25.4	27.3	58	59.5	0	0	0	0
53		53	24.5	26.4	28.3	59	60.5	0	0	0	0
54		54	25.5	27.4	29.3	60	61.5	0	0	0	0
55		55	26.5	28.4	30.3	61	62.5	0	0	0	0
56		56	27.5	29.4	31.3	62	63.5	0	0	0	0
57		57	28.5	30.4	32.3	63	0	0	0	0	0
58		58	29.5	31.4	33.3	0	0	0	0	0	0
59		59	30.5	32.4	34.3	0	0	0	0	0	0
60		60	31.5	33.4	35.3	0	0	0	0	0	0

Figure 73-5   Two-way data table computes optimal two-part tariff

To highlight the profit-maximizing two-part tariff, I used conditional formatting, selecting the range L10:BE60. We choose Conditional Formatting from the Home tab of the Ribbon, click Top/Bottom Rules, and then click Top 10 Items. Then change the 10 in the dialog box to a 1, so only the largest profit is formatted. We find that a fixed fee of $56.00 and a price per ride of $2.50 earns us a profit of $63.50, which almost doubles the profit from linear pricing. A fixed fee of $59.00 and a price per ride of $2.30 also yields a profit of $63.50.

Because a quantity discount plan involves selecting three variables (cutoff, high price, and low price), we cannot use a data table to determine a profit-maximizing, quantity-discount plan. You might think we could use a Solver model (with changing cells set to cutoff, high price, and low price) to determine a profit-maximizing, quantity-discount strategy. Unfortunately, Solver often has difficulty determining optimal solutions when the target cell is computed by using formulas containing IF statements. Therefore, Solver might fail to find a profit-maximizing, quantity-discount plan. For details about how to set up Solver models involving IF statements, read Chapter 15 of my book *Introduction to Mathematical Programming* (Duxbury Press, 2003).

Problems

Both problems refer to the following situation: You own a small country club and have three types of customers who value each round of golf they play during a month, as shown in Figure 73-6.

Round #	Type 1	Type 2	Type 3
1	$60	$50	$40
2	$50	$45	$30
3	$40	$30	$20
4	$30	$15	$10
5	$20	$0	$0
6	$10	$0	$0

Figure 73-6 Data for golf problem

1. Find a profit-maximizing two-part tariff.

2. Suppose you are going to offer a pure bundle. For example, a member can play up to five rounds of golf for $60 per month. The member has no other option to choose from other than the pure bundle. What pure bundle maximizes your profit?

Chapter 74

Array Formulas and Functions

- What is an array formula?

- How do we interpret formulas such as *(D2:D7)*(E2:E7)* and *SUM(D2:D7*E2:E7)*?

- I have a list of names in one column. These names change often. Is there any easy way to transpose the listed names to one row so that changes in the original column of names are reflected in the new row?

- I have a list of monthly stock returns. Is there a way to determine the number of returns from −30 percent through −20 percent, −10 percent through 0 percent, and so on that will automatically update if I change the original data?

- Can I write one formula that will sum up the second digit of a list of integers?

- Is there a way to look at two lists of names and determine which names occur on both lists?

- Can I write a formula that averages all numbers in a list that exceed the list's median value?

- I have a sales database for a small makeup company that lists the salesperson, product, units sold, and dollar amount for every transaction. I know I can use database statistical functions to summarize this data, but can I also use array functions to summarize the data and answer questions such as how many units of makeup a salesperson sold, how many units of lipstick were sold, and how many units were sold by a specific salesperson or were lipstick?

- What are array constants and how can I use them?

- How do I edit array formulas?

- Given quarterly revenues for a toy store, can I estimate the trend and seasonality of the store's revenues?

What is an array formula?

Array formulas often provide a shortcut or more efficient approach to performing complex calculations with Microsoft Office Excel. An array formula can return a result in either one cell or in a range of cells. Array formulas perform operations on two or more sets of values, called *array arguments*. Each array argument used in an array formula must contain exactly the same number of rows and columns.

When entering an array formula, you must first select the range in which you want Excel to place the array formula's results. Then, after entering the formula in the first cell of the selected range, *you must press Ctrl+Shift+Enter*. If you fail to press Ctrl+Shift+Enter, you'll obtain incorrect or nonsensical results. I'll refer to the process of entering an array formula and then pressing Ctrl+Shift+Enter as *array-entering* a formula.

Excel also contains a variety of *array functions*. You met two array functions (LINEST and TREND) in Chapter 47, "Introduction to Multiple Regression" and Chapter 48, "Incorporating Qualitative Factors into Multiple Regression." As with an array formula, to use an array function you must first select the range in which you want the function's results placed. Then, after entering the function in the first cell of the selected range, you must press Ctrl+Shift+Enter. In this chapter, I'll introduce you to three other useful array functions: TRANSPOSE, FREQUENCY, and LOGEST.

As you'll see, you cannot delete any part of a cell range that contains results computed with an array formula. Also, you cannot paste an array formula into a range that contains both blank cells and array formulas. For example, if you have an array formula in cell C10 and you want to copy it to the cell range C10:J15, you cannot simply copy the formula to this range because the range contains both blank cells and the array formula in cell C10. To work around this difficulty, copy the formula from C10 to D10:J10 and then copy the contents of C10:J10 to C11:J15.

The best way to learn how array formulas and functions work is by looking at some examples, so let's get started.

How do we interpret formulas such as *(D2:D7)*(E2:E7)* and *SUM(D2:D7*E2:E7)*?

In the *Total Wages* worksheet in the Arrays.xlsx file, I've listed the number of hours worked and the hourly wage rates for six employees, as you can see in Figure 74-1.

	C	D	E	F	G
1		Hours	wage rate	total owed each person	grand total owed
2	John	3	$ 6.00	$ 18.00	$ 295.00
3	Jack	4	$ 7.00	$ 28.00	
4	Jill	5	$ 8.00	$ 40.00	
5	Jane	8	$ 9.00	$ 72.00	
6	Jean	6	$ 10.00	$ 60.00	
7	Jocelyn	7	$ 11.00	$ 77.00	

Figure 74-1 Using array formulas to compute hourly wages

If we wanted to compute each person's total wages, we could simply copy from F2 to F3:F7 the formula *D3*E3*. There is certainly nothing wrong with that approach, but using an array formula provides a more elegant solution. Begin by selecting the range F2:F7, where you want each person's total earnings to be computed. Then enter the formula *=(D2:D7*E2:E7)* and press Ctrl+Shift+Enter. You will see that each person's total wages has been correctly computed. Also, if you look at the formula bar, you'll see that the formula appears as *{=(D2:D7*E2:E7)}*. The curly brackets are the way Excel tells us that we've created an array formula. (You don't enter the curly brackets that show up at the beginning and end of an array formula, but to indicate that a formula is an array formula in this chapter, we'll show the curly brackets.)

To see how this formula works, click in the formula bar, highlight *D2:D7* in the formula, and then press F9. You will see *{3;4;5;8;6;7}*, which is the way Excel creates the cell range D2:D7 as an array. Now select E2:E7 in the formula bar, and then press F9 again. You will see *{6;7;8;9;10;11}*, which is the way Excel creates an array corresponding to the range E2:E7. The inclusion of the asterisk (*) tells Excel to multiply the corresponding elements in each array. Because the cells' ranges we are multiplying include six cells each, Excel creates arrays with six items, and because we selected a range of six cells, each person's total wage is displayed in its own cell. Had we selected a range of only five cells, the sixth item in the array would not be displayed.

Suppose we want to compute the total wages earned by all employees. One approach would be to use the formula *=SUMPRODUCT(D2:D7,E2:E7)*. Again, however, let's try to create an array formula to compute total wages. We begin by selecting one cell (I chose cell G2) in which to place our result. Then we enter in cell G2 the formula *=SUM(D2:D7* E2:E7)*. After pressing Ctrl+Shift+Enter, we obtain *(3)(6)+(4)(7)+(5)(8)+(8)(9)+(6)(10)+ (7)(11)=295*. To see how this formula works, select the *D2:D7*E2:E7* portion in the formula bar and then press F9. You will see *SUM({18;28;40;74;60;77})*, which shows that Excel created a six-element array whose first element is *3*6(18)*, whose second element is *4*7(28)*, and so on, until the last element, which is *7*11 (77)*. Excel then adds up the values in the array to obtain the total of $295.

I have a list of names in one column. These names change often. Is there any easy way to transpose the listed names to one row so that changes in the original column of names are reflected in the new row?

In the *Transpose* worksheet in the Arrays.xlsx file, shown in Figure 74-2 on the next page, I've listed a set of names in cells A4:A8. We want to list these names in one row (the cell range C3:G3). If we knew that the original list of names would never change, we could accomplish this goal by copying the cell range and then using the Transpose option in the Paste Special dialog box. (See Chapter 13, "The Paste Special Command," for details.) Unfortunately, if the names in column A change, the names in the row 3 would not reflect those changes if we use Paste Special, Transpose. What we need in this situation is the TRANSPOSE function of Excel.

	A	B	C	D	E	F	G
3			Julie	Jason	Jack	Jill	Jane
4	Julie						
5	Jason						
6	Jack						
7	Jill						
8	Jane						

Figure 74-2 Using the TRANSPOSE function

The TRANSPOSE function is an array function that changes rows of a selected range into columns and vice versa. To begin using TRANSPOSE, we select the range C3:G3, where we want our transposed list of names to be placed. Then, in cell C3, we array-enter the formula =TRANSPOSE(A4:A8). The list of names is now displayed in one row. More importantly, if we change any of the names in A4:A8, the corresponding name will change in the transposed range.

I have a list of monthly stock returns. Is there a way to determine the number of returns from –30 percent through –20 percent, –10 percent through 0 percent, and so on that will automatically update if I change the original data?

This problem is a job for the FREQUENCY array function. The FREQUENCY function counts how many values in an array (called the *data array*) occur within given value ranges (specified by a bin array). The syntax of the FREQUENCY function is FREQUENCY(*data array,bin array*).

To illustrate the use of the FREQUENCY function, look at the *Frequency* worksheet in the Arrays.xlsx file, shown in Figure 74-3. I've listed monthly stock returns for a fictitious stock in the cell range A4:A77.

	A	B	C	D
1	min	-43.84%		
2	max	52.56%		
3	Returns			
4	43.81%		Total	
5	-8.30%			74
6	-25.12%		Bin values	
7	-43.84%		-0.4	1
8	-8.64%		-0.3	1
9	49.98%		-0.2	2
10	-1.19%		-0.1	5
11	46.74%		0	13
12	31.94%		0.1	11
13	-35.34%		0.2	13
14	29.28%		0.3	12
15	-1.10%		0.4	11
16	-10.67%		0.5	4
17	-12.77%		0.6	1
18	19.17%			0
19	25.06%			
20	19.03%			
21	35.82%			
22	-8.43%			
23	5.20%			
24	5.70%			
25	18.30%			
26	30.81%			
27	23.68%			
28	18.15%			

Figure 74-3 Using the FREQUENCY function

We found in cells A1 and A2 (using the MIN and MAX functions) that all returns are from −44 percent through 53 percent. Based on this information, I set up our bin value boundaries in cells C7:C17, starting at −0.4 and ending at 0.6. Now I select the range D7:D18, where I want the results of the FREQUENCY function to be placed. In this range, cell D7 will count the number of data points less than or equal to −0.4, D8 will count the number of data points greater than −0.4 and less than or equal to −0.3, and so on. Cell D17 will count all data points greater than 0.5 and less than or equal to 0.6, and cell D18 will count all the data points that are greater than 0.6.

I enter the formula =FREQUENCY(A4:A77,C7:C17), and then press Ctrl+Shift+Enter. This formula tells Excel to count the number of data points from A4:A77 (the data array) that lie in each of the bin ranges defined in C7:C17. We find, for example, that one return is greater than −0.4 and less than or equal to −0.3. Thirteen returns are greater than 0.1 and less than or equal to 0.2. If you change any of the data points in the data array, the results generated by the FREQUENCY function in cells D7:D17 will reflect the changes in your data.

Can I write one formula that will sum up the second digit of a list of integers?

In the cell range A4:A10 in the *Sum Up 2nd Digit* worksheet in the Arrays.xlsx file, I've listed seven integers. (See Figure 74-4.) We would like to write one formula that will sum up the second digit of each number. Of course, we could obtain this sum by copying from B4 to B5:B10 the formula *VALUE(MID(A4,2,1))*. This formula returns (as a numerical value) the second character in cell A4. Then we could add up the range B4:B10 and obtain the total of 27.

	A	B	C	D	E	F
1		Total				
2		27				
3						
4	140	4				
5	85	5				
6	76	6				
7	1610	6	27		Error trapped	
8	302	0			27	
9	434	3				
10	13	3				
11		1 #VALUE!				

Figure 74-4 Summing second digits in a set of integers

An array function makes this process much easier. Simply select cell C7 and array-enter the formula =SUM(VALUE(MID(A4:A10,2,1))). Your array formula will return the correct answer, 27.

To see what this formula does, highlight *MID(A4:A10,2,1)* in the formula bar and then press F9. You will see {"4";"5";"6";"6";"0";"3";"3"}. This string of values shows that Excel has created an array consisting of the second digit (viewed as text) in the cell range A4:A10. The VALUE portion of the formula changes these text strings into numerical values, which are added up by the SUM portion of the formula.

Notice that in cell A11, I entered a number with one digit. Because this number has no second digit, the MID portion of our formula returns #VALUE. How can we modify our array formula to account for the possible inclusion of one-digit integers? Simply array-enter in cell E8 the formula {SUM(IF(LEN(A4:A11)>=2,VALUE(MID(A4:A11,2,1)),0))}. This formula replaces any one-digit integer with a 0, so we still obtain the correct sum.

Is there a way to look at two lists of names and determine which names occur on both lists?

In the *Matching Names* worksheet in the Arrays.xlsx file, I've included two lists of names (in columns D and E), as you can see in Figure 74-5. We want to determine which names on List 1 also appear on List 2. To accomplish this, we select the range C5:C28 and array-enter in cell C5 the formula {MATCH(D5:D28,E5:E28,0)}. This formula loops through the cells C5:C28. In cell C5, the formula verifies whether the name in D5 has a match in column E. If a match exists, the formula returns the position of the first match in E5:E28. If no match exists, the formula returns #NA (for not available). Similarly in C6, the formula verifies whether the second name on List 1 has a match. We see, for example, that Artest does not appear on the second list but Harrington does (first matched in the second cell in the range E5:E28).

	B	C	D	E
4			List 1	List 2
5	NO	#N/A	Artest	BMiller
6	NO	#N/A	Artest	Harrington
7	YES	2	Harrington	BMiller
8	NO	#N/A	Artest	Harrington
9	NO	#N/A	Artest	Harrington
10	NO	#N/A	Artest	BMiller
11	YES	2	Harrington	BMiller
12	NO	#N/A	Artest	Mercer
13	NO	#N/A	Artest	Harrington
14	NO	#N/A	Artest	Harrington
15	YES	8	Mercer	BMiller
16	NO	#N/A	Artest	Mercer
17	NO	#N/A	O'Neal	RMiller
18	NO	#N/A	O'Neal	BMiller
19	NO	#N/A	O'Neal	RMiller
20	NO	#N/A	O'Neal	RMiller
21	YES	13	RMiller	BMiller
22	NO	#N/A	O'Neal	RMiller
23	NO	#N/A	O'Neal	RMiller
24	YES	13	RMiller	BMiller
25	NO	#N/A	O'Neal	Mercer
26	NO	#N/A	O'Neal	BMiller
27	NO	#N/A	O'Neal	RMiller
28	NO	#N/A	O'Neal	BMiller

Figure 74-5   Finding duplicates in two lists

To enter Yes for each name in List 1 with a match in List 2, and No for each List 1 name without a match, select the cell range B5:B28 and array-enter the formula {IF(ISERROR(C5:C28),"No","Yes")} in cell B5. This formula displays *No* for each cell in C5:C28 containing the #NA message and *Yes* for all cells returning a numerical value. Note that =ISERROR(x) yields *True* if the formula x evaluates to an error and yields *False* otherwise.

Can I write a formula that averages all numbers in a list that are greater than or equal to the list's median value?

In the *Average Those > Median* worksheet in the Arrays.xlsx file, shown in Figure 74-6, the range D5:D785 (named *Prices*) contains a list of prices. We'd like to average all prices that are at least as large as the median price. In cell F2, I've computed the median with the formula *Median(prices)*. In cell F3, I compute the average of numbers greater than or equal to the median by entering the formula *=SUMIF(prices,">="&F2,prices)/COUNT-IF(prices,">="&F2)*. This formula adds up all prices that are at least as large as the median value (243) and then divides by the number of prices that are at least as large as the median. We find that the average of all prices at least as large as the median price is $324.30.

	D	E	F	G
2		median	243	
3		answer	324.2977	with formula
4	Price			
5	224			
6	321		324.2977	with array
7	133			
8	310			
9	370			
10	223			
11	380			
12	253			
13	211			
14	248			
15	146			
16	334			
17	393			
18	295			
19	398			
20	166			
21	162			
22	340			
23	392			
24	370			
25	224			
26	258			
27	385			

Figure 74-6   Averaging prices at least as large as median price

An easier approach is to select cell F6 and array-enter the formula *=AVERAGE(IF (prices>=MEDIAN(prices),prices,""))}*. This formula creates an array that contains the row's price if the row's price is greater than or equal to the median price or a space otherwise. Averaging this array gives us the results we want.

I have a sales database for a small makeup company that lists the salesperson, product, units sold, and dollar amount for every transaction. I know I can use database statistical functions to summarize this data, but can I also use array functions to summarize the data and answer questions such as how many units of makeup a salesperson sold, how many units of lipstick were sold, and how many units were sold by a specific salesperson or were lipstick?

The Makeuparray.xlsx file contains a list of 1900 sales transactions made by a makeup company. For each transaction, the transaction number, salesperson, transaction date, product sold, units sold, and dollar volume are listed. You can see some of the data in Figure 74-7.

Trans Number	Name	Date	Product	Units	Dollars
1	Betsy	4/1/2004	lip gloss	45	$ 137.20
2	Hallagan	3/10/2004	foundation	50	$ 152.01
3	Ashley	2/25/2005	lipstick	9	$ 28.72
4	Hallagan	5/22/2006	lip gloss	55	$ 167.08
5	Zaret	6/17/2004	lip gloss	43	$ 130.60
6	Colleen	11/27/2005	eye liner	58	$ 175.99
7	Cristina	3/21/2004	eye liner	8	$ 25.80
8	Colleen	12/17/2006	lip gloss	72	$ 217.84
9	Ashley	7/5/2006	eye liner	75	$ 226.64
10	Betsy	8/7/2006	lip gloss	24	$ 73.50
11	Ashley	11/29/2004	mascara	43	$ 130.84
12	Ashley	11/18/2004	lip gloss	23	$ 71.03
13	Emilee	8/31/2005	lip gloss	49	$ 149.59
14	Hallagan	1/1/2005	eye liner	18	$ 56.47
15	Zaret	9/20/2006	foundation	-8	$ (21.99)
16	Emilee	4/12/2004	mascara	45	$ 137.39
17	Colleen	4/30/2006	mascara	66	$ 199.65
18	Jen	8/31/2005	lip gloss	88	$ 265.19
19	Jen	10/27/2004	eye liner	78	$ 236.15
20	Zaret	11/27/2005	lip gloss	57	$ 173.12
21	Zaret	6/2/2006	mascara	12	$ 38.08
22	Betsy	9/24/2004	eye liner	28	$ 86.51
23	Colleen	2/1/2006	mascara	25	$ 77.31
24	Hallagan	5/2/2005	foundation	29	$ 88.22
25	Jen	11/7/2004	mascara	-4	$ (9.94)
26	Emilee	12/6/2006	lip gloss	24	$ 74.62
27	Jen	4/12/2004	lipstick	38	$ 115.99
28	Cristina	9/22/2005	foundation	77	$ 233.05
29	Betsy	10/23/2006	foundation	77	$ 233.36
30	Hallagan	11/16/2005	foundation	60	$ 182.25

Figure 74-7   Makeup database

This data can easily be summarized by using database statistical functions, as I described in Chapter 39, "Summarizing Data with Database Statistical Functions," or by using COUNTIFS and SUMIFS functions (see Chapter 18, "The COUNTIF, COUNTIFS, COUNT, COUNTA, and COUNTBLANK Functions," and Chapter 19, "The SUMIF, AVERAGEIF, SUMIFS, and AVERAGEIFS Functions"). As you'll see in this section, array functions provide an easy, powerful alternative to database statistical functions.

How many units of makeup did Jen sell?   We can easily answer this question by using the SUMIF function. In this worksheet, I named the cell range J5:J1904 *Name* and the cell range M5:M1904 *Units*. I entered in cell E7 the formula *SUMIF(Name,"Jen",Units)* to sum up all the units sold by Jen. We found that Jen sold 9537 units. We can also answer this question by array-entering in cell E6 the formula =SUM(IF(J5:J1904="Jen",M5:M1904,0))}. This formula creates an array that contains the units sold for a transaction made by Jen and a 0 for all other transactions. Therefore, summing this array also yields the number of units sold by Jen, 9,537, as you can see in Figure 74-8.

	A	B	C	D	E	F	G
5					units sold by jen	units lipstick sold by jen	units sold by Jen or lipstick
6				Array function	9537	1299	17061
7				other functions	9537	1299	17061
8							
9							
10					Name	Product	
11					Jen	lipstick	
12							
13					Name	Product	
14					Jen		
15						lipstick	
16		eye liner	foundation	lip gloss	lipstick	mascara	
17	Ashley	1920	1373	1985	1066	2172	
18	Betsy	1987	2726	1857	1305	1582	
19	Cici	1960	2031	1701	1035	2317	
20	Colleen	1107	2242	1831	765	2215	
21	Cristina	1770	1729	1734	788	1790	
22	Emilee	2490	1803	1725	720	1545	
23	Hallagan	2288	2387	1840	1045	1873	
24	Jen	2302	1883	1792	1299	2261	
25	Zaret	2715	2117	1868	800	1268	

Figure 74-8   Summarizing data with array formulas

How many units of lipstick did Jen sell?   This question requires a criterion that uses two columns (Name and Product). We could answer the question by using the database statistical function formula =DSUM(J4:N1904,4,E9:F10), which is entered in cell F7. This formula shows that Jen sold 1299 units of lipstick. We can also obtain this answer by using the array formula entered in cell F6, =SUM((J5:J1904="jen")*(L5:L1904="lipstick")*M5:M1904)}.

To understand this formula, you need to know a bit about Boolean arrays. The portion of this formula that reads (J5:J1904="jen") creates a Boolean array. For each entry in J5:J1904 that equals *Jen,* the array includes the value *True,* and for each entry in J5:J1904 that does not equal *Jen,* the array contains *False.* Similarly, the (L5:L1904="lipstick") portion of our formula creates a Boolean array with a *True* corresponding to each cell in the range that contains the word *lipstick* and a *False* corresponding to each cell in the range that does not. When Boolean arrays are multiplied, another array is created using the following rules:

- *True*True=1*
- *True*False=0*
- *False*True=0*
- *False*False=0*

In short, multiplying Boolean arrays mimics the AND operator. Multiplying the product of our Boolean arrays by the values in the range M5:M1904 creates a new array. In any row in which Jen sold lipstick, this array contains the units sold. In all other rows, this array contains a 0. Summing this array yields Jen's total lipstick sales (1299).

How many units were sold by Jen or were lipstick?   In cell G7, I used the database statistical function =DSUM(J4:N1904,4,E12:F14) to find that all units that were sold by Jen or that were lipstick total 17,061. In cell G6, I computed the number of units that were sold by Jen or that were lipstick by array-entering the formula {SUM(IF((J5:J1904="jen")+(L5:L1904= "lipstick"),1,0)*M5:M1904)}.

Again, the portion of our formula that reads (J5:J1904="jen")+(L5:L1904="lipstick") creates two Boolean arrays. The first array contains *True* if and only if Jen (the formula is not case sensitive) is the salesperson. The second array contains *True* if and only if the product sold is lipstick. When Boolean arrays are added, the following rules are used:

- *False+True=1*
- *True+True=1*
- *True+False=1*
- *False+False=0*

In short, adding Boolean arrays mimics the OR operator. Therefore, our formula will create an array in which each row where Jen is the salesperson or lipstick is the product sold has the number of units sold multiplied by 1. In any other row, the number of units sold is multiplied by 0. We obtain the same result as the database statistical formula (17,061).

Can I summarize the number of units of each product sold by each salesperson?

Array formulas make answering a question such as this a snap. We begin by listing each salesperson's name in the cell range A17:A25 and each product name in the cell range B16:F16. Now we array-enter in cell B17 the formula {SUM(($J$5:$J$1904=$A17)*($L$5:$L$1904=B$16)* $M$5:$M$1904)}.

This formula counts only units of eye liner sold by Ashley (1920 units). By copying this formula to C17:F17, I compute the units of each product sold by Ashley. Next, I copy the formulas in C17:F17 to C18:C25 and compute the number of units of each product sold by each salesperson. Notice that I add a dollar sign to A in the reference to cell A17 so that I always pull the person's name, and I add a dollar sign to the 16 in the reference to cell B16 so that I always pull the product.

> **Note** The astute reader might ask why I simply didn't select the formula in B17 and try to copy it in one step to fill in the table. Remember that you cannot paste an array formula into a range that contains both blank cells and array formulas, which is why I first copied the formula in B17 to C17:F17 and then dragged it down to complete the table.

What are array constants and how can I use them?

You can create your own arrays and use them in array formulas. Simply enclose the array values in curly brackets, { }. You need to enclose text in double quotation marks (" ") as well. You can also include the logical values *True* and *False* as entries in the array. Formulas or symbols such as dollar signs or commas are not allowed in array constants.

As an example of how an array constant might be used, look at the *Creating Powers* worksheet in the Arrays.xlsx file, shown in Figure 74-9.

	C	D	E	F
3	Sales	Sales^2	Sales^3	Sales^4
4	2	4	8	16
5	4	16	64	256
6	8	64	512	4096
7	10	100	1000	10000
8	14	196	2744	38416
9	20	400	8000	160000

Figure 74-9 Creating second and fourth powers of sales

In this worksheet, we're given sales during six months, and we want to create for each month the second, third, and fourth power of sales. Simply select the range D4:F9, which is where we want the resulting computation to be placed. Array-enter in cell D4 the formula =C4:C9^{2,3,4}. In the cell range D4:D9, this formula loops through and squares each number in C4:C9. In the cell range E4:E9, the formula loops through and cubes each number in C4:C9. Finally, in the cell range F4:F9, the formula loops through and raises each number in C4:C9 to the fourth power. The array constant {2,3,4} is required to let us loop through different power values.

How do I edit array formulas?

Suppose we have an array formula that creates results in multiple cells and we want to edit, move, or delete the results. You cannot edit a single element of the array. To edit an array formula, however, you can begin by selecting all cells in the array range. Then pick one cell in the array. By selecting F2 to edit a cell in the array, you can make changes in that cell. After making the changes, select Ctrl+Shift+Enter to enter your changes. Now the entire selected array will reflect your changes.

Given quarterly revenues for a toy store, can I estimate the trend and seasonality of the store's revenues?

The Toysrustrend.xlsx file, shown in Figure 74-10 on the next page, contains quarterly revenues (in millions of dollars) for a toy store during the years 1997–2002. We would like to estimate the quarterly trend in revenues as well as the seasonality associated with each quarter (first quarter equals January–March; second quarter equals April–June; third Quarter equals July–September; fourth Quarter equals October–December). A trend of, for example, 1 percent per quarter means that sales are increasing at 1 percent per quarter. A seasonal index for the first quarter of, for example, 0.80 means that sales during Quarter 1 are approximately 80 percent of an average quarter.

The trick to solving this problem is to use the LOGEST function of Excel. Suppose that we are trying to predict a variable y from independent variables $x1, x2,..., xn$, and we believe that for some values of $a, b1, b2,..., bn$, the relationship between y and $x1, x2,..., xn$ is given by $y = a(b1)^{x1}(b2)^{x2}(bn)^{xn}$. (I'll call this Equation 1.)

	C	D	E	F	G	H	I	J
1								
2								mean quarter
3								
4					1	2	3	index
5	Year	Quarter	Sales	Quarter#	Q1 dummy	Q2 dummy	Q3 dummy	Forecast
6	1997	1	1646	1	1	0	0	1853.104665
7	1997	2	1738	2	0	1	0	1826.702203
8	1997	3	1883	3	0	0	1	2025.018084
9	1997	4	4868	4	0	0	0	4366.196216
10	1998	1	1924	5	1	0	0	1917.500329
11	1998	2	1989	6	0	1	0	1890.180377
12	1998	3	2142	7	0	0	1	2095.387765
13	1998	4	4383	8	0	0	0	4517.922188
14	1999	1	2043	9	1	0	0	1984.133752
15	1999	2	2020	10	0	1	0	1955.864428
16	1999	3	2171	11	0	0	1	2168.202803
17	1999	4	4338	12	0	0	0	4674.920659
18	2000	1	2186	13	1	0	0	2053.082697
19	2000	2	2204	14	0	1	0	2023.83101
20	2000	3	2465	15	0	0	1	2243.548175
21	2000	4	5027	16	0	0	0	4837.374851
22	2001	1	2319	17	1	0	0	2124.427627
23	2001	2	1994	18	0	1	0	2094.15944
24	2001	3	2220	19	0	0	1	2321.51181
25	2001	4	4799	20	0	0	0	5005.474351
26	2002	1	2061	21	1	0	0	2198.251805
27	2002	2	2021	22	0	1	0	2166.931793

Figure 74-10 Toy revenue trend and seasonality estimation

The LOGEST function is used to determine values of a, $b1$, $b2$,..., bn that best fit this equation to the observed data. To use the LOGEST function to estimate trend and seasonality, note the following:

- y equals quarterly revenues.
- $x1$ equals the quarter number (listed in chronological order, the current quarter is Quarter 1, the next quarter is Quarter 2, and so on).
- $x2$ equals 1 if the quarter is the first quarter of the year, and 0 otherwise.
- $x3$ equals 1 if the quarter is the second quarter of the year, and 0 otherwise.
- $x4$ equals 1 if the quarter is the third quarter of the year, and 0 otherwise.

We need to choose one quarter to leave out of the model, and I've arbitrarily chosen the fourth quarter. This approach is similar to the one we used with dummy variables in Chapter 48. The model we choose to estimate is then $y=a(b1)^{x1}(b2)^{x2}(b3)^{x3}(b4)^{x4}$. When the LOGEST function determines values of a, $b1$, $b2$, $b3$, and $b4$ that best fit the data, the values are interpreted as follows:

- a is a constant used to scale the forecasts.
- $b1$ is a constant that represents the average per quarter percentage increase in toy store sales.
- $b2$ is a constant that measures the ratio of first quarter sales to the omitted quarter's (fourth quarter) sales.

❑ *b*3 is a constant that measures the ratio of second-quarter sales to the omitted quarter's sales.

❑ *b*4 is a constant that measures the ratio of third-quarter sales to the omitted quarter's sales.

To begin, I created the dummy variables for Quarters 1–3 in the cell range G6:I27 by copying from G6 to G6:I27 the formula *IF($D6=G$4,1,0)*. Remember that a fourth quarter is known to Excel because all three dummy variables equal 0 during the fourth quarter, which is why we can leave out the dummy variable for this quarter.

We now select the cell range K6:O6, where we want LOGEST to place the estimated coefficients. The constant *a* will be placed in the right-most cell, followed by the coefficients corresponding to the ordering of the independent variables. Thus, the trend coefficient will be next to the constant, then the Quarter 1 coefficient, and so on.

The syntax we will use for the LOGEST function is *LOGEST(y range,x range,TRUE, TRUE)*. After array-entering in cell K6 the formula *=LOGEST(E6:E27,F6:I27,TRUE, TRUE)}*, we obtain the coefficient estimates shown in Figure 74-11. Our equation to predict quarterly revenues (in millions) is as follows:

$$4219.57*(1.0086)^{\text{quarter number}}*(.435)^{\text{Q1dummy}}*(.426)^{\text{Q2dummy}}*(.468)^{\text{Q3dummy}}$$

	J	K	L	M	N	O
2	mean quarter	0.582197	q4	172%		
3						
4	index	80%	73%	75%		
5	Forecast	q3	q2	q1	trend	const
6	1853.104665	0.467772	0.425581021	0.435435	1.008577	4219.566
7	1826.702203					
8	2025.018084					
9	4366.196216					
10	1917.500329					
11	1890.180377					
12	2095.387765					
13	4517.922188					
14	1984.133752					
15	1955.864428					
16	2168.202803					
17	4674.920659					
18	2053.082697					
19	2023.83101					
20	2243.548175					
21	4837.374851					
22	2124.427627					
23	2094.15944					
24	2321.51181					
25	5005.474351					
26	2198.251805					

Figure 74-11   LOGEST estimates trend and seasonality

During the first quarter, the Q1 dummy equals 1 and the Q2 and Q3 dummies equal 0. (Recall that any number raised to the power 0 equals 1.) Thus, during a first quarter, we predict quarterly revenues to equal $4219.57*(1.0086)^{\text{quarter number}}*(.435)$.

During a second quarter, the Q1 dummy and the Q3 dummy equal 0 and the Q2 dummy equals 1. During this quarter, we predict quarterly revenues to equal $4219.57*(1.0086)^{\text{quarter number}}*(.426)$. During a third quarter, the Q1 dummy and the Q2 dummy equal 0 and the Q3 dummy equals 1. We predict quarterly revenues during this quarter to equal $4219.57*(1.0086)^{\text{quarter number}}*(.468)$. Finally, during a fourth quarter, the Q1, Q2, and Q3 dummies equal 0. During this quarter, we predict quarterly revenues to equal $4219.57*(1.0086)^{\text{quarter number}}$.

In summary, we have estimated a quarterly upward trend in revenues of 0.9 percent (around 3.6 percent annually). After adjusting for trend, we find the following:

- Quarter 1 revenues average 43.5 percent of Quarter 4 revenues.

- Quarter 2 revenues average 42.6 percent of Quarter 4 revenues.

- Quarter 3 revenues average 46.8 percent of Quarter 4 revenues.

To create a seasonal index for each quarter, we give the omitted quarter (Quarter 4) a value of 1, and we find an average quarter has a weight equal to the following (see cell K2 in Figure 74-11):

$$\frac{.435 + .426 + .468 + 1}{4} = .582$$

Then we can compute the relative seasonal index for Quarters 1–3 by copying from K4 to L4:M4 the formula *K6/$K$2*. The Quarter 4 seasonality is computed in cell M2 with the formula *1/K2*. After adjusting for trend, we conclude that:

- Quarter 1 sales are 80 percent of a typical quarter.

- Quarter 2 sales are 73 percent of a typical quarter.

- Quarter 3 sales are 75 percent of a typical quarter.

- Quarter 4 sales are 172 percent of a typical quarter.

Suppose we want to generate the forecast for each quarter corresponding to our fitted equation (Equation 1). We can use the Excel GROWTH function to create this forecast. The GROWTH function is an array function with the syntax *GROWTH(known ys,known xs,new xs,True)*. This formula will give the predictions for the new *xs* when Equation 1 is fitted to the data contained in the ranges specified by *known ys* and *known xs*. Thus, selecting the range J6:J27 and array-entering in cell J6 the formula ={*GROWTH(E6:E27, F6:I27,F6:I27,TRUE)*} generates forecasts from Equation 1 for each quarter's revenue. For example, our forecast for Quarter 4 of 1997 using Equation 1 is $4.366 billion.

Problems

All data for Problems 1–5 is in the Chapter74data.xlsx file.

1. The *Duplicate* worksheet contains two lists of names. Use an array formula to count the number of names appearing on both lists.

2. The *Find Errors* worksheet contains some calculations. Use an array formula to count the number of cells containing errors. (Hint: Use the ISERROR function in your array formula.)

3. The *Sales* worksheet contains 48 months of sales at a toy store. Create an array formula to add (beginning with Month 3) every fifth month of sales. (Hint: You might want to use the Excel MOD function. *MOD(number,divisor)* yields the remainder after the number is divided by the divisor. For example, *MOD(7,5)* yields 2.)

4. Use an array function to compute the third, fifth, and seventh power of each month's sales.

5. The *Product* worksheet contains sales during April through August of products 1–7. Sales for each month are listed in the same column. Rearrange the data so that sales for each month are listed in the same row and changes to the original data are reflected in the new arrangement you have created.

6. Use the data in the Historicalinvest.xlsx file to create a count of the number of years in which stock, bond, and T-Bill returns are from –20 percent through –15 percent, –15 percent through –10 percent, and so on.

7. An *m* by *n* matrix is a rectangular array of numbers containing *m* rows and *n* columns. For example,

$$\begin{bmatrix} 1 & 2 & 3 \\ 4 & 5 & 6 \\ 7 & 8 & 9 \end{bmatrix}$$

is a 3-by-3 matrix. Consider two matrices, *A* and *B*. Suppose that the number of columns in matrix *A* equals the number of rows in matrix *B*. Then you can multiply matrix *A* by matrix *B*. (The product is written as *AB*.) The entry in row I and column J of *AB* is computed by applying the SUMPRODUCT function to row I of *A* and column J of *B*. *AB* will have as many rows as *A* and columns as *B*. The Excel MMULT function is an array function with which you can multiply matrices. Use the MMULT function to multiply the following matrices:

$$A = \begin{bmatrix} 1 & 2 & 3 \\ 4 & 5 & 6 \\ 7 & 7 & 0 \end{bmatrix} \text{ and } B = \begin{bmatrix} 1 & 2 & 3 \\ 1 & 2 & 0 \\ 3 & 3 & 0 \end{bmatrix}$$

8. A square matrix has the same number of rows and columns. Given a square matrix A, suppose there exists a matrix B whereby AB equals a matrix in which each diagonal entry equals 1 and all other entries equal 0. We then say that B is the inverse of A. The Excel array function MINVERSE finds the inverse of a square matrix. Use the MINVERSE function to find the inverse for matrices A and B in Problem 7.

9. Suppose we have invested a fraction f_i of our money in investment i ($i=1,2,...,n$). Also, suppose the standard deviation of the annual percentage return on investment i is s_i and the correlation between the annual percentage return on investment i and investment j is $\tilde{n}_{ij}$. We would like to know the variance and standard deviation of the annual percentage return on our portfolio. This can easily be computed by using matrix multiplication. Create the following three matrices:

   ❏ Matrix 1 equals a 1 by n matrix whose ith entry is $s_i f_i$.

   ❏ Matrix 2 equals an n by n matrix whose entry in row i and column j is $\tilde{n}_{ij}$.

   ❏ Matrix 3 is a n by 1 matrix whose ith entry is $s_i f_i$.

   The variance of the annual percentage return on our portfolio is simply *(Matrix 1)*(Matrix 2)*(Matrix 3)*. The data in Historicalinvest.xlsx gives annual returns on stocks, bonds, and T-Bills. Use the MMULT and TRANSPOSE functions to estimate (based on the given historical data) the variance and standard deviation of a portfolio that invests 50 percent in stocks, 25 percent in bonds, and 25 percent in T-Bills.

   Problems 10–13 use the data in the Makeupdb.xlsx file.

10. How many dollars' worth of lip gloss did Jen sell?

11. What was the average number of lipstick units sold by Jen in the East region?

12. How many dollars of sales were made by Emilee or in the East region?

13. How many dollars' worth of lipstick were sold by Colleen or Zaret in the East region?

14. Use the data in the Chapter52data.xlsx file to estimate the trend and seasonal components of the quarterly revenues of Ford and GM.

15. In the toy store example (using the Toysrustrend.xlsx file), use the data for 1999–2001 to forecast quarterly revenues for 2002.

16. The Lillydata.xlsx file contains information from a market research survey that was used to gather insights to aid in designing a new blood pressure drug. Fifteen experts (six from Lilly and nine from other companies—see column N) were asked to compare five sets of four potential Lilly products. The fifth choice in each scenario is that a competitor's drug is chosen over the four listed Lilly drugs.

   For example, in the first scenario, the second option considered would be a Lilly drug that reduced blood pressure 18 points, resulted in 14 percent of side effects, and sold for $16.

The range I5:N21 contains the choices each expert made for each of the five scenarios. For example, the first expert (who worked for Lilly) chose a competitor's drug when faced with Scenario 1 and chose the first listed drug when faced with Scenario 2. Use this information to answer the following:

- ❑ Enter a formula that can be copied from I2 to I2:M5 that calculates the price for each scenario and option in I2:M5.

- ❑ Enter an array formula in I23 that can be copied to I23:I32 and then to J23:M32 that calculates for each question the frequency of each response (1–5), broken down by Lilly and non-Lilly experts. Thus for Question 1, one Lilly expert responded 1, three responded 2, and two responded 5.

17. The Arrayexam1data.xlsx file contains sales by company and date. Your job is to break sales down on a quarterly basis by using array formulas.

    I want the data summarized (using only array formulas) by company and by quarter as shown in Figure 74-12.

	K	L	M	N	O	P
6		1/1/2004	4/1/2004	7/1/2004	10/1/2004	1/1/2005
7	ACS					
8	ActSys Medical, Inc.					
9	Baxter Healthcare Corporation					
10	BioMed Plus, Inc.					
11	Blood Diagnostics, Inc.					
12	Briggs Corporation					
13	Cardinal Health					
14	Gentiva Health Services					
15	Priority Healthcare					
16	Tri State Distribution, Inc.					
17						

Figure 74-12   Format for Problem 17 answer

For example, L7 should contain Quarter 1 (January 1 through March 31) ACS sales, and so on. Verify your answer with a PivotTable.

18. Explain why array-entering the formula $=SUM(1/COUNTIF(Info,Info))$ will yield the number of unique entries in the range Info. Apply this formula to the data in the Unique.xlsx file and verify that it returns the number of unique entries.

19. The Salaries.xlsx file contains the salaries of NBA players. Write an array formula that adds the four largest player salaries. Hint: Use the array constant {1,2,3,4} in conjunction with the LARGE function. Then generalize your formula so that you can enter any positive integer n and your formula will add the n largest salaries. Hint: If cell G9 contains an integer n, then when you array-enter a formula $ROW(Indirect("1:"\&G9))$, Excel will create an array constant {1,2,...,n}.

Index

Symbols and Numbers

#DIV/0 error, 84
#N/A errors, 83–84
#NAME? error, 84
#NUM! error, 84
#REF! error, 84
#VALUE! error, 84
& operator, 31
4 period moving average, 427
95 percent confidence interval for mean profit, 482
95 percent service level
    defined, 538
    reorder point calculation using, 540–541

A

abandonment options, 523
Add Constraint dialog box, 224
adding numbers when pasting, 99–101
allocating assets, with bootstrapping, 495–498
alternative hypothesis, 411
American stock options, 514. *See also* call options; put options
    comparing with European options, 514
analysis of variance, one-way. *See* ANOVA
AND formulas, 78
annual revenue, predicting, 114–116
annuities
    valuing. *See* PV function
    valuing, in future dollars. *See* FV function
ANOVA
    analyzing data with, 412–413
    defined, 411
    dependent variable analysis with, 417
    forecasting with, 414–415, 419–420
    hypotheses, testing, 411–412
    term origin, 413–414
    two-way model, 418
    two-way model with replication, 420–422
    two-way model without replication, 418–419
array arguments, 572
array constants, 580–581
array formulas, 572
    editing, 581
    entering, 572
    example of, 572–573
    pasting, 572
    summing second digit of list of integers with, 575–576
array functions, 572. *See also* specific functions
    summarizing data with, 577–580
ASCII characters, returning number for, 32

asset allocation, determining with bootstrapping, 495–498
auditing tool, 103. *See also* dependents; precedents
    multiple worksheets and, 106–107
AutoComplete
    implementing, 194–195
    and named ranges, 7
AVERAGEIF function, 140, 142
AVERAGEIFS function, 140, 142–143
averages, determining for flagged rows, 334
averaging numbers greater or equal to median value, 577

B

best-case scenarios. *See* Scenario Manager
Beta random variable. *See also* BETADIST function
    defined, 471
    duration modeling with, 473–474
BETADIST function, 474. *See also* Beta random variable
bidding, simulating, 486–488
bin ranges (histograms), 277
    defining, 278
binary changing cells, 241
BINOMDIST function, 453–454
binomial random variables
    defined, 451
    examples of, 452–453
    negative, 455
    simulating, 485
Black-Scholes formula
    history of, 513
    implementing, 516–518
    parameters determining put/call value, 515
    stock volatility estimating with, 519–520
blank cells, counting. *See* COUNTBLANK function
Boolean arrays, 579–580
bootstrapping. *See also* RANDBETWEEN function
    allocating assets with, 495–498
    data tables for, setting up, 493–494
    defined, 491
    demonstration of, 492–494
Bottom 10 Items conditional formatting rule, 165–166
break-even analysis, 120
bundling products, 564–566

C

call options
    defined, 513
    parameters, changing, 518–519
    parameters determining value, 515
capital budgeting with Excel Solver, 241–243

About the Author

Wayne L. Winston is a professor of decision sciences at the Indiana University Kelley School of Business. He has earned an MBA teaching award for 26 consecutive years and regularly teaches business analysts how to use Microsoft Office Excel to make better decisions. Wayne also consults for several Fortune 500 clients, including 3M, Bristol-Myers Squibb Company, Cisco Systems, Eli Lilly and Company, Ford Motor Company, General Electric Company, General Motors Corporation, Intel Corporation, Microsoft Corporation, NCR Corporation, Owens Corning, Pfizer, Proctor & Gamble, the U.S. Army, U.S. Department of Defense, Verizon, and WellPoint. He and business partner Jeff Sagarin developed the statistics tracking and rating system used by the Dallas Mavericks professional basketball team. Wayne is also a two-time Jeopardy! champion.

What do you think of this book?

We want to hear from you!

Do you have a few minutes to participate in a brief online survey?

Microsoft is interested in hearing your feedback so we can continually improve our books and learning resources for you.

To participate in our survey, please visit:

www.microsoft.com/learning/booksurvey/

...and enter this book's ISBN-10 number (appears above barcode on back cover*).
As a thank-you to survey participants in the United States and Canada, each month we'll randomly select five respondents to win one of five $100 gift certificates from a leading online merchant. At the conclusion of the survey, you can enter the drawing by providing your e-mail address, which will be used for prize notification only.

Thanks in advance for your input. Your opinion counts!

* Where to find the ISBN-10 on back cover

ISBN-13: 000-0-0000-0000-0
ISBN-10: 0-0000-0000-0

0 0 0 0 0

0 000000 000000

Example only. Each book has unique ISBN.

Microsoft®
Press

No purchase necessary. Void where prohibited. Open only to residents of the 50 United States (includes District of Columbia) and Canada (void in Quebec). For official rules and entry dates see:

www.microsoft.com/learning/booksurvey/